Beyond Acts...

A Challenging Research . . .

Beyond Acts

New Perspectives in New Testament History

by

Paul R. Finch

© COPYRIGHT 2003 by Paul R. Finch

All rights reserved. No part of this publication may be reproduced, stored in a retrieval system, or transmitted in any form or by any means, electronic, mechanical, photocopying, recording or otherwise, without the prior permission of the copyright owner. Brief quotations in printed reviews and scholarly publications are permitted.

Unless otherwise noted, biblical quotations are from the *New Revised Standard Version* of the Bible, copyright © 1989, Division of Christian Education of the National Council of Churches of Christ in the United States of America. Used by permission. All rights reserved.

Library of Congress Cataloging-in-Publication Data

Finch, Paul Richard, 1944-
Beyond Acts: new perspectives in new testament history/ Paul R. Finch
p. cm.
Includes bibliographical references.
ISBN 1-4120-0364-4 (pbk.)
1. Bible, N.T. — Canon. 2. Bible, N.T. — History of Biblical events.
3. Bible, N.T. — History of contemporary events. I. Title.
BS2407.F55 2003
C2003-902880-1
225.9'5

Picture on cover is an original painting made specifically for this book by James A. Finch of Burbank, California (the author's son), entitled "The Last Work of Peter and Paul." It depicts the Apostles Peter and Paul editing their writings in prison at Rome in the autumn of 66 C.E. as perceived by the author.

This book was composed on Adobe Framemaker, version 7.0, by the author, using 11 pt. Garamond-Normal font.

First edition printed and bound in Canada by Trafford. Second edition printed and bound in the United States of America by United Graphics Inc. for Sunrise Publications, P.O. Box 155, Palm Bay, Florida, 32911-0155. All correspondence to be addressed to the author at this address or emailed to same at pfinch1@cfl.rr.com.

To the Memory of Ernest L. Martin (1932-2002)
Friend, Teacher, Mentor

Contents

Appendix 2

Appendix 3

Appendix 4

Appendix 5

Preface

THE IDEA FOR THIS BOOK CAME ABOUT BACK in 1995 when I first became acquainted with the "world wide web" and the newsgroup "soc.religion.christian.bible-study." I had then submitted to that newsgroup a series of articles that I named "Beyond Acts." At that time, I did not have a home computer and what I had written was done at work during my lunch breaks. A number of people showed interest in what I was writing because it answered many important questions that some had been wondering about regarding the history of the New Testament. Some who were new to the newsgroup requested the first parts of the series that they had missed. From the response and feedback that I received, I knew that a number of people out there had their interest piqued, and for a while I received comments and questions on that series.

It was also at this time that I was working on another book titled: *The Passover Papers*. As I got more involved with that project, I never did bring my *Beyond Acts* series on the web to a conclusion. Now here is where the story gets interesting. I had backed up all my parts of that series to a local home folder, but when the company that I worked for switched to new servers, unbeknownst to me, my material got archived somewhere. Fortunately, I had made a hard copy for myself.

In February of 1998 I had self-published my book, *The Passover Papers*. Then, in March, I went to California to visit my son, James, and also to attend the *Biblical Archaeology Society Seminar* that was conducted on the *Queen Mary*, in Long Beach. For some strange reason I had brought along with me my series on *Beyond Acts*.

It was at this seminar that I heard one the most noted biblical scholars of today, professor David Noel Freedman, give two lectures on "First Temple Jerusalem and the Babylonian Conquest" and "Second Temple Jerusalem and the Roman Conquest." I was enthralled with professor Freedman's second topic, especially because he was in agreement with the conclusions that I had made concerning the dates of the New Testament books.

Dr. Freedman pointed out that "prediction," "event," and "confirmation" is a repeated pattern in many prophetic writings. Now the interesting point about what Dr. Freedman had brought out was that, if an "event" is different than the prophecy of that "event" — that confirms the prophecy. What a brilliant analysis! In other words, who would ever invent a false prophesy having known the outcome of that prophecy?

Now, what does this mean in terms of the New Testament writings and the destruction of the second temple? If the Gospel writers and Paul had any knowledge about the destruction of the temple, they would have said so. Yet, no New Testament writer seems to have made any attempt to confirm the olivet prophecy of Jesus. This would mean that all of the New Testament writings are to be dated prior to the destruction of the temple. And this is exactly what I had believed and had brought out in my *Beyond Acts* series. I was so elated by what I had heard that I felt that I had to share with Dr. Freedman some of my views that were in line with his.

After Dr. Freedman's lecture, I was able to corral his attention for a few moments to discuss with him my thoughts on the subject. In talking with him I remembered that I had brought along the *Beyond Acts* folder. I wanted Dr. Freedman to read my paper. I asked my son, James, to run back to our room (cabin) and get it. I then gave Dr. Freedman the paper to read. It was at that time that I realized that I had to make this paper the subject of another book.

When I returned home and to work, I tried to find my soft copy of the *Beyond Acts* series, but could not find it. I asked the system administrator at work if he could recover the material that he had archived. He said that if I could provide him with a date, then he could restore it. I gave him what I thought was the correct time frame that those files should have been on the system. But when he restored the data for the dates that I gave him, my paper was not to be found among the files.

Now I became concerned. I thought for sure that I had made another hard copy. Yet, when I searched high and low for one, I could not find it. In other words, I had given my one and only copy to Dr. Freedman. Now I was in the embarrassing position of getting in touch with him and asking for the paper back.

So, I mustered up my courage and I timidly called the University of California, San Diego, and asked to speak with professor Freedman. When he got on the line I asked him if he remembered me, and he said yes, he did. I will never forget his reaction when I asked him to please return the only copy I had of that paper. In a rather angered and annoyed tone he said, "I am right in the middle of grading term papers, and if you could just see my desk right now — your paper is buried somewhere within that mountain of work." Nevertheless, he promised that he would look for my paper and would send it back to me, if he could find it.

Now, it was just a matter of waiting to see if I would ever see that paper again. I waited nervously for the next few days. Then, about a week later, the paper was back in my hands. Phew, what a relief. I saw this as a providential sign that this book was intended to be a reality, someday.

In November of 1998 there was a *Bible and Archaeology Fest*, also sponsored by the *Biblical Archaeological Society*, right here in Orlando. I attended that seminar particularly because of some of the noted scholars that would be there, such as Bart Ehrman, Steven Friesen, Ronald Hendel, James Strange, and of course, once again our beloved Dr. David Noel Freedman, to name just a few. It was there that I had many more of my questions answered.

I then started to collect the books and papers that I needed to document my thesis. I went to Wesleyan University's Olin Library, Yale's Sterling Library, and our own local library, the Franklin T. DeGroodt Public Library here in Palm Bay, Florida. In the summer of 2000 I bought a home computer and began the task of writing this book. As it turned out, this was not an easy task. In between computer crashes, software problems, lost data, etc., I still had to deal with the problems of daily life. On top of that, I had a full time job working for a large space communication company, and they went on overtime for the next two years, leaving me with few precious moments to tend to my book.

It wasn't until March of 2000 that I attended another BAR Seminar, which also happened to be close to me, in Fort Lauderdale, Florida. Bart Ehrman again was there and he spoke on topics that I had great interest in for my book, e.g., "The Text of the New Testament: Do We Have the Original Writings?", "The Canon of the New Testament: Why These Twenty-seven Books?", and "The Writings of the New Testament: Were Any of the 'Apostles' Works Forged?"

When putting together the material for this book it became obvious by the nature of the subject that so many issues had to be addressed that I soon realized that one can get in over their head real fast. After all, critics are totally unforgiving when it comes to challenging old ideas without scrupulous documentation. But to do that might have put the publication of this book far off into the future. Therefore, I made a decision that I would publish my general thesis without the mass of data that would have been a detriment to the overall story flow, but I would provide at least a fair amount of reference material of many issues discussed in recent important works.

I also know that reader reaction will play no small part in a future "revised edition." Hopefully, criticism will serve as the impetus for a refinement of the overall premises. In the event that some of my ideas participate in any revised thinking on the part of present day scholarship, then I feel that I have at least made a contribution that will engender a new generation of scholarship that is not afraid to challenge the status quo. Indeed, any new work on the subject of New Testament history and canonization cannot ignore the challenges made in this book.

I have chosen to dedicate this book to the memory of the late Dr. Ernest L. Martin, whose material can be obtained online at www.ernestlmartin.com. I had known Dr. Martin since the late 1950's, and last saw him in November, 2000, at the *Grand Ol' Opry Convention Center*, where he attended the *Society for Biblical Literature* convention. He was there promoting his new book, *The Temples that Jerusalem Forgot*. When he got a break from his booth, we had a chance to sit down and discuss, as usual, some of the points that we agreed and differed on, as well as issues I intended to treat in my book. Specifically, I wanted to know what he thought about my idea for the dating of the *Epistle of First Clement.* I told him that I believed that its date should be lowered from around 95 to 69 C.E. When I explained to him my reasoning, he remarked: "I see where you are coming from." I could see those wheels turning and I knew that I had sparked his intellectual curiosity. He said that he was going to look into the matter thereafter. That was the last time that I saw him.

Dr. Martin died in January of 2002 (a tribute to him by James D. Tabor can be seen online at http://ernestlmartin.com/tribute.htm). Dr. Martin was indeed a giant among biblical researchers. His influence on me and my thinking is reflected in many pages of this book.

In a real sense, Dr. Martin's death inspired me to push on with my project more than ever. Therefore, it is in the spirit of Dr. Martin's incredible insight, inspiration, and his dedication to the truth, that I feel that we who are his students and who have been shaped by his teaching, have a responsibility to carry on the task that he has dedicated his life to — research that enriches the knowledge of the biblical revelation. And it is in this spirit that I dedicate this book to his memory.

P. R. F.
Palm Bay, Florida
July, 2003

Preface to the Second Edition

ONLY FIVE MONTHS HAVE TRANSPIRED SINCE I published the first edition, but since I have received a number of good comments and suggestions already, I decided to incorporate them at this time.

It is gratifying to know that so many have encouraged me to move forward with this project, and that this book is a needed supplement to the ever growing mountain of confusing literature that is continually being pumped out *en masse* to the general public. It would appear that scholars are dedicated to the proposition that it is imperative for them to "publish or perish," and so, as a result, the amount of literature is becoming so bewildering on the subject of New Testament history, that it boggles the mind.

When I attended the SBL conference this last November in Atlanta, the publisher displays covered two floors of books that seemed to go on forever. How does one keep up with all of this staggering amount of literature? And with it all, one has to ask, is there anything really new to the contribution of our knowledge base?

That's a very good question because one scholar has written to tell me that my book really contributes nothing new to the subject of New Testament history. What an incredible statement! I turn the world upsidedown with page after page of new data that overthrows the entire canonization model maintained by just about everyone, and this is considered as nothing new. Its almost as if this scholar wishes this to be the case and would like my book to just vanish somehow rather than face reality. My book is breakthrough research if ever there was one, and it will not go away, it will overthrow the outdated ideas that have for too long gripped the thinking of New Testament scholarship!

To address another criticism of my book leveled at me is that I engage in too much scholar bashing. Certainly my book points out a number of errors of many current theories held by leading scholars, but one has to read the context. I have the utmost respect for true scholarship, but I have very little time and patience for some of the nonsense theories that masquerade under the pretence of scholarship.

The important theses of my book should not be obscured by the fact that I take scholarship to task on a number of important issues. I am not about scholar bashing, believe it or not. I have the greatest respect for the painstaking dedication that many a true "scholar" has contributed to an ever increasing knowledge base about biblical issues. In fact, in case anybody hasn't noticed, my book is filled with legions of scholarly quotes. Page after page, my opinions have been fortified by the very words of many a leading scholar on the subject. But I also am not intimidated by the critical reviews that I have already seen that merely appear to be some sort of self preserving, damage control. If scholars, such as the stature of David Noel Freedman, can personally write me and praise my work, then I can not be bothered by the pettiness of those who treat the Bible with about as much respect as a comic book.

Don't you sometimes get the feeling that certain scholars, some of which are total, unabashed atheists, feel that their opinions rise above the subject of which they write? Indeed, it is just because of such sentiments that I was prompted to write this book in the first place. Why are these scholars given a place in the spotlight and their vaunted opinions dominate the entire perspective on New Testament history, when in fact they are hostile to the notion of the New Testament being considered as sacred literature? Indeed, it is just because of the belligerent attitude maintained by a certain group of "Jesus" scholars that I was prompted to write a book of my own opinions with the attitude that their so-called scholarship to the contrary be damned! The gloves are off. It is time that we stop molly codling a bunch of Bible critics whose only purpose is to destroy the faith of millions who have come to believe that the Bible is indeed sacred literature based upon its own internal evidence!

But what about Christian scholars who take exception with me. I've had "Christian" scholars tell me that I am not qualified to form an opinion on many of the topics within this book. In fact, the criticism goes far deeper than that. My book may have garnered the distinction of being placed in that new category of "pseudo-scholarship," where some scholars now feel the need to alert other scholars about such an alarming trend and dangerous phenomenon as books such as mine, simply because the average reader has no way of distinguishing between "real" scholarship and "pseudo" scholarship. Really! One has to wonder, however, who are such scholars really trying to protect—the general public—or are they more concerned with protecting their own reputations whose theories may go up in smoke and would be made to look foolish if they are shown up by some outsider who is not a member of their elitist inner circle? Are we to believe that no one is qualified to form an opinion on the Bible, unless, of course, they are all a full fledged Ph.D. in New Testament studies? Do scholars think that they own the Bible and that the Bible is what only they say it is, and nothing more? How did such a situation arise that scholars have kidnapped the Bible for their own pedantic purposes?

Don't these scholars feel that they have a responsibility to the general public and are answerable to them if they betray our trust and go off on tangents that are based upon nothing but outrageous theories? Frankly, I feel that many a scholar has betrayed the trust of the general public in foisting on us all historical scenarios that rest not upon scholarship, but on an inner desire to bring down the authority of the Bible to a level that they can look down upon.

It is one thing for scholars to use their expertise in language and archaeology to help us see and understand some amazing things about the past. For this, we should be all extremely indebted and thankful. But it is quite another thing for them to use their "chair" for purposes of pontificating a host of outrageous historical scenarios that are not based on legitimate evidence, but merely their own bias that invariably is a rejection of the internal evidence to the contrary. Maybe the general public has given some of these scholars too much benefit of the doubt. Maybe its time to bring many a such scholar to task about some of the most outrageous and egregious theories imaginable, backed up by nothing other than their own vaunted opinions.

What do we mean by the term "scholarship" anyway? Is it just a means to block the entrance of new ideas that finally break through the madness under the guise of scholarship? We can be sure that if the apostle Paul or Peter were sitting in some of the classrooms taught by many of these scholars, their opinions would be denounced by these professors as being ignorant and totally unqualified. That's a problem! But we all know that that's just the way it is, isn't it? But scholars should realize that it is just because of this problem that books like mine are more likely to be written, and will continue to be written, in the future. It is not as if I haven't done my homework. I have. And what I have found is that much of scholarship has not reported to the general public all the facts. And if scholars refuse to do it, who will? Enter, *Beyond Acts!*

Indeed, scholars are going to have to realize that the average lay person is no longer the ignorant, gullible person of years ago, much to their chagrin, I'm sure. Many a scholar would like to return to the good old days of yesteryear. Today, more and more people are becoming well read than ever before. People are studying on their own Greek and Hebrew. We now have the World Wide Web, with more information available to us than ever before. The sophistication of many lay people should be a welcome change to scholars, not a threat. But, it seems, it is only welcomed, as long as it does not attempt to provide a cross check on some of their own cherished positions.

But let us not bicker amongst ourselves and get bent all out of shape over petty issues that tend to obscure these very important issues. The subject of this book transcends the pettiness of such criticisms and the success of this book will not depend on them in the long run, we can be all thankful for that.

What the reader needs to understand is that my book is not based upon pure speculation! It is based upon the rejected internal evidence that must now be given a chance to speak. Therefore, if anything, we must come to understand that the gradual acceptance theory is in reality nothing more than a mirage that is like people admiring the non-existent emperor's new cloths, which a young lad could see was absolutely invisible! Canon scholarship today appears to be wrapped in just such fabric. Maybe scholars think that they can see something, but in reality there is nothing at all to behold. We can be sure it only exists in the halucinations of their own minds, and nothig more.

Fortunately, the time has come to strip away the thin veil of non-existent material and look at the bare facts. *Beyond Acts* does this very thing. It will end up as the book that many a scholar will have wished that they had written. Maybe, someday, many will. But for now, like the young lad of the Emperor's new cloths story, it is only fitting that out of the mouths of babes comes the truth. *Beyond Acts* will be your guide in one of the greatest advances in New Testament research to date!

Another criticism that I received is that "to think that Peter and John produced the New Testament is a lot of wishful thinking." When I read this, I sat back and realized that this scholar had the genius to put his finger on the most important theme of my entire book. In one simple statement he condensed my entire thesis into the very crux of the problem. Even I didn't realize how important my book was until I saw it through the eyes of a critical scholar, who nailed it to a tee. When I saw those words, I immediately opened the pages of my book to chapter 15, which was entitled: "The Responsibility to Canonize Scripture." Now it became obvious that this title needed to be changed. The word "Responsibility" was not strong enough, it had to be changed to "Authority."

As I said, this brings up the most crucial point of my book. Who had the "authority" to canonize the books of the New Testament? Scholars seem never to really address this important issue. In fact, if one goes to the latest book on canonization, *The Canon Debate*, by Lee Martin McDonald and James A. Sanders, none of the authors writing in this 600 plus page book even addresses that fact. Apparently, they, like this scholar who wrote me, just naturally assume that clerics in the later church had the authority to canonize Scripture. They talk about the books that didn't make it, and canon expansion today, and all kinds of nonsense, but they all get an "F" on their report card in the most important aspect of canonization of all. Maybe its time that students in the classes of these scholars raise their hands and ask this simple question. Once again, the entire subject rests upon *a priori* assumptions. But the answer to the question vanquishes all notions of "wishful thinking!" Indeed, it is because scholars believe that anyone in the post-apostolic era had the "authority" to canonize Scripture is the wishful thinking that the entire problem rests. Scholars need to be stopped in their tracks if they continue to venture theories of post-apostolic canonization. They should no longer be allowed to get away with murder in foisting theories that ignore the most basic answer to the entire question. No one in post apostolic times had the authority to canonize Scripture! End of story!

Beyond Acts will turn out to be the very best book you will ever read on the subject of canonization anywhere, bar none. It is just as good as scholarship as one will ever find on the subject, and in many respects, even better. There is nothing "pseudo" about the scholarship of ths book. Let the reader be the judge.

One of the favorable comments that I received about my book is that it is very "readable" for the lay person, and is not filled with a lot of pedantic, esoteric language that only serves to separate the average reader from the scholarly community. All that is needed in order to derive anything out of my book is to have an open mind. The reader now has the means to experience, for a refreshing change, just what the subtitle of this book has intended that it should be: *New Perspectives in New Testament History*.

All this being said, I can only reflect upon the sentiments of Mahatma Ghandhi, who is reported to have said that "first they will try to ignore you, then they will try to ridicule you, but in the end, they will be forced to recognize you as a force to be contended with." The future will confirm this axiom in regard to this book. And for that, I am truly proud of my efforts.

P. R. F.
Palm Bay, Florida
December, 2003

Acknowledgements

I HAVE CHOSEN TO EXPRESS MYSELF IN THE body of this book by an editorial "we/our" instead of the usual "I/my" phraseology. I wanted to make this fact plain, because at no time in the production of this book had there ever been a co-writer. This book is a complete production by myself, of which I never had any help from anyone else, except for proofreading. No one has guided me in this task, nor given me helpful suggestions, and no Church, nor educational institution, has prompted, endorsed, nor underwritten this project in any way.

That being said, I don't have a list of acknowledgements that one usually finds in the beginning of most books. The only help that I have received is from the people mentioned below. My only reason for writing in this manner was prompted by the desire to adopt a style that appeared less offensive than that of an egocentric, know-it-all. Maybe, as time goes on, the positions taken in this book will be adopted by a group of like-minded individuals who will fall in the category of "we." At that time, then, "we" will unitedly proclaim the truths herein advocated.

First of all, I wish to give a special thanks to my son, James Aaron Finch, an exceptional artist, for recreating the scene of Peter and Paul on the front cover.

I have a special indebtedness to the genius of Amy Young (LadyWriter0227@cfl.rr.com) for her excellent proofreading skills and her keen sense of knowing what I wanted to convey. She has surely saved me from the excruciating embarrassment of bad grammar and misspellings.

I wish to thank the superb library staff of the Olin Library at Wesleyan University in Middletown, Connecticut, for their help in gaining access to many of the materials used in this book, as well as the helpful staff at the Sterling Library, and the Beineke Rare Book and Manuscript Library at Yale University, in New Haven, Connecticut.

And last, but certainly not least, I most sincerely want to thank the inter-library loan staff of the Franklin T. Degroodt Library in Palm Bay, Florida, viz., Marie Mercer, Chris Sullivan, Lorraine Concha, and Jeanne Hillenbrand, who tirelessly obtained the many technical journal articles that I plagued them with for the past five years.

Introduction

DOWN THROUGH THE CENTURIES STUDENTS OF New Testament history have lamented over the fact that the New Testament Book of the "Acts of the Apostles" ends abruptly and was never finished — it breaks off right at the most crucial point in apostolic history — only three decades after the Resurrection of Jesus. If ever the missing conclusion of this amazing story could be found, it would revolutionize our understanding of the history of the New Testament Church leading up to the destruction of Jerusalem in 70 C.E. — and *BEYOND!*

The *Book of Acts* cuts short the later history of, not only the work of the Apostle Paul, but also that of Peter and John. It is for this reason that scholars have been cast adrift in a hopeless sea of speculation concerning the history of how the New Testament came to be. Yet, there are valuable internal clues to what these apostles were doing that help us construct what was really going on.

Don't we wish we could just somehow lift the veil of mystery that surrounds the final days of the apostles and finally get some straight answers on some of the biggest questions surrounding the New Testament itself? Well, hang on to your seats. This book intends to do just that. It will be your guide into that great adventure, and it will be the next best thing to actually having the final chapter of the *Acts of the Apostles*.

It is not only beyond the *Book of Acts* that we journey in time, but beyond the sphere of the Judean world, and in the footsteps of those disciples that Jesus sent far and wide to spread his message.

There is much information besides the missing ending of the *Book of Acts*, which, when pieced together, help us reconstruct the events that followed. When we look into these events, a story unfolds that is as gripping and inspiring as any that you have ever read or, for that matter, dare we say, ever will read? Those who seek to find answers to the validity of the message that Jesus brought should examine for themselves this new evidence with renewed zeal. All of the pieces of the puzzle that we present must be studied in their entirety before a final conclusion can be made. If we criticize any one piece of the puzzle before we see the whole picture, we will only allow our own preconceptions and biases to lead us away from the truth.

This book will also present poignant data that will show us how a correct understanding of the later years of the apostles, specifically, Paul, Peter, and John, is the very key to unraveling the mystery of how the New Testament came into being. Scholars really haven't a clue as to how the New Testament was decided upon because they have rejected the clues that are so abundantly obvious to those who have not been fed a diet of skeptical, modern day malarkey.

The amount of scholarly literature on canon history abounds today, yet the majority of these books wind up with the conclusion that the New Testament is really nothing more than a collection of works by post-apostolic fakes. The reader is therefore enjoined to read carefully what we are going to present here, for it will break down those false notions which are being foisted on the general public under the guise of scholarship.

This book, therefore, intends to be controversial. It takes a stand against many of the false teachings that the Orthodox Church has adopted down through the ages that is a departure from the pure message of the New Testament. It also takes much exception to the majority of scholarly works on the subject of New Testament history. Since most scholars look at the New Testament writings as works by later writers who merely invented legends about Jesus, then they will find no sympathy for their theories in the pages of this book. The present author presents a different story than what is usually propagated under the guise of scholarship. The reader will, therefore, find a refreshing retelling of the story that is in alignment with history, the biblical record, and the strong traditions that have been handed down in rare writings.

One of the most inspiring aspects of our journey will be discovering the true history of how the New Testament canon came into existence. It is far different than the scenarios put forth by most modern scholars. Indeed, this is one of the most important aspects of this book: it is the real story of the circumstances that prompted the Apostles to put together a New Testament.

The time period from 58 C.E. to 70 C.E. is indeed the most important time period in Apostolic history. It is a story that few really comprehend — filled with intrigue, betrayal — even rejection of apostolic authority, and of disillusionment in the early Church and yet, it culminates in *THE* most inspiring literary undertaking of the last two millennia.

Again, it cannot be over emphasized that there is a modern myth prevalent among New Testament scholarship, as well as the broad majority of orthodox clerics, that the New Testament, as we know it, is the product of the post apostolic Catholic Church. Yet the biggest reason why this idea is totally false is that if it were true, then the New Testament would have taken on a form far different than what has come down to us, and scholars should realize and admit that this is a fact that cannot be denied. It would appear that scholars interpret the history of the apostolic age through the prism of their own theories rather than letting the internal evidence of the New Testament itself tell its own story. It is therefore the purpose of this book to boldly tell the story that is ignored in the very pages of the New Testament that confirm its own inspiration.

In a very real sense of the word, there is no more important New Testament study than how the New Testament itself came into existence. Indeed, it is pointless to study this or that aspect of the New Testament without knowing the true basis of its very own existence. It is for this reason that we need to go beyond the testimony of the *Book of Acts* and look very carefully at the period of time between its conclusion and the end of the first century.

The apostles Peter and Paul had warned their congregations that after they would depart from this world, the faithful followers of the "Way" would be led astray into apostasy, heresy, and doctrinal error by those in authority within the Church itself. If we truly believe that these apostles felt that this was in any way true, then we must be guided by this fact, go down this path, and follow the direction that it leads us. And by so doing, we are already out of the hopeless alley of the so-called "gradual acceptance theory" of how the New Testament was formed. In other words, if we know and accept the fact that after the time of the apostles there would be a time of heresy, then we have to only ask some very important questions that finally bring fresh air to the entire study. And question number one has to be whether the apostles themselves would have knowingly left their writings in the hands of later church apostates to decide upon what should be the authoritative word for the later Church.

Most scholars of today believe that the canon of Scripture is the product of post-apostolic times. But we have to realize that if this thesis is in any way true, then the apostles failed to curtail what they foresaw as a detriment to maintaining the truth they once delivered. The main premise of this book stands upon that fact that the Apostles not only did in fact see to it that their writings would be bound in an authoritative body of literature for the future Church, but that they would have seen to it that their writings would have been protected in a way not generally understood even by scholars who have written volumes on the subject. This fact too is one that provides new vistas in understanding the entire subject.

Many today seem confident in the idea that some of the books within the New Testament, which bear the names of apostles themselves, are in fact pseudonymous — a clever term that is supposed to cover up the fact that these documents were total forgeries — written in the name of the apostles, yet decades after they lived. The implication of this theory is that, not only did the New Testament slowly evolve, but that Christian doctrine continued to slowly evolve and develop over the course of three centuries. Therefore, using this reasoning as a guide, for example, and since the development of the doctrine of the Holy Trinity took three centuries to develop, then it is this argument that is used to prove that the canon likewise slowly developed. Or conversely, if the canon took three centuries to develop, then certainly slow doctrinal development is to be taken as a matter of fact. Such is the circular reasoning exercise that continues to plague the truth of the story *Beyond Acts*.

As we have already said, scholars look vainly for evidence of how the canon was developed in post apostolic times and they cannot produce anything that is credible history on the matter. Where are the conferences? Where are the debates? Where is the evidence that the Church at Rome was at all concerned with what the canon should consist of until the end of the fourth century?

It was some 300 years after the death of the last apostle — the Apostle John — that the church finally agreed upon what already was in existence. Yet, the canon was not established in 397 C.E. — it was only reaffirmed at that time! Anyone who says that the canon was only established in the fourth century is way off base. This is why it is time that the truth of what the apostles were doing, after the *Book of Acts* closed, be made known from the internal evidence that scholars have for so long ignored and/or rejected.

Therefore, what this book intends to do is to lay at the feet of those who wish to get another perspective on post-Acts history. It is here, hopefully, that this work will stimulate new research that finds renewed direction into areas not generally explored. I am confident that many will be inspired to find a new dimension in biblical understanding that is far more refreshing than what is being taught by scholars and even clerics today. Once this is seen, then the New Testament books themselves will take on new meaning.

Moreover, the purpose of this book is to investigate alternative scenarios to New Testament history based on the internal evidence, as well as the many neglected and spurned external sources that have not been generally given much attention.

This book is dedicated to new readers with open minds that are uncluttered with traditional false teachings, as well as the more menacing modern mythologies that are beginning to spread in some circles. In stating this, therefore, it is important to realize that it is not the purpose of this book to somehow convince scholars or clerics or adherents of traditional orthodoxy, of the truthfulness that we are here proposing. Indeed, it is anticipated that this book will receive a fair amount of criticism from both the scholarly community and the orthodox Christian community. This is to be expected, since this book intends to be controversial in nature and intends to upset the apple cart of prevalent and dominant theories to the contrary. Nevertheless, this author stands firm on his own scholarship. I have done my homework.

The readers of this book are therefore challenged from the start to keep an open mind to what they may encounter within its pages. The reader may choose to believe or disbelieve what is presented herein, but, at least now, the truth seeking student of New Testament history will be given some additional food for thought in settling on a credible history that this author feels has just as much right and merit to being imparted as anything yet proposed.

Another very important aspect that will be addressed is that New Testament History stretches far beyond the borders of Palestine. Where it will lead us is far more amazing than what we read in most conventional histories of the New Testament. Let the reader judge for themselves what we are about to embark upon and its revolutionary impact on New Testament studies.

The author feels that had this book not been written, the general public would have been denied some of the most fascinating alternative theories that are being discussed in literature that rarely makes its way to them. These alternative ideas are just as viable as those proposed by most mainstream scholars today. In fact, the pieces of the puzzle far better fit a realistic, cohesive picture presented herein than what is generally offered. Indeed, it is essential to the accurate understanding of New Testament doctrine that this story be told.

This being said, it is time that we take a brave new look at the history of the first century "Christianity" as we journey *Beyond Acts*. Our journey begins now.

P. R. F.
Palm Bay, Florida
July, 2003

CHAPTER 1

The Apostolic Drama Begins

AFTER THE RESURRECTION AND ASCENSION OF Jesus, on the day of Pentecost in the year of 30 C.E., the apostles, along with the relatives and followers of Jesus, witnessed a tremendous growth of those who followed what they called at that time "The Way" (Acts 2:47).[1] Indeed, Luke records that shortly after this miraculous event had occurred, the number of believers had reached a staggering 5000 (Acts 4:4).

This incredible growth was more than the Jewish authorities, who had thought that they exterminated the Messianic cult of Jesus with Jesus' crucifixion, could stand. As a result, it didn't take long before the Apostles Peter and John were apprehended by these Jewish religious authorities and thrown into prison. But they could not be held for very long because of the great support that the apostles now had with the majority of the people.

Acts 5:14 goes on to say that "Yet more than ever believers were added to the Lord, *great numbers* of both men and women." Again, the High Priests "took action" (Acts 5:17) to do something about this threatening trend. The apostles were rounded up and again put into public prison. But

---

[1] Luke carefully calls the followers of Jesus, those who were adhering to his teachings, as those who followed "The Way," echoing back to numerous Old Testament references, such as 2 Sam 22:31: "This God – his *way* is perfect;" Prov 6:23: "For the commandment is a lamp and the teaching a light, and the reproofs of discipline are the *way* of life;" Isa 30:21: "This is the *way*, walk ye in it." Jesus is quoted as saying in John 14:6 "I am the *way*, and the truth, and the life." Notice further that Luke's distinction is marked by the fact that the followers of Jesus were not called "Christians" until Acts 11:26, by outsiders in Antioch, where it appears to be a slur word, a derogatory term for the followers of Jesus that was all but flattering. F.F. Bruce, *New Testament History* (New York: Doubleday, 1969), 213, notes: "If we call the early disciples 'Christians', we may use this as a term of convenience, but such use at this stage is an anachronism. The name 'Christian" did not come into use until the Gentile mission began, several years later; it was Greek-speaking inhabitants of Syrian Antioch who coined it. The disciples themselves called their movement 'The Way'; to their fellow-Jews they were known as Nazarenes…" For a good discussion concerning the Nazarene phenomenon, see Ray Pritz, et al., *Nazarene Jewish Christianity: From the End of the New Testament Period until its Disappearance in the Fourth Century* (Jerusalem: Magness Press, 1995).

this plan was once again thwarted, we are told, because an angel supernaturally released the apostles. And what did the apostles do? They boldly went right back and taught in the temple in utter defiance to the Jewish religious authorities. There is a sense here that the apostles felt that they were untouchable and had the backing of divine protection on their side.

Again, the apostles were apprehended by the Jewish authorities and thrown into prison. However, this time the famous Pharisee Gamaliel[2] warned the Sanhedrin with his ever so memorable wise admonition that if this phenomenon was a matter of men, then it will amount to nothing, but if it is truly of God, no one can fight it (Acts 5:33-9). In other words, don't tempt the hand of fate until you are sure that this is not a real movement from God. Why would he say such a thing? One almost senses that even Gamaliel was beginning to question his own conscience concerning the miraculous events, and he feared that the Jewish authorities might be witnessing something that was far more than they were willing to acknowledge.[3]

The Council, respecting Gamaliel's advice, reluctantly acquiesced for the time being, and allowed the apostles once again to go free. And no sooner were Peter and John released than they were right back at the temple to "proclaim Jesus as the Messiah" (Acts 5:42). Additionally, the *Book of Acts* tells us that at this time

> the word of God continued to be spread; the number of the disciples increased greatly in Jerusalem, and a great many of the priests became obedient to the faith (Acts 6:7).

Now, even some within the priesthood of the temple were beginning to follow the teaching of the apostles. If the Sanhedrin were willing to give Gamaliel's advice a little time in deference to his authority, time had now run out. It appears that the advice of Gamaliel must now be abandoned because unless this unprecedented growth were to be checked, then the entire religious establishment of the Jews would be threatened.

Isn't it surprising that so many within the Jewish religious community

---

[2] Gamaliel the Elder (Rabban Gamliel ha-Zaken) was the son of Shimon and grandson of Hillel the Elder, who was a descendant of King David (*JT Taan.* 4:2; cf. *Kes.* 62, BR 33.3, *Tos.* to *Sanh.* 5). He is said to have taught and judged in the *Lishkas ha-Gazis* (Chamber of Hewn Stones) in the temple (*Mish. Peah* 2:6). He was president of the Sanhedrin at this time, and thus his opinions carried the weight of the Pharisaic School that counter-balanced that of the priesthood (the School of Shammai). The Mishnah relates that "when Rabban Gamliel ha-Zaken died, the glory of the Torah ceased and purity and separation [*perishus*] perished" (*Mish. Sota* 9:15, 49). Luke tells us that the Apostle Paul had studied under him (Acts 22:3).

[3] Robert Eisenman, *James, the Brother of Jesus* (New York: Viking Penguin, 1997), 607, notes: "In Acts 5:38, Gamaliel is someone who urges a more deliberate policy in dealing with 'these men', while in *Recognitions* 1.65, he is a secret supporter."

would accept Jesus as the Messiah of the Hebrew Scriptures, in the light of his ignominious crucifixion?[4] This must point to the fact that many of these people, including the priesthood, were eyewitnesses to the most extraordinary event in human history – the resurrection and ascension of Jesus. Either that, or they personally knew people whose united testimony convinced them of that fact.

F. F. Bruce has some insightful remarks concerning what the apostles were up against at this time:

> The handicap with which the disciples embarked upon their public witness to Jesus can scarcely be exaggerated. They were bound to compromise themselves in the eyes of the Romans by proclaiming themselves the followers of a man whose execution had followed his conviction in a Roman court on a charge of sedition. And the idea of commending to their fellow-Jews as the long expected Messiah of Israel a man who had been crucified would, on all rational grounds, have been ruled out as absurd and scandalous. A crucified Messiah was a contradiction in terms. Practically by definition, the Messiah of Israel was one on whom the divine favour rested in an unparalleled degree; equally by definition, a crucified man was one on whom the divine disfavor rested, for the sentence stood unambiguously in the Torah: 'a hanged man is accursed by God' (Deut. 21:23). To many Jews the suggestion that the crucified Jesus was the Messiah must have been intolerably blasphemous. Yet the followers of Jesus, freely acknowledging that their Master had been crucified, maintained that, by raising him from the dead, God had reversed the death-sentence passed upon him together with all that that death-sentence implied. To Jesus' resurrection they themselves could bear first-hand witness, and Old Testament *testimonia* were available to prove that his resurrection marked him out as the promised Messiah.[5]

[4] What an amazing testimony to the resurrection of Jesus that many in the priesthood were now becoming believers. It is interesting that Luke punctuates this section of Acts (the growth of the church) with the fact that many in the priesthood became followers of the faith just before the story of Stephen. Stephen denounced the efficacy of the temple. If the priesthood accepted the resurrection story, the very sole of Judaism was now on the line.

[5] F. F. Bruce, *New Testament History* (New York: Doubleday, 1971), 211-12.

The Resurrection Faith

HOW DO WE EXPLAIN THE PHENOMENAL GROWTH that the early Church experienced? In order to understand what was happening, we have to put ourselves back to the time when these events occurred.

The disciples of Jesus had forsaken their prior professions and followed Jesus for some three years. But when Jesus was arrested just before Passover in the year of 30 C.E. by a blood-thirsty mob, then brought before a Roman governor, tried by Jewish authorities, then whipped, stoned, beaten, spat upon, jeered at, mocked at with a crown of thorns, and finally speared to death, the disciples "forsook him and fled" (Mark 14:50).

Jesus had been crucified on a tree and hung as the ignominious "cursed thing" (cf. Deut 21:23; Gal 3:13). He had been convicted of the crime of blasphemy; therefore, worthy of the most disgraceful punishment that was possible. Now, the story of Jesus as the predicted Messiah of the Hebrew Scriptures had ended in total disgrace and humiliation. The disciples must have asked themselves, how could this be? Didn't Jesus have the power to heal the sick, walk on water, feed thousands, calm raging storms, and raise people from the dead? Why could not Jesus muster up divine power and thwart his enemies? The disciples of Jesus had banked all of their hopes and their very lives on Jesus. Now, everything seemed to be for nothing. They must have been in a state of total shock over the events that had just transpired.

Peter, only days before all of this, said to Jesus:

> 'Even though I must die with you, I will not deny you.' AND SO SAID *ALL* THE DISCIPLES (Matt 26:35).

Jesus, of course, knew that Peter not only would deny his master, but would in fact do so on three separate occasions (v. 34). It wasn't long afterward that Peter was put to the test on the night that Jesus was arrested. Peter was spotted by a hand-maiden of the Priests who said to him:

> "You also were with Jesus, the man from Nazareth." But he denied it, saying, "I do not know or understand what you are talking about." ...[Later on] the servant girl, on seeing him, began again to say to the bystanders, "This is one of them." But again he denied it. Then after a little while the bystanders again said to Peter, "Certainly you are one of

> them, for you are a Galilean." But he began to curse, and he swore an oath, "I do not know this man you are talking about" (Mark 14:67-71).

The story would have been over at the crucifixion of Jesus, except for the fact that something out of the ordinary happened that was so profound upon the apostles and witnesses to the crucifixion and burial of Jesus, that in less than two months time, these frightened and humiliated men returned back to the public's eye as bold champions of a newly established faith.

Jesus had returned to life, just as he said he would, after three days of being dead. How could this be possible? This not only defies the laws of nature and science, but it can only be seen as something that could never be explained by human reasoning or science. Yet, as a result of Jesus' reappearances to the disciples and to no less than five hundred witnesses (1 Cor 15:6), many became believers.

What a Difference 50 Days Makes

THE 11 DISCIPLES OF JESUS WERE NO LONGER frightened little lambs. They now had been transformed into mighty and bold lions of a new religious faith. They no longer feared the Romans. They no longer feared the Jews. They boldly went straight on with the utmost sense of mission than anyone could ever have. They were all unified with no hesitancy on any of the disciple's part. Why?

Leon Morris observes:

> It is important to realize the depths out of which faith came. The crucifixion had crushed the disciples. One may argue that the appearances engendered a contagious and growing enthusiasm. But how did it start? Apparently no follower of Jesus retained faith and optimism after the crucifixion. Only gloom and emptiness prevailed, and these elements did not produce a contagious faith. But what happened on Easter morning made the difference.[6]

It was on the day of Pentecost in 30 C.E. that the church of Jesus was born. And not long after that event, the apostles went on a world-wide campaign to preach the gospel message concerning the resurrection of

[6] Leon Morris, "The Resurrection of Jesus Christ," in *The International Standard Bible Encyclopedia* (Grand Rapids: Eerdmans, 1979), 4:151.

Jesus and what it meant to everyone in the plan of God.

Ernest L. Martin observes:

> All eleven of the original apostles were consistent in their teaching. Is it possible to believe that they were all lying? The understanding of basic human psychology suffices against our believing that eleven individual men could one after another deceptively tell a crowd they once feared that Christ was now alive from the dead. They were jeopardizing their lives before that crowd by preaching Christ's resurrection.[7]

By the end of the first century, the momentum had gained such strength by these apostolic campaigns far and wide that it resulted in the birth of a new world religion. By the second century, churches were established all over the Roman Empire. Millions became believers in the fact of the resurrection of Jesus. It would certainly defy all rationale to believe that such a phenomenon could take hold so quickly, if not for the fact that the original message of the apostles had shown everyone of their absolute conviction concerning this fact – especially as expressed in their writings.

Peter lived nearly four decades after the resurrection of Jesus, as well as many of the other apostles. Their continued conviction all the rest of their lives resulted in one thing: people were at least satisfied that the apostles were absolutely convinced about the resurrection of Jesus.[8] Indeed, the Apostle Paul, writing twenty-four years after the resurrection, challenged the Corinthian congregation to look up some of the living 500 witnesses to the resurrection (1 Cor 15:6) in order to verify the veracity of his testimony of the resurrection of Jesus.[9] How could he leave himself so wide open to censure if what he wrote was not true?

Leon Morris notes:

---

[7] Ernest L. Martin, "Design and Development of the Holy Scripture" (Ph.D. diss., Ambassador College Graduate School of Theology, 1965, 1971), 20-21.

[8] William Lane Craig, "Did Jesus Rise from the Dead?" in *Jesus under Fire: Modern Scholarship Reinvents the Historical Jesus.* Michael J. Wilkins and J. P. Moreland, eds. (Grand Rapids: Zondervan, 1995), 154, notes: "Roman historian A. N. Sherwin-White remarks that in classical historiography the sources are usually biases and removed at least one or two generations or even centuries from the events they narrate, but historians still reconstruct with confidence what happened (A. N. Sherwin-White, *Roman Society,* 190). In the Gospels, by contrast, the tempo is "unbelievable" for the accrual of legend; more generations are needed (Vincent Taylor, *The Formation of the Gospel Tradition,* 2d ed. [London: Macmillan, 1935], 92-92). The writings of Herodotus enable us to test the tempo of myth-making, and the test suggests that *even two generations are too short a span to allow the mythical tendency to prevail over the hard historic core of oral tradition.* Such a gap with regard to the Gospel traditions would land us in the second century, precisely when the apocryphal Gospels began to originate."

> Importantly Paul made the claim early, for his letters, the oldest available documents that record this claim, were written within twenty or thirty years of Jesus' death. Paul says that "most" of the five hundred to whom Jesus appeared were still alive (1 Cor. 15:6); thus they could be interrogated. That there is no evidence of any serious attempt to refute the testimony to the resurrection is significant.[10]

The Apostle Peter, on the day of Pentecost and the birthday of the church, could now go daringly before all of Jerusalem and give a powerful testimony to what he had seen happen:

> Jesus of Nazareth, a man attested to you by God with deeds of power, wonders, and signs that God did through him among you, AS YOU YOURSELVES KNOW – this man, handed over to you according to the definite plan and foreknowledge of God, you crucified ...But GOD RAISED HIM UP, having freed him from death. ...David spoke of the resurrection of the Messiah, saying, 'He was not abandoned to Hades, nor did his flesh experience corruption [Ps 16:10].' THIS JESUS GOD RAISED UP, AND OF THAT ALL OF US ARE WITNESSES (Acts 2:22, 23, 24, 30-32).

Now we see the disciples, instead of being like the cowering bunch that they were when they had fled the crucifixion scene, had the courage to come back and face the Romans and the Jews head on. They could now, undauntedly, face beatings, jail, torture, and ultimately martyrdom. Why? Why on earth would anyone do so to support a myth? What

---

[9] The fact that Paul ends this passage with "most of whom are still living" begs the invitation for people to go and check Paul out on this fact. Again, William Lane Craig (ibid.) notes: "The witnesses listed in 1 Corinthians 15 continued to live and move in the early community and would exercise a control over the appearance traditions. Similarly, if persons like Mary Magdalene and the women did not see Jesus, it is difficult to see how the early tradition could arise and continue in opposition to the better knowledge of first generation believers." Obviously, the Apostle Paul would not subject himself to the ridicule of being exposed as a liar if he were trying to promote a myth. Nevertheless, we cannot help ourselves in citing Burton Mack's strange appraisal of Paul's resurrection conviction: "It was Paul who focused attention on 'the cross' (1 Cor. 1:18) instead of the resurrection and who added an apocalyptic framework to the mythology of Jesus Christ as lord. He did this to counter a fascination with the mythology of the resurrection he thought dangerous." It should be apparent to anyone who has the ability to read and understand the thrust of First Corinthians 15 that the Jesus Seminar revisionists are completely out of touch with the message of the Apostle Paul. The relationship between Paul's understanding of the cross and the resurrection is: "For while we were enemies, we were reconciled to God through the death of his Son, MUCH MORE SURELY, having been reconciled, will we be SAVED BY HIS LIFE" (Rom 5:10).

[10] Leon Morris, ibid.

possible motivation would there be on their part (or anyone's for that matter) to risk death for a myth? Are we to believe that every one of them did such an amazing turn of about face because of what they all knew to be a total lie? Indeed, after being flogged by the Jewish authorities, we see that

> Peter and the apostles ...rejoiced that they were considered worthy to suffer dishonor for the sake of the name [Jesus]. And every day in the temple and at home they did not cease to teach and proclaim Jesus as the Messiah (Acts 5:29, 41-2).

Again, Leon Morris notes:

> What caused this astounding transformation? It must have taken hard evidence to convince people like Peter, Thomas, and Paul. Yet they were convinced that Jesus had risen. That people were imprisoned and that Stephen and James suffered death is significant. People do not usually run such risks unless they are very sure of themselves. When confronted with such great perils they are apt to look for an alternative explanation of that for which they may be put to death. But the disciples were quite firm. They were sure of the Resurrection.[11]

The growing phenomenon of the follower's of the Way was due to the fact that the resurrection of Jesus was seen as a reality by hundreds of witnesses. As witnesses to these events that the apostles wrote about, they spread the "Word" fully aware that they would be facing martyrdom. What greater testimony to the truth of their message can there be?

THE RESURRECTION AND MODERN CRITICS

TODAY, THERE ARE MANY WHO BELIEVE THAT the gospel message of the resurrected Jesus is all a fabricated myth. They would not only have you believe that the disciples died for a lie, but that they did it KNOWINGLY. But is this truth, or are modern critics, who were certainly not there to witness the facts, guilty of creating their own modern myths in order to justify their predisposed agnosticism? One thing is certain. Critics cannot be said to have the persuasive argument on

[11] Leon Morris, ibid.

their side in this debate. Let us see why.

What modern critics believe is that the gospel writers consistently lied (a vice that they totally condemned, by the way), yet, they all were willing to give up their lives in order to sustain this lie. Even if we were to imagine that one or two of the disciples would be guilty of such a thing, what are the chances that all of the disciples would go in on this farce, all the while facing martyrdom? Would you? Certainly, the reality is that the apostles were not a bunch of liars, but eyewitnesses to historical truth!

Let us understand that the execution of Jesus was not done in a vacuum. It was done in the capital of the Roman province of Judea at the time of one of the great Jewish pilgrimage feasts known as Passover. Josephus tells us that in the first century, as many as two million people would throng the city of Jerusalem just to attend one of these annual festival gatherings (Josephus, *B.J.* 6.9.3 [422-26]). This means that there were multiple thousands of eyewitnesses to Jesus' crucifixion from all over the Empire. And, these same people were well aware of the fact that the disciples of Jesus had fled the scene, had abandoned their mentor, and went into seclusion.

The next annual festival gathering that was to occur in the Jewish religious calendar was the Feast of Shavuoth (Pentecost), which occurred 50 days after the Sabbath within the Feast of Unleavened Bread. Many of the same pilgrims that were there at Passover returned to Jerusalem for Shavuoth. These same witnesses must have been startled to see all eleven of Jesus' disciples back in total visual display, but now completely transformed.[12]

The Synoptic Gospels record the fact that Peter and the rest of the apostles all fled as cowards at the crucifixion of Jesus. This is important to realize because the printed gospel accounts were distributed within the lifetime of many of these pilgrims who could verify the authenticity of the statements that the apostles were making.

Even critical scholars concede that the *Book of Acts* was written within the contemporary lifetime of thousands of eyewitnesses to the testimony given therein. Luke would have exposed himself as a complete charlatan of the highest caliber if he dared record anything that could be challenged by those who knew the facts to be otherwise. Indeed, Luke goes out on a limb by initially stating that

> since many have undertaken to set down an orderly account of the events that have been fulfilled among us, just as they

---

[12] These witnesses consisted of devout Jews from "every nation" (Acts 2:5) i.e., Parthia, Media, Elam, Mesopotamia, Judea, Cappadocia, Pontus, Asia, Phrygia, Pamphylia, Egypt, Libya, Cyrene, Rome, Crete, and Arabia (Acts 2:9-11).

> were handed on to us by those who from the beginning were EYEWITNESSES and servants of the word, I too decided, AFTER INVESTIGATING EVERYTHING CAREFULLY from the very first, to write an orderly account (Luke 1:13).

This fact in itself makes the testimony of *Luke-Acts* a reliable document. Again, Leon Morris notes:

> C. F. D. Moule argued this convincingly. He pointed to the fact that the Church was created by the preaching that the Messiah Jesus had been crucified but had risen from the dead. Moule asked, "If the coming into existence of the Nazarenes, a phenomenon undeniably attested by the NT, rips a great hole in history, a hole of the size and shape of the Resurrection, what does the secular historian propose to stop it with?" (*Phenomenon of the NT* [1967], p. 3).[13]

The fact of the matter is that critical scholarship, with all of its intellect, has never been able to adequately account for the fact of the phenomenon of the testimony of the Apostle's conviction about the resurrection. It is not something that can ever be tested to scientific satisfaction. And that is just the point. It is the New Testament itself that confidently spurns such evidence. It unabashedly demands belief in the testimony of Jesus' disciples. This is why it is important to understand the story of *Beyond Acts* and the reason why the writings of the New Testament are trustworthy. And this is the very story that we will be telling within the following pages.

THE TESTIMONY OF THE APOSTLE PAUL

NO GREATER TESTIMONY TO THE RESURRECTION of Jesus is there than that of the Apostle Paul. He was originally the great persecutor of the church (Acts 8:3; 9:1). From the accounts, it is obvious that no one was more convinced of the unresurrection of Jesus than he was. He was not only trained in Judaic theology, but being from Tarsus, a center for stoic philosophy, he was well acquainted with the classical works of the Gentiles. No one was more unlikely to accept the fact of Jesus' resurrection than he was.

[13] Leon Morris, ibid., 152.

Yet, this man of lofty intellect had his mind changed for him in a miraculous way (Acts 9:3-5). And his well trained mind could now accept the many proofs that were right there in the Hebrew Scriptures from which he was taught. From being the chief persecutor of the church, now Paul became the best propagator of Jesus' resurrection than anyone else. Indeed, Paul became so fervent in the belief of the resurrection of Jesus, that he "turned the world upside down" (Acts 17:6) in order to demonstrate this fact. Therefore, Paul is probably the greatest testimony to the truth of the resurrection than anyone in the entire New Testament.

Nevertheless, prior to his conversion, the Apostle Paul was the chief antagonist to the "Way." His persecution of the early believers had driven many of them out of the Jerusalem area. And this brings up a very important question: What happened to the closest friends and relatives of Jesus, such as the Mother of Jesus, Joseph of Arimathea, Lazarus, Mary Magdalene, Martha, and others? They totally disappeared without a trace in the *Book of Acts* and the entire New Testament. What happened to them? Can we know? In order for us to answer this question, we have to do what the title of this book impels us to do – to go *Beyond Acts*. There are persistent traditions that we must address that tell a story of their own. Therefore, this will be the subject of our investigation in the next chapter.

CHAPTER 2

The First Scattering

THE SAULIAN PERSECUTION BRINGS US TO THE shores of lands far beyond the dusty roads of Judea. The closest inner circle of Jesus' friends, lead by Jesus' uncle and adopted father, Joseph of Arimathea,[14] were a part of the first scattering of the faithful due to persecution.

After Joseph of Arimathea's brief appearance in the Bible, he disappears from biblical tradition and steps into the romantic legends of the Holy Grail, King Arthur and Glastonbury, England. The summary legends involved the following:

> The Glastonbury Legend asserts that the Christian faith was brought by St. Joseph of Arimathea in the year A.D. 63 (or even earlier, between A.D. 40 and 50, as one version claims). Joseph had been sent by his friend and leader, the Apostle Philip, who had just completed the conversion of Gaul, to carry the faith to the neighboring Britons. Accompanied by a band of followers, he brought with him the Holy Grail, the sacred chalice of the last Supper, which Pontius Pilate had given to him, and in which, at the Crucifixion, he had collected Christ's blood, which had remained miraculously uncorrupted throughout his long journeyings. After many perils and adventures, Joseph and his companions landed

---

[14] We believe that Joseph of Arimathea was actually the brother of Mary, the mother of Jesus. After Joseph, the father of Jesus died [whose genealogy is given in Matthew 1], the elder male member of the family and a brother had to adopt his sister's unheired sons. Therefore, the genealogy given in Luke 3 is that of Jesus' adoptive father, Joseph of Arimathea. Luke preserves the adoption papers of Jesus to Joseph of Arimathea. Joseph was the son of Heli, the grandson of Matthat. Joseph's name betrays the fact that he came from the city of Matthat (Ir-Matthea). It may be that when Matthew wrote his gospel around 40 C.E., he gave the legal lineage of Joseph the "Carpenter." However, later criticism at that time about the lineage of Joseph the Carpenter, although a descendent of David, was that he was of the line of Jeconiah, whose descendents were cursed from sitting on the throne of David (Jer 22:24-30). The honored seat that Joseph of Arimathea held on the Council may have been the seat of the house of David, and thus his lineage (as well as Mary's) provides the legal path for Jesus to also sit upon the throne of David.

> somewhere in South-Western Britain, possibly on the Somerset coast, and made their way eastwards towards Glastonbury Tor, without attempting to find any earlier abiding-place. At length, approaching the Tor across the marsh, all weary with their long journeying, they rested on the rise about a mile to the south-west of Glastonbury, and ever since their halting-place has been called 'Wearyall Hill'. At the foot of the Tor, St. Joseph stopped to pray: before he knelt, he thrust his staff into the ground, and lo!, a miracle! The staff immediately took root and budded; it was a sign from heaven that he had reached Journey's end.[15]

Obviously, a certain amount of mythology has evolved around the story,[16] but there are ancient sources which attest to the central core of the tradition.[17] Much of the material has been collected by the former Vicar of the Glastonbury Abbey, Reverend Lionel Smithett Lewis.[18] Laurence Gardner also brings together some of the most notable sources that affirm these legends:

> John of Glastonbury (14th-century compiler of *Glastoniencis Chronica*) and John Capgrave (Principal of the Augustinian Friars in England 1393-1464) both quote from a book found by the Emperor Theodosius (ruled 375-395) in the Pretorium in Jerusalem. Capgrave's *De Sancto Joseph ab Arimathea* tells how Joseph was imprisoned by the Jewish elders after the Crucifixion. This is also described in the apocryphal *Acts of Pilate*. The historian Bishop Gregory of Tours (544-595) similarly mentions the post-Crucifixion imprisonment of Joseph in his *History of the Franks*. And in the 12th century it was recounted yet again in *Joseph d'Arimathie* by the Burgundian Grail chronicler Sire Robert de Boron.[19]

---

[15] R. F. Treharne, *The Glastonbury Legends* (London: The Cresset Press, 1967), 5.

[16] For an interesting study on the subject, see Valerie M. Lagorio, "The Evolving Legend of St. Joseph of Glastonbury" *Speculum* 44:2 (April, 1971): 209-32.

[17] Before we give in to the temptation of rejecting these traditions out of hand, it should be noted that many of the so-called recognized sources of ancient history, if we were to subject them to the same scrutiny, might be on shakier ground than we realize. For instance, scholars look at Dio Cassius as a recognized source of Roman history. However, as Albert A. Bell, Jr. ("The date of John's Apocalypse: The Evidence of Some Roman Historians Reconsidered" *New Testament Studies* 10 [1977-78]: 94) has noted: "About two-thirds of his work survives only in an eleventh-century epitome by the Byzantine monk Xiphilinus and a twelfth-century summary by Zonaras, secretary to the emperor Alexis I Commenus. According to E. Cary, Xiphilinus' epitome, the chief source for the Domitianic period, was made 'very carelessly'. Even in the extant portions of Dio's original work his tendency to sacrifice accuracy for rhetorical flourish is everywhere evident ..."

[18] Lionel Smithett Lewis, *St. Joseph of Arimathea at Glastonbury* (Cambridge: James Clark, 1922).

[19] Laurence Gardner, *Bloodline of the Holy Grail* (Boston: Element Books, 1997), 134.

The English historian, William of Malmesbury (ca. 1130) also makes mention of Joseph's coming to Britain:

> Now St. Philip, as Freculphus [Bishop of Lisieux, France, 825-51] testifies in his 2nd book, chapter IV, coming into the country of the Franks to preach, converted many to the Faith, and baptized them. Therefore, working to spread Christ's word, he chose twelve from among his disciples, and sent them into Britain to bring thither the good news of the Word of Life, and to preach the Incarnation of Jesus Christ after he had most devoutly spread his right hand over each. Their leader, it is said, was Philip's dearest friend, Joseph of Arimathea, who buried Our Lord.[20]

Also, a long marginal note to the first original section of William's *De Antiquitate* states

> that Joseph of Arimathea, the noble counsellor, with his son Josephes and many others, came to Greater Britain (which is now called Anglia) and there ended his life, is attested by the book of The Deeds of the famous King Arthur.[21]

Cardinal Caesar Baronius (1538-1607), who was a librarian at the Vatican, documents that he found a most ancient manuscript in which was described the exodus of Joseph and his companions. Under the section for the year 35 C.E., in his magnum opus, *Ecclesiatical Annals*, he records:

> In that year the party mentioned was exposed to the sea in a vessel without sails or oars. The vessel drifted finally to Marseilles and they were saved. From Marseilles Joseph and his company passed into Britain, and after preaching the Gospel there, died.[22]

Cardinal Baronius elsewhere lists "the party mentioned" (taken from a work from Mistral, and another ancient document supposedly in the Vatican Library during his time). The exiles with Joseph are said to have included the following people:

---

[20] As quoted in Lionel Smithett Lewis, *St. Joseph of Arimathea at Glastonbury* (Cambridge: James Clark, 1922), 185-6. See further, William of Malmesbury, *De Gestis Regum Anglorum* (J.-P. Migne, *Patrologia Latina* 174:991).

[21] As quoted in J. Armitage Robinson, *Two Glastonbury Legends* (Cambridge: Cambridge University Press, 1926), 28-9. See further, William of Malmesbury, *De antiquitate glastoniensis ecclesiae*, 1 (J.-P. Migne, *Patrologia Latina* 174:1683-1734).

[22] Caesar Baronius, *Ecclesiastical Annals*, ad annum 35, as quoted in John D. Keyser, "Joseph of Arimathea and David's Throne in Britain," online at http://hope-of-Israel.org/i000111a.htm.

St. Mary, wife of Cleopas;
St. Martha;
St. Lazarus;
St. Eutropius;
St. Salome;
St. Clean;
St. Saturninus;
St. Mary Magdalene;
Marcella, the Bethany sisters' maid;
St. Maximim;
St. Martial;
St. Trophimus;
St. Sidonius (Restitutus);
St. Joseph of Arimathea.[23]

Here we have information that is beyond the *Book of Acts* indeed and has survived only in traditional accounts. Yet, it is information that demands the attention of those who have wondered about the disappearance of these notable friends of Jesus and relatives of Jesus.

R. W. Morgan further elaborates on the Baronius quotation:

> The Vatican manuscript, quoted by Baronius in his "Ecclesiastical Annals," *ad annum* 35 (the same year in which the Acts of the Apostles state all, except the apostles, were scattered abroad from Judea). The manuscript records that in this year Lazarus, Maria Magdalene, Martha, her handmaiden Marcella, Maximin a disciple, Joseph the Decurion of Arimathea, against all of whom the Jewish people had special reasons of enmity, were exposed to the sea in a vessel without sails or oars. The vessel drifted finally to Marseilles, and they were saved. From Marseilles Joseph and his company passed into Britain, and after preaching the Gospel there, died.[24]

In another old manuscript in the Magdalen College Library at Oxford entitled *Life of St. Mary Magdalen*, originally ascribed to the French bishop of Mayence, Rabanus Maurus (776-856 C.E.), a similar story in chapter 37 is described:

> Leaving the shores of Asia and favoured by an east wind, they went round about, down the Tyrrhenian Sea, between Europe and Africa, leaving the city of Rome and all the land of Italy to the right. Then happily turning their course to the right, they came near to the city of Marseilles, in the

[23] George F. Jowett, *The Drama of the Lost Disciples* (London: Covenant Publishing Co., 1961), 70.

[24] R. W. Morgan, *St. Paul in Britain* (London: Covenant Publishing Co., 1948), 118.

> Viennoise province of the Gauls, where the River Rhone is received by the sea. There, having called upon God, the great King of all the world, they parted; each company going to the province where the Holy Spirit had directed them; presently preaching everywhere, 'the Lord working with them, confirming the word with signs following.'[25]

As the story goes, the British king, Arviragus, had become acquainted with Joseph years earlier when Joseph had administered his mining interests in Cornwall and Devon. As a result we are told that

> King Arviragus is recorded as having granted to Joseph and his followers, "twelve hides" of land, (about 1900 acres) tax free, in "Yniswitrin," described as a marshy tract – afterwards called the "Isle of Avalon." Confirmation of the Royal Charter is found in the official Doomsday Book of Britain (A.D. 1086) which states: "The Domus Dei, in the great monastery of Glastonbury, called the Secret of the Lord. This Glastonbury Church possesses, in its own villa XII hides of land which have never paid tax." (Doomsday Survey folio p. 249 b). This notable act of the King gave the recipients many British concessions, including the right of citizenship with its privileges of freedom to pass unmolested from one district to another in time of war. The grant was given to them as "Judean refugees." (Quidam advanae-' certain strangers' – old Latin – in Later Latin, "Culdich" or Anglicized, "Culdees").[26]

Tradition also informs us that Joseph, having gained legal title to the land from King Arviragus, built the first Christian church, made from wattle[27] daubed with mud. Joseph is said to have been ordained by the Apostle Philip, and, thereafter, Joseph became the apostle to the Britons.

A further tradition is recorded in Maelgwyn of Llandaff (ca. C.E. 450, uncle of St. David):

> Joseph of Arimathaea, the noble decurion, received his everlasting rest with his eleven associates in the Isle of Avalon. He lies in the southern angle of the bifurcated line of the Oratorium of the Adorable Virgin. He has with him the two white vessels of silver which were filled with the blood and the sweat of the great Prophet Jesus.[28]

---

[25] As quoted by J. W. Taylor, *The Coming of the Saints* (London: Covenant Publishing Co., 1969), 90.

[26] E. Raymond Capt, *The Traditions of Glastonbury* (Thousand Oaks, Calif.: Artisan Sales, 1983), 41.

[27] Wattle: "1. A woven work of sticks intertwined with twigs or branches" *Webster's New World Compact Desk Dictionary and Style Guide*. Michael Agnes, ed. (New York: MacMillan, 1998), 486.

APOSTLES IN FRANCE?

AS TO THE TRADITION OF LAZARUS BECOMING the first bishop of Marseilles, it is found in other manuscripts in the Bodleian. Roger of Hovedon (ca. 1174-1201) recorded:

> Marseilles is an Episcopal city under the dominion of the King of Aragon. Here are the relics of St. Lazarus ...who held the Bishopric here for seven years after Jesus had restored him from the dead.[29]

Marseilles is not all that far from Rome. If it is possible for the apostles to reach Rome, it is a small step to reach Marseilles. The traditions tell us that in the three years that Joseph and his companions spent in France, they progressed up the Rhone valley through Figeac, Roc Amadour, Limoges and finally to Morlaix on the Britanny coast. From there they sailed to what is now Falmouth, England. And then travelled to the west coast of Britain.

Gladys Taylor writes:

> Irenaeus, born c. 120 in Asia Minor, came closer to us than any others of his contemporaries. He was a pupil of Polycarp, Bishop of Smyrna, who was himself the pupil of St. John the Apostle. He travelled to France where he took the office of Pothinus, the martyred Bishop of Lyons. Dr. Leighton Pullan tells us, 'S. Irenaeus is himself the best evidence of Christianity in the south of Gaul. The faith had come thither from Asia Minor and found a home among people of Greek speech. Greek, it must be remembered, was the official language of Marseilles until the fifth century, and even now it has left traces in the dialects of southern France. Irenaeus, however, was surrounded by Celtic converts, and diligently spoke the Celtic language for their benefit. He spoke with authority of 'the apostles planting churches among the Celts.'[30]

That Gaul was early the object of an evangelizing undertaking by the

---

[28] Quoted from Morgan, *Paul in Britain,* 117. The vessel, of course, is what has become known in tradition as the "Holy Grail."

[29] Quoted from E. Raymond Capt, *Traditions,* 38. Ivor Fletcher, *Incredible History,* 50, relates that John Bloom of London, conducting excavations under a license granted by Edward the Third, claimed to have discovered Joseph's body at Glastonbury in 1345.

[30] Gladys Taylor, *Our Neglected Heritage: the Early Church* (London: Covenant Publishing Co., 1969), 1:17.

apostles, we should also consider the following: When the Apostle Paul stated that Crescens[31] had gone to Galatia (2 Tim 4:10), he was making this statement during his imprisonment at Rome (not in Caesarea, as some believe). If that is the case, then Crescens would certainly have been a lot closer to Gaul than the Roman Province of Galatia.[32] And, in fact, there is testimony that Crescens indeed went to Gaul, and not to Galatia. L. S. Lewis concurs with this assessment:

> It is quite important to know that the Churches of Vienne and Mayenence in Gaul claim Crescens as their founder. This goes far to corroborate that Galatia in II Timothy iv, 10, means Gaul, and not its colony Galatia in Asia, and that Isodore meant to say that St. Philip preached to the Gauls, and not to the Galatians of Asia.[33]

Also, Reverend Lewis again notes that the church Father, Epiphanius (315-407 C.E.), bishop of Salamis, understood that the term Galatia in the Gospels actually referred to Gaul and not to the Asia Minor Roman Province of Galatia in Asia Minor. Epiphanius wrote:

> The ministry of the divine word having been entrusted to St. Luke, he exercised it by passing into Dalmatia, into Gaul, into Italy, into Macedonia, but principally into Gaul, so that St. Paul assures him in his epistles about some of his disciples – 'Crescens,' said he, 'is in Gaul.' In it must not be read in Galatia as some have falsely thought, but in Gaul (Epiphanius, *Pan.* 51.11).[34]

Notice that even in Epiphanius' time there was already confusion as to where Crescens went. Epiphanius cleared up that confusion, as did Eusebius: "Paul testifies that Crescens was sent to Gaul" (*Hist. eccl.* 3.4.9).[35]

Reverend Lewis again adds:

> We have seen that the *Recognitions of Clement* (2nd century) stated that St. Clement of Rome, going to Caesarea, found St. Joseph of Arimathea there with St. Peter, Lazarus, the

---

[31] An apparent co-worker of Paul during his Roman imprisonment.

[32] Florence Morgan Gillman, "Crescens," *The Anchor Bible Dictionary,* David Noel Freedman, ed., [New York: Doubleday, 1992], 1:1206, writes "If the imprisonment it portrays was Rome, proximity to Gaul makes it the more probable destination of Crescens; a Caesarean imprisonment, in contrast, would favor reading 'Galatia.' "

[33] L. S. Lewis, *Traditions,* 113.

[34] Quoted from L. S. Lewis, *Traditions,* 114.

[35] Although the manuscript tradition for the most part favors "Galatia," the Codex Sinaiticus and Codex C actually read Gaul, rather than Galatia.

> Holy Women and others, a quite likely place for the start of the voyage of St. Joseph and the home of St. Philip in the Bible story. Afterwards tradition brings him to France, whence he sent St. Joseph to Britain. William of Malmesbury, quoting Freculphus, calls Joseph, St. Philip's "dearest friend". They must have been in close association. Tradition brings the Holy Woman and St. Joseph to France. All the way up the Rhone Valley, as we have seen, from Marseilles to Mortaix [sic: Morlaix], we find constant memories of the occupants of that boat without oars and sails. From Morlaix in Brittany it is a short step to Cornwall in Britain. The route from Marseilles must have been known well to St. Joseph. It was that of his fellow traders, seeking ore. From Cornwall an ancient road led to the mines of Mendip, remains of which exist. Arviragus's reception of St. Joseph, though unconverted, suggests a very possible previous acquaintance."[36]

From the above information we have traditions that make Joseph of Arimathea a Nobleman, a Decurion, a prominent individual within the Roman Empire. He was able to freely move about the Roman Empire and had official connections that allowed him to bring with him his entourage of closest friends. He was rich and respected among Roman officials and was a protected Roman citizen, once he was out of the sphere and grasp of the High Jewish authorities.

The traditions are strong that Joseph of Arimathea, along with many of the closest friends of Jesus and some of his disciples had left Judea during the Saulian Persecution around the year of 35 C.E. and first went to Marseilles, France, and then Joseph went on to Britain in the year of 37 C.E.

The "Saulian Persecution," as we should refer to it, was far more severe than has been generally recognized. It was severe enough to cause a widespread dispersion of Jesus' closest friends and relatives. As a result, the first spreading of the gospel message took place.[37] The famous church historian, Eusebius of Caesarea, tells us that the apostles had penetrated Rome, Persia, Armenia, Parthia, Scythia, India, "and some crossed the Ocean and reached the Isles of Britain."[38]

---

[36] L. S. Lewis, *Traditions*, 115-116.

[37] Jack Finegan, *Handbook*, 373, notes: "Acts relates that the subsequent general persecution [after Stephen's martyr] actually gave a new impetus to Christian missionary activity." E. Glenn Hinson, *The Early Church* (Nashville: Abingdon, 1996), 44, writes: "Christianity might have sundered its bonds with Judaism more slowly had persecution not scattered the Jerusalem community far and wide (Acts 8:1). The leader of the onslaught was the Pharisee Saul of Tarsus (Acts 8:3; 9:1-2; 1 Cor. 15:9; Gal. 1:13; Phil. 3:6; 1 Tim. 1:13), zealous to conserve his ancestral faith now threatened by the growth of Christianity. There can be little doubt that the faith was taking hold rapidly in Jerusalem and beyond."

The tentacles of the Arimathean traditions that reach all the way into France and Britain may have become embellished through the religious monks of the medieval period, but we have to admit that they do answer some important questions. They give us a plausible reason for the disappearance of Jesus' closest friends. We should at least allow more respect for such information for lifting our attention to *beyond* the dusty roads of Judea. If the apostles made it all the way to Rome, and the Apostle Paul as far as Spain, then there is nothing in these traditions that are so fabulous as to dismiss them out of hand. Furthermore, the British connection to the early church plays directly into the story of what the apostles were later doing *Beyond Acts*, which we will look at in a later chapter.

[38] Eusebius, *The Proof of the Gospel*, ed. and tr. by W. J. Ferrar (Grand Rapids: Baker, 1981), 130.

CHAPTER 3

The Last Days of the Temple

THE TEMPLE IN JERUSALEM WAS THE MAIN component of Mosaic religion. No understanding of first century Judaism can be gathered without a good understanding of what the temple stood for and meant to the Jewish people at that time. In the early 60's, the temple was incredibly still going on strong. The priesthood was still conducting sacrifice. There seemed to be no change in the status quo, even 30 years after the death and resurrection of Jesus.

The nagging question as to whether God's presence was still connected with the temple structure had to be on the mind of the Apostle Paul. However, the Jerusalem church at this time seems to have had no real struggle with the apparent paradox. But to the Apostle Paul, this must have been a question on his mind as to why such a paradox continued to exist.

It was probably just before the crucial year of 63 C.E. that the Apostle Paul set out to try to deal with the entire question of the temple by commissioning one of his fellow ministers (most likely Apollos) to write a reasoned argument to send to the Jerusalem-based apostles to answer some important questions in this regard. After adding some editorial remarks of his own, Paul sent this letter on to Jerusalem. This letter simply bears the title in the canon of: "To the Hebrews." But even in this treatise, it is apparent that Paul still did not have all the answers yet, as he would have later on.

Paul was probably the first apostle to come to the conclusion that the end time was far into the future. But were the apostles in Jerusalem convinced, right in the midst of temple worship, and a growing fervor of overthrowing the Roman government? Did not the prophecies say: "The Lord whom you seek will suddenly come to his temple" (Mal 2:1)? If Jesus was to return in the generation of the apostles, then it made perfect sense to the Jerusalem-based apostles that the structure of the temple had to be still standing, as they may have believed at that time.

THE SIGNIFICANCE OF THE TEMPLE

THE TEMPLE, AS A RELIGIOUS INSTITUTION, WAS where the Shekinah Glory of God of Israel dwelt. It stood for the religion of their ancestors, of Moses, and of all the holy prophets of old. No religious Jew of the first century could help but start questioning what on earth was going on with so many people turning to be followers of Jesus? The tension that was produced between the Jesus movement and the temple establishment can hardly be ignored. If God were starting a new religious order, why was the temple still allowed to carry on and function? We must pursue this question further before we can understand what was going on.

The temple was the center of first century Judaism. But Stephen suddenly comes on the scene to boldly insist that "Jesus of Nazareth will destroy this place [the temple] and will change the customs that Moses handed unto us" (Acts 6:13) and that "the Most High does not dwell in houses made with human hands" (Acts 7:48). How Jesus could destroy the temple if he was put to death was a question that no doubt was on the minds of the Jewish authorities. The conviction of the apostles was undoubtedly that the risen Jesus was soon to return as the Messiah.

Stephen certainly was ahead of his time and certainly went beyond what Peter and John dared to even address. He began attacking the very core of Judaism. We can only wonder what course the Jerusalem church would have taken if Stephen had remained alive throughout that generation. This is because Stephen's attitude was diametrically opposite with that of James the Just, who shortly afterward assumed the leadership of the Jerusalem church. James was a staunch defender of Jewish customs and temple worship.[39]

The Jewish authorities, outraged at Stephen's sermon against the holiest structure of their faith, immediately arrested Stephen on trumped up charges of speaking against Moses and God (Acts 6:11). But what they really could not tolerate is anyone daring to speak against their temple, where God's Shekinah glory was seen to still reside. Luke records Stephen's long and impassioned speech which so enraged the Jewish religious

[39] James is traditionalized as being able to enter the holy of holies on the day of Atonement (Eusebius, *Hist. eccl.* 2.23.6; Epiphanius, *Pan.* 29.4.1-3; 78.13.5-8). Thus we have a stark enigma within the early church. If Jesus' sacrifice was the sacrifice to end all sacrifices, then why was James continuing in the function of outright Judaism? It wasn't until after the death of James that the Jerusalem-based apostles, specifically Peter and John, began to move away from the influence of James the Just and finally accepted the work of the Apostle Paul. But, lest we get ahead of ourselves here, that will be discussed later on.

authorities. Arresting Stephen was not enough. In a fit of mob violence, they drug him outside of the city and stoned him to death (Acts 7:54-60).

Luke is careful to record that Stephen dies at the feet of one who is first introduced into the scriptural record by the name of Saul (v. 58).[40] It would seem that the Jewish authorities, unable to squash the apostle's growing success, had already enlisted an outside henchman to take care of the matter once and for all.

Who was this Saul? He was an influential Pharisee and a Roman citizen that apparently had the authority to be an executioner within the Roman Empire. He must have been able to operate as a freelance vigilantly, hired by the Jerusalem authorities to rid themselves of this new Messianic movement that was sweeping the Jerusalem environs.[41]

Now, persecution of the faithful to the gospel message of the Kingdom of God, as preached by Jesus and his apostles, turned into an outright crackdown which lead to the church's first martyr, Stephen. On the very day of Stephen's death, a whole turn around of events took place and a pogrom was now fully launched and underway against the followers of the "Way." This was the beginning of the first great persecution of the church.[42] And the chief executioner was this man named Saul.

> That day (the day of Stephen's murder) a severe persecution began against the church in Jerusalem, and all except the apostles were scattered throughout the countryside of Judaea and Samaria. Devout men[43] buried Stephen and made loud lamentation over him. But Saul was ravaging the church by entering house after house; dragging off both men and

---

[40] The link between the brief work of Stephen and the long career of Paul in a biography dedicated mainly to the life of the Apostle Paul seems intentional. M.-É. Boismard, "Stephen" in *The Anchor Bible Dictionary*, David Noel Freedman, ed., [New York: Doubleday, 1992], 6:210, writes: "When the author [of Acts] insists in this way on Paul's presence, might this not be to suggest that there is a link between Stephen's martyrdom and Paul's conversion (Acts 9)? ...Stephen gave his life to defend the ideal...[that] Christianity could not develop except by separating from Judaism and by putting distance between itself and the Mosaic law and the Jerusalem temple. This is the principle which Paul, having become a Christian after he had persecuted the church, would defend with tenacity (Galatians 1-2). We might say, then, that Stephen was the precursor of the apostle to the Gentiles." Indeed, Paul may have even viewed his own work as that of a reincarnation of Stephen's in view of Paul's own dedication to Stephen's dying breath (cf. Acts 7:48 with 17:24).

[41] At the time of Stephen's death, there was a virtual interregnum in the procuratorships. The powerful Pontius Pilate was no longer on the scene and was replaced by Marcelus, who apparently had less power than even the high priest. See E. Mary Smallwood, *The Jews under Roman Rule from Pompey to Diocletian: A Study in Political Relations* (Boston: Brill Academic Publishers, Inc., 2001), 172.

[42] Many believe that the great persecutions against the first Christians were carried out by Rome under Claudius, Nero, and Domitian, but hardly mention the Saulian Persecution. However, from what we see here in Acts, the Saulian Persecution was probably one of the fiercest of persecutions of the entire first century church.

women, he committed them to prison (Acts 8:1-3).

The long discourse of Stephen that is recorded in Acts shows us what a brilliant mind was lost to us in the development of Christian thought. Stephen appears to be the kind of individual who could have reshaped the direction of the Jerusalem church. Luke tells us that Stephen

> was full of grace and power, did great wonders and signs among the people. Then some of those who belonged to the synagogue of the Freedmen (as it was called), Cyrenians, Alexandrians, and others of those from Cilicia and Asia, stood up and argued with Stephen. But they could not withstand the wisdom and the Spirit with which he spoke (Acts 6:8-10).

On the heals of this we see the ministry of Philip to the Samaritans, and the beginning of the Samaritan magician Simon, who feigned conversion in order to obtain the power of the Holy Spirit (Acts 8). This is the infamous Simon Magus, who will be given attention later on. Nevertheless, the persecution of Saul now had widened to areas outside of the Jerusalem area:

> Meanwhile Saul, still breathing threats and murder against the disciples of the Lord, went to the high priest and asked him for letters to the synagogues at Damascus, so that if he found any who belonged to the Way,[44] men or women, he might bring them bound to Jerusalem (Acts 9:1-2).

It is important to realize that after about three or four years of abundant growth, now the church was experiencing unprecedented persecution and even extermination. It was nothing less than a full blown war against those who followed the teachings of Jesus. What on earth was happening to this growing phenomenon that was miraculously expanding in leaps and bounds, but was now on the run? This first great persecution of the church was resulting in the Jerusalem church being now scattered in all directions.

Saul then sought to attack those who "belonged to the Way" (Acts 9:2) to areas even outside of Judea. Was this the beginning of the persecution of the faithful that Jesus predicted would be the beginning of the events

---

[43] Who were these unnamed "devout men?" Could they have been none other than the same men behind the scenes of Jesus' own burial, i.e., Lazarus, Nicodemus and Joseph of Arimathea? Shortly after this, these people disappear from biblical history and into ancient legend. This was discussed in chapter 2.

[44] Again, the apostolic movement at first is referred to as "the Way" (see footnote 1). At this point in time the word "Christian" appears to unknown.

that signalled his return to this earth (Matt 24:9-11)? If this was so, then the apostles knew that the gospel had to be preached to all the world first as a witness. And if the end was near, then the followers of Jesus' message about the Kingdom of God coming had to be spread far and wide by his followers. This must have certainly been on the minds of the apostles at that time.

THE TEMPLE AND FIRST CENTURY JUDAISM

THE TEMPLE WAS THE KEY ELEMENT TO THE Judaic religion at the time. It is necessary to fully understand how important this structure was in order to better understand the events that lead up to the destruction of that all important structure in 70 C.E. Indeed, we must build an appreciation of that structure in the same sense that first century Jews had for it.

Herod the Great began a restoration of the second temple in his eighteenth year (18 B.C.E.).[45] The Jews told Jesus, just before Passover in 28 C.E., that the temple had been under reconstruction for a period of 46 years (John 2:20).[46] Another 36 years were spent on completing the

[45] Josephus, *A.J.* 15.11.1 [380]: "Now Herod, in the eighteenth year of his reign, ... undertook a very great work, that is, to build of himself the temple of God and make it larger in compass, and raise it to a most magnificent altitude." In *A.J.* 15.10.3 [354], he states: "Now when Herod had already reigned seventeen years, Caesar came into Syria." According to Dio Cassius, *Roman History* 54.7.4-6, Caesar came to Syria in 20 B.C.E. See Finegan, *Handbook*, 347.

[46] Counting forty-six years from 20 B.C.E. brings us to 27/28 C.E. Since this statement occurs at Passover, then it was made in 28 C.E. See Emil Schürer, *The History of the Jewish People in the Age of Jesus Christ*, (rev. and ed. Geza Vermes and Fergus Millar; Edinburgh, T&T Clark, 1973), 1:292, f.n. 12, as well as Raymond E. Brown, *The Gospel according to John* (New York: Doubleday, 1970), 1:116, and William Hendriksen, *John* (NTC 1; Grand Rapids: Baker, 1953), 126. However, the matter appears not to be such a simple one. The discussion of John P. Meier, *Marginal Jew*, 1:380-382, with notes on 417-18, is interesting, but with a disappointingly cautious conclusion: "Granted all the question marks that a study of John 2:20 unearths, my opinion is that we cannot use John 2:20 to fix an exact date for the first passover of Jesus' ministry. ...John 2:20, while plagued with too many problems to give us an exact date, does confirm the years around A.D. 27-30 as the general time span of Jesus' ministry" (382). We believe, however, that since John 2:20 is relating events of Jesus' first Passover, the simple reading of the lower date is preferred and best coincides with Josephus' statement above. Nevertheless, two leading New Testament chronologists, Jack Finegan (*Handbook*, 346-9) and Harold Hoehner, *Chronological Aspects*, 38-43, disagree and believe that the 46 years should be counted when the priests completed the initial structure of the temple in 18/17 B.C.: "*After* 18/17 B.C., forty-six years brings us to A.D. 29/30. The conversation in question between Jesus and the Jews took place at the Passover described in John 2:13-21, and this Passover is therefore to be dated in the spring of the year A.D. 30" (349).

temple, and in 64 C.E.,[47] the temple reconstruction project, which began way back by Herod the Great, finally was completed. The 26 acre complex was now one of the greatest and most beautiful structures on earth.

But besides being beautiful, there was also a certain holiness attached to that structure that, even to this day, is revered by devote Jews all around the world. This area, once the temple's holy of holies, is still believed to be sacred ground by many Jews today. And many modern Jews are still looking forward to when a new temple can be rebuilt on that very spot, and the religion of Moses be restored as it once originally was.

THE HOLINESS OF THE TEMPLE

WHAT WAS IT THAT MADE THE TEMPLE "HOLY?" What do we mean when we say that there was a certain "holiness" attached to that structure? Let us understand the principle involved here that will guide us to the correct answer. When YHVH introduced himself to Moses from a bush that appeared to be burning, God called to Moses and said

> come no closer! Remove the sandals from your feet, for the place on which you are standing is holy ground (Exod 3:5).

What made the ground that Moses stood on "holy?" The ground could only be considered holy because of the presence of God on it. And God's presence was manifested by a bright light that appeared like a fire in the bush.[48]

Consider also that when the Israelites came to the foot of Mount Sinai, they were told not to touch the mountain, including their animals, or they would face death (Exod 19:12-13; 34:3). What was it about Mt. Sinai that gave it such powers?

When Moses came down from the "Mountain," after being in the presence of God for forty days, his skin was said to shine so brightly that he had to put a veil over his face so that people could even come near him (Exod 34:29-35).[49] This "bright light" was called by later Jews the "Shekinah" – the "dwelling of God." It was so bright that it was impossible for humans to look at it, and in the time of Moses, God had to subdue its manifestation within a thick cloud (Exod 19:16). It hid the

---

[47] Finegan, *Handbook,* 348.

[48] The purpose of the bush seems to have been to subdue the brightness of the light so that it was not so blinding that it could not be seen.

Israelites from the pursuing Egyptians during the day and lighted the way at night for Israel in their march through the wilderness (Exod 13:21; 14:19-20). To the Egyptians it was a cloud of darkness, but to Israel a cloud of light. When God spoke to Moses, this thick cloud covered all of Mount Sinai (Exod 24:15-18). The purpose of the cloud was to subdue the sun's strong brightness of the Shekinah Glory of God.

The tabernacle (which was a rectangular tent with three compartments with entrances to the East) was to be set up where the Shekinah glory of God would designate a location of sojourn by ceasing to move and becoming stationary (Num 9:15-23). When the cloud (or the bright light within the cloud) began to move, it signaled that it was time for the Israelites to pack up their tents and move on to the next resting spot that the "Shekinah" would designate (Num 9:22; Exod 40:34-8).

The Tabernacle was divided into three compartments, the outer court, the holy place, and the most holy place or, as it has been later designated – "the holy of holies" (Exod 26:23). The Ark of the Covenant was situated within the holy of holies and the Shekinah hovered directly over the Ark (1 Sam 4:21-2). Later, when Solomon built the "first" temple, the Shekinah came to fill that temple (2 Chron 7:1).

Notice also, that when Jesus took Peter, James and John up to the "high Mountain," they saw a vision of the way Jesus will look in the Kingdom, with his face shining as the sun and his cloths beaming in radiant white light (Matt 17:2). During this vision a bright cloud overshadowed them (to protect their eyes) and a voice boomed out of heaven

> This is my beloved Son, in whom I am well pleased; Listen to Him (Matt 17:5).

And when Jesus ascended into Heaven after his resurrection, he was received in a "cloud," and disappeared out of their sight (Acts 1:9). We are told that when Jesus returns to this earth it is prophesied that he will return "in a cloud with power and great glory" (Luke 21:27).[50] The vision that John received depicted the risen Jesus with eyes like fire (Rev 1:14).

When King Solomon built the first temple, God consecrated that structure by having his Shekinah glory enter it in a miraculous way (2 Chron 7:1-3). When Solomon dedicated the temple God gave the nation

[49] This brightness of Moses' face was the result of being in the presence of God. In the story of Adam and Eve it is apparent that they were clothed in the glory of their maker and their bodies glowed brightly until they sinned. It would appear from the story that their sin stripped them of the cloak of God's radiant covering, and this is why they suddenly felt naked and needed to seek some other covering to hide their shame.

[50] The cloud appears to be an eye protection device.

of Israel a warning. If they were to return from God and worship other gods then God would take them out of the land. In other words – captivity. It was thus prophesied:

> And this House, which I have consecrated for my name, I will cast out of my sight, and will make it a proverb and a byword among all peoples (2 Chron 7:19-22).

THE THREE-FOLD WARNINGS

THE HISTORY OF ISRAEL SHOWS US WHAT happened concerning the above prophecy. Captivity was indeed the result of Israel turning away from the true God. Yet many do not realize that there is a biblical principle regarding punishment from God that follows a three-fold scenario of warning and final judgment. This principle is important, especially in understanding the judgments against the temple.

Ezekiel foretold that a great trial by the sword would come upon the temple. He was instructed to hold his hands together with a double sword on *THREE* different occasions (Ezek 21:14). This three-fold warning was to tell the Jewish people that a three-fold sign of overturning the Davidic kingdom would occur until a single Davidic King would arise whose right it was to wear the crown permanently (Ezek 21:25-7).

Notice also in Jeremiah this three-fold judgment of God:

> O Land, Land, Land, hear the word of the LORD (Jer 22:29).

When the people heard Jeremiah's predictions about the temple being overthrown, they responded by saying that the temple would never be overthrown. But Jeremiah rebuked them by saying

> do not trust in these deceptive words: "This is the temple of the LORD, the temple of the LORD, the temple of the LORD" (Jer 7:4).

Do notice the curious three-fold wording again here. Jeremiah's deliberate three-fold wording was to emphasize the people's final response. We observe that it was three separate occasions that the temple was profaned.

The first occurrence was during the reign of Ahaz. This king cut to pieces the ordained furniture of the temple, closed the temple and set up numerous altars for Baal worship all over his kingdom (2 Chron 28:19-

25). But, because Hezekiah, Ahaz's son, led a reform among the Jewish people, Divine wrath was satisfied, and the Kingdom was allowed to continue further (Isa 38:1-22).

A second outrage against the temple occurred during the reign of Hezekiah's son, Manasseh, followed by his grandson, Amon. These two kings even went beyond the abominations of Ahaz (2 Chron 33:1-25). King Manasseh turned the temple into a heathen shrine (2 Chron 33:7). He made the people to be worse than the heathen Canaanites, which Joshua was told to utterly eradicate from the land (v. 9).

Once again God was about to destroy the temple (2 Chron 34:27-8). Yet, the young King Josiah, son of Amon, and the great-grandson of Hezekiah, turned the nation of Judah back to the religion of Moses and the wrath of God was again assuaged. And thus, as long as Josiah remained alive, there would continue to be peace in the land (2 Chron 34:27-8).

In the thirteenth year of Josiah (627 B.C.E.), God raised up the prophet Jeremiah (Jer 1:2). Jeremiah prophesied that the temple, which the Jewish nation trusted in, eventually would be destroyed (Jer 7:8-14). And it is worthy of notice that Jeremiah prophesied for exactly forty years, after which the temple was indeed destroyed in the year of 587 B.C.E. Thus, we can look back on history and see the obvious parallel with the second temple with a similar 40 year period of warning from 30-70 C.E.

The prophet Ezekiel also prophesied during the time of Josiah (a later contemporary of Jeremiah). He was given a significant vision concerning the future of that first temple. Ezekiel had a vision which constituted part of the third, and thus a final warning concerning the down fall of the first temple. This vision occurred in the year 592 B.C.E and is recounted in chapters eight through eleven of Ezekiel's book of Prophecy.

Ezekiel, who was a Jewish exile in Babylon, was transported in vision to Jerusalem by Cherubim in vision and saw an image of "jealousy" at the North Gate. He also saw the Shekinah – "the Glory of the God of Israel" (Ezek 8:4). God warned that if the abominations that were being conducted there were to continue, then God would go far off from the Sanctuary (v. 6).

Then Ezekiel was shown even greater abominations (vv. 7-14). In the holy place there were twenty-five priests with their backs to the holy of holies worshipping the sun toward the East (vv. 15-16). The Shekinah then entered into the holy of holies and a cloud and bright light filled the inner court (Ezek 10:1-5).

Ezekiel was next taken in vision to the East Gate of the temple where he conversed with the elders of Judah (Ezek 11:1-21). Here he told them that God was about to leave the temple precincts and would dwell in a "little sanctuary" (*mikdash me-at*) among the Israelites in captivity (v. 16). Then Ezekiel saw "the glory of the God of Israel" leave the temple and Jerusalem and retreat to the "mountain which is on the east side of the city" (vv. 22-3). What in fact Ezekiel saw in vision was the abandoning of the Shekinah glory from the Jerusalem temple and then moving to the top of the Mount of Olives, directly east of the temple. And with this, the vision ends.

The temple structure certainly could not move with the movements of the Shekinah, as did the tabernacle during Moses' time. With the Shekinah glory repositioning itself away from the temple, a major sign that God was abandoning Mount Moriah and the temple structure, was to occur.

Ezekiel wrote that it would be God himself that would profane his sanctuary (Ezek 24:21). Jeremiah, writing around the same period as Ezekiel also wrote:

> The Lord has cast off his altar, he has abhorred his sanctuary (Lam 2:7).

THE FIVE YEAR GRACE PERIOD

NOW NOTICE THAT EZEKIEL DATED THIS SERIES of visions to the year 592/591 B.C.E. (Ezek 8:1).[51] And in five years the temple was utterly destroyed by Nebuchadnezzar in 587 B.C.E. Also, note similarly that from the time of Jeremiah's commission in 627 B.C.E. to the time of Josiah's reform in 622 B.C.E., was also a period of five years. It would seem from this that a period of five years of grace is given to the nation of Israel for repentance before the final destruction is to occur. But after Ezekiel's warning at the end of that five year period, there was no forthcoming repentance, and the temple and city of Jerusalem were totally destroyed in the year of 587 B.C.E.

Even though the temple was destroyed, and its vessels were carried away to Babylon, Jeremiah prophesied that they would only be there

> until the day I visit them, says the Lord; then will I bring them up, and restore them to this place (Mt. Moriah) (Jer 27:21-2).

[51] Finegan, *Handbook*, 265.

The temple was to be rebuilt and "the glory of this latter house (the second temple)" was to be even more glorious than that of Solomon's original temple (Haggai 2:9). But in spite of this, even this temple was prophesied to be destroyed once again in the future (Dan 9:26; Zech 11:1).[52]

The reason that the first temple was destroyed was due mainly to God's people turning to idolatry. Yet, after the Jews returned from the Babylonian captivity, they became very strict in not allowing the slightest form of idolatry ever to surface again. Even though during the time of Antiochus Epiphanes, the temple was desecrated with the setting up of the image of Zeus, this desecration doesn't count as a desecration of the Jews because they had nothing to do with it and, in fact, they lamented over it.

The Jews finally retook the second temple in 165 B.C.E. The only other outrages that the Jews suffered were in 63 B.C.E., when the Roman General Pompey entered the temple, and in 54 B.C.E., when Crassus plundered it. But again, these were not Jewish desecrations.

History also records that in the year that Herod the Great had died – 70 years before the temple was destroyed – Herod's successor, Archelaus, stormed the temple during Passover sacrifices and 3000 worshippers were killed (Josephus, *A.J.* 17.9.3, [213-18]). But these desecrations were the actions of Gentiles, not of the Jews, so apparently they also did not count as far as God's judgements upon his people was concerned.

The Three Outrages of the Second Temple

FROM THAT TIME ON UNTIL THE WAR WITH THE Romans (between 66-73 C.E.), there were no further defilements that were attributed to the Jews. So, on what grounds would the second temple be destroyed? The key may be found in what Ezekiel wrote concerning what he saw in his vision. He said that the Shekinah was to leave the temple

[52] The latter Rabbis could not adequately explain why the second temple was destroyed when they believed that the Jewish people were not guilty of the sins that brought down the first temple, so they offered the following reasoning: "The first temple was destroyed because of the sin of idolatry, sexual licentiousness and murder. ...But during the time of the second temple, the people were engaged in the study of Torah, and the performance of commandments and deeds of loving kindness. Why, then, was the second temple destroyed? Because the people were guilty of groundless hatred. This teaches that the sin of groundless hatred is considered to be as grave as the sins of idolatry, sexual licentiousness and murder" (*Yoma* 9b).

and then dwell in a little sanctuary among the people of God (Ezek 11:16). This could mean that God's "Spirit" (not a separate divine "person" in some Trinitarian connotation, but rather a form of God's Shekinah glory) would continue to dwell in the minds of those who continued to trust in God. The key to understanding this is in what Paul told the Corinthians:

> Do you not know that you are God's Temple and that God's spirit dwells in you? If anyone destroys God's Temple, God will destroy that person. For God's Temple is holy, and you are that Temple (1 Cor 3:16).

The biblical teaching is simply this: An individual, whom God has chosen, called, and given his divine Spirit to reside within, is considered a vessel more precious than any temple made by human hands. And the one individual in history, who was given God's Spirit without measure, was Jesus Christ (John 3:34). After Christ's resurrection, on the Day of Pentecost in 30 C.E., God poured out His "Spirit" to his church in a dynamic way (Acts 2:1-4). Now, the disciples of Jesus then became "filled with the Holy Spirit" (v. 4). With this insight we can now understand what the outrages were that brought down the second temple.

It was forty years before the second temple was destroyed that the first outrage occurred. Jesus was tried right in the precincts of that temple by the Jews. The Sanhedrin at this time still prosecuted cases in the "Chamber of Hewn Stones" in the court of the temple. This is where Jesus in reality met his judicial death. And, at the exact moment of his physical death, something happened that had a startling affect on the whole area of Jerusalem. An earthquake occurred and violently shook the city of Jerusalem. Darkness had already been cast over the land[53] and the great veil of the temple was torn in two (Matt 27:51-6; Mark 15:38; Luke 23:45-9).[54]

The eastern entrance to the holy place was known as the "Hekel." Josephus said that it was over 55 cubits tall (80 feet) and 16 cubits wide (24 feet) (Josephus, *B.J.* 5.5.4 [210-214]). It is obvious that if an earthquake occurred at this time, the breaking up of this massive stone lintel over the Hekel is was what caused the curtain to split from the top to the bottom.

---

[53] This darkness could not have been a solar eclipse because it was the time of Passover and therefore a full moon, meaning that the moon was opposite the sun due to its full reflection of the sun. In other words, the moon could not eclipse the sun if it was not in line with it. Also, eclipses do not last for three hours in duration. Obviously, the darkness was due to thick clouds that shrouded the sun's brightness.

[54] It is also recorded in a Jewish Christian work entitled the *Gospel of the Nazarenes* that the large stone lintel that supported the huge curtain which hung before the "Hekel" broke in two. See Edgar Hennecke and Wilhelm Schneemelcher, *New Testament Apocrypha* (Philadelphia: Westminster Press, 1965), 1:150, 153.

The earthquake caused severe structural damage to the temple itself, so that no longer could the Chamber of Hewn Stones be safe to use again. The Sanhedrin had to now use the Trading Station to conduct court instead of the prestigious Chamber that they formerly occupied. The Talmud says that:

> Forty years before the destruction of Jerusalem, the Sanhedrin was banished (from the Chamber of Hewn Stones) and sat in the Trading Station.[55]

The temple was destroyed in 70 C.E. Forty years before this time brings us to the very year that Jesus was crucified, in 30 C.E., the year of this great earthquake that caused the Sanhedrin to abandon the Chamber of Hewn Stones.

Recorded also at this time was another cryptic reference to the events of 30 C.E.:

> Forty years before the Temple was destroyed, the gates of the Hekel opened of themselves, until Rabbi Yohanan ben Zakkai rebuked them saying: Hekel, Hekel, why alarmest thou us? We know that thou are destined to be destroyed. For of thee hath prophesied Zechariah ben Iddo: "Open thy doors, O Lebanon, and the fire shall eat thy cedars" (*Yoma* 39b).

Notice that this would indicate that in the very year of the crucifixion of Jesus, the Jewish authorities were receiving a divine oracle that their temple was to be destroyed and they were quite aware of that fact! Rabbi Yohanan ben Zakkai admitted such when he said "*We* know that you are destined to be destroyed."[56]

The great curtain that separated the holy of holies from the holy place was now destroyed. Certainly, if the doors behind the curtain remained closed, then the tearing of the veil would have had no meaning. But the veil being rent and the mighty doors thrust open was a sign of the end that the Jews recognized and fully understood. The Sentence of Jesus in the Chamber of Hewn Stones was the last sentence it would ever make in that authorized place. The court was banished from that majestic hall and forced to meet at the Trading Station from thence forward. This was the first of three signs that the second temple was coming under the judgment of God.

---

[55] *Shabbath* 15a; see also *Rosh ha-Shanah* 31a, b.

[56] Similar to the destruction of the first temple, which had a 40 year period of warning (627-587 B.C.E.) before it was destroyed, the Jews were given ominous warnings that they themselves knew predicted the fall of the second temple forty years hence.

The second outrage was the trial and condemnation of Stephen a few years later. Stephen's trial was also held in the temple precincts, but now in the Trading Station (Acts 6:8-14; 7:1-60). Stephen was a newly ordained minister who was filled with God's Spirit (Acts 6:3; 7:55). Stephen stirred up the people and the elders of Judah with signs and wonders. He was then stoned to death outside the city (Acts 7:58-60). This second condemnation of one who had God's Spirit dwelling within him (the "little" temple of Ezekiel's prophecy) was a sign that even Rabbi Gamaliel must have been taken aback by, considering his comments to the Sanhedrin (Acts 5:33-9).

It was during this stirring sermon that Stephen told the Jews that God does not dwell in "Temples made with hands." Stephen died at the feet of the persecutor of early Christians, Saul (v. 58, later on to become the Apostle Paul). This event had left a marked impression on Paul and those words he would remember the rest of his life – indeed, they became fundamental to Paul's theology, and he would recall these words in his own stirring remarks to the Athenian philosophers (Acts 17:24).

The third temple outrage was the martyrdom of James the Just, brother of Jesus. He was thrown off the wall of the temple and then clubbed to death by an angry mob. Eusebius records this event:

> So remarkable a person must James have been, so universally esteemed for righteousness, that even the more intelligent Jew felt that this was why his martyrdom was immediately followed by the siege of Jerusalem, which happened to them for no other reason than the wicked crime of which he had been the victim. And indeed Josephus did not hesitate to write this down in so many words. "These things happened to the Jews in requital for James the Righteous, who was a brother of Jesus known as Christ, for though he was the most righteous of men, the Jews put him to death" (Eusebius, *Hist. eccl.* 2.23.19-20).[57]

Thus, we can see that these three men of God, filled with God's Spirit, died or were condemned to death within the temple precincts during the forty year period of warning.

Other Signs that the Temple Would Fall

THE DAYS BEFORE THE DESTRUCTION OF THE

[57] This event occurred near Passover of 62 C.E.

second temple were also marked by a degeneration of the moral fabric of the city. Josephus recorded that by 54 C.E. the whole state of Judea was now virtually crime ridden and that

> God out [of] his hatred to these men's wickedness, rejected our city; and as for the temple, he no longer esteemed it sufficiently pure for him to inhabit therein, but brought the Romans upon us, and threw a fire upon the city to purge it; and brought upon us, our wives, and children, slavery, – as desirous to make us wiser by our calamities (Josephus, *A.J.* 20.8.5 [166]).

In the year 66 C.E., a great Passover celebration was planned to occur in commemoration of the newly rededicated temple. The Jewish elders must have wished to turn the nation to repentance and ask God to spare them for their sins and show them that he was still their God by some miraculous sign. Over two and a half million pilgrims attended this festival, the largest gathering ever witnessed at the temple. Josephus called it a "vast multitude" because it was so large (Josephus, *B.J.* 6.9.4 [428]). If God was going to reveal his intentions to the Jewish nation, this, indeed, was the precise time to do so. And this is exactly what happened in a supernatural and miraculous way.

On Nisan 8 of that year, when the people began to assemble for their purification rites in preparation for the Passover, a supernatural light was seen (Shekinah!) at three o'clock in the morning for about a half hour at the altar in the temple and then suddenly disappeared (Josephus, *B.J.* 6.5.3, [289-91]). Josephus also refers to it as a "star resembling a sword, which stood over the city, and a comet, that continued for a year" (*B.J.* 6.5.3 [289]). Then the Nicanor Gates in the temple, which twenty men could barely move, opened up during the night (*B.J.* 6.5.3 [293-6]).

Were these the signs that Jesus foretold that were to precede the destruction of the temple and the "Time of the End?" Peter and John, still in Jerusalem at this time, may have wondered if this were the case. Notice also that during the second Passover season of that same year (66 C.E.) the following is recorded by Josephus:

> For, before sunsetting, chariots and troops of soldiers in their armor were seen running about among the clouds, and surrounding of cities (Josephus, *B.J.* 6.5.3 [298-99]).

Is this not what Jesus exactly foretold would happen and what he predicted that the faithful should watch for (Luke 21:20-25)? When these signs were to occur, Jesus told his disciples to then flee from the city of Jerusalem to the mountains. And all these signs Jesus himself connected with the destruction of the temple. Jerusalem was surrounded by a heavenly army and that was the prime signal to escape from the city.[58]

The entire forty-year period preceding the destruction of the temple also witnessed other strange occurrences associated with it. On the Day of Atonement each year the High Priest would select the Azazel goat by lot. The Babylonian Talmud informs us that for forty straight years "the lot 'for the Lord' did not come up in the right hand" (*Yoma*, 39b). The odds of this happening consistently for a forty year period comes out mathematically to be about a trillion to one.[59] In other words, this was a miraculous event that could not be explained by mere chance or happenstance.

Also, the light from the western Menorah, which was to never go out, is said to have gone out consistently for forty years every single night of its own accord, despite the efforts of the Priests to keep it going (Josephus, *C. Ap.* 1.22 [199]; *Tamid* 3.9; 6.1; *Sifra*, *Emor* 13,7; *Sifra Num.* 59; *Yoma* 33a). Furthermore, beginning in 30 C.E., the crimson thread, also associated with the Day of Atonement since the days of Simon the Righteous (third century B.C.E.), never turned white again (*Yoma*, 39b). Such happenings defy any rational explanations.

Josephus further records that at the Festival of Pentecost in the year of 66 C.E.

> as the priests were going by night into the inner [court of the] temple, as their custom was, to perform their sacred ministrations, they said that, in the first place, they felt a quaking, and heard a great noise, and after that they heard a sound as of a great multitude, saying, "Let us remove hence" (Josephus, *B.J.* 6.5.3, [299-300]).

Think about what this means! The announcement that the Shekinah was leaving the temple would render that entire structure, even including the holy of holies, as profane. The only reason why the "holy of holies" was so designated was for the fact that the Shekinah glory dwelt therein. But once gone, after the departure of the Shekinah, the structure became an empty shell.

Where did the Shekinah depart to? Exactly as in Ezekiel's vision, when the Shekinah left the first temple, it departed then and hovered over the Mount of Olives for a time. Rabbi Jonathan recorded that the Shekinah

[58] We should note that if Jerusalem were actually surrounded by literal Roman Legions, how would anyone be able to escape? Indeed, Rabbi Johannan ben Zakkai had to be smuggled out of the city in a coffin. However, a heavenly army would be able to dismay any surrounding army while allowing the escapees a way out.

[59] One only has to take 2 to the 40th power to arrive at this result. The exact number equals to: 2^{40} = 1,099,511,627,776.

> abode on the Mount of Olives hoping that Israel would repent, but they did not; while a Bet Kol issued forth announcing, "Return, O Backsliding children" (Jer 3:14). "Return unto me, and I will return unto you (Mal 3:7)." When they did not repent, it said, I will return to my place [in heaven] (Eusebius, *Dem. ev.* 2:6.18.28).[60]

Eusebius also attested to this fact:

> Believers in Christ all congregate from all parts of the world, not as of old time because of the glory of Jerusalem, nor they may worship in the ancient Temple at Jerusalem... (but) that they may worship at the Mount of Olives opposite to the city, whither the glory of the Lord (Shekinah) migrated when it left the former city (Eusebius, *Dem. ev.* 1:3.5.124d).[61]

Eusebius also said that Christians later built a church on the Mount of Olives.[62] Jerome mentioned that

> Here also (the Mount of Olives) according to Ezekiel the Cherubim after leaving the temple founded the church of the Lord (Jerome, *Epist.* 108.12 [*NPNF*[2] 6:200]).[63]

This striking event occurred exactly 36 years after God poured out his Spirit to his church – to the very day in fact – on the day of Pentecost! And on the Day of Pentecost in 66 C.E., God withdrew his Spirit from the temple of his people. This signalled the beginning of the end of temple worship. The temple had less than a five-year grace period before it would be destroyed. The apostles knew by these events that it was time to get out of Jerusalem. But notice further some other intriguing events.

Ezekiel's Prophecy Fulfilled

The Holy Days were days in which all 24 priests administered along with the High Priest. And these combined 25 priests certainly represented those 25 priests of Ezekiel's prophecy (Ezek

[60] *Midrash Rabbah: Deuteronomy and Lamentations,* ed. H. Freedman and Maurice Simon, (London: Soncino Press, 1961), 7:51.

[61] Quoted from Eusebius, *Proof of the Gospel,* ed. W. J. Ferrar (Grand Rapids: Baker Book House, 1981), 29.

[62] Ibid., 143.

[63] The prophesy that Jerome referred to is found in Ezek 10:18, 19.

8:15-16). God could not have given his priesthood, his people, and even the Jerusalem church, a greater witness as to what was happening. There could be no question that the destruction of the temple would soon occur, certainly within less than five years. Those that had eyes to see and were aware of the prophecies involved could see this as plain as the hand in front of their face. And just like the vision of Ezekiel, in less than 5 years from these occurrences, the temple indeed was utterly destroyed.

After all these striking events, there was now no question in the minds of Peter and John that the prophecies concerning the abomination of desolation could not occur, since, even though the temple still stood, the holy of holies had now become, in reality, an empty shell.

The sacrifice of Jesus indeed nullified the existence of temple worship. Now Peter and John had to agree that what the Apostle Paul was preaching and writing about was exactly right after all. Indeed, Peter at this time must have come to the conclusion that he had to go to Rome to confer with Paul about these very theological issues, certainly before Paul would meet his death.[64] There was no doubt that the preservation of the body of Christ – the church – down through the centuries to the last generation now must have been the number one concern of the apostles.

As far as what the Jews themselves believed at this time concerning the temple and the miraculous events, Josephus speaks of "the aversion God had already at the city and the sanctuary" (Josephus, *B.J.* 2.19.6 [539]), and that the temple was "no longer a place fit for God" (*B.J.* 5.1.3 [19]), because "God is fled out of his sanctuary" (*B.J.* 5.9.4, [412]).

The church in Jerusalem did flee according to Eusebius, to a town some 60 miles north of Jerusalem and across the Jordan known as Pella. It should be noted, though, that Jesus told his disciples that when they see these signs that he was talking about, then they should flee to the mountains. The fact that the church did not flee to the mountains, but rather to the northern plains of Judaea, tells us that the Jerusalem church certainly now understood that these times were not when the signs that Jesus referred to would happen.

Clearly, the destruction of the temple and Jerusalem would soon occur. But the key sign that Jesus gave to his disciples concerning the abomination of desolation (Matt 24:15) must refer to some future temple beyond the lifetimes of those in the apostolic church. It would be some future Antichrist that would place the "abomination of desolation" within a newly reconstructed third temple.

It appears that the Apostle Paul had already adopted a position that

[64] We maintain that it is right at this time that John Mark comes to Jerusalem from Rome to bid Peter to come back to Rome with him and help the Apostle Paul with his plans to create a Christian body of Scriptural writings, as we will bring out later on.

the prophesies of the end time were for a later generation. Now it became obvious to the Jerusalem-based apostles that the assessment of Paul was indeed correct.

After the miraculous signs of Pentecost in the year of 66 C.E., the events in Judaea further persuaded the Jerusalem apostles that war with Rome would be inevitable and futile. With this realization it was evident that steps had to be taken to secure the future of the church. What steps were these? We will pursue this question in the chapters that await us.

CHAPTER 4

The Jerusalem Church under James the Just

THE BOOK OF ACTS STARTS OFF THE STORY OF the Christian church with a bang and, ideally, we would expect it to tell us the details of how it grew, the works of all the apostles and the glorious spread of the gospel. But, unfortunately, it only took seven chapters to see that the Jerusalem church almost fell apart by persecution. Then the story seems to center around Luke's account of the work of the Apostle Paul, but even that story breaks off right at the most crucial point in apostolic history. Indeed, it didn't even carry through with some of the most significant events of the story, not the least of which is the martyrdom's of James the Just, Peter and Paul. This is why this work must go beyond the *Book of Acts* to understand these important matters.

By the early sixties C.E. the apostles who were still in Jerusalem were to witness some horrendous internal developments within the church that would alter its entire direction and focus. It is important to understand the nature of these occurrences in our survey of New Testament history. Unfortunately, since the *Book of Acts* breaks off just before these events occurred, we will have to piece together the story from other material, internal and external, to the New Testament.

Initially, Christianity was basically still a modified form of Judaism and not in anyway the divergent religious system that we witness today. Today, Christianity is so totally different than what it was in the first century that anyone from the first century would hardly recognize it as anything like what the original apostles preached. The main difference between then and now, of course, is in the fact that the original Jewish followers of Jesus believed that he was the prophesied Jewish Messiah of Hebrew prophecy and that this physical son of David would soon return in their lifetime, as Jesus himself had explicitly told them, within their own generation, to become the messianic ruler of the Kingdom of God on earth.

We must not forget that Jesus was indeed thoroughly Jewish in his cultural and religious background. He kept the Law, confirmed the Shema, reiterated the prophecies of the Hebrew Scriptures, observed the Sabbath (not in a Pharisaic sense, for which Jesus was criticized), as well as all of the Holy Days of Leviticus 23, ate clean foods, and so on.[65]

There was not an inkling among the initial disciples of Jesus that he intended to lay aside the Law of Moses for his own followers. Indeed, all of the disciples considered the Mosaic institutions to be the very Law of God. All of Christ's disciples were thoroughly Jewish. They knew nothing other than Judaism as it was practiced in the first century. And the *Book of Acts* even shows us that they kept right on observing the Feasts of Leviticus 23 after Christ's resurrection and throughout the period embraced within the *Book of Acts.*

There can be no doubt that the first three decades after the resurrection the church was indeed a "Jewish" Christian church. We need to understand the significance of this because many see the work of Paul among the Gentiles as the main focus of the New Testament. However, we must not let Paul's work obscure what was going on within the church at Jerusalem during this period.

One of the most significant players in the apostolic church (if not one of the most enigmatic) was the Apostle James, the [half] brother of Jesus.[66] His death at Passover, in the year of 62 C.E., was, no doubt, a pivotal factor in changing the course of history of the church for this period.

It appears that the Apostle James was the leader of the early church in Jerusalem and governed it with almost a monarchial type of rule. Ernest L. Martin notes:

> The death of James at Passover A.D. 62 was a major turning point in the history of Christianity. As long as James was alive he headed the government of the Christian community from Jerusalem with practically a sovereign type of rule. The New Testament states that it was James to whom reports were given (Acts 12:17), to whom most apostles gave obeisance (Galatians 2:11-14), from whom executive

---

[65] It may be that Jesus even wore the traditional Jewish fringes (*tzitzit*) commanded in Numbers 15:38-41 and Deuteronomy 22:12. David H. Stern translates κρασπέδον in Matt 9:20 and 14:36 as *tzitzit.* See *Jewish New Testament* (Jerusalem, Israel: Jewish New Testament Publications, 1989), 12, 21.

[66] Recent studies have assembled a wealth of information concerning James. See Robert Eisenman, *James, the Brother of Jesus* (New York: Viking, 1997); John Painter, *Just James: The Brother of Jesus in History and Tradition* (Minneapolis: Fortress, 1999); Bruce Chilton and Jacob Neusner, eds., *The Brother of Jesus: James the Just and His Mission* (Louisville: Westminster, 2001). Also, an ossuary has been recently found with the inscription "James, son of Joseph, brother of Jesus" which has all the appearances of being an authentic confirmation of the existence of Jesus and James. See André Lemaire, "Burial Box of James the Brother of Jesus," *Biblical Archaeology Review* 28:6 (Nov/Dec, 2002): 24-33, 70.

> doctrinal decisions were once rendered for Christians (Acts 15:13-19). Even Paul reported to James and complied with him regarding doctrinal issues (Acts 21:18-26). Paul even stated that his preaching among the Gentiles would have been in vain had he not gained the approbation of James and the other Jerusalem based apostles (Galatians 2:1, 2, 9, 10).[67]

The legends in the church regarding James' role as leader of Judaean Christianity were amplified in later traditions, specifically in the memoirs of Hegesippus and Pseudo-Clementine literature. They offer us a glimpse of this enigmatic individual that is not reported in the New Testament. F. F. Bruce writes:

> The type of argument by which his (James') primacy was supported in later generations is illustrated by one of the logia in the Gospel of Thomas, where, in reply to the disciples' question who will be chief among them after he himself has gone away, Jesus says: 'In the place to which you have gone, you will go to James the Just, for whose sake heaven and earth came into being.'[68]

It is interesting that James was not recorded as being even one of the disciples of Jesus during his ministry and yet, sometime after Christ's resurrection, James is the one who emerges as the leader of the Jerusalem church.[69] This curious circumstance may be revealed in the fact that after Jesus appeared to the 500 "brethren," Jesus then appeared to James first of all, and then to all of his disciples. A second century embellishment of this account is recorded in the *The Gospel according to the Hebrews,* where James swears an oath that he will eat no bread until he sees Jesus "rising from those who sleep." Jesus next appears to James and then the following is recorded:

> But when the Lord had given the linen cloth to the servant of the [High] priest, he went to James and appeared to him. For James had sworn that he would not eat bread from that hour in which he had drunk the cup of the Lord until he should see him risen from among them that sleep. And shortly thereafter the Lord said: Bring a table and bread!

---

[67] Ernest L. Martin, *Restoring,* 266.

[68] F. F. Bruce, *New Testament History* (New York: Doubleday, 1971), 369.

[69] James may have not assumed the leadership of the church until Peter and the rest of the apostles went forth to spread the gospel far and wide throughout the known world. This may have been in the year of 41/42 C.E., since traditionally, the apostles remained in Jerusalem for 12 years after the resurrection (*Acts of Peter,* 5:22). For a discussion on this dating, see Rainer Riesner, *Paul's Early Period* (Grand Rapids: Eerdmans, 1998), 119-22.

> And immediately it is added: he took the bread, blessed it and brake it and gave it to James the Just and said to him: My brother, eat thy bread, for the Son of man is risen from among them that sleep.[70]

JAMES — A NAZARITE?

ACCORDING TO THE EARLY CHURCH HISTORIAN, Eusebius, quoting from an earlier church historian, Hegesippus (90-180), we have testimony which describes James in terms that portray him as being a life long Nazarite:

> James, the brother of the Lord, succeeded to the government of the Church in conjunction with the apostles. He has been called the Just by all from the time of our Saviour to the present day; for there were many that bore the name of James. He was holy from his mother's womb; and he drank no wine nor strong drink, nor did he eat flesh. No razor came upon his head; he did not anoint himself with oil, and he did not use the bath. He alone was permitted to enter the holy place; for he wore not woolen but linen garments; And he was in the habit of entering alone into the temple, and was frequently found upon his knees begging forgiveness for the people, so that his knees became hard like those of a camel, in consequence of his constantly bending them in his worship of God, and asking forgiveness for the people. Because of his exceeding great justice he was called the Just, and Oblias, which signifies in Greek, 'Bulwark of the people' and 'Justice,' in accordance with what the prophets declare concerning him (Eusebius, *Hist. eccl.* 2.23.4-7).

Epiphanius, also basing his description of James on Hegesippus, tells us that James

> wore *no second tunic*, but used only a linen cloak, as it says in the Gospel, 'The young man fled, leaving behind the linen cloth which he had around him.' For it was John and James and James, these three, who practised (sic!) this Way of life: the two sons of Zebedee and James the son of Joseph and brother of the Lord. ...But to James alone, it was allowed to

[70] Edgar Hennecke, *New Testament Apocrypha.* Wilhelm Schneemelcher, ed., (Philadelphia: Westminster Press, 1963), 165. This fragment is preserved by Jerome, *Vir. ill.* 11 (*NPNF*[2] 3:363).

> enter once a year into the Holy of Holies, *because he was a Nazarite* and *connected to the Priesthood.* Hence Mary was related in two ways to Elizabeth and James was a distinguished member of the Priesthood, because the two tribes alone were linked to one another, the royal tribe to the priestly and the priestly to the royal, just as earlier in the time of the Exodus, Nahshon, the scion from the tribe of Judah, took to wife a previous Elizabeth daughter of Aaron. [Exod 6:23] (Epiphanius, *Pan.* 29.4.1-3; 78.13.5-8).[71]

JAMES — A PRIEST?

THAT JAMES WAS ALLOWED INTO THE SANCTUARY of the temple is most interesting, since only priests could enter therein. Could James fall into the category of an Opposition Priest? His genealogy indicates that he was in fact a member of a priestly family, as Epiphanius brings out. Mary (the mother of Jesus and James) was a relative of Elizabeth, mother of John the Baptist, who was married to Zechariah, a priest in the course of Abijah (Luke 1:5). So we learn from this that James, and of course Jesus, were of priestly ancestry, as well as being a part of the line of David.[72]

James' priestly ancestry could explain why James could enter into the sanctuary. In any event, the language of Hegesippus conveys the idea that James' ministry even superseded that of the legitimate priesthood, i.e., the Godly representative on earth being transferred from Caiaphas and his colleagues to James and his successors. Indeed, we might ask, as those of the time might have done, if Jesus was the prophet like Moses, was not the brother of Jesus also cast in the role of Moses' brother, Aaron? And if so, the implication is that James' priesthood superseded even that of the existing establishment – specifically, the High Priest Caiaphas.

As we have already pointed out in a previous chapter, even "a *great many* of the priests became obedient to the faith" (Acts 6:7). Hegesippus said that the ruling class of the Jews believed in Christ and that some of

---

[71] Quoted from Robert Eisenman, *James, the Brother of Jesus* (New York: Viking Penguin, 1997), 369.

[72] If we may speculate here, James' grandmother, on his mother Mary's side was the wife of Heli and apparently sister to Zechariah the Priest, husband of Elizabeth and parents of John the Baptist. This explanation would assume, of course, that Zechariah was elderly and his wife Elizabeth was very young. This may have been the same situation with Joseph the Carpenter, who appears to have passed from the scene early, while Mary appears to have lived on into the seventies of the first century.

the Scribes and Pharisees thought that the popularity and influence of James was so immense that there was even the "danger that the whole people would be looking for Jesus as the Christ" (Eusebius, *Hist. eccl.* 2.23.10). Remember, that it was James who stated in the mid 50's that there were "many tens of thousands of Jews who believed, and they are all zealots for the Law" (Acts 21:20).

JAMES — THE FIRST POPE?

JAMES APPEARS TO HAVE EXERCISED VIRTUAL pontifical authority within the early Jerusalem church. He obviously had the authority to demand of the Apostle Paul, with four other Jewish followers, that they offer animal sacrifices in the temple to prove that "you are walking orderly and also keeping the Law" (Acts 21:24). James appears to be trying to defuse a situation that could have given the reason for the Pharisees to finally get the advantage over James and justification for them to finally destroy him.

The Apostle Paul, probably understanding the significance of the situation, dutifully obeyed James' instruction. All this points to the fact that the primitive Jerusalem-based church, when James was alive, was entirely within the Jewish sphere and James was certainly the head of that church.

The account in Acts 21, concerning Paul's submission to James, is astonishing considering the fact that the sacrifice of Christ should have been the ultimate sacrifice which made any subsequent sacrifices redundant and superfluous. Yet, here we see Jewish Christians performing temple ritual. And notice that James was deeply concerned that Paul's ministry had garnered a reputation of being anti-Law in nature. We can see this in James' statement to Paul:

> You observe, brother, how many thousands of converts we have among the JEWS, all of them staunch upholders of the Law. Now they have been given certain information about you: it is said that you teach all the Jews in the Gentile world to turn their backs on Moses, and tell them not to circumcise their children or follow our way of life (Acts 21:20).

From James' point of view Paul had to be made an example of. Paul must have understood the overtones of this delicate situation and the implication of what would happen if he did not comply with James' order. The Jewish authorities were trying to entrap James, like they did with his brother Jesus. Paul was not about to give these Pharisees an excuse that would jeopardize James' standing in the community. So, James decides to order Paul to go through a seven day purification period in the temple with four other Jewish Christians. On the seventh day Paul was identified in the temple by Jewish Christians from Asia, where they shouted

> Fellow Israelites, help! This is the man who is teaching everyone everywhere against our people, our law, and this place; more than that, he has actually brought Greeks into the temple and has defiled this holy place (Acts 21:27, 28).

The accusation that Paul brought Gentiles into the temple was false, but the important point here to notice is that obviously, we are still at a period of time when it was not only desirable to be a law abiding Jew within the church, it appears to be a virtual necessity.

Paul's message to the Gentiles was not well accepted in Jerusalem and it rubbed the Jewish Christians the wrong way because it dangerously teetered on the edge of lawlessness as understood by most of these Jerusalem believers.

Paul was also falsely accused of bringing Gentiles into the temple (v. 29). This accusation stirred up the crowd and Paul was, as a result, literally thrown out of the temple, with the temple doors being slammed shut behind him (v. 30). Then an angry crowd turned on him and began to beat him, until the garrison commander intervened (v. 31-33). Paul, in his defense, later explained to the Jews that he was once so zealous for the Law that he was the one who killed Christians in defense of it, until he was struck down on the road to Damascus and converted (Acts 21: 34-40; 22:1-21). The point of all this is that we see here, some quarter of a century after the resurrection, that the Jerusalem church was still deeply rooted in Judaism as a religious form of worshipping God. And as long as James was alive, Christianity in Jerusalem was without question, Judaic to the core.

Catholic tradition may speak of the "Primacy of Peter" beginning at Antioch and then Rome, but the original primacy of the church certainly rested at Jerusalem, which was undeniably the mother-church in the first three decades after the resurrection.[73] Peter only emerges as the leader of the church after the death of James, and that did not happen until after Passover, 62 C.E. Before that time it was the Apostle James who appears to be a President of the elders of the primitive Jerusalem-based church. And as long as James was alive, there was a general stability and a unanimity of belief among the followers of Jesus – albeit not always unflawed – and that original Christian belief was almost entirely Jewish to the core! We can see this in the fact that in the original Jerusalem church, there was a strong emphasis on keeping the Law and the Feast Days, such as the Days of Unleavened Bread (Acts 12:3-4; 20:6), Pentecost (Acts 18:21), Atonement (Acts 27:9), and, of course, the weekly Sabbath (Acts 13:27, 42, 44; 16:13; 17:2; 18:24).

JEWISH CHRISTIANITY

THERE CAN BE NO DOUBT THAT CHRISTIANITY in its earliest form was unquestionably what we would today call "Jewish Christianity." And belief in the return of Jesus within the 40 year generation after the resurrection was the driving force of the apostles and that early church. Indeed, it was the great expectation of the Messiah among all of the Jews that was at an all time peek in the generation after Christ's resurrection.

The original Christianity of the apostles focused on the faith of Abraham, and the covenant made with him, which had been fulfilled in part, but was still waiting to be filled at the *Parousia*. The New Testament faith grew from the roots of the Hebrew Scriptures "As [God] spoke to Abraham and his seed in view of the (Coming) age (εἰς τὸν αἰῶνα)" (Luke 1:55). Even Paul emphasized the Christian faith was the confirmation of the promises made to the fathers (Rom 15:8).

The Old Testament canon was the essential basis of what Christ and the apostles interpreted and expounded their faith to be. But the post-apostolic age of the second century (and beyond) witnessed a complete turn-about from these Jewish roots. It took on a Gentile complexion that was alien to the original followers of Jesus. Indeed, in the second century we see virtually an anti-Semitic transformation in the church which turned Christianity away from its "Jewish" heritage to a Gentile church rooted in a Greek philosophical legacy as opposed to the Jewish patrimony of the

---

[73] If anything, James the Just should have been honored with the title of being the first Pope. See Martin Hengel, "Jacobus der Herrenbruder – der erste 'Päpts?'" in *Glaube und Escatologie: Festschrift für W. G. Kümmel zum 80. Geburtstag*, ed. by E. Grässer and O. Merk. Tübingin: J. C. B. Morh (Paul Siebeck), 1985. Obviously, the church of Rome certainly divorced itself from James, and the canon of Athanasius displaced the prominent position of James as being the first Epistle after Acts to a position after Paul's, whose Epistle to the Romans now stands first after Acts. Obviously, the church at Rome had clearly divorced itself from its Jewish roots after the first century.

Hebrew Bible.

Gentile Christianity eventually emerged on the scene in the second century. The transformation was the result of the Gentile preference to the speculative, neo-platonic Greek mind of the ancient philosophers of Plato and Socrates rather than the Hebrew mind set of the expectation for an anointed Jewish King ruling in Jerusalem as a fulfillment of the land-promise made to Abraham. The circumstances that brought about this sharp contrast in Gentile versus Jewish Christianity is one of the most important phenomenons in the entire history of the church at this period, and we must pursue this aspect even further.

THE DESIRE TO BE JEWISH

BACK WHEN JOHN HAD WRITTEN IN THE INITIAL draft of the *Book of Revelation* around 56 C.E., he said that it was a desirable and an honorable thing to be a "Jew" (Rev 2:9).[74] One of the biggest problems that Paul had to deal with among his Gentile converts was their persistent longing also to become "Jewish." They wanted to adopt Jewish religious practices, and even wishing to be supervised by Jewish Christian authorities (2 Cor 11 and 12). What we must come to realize is that this was a phenomenon that would only be possible during the pre-Jewish War of 66 to 73 C.E. But after that War, all of this changed.

We can see the change in attitude by some of the writings that appeared after the Jewish War. In the second century the *Epistle of Barnabas* appeared which was decidedly anti-Jewish in its themes. And even John, in his Gospel, written after the War, writes in a manner which is not all that flattering to the Jews. And if we believe that John was the same author of both the *Book of Revelation* and the *Gospel of John*, then this marks a decisive change in attitude on his part.

Now we must note and re-emphasize a most significant event that occurred right at this time in our story in 62 C.E. This event was so tremendous in impact, that no other single circumstance in all of apostolic history could compare to the major blow to the apostles that

[74] John was referring to the desire of some people within the church who wanted to be identified as "Jews," even though they were, in actual fact, not. This was certainly a reflection of the pre-Jewish/Roman War mentality, which wanted to be identified with the Jewish people, even though they were Gentiles. In no way would this statement be possible after the year of 70 C.E. This also goes a long way in establishing the fact that the *Book of Revelation* was initially a pre-Jewish War production.

this incident had – even to the entire future of the church. It was the martyrdom of the Apostle James the Just in Jerusalem. It is that event, more than has been generally recognized (nor conceded), which was no doubt the most significant occurrence in the history of the apostolic church. It signaled the beginning of the end of so-called "Jewish Christianity."

Let us understand the significance of this monumental event. If the Jewish leaders perceived that James and the apostles were in fact being recognized as the spiritual successors to the priesthood, then it becomes understandable that the Jewish leaders may have become threatened by such an idea and would want to eliminate James, the leader of the followers of Jesus. Even though they recognized that James was a righteous man, they could not afford to allow their prestige to be sublimated by the brother of the one they felt was put to death for blasphemy. It was, therefore, inevitable that a clash between the Jewish religious leaders and James would eventually occur.

THE MARTYRDOM OF JAMES

IN WHAT APPEARS TO BE A MOMENT OF DECISION for the Jewish religious authorities upon the death of the Roman Procurator Festus in 62 C.E., the opportunity for the Jewish religious leaders to take action on their own had to have been executed soon and expeditiously. The political instability of Festus' death afforded an opportunity to take action during this time. Josephus relates that

> when, therefore, Ananus was of this disposition, he thought he had now a proper opportunity [to exercise his authority]. Festus was now dead, and Albinus was but upon the road, so he assembled the sanhedrin of judges, and brought before them the brother of Jesus, who was called Christ, whose name was James, and some others, [or, some of his companions]; and when he had formed an accusation against them as breakers of the law, he delivered them to be stoned (Josephus, *A.J.* 20.9.1 [200]).

What "law" did James break? Josephus does not tell us but, instead, tells us that the High Priest's action offended "those citizens who were reputed to be most fair-minded and to be strict in their observance of the law" (*A.J.* 20.9.1 [201-3]). Obviously, James and his associates compromised themselves in the eyes of Annus by receiving Paul when he came to Jerusalem and, of all things, allowing a Gentile into the temple precincts, as they had wrongly still believed. This is the only reason that Annus could justifiable condemn James.

Paul escaped from the clutches of Annus, but only narrowly, by his appeal to Caesar. But James and his associates still lay within the jurisdiction and grasp of these incensed Jewish leaders. And, although James had originally won the esteem of the Jewish community by his asceticism and his holiness of life, his association with Paul, the "ringleader of the sect of Nazarenes" (Acts 24:5), may have turned many against him, despite James' attempt in having Paul comply with the Law of Moses in order to demonstrate to all of the Jewish community that he was a law keeper.

Eusebius, via Hegesippus, tells us that the "Scribes and Pharisees" staged a public debate with James at Passover and set him on the "pinnacle" of the temple so that he might be seen and heard by all who had come up for the festival.[75] When he was asked "What is the gate of Jesus?" James replied in a loud voice:

> Why do you ask me concerning Jesus, the Son of Man? He himself sitteth in heaven at the right hand of the great Power, and is about to come upon the clouds of heaven" (Eusebius, *Hist. eccl.* 2.23.13).

Notice that James, in the year of 62 C.E., was still of the firm conviction that Jesus is "about to come upon the clouds of heaven." The faith of James most likely represented the belief of the Jerusalem-based apostles, Peter and John, and was still strong in the belief that Jesus was to return within their lifetime. At this the crowd cried out "Hosanna to the Son of David," and James's enemies, realizing that their plan to discredit him had misfired, threw him down and began to stone him, and then finally, he was beaten to death with a fuller's club (ibid., 2.23.14-18).

The account even goes on to say that the destruction of Jerusalem in 70 C.E. was the direct result of God punishing the Jews for killing James the Just (ibid., 2.23.19). Consider the ramifications of this fact. If such an assessment were the true sentiments of the church and the Jewish community in Jerusalem at that time, then there can be no doubt that the death of James had a tremendous impact on the church and certainly sent

---

[75] Although, by our chronology Paul was arrested in 55 C.E., James was martyred seven years later. Eusebius (*Hist eccl.*, 2.23.1-3) makes it appear that the two events were consecutive. But Eusebius also tells us that the Jews waited until Festus had died and Judea was in between Procurators. In other words, they held out until there was a period when Roman officials could not interfere with their treacherous plot against James, so we see no contradiction in this narrative.

a shock wave of astonished bewilderment among the entire Jerusalem community.

It is right at this time in church history that Jesus' followers may have been preparing for the beginning of the end-time events that Jesus spoke about – the last seven years of Daniel's prophecy (and now John's) climatic period that would signal the return of Jesus, the Messiah. It probably never occurred to the apostles, nor the rest of the church, that James would have been cut off right at this crucial time in prophetic history. There was no idea of a designated successor. And whenever a strong monarchial type of leader dies without a designated successor, there usually is a break down in authority and direction. And such was the case within the Jerusalem church soon thereafter.

Eusebius tells us that the uncle of Jesus and James succeeded James' chair as bishop of the Jerusalem church, Symeon, the son of Clopas,[76] and brother of Jesus' father, Joseph (Eusebius, *Hist. eccl.* 3.11.1-2; 3.22; 3.32.1-6, 35; 4.5.3; 4.22.4). Symeon was 76 years old when he took office and is reported to have held office for the next 44 years, until at the age of 120. He was tortured and martyred during the reign of Emperor Trajan, which Eusebius, in his chronicle, places in the year of 106/7 C.E.[77] During the next 28 years the bishops of Jerusalem that succeeded Symeon were all Jewish until the time when Emperor Hadrian destroyed Jerusalem in 135 C.E. and forbade any Jews to return to Jerusalem, which was renamed Aelia.[78] After the second destruction of Jerusalem, Jewish Christianity was

---

[76] Concerning Clopas, John records: "Standing near the cross of Jesus were his mother, and his mother's sister, Mary the wife of Clopas, and Mary Magdalene" (John 19:25). It is not clear from the Greek whether there were four women or three. "If one takes 'Mary of Clopas' to stand in apposition to 'the sister of his mother,' then Clopas could be Jesus' cousin or grandfather or uncle on his mother's side" (Jon B. Daniels, "Clopas" *The Anchor Bible Dictionary,* David Noel Freedman, ed., [New York: Doubleday, 1992], 1:1066). Was this Clopas the same as the Cleopas who was one of the two travellers to Emmaus with whom Jesus conversed after the resurrection according to Luke 24:18? Most scholars think not, even though Origen (*Cles.* 2.62, 68) preserves a tradition that they were one and the same.

[77] How interesting it is that the chair of James was passed on to someone whom we know nothing of from the New Testament and not passed on to Peter or John, the other two pillars of the Jerusalem church. Obviously, Peter and John must have felt that the family of Jesus had priority in leading the church in Jerusalem. Andrew Louth, (*Eusebius: The History of the Church from Christ to Constantine* [New York: Penguin, 1965)], 418, states that this Symeon, who left no writings, "suffered martyrdom at the age of 120 at a date which would seem to be ca. 106/7."

[78] The 13 Jewish Jerusalem bishops who succeeded Symeon did not fair very well in the annals of history – being merely names on an episcopal list. Symeon was succeeded by Justus I, Zacchaeus, Tobias, Benjamin, John, Matthias, Philip, Seneca, Justus II, Levi, Ephres, Joseph, and Judas (Eusebius, *Hist. eccl.* 4.5.3). Thirteen bishops in 28 years works out to an average of 1 to 2 years a piece, which may reflect the instability of the times. Another possibility is that these names represented a council of twelve ruling at the same time, where, in that whole time, only one member had to be replaced, thus, thirteen altogether.

virtually snuffed out.

A few years after James' death, the Apostle John writes that many – not a few – but many rebels were now emerging within the ranks of the church itself (1 John 2:18, 19). Many of them who had formerly accepted and believed in Jesus were now beginning to deny his name (1 John 4:1, 2), and even then these people were no longer submitting to the original apostles. Indeed, some of the Gentile church elders began to reject the authority of the Apostle John himself (1 John 4:6).

The Apostle Peter predicted that destructive sects were to arise within the pale of the church, feasting with Christians themselves, committing abominable acts and now were denying that Christ would return to earth (2 Pet 2:1, 2, 13; 3:3, 4). The Apostle Jude (James' and Jesus' brother), began to write about the common salvation that the faithful share in, but was forced to break off from that topic and "write and appeal to you to contend for the faith that was once for all entrusted to the saints" (Jude 1:3). Jude was now witnessing what Peter had predicted would happen.

Even Paul was witnessing a breakdown in the church when he wrote "all men in Asia have turned away from me" (2 Tim 1:15). Up to the time of James' martyrdom, the *Book of Acts* portrays a basically unified church (albeit strains here and there), but afterward we see insurrection, dissension, and many doctrinal doubts beginning to surface.

Then, all of a sudden, the story of Acts seemingly comes to an abrupt halt right at the verge of some of the greatest events in apostolic history. It is almost as if the Apostle Paul (or possibly Peter) could not bear to record the unfortunate events which followed in church history. Could they have removed the last chapters when these letters were edited for inclusion within the Christian canon? Who else would have had the authority or the reason to do so? Indeed, Peter may have deliberately wished not to include within a future canon for the church the events that would have been either superfluous or even distressful. In any event, the final chapters of Acts appear to be a deliberate deletion.

The death of James must have been so unexpected that it never occurred to the apostles that James would not be alive when Christ returned to his church. But after the death of James, coupled with the failure of the end-time prophecies occurring as expected, the disillusionment of Jewish Christianity was becoming widespread. Eusebius tells us that many of the Christians at this time "were driven out of Judaea" (Eusebius, *Hist. eccl.* 3.5.2).

The many thousands of Jews that James said were believers in Christ had by now either renounced Christianity, moved out of Judea, or joined the Zealots to fight Rome, or just gave up on the faith altogether. Even though events were not shaping up as were expected, Peter, John and Jude, who were still in Jerusalem where the temple was still operating, no doubt, following the influence of James, remained staunch believers in the law and the expectation of Jesus' soon return.

The Apostle Paul, on the other hand, certainly felt that something was wrong in all of this, but still could not put his finger on what the exact answer was. Why did James die? Why was the temple still functioning? Was Jesus really going to return in their generation or not? These are questions that Paul must have been wrestling with at this time. Whatever the case, the year 62 C.E. was no doubt another phenomenal turning point in the history of the apostolic church, and was another significant event that had a great bearing on the prophetic outlook of Paul.

One thing seemed certain. Without James, the Jerusalem church suffered an extremely hard blow. They may have not realized it at the time, but in reality, it signaled the beginning of the end of "Jewish Christianity." This in turn was the door that broke the Judaic character of the initial followers of Jesus. The "Jewish" apostles appear to not have been able to correctly deal with this phenomenon.

The Apostle Paul, however, was prepared and would thus be used to produce more New Testament writings than anyone else in order to deal with these important matters. However, even Paul didn't have all the answers that he was seeking yet at this time. But the answers would soon be revealed to him, which we will look at in an upcoming chapter.

CHAPTER 5

The Expectation of the Apostolic Church

WHEN WE LOOK AT THE APOSTOLIC WRITINGS penned prior to the year of 63 C.E., it is evident that the apostles originally viewed the second coming of Jesus to be very imminent and within their own generation. Their Epistles reveal that they believed that the return of Christ would be within the time period that embraced their very own life time. This fact is one of the most important factors in comprehending the background to the series of events in the later years after 63 C.E.

Unfortunately, scholars have completely missed the significance of the year 63 C.E. and, therefore, have assumed that Peter, John and Paul all believed (until their dying breath) that the second coming would occur during their lifetime.[79] What this false assumption has done is to only give scholars another reason to bolster their own view that the latter writings were not written by the apostles.

However, could it be that in the years after 63 C.E. the apostles made a complete turn-about in their thinking and, as a result, took emergency steps in order to preserve their testimony for a future age? Of course it is! It is time that we look at the internal evidence and understand what was really going on in the minds of the apostles. The pre-63 mentality was expectancy. The post-63 C.E mentality was settling in for the long term. The pivotal year of 63 C.E. is the key to understanding the period of *Beyond Acts*. Let us now study this in further detail.

First of all, the Apostle Paul, based upon what he himself wrote, in all of his Epistles written before 63 C.E., believed that the imminence of all end-time prophetic events was about to soon occur. Paul also believed that the initial readers of his Epistles would be alive to observe the second

---

[79] The *Book of Revelation* was also a part of the pre-63 C.E. environment, as the internal evidence clearly shows (see appendix 5). The damage that has been done by placing it in the mid-90's C.E. has caused scholars to totally misunderstand the entire apostolic era and especially, the picture of canon history as well.

coming of their Lord themselves (1 Cor 15:15, 52; 1 Thess 4:15-17). We can surely see this in such sentiments like

> the appointed time has grown short... for the present form of this world passes away (1 Cor 7:29, 31).

So convinced was the Apostle Paul concerning the imminence of the end-time events that he even admonished the Corinthians in the year 54 C.E. that they should refrain from marriage due to the "impending crisis" (1 Cor 7:26). Why would Paul give such drastic cautioning? Certainly because he believed that the anticipated end-time events were soon to occur (1 Cor 7:1-32). A year later he wrote to the Congregation in Rome with even more strenuous anticipation of end-time events:

> Now it is high time to awake out of sleep: for now our salvation is nearer than when we first believed. The night is far spent, the day is at hand (Rom 16:20).

Paul had a solid conviction that Satan would soon be crushed under the feet of the saints (Rom 16:20). And as late as 58 C.E., Paul was still of the conviction that "the Lord is at hand" (Phil 4:5). Paul's fervent expectancy of Christ's return was expressed to the believers in the church at Thessalonica when he told them

> for since we believe that Jesus died and rose again, even so, through Jesus, God will bring with him those who have died. For this we declare to you by the word of the Lord, that we who are alive, who are left until the coming of the Lord, will by no means precede those who have died (1 Thess 4:14-15).

Notice Paul's emphatic declaration "we who are alive." Paul was absolutely convinced that these are the believers who "are left until the coming of the Lord." There can be no doubt that the Apostle Paul at this time in his life believed that he and all of those that he wrote to were included in the statement that they would be "alive" and that they would see "the coming of the Lord." Paul also said that these are the ones who "certainly" will "not precede" those who have fallen asleep. This certainly was the basis of Paul's teaching in this context in the years prior to 63 C.E.

When we look at the writings of the Apostle James, the (half) brother of Jesus, writing probably in the early forties, we likewise see that he warned his audience that it was "the last days" and that they should remain patient "until the coming of the Lord... for the coming of the Lord is near" and "the Judge is standing at the doors" (James 5:7, 8, 9). These statements represent the absolute conviction that Jesus was soon to come to the living recipients of these letters.

Again, the Apostle John, who most likely wrote after 63 C.E., appealed to his readers with the following words:

> Children, it is the last hour! As you have heard that antichrist is coming, so now many antichrists have come. From this we know that it is the LAST HOUR (1 John 2:18).

We can see here that John is not just talking about the "last days," but now the "last hour" – imminency in the extreme.[80] Also, we can see from such fervent statements as these that there can be no doubt that these quoted apostles were absolutely convinced, with all of their being, their might, and their total conviction, that they were living in the very last generation that would witness the return of Christ to this earth.

Why did the apostles believe in the soon return of Christ so fervently? First of all, their belief was the direct result of Jesus' very own words. Listen carefully to what Jesus himself said:

> Truly I tell you (speaking to his disciples), THIS GENERATION will not pass away, until all these things have taken place (the end-time events that Jesus had been predicting that would usher in his second coming, Matt 24:34).

Jesus had been predicting, throughout the twenty-fourth chapter of Matthew, the type of events that would precede his coming. He was telling his disciples to look for the events that he was describing. He further told his disciples that judgments upon evil people from the time of Abel to the close of the Old Testament age would take place on that very generation which existed in the first century. And again, Jesus reiterated to his disciples that

> truly I tell you, all this will come upon this generation (Matt 32:36).

Obviously, the use of Jesus' term "this generation" certainly limited these events to within the lifetime of Jesus' listeners. But we should ask ourselves at this point, if the term "this generation" was specific enough to be a definite period of time? Or was this term just some loose phrase that only vaguely gave a rough indication that Jesus would return

[80] The Apostle John, and some of the other Jerusalem-based apostles, may have not changed their mind in 63 C.E., as did Paul, based upon the apocalyptic vision that John was already given. The language that John uses in his first Epistle would seem to indicate that he was writing in 69 C.E. or early 70 C.E., just prior to the destruction of the temple.

sometime within the lifetimes of his listeners?

At first, the disciples thought that the return of Christ could be soon after his resurrection (Acts 1:6). Then after four years of abundant growth, the church witnessed its first martyr, Stephen, and severe persecution ensued thereafter. Was this persecution the beginning of the end time events predicted by Jesus?

As the first decade came and went, there was no sign that the end was to occur. After this, the apostles may have begun to understand the term "generation" in the same sense as the generation of the Israelites that wandered for forty years in the desert before entering the land of promise. This makes perfect sense because, if Jesus was the prophet like Moses, and the children of Israel did not enter the promised land for an additional 40 years, would not there be a similar 40-year period prior to the second coming of Jesus?

It seems that this belief in the 40 year period became the basis for the apostles to be able to move from statements about the last days to statements about the last hour. Certainly, it appears that the apostles must have adopted a definite time table of events to occur in the same manner as Jesus had predicted. A progression in time of forty years was therefore apparently seen as the measure for the apostle's understanding of the fulfillment of end-time events.

This fact is *extremely* important in New Testament studies, because it has a great bearing on interpreting correctly the events of all New Testament history. The importance of understanding this point cannot be underestimated, nor stressed enough. Many have tossed the statements of Jesus on this matter aside and, as a result, have not correctly reconstructed what was going on in the minds of Jesus' faithful disciples in the years thereafter.

The fact of the matter is that in this context, the term "this generation" does in fact mean a very specific span of time in the minds of the apostles. The apostles could see the parallel between the "generation" of the ancient Israelites that wandered for forty years in the desert from the time of the Exodus to the entry into the land of Canaan, and the generation from the time that Jesus predicted the end until his return – a type of entering into the promised Kingdom of God. We can certainly see this in such statement as

> your ancestors put me to the test, though they had seen my works for FORTY YEARS. Therefore I was angry with THAT GENERATION (Heb 3:9, 10).

"That generation" was, in this very context, defined as a period of 40 years. And when "that generation" is compared to "this generation" in which the apostles were then living in, then they could see that if Christ died in the year that we call 30 C.E., it is simple arithmetic for the apostles to conclude that the culmination of all end-time prophecies would occur by 70 C.E. And since the prophet Daniel spoke of a period of seven years to complete the events leading up to the coming of the Messiah, and Jesus himself referred to Daniel's prophesy as a gauge to measure those events, then counting backwards seven years from 70 C.E. brings us to the crucial year of 63 C.E. for these events to begin happening.

However, we can now look back with 20/20 hindsight and see that Jesus did not return at this time. But we do know that the city of Jerusalem was in fact destroyed exactly as Jesus had predicted, within the forty years that made up the generation after Jesus' prediction. In fact, Daniel had prophesied that there would be a final week of years – seven years – before the end would come (Dan 9:27; 11:31). During this time (63-70 C.E.) the apostle's now believed that this is when all of end prophecy would take place.

And Daniel also said that in the midst of this period the sacrifice and oblation would cease due to the "abomination of desolation." This would be three and a half years into the midst of this period and would bring us to the year of 67 C.E. Jesus himself referred to this prophecy (Matt 24:15) as a time for the faithful to flee out of Jerusalem into the mountains for safety. It is significant to understand that the *Book of Revelation* also foretold that the church would flee at this time for a period of three and a half years (Rev 12:14).[81]

There is still another point to consider in understanding that the apostles came to realize that the period of the generation that they were living in was at least forty years from the prophecies of Jesus. The Apostle Peter had been told that he would die an old man before the return of Christ (John 21:18, 19), whereas John himself would "tarry until I come" (John 21:21-3).[82]

If Peter was around Jesus' age of 30 and Jesus was to return another forty years thereafter, then Peter would have died just before Jesus' return around the archetypical age of 70 years. This then could be interpreted as Peter living until the late sixties C.E., whereas the Apostle John would live until the return of Christ in 70 C.E. And indeed, Peter did die in the late sixties and John was still alive past the destruction of Jerusalem. But again, it is important to realize that Jesus did not return when Jerusalem was destroyed in 70 C.E.

---

[81] This fact tells us explicitly that this time period, which, when this was penned, was still a foreseen event, and therefore was a period that was prior to 67 C.E. The date of the writing of the *Book of Revelation* is fully discussed in Appendix 3.

[82] See Ernest L. Martin, *Restoring*, 196, for further insight on this subject.

Now, here is the significance of this entire line of discussion. Many scholars believe in what we are here saying – that the first century Christians believed in the fact that the return of Christ would occur within their lifetimes. And since a number of scholars place the Apostle Paul's death around 62 C.E.,[83] and we have Paul stating as late as 57/58 C.E. that the end is near, then these scholars also believe that Paul, all through his lifetime, never swerved from this belief. And if that is the case, then the so-called Pastoral Epistles of Paul, which have a very different tone and message, were supposedly written long after the lifetime of Paul by some other unknown author and therefore certainly could not have been written by the Apostle Paul himself.

Indeed, most scholars maintain that the expectation of the first century Christians – that Jesus would return soon – was held all the way down to the end of the first century. And it is because of this premise that many scholars have concluded that those New Testament books, which do not emphasize the imminence of Jesus' return, were written after the time of the apostles. And since the *Book of Revelation* is erroneously dated to around 96 C.E., then this also confirms the idea that the first century church still held onto the belief of Jesus' soon return right on down to the end of the first century. Yet, nothing could be further from the truth. Indeed, this false interpretation of the data must be overturned once and for all if we are to ever come to a correct reconstruction of first century apostolic history. It is therefore important that we understand that "this generation" was limited to the 40 years after Jesus as the apostles must have understood it.

Jesus had also predicted that certain other events must take place before his return. Then, and only then, can we see that as the time grew nearer to the end of this 40 year span, it became obvious to the apostles that those events were not happening as predicted. And as a result, could it be that the apostles, as the time approached the crucial year of 63 C.E., were weighing the events carefully and could see soon after 63 C.E. that the events that they had been expecting were not panning out as originally believed? Could it be that the apostles themselves changed their mind when it became obvious to them that the end was not near? Of course it is, and we maintain that this is exactly what was happening in the minds of the apostles. It is time that modern scholars project themselves back into the sandals of the apostles. Scholars seem to have a lot of theories, but none of them, it seems, are able to place themselves surrounded by the actual historical events of the first century.

We will show that the Apostle Paul lived at least another 5 years

---

[83] So, e.g., Robert Jewett, *A Chronology of Paul's Life* (Philadelphia: Fortress, 1979), 102.

beyond his supposed death in 62 C.E. And, we will show that it was during this period of time that Paul changed his conviction that Jesus would soon return. This fact is extremely important in order to understand New Testament history correctly and even the true circumstances behind the canonization of the New Testament.

We will trace the history of the New Testament and show that even though the apostles early believed that Jesus would return in their generation, as the years approached the end of the forty year span, it became evident to some (but maybe not all) of the apostles that Jesus would NOT return within their generation.

That is the conclusion that we are compelled to make when we finally see the events that transpired as the apostles saw them. This we will do and this is why the story of *Beyond* the *Book of Acts* – the period of beyond 58 C.E. – is so important to understand. It is after this period that we must reconstruct the story in its true light.

We will show why modern theories that claim that during the entire first century the church believed that Jesus would return are wrong. Most scholars believe that it was not until the second century that the church looked at the return of Jesus as a futuristic event. And it is because of this faulty reasoning that many scholars, who look at the Pastoral Epistles as not being the work of Paul, do so because these letters speak of establishing churches and setting forth guidelines for selecting Pastors and Elders for a church that is to continue past their time. Works such as these, (so conclude these scholars), could not be the work of the Apostle Paul. Why? Because Paul fervently believed (so say these scholars) to his very dying day that the end was near.

It is therefore reasoned that if all during the first century the faithful were awaiting for Jesus' return, then there would be no reason to establish churches with a hierarchal administration. Why would the apostles be concerned with establishing churches if Jesus was soon to return? Good point. So good in fact that scholars find it too irresistible for it not to be the actual case. But the reader should not be fooled into accepting this line of reasoning. Why? Because it is entirely deceptive for the following reasons.

First of all, many scholars have gotten their chronology wrong. It is therefore impossible for us to move forward in the correct direction until this is straightened out.[84] Paul did not die in the early sixties, nor did Peter. They died in the late sixties. This is crucial to understanding the history of *Beyond Acts*. Once we are clear on this, then we can see that the time of disillusionment was not during the second century, but soon after

---

[84] New Testament chronology is discussed in appendix 2.

the year of 63 C.E. And, as a result, the Apostle Paul, who in his earlier writings believed in Christ's return during his lifetime, changed his mind toward the end of his ministry. Peter, as well, did the very same thing. Why did they change their minds? This is the theme that we will develop throughout our story, but we can see here that Paul definitely changed his mind for the following reasons.

There are definite clues that show us that the year 63 C.E. was indeed the turning point in the prophetic scenario of the first century. Many have ignored this pivotal year in their analysis of the prophetic run down as the apostles themselves must have analyzed the events that transpired. As a result, many simply believe that the apostles maintained a constant belief to their dying day that Jesus would return in their lifetime. That notion has had a disastrous effect on the interpretation of the development of the New Testament.

We maintain, however, that the year of 63 C.E. was the year that the Apostle Paul, at least, had now changed his tune. It is as a result of his influence that, not long after, the Apostles Peter and John finally changed their minds as well. The significance of this fact should revolutionize the entire understanding of New Testament development.

We have placed a lot of emphasis on the year of 63 C.E. as a turning point in the New Testament history. This point is so significant to the overall story, and one that has not caught the eye of scholars in general, that we will now look into it in depth in the next chapter. Understanding this significant key alone is as crucial as any point in the entire history of the first century church. This will help us fill in the true story after the final chapter of the *Book of Acts* and *beyond...*

CHAPTER 6

The Mystery of the Year 63 C.E.

IN THE THREE DECADES AFTER THE RESURRECTION of Jesus, the *Book of Acts* records that there had been thousands of Jews who turned to Christianity. Yet, when the last remnants of Christians retreated to the area around the small city of Pella by 66 C.E., there were only hundreds. Although many had left the Jerusalem area initially due to the Saulian persecution in the mid-thirties, many who remained eventually had left the faith entirely. Luke's account in Acts breaks off just before we could read the details of what was actually happening in the subsequent years after Paul's release from his first imprisonment at Rome in 58 C.E.

The most monumental events of apostolic church history were about to occur, and yet the *Book of Acts* breaks off right at the most crucial point in all of New Testament history. It is one of the greatest enigmas of all time as to why Acts is silent about future events after this point. It almost seems that a conscious decision was made not to incorporate the events that were occurring because they were showing the disintegration of the church. The later letters of Peter and Paul, however, give us clues as to what was happening that help us fill in the blanks during this important period.

The air of messianic expectation that Jesus would return at the end of the fourth decade after the resurrection was early believed by all the apostles (based on their writings), but as the time approached near the crucial year of 63 C.E., it was becoming apparent, first by the Apostle Paul, at least, that the prophetic scene was not shaping up as should be expected. The Apostles Peter and John may have waited to the mid-point of the Sabbatical cycle (65/66 C.E.) that began in the autumn of 61 C.E. to see if Daniel's prophecies would at all shape up as they believed that they should in order to signal the events that Jesus, Daniel and even the Revelation of John had foretold. But after some monumental events in 66 C.E. (which was discussed on pages 34-7), it appears that these apostles too would have had to abandon their hope in Christ's return within their own generation. This is a significant point in understanding how the New

Testament canon was to take shape.

Ironically, it was around this same time that most of the Jews were becoming more fervent in their belief that the promised Messiah would soon appear on the scene. As one noted New Testament scholar writes concerning this time:

> Josephus, Tacitus and Suetonius combine to tell how they [the Jews] were encouraged by an ancient oracle in their sacred writings to the effect that 'at that very time' a man or men from Judaea would gain supreme world-dominion. The oracle is probably the angelic prophecy in Dan. 9:24-7 announcing that seventy heptads of years would elapse before the establishment of everlasting righteousness. ...calculations in the sixties evidently led some to believe that this period was approaching completion.[85]

Jesus referred to Daniel's prophecies (Matt 24:15) in connection with the events "at the end of the age" (v. 3) and that "this generation shall not pass, till all these things be fulfilled" (v. 34). Even the Romans viewed Daniel's prophecies as pointing to fulfillment within their generation. The great fire of Rome of July 19, 64 C.E. was blamed on those expecting the arrival of the "New Age" of the Messiah, especially those Jews and Gentiles aligned with the Jesus movement.

Nero, near this time, was even advised by his astrologers to move his capital from Rome to Jerusalem because they said that sovereignty over the world was destined to arise in Judaea at that period of time (Suetonius, *Nero*, 40). Both the Roman historians Tacitus (*Histories*, 5.13) and Suetonius (*Vespasian*, 4) mentioned the general feeling of the people throughout the Empire who looked for the soon emerging "New Empire."

A new Sabbatical cycle began in the autumn of 61 C.E. This cycle may have been considered the last Sabbatical cycle of Daniel's prophecy. If the apostles looked at this prophecy in this way, then they knew that the gospel had to be preached in all the world before the "abomination of desolation" would be set up in the temple in Jerusalem.

The last seven years of Daniel's prophecy was divided into two sections of three and a half years. In the middle of that period the "abomination of desolation" would be set up (Dan 9:27) and at the end of this period Michael, the Archangel, would stand up to defend Israel (Dan 12:1). Thus, if the timing was right, then by the end of the year 66 C.E., the abomination of desolation had to be in place or the prophecy must refer to some other seven year period still lying in the future. And, indeed, none of this was taking place at this time. It is the failure of this

---

[85] F. F. Bruce, *New Testament History* (New York: Doubleday, 1969), 380.

event that must have finally hit home with Peter and John, who were still in Jerusalem at this time and could witness first hand what was going on. We will shortly show why the apostles now finally came to the conclusion that the prophecies were yet future. For now, however, let us see why the year 63 C.E. was so significant prophetically.

DANIEL — KEY TO PROPHECY RUN-DOWN

DANIEL, THE NINTH CHAPTER, MADE IT CLEAR that the city of Jerusalem and the temple were to be destroyed before a covenant involving one Sabbatical cycle could commence (Dan 9:26-7). The latest that this could have happened, and still have the last seven years of Daniel's prophecy remain within the 40 years' generation from Christ's resurrection, was in the year of 63 C.E. Then the temple and the city had to be hurriedly rebuilt in order for the "abomination of desolation" to be placed in the holy of holies after the first three and a half years (Rev 11:1).[86]

Also, we read in the *Book of Revelation* that

> there are seven kings: five are fallen, and one IS (the sixth king), and the other is NOT YET COME; and when he comes, he must continue a short space (Rev 17:10).

Who were these seven kings? This is a question that even the apostles wondered about. The clue was that "one is" and the last king had not materialized yet. Did John know which kings he was referring to? If John had in mind the Roman Emperors, then the "king" that "now is" could be Nero (54-68 C.E.), since Nero was in fact the sixth Roman Emperor since Julius Caesar.[87]

Even if John was referring to the rulers of Jerusalem, then Herod the Great could have been considered to be the first king of the prophecy, then Archelaus would be the second, then the third would be the Roman Government, then fourth, Agrippa the First (37-45 C.E.), then fifth would again be Rome (45-56 C.E.), and the sixth government would be that of Agrippa II (56-70 C.E.). At any rate, the change in government in Rome in

---

[86] Revelation describes a measuring reed associated with the prophecy of the two witnesses which may imply a rebuilding project.

[87] 1. Julius Caesar, 2. Augustus, 3. Tiberius, 4. Caligula, 5. Claudius, 6. Nero (54-68 C.E.). See Kenneth L. Gentry, Jr., *Before Jerusalem Fell: Dating the Book of Revelation* (Tyler, Tex.: Institute for Christian Economics, 1989), 158.

54 C.E. and in Jerusalem in 56 C.E. may have been looked on as significantly prophetical.[88]

At the beginning of Nero's reign many false Messiahs came on the scene. In the first year of Nero's reign (54 C.E.), Josephus records that

> imposters and deceivers persuaded the multitude to follow them into the wilderness, and pretended that they would exhibit manifest wonders and signs, that should be performed by the providence of God. And many that were prevailed on by them suffered the punishments of their folly; for Felix brought them back, and then punished them (Josephus, *A.J.* 20.8.6 [167-8]).

Things were beginning to stir up. Indeed, at this time, arose a false Messiah who was simply known as "the Egyptian." If the reports are true, his influence was far greater than even the Christian movement, for then he is said to have led some 30,000 people to the Mount of Olives and then to the desert, proclaiming that he would cause the walls of Jerusalem to be destroyed. The reason for his popularity is obvious. He, unlike Jesus, definitely did have political designs against the Roman establishment, and the fanaticism of zealots always had an appeal among those who showed promise in overthrowing Rome. Therefore, "the Egyptian" was one messianic pretender that was not to be ignored.

The Roman Procurator, Felix, was able to quickly put an end to the sedition aroused by this "Egyptian" and rout the people back under his control, even though the Egyptian himself escaped. About two years later, the Roman authorities thought that this Egyptian renegade reappeared back on the Jerusalem scene, since they thought that it was the Apostle Paul who was "the Egyptian" returning to cause trouble (Acts 21:38; Josephus, *A.J.* 20.8.6 [169-172]).

Interestingly enough, Jesus had actually predicted that this false prophet would come on the scene to lead people into the desert, claiming that Jesus was there. Note that Jesus warned his disciples "Wherefore if they shall say unto you, Behold he is in the desert... believe it not" (Matt 24:26). The apostle's of Jesus must have viewed all of this as a direct fulfillment of what Jesus had warned.

Another indication that the time of the end grew close at hand is that Josephus said that so many false Christs began to appear among the Jews in Judaea that hardly a day went by that the Roman Procurator did not

[88] Martin, *Restoring*, 324-5. Based upon this, the initial vision given to the Apostle John in Jerusalem would have to have been around 56/7 C.E. Gentry (ibid.) states: "It seems indisputably clear that the *Book of Revelation* must be dated in the reign of Nero Caesar, and consequently before his death in June, A.D. 68. He is the sixth king; the short-lived rule of the seventh king (Galba) 'has not yet come.' "

put some of them to death (Josephus, *A.J.* 20.8.5 [160-1]). As early as 49 C.E., the Jews in Rome were expelled from the capital because of the commotion caused by a Messianic pretender named "Chrestus" (Suetonius, *Claudius*, 25).[89]

SIGNIFICANT FACTORS CONCERNING 63 C.E.

THE APOSTLES AT THIS TIME MAY HAVE ALSO been evaluating the prophecies of Daniel. Daniel had said that the Kingdom of Nebuchadnezzar was the "head of gold" which represented the Babylonian (Gentile) system of government. It lasted from 604 B.C.E. to 538 B.C.E. – a period of 66 years. Interestingly enough, 666 years later from the beginning of Nebuchadnezzars rule lands squarely on the year of 63 C.E.

Also note that Josephus stated that 600 years was looked upon by the Jews as an astronomical/historical cycle of time called "The Great Year" (Josephus, *A.J.* 1.3.9 [106]). Counting from the start of the silver portion of Daniel's image in 538 C.E., 600 years later falls exactly on 63 C.E. A third world empire was represented in Daniel's brass portion of the image. This was to commence with a he-goat from the West pushing at the silver portion in the East. This was recognized to be Alexander the Great, who

[89] If we take this passage at face value, *Chrestus* appears to be an agitator who is alive during Claudius' time and there in Rome. Rainer Riesner, *Paul's Early Period* (Grand Rapids: Eerdmans, 1998), 162-7, however, along with most scholars, recently argues that "*Chrestus*" refers to Christ. Eisenman, *James*, 787, also states that *Chrestus* "obviously intended to mean 'Christ' – the Romans not distinguishing between Jews and Christians at all at this point." Yet, F. F. Bruce, *History*, 297, states: "Although Christianity was indistinguishable from Judaism in the time of Claudius, it was perfectly distinguishable by the time Suetonius wrote (*c.* A.D. 120), and it was well known that it had been founded by Christ (*Christus*, not unnaturally confused with the common slave-name *Chrestus*, which was pronounced in practically the same way)." We should not overlook the fact that Suetonius was later on referring to Christianity as *Christiani* (*Nero* 16.2). The motivation for finding historical references of Jesus in the Roman records may be the basis of many scholarly conclusions on this. It could also be that the term *Chrestus* was referring to expectations of the Jews of a coming Messiah other than referring to the "Christian" movement. Furthermore, should we always jump to the conclusion that this riot was due to a religious movement? *Chrestus* could have been a sort of Spartacus, leading a Jewish slave uprising against Rome, and therefore a civil Messiah in the eyes of his adherents. Besides this, are scholars forgetting Jesus' admonition: "For many will come in my name, saying, 'I am the Christos'" (Matt 24:4)? Certainly, Simon Magus would have adopted such a title if it were a magic formula that gained him a following. It therefore seems that Claudius was nipping in the bud a new movement instigated by a new messianic pretender rousing up the Jews in the city of Rome and not a reference back to Jesus.

began to conquer the Persian Empire with his victory at the Battle of Granicus in 334 B.C.E. Counting from this date, 6 times 66 years (396) brings us again to 63 C.E. Everything seemed to converge on this important year as a significant turning point in Daniel's prophecy.

We have to remember that it was the *Book of Revelation* that made the connection of the ominous number of 666 with the Beast. This "beast" was derived from Daniel's prophecy. It was Daniel who described the Babylonian system in terms that likened it to a wild animal or a "beast." The *Book of Revelation* makes the same comparison and this comparison points to the scrutiny of the apostles in attempting to apply Daniel's prophecies to their own generation.

It could be construed that when Jesus told his disciples that "Verily I say unto you, ALL THESE THINGS shall come upon THIS GENERATION" (Matt 23:35, 6), that the apostles believed that all the prophecies of the Old Testament would be fulfilled in their own generation – "upon whom the ends of the age are come" (1 Cor 10:11). The *Book of Revelation* certainly adopted this style of interpretation. It assembled dozens of prophecies from all parts of the Old Testament with little attention to the details of those prophecies or the people to whom the prophecies were first given. It simply focused the combined fulfillment of all prophecy into a single generation – indeed, even into a single seven-year period (divided into two halves, as Daniel had done earlier) and placed their fulfillment in the "Lord's Day"– or rather, "the Day of the Lord (Rev 1:10). Ernest Martin comments in this regard:

> The Book of Revelation drew prophecies from all over the Old Testament and combined them into a single prophetic framework which was destined to occur within one generation of 40 years and with a final period of 7 years. This resulted in ancient prophecies referring to Babylon, Tyre, Assyria, Egypt, Edom, etc., being combined together into one prophetic scenario to occur in a single generation just prior to Christ's second advent. Indeed, this type of prophetic interpretation was not limited to Christians alone. When one surveys the apocalyptic literature that was being written around the time of Christ, one sees much evidence of this type of explanation being in vogue. People were identifying all types of ancient nations with political entities existing in the first century. There were the Dead Sea sectarians who lived just before and during the time of Christ who interpreted the prophecies of Habakkuk about early Chaldeans as being the people of Chittim (which they acknowledged as the Romans of their day). After all, it was evident that many of the ancient prophecies had not yet found fulfillment but it was firmly expected that all of them would occur. The generation of fulfillment was

> anticipated to last for 40 years (with the final 7 years being most crucial) before the Kingdom of God would be established on earth. And to the apostles that strategic end-time period was presumed to occupy the period of 40 years after Christ's resurrection.[90]

John believed that this collection of prophecies (along with new ones revealed to him) were "things which MUST SHORTLY come to pass" (Rev 1:1), and not in any generation which followed, for he says that even the ones who crucified Jesus would be alive to witness the second advent (Rev 1:7; Matt 26:64).[91]

Another important fact to consider is that the apostles identified the virgin birth of Immanuel of Isaiah 7:14 with the virgin birth of Jesus (Matt 1:23). It is significant that this prophecy says in Isaiah 7:8 that there would be a period of 65 years associated with Immanuel that must transpire before the Syrians and Ephraimites could be overthrown and the Messianic kingdom described in Isaiah 11 and 12 could begin to be set up. Consider this! The early church fathers were nearly unanimous in their belief that Jesus was born in what we consider 3 B.C.E.[92] This understanding was no doubt that of the apostles, who may have counted the 65 years from Jesus' birth to the year of 63 C.E. As this year approached, the church no doubt expected the unfolding of all end-time prophecies to commence.

Thus, the year 63 C.E. was obviously a turning point in the apostolic interpretation of prophecy. After it had come and gone without anything significant prophetically, is when some attitudes began to change, specifically in the mind of the Apostle Paul, as we shall see in the next chapter.

---

[90] Ernest L. Martin, *Restoring*, 222-3.

[91] This certainly would be a stretch if John was writing in the 90's. A 50's date for Revelation, however, makes all this perfectly possible.

[92] See Jack Finegan, *Handbook*, 288-91.

CHAPTER 7

The Post Years of Acts

THE BOOK OF ACTS MYSTERIOUSLY AND ABRUPTLY ends its narrative near the summer of 58 C.E., without even as much as the customary closing "Amen." As to why this is the case has been a matter of speculation down through the centuries. The ironic thing of it, however, is that it stops right at the point in time when some of the most monumental events of the entire New Testament period were about to transpire. These events were so profound in nature that they greatly affected the writings of the last letters of the apostles – specifically those of the Apostles Peter and Paul.

Had the *Book of Acts* been completed, then we would not be in any doubt as to what was truly transpiring during this time. One thing to remember (in order to come to a correct understanding as to what the apostles were doing in their last days), is to realize that although the apostles reflected expectation in the soon return of Christ within their lifetime, as seen within their earlier writings, their later writings show a definite switch in mentality. As such, many biblical critics of today have rejected the latter New Testament writings as not being authored by the apostles which bear their names. They have opted to simply assign different authorship rather than investigate the factors that would have changed the apostle's outlook as they reached the end of their generation.

Scholars thus have concocted theories that the New Testament documents were written by unknown writers who lived, in some cases, long after the apostles. Why is this? Because the latter writings of the apostles changed so dramatically in character and in tone that scholars can see no other choice other than to opt for different, post-apostolic authorship. But we must legitimately ask, if there is something about what the apostles wrote in their latter writings that seemed so different, is it due to different authorship or is it due to different circumstances that caused these writers to change their minds? Scholars have never adequately addressed this possibility. Our investigation into this subject is crucial in understanding how the New Testament itself came into being, and why.

As it has already been shown, the Epistles of Paul show a marked change after the year 63 C.E. We see this not only in the Apostle Paul's writings, but also in the Apostle Peter's as well. The differences between the Epistles of First and Second Peter are so marked that many scholars reject Petrine authorship of Second Peter.[93]

Jesus had actually prophesied that people, especially those of the faithful, would eventually be wondering why Jesus was not intervening in world affairs and begin saying: "My Lord delays his coming" (Matt 24:48). He then immediately taught the parable of the Ten Virgins which instructs us that no one would know the precise time of Christ's return (Matt 25:1-13). But if people were beginning to say that "Christ delays his coming," does that not imply that there was a date of expectancy surrounding that promise? How can one be delayed if there is no appointed time for an arrival?

Also, were the Christians of the first century any different than any of those down through the centuries who have set their hopes on a particular date for the return of Christ and then experienced a period of "great disappointment" when the time came and went without the Parousia?

Did not the first century Christians and apostles look to the writings of the prophets in order to try to understand how the prophecies would come to pass in their generation? Did not Daniel provide chronological information that allowed, not only the messianic believers of the first century, room for speculation, but the entire Jewish community in general? The coming of the Messiah was no doubt paramount in the minds of the Jews, as well as Christians, in the sixth decade of the first century.

Significant Post Acts Events

AFTER THE *BOOK OF ACTS* CLOSES, THE FIRST major event that happened in the church was the martyrdom of the Apostle James, the (half) brother of Jesus, and head of the Jerusalem church, in the year of 62 C.E. (Eusebius, *Hist. eccl.* 2.23.1-25). There can be no doubt of the tremendous impact which that event must have had on the Christian community in Jerusalem. Let us run down some other events that also had an impact on the mood of the time.

---

[93] The subject of Petrine authorship of Second Peter is dealt with in Appendix 1.

The year of 61/62 C.E. was a Sabbatical year. It was in this year that Josephus records the commencement of a prophetic dirge against Jerusalem and the temple by a man named Joshua ben Ananias (Josephus, *B.J.* 6.5.3 [300-9]). Josephus also records that at this time that "sickness fell upon our city, and everything went from bad to worse" (*A.J.* 20.9.4 [214]). This epidemic started at the Feast of Tabernacles of that year – "from this date were sown in the city the seeds of its impending doom" (*B.J.* 2.14.1 [276]).

Many Jews and Christians became fearful of these events and because of this, many began migrating out of that area and sought refuge in other Provinces of the Roman Empire. So great was this emigration that by the year 64 C.E., when the Roman Procurator Florus took rule in Judaea, even whole cities and regions were moving out in droves (*B.J.* 2.14.2 [278-9]).

Eusebius also tells us that at this time the apostles and disciples who were in Judea began to be scattered around the world (Eusebius, *Hist. eccl.* 3:1.1). Thomas went to Parthia, Andrew went to Scythia, and the Apostle John went to the western parts of Asia Minor, settling in the city of Ephesus, where he remained until his death. The Apostle Phillip and his virgin daughters went to Hieriopolis near the city of Laodicea in Asia Minor. Eusebius makes note that the apostles were actually "driven out of Judea" not long after James' death (ibid. 3.5.1).

The death of James was indeed the most significant event after the *Book of Acts* concluded. This event, coupled with the prophetic dirge, which was begun by Joshua ben Ananias in the fall of 62 C.E., may have impelled the apostles to start on a world-wide evangelistic campaign to preach the gospel to the whole world as a witness before the end of the age, just as Jesus had foretold would be done (Matt 24:14).

After Paul's release from his first Roman imprisonment in 58 C.E., he too felt compelled to spread his work to the far "West." Tradition tells us that he went to Spain, and then went to Gaul, and further traditions hold that he even went on to the British Isles. Indeed, Clement, the first bishop of Rome after the deaths of Peter and Paul, stated that Paul "taught righteousness to the WHOLE WORLD, having travelled to the LIMITS of the west" (1 Clem 5:7). The significance of the words "whole world" and "limits of the west" cannot be dismissed as mere hyperbole.

When Paul wrote to the Evangelist Timothy after his return from the west around the year of 64 C.E., he said that Christ "was preached among the nations and was believed on *IN THE WORLD*" (1 Tim 3:16). This is exactly what Clement had referred to. Paul also told the Colossians:

> Do not be shifted away from the hope of the Gospel which you heard, and which was preached IN ALL CREATION under heaven, of which Gospel I Paul became a minister

(Col 1:23).

Paul himself admits that he had been a part of the ministry that preached the gospel to the utter most parts of the known world. This statement is a key to understanding that Colossians was written after Paul's western campaign. And since it is a Prison Epistle, it indirectly refers to an imprisonment after Paul's two year Roman imprisonment where Paul had written to the Philippians. In this Epistle Paul tells the Colossians:

> You have heard of this hope before the word of truth, the gospel that has come to you. Just as it is bearing fruit and growing IN THE WHOLE WORLD (Col 1:6).

This statement is most interesting and worthy of further scrutiny because it shows us that Paul had already returned from his western campaign by the time he wrote this letter and penned this "Prison Epistle" in an imprisonment subsequent to his Roman imprisonment which ended in 58 C.E.

Some scholars are of the opinion that Paul lost his life during an imprisonment at Rome, which is typically dated to 62 C.E. This is supposedly seen as the reason why Paul could not have written the Pastoral Epistles. But this concept is false for the following reasons which we will now explain.

Correctly Placing the Prison Epistles

THE "PRISON EPISTLES" ARE GENERALLY BELIEVED all to have been composed during Paul's first imprisonment at Rome during the two years from 56-58 C.E. (which is generally dated 60-62 C.E.). We can accept the fact that Philippians was no doubt composed during this time because, for one thing, Paul was still expecting the soon return of Christ (Phil 4:5). This is significant because this places the Epistle back at a time prior to Paul's western campaign when he still held to the conviction that Daniel's prophecies would start around the significant year of 63 C.E.

Another significant fact that ties the letter of Philippians to Paul's first Roman imprisonment is the fact that he also refers to "those of the emperor's household" (Phil 4:22).

But closer examination of the other imprisonment Epistles appear to be of some later imprisonment after Paul's western campaign. Indeed, it is because scholars have incorrectly placed the letters of *Ephesians*, *Colossians*, and *Philemon* to Paul's first Roman imprisonment, or even earlier, that explains why scholars have been side-tracked into a ditch of their own making. This unfortunate circumstance has once again contributed to a false reconstruction of New Testament history and canon history as well. Let us now look at the internal evidence for the clues that will guide us in correctly reconstructing the true placement of these Epistles.

The *Book of Acts* ends with Paul under house arrest in Rome in the year of 58 C.E. Many scholars see no need to believe in any subsequent imprisonments. Yet, tradition tells us that Paul left Rome after his first imprisonment there and went to the far west for probably a four to five year "missionary" journey. It was his return to Asia Minor, that he was then imprisoned in the city of Ephesus.[94]

There is a point here to consider. The Marcionite Prologue to *Colossians* states also that it was written from the city of Ephesus.[95] This is an important clue that we should not just dismiss out of hand because the implication is a very simple one. If the *Epistle to the Colossians* is a Prison Epistle, and it was written from the city of Ephesus, then we have to conclude that Paul's imprisonment was one there at Ephesus,

---

[94] George S. Duncan has made a full study of Paul's Ephesian imprisonment in *St. Paul's Ephesian Ministry* (London: Hodder and Stoughton, 1929). One interesting observation that he makes is: "In Ephesus there is still shown a building which tradition declares to have been Paul's prison" (70). The only problem with Duncan's entire hypothesis is that he tries to place the Ephesian imprisonment before Paul's first Roman imprisonment. Even recently, Jerome Murphy-O'Connor, (*Paul: A Critical Life* [Oxford: Clarendon Press, 1996], 182-4], makes the same mistake. This assumption, of course, is impossible, and therefore has only given other scholars reason to shoot down the entire theory. See, for example, Donald Guthrie, *New Testament Introduction* (Downers Grove: InterVarsity Press, 1990), 493, 4, who stated: "When the evidence is carefully sifted it cannot be said to point very strongly to an Ephesian imprisonment, and there is still the silence of Acts to consider. ...It is impossible, without ignoring the plain meaning of Acts 20:1, to fit in an imprisonment at Ephesus subsequent to the riot." Such an objection, however, evaporates when we understand that the Ephesian imprisonment was subsequent to the story in *Acts*. A second mistake that scholars make is to lump together the letters of *Philippians, Colossians,* and *Ephesians* all under the same imprisonment (so Ben Witherington III, "An Ephesian Imprisonment?" in *New Testament History: A Narrative Account* [Grand Rapids: Baker, 2001], 285-7). Since *Philippians* is definitely written from a Roman incarceration, Witherington uses that argument to shoot down the entire theory of the Ephesian imprisonment. Thus, he has no choice other than to say that "the theory of an Ephesian imprisonment, while not totally impossible, is without a firm foundation in any of the evidence we have at hand" (287). Yet, *Philippians* has an entirely different complexion than the other Prison Epistles, which has seemed to escaped the scrutiny of many a scholar, as we have noted above. Thus, from our point of view, the two major king pin objections to an Ephesian imprisonment have now been answered, making just about every scholarly objection on the subject in the past now obsolete!

[95] Guthrie, *Introduction*, 490.

subsequent to his first imprisonment at Rome, and not before it.

But there is an even stronger point to consider that scholars seem to be totally oblivious to. It bears on the contents of what is written. Obviously, *Colossians, Ephesians,* and *Philemon* were written under the same circumstances. But there are two very important points that separate these Epistles from that of *Philippians.* Since scholars do not understand that the year 63 C.E. was the crucial year that Paul changed his mind on prophetic events, a simple comparison of what Paul writes in these Epistles shows us that in *Philippians* Paul was still of the belief that the end was near (Phil 4:5), but in the other Prison Epistles, there is none of this emphasis. But there is something even more important to consider and that has to do with the revelation that Paul received in the year of 64 of what he calls the "Mystery." This is the clincher that positively separates *Philippians* from the other Prison Epistles (which again, scholars seem to be totally oblivious to). The *Epistles of Colossians* and *Ephesians* were specifically written to explain this new teaching. Yet, lest we get too far ahead of ourselves in our story, that will be fully explained in the next chapter.

But, there is a third reason for accepting an Ephesian imprisonment. The circumstances within the Epistles demand it. Notice Ernest L. Martin's solution to the problem:

> In what area of the world was Paul's imprisonment when he wrote the epistles of Colossians, Ephesians, and Philemon? We have a good clue to the location when we read Paul's second letter to Timothy which he wrote from Rome. He mentioned that Onesiphorus had proved to be of great service to him while he was in Ephesus and that Timothy had been well aware of the help given him by Onesiphorus (II Timothy 1:16,17). Indeed, if one reads II Timothy 1:15 through 18 carefully, it will be seen that those four verses speak about Paul's experiences while he was in the Roman province of Asia (v. 15), particularly of Ephesus (v. 18). And in the midst of speaking about the events that happened to him at Ephesus, Paul said that Onesiphorus helped him while he was in chains (v. 16). Paul also put into the same context a parenthetical reference that Onesiphorus had ALSO sought him out in Rome (v. 17). Paul, however, was informing Timothy about Onesiphorus' help when he was in an Ephesian imprisonment, not his current incarceration that he was then enduring at Rome.[96]

What we are faced with here clearly, then, is a direct reference by Paul

[96] Ernest L. Martin, *Restoring,* 239-40.

to an imprisonment at Ephesus that was after his first imprisonment at Rome, but previous to his final imprisonment at Rome later on.

The *Epistles of Colossians*, *Philemon*, and *Ephesians*, based upon contents, appear to fit better the Ephesian imprisonment, rather than the earlier imprisonments at Caesarea and Rome, or even his final imprisonment at Rome. Also, note that Paul describes himself in Philemon as "an old man" (Phlm 1.9). This would fit better with a later imprisonment than one of the earlier ones.

The best piece of evidence for an Ephesian imprisonment, however, comes from Clement of Rome, who stated that Paul was imprisoned seven times (1 Clement 5:6). Scholars who believe that Paul lost his life in his first imprisonment at Rome cannot account for seven imprisonments within the time frame of Acts. But now, we can identify these seven imprisonments as follows:

1) In the summer of 49 C.E. at Philippi (Acts 16:11-23);

2) In custody before Gallio, July 51 (Acts 18:12);

3) Apprehended by mob at Ephesus (Acts 19:37; cf. 2 Cor 11:23; Rom 16:7);

4) The one month [not a two year!] incarceration at Caesarea in June/ July of 55 C.E. (Acts 26:29);

5) The first Roman imprisonment lasting "two whole years" (Acts 28:30) from 56-58 C.E.;

6) The Ephesian imprisonment of ca. 64-65 C.E.;

7) Paul's final imprisonment at Rome, during which he was executed in 67 C.E. (2 Tim 1:8; 2:8,9; 4:16).

We are now in a position to understand something that is very important in trying to unravel the mystery of who wrote the latter writings of the Prison and Pastoral Epistles. They were indeed written by Paul and after the crucial year of 63 C.E. This is significant to the story of *Beyond Acts*. *Philippians* was written during Paul's first Roman imprisonment, most likely toward the end of his two years there, say 58 C.E, whereas *Ephesians*, *Colossians*, and *Philemon* were written some six years later during an Ephesian imprisonment, which we will set a date of around 64 C.E.

Now that we have straightened out the correct chronology of these Epistles, we can understand something about the Apostle Paul's later writings that are missed by just about everyone who has written on the subject. Yet, it is probably one of the most important theological revelations in the entire New Testament. As we have just mentioned, after the year 63 C.E., Paul had received a new revelation concerning what he called the "Mystery." This "Revelation" of the Apostle Paul is a very important subject to the overall story and we will now look at this in the next chapter.

CHAPTER 8

The "Revelation" of the Apostle Paul

WHEN THE APOSTLE PAUL HAD FINISHED his western campaign and returned to Crete and then Asia Minor, he stated that the gospel had been taken to "all the world" (Col 1:6) and indeed to "every creature under heaven" (Col 1:23). He had fulfilled his threefold commission of taking the gospel to the Gentiles, to Kings, and to Israel (Acts 9:15).

All of the apostles spread themselves throughout the civilized world with the gospel message and now it was the crucial year of 63 C.E. Would Daniel's prophecies now start to take place? What about the "Revelation" that the apostle John had received a few short years earlier? Why were things not shaping up prophetically, as had been expected, by this date? Why was the Apostle James martyred? Paul may have been very perplexed about the prophetic conditions, but there were still some other nagging doctrinal issues that needed clarifying.

The prophetic Revelation that Jesus gave to the Apostle John in the late 50's C.E. was a powerful and graphic vision which, to this very day, is a source of inspiration for Christ's second coming. The stirring events that John recorded were thought to be for the generation of the apostles. Yet, by the year of 63 C.E., it became apparent (to the Apostle Paul at least) that the conditions on the world scene were not taking shape as expected and that the church would be continuing beyond his day into a future end-time generation.

Respect for the *Book of Revelation* no doubt went down in the eyes of some and John may have lost considerable standing with many, even within the congregation of the faithful. When prophecies fail, the zeal which drove the people to expectation plummets and the disheartening effect is that many lose interest and fall away.

The year 63 C.E. must have been a great year of disappointment to many who yearned for the long overdue return of Jesus as *King of Kings*. Many started to become disillusioned by what they felt was a prophecy failure. As a result, many even started to abandon the faith altogether.

The year 63 C.E. must have been a year of disappointment for the Apostle Paul as well. When Paul returned from his western campaign, he first went to the island of Crete, where he left Titus to evangelize and raise up churches there. Already we are witnessing a different Paul in this fact.

When Paul left Rome five years earlier his belief in the soon return of Christ was still vigorous. But now he could see that the Roman Empire (the "iron legs" of Daniel's image) was not going to collapse to allow the prophesied ten kings to emerge on the scene. Also, with the news of the death of the Apostle James, Paul must have realized that this event also was something never expected to occur before the return of Christ.

Then, there was a dramatic change in events in Rome itself. With the death of the Praetorian Prefect Burrus and the wife of Nero, Octavia, as well as the fall of Seneca, a new Nero emerges who was now influenced by his new wife, Poppaea, and the new Praetorian Prefect, the ruthless Tigellinus. This dramatic change at Rome marked the beginning of the era of persecution toward the Christian movement. This all occurred in the year of 62 C.E. This is the same year that the Apostle James was martyred. And this is the same year that the Romans defeated the British Queen, Boadicea. Paul may have been in Britain at this time and witnessed first hand the subjugation of the British.

Once the year of 63 C.E. had past, the last possible year for Daniel's seven-year prophecies to commence within the 40 year generation from Christ's prophecy, then it became obvious to the Apostle Paul that the Parousia was now beyond his own day. Nothing prophetically was occurring to show him that this year marked the last seven years as the one's referred to by Daniel.

A New and Different Apostle Paul

THE FIRST EPISTLE THAT PAUL WROTE AFTER his return from the West was to "Titus." It is in this letter that Paul discusses leaving Titus in Crete for the purpose of ordaining elders to pastor the churches there. Paul there speaks of the need to refute false teachers (Titus 1:10-16). He gives regulations for Christian behavior (Titus 2:1-10). He admonishes loyal citizenship, honest toil and a courteous approach to others (Titus 3:1-2). And remarkably, not a single mention is made of Christ's imminent return. Paul was now a changed man. His concerns were all different. He now thought in terms of the needs of congregations and a future church structure.

The context of the *Epistle to Titus* shows us that Paul now was more concerned with setting up church government in the various congregations and getting about the business of living by Christian principles within the community. The change in style of the "Pastoral" letters is so marked that numerous scholars do not even believe that Paul could have been the author, and that they were written by some unknown church leader much later on after the death of Paul, when the church was organized and structured. This view fails to take into account the bearing that world events had on the thrust of the apostolic church and the about face that the apostles took because of these events.

Paul wintered in Nicopolis in Western Greece (Titus 3:12). In the spring of 64 C.E., he journeyed north to Macedonia with a brief stop in Ephesus to see Timothy (1 Tim 1:3). Then, after spending some time in Macedonia, he writes to Timothy in the summer of 64 C.E. Here again Paul is concerned with setting up church organizations. But one thing that we should notice is that doctrinally he mentions a particular new "revelation." What is this new "revelation?" Let us come to understand one of the most significant insights that the Apostle Paul has contributed to the correct understanding of the entire plan of God.

THE REVELATION OF THE "MYSTERY"

THE APOSTLE PAUL WRITES TO THE EVANGELIST Timothy with excitement about a new doctrine that has been revealed to him which he simply calls "the Mystery" (1 Tim 3:16). Later on he expounds this new doctrine in his Epistles to the Colossians and Ephesians, which he there says had never been "revealed" in previous ages (Eph 3:1-11; Col 1:26).[97]

Apparently, this new "revelation" must have occurred to Paul between his letters to *Titus* and *First Timothy*, probably in the spring of 64 C.E. It may be that this "revelation" was given to Paul at this time to help explain why Christ was not returning to that generation and as an encouragement to him to continue with his work.

After Paul had written *First Timothy* in Macedonia, he returned to Ephesus in 64 C.E. He spent some time there preaching and was then apprehended and thrown into prison there. This was Paul's sixth imprisonment. It was during this imprisonment that he wrote the Epistles of *Colossians, Ephesians,* and *Philemon.*[98]

In the spring of 64 C.E. Paul may have desperately been seeking an explanation concerning the future course of events. Even though Christ's sacrifice was supposed to be the sacrifice to end all sacrifices, the temple was still very much continuing to function. Why was this? Indeed, it was in that very year that the temple was completed.

Renovation began back in the days of Herod the Great and continued for a period of eighty years (Josephus, *A.J.* 20.9.7 [219]). There must have been great celebrations at the completion of this long renovation, since now that the temple was completed, the prophesied Messiah could finally appear. To Peter and John in Jerusalem, they witnessed this completion of the temple and may have been still wondering if the return of Christ was very close. John now believed that it was the "last hour" (1 John 2:18). To the Apostle Paul in Asia Minor, however, none of this quite set right. Indeed, something was not making sense about the temple still functioning with the Shekinah glory of God still resident therein. That was the stickler.

Temple ritual was as strong as ever among the Jews in the summer of 64 C.E. Even Jewish Christians continued to look to the temple where God's Shekinah glory still remained. Many were looking to such prophecies as, "the Lord whom you seek will suddenly come to his Temple" (Mal 2:1). If Jesus was soon to appear, the temple had to be in existence. Even Jesus upheld the sanctity of the temple (Mark 11:17). Yet, Paul's position was, as he told the philosophers of his day, that "God... dwells not in Temples made with hands" (Acts 17:24-5). Stephen had earlier made this same statement (Acts 7:47-50).

---

[97] Raymond Brown, *Introduction to the New Testament* (New York: Doubleday, 1997), 607, in discussing the "mystery" and possible connections with "Mystery Religions," sums up his thoughts as follows: "If these observations leave a picture filled with uncertainties, that is an honest estimate of the state of our knowledge of the teaching [of the mystery]." Ben Witherington III, in his 347 page book, *The Paul Quest* (Downers Grove, Ill.: InterVarsity Press, 1998), has no listing in his index for the term "mystery." In other words, scholars admit that they don't have a clue as to what Paul was writing about concerning the "mystery," and therefore, miss the boat on a very important key to understanding New Testament history. Indeed, they get an "F" on their report card for their failure to see one of the most significant theological contributions of the Apostle Paul. Peter most certainly had in mind Paul's doctrine of the "mystery" when he wrote there are some things in Paul's letters that are "hard to understand, which the ignorant and unstable twist to their own destruction" (2 Pet 3:16).

[98] The Marcionite Prologue to Colossians states that it was written from Ephesus, (Donald Guthrie, *New Testament Introduction* [Downers Grove: InterVarsity Press, 1990], 577). Colossae was devastated around 60 or 61 by an earthquake, however "that a Christian community could have survived in Colossae after the devastation is quite possible; unfortunately the area of Colossae has not been the subject of archaeological investigation, so there is no help from that direction" (Paul J. Achtemeier, Joel B. Green and Marianne Meye Thompson, eds., *The New Testament: Its Literature and Theology* [Grand Rapids: Eerdmans, 2001], 419).

To Paul, Christians themselves were considered as being "Temples" because God's Spirit dwells within them (1 Cor 3:16, 17; 6:19; 2 Cor 6:16). The perplexing thing was that the Shekinah glory of God was still present in the holy of holies and that alone meant that Paul was going out on a limb by stating that the temple sacrifices were unnecessary. It was probably just before this time that Paul commissioned most likely Apollos, or some other companion, to write the *Book of Hebrews* which demonstrates the superiority of the priesthood of Christ to that of Levi. But in this treatise there is still emphasis on the New Covenantal relationship in Christ (Heb 12:24). However, the irony is that the New Covenant was to be made with Israel in exclusion of the Gentiles. This also was something that didn't quite fit the overall picture because the Apostles Peter and Paul witnessed Gentile believers receive the Holy Spirit – a sign of conversion (Rom 8:9-11) – without being literally circumcised (Acts 10:44-48; Gal 2:3).

So what is going on here? To the Apostle Paul something still wasn't right. Finally, however, while Paul was sitting in his Ephesian cell, a revelation came to him that put it all together in an entirely new light. Now Paul could understand something about the plan of God that had never been revealed before. What was it? This "Revelation" and its importance has been missed by so many scholars and clerics alike that it is amazing. Yet, we need to look at this revelation in the light of what the Apostle Paul was privileged to have been revealed. And, what did this new revelation mean in relation to the New Covenant? Let us understand.

THE NEW COVENANT VERSUS THE "MYSTERY"

THE NEW COVENANT WAS PROPHESIED BY THE prophet Jeremiah, and it is to be made only with the House of Israel and Judah (Jer 31:31-4; Heb 8:8-12). But what does it mean to be under the "New Covenant?" Many have completely missed what the New Covenant is all about. We are now hitting upon a most significant subject in all of Scripture, yet one of the least understood. To be under the New Covenant means:

1) that God's laws would be put into people's hearts (Jer 31:33);
2) that people would be instructed in spiritual matters (v. 34);
3) that their sins would be forgiven (ibid.), and finally;
4) that they were to inherit the land of Palestine (Jer 32:40-1).

This final promise of the New Covenant was merely an extension of the promise originally made to Abraham and his seed (Gen 17:1-8). And

Paul affirmed that Abraham was assured not only the land of Palestine, but the entire world as his possession through his seed (Rom 4:13). This would be fulfilled in the establishment of the "Kingdom of God," which was the entire focus of the message of John the Baptist and of Jesus Christ.

One thing that is certain about the New Covenant that many do not realize, or for that matter, believe in, is that the New Covenant was for the nation of Israel and that its promises were physical land inheritances and had nothing whatsoever to do with "salvation" or some kind of heavenly reward in a spiritual kingdom. Those who have blended the teaching of Salvation with the Kingdom of God/New Covenant have not rightly "divided the truth" (2 Tim 2:15).

Also, there is not one word in Scripture which says that the New Covenant was, or indeed ever will be, made with Gentiles. The only path to the Old Covenant was for Gentiles to reject their own national identity and heritage and become "Israelite." The same applies to the New Covenant. In other words, all male Gentiles had to be circumcised (Exod 12:48).

Those who equate the Kingdom of God with a heavenly reward do not understand that the Kingdom of God is in fact the thousand year reign of Jesus on this earth. But the Kingdom phase of God's plan is only part of the entire story of God's overall plan of Salvation. And, the Apostle Paul was now given a new "revelation" that would explain all the missing pieces to the puzzle that he so desperately sought to understand. And this new revelation that Paul received he simply called "the Mystery."

But what did the temple, the New Covenant, and even circumcision mean to the fast growing Gentile body of believers? Paul still had nagging questions that had to be resolved. He had witnessed the fact that when Gentiles after Christ's resurrection expressed faith in Christ, at first even the apostles demanded all males to be circumcised (Acts 15:1). He knew that Jesus had confirmed the New Covenant that night before his crucifixion at his Last Supper (Matt 26:28). He also knew that a circumcised Gentile male could partake of the Passover in the Old Testament (Exod 12:48) and that this was a sign that he had entered a "covenant" relationship with the God of Israel. But somehow, temple worship with a levitical priesthood still seemed to be an anomaly to the entire plan of God. Either Christ's sacrifice superseded temple sacrifices, or what did his sacrifice mean? Can we even begin to put ourselves in the place of the Apostle Paul at this time?

How was it that Gentiles were receiving the spirit of God without being circumcised? The only explanation to this was that since these converted Gentiles were considered to be "in Christ," and they formed a part of the very "body of Christ," it was accepted that the circumcision performed on Jesus, when he was an eight-day-old infant, must be considered a substitution for all new Gentile converts (Col 2:11; Phil 3:3).

Indeed, the whole concept of "substitution" was the basis of the entire sacrificial system in the first place and in the same manner Christ's death is substitutionally applied to all who believe in his sacrifice. Is not the concept of "substitution" one of the most fundamental teachings of all of Christianity? And it is this concept of substitution that allowed Paul to develop his interpretation that the Gentiles were now grafted in (Rom 11:17) and that they were now Abraham's seed and also heirs according to the promise (Gal 3:29), and that they are the "Israel of God" (Gal 6:16) and were able to partake of a Christian Passover (1 Cor 10:16-21; 11:20-34), being no longer strangers to the covenant of promise (Eph 2:12).

It appears that the Apostle Paul now had the missing key. Paul now hit upon something that he could only call "the Mystery." While Paul sat in an Ephesian prison in 65 C.E., he wrote that he became a servant of the church

> according to God's commission that was given to me for you, to make the word of God FULLY KNOWN, the MYSTERY that has been hidden throughout the ages and generations but has now been REVEALED to his saints. To them God chose to make known how great among the Gentiles are the riches of the glory of the MYSTERY, which is Christ in you, the hope in glory (Col 1:25-7).

What did Paul mean "Christ in you?" Paul explains elsewhere:

> Anyone who does not have the Spirit of Christ does not belong to him. But if Christ is in you, though the body is dead because of sin, the Spirit is life because of [his] righteousness. If the Spirit of him who raised Jesus from the dead dwells in you, he who raised Christ from the dead will give life to your mortal bodies also through his Spirit that dwells in you (Rom 8:9-11).[99]

[99] One wonders if this mature teaching was not added to the letter of Romans by Paul when he finally edited his letters for the purpose of canonization. Obviously, the "doxology" at the end of the *Epistle of Romans,* which in some manuscripts occurs in different locations, was added by Paul after he had received the revelation of the Mystery, for he writes: "Now to God who is able to strengthen you according to my Gospel and the proclamation of Jesus Christ, according to the REVELATION OF THE MYSTERY that was kept secret for long ages but is now disclosed, and through the prophetic writings is made known to all the Gentiles, according to the command of the eternal God, to bring about the obedience of faith – to the only wise God, through Jesus Christ, to whom be the glory forever! Amen" (Rom 16:25-27).

What Paul is saying is not what many "Christians" of today believe. What Paul is saying is that a Christian is not one, who, on his or her own initiative, decides the follow Christ during this present age, but one who has been given the Spirit of God. This is what Stephen had so long ago testified back in the mid-thirties that still must have resounded in the Apostle Paul's ears. In other words, it is not a decision of the individual to become a Christian – God calls those whom He chooses to implant His Spirit. This agrees with what the Apostle John had recorded:

> No one can come to me unless drawn by the Father who sent me, and I will raise that person up on the last day (John 6:44).

The thing to understand is that God has different time phases for his overall plan and this age is only one in which he is calling just a few. Although this goes beyond what we can address in this volume, it is a fact of Scripture that many are completely oblivious to. The overwhelming vast majority of the world is blinded in total spiritual darkness – especially many who profess "Christianity." These people live and die in this age only to be later resurrected in a future age in order to be dealt with on a scale where the spiritual influences of the god of this world [Satan] will be removed. This is all within the pages of Word of God. Of course, since the god of this world is presently head of all principalities, dominions, and governments – including, and especially, organized religion – then those very organizations will fight tooth and nail against this message and the entire message of the Mystery.

Religious Ritual versus "The Mystery"

TO PAUL, NOW, RELIGIOUS RITUAL HAS BECAME totally meaningless. What was important was not what you do to gain favor with God, but what Jesus already has accomplished within his own flesh that is applied to you, if, and only if, the spirit of Christ is in you. It is his (Christ's) righteousness that counts, not ours. Yet, this goes entirely against the grain of what religionists will have us believe. This is why Paul was careful to warn his audience:

> See to it that no one takes you captive through philosophy

> and empty deceit, according to human tradition, according to the elemental spirits of the universe, and not according to Christ (Col 2:8).

In other words, professional religionists are stuck in "human tradition" and so they will try to make you follow their own "empty deceit," but none of this is "according to Christ." Paul goes on:

> For in him the whole fullness of deity dwells bodily, and you have come to fullness in him, who is the head of every ruler and authority (Col 2:9).

What an amazing declaration! What Paul is saying is that the "deity" that was invested in the human being Jesus (1 Tim 2:5), "the pioneer" of our salvation (Heb 2:10), as a result of him being raised from the dead and then God "exalted him and gave him the name that is above every name" (Phil 2:9), will be our reward as well – "you have come to fullness [of deity] in him." This fact is reiterated two other times – that those who have been called by God and given his Spirit will be "filled with ALL the fullness of God" (Eph 3:19, see also Eph 1:23). What the human being Jesus received for his reward is what is destined to be exactly what God has in store for the rest of the human race. Paul also states that

> for in him [Jesus] ALL the fullness of God was pleased to dwell, and through him God was pleased to reconcile to himself ALL things, whether on earth or in heaven, by making peace through the blood of his cross (Col 1:19-20).

Now continuing the thought line that Paul was making in Colossians, the second chapter:

> In him also you were circumcised with a spiritual circumcision, by putting off the body of the flesh in the circumcision of Christ; when you were buried with him in baptism, you were also raised with him through faith in the power of God, who raised him from the dead (Col 2:11-12).

Paul is stating that the perfect, sinless life of Jesus on this earth are the works that count, not ours! Thus, when Jesus was literally circumcised – "in him also you were circumcised with a spiritual circumcision (being a spiritual principle, this applies spiritually to male or female)... in the circumcision of Christ." When he was literally baptized by John the Baptist, that physical "work" of baptism was applied to God's called out ones in a substitutionary sense. And likewise, when Jesus was raised from the dead by God the Father, the faithful are already accorded with the fact that "you were also raised with him." How? "Through faith in the power of God."

Now Paul finally understood the real reason why the Gentile converts did not have to be circumcised. It was not their law keeping that mattered at all. It was the keeping of the law by Jesus that mattered. And if Christ is in them, then legally, his entire life of righteousness is applied to them. Indeed, Paul said that

> we were reconciled to God through the death of his Son, much more surely, having been reconciled, will we be saved by his life (Rom 5:10).

Even Christ's death is applied to us so that the debt of sin can be "reconciled," i.e., paid off. But notice that salvation is not the result of Christ's death, but "by his life."

> For you have died, and your life is hidden with Christ in God. When Christ WHO IS YOUR LIFE is revealed, then you also will be revealed with him in glory (Col 3:3).

Now we can fully appreciate Paul's enthusiasm about the Mystery revelation that he received:

> For surely you have already heard of the commission of God's grace that was given me for you, and how the MYSTERY was made known to me BY REVELATION, as I wrote above in a few words, a reading of which will enable you to perceive my understanding of the MYSTERY of Christ. In former generations this MYSTERY was not made known to humankind, as it has now been revealed to his holy apostles and prophets by the Spirit:[100] that is, the Gentiles have become fellow heirs, members of the same body, and sharers in the promise in Christ Jesus through the Gospel (Eph 3:3-6).

This new "Revelation" to Paul (and "other" apostles) completely revolutionized the direction of Christian theology. It did not supersede the New Covenant message about the Kingdom of God, but it did explain the message of God's ultimate plan as never understood before.

Paul felt that the "Word of God" was now "fully known" and that it had been hidden from former generations. Notice that since this new teaching might be considered a departure from the message of Christ, Paul was very careful to qualify his remarks by first stating that the authority that he had was "according to God's commission," lest anyone take

[100] Obviously, this same revelation Paul felt was given to his fellow apostles and "prophets," i.e., Peter and John. See 2 Pet 3:9; 1 John 2:1, 2; 3:8; 4:14.

exception to his apostleship and what might be called his new fangled teachings.[101]

Paul now taught that all barriers that separated Israel and the Gentiles were completely removed, especially the middle wall of partition in the temple (Eph 2:14), and that the only mediator left between God and humankind was Jesus Christ and him alone (1 Tim 2:15). And through Jesus, all were to have access to the Father (Eph 2:15) because a converted person is now considered a new creature, neither Jew nor Gentile. Human ethnicity no longer has any significance.

The curtain that separated the holy place from the holy of holies in the temple into which only the High Priests of Levi could enter was reckoned as being torn in two (Heb 10:19-20). In Paul's earlier writings [102] it was still necessary for Gentiles to become Israelites if they hoped to be saved. But in *Ephesians* and *Colossians*, it is far different. Paul talks about the NEW MAN who has no national, social, nor racial characteristics. Paul now says:

> Put on the New Man ...where there is neither Greek nor Jew, circumcision nor uncircumcision, Barbarian, Scythian, bond or free; but Christ is all, and in all (Col 3:10-11).

This new teaching of "the Mystery" was quite a contrast between the teaching of the New Covenant. With the New Covenant the Apostle Paul had to begin his message of salvation with the history of Abraham, because that is as far back as he could go in a covenantal sense. But with the Mystery he said it had its origin: "before the foundation of the world" (Eph 1:4). And while the message of the New Covenant required water baptism to enter a covenant relationship with God,[103] the "Mystery" has only one baptism (Eph 4:5) and the context shows us that the particular baptism of the Mystery was of the Spirit – not of water.

The New Covenant prophesied by Jeremiah was not abolished. One could (and still can) enter a New Covenant relationship with Christ. But to do so one must be prepared to partake of the bread and the wine in a yearly Passover service, as Jesus had instructed at the Last Supper, in order to renew yearly one's "covenant" relationship with Christ. There is nothing wrong with this. In fact, it has the benefit of strengthening the somber reality of the magnitude of what Jesus did for us. But we must realize also that this puts us in a situation that we become debtors to the whole law instead of Christ. In other words, in attempting to honor Jesus

---

[101] In both his letters to the *Ephesians* and *Colossians*, Paul made sure that he emphasized his own authority and apostleship before expounding the Mystery (Eph 1:1; Col 1:1).

[102] *Romans, Corinthians,* and *Galatians,* written between 50-55 C.E.

[103] "Repent and be baptized" – Acts 2:38.

by keeping a "Christian Passover," we in fact turn our backs on everything that he did – his baptism, circumcision, Sabbath keeping, Passover keeping, and his crucifixion and resurrection.

But on the other hand, with the revelation of the teaching of the "Mystery," another relationship with God was now made possible. In this relationship, Christ has already come to us and believers are presently considered to be "IN HIM" (Eph 1:3). Indeed, Paul even believed that those of the "Mystery" are even presently sitting with Jesus in the heavens in a spiritual sense (Eph 2:6).

And while the covenants applied only to Abraham's seed and salvation was invested solely in Israel under the covenants, the "Mystery" was to extend salvation to the totality of the human race, without the slightest need for one to become an Israelite. And while all the promises in the Old and New Covenants are exclusively confined to this earth, the "Mystery" went beyond and promised "spiritual blessing in heavenly places in Christ" (Eph 1:3; 2:6).

So the question remains, did this new revelation of the Apostle Paul do away with the Old and New Covenants? Not at all! All the promises that God made to those under the covenants God will surely keep. All those under the Old and New Covenants, that have faithfully kept the requirement of those covenants – the patriarchs, prophets, kings, priests, and even Christians who died before and after the revelation of the "Mystery" will indeed be resurrected at Christ's coming and receive all the rewards to rule with Christ in his earthly, one thousand year reign here on this earth.

But those who have entered into a "Mystery" relationship will receive a heavenly reward during the periods of the Millennium and the Great "White Throne" judgement. After that all of the redeemed in heaven and on earth will join to become "all in all" (1 Cor 15:28).

Paul dispatched his new revelation with first the writing of the Epistle which we call "Ephesians." This was an encyclical letter intended to be sent and read to the very same seven churches of Asia that John had sent his revelation. Paul then wrote the Epistle to the Colossians, which had a similar theme and mentioned at the end of it that it should be read to the congregation at Laodicea and the one from Laodicea be read to the Colossians (Col 4:16). Just as John had sent his "Revelation" to the seven churches in Asia a few years earlier beginning with Ephesus and ending with Laodicea, Paul similarly, most likely, sent his revelatory Epistles to these very same congregations.[104]

[104] That Paul was following John's precedence in writing to the seven churches of Asia was noted by Cyprian [*Exhortation for Martyrdom,* 11] and Victorinus of Pettau [*On the Apocalypse,* 1.7, on Rev. 1:20].

THE REACTION TO PAUL'S REVELATION

WHAT WAS THE REACTION TO THIS NEW revelation that was given to Paul? Were people overjoyed with excitement about it? The answer is an emphatic no! Why? Because it goes against the grain of what people think religion is all about. When it comes to matters of religion, people everywhere want to believe that, in order to be religious, and in the right standing with God, you must constantly show your devotion to Him by ritualistic ceremonies that somehow are pleasing to Him. But look at what the Apostle Paul was saying. He was now advocating doing away with all forms of this kind of religion entirely because, in his mind, they are totally unnecessary. Indeed, they stood in the way of what Jesus himself did for us. According to Paul's new "Revelation," Christ alone is our mediator now. Therefore, the need for Pontiffs, a priesthood, and indeed, all forms of human mediators to perform ritualistic ceremonies on our human behalf became totally superfluous.

So what was to be the role of the ministry? The role of the ministry was to become teachers, not religious mediators. They were given the authority to be guidance counselors, ordain, anoint the sick, perform marriages, preach the word – but not to be a human mediator on behalf of Christians. It is in the context of this new revelation that Paul instructed Timothy to now rightly "divide" the truth (2 Tim 2:15). In other words, rightly dividing between pre-mystery versus post-mystery truth.

Many, who blend all kinds of earlier writings with the latter revelation of the Mystery, come up with a mish-mash of religious ideas which are inconsistent with the final message revealed to Paul. Thus, Christianity has, as a result, splintered into every conceivable opinion as to what Christianity should be. But in reality, it was never God's intention to set up any ritualistic form of religion, such as the sacrificial system, in the first place. The Bible itself reveals that such a circumstance came about due to man's rebellion against God, not because of God's love toward man (Jer 7:22-27).

The Christian message suddenly became a lot simpler than many religious people would, and still will, ever admit. It is they who have added stumbling blocks to the pure beauty of this simplicity of the final message revealed to Paul. It is they who have made religion a concoction of ceremony, candle lighting, bead counting, incense burning, holy water sprinkling, and on and on, by some human mediator that stands between them and God. David was absolutely right when he said that God did not desire sacrifice and did not delight in burnt offerings, but that the sacrifices of God were in reality a contrite, humble attitude (Ps 51:16-17).

But to Paul's audience, and even some fellow apostles, it may have been interpreted as Paul going too far with his already infamous anti-law stance. Peter and John probably didn't even go along with this new "Revelation" at first. After all, it was one thing to say that the Gentiles did not have to keep the Law, but Paul was now saying that even Jewish Christians did not have to keep it (Eph 2:14-22). That was something that was not only entirely new, but was something that James would never have accepted, pure and simple. But now that James was dead, was Paul taking advantage of this fact and pulling out all stops, defying everything that seemed previously right to the remaining Jerusalem apostles, namely Peter and John?

Right at the time that the temple was being completed and the Jewish nation was looking for signs that the Messianic Kingdom would soon occur, Paul was going off and turning the entire world upside down with his new teachings which just went against the grain of those who were zealous for the Law.

Paul encountered intense hostility toward his revelation of the Mystery and he mentioned this in his second letter to Timothy (2 Tim 3:11). Even Demas, Paul's close associate and friend, found it impossible to side with Paul in these matters (2 Tim 4:10). Eventually Paul's rejection was so replete that he told Timothy that "*all* men in Asia have turned away from me" (2 Tim 1:15). This is where the seven churches of Asia were located. And this is where the Apostle John had settled, in the city of Ephesus, the very city where Paul had been given his revelation of the Mystery. But what did John write about?

The Apostle John, writing around this time in his three small Epistles insisted his readers to recapture the teachings which were given "from the beginning" (1 John 2:7, 13; 3:8, 11; 2 John 1:5). The wording of these Epistles appears to decry any new type of teachings which were emerging on the scene. And we know from history, as we shall see later on, that the Apostle John continued to keep the Passover and teach Polycarp and others to do so years after the revelation of the "Mystery." This amazing story will be told later on, but for the moment we need to understand the Apostle Paul's view on prophecy. It is pivotal to a correct understanding of New Testament history. This we will do in the next chapter.

CHAPTER 9

The Prophetic Viewpoint of the Apostle Paul

WE HAVE SEEN THAT THE APOSTLES, IN THE FIRST three decades after the resurrection, believed that they were living in the last days, prior to Jesus returning in full glory. Since the apostles believed that Jesus was the Messiah of the Hebrew Scriptures, then it followed that the entire panorama of prophecy would have to transpire leading up to the return of the Messiah, especially the prophecies that were uttered by the ancient Hebrew prophet Daniel.

One of the most important things that Daniel said was to happen was that the structures of the temple and Jerusalem would have to be first destroyed before a covenant involving one Sabbath of years could commence (Dan 9:27). If the last seven years of Daniel's seventy-week prophecy could not begin until the temple were to lay in ruins, then some power had to arrive on the scene which would be mighty enough to cause such a destruction.

There was another major event that had to take place before the last seven years of Daniel's prophecy could begin. The Roman Empire had to be overthrown. In Daniel's image the Roman Empire was represented by "legs of iron." Daniels's interpretation of the image made it clear that the "iron legs" would break up into ten divisions, some strong as iron and others weak as miry clay. Since these ten kingdoms were to be associated with the "little horn" (the new "Nebuchadnezzar"), Rome had to disintegrate into the ten kingdoms. It would be in "the days of these kings that the God of heaven would set up a kingdom which shall never be destroyed" (Dan 2:44). Jesus, himself, alluded to the breakup of the Roman Empire into segments when he stated that nation shall rise up against nation and kingdom against kingdom (Matt 24:6, 7).

When the "little horn" was destined to come on the scene, the nation of Egypt would have broken away from its political allegiance to Rome and then be a free and independent power, along with the Libyans and Ethiopians (Dan 11:43). Moab, Ammon, and Edom would also be independent countries and no longer a part of Rome (v. 41). The nation of Edom was to become the prime force among the ten nation alliance, with the armies from all the nations of the world gathered within it for a major showdown with the Messiah at the time of his arrival (Isa 34; 63:1-4).

But in the days of the apostles, there was no specific nation of Edom any longer, so what nation could Edom be in a prophetic sense? Could Edom be Judea under the rulership of the Idumaean (Edomite) Herods? Or could Edom be Rome itself? Or could Edom mean just the final Kingdom of Man (since the word "Edom" can mean "man" or "mankind" as James interpreted it in Acts 15:17 when quoting Amos 9:11)? This is the scenario that faced the apostles and their understanding of the events that must take place, if, indeed, they were witnessing the beginning of the end-time prophecy rundown.

The Apostle Paul no doubt referred to the collapse of the Roman Empire when writing to the Thessalonians in 50 C.E., where he told them about the coming apostasy which had not yet occurred because it was being "restrained" (2 Thess 1-7). The arrival of the Man of Sin and the Great Apostasy was being delayed or "hindered" by some power. Obviously, the Roman Empire had to collapse if the apostasy were to occur. Since it is clear from Paul's comments that he is giving the Thessalonians a commentary on Daniel 7:25, the only real "hinderers" mentioned in the prophecies of Daniel were the angelic powers who had control over the nations. The angel Gabriel informed Daniel that "the Prince of Persia withstood me (restrained or hindered me) one and twenty days" (Dan 10:13).

The angelic prince over the Empire of Alexander was also a "hinderer" to Gabriel (Dan 10:20). The apostles certainly believed that all the nations had angelic powers ruling over them and that all of them were ultimately under the control of Satan (Matt 4:8-11, Eph 6:12). Michael, the Archangel, had charge of the affairs of Israel and was the only power to overcome the "hinderers" of the other nations of the earth. John wrote that these mighty angelic powers actually battled one another in heavenly spheres and the outcome of those wars was reflected in the history of nations on earth (Rev 12:7-17).

It was evident in Paul's mind in 50 C.E. that the angelic powers in charge of the Roman Empire were still clearly in control with no evidence that the powerful "iron legs" would soon break up. And as long as the Romans were still strong and in solid control of Palestine, there could be no Antichrist arising in the East.

Zechariah prophesied that before the introduction of the Kingdom of God, the people of Judah would once again rise to power and be an independent nation of the Middle East (Zech 12-14). The revival of the Davidic Kingdom was part of the work of a future "Elijah" who was prophesied to restore "all things" (Mal 4:5, 6). Peter mentioned this "restoration" as something that must occur before the return of Christ (Acts 3:19-21). Therefore, the apostles must have looked to what was happening in the Roman Empire to see if, indeed, prophecy was shaping up for the return of the Davidic dynasty, followed by a Great Tribulation upon Judea, the Man of Sin, the holocaust and the return of Jesus.

But as things were shaping up in the late 50's C.E., it appeared more and more obvious that events were going in the wrong direction for the stage of end-time prophesies to play out its drama. This sobering realization had to be on the mind of the Apostle Paul, for in his first Epistle to the Thessalonians he tells us that the "day" will not surprise those who are in the light and are "sober" concerning the fulfillment of these prophesies (1 Thess 1:5-8). Therefore, if Paul was trying to heed his own instruction to be sober and not be surprised, then he was indeed diligent in studying the prophecies in the light of what was happening in the world. So, what was occurring within the Roman Empire and surrounding nations at this time?

In 54 C.E. Nero became Emperor in Rome. Rome at that time entered war with Parthia in the East where anciently the nations of Assyria and Babylon once existed. Isaiah mentions the Lord will do battle with the "Assyrian" at the coming of the Messiah (Isa 30:31; 31:8). If this was to be one of the signs that the apostles were looking for, then could the Parthian wars be what would bring down the Roman Empire? Over a half a century earlier, Parthian Magi had paid homage to the infant Jesus with expensive gifts. Parthia, in fact, was the only nation at that time that was strong enough to drive the Romans out of Palestine.

The Parthian/Roman wars lasted 9 years. If the apostles looked to the last possible year for the sequence of events to begin and still have their fulfillment by the end of the 40 years' generation from Christ's resurrection – 63 C.E. – then the events of that year would have to be decisive in their eyes.

But war with the Parthians finally came to an end in the spring of 63 C.E., with the Parthian envoys appearing in Rome with a proposal that offered terms of capitulation to the Romans.[105] Also, in Britain, the Romans defeated the last opposition in the Boadicean war.

Instead of a Roman collapse, Rome had become stronger than ever. Indeed, throughout the period from Christ's resurrection the absorption of client-kingdoms continued.[106] Also, Britain was beaten down in the

---

[105] *Cambridge Ancient History,* 10:770-73.

Boadicean debacle, which the Apostle Paul could have witnesses first-hand.

The political environment in 63 C.E. was also not shaping up as would be expected for a "this generation" come-back of Jesus. Paul could see that what he had written in his letters to the church of Thessalonica was not going to happen. He had no course of action other than to abandon those ideas in favor of accepting the fact that the prophecies were for the future and not for the generation that he was living in.

The Apostle Paul was intent on going to Spain and ultimately Britain in order to not only spread the gospel, but to see first hand if the British could also be the ones who could bring down Rome. That the Apostle Paul did go to Britain will be the focus of our next chapter in the continuing saga of *Beyond Acts.*

---

[106] "Cappadocia was annexed by Tiberius, Mauritania by Caligula, Thrace by Claudius and Pontus by Nero. The Iturean principalities were divided between the Province of Syria and the surviving Herodian tetrarchy, that of Agrippa II. Commagene, though annexed by Tiberius, was restored and enlarged (by the addition of part of Cilicia) by Caligula" (Colin McEvedy, *The Penguin Atlas of Ancient History* [London: Penguin, 1967], 78).

CHAPTER 10

The Gospel unto Britain

THE NEW TESTAMENT TELLS US LITTLE ABOUT the activities of Jesus' disciples, but one thing is for sure. To the original twelve disciples Jesus had instructed them to

> go nowhere among the Gentiles, and enter no town of the Samaritans, but go rather to the lost sheep of the house of Israel (Matt 10:6).[107]

Such a profound statement is largely ignored by scholars today. But to us, it should be our guiding light in understanding the mission of not just the twelve, but to Jesus' other 72 disciples.[108] Tradition does support a far-flung evangelizing activity by Jesus' disciples and it should be no surprise that some of them made it to Britain, as is handed down to us from various sources. These disciples were to go to far off areas where pockets of Israelite descendants were scattered throughout the nations. Nevertheless, modern scholarship refuses to expand their research into these areas and only confines itself with the ministry of Jesus in Galilee and Jerusalem, and the travels of the Apostle Paul. Yet, our quest must go

---

[107] Certainly, many could argue that the term "lost sheep" means "spiritually lost" souls and that the House of Israel was only meant to convey the Jews in the dispersion. However, the prophet Ezekiel (Ezek 34:2, 4, 6) not only used the term "lost sheep" in reference to Israel, but makes a distinction that one day Judah (the Jewish people) and Joseph (the House of Israel) would be united (Ezek 37:15-28).

[108] Luke 10:1,17 speaks of seventy or seventy-two disciples who were sent out in pairs. Even though the weight of evidence and modern opinion is that the number should be 70, the chief Alexandrian witnesses (B, P^{45}, D, L, 1071), the Old Latin and the Sinaitic Syriac support the numeral 72. It is tempting to prefer 72, if for no other reason than the symbolism involved. This would make a total of 12 original disciples plus 72 equals 84, or 12 times 7. The symbolism of twelve (a number of organized beginnings) and seven (a number denoting completeness) appears significant. But it may be just for such a reason that some copyists inserted "*duo*" after "*hepdomekonta*." Hippolytus, in his list of these disciples only knows of seventy. For further discussion, see Metzger, *Commentary*, 126-7 and "Seventy or Seventy-two Disciples?" in *New Testament Studies* 5 (1959): 299-306, and now in his *Historical and Literary Studies, Pagan, Jewish and Christian* (Grand Rapids: Eerdmans, 1968), 67-76.

to where the disciples of Jesus went, which is outside the boundaries delineated by modern scholars who teach that Jesus was merely a poor Galilean peasant, a humble carpenter who played a small part in the messianic movement of the political factions of his day. This picture is far from the truth. The impact of the message of Jesus in the first century was far and wide.

The *Book of Acts* tells us that when the Holy Spirit descended upon the followers of Jesus, who were all together in one place, that there were:

> Devout Jews from every nation under heaven living in Jerusalem and that they heard Peter speak in their own native language, which included Parthians, Medes, Elamites, and residents of Mesopotamia, Judaea and Cappadocia, Pontus and Asia, Phrygia and Pamphylia, Egypt and the parts of Libya belong to Cyrene, and visitors from Rome, both Jews and proselytes, Cretans and Arabs (Acts 1:5, 9-11).

These devout Jews from these scattered nations who had made the pilgrimage to Jerusalem were representatives from all over the Roman Empire. These people alone were spreading the word when they returned to their respective homelands.

Tertullian (ca. 160-240 C.E.), the Carthaginian lawyer who is famous for coining the term "Trinity," also informs us likewise:

> For upon whom else have the universal nations believed, but upon the Christ who is already come? For whom have the nations believed, – Parthians, Medes, Elamites, and they who inhabit Mesopotamia, Armenia, Phrygia, Cappadocia, and they who dwell in Pontus, and Asia, and Pamphylia, tarriers in Egypt, and inhabiters of the region of Africa which is beyond Cyrene, Romans and sojourners, yes, and in Jerusalem Jews, and all other nations; as, for instance, by this time, the varied races of the Gaetulians, and manifold confines of the Moors, all the limits of the Spains, and the DIVERSE NATIONS OF THE GAULS, and the HAUNTS OF THE BRITONS – inaccessible to the Romans, but subjugated to Christ, and of the Sarmatians, and Dacians, and Germans, and Scythians, and of many remote nations, and of provinces and islands many, to us unknown, and which we can scarce enumerate? In all which places the name of the Christ who is already come reigns, as of Him before whom the gates of all cities have been opened, and to whom none are closed (Tertullian, *Answer to the Jews* 7 [*ANF* 3:157-8], emphasis the authors).

The list of nations almost sounds like the one we read in Acts, the first chapter. Interestingly, Tertullian here tells us that the gospel had reached "the haunts of the Britons – inaccessible to the Romans." We know that the Romans had not penetrated the western parts of Britain, where lay Glastonbury, the traditional burial place of Joseph of Arimathea.[109] And tradition also tells us that the Apostle Simon, the Zealot, is the one who had taken up the ministry to Britain after the decease of Joseph of Arimathea. After the death of Simon, then Aristobulus takes up the mission in Britain. It is important for us to look into these matters for the overall bearing on the story of *Beyond Acts.*

SIMON ZELOTES

SIMON ZELOTES WAS ONE OF THE ORIGINAL twelve apostles. We do not know much about him from the New Testament, but tradition tells us that he was one who traveled far and wide, and eventually ended up in Britain. R. W. Morgan tells us concerning Simon Zelotes:

> The next missionary after Joseph [of Arimathea] was Simon Zelotes the apostle. There can be little doubt, we think, on this point. One menology assigns the martyrdom of Zelotes to Persia in Asia, but others agree in stating he suffered in Britain. Of these the principal authority is Dorotheus, Bishop of Tyre, in the reigns of Diocletian and Constantius (A.D. 300). His testimony we consider decisive: 'Simon Zelotes traversed all Mauritania, and the regions of the Africans, preaching Christ. He was at last crucified, slain and buried in Britain' (Dorotheus, *Synod. de Apostl.; Synopsis ad Sim Zelot.*). Crucifixion was a Roman penalty for runagate slaves, deserters, and rebels; it was not known to the British laws. We conclude Simon Zelotes suffered in the east of Britain, perhaps, as tradition affirms, in the vicinty [*sic*] of Caistor, under the prefecture of Caius Decius, the officer whose atrocities were the immediate cause of the Boadicean war.[110]

Traditions concerning Simon Zelotes are varied, as Otto Hophan points out below. However, the dominant opinion that the Greek commentators in particular followed

[109] The traditions are collected and elucidated in Lionel Smithett Lewis, *St. Joseph of Arimathea at Glastonbury* (Cambridge: James Clark, 1922), 117.

[110] R. W. Morgan, *St. Paul in Britain* (London: Covenant Publishing Co., 1948), 127-8.

placed the region of Simon's apostolic labors in Egypt, Libya, Mauritania (an ancient kingdom in northwestern Africa, and later a Roman province), and even Britain. The Roman Breviary also mentions Simon's missionary labors in Egypt, and after this portrays Simon working with Jude Thaddaeus in Persia.[111]

Lionel Smithett Lewis records that there are three main sources of tradition that Simon preached in Britain:

(1) DOROTHEUS, Bishop of Tyre (A.D. 303), or the writer who attributed the Synopsis to him, in his *Synopsis de Apostol.* (9. Simon Zelotes) says: "Simon Zelotes preached Christ through all Mauitania [sic], and Afric [sic] the less. At length he was crucified at Brittania, slain and buried."

(2) NICEPHORUS, Patriach [sic] of Constantinople and Byzantine historian, A.D. 758-829, wrote (Book II, c. 40): "Simon born in Cana of Galilee who for his fervent affection for his Master and great zeal that he showed by all means to the Gospel, was surnamed Zelotes, having received the Holy Ghost from above, travelled through Egypt and Africa, then through Mauretania [sic] and all Libia [sic], preaching the Gospel. And the same doctrine he taught to the Occidental Sea, and the Isles called Britannia."

(3) GREEK MENOLOGY. The Menology of the Greek Church celebrates St. Simon's Day on May 10, and supports the statement of his having preached and been martyred in Britain (Baronius, *Annales Ecclesiastici,* under A.D. 44. Sec XXXVIII).[112]

Dorman Newman further relates that

he (Simon Zelotes) is said to have diverted his journey towards Egypt, Cyrene, Africa, Mauritania, and Libya. Nor could the coldness of the climate benumb his zeal or hinder him from shipping himself over into the Western Islands, yea even to Britain itself. Here he is said to have preached and wrought many miracles, and after infinite troubles and difficulties which he underwent, suffered martyrdom for the faith of christ, being crucified by the infidels and buried among them.

Others indeed affirm that after he had preached the gospel

[111] Otto Hophan, *The Apostles* (Westminster, Md.: The Newman Press, 1962), 285.
[112] Lewis, *St. Joseph,* 117.

> in Egypt he went to Mesopotamia, where he met with St. Jude the Apostle and together with him took his journey into Persia where, having gained a considerable harvest to the Christian Faith, they were both crowned with martyrdom: but this is granted by all learned men to be fabulous, wanting all clear foundation in Antiquity to stand on.[113]

Since tradition places one of the original disciples of Jesus in Britain at the end of his career, this fact places further weight on the argument it was not out of the question that Jesus and some of his faithful followers could have and indeed, did travel to Britain.

ARISTOBULUS

IN ROMANS 16:10, PAUL GREETS THOSE OF THE family of Aristobulus. Who was this Aristobulus?

> According to tradition, Aristobulus was the brother of Barnabas, one of the 70 disciples, ordained a bishop, and was eventually a missionary to Britain.[114]

Hippolytus, in his list of the 70 disciples, puts Aristobulus at number 29 with the comment "bishop of Britain" (Hippolytus, *Hippolytus on the Seventy Apostles* [*ANF* 5:256]). Again, R. W. Morgan gives us the traditional sources that Aristobulus was a missionary in Britain:

> The Martyrologies of the Greek Churches: "Aristobulus was one of the seventy disciples, and a follower of St. Paul the Apostle, along with whom he preached the Gospel to the whole world, and ministered to him. He was chosen by St. Paul to be the missionary bishop to the land of Britain, inhabited by a very warlike and fierce race. By them he was often scourged, and repeatedly dragged as a criminal through their towns, yet he converted many of them to

[113] Dorman Newman, *The Lives and Deaths of the Holy Apostles* (London: Kings Arms in the Poultry, 1685), 94, as quoted in William Steuart McBirnie, *The Search for the Twelve Apostles* (Wheaton, Ill.: Tyndale, 1973), 207-8.

[114] Scott T. Carroll, "Aristobulus" *The Anchor Bible Dictionary*, David Noel Freedman, ed., [New York: Doubleday, 1992], 1:383. M. O. Evans, (*The International Standard Bible Encyclopedia*, article: "Aristobulus:5" [Grand Rapids: Eerdmans, 1979], 1:290), on the other hand believes: "He was probably a grandson of Herod and brother of Herod Agrippa, a man of great wealth, and intimate with the emperor Claudius."

Christianity. He was there martyred, after he had built churches and ordained deacons and priests for the island (*Greek Men., ad 15 March*).

Haleca, Bishop of Augusta, to the same effect: "The memory of many martyrs is celebrated by the Britons, especially that of St. Aristobulus, one of the seventy disciples" (*Halecae Fragments in Martyr*).

Dorotheus, A.D. 303" "Aristobulus, who is mentioned by the Apostle in his Epistle to the Romans, was made bishop in Britain" (*Synopsis ad Aristobulum*).

Adonis Martyrologia: "Natal day of Aristobulus, Bishop of Britain, brother of St. Barnabas the Apostle, by whom he was ordained bishop. He was sent to Britain, where, after preaching the truth of Christ and forming a Church, he received martyrdom" (*In Diem Martii* 17).

The British Achau, or Genealogies of the Saints of Britain: "These came with Bran the Blessed from Rome to Britain – Arwystli Hen (*Senex*), Ilid, Cyndaw, men of Israel; Maw, or Manaw, son of Arwystli [Aristobulus] Hen" (*Achau Saint Prydain*).[115]

From these sources, Reverend Morgan reconstructs the following:

Aristobulus was sent into Britain by St. Paul before St. Paul came himself to Rome, and even before the Epistle to the Romans was written, for Aristobulus, when St. Paul wrote it, had left for his mission. The large space given by the Roman historians to the wars in Britain demonstrates the interest felt in them by the whole empire. Britain was a familiar term in every household. Upon it the whole military attention had for some years been concentrated. The name of Arviragus had by this time attained as great a celebrity as that of his cousin Caractacus – it was in every one's mouth; and Juvenal could suggest no news which would have been hailed by the Roman people with more intense satisfaction than that of his fall: "Hath our great enemy Arviragus, the car-borne British king, Dropped from his battle-throne?"[116]

New Testament scholars are certainly amiss in not addressing the

[115] Morgan, *St. Paul,* 129-30. See further on Dorotheus, *De septuaginta domini discipulis* (J.-P. Migne, *Patrologia Graeca,* 92:1063, 1074) and on Theodoretus, *Interpretatio epistolae II ad Timotheum 4.17,* (J.-P. Migne, *Patrologia Graeca,* 82:855).

[116] Ibid., 131.

significance of the events and leading characters of the British/Roman connection. It is our task to not ignore the importance of this association, for as we have seen already, there is strong tradition that Britain and Gaul were one of the earliest evangelized regions at that time.

After the Saulian persecution, the chief persecutor of the church, Saul of Tarsus, was struck down by a great light and blinded on the way to Damascus, Syria, where he had been granted authority to seek out followers of the Jesus cult there. The story of Paul's dramatic conversion is recounted in Acts, the ninth chapter. And with the conversion of Paul, the direction of events for the New Testament church changes dramatically.

THE APOSTLE PAUL'S THREEFOLD COMMISSION

BECAUSE THE APOSTLE PAUL MINISTERED IN THE Gentile cities of Asia Minor, he is generally thought of as strictly the apostle to the Gentiles. But one of the most interesting aspects of this story is the fact that Saul (whose name was changed to Paul) was given a threefold commission (Acts 9:15). Many scholars have completely overlooked this important detail concerning the Apostle Paul's biblical commission. That commission was:

1) To spread the gospel among the Gentiles;
2) To announce it before Kings;
3) To deliver it "to the people of Israel."

Many merely focus on the fact that Paul was the Apostle to the Gentiles, but miss out on the fact that he did appear before kings (plural) and that he did travel to the scattered people of Israel. The *Book of Acts* indeed tells us that Paul was informed by an angel:

> Take courage, For just as you have borne witness to my cause in Jerusalem, so you must also bear witness in Rome (Acts 23:11).

It was Paul's appeal to Caesar that would bring him to Rome and before the Emperor. That Paul's journey to Rome to go before Caesar was part of Paul's fulfillment of his second commission is reaffirmed by an Angel who tells him:

> Do not be afraid, Paul; you must stand before the Emperor

(Acts 27:24).

And, of course, the Emperor that Paul was to stand before was none other than Nero himself. As we have thus far established, the Apostle Paul came to the city of Rome in 56 C.E. Paul indeed was there exposed to the Roman authorities, if not Nero himself. But the Apostle Paul also made contact with another class of royalty that is little understood and barely mentioned in most studies on the subject. It is time that this story be told to a new generation of biblical inquirers.

PAUL AND THE BRITISH WAR CAPTIVES

WHEN THE APOSTLE PAUL SENT GREETINGS TO the church at Rome in the spring of 54 C.E., he listed the longest group of salutees of any of his letters, and yet he had never been to Rome.[117] Among those greeted he says: "Greet Rufus, chosen in the Lord, and his mother and mine" (Rom 16:13, NAB). What? His mother and MINE?[118] In this tiny verse we are given a key as to why Paul had an interest to go to Spain (and Britain).[119] Since Paul was a Benjamite (Rom 11:1), it would appear from this that his father was of the Hebrew tribe Benjamin, but that his mother had remarried a second time to the father of this Rufus.

Again, when Paul writes his last Epistle from Rome, he gives us a further clue to this family relationship. He there sends greetings to Timothy and "Eubolus sends greetings to you, as do Pudens and Linus and Claudia and all the brothers and sisters" (2 Tim 4:21).[120]

Who was this "Rufus" of Rom 16:13 and who was this "Pudens" of 2

---

[117] Acts 2:10 mentions that there were many visiting Jews and proselytes from Rome that may have been converted on the day of Pentecost. However, we maintain that those that Paul is writing to were British war captives from the Claudian expeditions in the 40's and into the 50's. Since Aristobolus and Simon Zealotes are said to have traveled to Britain earlier, these people apparently are Christian converts as a result of these missionary activities.

[118] A number of translations attempt to make this mother a sort of spiritual mother, e.g., NRSV: "his mother — a mother to me also"; REB: "to his mother, whom I call mother too"; NJB: "to his mother — a mother to me too." But why would Rufus' mother be a literal mother, but in the same breath, she is a spiritual mother to Paul?

[119] Spain may have been the general designation for the entire western area and possibly Paul's code word for Britain, being careful not to tip off Roman officials that he intended to go to an area of the Roman Empire that was still technically a sensitive war zone.

[120] Eubolus is no doubt a shortened version of Aristobulus in the Romans 16:13 passage.

Tim 4:21. It would appear from ancient testimony that they are actually one and the same person, in other words: "Rufus Pudens." A. S Barnes notes the following concerning this Pudens:

> He was married, according to Christian tradition, to a lady of the name of Claudia, and this is supported by the mention of the two names in the salutations at the end of St. Paul's Second Epistle to Timothy, "There salute thee ...Pudens and Linus and Claudia". Now there is extant among the epigrams of Martial, one (4:13) which records the marriage of a distinguished Roman of the name of Pudens to a foreign lady (*peregrina*) named Claudia. From another epigram (11:54) we learn that she was a Briton.[121]

Cardinal Baronius records:

> It is delivered by a firm tradition of antiquity that the house of Pudens at Rome was the place of the first entertainment of S. Peter Prince of the apostles: and that there new converted Christians began their assemblies to celebrate divine mysteries: Which house was erected into a church, by the most ancient title of Pudens.[122]

A Latin inscription has been found at the church of Pudenziana in the Palatium Britannicum in Rome, which reads:

> In this holy and most ancient Church dedicated by the Holy Pope Pius, by the title of Pastor, heretofore the house of Saint Pudens a Senator, and the Hospice of the Holy Apostles, there rests the bodies of three thousand martyrs, which the Holy virgins of Christ, Pudentiana and Praxedes, buried with their own hands.[123]

We also know from an excavation of an ancient Roman temple in Chichester, England, dug up in 1723, a stone tablet was unearthed bearing an inscription in Latin that identifies one "Pudens, son of Pudentinus."[124] We can only speculate that this Pudens is the same as the "Aulus [Rufus] Pudens," the soldier, and later senator, who became the husband of a British woman, Claudia Rufina, and who was immortalized in the Roman Poet Martial's (29-104) Epigrams, wherein we read:

---

[121] A. S. Barnes, *St. Peter in Rome* (London: Swan Sonnenschein & Co., 1900), 42.

[122] Baronius, *Annales Ecclesias,* in "Notis ad 19 Maii." Quoted from R. F. Serenus Cressy, *The Church History of Brittany* (Rouen, France: Printed for the Author, 1668), 11.

[123] Cressy, ibid.

[124] This is the restoration of Horsley and Gale, as reported in Morgan, *St. Paul,* 104. H. H. Scullard, *Roman Britain* (London: Thames & Hudson, 1979), 50-51, on the other hand, translates the donor as "Clemens, son of Prudentinus."

> Claudia's to marry Pudens, so they say. God's blessing, Rufus, on their wedding day.[125]

Now if Pudens is the son of Pudentinus, then we might infer from this that the Apostle Paul's mother had married secondly this Pudentinus and that is why Paul and Rufus had the same mother.

Cressy also notes, quoting from the *Martyrology of England*, against the date of the seventh of August:

> A commemoration of S. Claudia, A British woman, who was carried to Rome during the reign of the Emperor Claudius, and afterward in the year of our Lord one hundred and ten, died at Sabinum, a city of Umbria.[126]

Obviously, if Claudia is British, then the name "Claudia" is one in which she adopted when her family was exiled to Rome and the royal British family of Caractacus lived in a palace provided them in Rome by Emperor Claudius.[127] What was Claudia's British name? R. W. Morgan maintains, from British sources, that Claudia's British name was Gladys and that she was a daughter of the captured British King, Caractacus, who was then living in Rome.[128]

The *Apostolic Constitutions* informs us of the relationship of Linus and Claudia:

> Now concerning those bishops which have been ordained in our lifetime, we let you know that they are these: ... Of the church of Rome, Linus the son of Claudia was the first, ordained by Paul; and Clemens, after Linus' death, the second, ordained by me Peter (*Constitutions of the Holy Apostles* 7:46 [*ANF* 7:477-8]).[129]

---

[125] A. L. Francis and H. F. Tatum, *Martial's Epigrams* 4.13 (Cambridge: Cambridge University Press, 1924), 58.

[126] Cressy, *History*, 12.

[127] We should remember that the Chichester Inscription shows a British noble with the name of Tiberius Claudius Cogidunus, demonstrating a practice that is similar to that of Josephus, who adopted the name of the Flavian Caesars. A. S. Barnes, *St. Peter*, 42, observes: "Tacitus (*Agricola* 14) records that one Cogidunus, a British king in the time of Claudius, was rewarded with certain lands in recognition of his fidelity to Rome. Now there was dug up at Chichester, in 1723, a marble, which bore an inscription telling how the king, Tiberius Claudius Cogidunus, had permitted a temple to be erected in honour of Neptune and Minerva, on land that had been presented by Pudens, the son of Pudentinus. This inscription shows us that this British king had adopted as his own the name of his patron Claudius the emperor. Claudia according to Roman usage, and the occurrence in this inscription of the name of Pudens in addition to that of the father of Claudia suggests at once that we have here the Pudens and Claudia of Martial's epigram, and perhaps also of St. Paul's Epistles."

[128] R. W. Morgan, *Paul*, 89, 164.

The thrust of all of this is that the Apostle Paul had spent two years at Rome, residing apparently in the royal palaces of the British exiled kings, to whom he had even family ties. Although we cannot pursue this line of discussion any further here, we believe that there is sufficient reason to believe that the Apostle Paul did witness, not only before Nero, but before the British royal house held captive in Rome. Indeed, when Paul writes to the church at Rome and greets "Andronicus and Junia, my kinsman, and my fellow-prisoners" (Rom 16:7) he uses the word "συναιχμαλώτουσ," which E. W. Bullinger translated literally as "war captives."[130] Andronicus (meaning "a man excelling others" or "conqueror") may be the very Pendragon Caractacus himself, along with his wife Junia. If so, they may be related due to the fact that Paul's mother, Priscilla, had married secondly Pudentinus, father of Rufus Pudens Pudentius, husband of Claudia, and daughter of Caractacus. Thus, the *Epistle to the Romans*, by virtue of the names listed, is in reality an Epistle to the British war captives in Rome, rather than strictly to Latin citizens of that city.

Therefore, we believe that the Apostle Paul did fulfill his second commission in witnessing before "Kings" and not just a single King, before fulfilling his third commission to witness before Israel. That third commission the Apostle Paul fulfilled upon his release from prison in Rome in 58 C.E.

Back in 54 C.E., Paul stated that he did plan on going from Italy into Spain (Rom 15:28). It was on this campaign that Paul was to bear the name of Jesus to the "children of Israel" (Acts 9:15). From Spain Paul could have easily continued on to Britain to work among the descendants of the ancient tribes of Israel who had migrated there.

In the year of 60 C.E., war flared up with Rome and Britain.[131] The British "client king" Prasutagus died in 60 C.E., and upon his death his

[129] The Greek simply reads "*Linos ho Klaudias,*" so it is uncertain from just this passage of whether the relationship of Claudia to Linus is son or husband. E. B. Redlich, *S. Paul and His Companions* (London, 1913), 222, commenting on the fact that in 2 Tim 4:21 the name of Linus is wedged in between Pudens and Claudia, stated: "If the order of names suggests anything, it points to a closer relationship between Linus and Claudia than between Pudens and Claudia." A. S. Barnes, *St. Peter*, 51, however noted: "The occurrence of the name of Linus between those of Pudens and Claudia, who there is every reason to suppose were husband and wife, has been a difficulty to commentators. If, however, we are right in supposing that Linus was actually living in Pudens' house, and that this was now the headquarters of the Christian community at Rome, the arrangement of the names is quite natural."

[130] E. W. Bullinger, *The Companion Bible* (London: Samuel Bagster & Sons, 1969), 1692.

[131] Following our chronology, Paul would have left Rome for the western campaign two years before, 58 C.E. It would seem most unlikely that Paul, or anyone, would be free to travel to Britain while Rome was engaged in war there after this time.

two daughters were raped by Roman officers. Their mother, the queen Boadicea, protested in vain at this outrage and was even flogged and jeered at for so doing. She thereupon stirred her tribesmen to unite behind her in an armed rebellion against the newly established Roman rule. Tacitus informs us that she was actually able to capture Camulodunum and Londinium and in the process killing some 80,000 Roman troops (Tacitus, *Ann.* 14.30-38).

Now here is the interesting thing to notice. If Paul knew that Britain was one of the nations that could bring about the defeat of Rome, along with Parthia and the Jewish rebels in Judea, then Paul certainly had an interest in going to Britain to see first-hand if prophecy was going to be fulfilled or not. Paul arrived in Britain just before the time of the Boadicean uprising. If Paul witnessed Britain vanquishing eighty thousand Roman troops, would he witness Britain to go on to bring Rome at its knees?

Parthia also had been at war with Rome since 54 C.E. Now the Roman Province of Britain was also fighting Rome. And with the uprising in Judea starting to occur, this could be the beginning of the end for Rome. Also, the Roman Emperor, Nero, was decadent and weak. All of these factors must have played upon the prophetic thinking of the Apostle Paul.

We have to place ourselves within the time frame of the apostles in the early 60's C.E., since the crucial year of 63 C.E. was just about to turn the corner and prophecy could be starting the end-time rundown if Rome was beginning to topple.

Would other client Kingdoms rebel and instigate the fall of the mighty Roman Empire which had to occur shortly if Daniel's prophecies were going to take place? It may be that this was on the mind of the Apostle Paul in viewing the international events that had to start occurring if indeed he was witnessing the fulfillment of end-time prophecy.

But in 62 C.E. the Britons were finally defeated in a great slaughter. If Paul was still there, then he must have come to the realization that the next year, 63 C.E., would not be the beginning of the prophet Daniel's seven year scenario that would usher in the end-time prophecies. The following year, Paul returned to the Isle of Crete.

It was now the crucial year of 63 C.E. And it was in this very year that news came that Parthia submitted terms of peace. Rome was not being overthrown at all. Indeed, Rome was all the while annexing and expanding territories and becoming stronger than ever. There was now no doubt in the mind of the Apostle Paul that the return of Jesus was for a future age. And with this recognition we witness a whole different Paul than what we have read up to now.

Paul now finally abandoned the idea of Christ's return in his generation. The other Jerusalem-based apostles may have still held out a little longer – to the mid-period of the 7 years of Daniel's prophecy, 66/67, but by then even Peter and eventually John finally began to see that "this generation" was not theirs, but a future one.

Whereas a few short years before John wrote, in his initial draft of the *Book of Revelation*, that there would be about 12,000 converts from each tribe of Israel before Christ's return, now, in the mid 60's, there were only a hand full of faithful believers. Further, the scattered Israelites had so long lived among the Gentile heathens that James had to deal with them in the most rudimentary way with stern language about their warring, adulterous, and murderous behavior (James 4:1-10).

Paul returned to Cyprus in the year of 63 C.E. As we have stated, this was the very year that he and the other apostles originally expected the breakup of the Roman Empire and the ushering in of Daniel's prophecies. But now Paul came to realize that everything that he expected to happen at that time was not at all panning out.

Nothing was shaping up to support the idea that Daniel's prophecies were going to be fulfilled within the 40 year generation from Christ's crucifixion. This stark reality finally hit home to the Apostle Paul after his journey in the "West." It was next for Peter and John to come to this same realization. And in the spring of 66 C.E. it was to be revealed in a miraculous way. Peter and John may not have accepted Paul's interpretation of prophecy at first, but something happened shortly thereafter which changed their minds in a most dramatic way. What that was will be explored in the next chapter.

CHAPTER 11

The Jerusalem Church Flees

THE MIRACULOUS EVENTS THAT OCCURRED IN Jerusalem in the spring of 66 C.E. were signs to the faithful believers of the prophetic warnings of Jesus that the God of Israel was abandoning the holy temple in Jerusalem. And in line with Jesus' Olivet prophecy, this was a clear signal to the church there for them to flee from that area because of the ensuing destruction of the city that was foretold to occur.

Furthermore, Jesus had told his followers that when they were to witness certain celestial signs, then they were to "flee" from the area of Jerusalem into the mountains (Matt 24:16). From Eusebius we are informed that the church did, in fact, flee from Jerusalem at this time (Eusebius, *Hist. eccl.* 3.5.3).[132] Yet, what has escaped most critical assessments of this fact is that Jesus had told his followers to flee to the mountains. Did the church obey the words of Jesus and flee to the mountains? No! They fled instead to the northern plain country of Judaea, to a small town called Pella.

What is staring us in the face here is not disobedience to the explicit directive of Jesus, but a fact that is most significant to the entire story. It tells us that the apostles knew something that many today fail to recognize. The church leaders and apostles there in Jerusalem – Peter, John, Jude, Simeon, Matthew, and so on – obviously had come to the conclusion by this time that their generation was not the end-time prophesied by Jesus because they did not do as Jesus had instructed them – to flee to the mountains. They rather fled to the northern plains of Judea, in the area of Pella.

It is important to understand the Olivet prophecy in the context of what Jesus told his disciples some thirty-six years before. When Jesus said to flee to the mountains, did his disciples understand just which mountains that they were to flee to? Is there anything within the text of the Olivet prophecy to give us a hint? Let's notice some interesting things

[132] So also Epiphanius, *De mens. et pond.* 15.

about Jesus' explicit teaching before going on. It will be truly illuminating.

Jesus said to his disciples that when he returns to Jerusalem it will be from the direction of the East in relation to the Olivet ridge where he addressed his disciples (Matt 24:27). His approach is therefore to be from the area of Jericho. Note that it is just east of the Jericho region, and directly across the Jordan River where Moses died and was given a secret burial (Deut 34:16). In this context, then, if we go back and look at the route that the Israelites took during the Exodus, after their encounter with Edom, they went on the King's Highway in Moab and turned north to Mount Nebo which overlooked the Promised Land opposite Jericho (Deut 34:1-6).

Using this information as a guide then, if Jesus, when he returns to this earth, were to follow this same route to the very place where Moses was buried, then Mount Nebo might just be the staging area where Moses and Elijah are the first two individuals to be resurrected out of their graves at that place, and then the "First Resurrection" of the righteous dead, along with those who are alive at that time and are changed in a twinkling of an eye, would occur.

It is at this point that the angels are to gather the spirit composed "Saints" from around the world and bring them to the very spot where Jesus had returned. And from that place Jesus and the entire assembly would proceed westward in the air to approach Jerusalem from the East.[133] Thus, just before the end, the church was to flee to those mountains where Jesus was to return. And the specific mountain in particular appears to be Mount Nebo.

Now notice what Luke brings out:

> For as the lightning [the sun] that lights out of one part under heaven, shines to the other part under heaven; so shall also the Son of Man be in His day (Luke 17:24).

This is telling us that the approach of Jesus to Jerusalem would be from East to West. The context here is the return of Jesus Christ "in His day" – not in the generation that he was then addressing. We can be sure that this is true because in the very next verse Jesus says

> but first He [Jesus] must suffer many things, and be rejected of THIS generation [in contrast to that generation that will be in "His day"] (Luke 17:25).

---

[133] Notice that Jesus and the Saints do not go to Megiddo to fight in a battle of Armageddon. Megiddo is simply the staging area where the Man of Sin will "assemble" (Rev 16:16) his armies and from there go to Jerusalem to fight Jesus there. Thus, there is no such thing as a battle of Armageddon.

Jesus then told his disciples about the unexpectedness of his coming by a reference to Noah. The very next thing Jesus mentioned was a long reference to Lot, the nephew of Abraham. Right after stating the examples of Lot, Jesus then said that at his coming some people would be in bed, others grinding, and others in the field – and that from each group there would be someone taken (Luke 17:34-6).[134] Taken to where? Jesus did not say. So, logically, the very next thing that the disciples then asked Jesus directly was: "Where Lord?" And instead of Jesus giving a definite answer, he rather gives them something akin to a riddle:

> And He [Christ] said unto them, "wherever the body is, there will the eagles be gathered together" (Luke 17:37, KJV).[135]

Christ's enigmatic answer must be understood in the context of what he was already saying. Jesus had taken five verses to tell us about the experiences of Lot and his escape from the destruction of Sodom. The clues to what Jesus meant are right within the context of what he was saying. Let's understand.

Lot fled Sodom to a small village east of the Dead Sea called Zoar and then he went "up to the mountain." What mountain did Lot go up?

It must have been a mountain that would have been prominent enough for the disciples to understand, for it did not need any further identification by Jesus. If Jesus told his disciples to pay heed to the example of Lot in regard to circumstances involving the Second Advent, then it is important to determine the identification of this mountain. The cities of the plain, where Lot lived, were in the northern parts around the Dead Sea region, not in the south. This is right in the vicinity of where Moses died and was buried on Mount Nebo.

There was no person in the entire Old Testament period more important than Moses. It was necessary that Moses' exact burial place be hidden so that people would not retreat to his sepulchre to worship him like the pagans did with their heros. Scripture also reveals that Satan wanted to make known to the world where Moses' body was buried, but the archangel Michael stepped in (Jude 1:9) and secured the command of

[134] Notice that this "taking," or snatching of people at Jesus' return, which many fundamental Christian groups have dubbed the "Rapture," really occurs right at Christ's second coming and not some seven or three and a half years earlier, as the Rapture theory erroneously maintains.

[135] Most translations say "vultures" instead of "eagles" because, after all, vultures do gather around dead bodies. However, if the body in question is that of Moses, as we suggest, then the gathering can be considered, not a gathering around a corpse, but a gathering of saints brought about by the eagles wings. The context favors this interpretation because it is talking about the saints being snatched and" taken" somewhere.

God regarding its secrecy (Deut 32:49).

Having said this, then the obvious question is: What was the one significant "dead body" of all the entire Old Testament that was buried somewhere on Mount Nebo? It was the body of Moses! And Jesus said that where that body was (the buried body of Moses), there would be a gathering place of the resurrected saints who would have been brought there by angelic beings, appearing like the wings of eagles. Therefore, the Mountain that the church was to flee to was obviously Mount Nebo.

Notice also that this mountain is where the prophet Elijah ended his career. It is also the exact area where Lot went to in order to escape the burning fires of Sodom. And what was the last official act of Elijah? It was to lead his successor Elishah from Bethel eastwards to the Jordan River, then to cross the Jordan dry shod by a miracle – similar to the miracle when the Israelites crossed into the Holy land under Joshua.

Many may not have realized this fact, but Elijah's departure was in the same direction as of Moses' burial place. Elijah was then taken up by a whirlwind into a cloud (2 Ki 2:11).[136] The completion of both Moses' and Elijah's careers was in the same area. The lifting up of Elijah into the clouds may be a type of the way the resurrected chosen ones will gather to meet the Lord in the air at Christ's return to this earth (1 Thess 4:17).

Now we should note something very significant to the entire story. When Jesus gave a vision of his Second Advent to three of his closest disciples, Peter, James, and John, he took them up to a mountain and showed them a vision of the future where Jesus is standing in glory with two other personages with him. And who was standing there with him? It was Moses and Elijah (Matt 16:27, 8 to 17:9).[137]

Moses, who was the most important individual of the Old Testament, may be the very first individual to be resurrected in the "first resurrection" right over the very spot that he was buried. Then we have Elijah, who may also have been buried in that area. The so-called "Transfiguration" was, in fact, a vision, which may be showing us the first two resurrections of the "First Resurrection" – that of Moses and Elijah – when Jesus returns to this earth. The vision shows Christ in his glorified appearance addressing

[136] Although we later hear of Elijah in 2 Chronicles 21:12, it is no doubt symbolic that Elijah's mission was completed on the east side of Jordan, opposite Jericho, near the burial place of Moses.

[137] This was a "vision," as the text plainly says it was (Matt 17:9), and not a situation where Moses and Elijah, who are supposedly alive in heaven, and came down at that time to talk to Jesus. In no way is the Transfiguration story a proof text to support the idea that departed loves ones are alive today in heaven. The biblical teaching is that departed ones are asleep, awaiting one of the resurrections mentioned in the Bible. The Bible only speaks of a resurrection from the state of death and does not support any such notion that dead people are not dead at all, but alive in heaven (or a place called hell) during this time period. The one exception, of course, is Jesus.

these two individuals in preparation to the gathering of the rest of the spirit-born children of God, who being transported to the same place from around the world by angels that appear like eagles.

Is it not significant that the very last prophecy in the Old Testament in Malachi couples Moses and Elijah together in the same context:

> Remember the Law of Moses, My servant, which I commanded him in Horeb for all Israel ...Behold, I will send you Elijah the prophet before the coming of the great and dreadful day of the Lord. And he will turn the hearts of the fathers to the children, and the hearts of the children to their fathers, lest I come and strike the earth with a curse (Mal 4:4-6, *NKJV*).

Here we see Moses, the great law giver and organizer, together with Elijah, who was prophesied to turn the hearts of the children back to the fathers. These two individuals are to be central figures in the future Kingdom of God on this earth, along with Jesus. In this vision, Jesus may be apprizing Moses and Elijah as to what is happening and giving them instructions in preparation to the meeting of those, who are chosen for the first resurrection, in the air which was soon to follow.

The resurrected saints from around the world are prophesied to gather together east of the city of Jerusalem. Christ shall then take Moses, Elijah and the resurrected saints and those who are alive and taken to changed into a spirit being at that time, with him to Jerusalem from the east. He then descends to stand on the Mount of Olives. In so doing, Jesus returns exactly as the Angel in Acts 1:11 prophesied, in the same manner as he left this earth, to the very spot that his feet last touched some two millennia before.

> Then the LORD will go forth and fight against those nations as when he fights on a day of a battle. On that day his feet shall stand on the Mount of Olives, which lies before Jerusalem ON THE EAST, and the Mount of Olives shall be split in two from east to west by a very wide valley on the LORD'S mountain. for the valley between the mountains shall reach to Azal and you shall flee as you fled from the earthquake in the days of King Uzziah of Judah. Then the LORD my God will come, AND ALL THE HOLY ONES WITH HIM (Zech 14:3-5).

Luke records Jesus' prophecy in the following words:

> There will be signs in the sun, the moon, and the stars, and on the earth distress among nations confused by the roaring of the sea and the waves. People will faint from fear and

> foreboding of what is coming upon the world, for the powers of the heavens will be shaken. Then they will see 'the Son of Man coming in a cloud' with power and great glory (Luke 21:25-7).

The apostolic church was looking for these events to transpire in their generation. But by 66 C.E., the Jerusalem church fled out of the area, not because that they believed that these prophecies were being fulfilled, but because they had come to see that the real fulfillment of these prophecies were not to occur for centuries later. They could easily stack up what Jesus predicted and see that there was no "abomination of desolation" standing in the holy place of the temple at that time. Indeed, they knew by the miraculous signs that were occurring then that God was abandoning the temple and turning his back on his people prior to war with the Romans.

The church at that time then fled Jerusalem. The fact that the church did not retreat to the immediate mountains of Nebo, but rather to the plains of northern Judaea, shows us that the church leaders had finally had come to the realization that the end was not during their generation. This is exactly just as the Apostle Paul had believed for some time now.

As the signs of war became closer, the remnant church in Jerusalem abandoned Judaea altogether later that year (66 C.E.). The Apostles John and Andrew went to Ephesus and Peter and Mark went to Rome where the Apostle Paul was in prison.

Peter wanted to meet up with Paul before he was executed in order to secure Paul's letters for posterity. And Second Peter 3:16 is abundant testimony that he did just that! It is thus apparent that the church of Jerusalem left that city before the Jewish/Roman War had already started in the summer of 66 C.E., to go to a less politically active area to the north.

It was now obvious that all the apostles remaining at Jerusalem, including Peter, Jude and John, knew that the return of Christ would not be in their lifetime, but would be future to their day. Paul was indeed right, after all. And with this new realization came a new mission of urgency that prompted the apostles to fulfill another aspect of the apostolic church. But before we get into this, it is necessary that we understand the events that were occurring in Judaea in the year 66 C.E. that lead to war. This we will cover in the next chapter.

CHAPTER 12

The Apostolic Church and the Roman War

AFTER PENTECOST IN 66 C.E., THE JERUSALEM church received signs to flee. The church then went to a town north called Pella (Eusebius, *Hist. eccl.* 3.5.3; Epiphanius, *Pan.* 29, 7; 30, 2; *de mens. et pond.* 15) There they stayed initially and then went on to safer areas. Josephus records the events of this fateful year which lead to open rebellion to the Roman government. These events are helpful in understanding, not only what led to war with the Romans, but also our understanding of what the early apostles were witnessing and commenting on in their letters.

To begin with, the Jewish population of Caesarea some years earlier had argued for citizenship and took their case all the way to Nero (Josephus, *B.J.* 2.13.7 [266-70]). The Jewish population had then increased in this area to the point that it outnumbered the Syrians, who were Roman citizens. The Roman Procurator, Antonius Felix (52-55 C.E.), had his hands full trying to keep the peace. Nero, of course, sided with the Syro-Greek population of Caesarea against the Jews for mainly political reasons. Despite this ruling, the Jews continued to antagonize the Syrians.

But in the Hebrew month of Iyyar (May/June) the Jews had the last straw when a certain Greek refused to sell property surrounding a synagogue and, as if to spite the Jews, he built buildings on that property which restricted access to the synagogue itself (*B.J.* 2.14.4 [284-288]). Physical violence broke out in order to try to stop the building. Appeals to the Governor, Gessius Florus (64-66 C.E.) were unsuccessful. One rich Jew even bribed Florus with eight talents, but Florus took the money and retreated to a town called Sebaste, abandoning the problem to the locals.

On the next Sabbath, when the Jews were walking to the Synagogue they had found that a Syrian had sacrificed birds on an upturned pot right in front of their place of worship. The acting commander, Jucundus, tried to prevent hostilities by removing the pot, but was overcome by the Caesareans, so the Jews took their copy of the Torah and withdrew to a place outside the city. A Jewish delegation went to Florus in Sebaste (Samaria) to gain his support for their cause, reminding him of the eight talents they had already given him beforehand, but Florus, instead of sensing the volatility of the situation, had the brazen gall to throw the delegation into prison on trumped up charges that they had stolen the books of the Law from their own synagogue (*B.J.* 2.14.5 [289-92]).

Next Josephus reports that Florus sent his men to Jerusalem to take seventeen talents from the temple treasury under the guise that it was ordered by Caesar (*B.J.* 2.14.6 [293-6]). The Jews were outraged and knew that it was Florus, not Caesar, who wanted the money for his own greed. As a result, many of the Jews publicly insulted Florus, and mocked him by acting like beggars for Florus (*B.J.* 2.14.7 [297-300]).

Although Florus should have returned to Caesarea to quell the disturbances that were taking place in that city, he was so outraged by the mockery of him in Jerusalem that he marched on Jerusalem with troops, refusing the greetings of the people. He thereupon set up a tribunal to punish those who had publicly insulted him, especially those who had pretended to beg for copper coins for Florus. The Jewish leaders refused to cooperate, of course, in identifying the culprits, saying that it was impossible to identify them. In retaliation for the Jew's refusal to cooperate, Florus sent his army to sack the upper city. Josephus reports that over 3600 Jews, men, women and children and even some of the Roman Equestrian rank were slaughtered or executed by crucifixion (*B.J.* 2.14.8-9 [301-308]).

At this time Queen Berenice, daughter of Herod Agrippa and wife of Agrippa Junior, had come to Jerusalem to perform a vow. Upon seeing all the violence going on there she appealed to Florus to stop it at once, but found that she too had to remain guarded in her own palace or run the risk of being slain (*B.J.* 2.15.1 [309-14]).

Florus further inflamed the situation with the Jews by informing them that two Roman Cohorts were marching into Jerusalem and that they were to be greeted by the chief priest and the leaders of the community. But unknown to the Jewish leaders was the fact that Florus had instructed the soldiers to rebuff the people's salutations and not return their greetings in order to excite the people further into violence. This gave the Romans an excuse to turn on the people. In the fighting that followed, Florus attempted to take the temple garrison, Fort Antonio, but was prevented by strong opposition that knew that he wanted to seize the temple treasury (*B.J.* 2.15.2-6 [315-332]).

It appears that Florus took this defeat in stride and even left a number of troops to keep order, deciding to return to Caesarea. From there Florus sent a report to the Syrian Governor, Cestius. Cestius also received a report of the Jerusalem massacre from the Jewish magistrates and Queen Bernice. Cestius, thereupon, sent a tribune, Neopolitanus, to investigate the matter. At the same time, Agrippa returned from a visit to Alexandra. King Agrippa and Neopolitanus met at Jamnia, along with the Jerusalem dignitaries. Neopolitanus went to Jerusalem to inspect the damage and hear the complaints from the Jews there first hand, and was convinced that the city was now basically calm.

Neopolitanus thus returned to Cestius with the belief that the situation had been stabilized, but nothing was done concerning the complaints against Florus. The Jews thus felt betrayed and they immediately appealed to King Agrippa that he should send a delegation to Emperor Nero to bring formal charges against Florus. Agrippa tried to diffuse the situation by giving a public speech which basically told the Jews how futile it would be for the Jews to go to war with Rome over this. In this speech Agrippa stated

> Will you not estimate your own weakness? Hath not your army been often beaten even by your neighboring nations, while the power of the Romans is invincible in all parts of the habitable earth? Nay, rather they seek for somewhat still beyond that; for all Euphrates is not a sufficient boundary for them on the east side, nor the Danube on the north; and for their southern limit, Libya hath been searched over by them, as far as countries uninhabited, as is Cadiz their limit on the west; nay, indeed, they have sought for another habitable earth beyond the ocean, and have carried their arms as far as such British islands as were never know[n] before. What therefore do you pretend to? Are you richer than the Gauls, stronger than the Germans, wiser than the Greeks, more numerous than all men upon the habitable earth? – What confidence is it that elevates you to oppose the Romans? (Josephus, *B.J.* 2.16.4 [362-4]).

Oddly enough, the initial response to Agrippa's appeal seems to have been a complete turn around in the actions of the Jews, at least for the time being, which even resulted in a collection of the outstanding taxes and repair of the damage done to the temple porticos. Agrippa was thus successful by his cautiously wise leadership, but still there was the unfinished business about Florus. When Agrippa told the Jews that they should obey Florus until he was to be replaced by the Emperor, the backlash was so great that Agrippa was shouted down, jeered at and even stoned by the people, resulting in him fleeing the city. And with the removal of Agrippa and Bernice, things got out of hand and events moved swiftly in the direction of war.

Lester Grabbe remarks at this point: "Up to this point wholesale war could probably have been avoided, however, things now moved rapidly."[138] The Sicarii, a band of zealots who had heard of the revolt in Jerusalem, decided that at last their hour had come and assaulted the Roman garrison at Masada, west of the Dead Sea. The leader of this band was Menahem, a descendant of Judas the Galilean. With the Roman weapons that were seized at the Masada arsenal, this band felt confident to march on to the city of Jerusalem.

At the same time, in Jerusalem, a man by the name of Eleazar ben Ananias, who was the custodian of the temple, took a bold step in forbidding all sacrifices by foreigners. This meant that the daily offerings for Caesar would thus be halted, and the chief priests and leading citizens appealed to get this decision reversed for fear of the consequences. Such a defiant gesture was tantamount to an open declaration of war against the Romans. For their own protection these Jewish magistrates even went to Florus, but Florus was only too eager to let the rebels have their way in order to let the situation get out of hand. So Florus simply did nothing.

Next, the Jewish leaders appealed to Agrippa and Agrippa supplied 3000 horsemen who occupied the upper city. The lower city was now firmly in the hands of Eleazar and the war party.

It was now around August of 66 C.E. At the festival of wood-gathering, the Sicarii, who had taken Masada, now slipped into the city and joined forces with the Jerusalem rebels. With this the zealots now had forces enough to expel Agrippa's troops from the upper city. The Palace was besieged and burnt down and Agrippa's troops fled or were allowed to leave unharmed, but the Romans were kept prisoner.

Menahem, leader of the Sicarii, assumed the leadership of all the insurgents. But he became abusive and took on the trappings of royalty and even slew the High Priest Ananias and his brother, Hezekiah, found hiding. This was too much for Eleazar and his followers, who turned on Menahem, killing him and a number of his gang. The rest of the Sicarii escaped back to Masada under the leadership of Eleazar ben Ananias.

The besieged Roman garrison finally agreed to surrender with the promise of safe conduct out of the city. Once the Romans delivered up their shields and weapons, however, they were brutally massacred by the rebels, except their leader, Metilius, who escaped by promising to become a circumcised Jew. Of course, once this act had occurred, then there could be only one consequence for it, for Rome certainly would not go unavenged in this total act of rebellion and war.

In Caesarea, Florus exterminated the Jewish population, with twenty

---

[138] Lester L. Grabbe, *Judaism from Cyrus to Hadrian* (Minneapolis: Fortress, 1992), 2:448.

thousand being slain on the same day as when the Roman soldiers were killed in Jerusalem. Josephus then records:

> Upon which stroke that the Jews received at Caesarea the whole nation was greatly enraged; so they divided themselves into several parties, and laid waste the villages of the Syrians, and their neighboring cities, Iphia, and Sebonitis, and Gerasa, and Pella, and Scythopolis (Josephus, *B.J.* 2.18.1 [458]).

Not all Jews were behind these Jewish raiding bands. In Scythopolis some of the Jewish citizens tried to fight back these rebels, although they were overcome. We note here that these bands had stormed the city of Pella, the city where the church had fled after the Pentecost signs. The apostles must have seen first hand that now the Jews were in total open rebellion against the Romans and that Judaea was no longer safe.

In September the Roman Governor Cestius finally commenced military operations against this revolt with two Roman legions and other auxiliaries, together with Agrippa's forces besides. First, Galilee and Joppa were pacified. Then they marched on to Jerusalem.

The Roman forces arrived in early October during the Feast of Tabernacles. Many of the festival pilgrims were enlisted to help halt the Roman advance. Agrippa attempted a negotiation, but the messengers were assaulted. The Romans thereby pushed on with their siege. The rebels were forced to withdraw from the outer city, retreating to the temple area and the inner city. Some of the citizens tried to secretly negotiate with the Romans, but these were halted when they were discovered by the war party.

Surprisingly, Cestius broke off the siege, apparently due to incorrect intelligence on the strength of the rebel forces. If Cestius only knew his advantage, he could have pressed the siege further and the war would have ended right then and there. The rebel insurgents looked on this, however, as a victory and even pursued the Romans, turning their withdrawal into a rout, with heavy losses on the Roman side.

This incident only deluded the war party into believing the fanciful notion that the Roman military machine could be beaten. The zealots may have also been encouraged by the memory of victories like that of Judas Maccabeaus and his brothers, who went to battle in the face of overwhelmingly larger forces, but were victorious because, as they believed, it was God who fought for them. Indeed, did not history repeat itself when the inferior forces of the Jews had just driven out the superior forces of the Romans under Cestius Gallus?

The ambush at Beth-horron recalled also the victories of Judas

Maccabaeus, the place where the famous Maccabean hero had won numerous victories at that very spot. With such a success against the Romans the peace party was discredited and the war party could now make the appeal to organize the Jewish population for a war of liberation (*B.J.* 2.19.9 [551-5).

The revolutionaries were now calling themselves "the patrons of liberty" (*B.J.* 4.4.4 [272]), to fight for the "preservation of ... liberty" (*B.J.* 4.4.4 [273]), to become "friends of liberty" (*B.J.* 4.4.4 [282]). The rebellion against Rome, although it promised liberty, was carried out by thugs who influenced the general population to the degree that many were following them into their degenerating conduct. Josephus records that at this time:

> Every law of man was trampled underfoot, every requirement of religion was ridiculed by those who scoffed at the oracles of the prophets as rogue's stories (Josephus, *B.J.* 4.6.3 [282]).

Josephus also tells us that

> that was a time most fertile in all manner of wicked practices, insomuch that no kind of evil deeds were then left undone; nor could any one so much as devise any bad thing that was new, so deeply were they all infected, and strove with one another in their single capacity, and in their communities, who should run the greatest lengths in impiety towards God, and in unjust actions towards their neighbors, the men of power oppressing the multitude and the multitude earnestly laboring to destroy the men of power (Josephus, *B.J.* 7.8.1 [259-60]).

The Apostle Peter warned those who were following the zealots,

> as there were false prophets in the past history of our people, so you too will have your false teachers, will insinuate their own disruptive views and, by disowning the Lord who bought them FREEDOM (liberty!), will bring upon themselves speedy destruction. Many will copy their debauched behavior, and the Way of Truth will be brought into disrepute on their account (2 Pet 2:1-2, NJB).

The entire second chapter of Second Peter was a stern warning of exactly what Josephus described was occurring at that time. It is evident that Peter left Judaea, probably soon after the Pentecost signs in the early summer of 66 C.E., and had traveled to Rome to meet with the Apostle Paul who was then in Prison (2 Pet 3:15).

When Paul wrote his last Epistle to Timothy from his Roman

imprisonment in the summer of 66 C.E., Peter was not yet in Rome. When Mark arrived in Jerusalem to tell Peter of Paul's imprisonment and his intention of collecting and binding his letters for the future church, Peter, no doubt, must have realized that Paul was correct in his prophetic understanding of the times after all. Peter then dispatches his first Epistle from Jerusalem, sending greetings from "Babylon" (Rome) via John Mark.[139] By the time Peter wrote his second Epistle the following year, Peter was in Rome and Paul was at that time dead.

When John Mark came to Peter to discuss the events that were occurring and what the plan of Paul was to produce a canon of inspired literature for the future church, Peter then knew that the "end" was not to be in their generation. He also knew that war with Rome was evident and would be disastrous. Since it was evident that war was inevitable and that many of the faithful were falling away, it was imperative that Peter should journey to Rome to visit Paul on what the future of the church would be after the apostles had departed. Paul also in his last Epistles warned of the apostasy that was soon to occur (1 Tim 4:1, 2; 2 Tim 4:3, 4).

When Peter's second Epistle was received back in Judea, the Apostle Jude may have been still there with the remaining faithful in the Pella area. The Apostle Jude intended to write about "our common salvation," but then had to break off from this theme because he now

> found it of urgent necessity to write you encouraging you to put up a hard fight (not against Rome, but for) the faith which was once delivered to the saints (Jude 1:3).

While Peter, writing from Rome in the summer of 67 C.E., prophesied that the apostasy would soon occur, now Jude, a brother of Jesus who was still holding out in the Judean hill country, dispatched his short Epistle that the things that Peter foretold were now occurring. It is as if Jude had a copy of Peter's Epistle and was confirming everything that Peter had written would occur.[140] But those who did not flee to Pella were turning away to fight with the zealots. Jude wrote that people were now "denying Jesus Christ" (Jude 1:4), that they "*are* defiling the flesh," and they "*are* disregarding high offices," and they "*are* blaspheming the ones of glory" (v. 8). They "*are* unreasoning animals" (v. 10), and "*are* corrupting

[139] There are three candidates for the appellation of "Babylon." 1) The literal city of Babylon in Mesopotamia; 2) Rome in a figurative sense; and 3) Jerusalem, also used figuratively. Traditionally, it has been thought to refer to Rome, and this is what we also believe. However, the Epistle itself was indeed written from Jerusalem. What most commentators miss is the fact that Peter is sending greetings from Rome [Babylon] via John Mark who just arrived from that city, and not from the city that Peter was then writing his Epistle. Ernest L. Martin, *Restoring*, 269-70, has gotten the city of composition right [Jerusalem], but he unfortunately believed that the term "Babylon" was a cipher for Jerusalem.

themselves" (ibid.). The present tense of Jude's language shows us that what Peter could foresee, Jude was now witnessing.

Notice also that Jude makes specific reference that these apostates were "feeding themselves without fear" at their "love feasts" (v. 12). And it was at the Feast of Tabernacles that many of the seditionists came into Jerusalem, feasting and recruiting many of them into war. Thus, Jude probably wrote sometime after the Feast of Tabernacles, after Cestius retreated, and when the marauding bands of seditionists had sacked the Judaean countryside, including Pella in late autumn of 66 C.E.

Jude, who was acting on Peter's behalf as an apostolic spokesman of the Jerusalem brethren in Pella, is specific that he was writing about the common salvation which people had in Christ, when all of a sudden disaster struck which caused him to put aside his original theme and address the immediate situation. This was in fact the outbreak of war among the Jews with the Romans.

One thing is for certain. The church of the second, third, and fourth century, if they had anything to do with the creation of the New Testament canon, would never have included either Jude or Second Peter. The issues of these Epistles certainly had no immediate relevance to the church at large in those later times. The very fact that church authorities in later times debated the authenticity and worth of these Epistles is testimony enough that these later church officials were far removed from the time that these Epistles were written and canonized.

Peter risked his life to go to Rome and visit with Paul, for he knew that he himself would surely be arrested and face martyrdom when he arrived in Rome. Why was it so necessary for Peter to accomplish this mission? It is obvious that Peter finally could see that Paul was right in so many things, prophetically and theologically. Peter had to see Paul just as much as Paul had to see Peter. The reason will be made even further clear as we move to the next chapter.

---

[140] Most scholar's believe that Peter borrowed from Jude, but the difference is that Peter was foretelling what would happen and Jude was confirming what Peter wrote. Indeed, Jude reminded his audience to remember the prediction of the apostles and then shows us specifically what apostles he was referring to by quoting virtually verbatim 2 Peter 3:3. Donald Guthrie *New Testament Introduction* (Downers Grove: InterVarsity Press, 1990), 921, addressing the opinion of Theodor Zahn, *Introduction to the New Testament*, 1909, 2:250-65, notes: "The used [sic] of the future tense in 2 Peter and the present tense in Jude with reference to the false teachers is also thought to point to the priority of 2 Peter. What 2 Peter foresaw, Jude has now experienced." Guthrie further comments that it is inexplicable why an 'apostolic' writer "should take over so much of the writing of an obscure man like Jude, whereas it is highly intelligible why the lesser man should be influenced by the greater" (ibid. 921-2).

CHAPTER 13

The Final Acts of the Apostle Paul

IN THE LAST LETTERS THAT THE APOSTLES PETER and Paul wrote, we can see that they were greatly concerned with the predicted heresy within the church that they now could clearly witness as beginning to happen. No longer do we see these apostles writing about the imminent return of Jesus in their lifetime, for it was now evident to them that the return of Jesus to this earth would be far into the future.

Rather than these latter letters being written by impostors after Peter and Paul's time, the different writing styles reflect different times and a very different understanding of prophecy than what the apostles maintained in their earlier years. And with that realization came the harsh reality that the church would soon become infected with false doctrine if, and only if, the apostles themselves did not do something to establish an official body of literature on the same par as that of the writings of Moses and the subsequent prophets.

If the church was to continue in the doctrines that Jesus established, then the responsibility fell squarely on Peter – the leading apostle still alive – to see to it that the pure message of the gospel would be preserved in such a way as to guide the faithful, as well as initiate new truth seekers into the authoritative word of the apostle's of Jesus. How else could the church survive down through the ages after the apostles had departed the scene? How else could they withstand the onslaught of the predicted coming heresy? The only possible way was to leave behind an official body of writings that the church could refer to in the same way as that of the Jewish canon of Scripture.

It is in this context that we must understand the final activities of the Apostles Peter, Paul and John. The concern of the Apostle Paul in what he told the Ephesian elders, was that "after I have gone, savage wolves will come in among you, not sparing the flock" (Acts 20:29). And in the context of this speech Paul told those elders that the remedy that would keep them through such times was God's word:

> And now I commend you to God and to the MESSAGE of his grace, a MESSAGE that is able to BUILD YOU UP and to give you the inheritance among all who are sanctified (Acts 20:32).

Paul knew full well the power of the Word of God. He had earlier written to the Thessalonian church that

> we constantly give thanks to God for this, that when you received the word of God that you heard from us, you accepted it not as a human word but as what it really is, God's word, which is also at work in you believers (1 Thess 2:13).

Paul also had told the Corinthians that

> now we have received not the spirit of the world, but the Spirit that is from God, so that we may understand the gifts bestowed on us by God. And we speak of these things in words not taught by human wisdom but taught by the Spirit (1 Cor 2:12-13).

It is obvious from Paul's letters that he was convinced of his own inspiration to write inspired Scripture. The mature teaching of "the Mystery" had finally been revealed to the Apostle Paul. He now knew that this revelation had to be passed on to the future church because he wrote that he became the servant of the church

> according to God's commission that was given to me for you, to make the WORD OF GOD fully known, the MYSTERY that has been hidden throughout the ages and generations but has now been revealed to his saints (Col 1:25-6).

Also, Paul knew that he had the authority to even write commandments as coming from God:

> If anyone thinks that he is a prophet or a spiritual person, he should recognize that what I am writing to you is a commandment of the Lord (1 Cor 14:37, *NAB*).

Then, in Paul's later years, he began to witness what he had predicted. He wrote Timothy that "all the men of Asia have turned away from me" (2 Tim 1:5). When the Apostle Paul wrote to Timothy in his second Epistle to him, he knew that his "time of departure has come" (2 Tim 4:6). Indeed, this was the last piece of literature that the Apostle Paul would pen before his imminent death. He further told Timothy that

> the time is coming when people will not put up with sound doctrine, but having itching ears, they will accumulate for themselves teachers to suit their own desires, and will turn away from listening to the truth and wander away to myths (2 Tim 4:3-4).

He had similarly written to Timothy in his first Epistle:

> Now the spirit expressly says that in later times some will renounce the faith by paying attention to deceitful spirits and teachings of demons, through the hypocrisy of liars whose consciences are seared with a hot iron (1 Tim 4:1).

These authoritative words fly in the face of those who believe that doctrine was to slowly develop in the centuries that followed after the apostles. Under no circumstance is this true. These words condemn such ideas. And they also condemn the idea that the New Testament writings would be a product of post apostolic times. Thus, "scholarly" works which advocate such theories have crossed over into speculative reasoning that has only produced an utterly false history of the first century church and especially the formation of the New Testament canon.

Prior to 63 C.E., the apostles gave little or no thought about leaving a collection of writings for future generations because they believed that Jesus would return within their own generation. What would be the point? And realize that Jesus never instructed his disciples to leave such a collection of writings for a future church. Professor James Barr writes:

> Jesus in his teaching is nowhere portrayed as commanding or even sanctioning the production of a written Gospel, still less a written New Testament. He never even casually told his disciples to write anything down, nor did he even, short of writing, command them to memorize his words exactly for future committal to the medium of writing.[141]

But now things were different. It was now evident to Peter and Paul that Jesus was not returning in their generation and that a great apostasy was now at work which threatened the existence of the future church. This circumstance caused an entire re-evaluation of the apostle's responsibility to "feed my sheep" (John 21:15-17, cf. Acts 20:28, 1 Pet 5:2). We must,

---

[141] James Barr, *Holy Scripture* (Philadelphia: Westminster Press, 1983), 12. This point is not to be pressed for claiming that the apostles were never guided by Jesus that they would be recipients of later revelation. Jesus told his disciples: "I have yet many things to tell you, but you are not able to bear [them] now. But when the Spirit of Truth has come, it will guide you in ALL THE TRUTH, for it will not speak of itself but what things it will hear and will declare to you the things that are to come" (John 16:12-13, translation the authors).

therefore, ask in the light of this fact whether the Apostle Paul simply faced martyrdom without seeing to it that his writings would somehow be formally established within the church as Scripture? Is it at all credible that the Apostle Paul passed from the scene without securing his own writings in a collection for future reference?

In the light of Paul's own testimony, such an idea would mean that Paul himself was derelict in his own duties as an apostle of Christ. Indeed, it would have been negligence of the highest order for him not to have had a personal hand in the "canonization" of his own writings. And we do not have to speculate on whether he did just that, for his last letter to Timothy leaves us with some very important testimony in this regard.

In Second Timothy, chapter 4, Paul first charges Timothy to proclaim the message of truth because the time was soon coming when many would turn to fables. Then Paul requests Timothy to

> do your best to come to me soon, for Demas, in love with this present world, has deserted me and gone to Thessalonica; Crescens has gone to Galatia, Titus to Dalmatia. Only Luke is with me. Get Mark and bring him with you, for he is useful in my ministry. I have sent Tychicus to Ephesus. When you come, bring the cloak that I left with Carpus at Troas, also the books, and above all the parchments (2 Tim 4:9-13).

Paul's urgent request was that Timothy was to come to him soon, *with speed*, to bring John Mark with him and *by all means* bring some important documents to him. In fact, there were three important things that Paul specifically requested. First, the cloak [Greek: φαιλόνην], secondly, the books or scrolls, and thirdly, the parchments.

It is not mere speculation that Paul's urgency was driving him to act upon a new endeavor that was certainly literary in nature. C. F. D. Moule explains:

> When ...Timothy is instructed bring the *biblia*, but particularly the *membranae*, what is meant by the biblia is the Jewish scrolls (in roll form), while the membranae meant the apostle's own notes (in codex form, whether in loose sheets or stitched together)– perhaps his sermons and disquisition, perhaps copies of letters, perhaps simply notes. If this is correct, the biblia and the membranae stand (in this particular context) for Jewish and Christian writings respectively.[142]

---

[142] C. F. D. Moule, *The Birth of the New Testament* (London: Adam & Charles Black, 1962), 183-4.

Dr. Moule has certainly captured what Paul was requesting. But rather than *membranae* being just some notes by the Apostle Paul, Paul more likely was requesting to bring all of his Epistles with him. These may have even included some Epistles that were not preserved in the New Testament.[143]

As far as the "cloak" that is mentioned is concerned, a number of commentators have explained that Paul was here asking for a winter cloak to keep him warm. But the meaning of "*phelonen*" had a broader meaning than that, as Marvin R. Vincent expertly describes:

> Hesychius, however, explains as a γλωσσόκομον, originally a case for keeping the mouthpieces of wind-instruments; thence, generally, *a box*. ...Phrynicus,[144] defines it as "a receptacle for books, clothes, silver, or anything else." Φαιλόνες or φαινόλης *a wrapper of parchments,* was translated figuratively in Latin by *toga* or *paenula* "a cloak," sometimes of leather; also the *wrapping* which a shopkeeper put around fish or olives; also the parchment cover for papyrus rolls. Accordingly it is claimed that Timothy is here bidden to bring, not a cloak, but a roll-case. So the Syriac Version.[145]

Chrysostom, in the fourth century, said that Paul here meant simply a book case. Notice what he wrote:

> The word here translated 'cloak' may mean a garment, or, as some say, a bag, in which the books were contained. But what had he to do with books, who was about to depart and go to God? He needed them much, that he might deposit them in the hands of the faithful, who would retain them in place of his own teaching. All the faithful, then, would suffer a great blow, but particularly those who were present at his death, and then enjoyed his society (Chrysostom, *Hom. 1 Tim. NPNF* 13:513-4).

We cannot help seeing what Chrysostom saw – that Paul needed these precious books in the time of his imminent martyrdom "that he might deposit them in the hands of the *FAITHFUL*, who would retain them in place of his own teaching." Therefore, we can dispense with the ridiculous idea that the cloak was nothing more than a winter jacket – it was a

---

143 Some believe that there may have been at least four Epistles to the Corinthians.

144 A Greek sophist of Vithynia in the second half of the third century, author of a selection of Attic verbs and nouns excluding all but the best Attic forms, and arranged alphabetically.

145 Marvin R. Vincent, *Word Studies in the New Testament* (Peabody, Mass.: Hendrickson, n.d., first published in 1886), 4:326.

specially made, heavy duty, leather carrying case made for transporting precious documents! Paul was now desperately on a mission in the pursuit of canonizing his own Epistles for the future church. Modern scholarship, as well as clerics down through the ages, have missed this vital key to understanding the true nature of what Paul saying here.

Since Paul used the word *phelonen* in context with scrolls and parchments, it is more likely that Paul needed this important protective receptacle to go with these items than to think that Paul needed Timothy to go all the way to Troas to fetch him a cloak in the face of his martyrdom. Are we to believe that there was not anyone there in Rome who could have given Paul some warm clothing?

Paul's urgent appeal was for a protective covering for the most important documents of the apostolic church. He certainly must have kept copies of his important letters secure in this special carrying case, and Timothy and John Mark would know exactly what Paul was here referring to.

Also, "*the* books" and "*the* parchments" certainly must have contained his own corpus of works. Some have assumed that Paul was requesting only a copy of the Old Testament Scriptures. But why would Paul need the Old Testament Scriptures when his service of ministry was about to end (as Chrysostom already pointed out in the above quote)? Luke, who was with Paul, certainly had a copy of the Hebrew Scriptures. No, the urgent appeal that Paul makes shows us that what Paul needed to accomplish before his death was one of the most important literary endeavors of his career. The responsibility for the canonization of Paul's writings needed to be set in order by the apostle Paul himself.

We should also note that in this context there was a significant drawing together of the leading writers of the New Testament works. There was the Apostle Paul, whose corpus of works numbered 14 Epistles, Luke who wrote his Gospel account and the Acts, and Mark, who also wrote another one of the Gospels. What we see here is Paul invoking a meeting with those who would be entrusted to carry out the completion of the first stages of a New Testament canon. These three men alone were responsible for 17 out of the 27 books of the New Testament. And when the Apostle Peter arrives there in Rome we can see that this conclave represented a meeting of the majority of the New Testament writers (with the exception of John, Matthew, James and Jude) and the one and only official series of meetings on the initial canon of the New Testament that scholars will ever find.

We should also understand why Paul needed the services of John Mark. Paul needed John Mark to perform a particular "service" or "ministry." The lame translations that simply imply that the personal secretary of Peter, i.e., John Mark, would be useful to Paul's ministry if he were to go and fetch him a winter jacket totally miss the thrust of what is being said here. The Greek actually says that Mark is useful for a particular "service" [Greek = διακονίαν]. And in the context of Paul's urgency which surrounded this literary activity, Paul certainly had some specific service in mind. We should remember that earlier Barnabas and Saul had taken John Mark on their missionary journey as "their helper" (Acts 13:5). Mark may have been still a young man at this period of time.[146]

Paul decided not to take Mark on his next missionary journey, since Mark had deserted them when in Pamphylia. As a result, two missionary parties were formed, with Mark assisting Paul's cousin Barnabas (Col 4:10) and Silas assisting Paul.

We are informed that Barnabas was a Levite (Acts 4:36) and therefore Mark may have been a Jew with Levitical connections and some prestige. Despite Paul's insistence not to take the young Mark on his second campaign, later Paul refer's to him as his "fellow-laborer" (Col 4:10-11). But tradition tells us that Mark became more of Peter's assistant later on and Peter affectionately calls John Mark "my son" (1 Pet 5:13).

Papias wrote that John Mark had become "Peter's interpreter" (Eusebius, *Hist. eccl.* 3.39.15). Mark may have become Peter's ministerial assistant who helped him in his literary efforts. As we see Mark mentioned as a co-worker with Paul, who is there recorded as one on the go (Col 4:10). Mark may have been a kind of liaison from Peter and the Jerusalem church to the field ministry and therefore could be relied upon for an official task that Paul had in mind for him to carry out.

Paul did not request Peter to come to Rome, but asking for Peter's personal assistant was tantamount to the same thing. Paul probably wrote second Timothy in the autumn of 65 C.E. He wanted Timothy to bring with him his "phelonen" – which we maintain was a type of suitcase which was sturdy enough to transport delicate documents on extended journeys – his books, and the parchments. He wanted Timothy and Mark to hurry to Rome before winter (2 Tim 4:21).

It could be that Paul wanted John Mark in Rome for the purpose of transporting his Epistles to Peter in Jerusalem in order that the Jerusalem church would safe-guard the permanency of his writings. At this time, the headquarters church in Jerusalem had still not seen the events that would ensue the following spring. It could be that John Mark did in fact transport Paul's writings to Peter by the spring of 66 C.E., and then, after

---

[146] Mark's mother's home was a house where worshipers gathered and Peter went to after he was delivered from prison, Acts 12:12.

the miraculous events took place there at Pentecost, the church flees from Jerusalem to Pella, and then in the summer retreats further to Asia Minor.

When Peter wrote his Second Epistle in Rome in the year of 67 C.E., he mentions "all his [Paul's] letters" as on the same par as other "Scripture" (2 Pet 3:15, 16). Peter certainly also realized the importance of the apostles leaving behind a collection of authoritative writings for the church. John Mark must have told Peter about Paul's imprisonment and that he was awaiting execution in Rome. Peter therefore needed to immediately journey to Rome to confer with Paul on the matter of creating an established set of documents for the future church, realizing that he himself would jeopardize his own life by going to Rome. Jesus had told Peter that he would suffer martyrdom and so Peter went to Rome head on, realizing the importance of his mission for the future of the church.

Once these two apostles came together, they would sanction which documents that they considered necessary for the initial canon and then they would dispatch John Mark (in continuation of his important service) with these documents to the Apostle John, who also left the Jerusalem area and settled in Ephesus.

When Peter writes his second Epistle, he defends Paul's writings, leaving us the supposition that Paul was no longer alive to counter his own gainsayers or to write additional letters. With Paul gone and Peter's own final days approaching, Peter is left with the work of completing the task of putting together the first semblance of an official church canon. That Peter did do this very thing, will be the subject of a future chapter. But now, we must look at the one of the greatest impetuses for the New Testament canon that certainly bore heavy on Peter, Paul, and John. This we will do in the next chapter.

CHAPTER 14

Heresy – Impetus for Canonization

IT IS INDEED UNFORTUNATE THAT THE *BOOK OF ACTS* ends with the events of 58 C.E. and does not continue the history of the apostolic church, at least down until the end of the first century. Had this vital piece of information been given us, it would have no doubt filled in our understanding of what the apostles were doing in their final days. But from the latter Epistles of the apostles, we are at least given testimony that helps us fill in the gaps and see what was truly on the minds of Peter and Paul.

Regrettably, since the *Book of Acts* depicts the early church as being blessed with growth, and it is evident from these earlier writings that the apostles expected Christ to return in their generation, critical scholarship has been lead to believe that the church continued in this fashion all through the first century.[147] If this is the case, as so many assume, then the so-called later writings of the apostles, which speak of Christ's return far into the future and also warn against the coming apostasy, must have been written long after the apostles, even though they bear the apostles' names. And if this is true, then the formation of the New Testament as a canon must have occurred at a time well after the apostles, so goes this whole line of reasoning.

But our survey of post-Acts history forces us to a different conclusion. The steps that we have carefully taken *beyond* the *Book of Acts* have shown us clearly that circumstances had come about to change the minds

[147] One of the reasons for this false assumption is that scholars believe that the *Book of Revelation* is the product of the mid-nineties, rather than the mid-fifties. Therefore, if the *Book of Revelation* is the product of the last decade of the first century, which speaks of the imminent return of Jesus, then the conclusion has to be that the first century church continued to believe this fact until the end of the first century. It is only once we realize that the *Book of Revelation* originally was composed in the fifties, and that Peter and Paul abandoned the idea of its theme just before they died, then we can proceed in the direction that the Apostles Peter and Paul changed their mind on these matters. This revolutionary concept needs to be seriously considered in understanding not only the true history of the apostolic church, but also the true history of the New Testament canon.

of the leading apostles concerning the return of Jesus in their generation. But there is another factor that needs serious consideration. It is the strong language that the Apostles Peter and Paul used in their latter Epistles against the coming heresy that they could see developing. They were adamant that this was a serious threat that needed some kind of attention.

Many scholars, however, pay no attention to the warnings of the apostles against the heresy that was beginning in their own time. Indeed, since many scholars believe that the later writings of the New Testament were written in the late first century or early second century, in a bit of circular reasoning, they feel that the heresy statements are proof that the writings were late. In other words, many scholars believe that the first century is too early for heretical sects to have evolved to threaten the apostolic church, and therefore, they feel justified in placing the writings of the latter Epistles into the second century, where evidence of heresy is clearly a problem that the "church fathers" had to deal with.

In short, the reasoning seems to be this: if heresy was a second century problem, then the Epistles denouncing heresy were second century Epistles. If such logic is valid, then should not the converse be equally valid, i.e., if heresy was a first century problem, then the Epistles which bear the names of the first century apostles were no doubt written in the first century and by the apostles whose name's they bear?

Scholars have made a serious mistake in assuming that Gnosticism was *only* a second century problem. They have wrongfully rejected ancient testimony that says Simon Magus, who came on the scene in the 30's C.E., was the father of Gnosticism. Yet, we can even see in the writings of Paul that he warned Timothy to

> guard what has been entrusted to you. Avoid the profane chatter and contradictions of what is falsely called knowledge [gnosis] (1 Tim 6:20).

Paul's reference here implies to more than simply a general reference to "knowledge," but to a particular belief system that is falsely called "gnosis." Paul had also written to Titus saying,

> They claim to *know* God, but by their actions they deny him (Tit 1:16, NIV).

Those who were claiming superior knowledge in Paul's day were sowing the seeds that fully blossomed the next century. In other words, scholars are only seeing the results in the second century of what the apostles were beginning to see develop in the first century.

> It was not until the mid-second century that the real showdown between the two [Christianity and Gnosticism] took place. By that time several systems of Gnostic thought had developed that called themselves Christian because they gave Christ a more or less central position. Such syncretistic Gnosticism, if successful, would have obliterated the distinctive historical features of Christianity, and it was not surprising that Irenaeus, Hippolytus, and other Church Fathers vehemently opposed these tendencies in order to protect Christianity from internal destruction.[148]

The belief of earlier scholars that Gnosticism was only a second century problem has also been challenged by Charles Kingsley Barret:

> Not only the origins but even the definition of Gnosticism are matters of dispute. Gnosticism is sometimes defined as the common trend and substance of a group of Christian heresies in the second century. Under this definition it is of course impossible to consider Gnosticism as part of the background of the New Testament; it did not come into existence until after the New Testament was complete. There is much to be said for this definition; it has the merit of objectivity, and the merit too of being dated. Yet it is not entirely satisfactory, for when this second-century Gnosticism is analyzed it shows a number of characteristics to which some New Testament writers appear to be reacting, so that we must conclude that though the developed Christian heresies arose after and to some extent on the basis of the New Testament writings there must already have been in existence, before at least some parts of the New Testament were written, a body of religious thought manifesting at least some of the characteristics of the second-century gnostic movement. Some describe the pre-Christian movement as Gnosticism, others retain that title for the later movement and describe the earlier as Gnosis, others again as Proto-Gnosticism, or some similar term.[149]

It was not only the church fathers of the second century who vehemently protested the error of Gnosticism, but in the writings of the apostles themselves we see alarm and concern over what was developing in their day.

> The derogation of existing apostolic sources was a necessary prelude to the substitution of pseudo-apostolic writings to bolster up contrary opinions.[150]

---

[148] Bruce M. Metzger, *The Canon of the New Testament* (Oxford: Clarendon, 1987), 76.

[149] Charles Kingly Barret, *The New Testament Background: Selected Documents* (San Francisco: HarperSanFrancisco, 1989), 92.

When Peter wrote his Second Epistle, there was already a twisting of Paul's "Scriptures" by some who were obviously denying the validity of the authoritative writings of the apostles.

> But the 'twisting' of apostolic writings and in particular those of Paul did not need to wait until developed Gnosticism. Rather was it a cause than an effect.[151]

We cannot, therefore, restrict the term "Gnosticism" to what we understand of the developed, second century systems of thought, if for no other reason than our knowledge of first-century problems is just too slight. The New Testament mentions the Nicolaitans of Asia and the Libertines of Corinth, but we know absolutely nothing of these groups as a system of thought.

Some new scholarship has now done much to see Gnosticism as an outgrowth of Jewish Sects. For example, G. Stroumsa writes:

> Time and again, I have insisted upon the importance of the Jewish elements, which were thoroughly reinterpreted or inverted in Gnosticism. These elements came not only from apocalyptic texts, but also from traditions later recorded in rabbinic literature; they appeared not as merely discrete mythologoumena, but rather pervaded all of early Gnosis, before its double encounter with Christianity and Middle Platonism. These Jewish elements could hardly be later influences upon a movement further and further estranged from anything Jewish; they must point to Jewish roots of Gnosticism, roots which appear to have run very deep. Every piece of evidence seems to confirm the conjecture that the cradle of some of the earliest Gnostic groups was among Palestinian or Syrian baptist sects of Jewish background.[152]

J. E. Fossum has been able to explain certain Gnostic terms and concepts as being directly derived from Samaritan tradition.[153] One phrase that he focuses in on is the expression that Simon Magus used:

---

[150] Donald Guthrie, *New Testament Introduction* (Downers Grove: InterVarsity Press, 1990), 849.

[151] Ibid., 848-849.

[152] Gedaliahu G. Stroumsa, "Aher: A Gnostic" in *The Rediscovery of Gnosticism,* ed. Layton Bently, Numen supplement 41 (Leiden: E.J. Brill, 1984), 170, 172. For further study on the fact that Christian Gnosticism was a further development of earlier Judaic Gnosticism, see Birger Pearson, *Gnosticism, Judaism and Egyptian Christianity* (Minneapolis: Fortress, 1990).

[153] J. E. Fossum, *The Name of God and the Angel of the Lord: Samaritan and Jewish Concepts of Intermediation and the Origin of Gnosticism* (Wissenschaftliche Untersuchungen zum Neuen Testament: Tübingen, 1985), 36: 162-91.

"the great power of God" (Acts 8:10). Fossum maintains that this was a Samaritan theological expression, and Simon's use of it "apparently was a claim to the office of being the Glory of God or the Angel of the Lord."[154]

Gnosticism, in its early stages, had Jewish/Samaritan roots and it might more rightly be called "proto-Gnosticism" to distinguish it from the forms that later developed.

> What is called "Jewish Gnosticism" was probably far removed from the radical dualism of developed systems, such as was taught by Valentinius or found in some of the Nag Hammadi documents. By contrast, to recognize the concept of "Jewish Gnosticism" is to recognize another strand within early Judaism that has largely disappeared from the known Jewish sources.[155]

However, the New Testament itself provides us with the essential data to guide our understanding here. In Acts 8:9-25, Luke relates to us one central figure who became known as the father of all heresy – Simon Magus.

Simon "the Magus" was a Samaritan who nominally converted to Christianity. Many of the church fathers of the second, third, and fourth centuries were virtually united in calling him the primary heretical influence that infiltrated the church of the first-century.

It was Peter and John who went to Samaria and confronted Simon face to face. Simon wanted to buy the ability to give converts the "Holy Spirit" as were the apostles. And when Peter told that Samaritan magician "You have no part or share in this" (Acts 8:21), it was like an uncanny echo of Nehemiah's words against the Samaritans of his day who mocked him, "you have no share or claim or historic right in Jerusalem" (Neh 2:20).

We should, in this light, consider the following insightful analysis:

> The mistake many scholars make is to assume that it was the Church of the Second Century which had to combat the Gnosticism. The truth is, Gnosticism had been around long before the Second Century. Simon Magus came on the scene as early as 33 A.D. It wasn't the Church of the Second Century which had to deal with the problem of Gnostic/ Samaritan heresy – it was the Church of the First Century, the apostles themselves. Like the controversy with the Samaritans that, at least in part, influenced Ezra to

[154] Ibid., 190.

[155] Lester L. Grabbe, *Judaism from Cyrus to Hadrian* (Minneapolis: Fortress, 1992), 2:518-519.

> canonize the Old Testament, so it was now the heresy arising from these same people – emerging in Christian garb five centuries later – that Peter had to counter in his canonization of the New Testament. Events which occurred in the former period were the pattern of those to occur in the latter. No wonder God tells us about the Samaritans in the Old Testament, and then about Simon Magus in the New.[156]

It is interesting that the same pattern of forces stemming out of Samaria that propelled Ezra the scribe to canonize the Hebrew Bible in the fifth century B.C.E., were the very same forces still extant that ignited Peter, Paul and John to lock down their writings in an effort to protect the future church from these same forces.

The secret nature of many of the Gnostic texts is merely a carry-over from the ancient Babylonian Mystery Religion handed down into the first century via Samaria and Simon the Magus. Paul stated that there was a "Mystery of Lawlessness" that was "already at work" (2 Thess 2:7). And he alluded to the "lawless one" who would be revealed (vs. 3-4). It is not hard to see the similarity of what Paul here writes about the "lawless one" and the testimony of what the church fathers wrote about Simon Magus. Simon was nothing less than a priest of the ancient Babylonian Mystery system of worship that was still prevalent in his day.

Jeremiah had described the Babylonian System as follows:

> Babylon was a golden cup in the Lord's hand, making all the earth drunken; the nations drank of her wine and so the nations went mad (Jer 51:7).

This false system of Babylon was similarly identified in the Apocalypse as

> the great whore who is seated on many waters, with whom the kings of the earth have committed fornication and with the wine of whose fornication the inhabitants of the earth have become drunk. ... in her hand a golden cup full of abominations and the impurities of her fornication; and on her forehead was written a name, a mystery: "Babylon the great, mother of whores and of earth's abominations" (Rev 17:1, 2, 4, 5).

The New Testament therefore points us in the right direction to understand the origin of the heresies that were developing in the first

---

[156] Ernest L. Martin, "Design and Development of the Holy Scripture" (Ph.D. diss., Ambassador College Graduate School of Theology, 1965, 1971), 279.

century. And it is none other than another form of that ancient apostasy accredited to Nimrod soon after the Flood, who is described in the Bible as the

> first on earth to become a mighty warrior... before [or against] the Lord. The beginning of his kingdom was Babel (Gen 10:9, 10).

Thus, the combined testimony of both Testaments is that "heresy" was begun with the ancient post flood character, Nimrod, who founded the original city of Babylon. It was then carried on down through the ancient Chaldean Mystery Religious system, then through the Samaritans in Ezra's day. It rises once again in the first century with the coming of Simon the Magus, the Samaritan high priest. The second century church father, Irenaeus, said that Simon Magus was the very person "from whom all sorts of heresies derive their origin" (Irenaeus, *Haer.* 1.23.2 [*ANF* 1:348]). Irenaeus further informs us further that

> this man [Simon Magus], then was glorified by many as if he were a god; and he taught that it was he himself who appeared among the Jews as the Son, but descended in Samaria as the Father, while he came to the other nations in the character of the Holy Spirit. He represented himself, in a word, as being the loftiest of all powers, that is, the Being who is the father over all, and he allowed himself to be called by whatsoever title men were pleased to address him (Irenaeus, *Haer.* 1.23.1 [*ANF* 1:348]).[157]

Paul said that the man of sin would declare himself to be God (2 Thess 2:4). This is something that Jesus never did, despite modern Christological arguments that attempt to make that so. Yet, Simon exploited this theology to his own advantage!

Notice also that to the Samaritans Simon wanted to be addressed as the "Father." Jesus forbade his disciples to call any man on earth by the religious title of "Father" (Matt 23:9). Yet, the Christianity that developed in the fourth century did that very thing. Indeed, to this very day this same kind of religious worship of men owes so much to the ancient priesthood of the Babylonian Mystery Religion, with men wearing gowns and robes and miters, looking like ancient Babylonian Priests, swinging incense lanterns, chanting in an ancient language, and performing

---

[157] We should note the astonishing triadic nature of Simon's representations: Son, Father and Holy Spirit. Now, for the first time in Christian literature, we have definite testimony of what later developed into the doctrine of the Trinity. Incredibly, it is linked with none other than Simon Magus, the father of ALL heresy!

ritualistic rites with "golden cups" (Rev 17), while calling themselves "Fathers," still thrives, and unbelievably, under the banner of the religion of Jesus. The New Testament clearly shows us that the apostles resisted this very thing and warned of it as a coming great apostasy. The final plea of the New Testament canon is to

> come out of her, my people, that you be not partakers of her plagues (Rev 18:4).

What Simon Magus did was to essentially change his message depending upon to whom he taught amongst. So when he worked among the Jews he taught that he was the "Son of God." This is the very title that was attributed to Jesus, and Simon Magus knew it. He ripped off this title and sought to use it to supplant himself as the true Messiah of Jewish hope. If he applied to himself the title of "Son of God," then he had effectively supplanted the role of Jesus. Was not Jesus the true "Son of God" as defined in the writings of the New Testament writers?

Then, when Simon taught amongst the Samaritans, he claimed to be the "Father." And when he taught amongst the Gentiles he claimed that he was the "Holy Spirit." This blending of different beliefs into one syncretic system was Simon's design to introduce a universal religion – indeed, a "Catholic Church." Ernest L. Martin notes:

> Though Simon Magus was unable to accomplish his goal in the first century, he was succeeded in his attempts by a fellow Samaritan by the name of Menander, and along side him emerged two other men by the names of Saturninus and Basilides. They all began to teach similar but variant doctrines under the common name of 'Gnosticism.' Other men soon followed in their footsteps, among them was a very important man from Pontus in Asia Minor named Marcion. He was a contemporary of Justin Martyr. Soon after the Christian writer Irenaeus wrote extensively against this Marcion and against Gnosticism itself in the middle and late second century (Irenaeus, *Haer.* 1.23.4).[158]

Irenaeus further recorded that

> they [the Gnostics] also have an image of Simon made in the likeness of Jupiter [Greek: Zeus], and of Helen in that of Minerva [Greek: Athena]; and they worship the statues; and they have a designation from their most impiously minded founder, being called Simonians, from whom the

---

[158] Ernest L. Martin, *The People that History Forgot* (Portland, Oreg.: ASK Publications, 1993), 25.

> Gnosis [knowledge], falsely so-called, derives its origins, as one can learn from their own assertions (Irenaeus, *Haer.* 1.23.4 [*ANF* 1:348]).

Notice that Irenaeus used the very same expression as did the Apostle Paul in First Timothy 6:20: "Gnosis, falsely so-called." The Gnosis System in Irenaeus' day was merely a carry-over from what Paul identified as gnostics in the first century. And Irenaeus' use of Paul's term, in direct reference to Gnosticism, points to a confirmation that Irenaeus was combating the very same system that Paul identified in the first century.

Notice again that another feature of Simon's religion was that "they worship the statues." Idolatry was a sin that was greatly condemned throughout the Old Testament. Yet, here we see just another hallmark of the kind of worship that Simon had inculcated into his religion. And the fact that the later church of Rome had inculcated such a practice into its liturgy has not escaped the notice of many a subsequent Protestant scholar.[159]

Also notice that the gnostic followers of Simon made images of him that made him resemble Zeus. In other words, they represented Simon Magus as having long hair and a beard, typical of Greek philosophers. Yet, the oldest extant representation of Jesus is that of a beardless face and moderate length hair.

Justin Martyr (ca. 100-165), himself a Samaritan, born only six miles from where Simon is said to have emerged, could speak for the traditions of the Samaritans:

> Nearly all the Samaritans, but few among the rest of the nations, confess him [Simon] to be the first god and worship him (Justin Martyr, *1 Apal.* 26).

---

[159] The primary work on the subject is, of course, the now dated, but still useful Alexander Hislop (1807-1865), *Two Babylons: Papal Worship Proved To Be the Worship of Nimrod and His Wife* (Edinburgh: Andrew Elliot, 1860). This work was written by the nineteenth century cleric, Reverend Alexander Hislop, in a pamphlet first published in Edinburgh in 1853. It was later expanded and has been reprinted many times and can be seen online: http://www.biblebelievers.com/babylon/ and also http://www.biblepreaching.com/twobabylons/00index.htm. Another work along these same lines is Ralph E. Woodrow, *Babylon Mystery Religion: Ancient and Modern* (Palm Springs, Calif.: Ralph Woodrow Evangelistic Assoc., 1966). However, Ralph Woodrow has now removed this book from print and replaced it with The Babylon Connection? (Palm Springs, Calif.: Ralph Woodrow Evangelistic Assoc., 1997). This book, written in a Woodrow vs. Woodrow format, has now overthrown Woodrow's original research. See online: http://www.ralphwoodrow.org/books/babylon.htm; http://users.clarkston.com/rcorson/2babylons.htm and http://www.wcg.org/wn/96jul23/woodrow.htm. Another important work to consider along these lines is C. Paul Meredith, *Satan's Great Deception*, online at http://www.giveshare.org/library/satandeception/index.html.

Such testimony must be regarded in trying to understand what was going on in the first century. Simon was a great religious leader in the first century – make no mistake about it. His religious system was nothing more than a reincarnation of the ancient Babylonian System. The New Testament writers condemned him as the "Man of Sin."[160]

Simon Magus was no figment of the imagination. He was a powerful religious leader of the first century that in fact had as much impact on the history of Christianity as Jesus himself. Indeed, in one sense, he had an even bigger impact when we realize that much of what was later adopted by the Orthodox church in fact was the religion of Simon, rather than the "Way" of Jesus. And it is this very fact that Peter and Paul foresaw which, if they were alive today, would most assuredly affirm.

Eusebius further tells us concerning Simon:

> Of such vices was Simon the father and contriver, raised up at that time by the evil power which hates all that is good and plots against the salvation of mankind, to be a great opponent of great men, our Saviour's inspired apostles. Nevertheless, divine and celestial grace worked with its ministers, by their advent and presence speedily extinguishing the flames of the Evil One before they could spread, and through them humbling and pulling down every lofty barrier raised against the knowledge of God [2 Cor 10:5]. Consequently, neither Simon nor any of his contemporaries managed to form an organized body in those apostolic days, for every attempt was defeated and overpowered by the light of the truth and by the divine Word Himself who had so recently shone from God on men, active in the world and immanent in His own apostles (Eusebius, *Hist. eccl.* 2.14.1-3).

Eusebius' testimony sheds light on the fact that Gnosticism could not spread its influence in the first century during the days of the apostles. Eusebius is giving us the very reason why Gnosticism, on the one hand, is accredited to Simon in the first century, but on the other hand, did not spread until the second century after the apostles had died. It could not spread in the first century due to the vigilance of the Apostles Peter, Paul, and John. Thus, the scholarly objections to what we have presented here should be balanced against such insight.

Eusebius goes on to tell us that the main reason why Mark wrote his Gospel (at the behest of Peter) was specifically to combat the false teachings of Simon Magus (Eusebius, *Hist. eccl.* 2.15.1-3). Tradition then

---

160 Simon Magus may well have been the "man of sin" that Paul may have had in mind when he wrote *Second Thessalonians* (2 Thess 2:3).

says that Mark later went on to Alexandria, the great city of science and philosophy, and the center of later Gnosticism. Later, at the end of the first century, a sect known as the Carpocratians circulated a "secret" Gospel of Mark, which Clement of Alexandria condemned.[161]

In the Nag Hammadi Library there are several Apocryphons – secret books – such as the Apocryphon of John and the Apocryphon of James. The so-called *Gospel according to Thomas* begins with these words:

> These are the secret words which Jesus the Living Jesus spoke and Didymus Judas Thomas recorded.[162]

"Secret knowledge" was the common thread of the ancient Babylonian Mystery religion and Gnosticism.

When Luke said that many gospel accounts were written before his account, he did not mean just Matthew's and Mark's. Peter tells us that these other accounts were "fables" that people were turning to (1 Pet 1:16) and needed to be rejected.

With the discovery of the Gnostic Library at Nag Hammadi, Egypt, in 1945, many of these spurious "Gospels" have come to light. Paul had written to Timothy concerning the beginning of some of the spurious beliefs that were popping up in his own time:

> Avoid profane chatter, for it will lead people into more and more impiety, and their talk will spread like gangrene. Among them are Hymenaeus and Philetus, who have swerved from the truth by claiming that the resurrection has already taken place (2 Tim 2:16-18).

The view that the resurrection had already taken place was the same view that was advocated in the "Treatise on Resurrection," the "Exegesis on the Soul," and the "Gospel of Philip," all of which are contained in the Nag Hammadi Library.[163] Many of these works fraudulently carry the names of the apostles. Therefore, who in the latter centuries would be able to decide which were the authentic works of the apostles and which were

---

[161] This letter of Clement of Alexandria was only recently discovered by professor Morton Smith in 1958 at the Mar Saba monastery, southeast of Jerusalem, and published 15 years later (see Morton Smith, *The Secret Gospel* [San Francisco: Harper and Row, 1973]). Clement of Alexandria refers to a "Secret Gospel of Mark" therein. Clement quotes excerpts of the text of this Gospel, which he claims was in the custody of the Church at Alexandria, but which was kept secret. This letter can be found online: http://www.gnosis.org/library/secm.htm.

[162] Quoted from Robert J. Millar, ed., *The Complete Gospels* (San Francisco: HarperSanFrancisco, 1992), 305.

[163] See James M. Robinson, *The Nag Hammadi Library* (San Francisco: Harper and Row, 1977), 5.

not? Indeed, if scholars of today can believe that the works of the apostles of the first century were actually works of frauds in the second century, based upon the widespread practice of pseudonymity in the second century, then how could people living in the second century themselves decide the authenticity of the many works passed off as apostolic?

The answer is clear once we understand that the apostles did something very ingenious that guarded their works in a collective body that separated their writings from those of the spurious frauds that they knew would appear after them. This will be brought out later, but for now, in the context of trying to understand the significance of heresy as the apostles saw it, they knew that they had to take extra measures to insure that their works would be kept out of the hands of heretics.

The challenge that we face is that if many of the church fathers themselves disputed whether or not some books were authentic or not (because they simply did not know one way or the other), then how are we to decide living centuries thereafter? We will satisfactorily meet this challenge in later chapters. But for now we submit that to imagine that those who were confused about the authorship of the apostle's writings were the one's responsible for deciding what constituted the authoritative words of the apostles in later times is to is postulate a theory that is altogether bankrupt of the historical facts and internal evidence! Indeed, such theories defiantly ignore the internal evidence to the contrary.

The entire concept that people have today concerning how the New Testament came to be – that it was formulated and gradually accepted by later church "Fathers" – is utterly and entirely false! It is time that serious students of the Bible question how bankrupt such theories really are.

We should note here the insightful remarks of George B. Caird in this regard:

> As long as the church was led by men who had known Jesus, and had as its nucleus a substantial number of Jewish Christians, educated in the strongly ethical religion of the Old Testament, the apostolic tradition was relatively safe from distortion. But henceforward the church was to be a predominantly Gentile institution, and there was an increasing danger that the originally Semitic Gospel should be diluted by an admixture of ideas drawn from the syncretistic religions of the Graeco-Roman world. Pliny's letter to Trajan indicates that Gentile converts had been received into the church in very large numbers, and that many of them had too slight a grasp of their new faith to withstand the pressure of persecution. From scattered references in Christian literature we can identify some of the pagan prejudices which kept these converts from a fuller appreciation of Christianity.[164]

In 66 C.E., the apostolic church was in a crisis. Heresy was knocking at the door and it was the responsibility of the apostle's of Jesus to act and do something about it. Indeed, had they not taken steps at canonizing their writings they would have been totally derelict in their responsibilities, especially so in the light of what they themselves had warned.

Are we to believe that the alarm that Peter and Paul expressed did not force them into some kind of action that would sustain future faithful believers in the truth, despite heretical encroachments into the Orthodox church that were beginning to introduce doctrines that were originated by the religion of Simon Magus (the ancient Babylonian Mystery Religion) and supplanting the teachings of Jesus and his apostles?

The Apostles Peter and Paul were witnessing a crises of no small magnitude arising on the horizon that threatened the purity of the future Church of God. We should, in this light, notice that there is one thing about a crisis – it forces upon those affected by it to make drastic decisions that otherwise would not have been made.[165] The many fables and myths that were beginning to be circulated about Jesus and the pure truth of the gospel was the cause that effected the initial New Testament canon. In other words, heresy is one of the key reasons why the New Testament was formulated in the first place by the Apostles Peter and Paul and John.

As one writer notes:

> What causes compelled the church to form a canon? One was the emergence of a host of Christian writings of dubious value and authority: the church had to decide which books contained true Christian tradition and teaching. More potent perhaps was the infiltration into the church of heresies like Gnosticism: If the church was to guard her members against this false teaching, necessity was laid on her to repudiate all such paganizing of the Faith, and to say where sound doctrine was to be found.[166]

It is at this point that we must interject another vital key to understanding the canonization of the New Testament. Since the apostles were suspicious of later church authorities as embracing heresy, then the church was the last place that the apostles would have deposited their

[164] George B. Caird, *The Apostolic Age* (London: Gerald Duckworth & Co., 1955), 143.

[165] During the time of Ezra, Judaism was threatened by the encroachment of Samaritan influence. Scholars have missed the entire endeavor of Old Testament canonization as a response to this encroachment. Likewise, they have missed the very same threat that reappeared in the days of the apostles as the primary motivation to codify their writings.

[166] A. M. Hunter, *Introduction to the New Testament* (London: SCM Press, 1957), 24.

writings for the future of Christianity.[167] Certainly, local churches had copies of writings of the apostles. But the master editions were archived within the great libraries of Caesarea and later, Alexandria. This is a fact that modern scholarship, as well as modern religious leaders, have failed (or refused) to see. But that is the irony of the entire history of the canon that has eluded everyone's notice down through the ages. This is a significant chapter in the story that awaits us in our investigation.

The apostle's themselves, realizing the problem of heresy that was initiated by Simon Magus, were impelled to form the "canon" – the "standard" for the future Church of God that was in the same vain as the canon of Hebrew Scriptures established by Ezra the Scribe in the fifth century B.C.E. The evidence that this was in fact accomplished by the apostles will be presented in the next chapter of this amazing story of *Beyond Acts.*

---

[167] Bart D. Ehrmann, *The Orthodox Corruption of Scripture* (London: Oxford University Press, 1993), has already shown that the "Orthodox" church was the chief corrupter of Scriptural transmission due to reasons of theology.

CHAPTER 15

The Authority to Canonize Scripture

IN THE SUMMER OF 66 C.E. THE APOSTLE PETER had journeyed from Jerusalem to Rome, just prior to the Apostle Paul's martyrdom, in order to confer with him matters concerning the organization of a body of literature that constituted what we call today the "canon of the New Testament."

Stop and realize these important facts. In the spring of 66 C.E., at Pentecost, miraculous events occurred in Jerusalem which culminated in revealing that the church there should flee out of that area. The church then fled north, to the area of Pella. But most of the faithful did not stay there, they migrated entirely out of the area of Judea, and went into the northern regions of Asia Minor. This is why we see the Apostle Peter writing to these areas in his Second Epistle. The point is that the church now knew that the end-time events were not going to happen in their generation, but was reserved for a future one.

Secondly, the motivating force that propelled Peter and Paul to concentrate on a canonizing effort before their martyrdom's was the expected coming apostasy that both apostles were warning about and were deeply concerned over. It is only when we look at canon history through the prism of these two factors that it is possible to come to a real historical scenario that makes sense and aligns itself with the truth.

In this light we must conclude that no other persons but the apostles themselves had the authority to produce such a body of literature that would have any authoritative quality, nor any real validity in the future Church of God. Indeed, the New Testament could have never carried the weight and authority as being "God's Word" without the endorsement and the approval of the two leading apostles, Peter and John. Why do we say this? This chapter is probably one of the most important chapters in the story of Beyond Acts and the true history of the canon that scholars have completely overlooked.

The two most important documents on the subject concerning the authority to canonize Scripture are the Epistle's of Second Timothy and

Second Peter.[168] But isn't it ironic that these two documents have been relegated by scholars into a post apostolic category that denies them the very authority that these letters carry? Instead, canon scholars have chosen to ignore the important testimony of these two documents and to wander around blindly in the second century and beyond, searching for any scrap of literature that would help them see how the New Testament came into being. Such a fruitless endeavor has only lead scholars to produce the nonsensical and entirely false notion of the "gradual acceptance" theory.

This book stands apart from those so-called "scholarly" works, in that its premise accepts the internal evidence that the New Testament itself provides us with for its own authority. Indeed, if we didn't follow this path, then we would have fallen into the same trap and loose sight of the words of the leading apostles on the subject. Let the reader digest the thrust of this chapter and judge if what Peter tells us is not far more compelling than what goes under the guise of present day scholarship on this subject.

Second Peter on Canonization

IT IS PETER'S SECOND EPISTLE WHICH EXPLAINS the canonizing activity that he had embarked upon. He begins by telling us about the "precious and very great promises, so that through them you may escape from the corruption that is in the world" (2 Pet 1:4).

Peter next tells his audience

> Therefore I intend to keep on reminding you of these things, though you know them already and are established in the truth that has come to you. I think it right, as long as I am in this body, to refresh your memory, since I know that my death will come soon, as indeed our Lord Jesus Christ has made clear to me. And I will make EVERY EFFORT so that AFTER MY DEPARTURE you may be able at any time to recall these things (2 Pet 1:12-15).

In order for this leading apostle of the first century church to be able to remind the future Church of God, in the face of his own imminent martyrdom, "to refresh your memory," and after his departure to make sure that "at any time to recall these things," points to the diligence that Peter was engaged in to leave an authoritative body of literature from

[168] The authorship of Second Peter is addressed in appendix 1.

Jesus' apostles for this very purpose. If words have any meaning at all, then "every effort" means Peter was serious about making available after his death the "precious and great promises," pure and simple.

It is utter foolishness to think that Peter was only referring to just this one Epistle, for within this Epistle he speaks of *all* of Paul's Epistles as having already attained the status of Scripture. And if Peter now recognized Paul's Epistles as Scripture in his time, then that in itself is "canonization," pure and simple![169]

The Epistle of Second Peter, rather than being some pseudonymous creation of the late second century, represents the very words of the Apostle Peter. Peter declares with the utmost authority that he was given, that he was seeing to it that there would be a body of authorized literature that would constitute the Word of God for the church that was on the very same par as the Hebrew Scriptures.

The true history of the New Testament canon begins with the canonizing efforts of Peter and Paul. It was Peter and Paul who first established their collections as Scripture already, and not some unknown church council decades or even centuries later. And certainly, we must maintain, that it was not created in some long, agonizing process of gradually accepting what should constitute a New Testament canon by scattered and bickering local churches of the second century and beyond. Such fatuous theories are baseless and devoid of any true historical support! It is time to say good-bye to such theories in the light of the internal evidence to the contrary.

Second Peter is not a second century fraud! Those who believe that it will never be able to present a credible history of the canon that reflects the true internal evidence. In order for Peter to say that the exceeding precious promises could be recalled at "each time" is Peter's clear statement that it was he who bound together the first compilation of apostolic writings into an organized "canon" for the purpose of future religious instruction.

Listen to the words of Peter, the "Chief of the apostles":

> For we did not follow cleverly devised MYTHS when we made known to you the power and coming of our Lord Jesus Christ, but we had been eyewitnesses of his majesty (2 Pet 1:16).

---

[169] The "gradual acceptance" theory is what forces many scholars to relegate the dating of Second Peter into a second century time frame. Such an assumption, however, forces us to then assume that some pseudonymous impostor had the authority to make such a claim as declaring Paul's writings as Scripture. The possibility that such a claim would not have been challenged by real authorities within the church is what defies such a theory.

On the one hand, we have scholars today claiming that the works of the New Testament are nothing but a pile of "cleverly devised myths" and on the other hand we have the thunderous words of an actual "eyewitness" to the Transfiguration tell us just the opposite. Who are the faithful to believe?

Could a fraud of the second century dare say that he did not follow "cleverly devised myths," that he was an eyewitness to the majesty of Christ, while all along knowing that he was the biggest liar on the face of the earth?[170] Has it never occurred to biblical exegetes why the Apostle Peter inserted this valuable piece of information concerning the vision of the Transfiguration? Let us understand the significance of this important piece of information in its relationship to Canon research.

THE TRANSFIGURATION AND THE PROPHETIC GIFT

THE APOSTLE PETER BRINGS OUT THE RELEVANCY of the Transfiguration for a specific reason that would have been totally lost on a future pseudo-Peter of the second century. Peter is here referring specifically to the vision that he witnessed, known today as the "Transfiguration."[171] This important detail is such a vital key in

[170] Nevertheless, Burton L. Mack, *Who Wrote the New Testament* (San Francisco: HarperSanFrancisco, 1995), 213, offers the following scathing appraisal of Peter's message: "So Peter is an apostle writing to remind his readers that they should remember the words of the apostles! The fiction should be clear ... Since the documentation for this tradition has always been these letters, it should be clear that the tradition is in reality a myth. The so-called Petrine tradition was created in the second century by means of pseudonymous writings attributed to the Peter pictured in Paul's letters and in the narrative Gospels. There is not a shred of historical evidence to support it." These unfortunate conclusions are given here to demonstrate the extremes that the gradual acceptance theory inevitably leads one. What should be clear is that no one in the known church of the second century could have been clever enough, indeed daring enough, to get away with such a fraud. When Peter says that "we did not follow cleverly devised myths," and now scholars conclude that the New Testament writings are nothing but "cleverly devised myths," then we should see this in the light of what Peter here states: "First of all you must understand this, that in the last days scoffers will come" (2 Pet 3:3) and "But false prophets also arose among the people, just as there will be false teachers among you, who will secretly bring in destructive opinions" (2 Pet 2:1). Rest assure, Second Peter has all the built in apostolic safe-guards to defend its own claim to authority.

[171] The Transfiguration was already a known tradition within the church and the accounts of it are contained in all three Synoptic Gospels (Matt 17:1-8; Mark 9:2-8; Luke 9:28-36). The church of the first century was fully aware of this important event. In one sense, it was *the* crowning moment in the career of Jesus on this earth.

understanding the matter of canonization that we must understand its significance. That this verse indeed refers to the Transfiguration, we continue to read:

> For he [Jesus] received honor and glory from God the Father when that voice was conveyed to him by the Majestic Glory, saying, "This is my Son, my Beloved, with whom I am well pleased." We ourselves [Peter, James and John] heard this voice come from heaven, while we were with him on the holy mountain (2 Pet 1:17-18).

This is first person testimony: "we ourselves heard this voice!" Only three apostles were given the privilege to witness this miraculous event. The significance of this is that it gave these three apostles a greater authority to testify to Jesus' Messiahship than anyone else, including the other apostles. This is a truly significant fact for the subject of canonization. Why do we say this? Notice what Peter himself says concerning this:

> We [the apostles who specifically witnessed that event] have the prophetic message more fully confirmed (2 Pet 1:19).

Peter is informing us that the eyewitnesses to the Transfiguration not only have the prophetic message, just as the prophets of old, but that they have it "more fully confirmed" than any of the Old Testament prophets, including Moses.

The Apostles Peter, John, and James [son's of Zebedee] were eyewitnesses to the vision of the future Jesus in the resurrection. No prophet of old had ever been given such a vision. These three apostles specifically heard the voice from on high ("the majestic glory") declare that Jesus was indeed the son of God and that God was well pleased with him. Thus, the message of Jesus as being the promised Messiah was confirmed more fully than ever before to these three disciples of Jesus. Indeed, this vision made those apostles even more "fully confirmed" than any prophet of God who had preceded them. Peter well understood this fact and we must not loose sight of it in understanding the subject of canonization.

Think of the significance of this very important point. The prophets wrote Scripture. It was now imperative on the apostles to record their actual and visionary experiences of Jesus with the same kind of authority that was invested in the Old Testament prophets.

It is obvious that Peter here sees himself as a "prophet" with the authority to write Scripture. It was Peter, John, and his brother James, that were selected to witness the momentous event which has been given the name of the Transfiguration. But when Peter wrote "we" as being the ones who have the message more fully confirmed, he was referring specifically to himself and the only other surviving witness to that great event, the Apostle John (James had been martyred in 44 C.E.). They were the witnesses to one of the most significant events of Christ's ministry.

This incident immediately gave Peter, James, and John pre-eminence over all the other apostles in regard to the prophetic message being more fully confirmed in them. That is why Peter bolsters what he is saying about having the New Testament prophetic message being available "at each time" beyond his death. Peter had, not only the responsibility, but the authority, to see to it that the message was not lost, but available in the future.

The body of literature that he was organizing was indeed set in order by one of the eyewitnesses to that monumental event who heard the shattering voice from heaven booming out of the cloud of the Shekinah glory of God, which totally enveloped them:

> This is my beloved Son in whom I am well pleased — Listen to him (Matt 17:5).

How on earth could we ever listen to the words of Jesus if his words were never recorded and preserved in an authoritative and codified body of literature? The significance of that visionary experience alone singled out these men to be the ones who would eventually be responsible for.[172]

THE "PROPHET" LIKE MOSES

THE GOSPEL MESSAGE IS THAT JESUS CHRIST IS not only the promised prophet like Moses, but also the future Messiah and saviour of the world. It was important that the New Testament writers were clear in their portrayal of Jesus as the "prophet" that Moses had predicted.

---

[172] We must remember that Peter, James, and John, were a limited group among the disciples of Jesus who were together on a number of significant occasions. It was they who witnessed the resurrection of Jairus' daughter (Matt 5:37). They heard the prophecy on the Mount of Olives (Mark 13:3). They were near Jesus in the Garden of Gethsemene (Mark 14:33; Matt 26:37). Also, when Jesus appeared after the resurrection at the Sea of Galilee, they are recorded as being all together there with him.

> For Luke especially, "prophet" is not a mistaken, preliminary, or minor category, but is one of his major categories of christological thought: Jesus is indeed the eschatological prophet promised in Scripture (Luke 24:19; Acts 3:22-23; 7:37; cf. Deut 18:15-18), who specifically identifies the Spirit that empowers him as the prophetic Spirit of Isa 61:1-2 (Luke 4:16-21). Jesus' authority is not the derived authority of the scribe, but the immediate authority of the inspired prophet (Matt 7:29).[173]

If Jesus was "that prophet" like Moses, then what does this mean in the light of canonization? Let us focus on this important question.

In the entirety of the Old Testament no single person stood out greater than Moses. He was the one chosen to deliver the nation of Israel out of Egyptian bondage by the greatest of all Old Testament miracles. Through him a whole new religious order was established. Whatever Moses said was accounted as coming from God himself (Exod 4:16, 7:1). Moses, indeed, saw God face to face. He delivered the "Law" to Israel, while all those succeeding him, it is said, only commented on that Law. He was so prominent, even in his day, that the place of his burial was kept secret, lest the people worship his tomb as the Egyptians did with their pharaohs.

Moses was indeed the greatest of God's prophets. A prophet is one who has been given a message from God and speak's to the people with the proverbial "Thus says the Lord...," and not merely one foretelling future events. Moses prophesied that a future great prophet would come "like unto me" (Deut 18:15-22). Therefore, in order to fulfill Moses' prediction, "that prophet" would have to perform similar mighty deeds and miracles. By the time of the last Old Testament prophets had left the scene (i.e., Ezra, Nehemiah, and Malachi), "that prophet" still had not come. And, all through the inter-testamental period, no one came on the scene fulfilling the prophecy of "that prophet."

Even the Jews of the first century had recognized the fact that the spirit of prophecy had died out with Ezra and Malachi. Josephus recorded that the spirit of prophecy had died out in the days of Artaxerxes – the time when Ezra and Malachi lived (Josephus, *C. Ap.* 1.8 [41]).[174] These were the great men who had completed the Old Testament canon of Scripture. Daniel had predicted, however, that from the time of a commandment to rebuild the city of Jerusalem would go forth, it would

---

173 M. Eugene Boring, "Prophecy (Early Christian)," in *The Anchor Bible Dictionary*, David Noel Freedman, ed., (New York: Doubleday, 1992), 5:498.

174 Lee M. McDonald, *The Formation of the Christian Biblical Canon* (Peabody, Mass.: Hendrickson, 1995), 50-52, discusses this tradition.

be 69 prophetic weeks of years (483 years) until the coming of the "Messiah" (Dan 9:25).

The prophecy stated that a count down of 483 years would begin to be counted from this commandment to rebuild the city of Jerusalem, which finally occurred in the reign of the Persian king Artaxerxes' seventh year (457 B.C.E.). This amazing prophecy actually pin-pointed the very year that the Messiah would come on the scene. And that year was 27 C.E. for the appearance of the Messiah – the precise year that Jesus began his ministry.[175]

Think of it! No other messianic pretender had appeared at that time to fulfill the prophecy of Daniel concerning the appearance of the Messiah in that very year.[176] We must realize that either the Messiah was to come at that time as predicted or there could not be another time for the Messiah to come thereafter.[177]

Jesus Was the Prophet Like Moses

During HIS MINISTRY, JESUS DEMONSTRATED that he, too, like Moses, can command the sea to obey him: "What manner of man is this, that even the winds and the sea obey him?" (Matt 8:27). Like Moses, Jesus founded an entirely new religious order. Moses said: "Behold the blood of the covenant" (Ex. 24:8), and Jesus says: "This cup is the *New* Covenant in my blood" (Luke 22:20). Like Moses, who brought the Law down from Mount Sinai, Jesus also, on the Mount of Olives, delivers a sermon that represents a fulfillment of the laws of God:

> Do not suppose that I have come to set aside the law or the prophets. I have not come to set them aside but to fill them up to the brim (Matt 5:17).[178]

[175] For a thorough discussion of this intriguing subject, see Siegrfied H. Horn and Lynn H. Wood, *The Chronology of Ezra 7* (Washington: Review and Herald Publishing Association, 1970).

[176] Indeed, the Magi of Parthia certainly knew of this prophecy and merely counted back 30 years to arrive at the time of birth for the Messiah. And these great sages of the east singled out the infant Jesus as being the one who fulfilled Daniel's 69 week prophecy.

[177] The later Rabbi's, realizing this dilemma, invented a chronology that relieved them of having to face this fact. Around the year of 200 C.E. they produced a chronology that claimed that the second temple only existed for a period of 420 years. Thus, they lowered the date of Daniel's prophecy some 235 years, which placed the coming of the Messiah around the year of 263 C.E. However, we have no indication that any other "Messiah" came at that time, so we are still left with the correct chronology that Jesus is the only messianic pretender who fulfilled Daniel's prophecy.

Jesus was to complete the Law, to go beyond Moses, to top it off, so to speak. And to those who heard this message, they

> were astounded at his teaching, for he taught them as one *having authority,* and not as the scribes (Matt 7:28).

Jesus had authority because he spoke in the following manner: "You have heard it said..., but I say unto you...," filling up and introducing new laws and in every sense acting as a prophet like Moses, for Jesus spoke with the same kind of authority as that of Moses. And like Moses, who climbed Mount Sinai to commune with God and return with his face shining in God's Shekinah glory, Peter, James and John witnessed Jesus "transfigured" on a mountain near Caesarea Philippi with the Shekinah glory of God covering not just Jesus, but Moses and Elijah standing in vision with Jesus.

Moses had predicted that a prophet would arise like him and the Transfiguration vision showed Jesus, standing in glory, conversing with Moses and Elijah – the summation of the Law and the Prophets – with the heavenly voice confirming that Jesus was indeed the beloved Son with whom the God of Moses and Elijah was well pleased. Jesus brought three witnesses with him to observe this event under the principle of "Every matter must be established by the testimony of two or three witnesses" (1 Cor 13:1, NIV, quoting from Deut 19:15).

THE SPIRIT OF PROPHECY RESTORED

THE JEWS OF THE FIRST CENTURY WERE OF THE belief that the spirit of prophecy had ceased in Israel at the time that Ezra the Scribe had completed the Old Testament canon.[179] Josephus recorded that

---

[178] Edith S. Williams, *The New Testament in the Language of the People* (Nashville: Hollman, 1936, repr. 1986), 18. Williams footnotes this verse with the following comment: "Picture of O. T. teaching as an unfilled cup, but filled by Jesus."

[179] Josephus *C. Ap.* 1.7-8 [37-41]; 1 Macc 4:44-46, 9:27-28, 14:41; Later sources express the same sentiment: *Seder Olam Rabbah* 30; t. *Sotah* 13.2; b. *Yomah* 9b and b. *Sotah* 48b. Scholars, of course, are reluctant to believe that the Old Testament canon was concluded by Ezra and the Great Assembly, because, for one thing, they believe that the *Book of Daniel* was written two centuries later, and therefore its presence in the canon would nullify Josephus' statement. Nevertheless, the reality is that the internal evidence of Daniel places it in pre-Ezra times and therefore in the sixth century B.C.E.

> from Artaxerxes [the time when Ezra lived] to our own time the complete history has been written but has not been deemed worthy of equal credit with the earlier records, because of the failure of the exact succession of the prophets (Josephus *C. Ap.* 1.8 [41]).

From such a statement it is obvious that the Jews knew one important thing about the spirit of prophecy: It was essential for the production of divinely inspired literature.[180] Yet, if there were no prophets from Ezra's time on to Josephus' day, then there could be no additional Scripture in the traditional sense. Yet, notice what Jesus instructed his disciples:

> Then he said to them, "These are my words that I spoke to you while I was still with you – that everything written about me in the law of Moses, the prophets, and the psalms must be fulfilled." Then he opened their minds to understand the scripture (Luke 24:44,45).

The grand, tri-part division of the Hebrew Scriptures is evident in this quote, but Luke, only a few verses earlier, had also recorded:

> Then beginning with Moses and ALL THE PROPHETS, he interpreted to them the things about himself in ALL the scriptures (Luke 24:27).

Notice here that "ALL the scriptures" is made up of Moses, the great Law-giver, and all the other writers of the Hebrew Bible, who were collectively put into a category of the "prophets" (whether or not they actually held the office of a prophet). In other words, all the later inspired writers of the Hebrew Bible were prophets in the sense that they had the spirit of divine revelation. In other words, the Jews had eventually connected the spirit of prophecy with the production of sacred literature.[181]

This is important to understand in the light of what Peter writes in his second Epistle. Peter not only claims to have the same prophetic spirit as the writers of the Hebrew scriptures, but he maintains that he even had it in an increased capacity:

---

[180] William Lee, *Lectures on the Inspiration of the Holy Scripture* (London: James Duncan, 1830), 60, long ago noted: "The invariable rule [is] that all witnesses of the Old Testament should be prophets." This sentiment was also expressed at nearly the same time by William Whitaker, *A Disputation on Holy Scripture* (London: Norgate, 1839), 49-50.

[181] For further discussion, see Sid Z. Leiman, *The Canonization of the Hebrew Scripture* (Hamden, Conn.: Archon, 1976), 130; Soloman Goldman, *The Book of Books: An Introduction* (New York and London: Harper and Brothers, 1948); Albert C. Sundberg, *The Old Testament of the Early Church* (Cambridge: Harvard University Press, 1964), 113-19, and David Aune, *Prophecy in Early Christianity* (Grand Rapids: Eerdmans, 1983).

> So we have the prophetic message more fully confirmed. You will do well to be attentive to this as to a lamp shining in a dark place, until the day dawns and the morning star rises in your hearts. First of all you must understand this, that no prophecy of scripture is a matter of one's own interpretation, because no prophecy ever came by human will, but men and women moved by the Holy Spirit spoke from God (2 Pet 1:19-21).

Peter is stating in the clearest of language that he and the other apostles were able to produce inspired writings that will be a lamp shining in a dark place, until the day dawns and the morning star rises (the return of Christ) in the hearts of the faithful. These words in themselves are words of a prophecy come true. Indeed, at the end of this Epistle, Peter can now claim that Paul's writings were classed with "the other scriptures" (2 Pet 3:15,16). And they were! Indeed, Paul, in his final editing of the Epistle to the Romans, stated with the utmost authority:

> Now to God who is able to strengthen you according to my gospel[182] and the proclamation of Jesus Christ, according to the REVELATION OF THE MYSTERY that was kept secret for long ages but is now disclosed, and through the PROPHETIC WRITINGS is made known to all the Gentiles, according to the command of the eternal God, to bring about the obedience of faith – to the only wise God, through Jesus Christ, to whom be the glory forever! Amen (Rom 16:25-27).

The Apostle Paul was keenly aware of his role to produce inspired scripture. He stated this in so many words that leave us no doubt about that fact:

> For surely you have already heard of the commission of God's grace that was given me for you, and how the MYSTERY was made known to me BY REVELATION, as I wrote above in a few words, a reading of which will enable you to perceive my understanding of the MYSTERY of Christ. In former generations this MYSTERY was not made known to humankind, as it has NOW been REVEALED TO HIS HOLY APOSTLES AND PROPHETS by the Spirit:[183] that is, the Gentiles have become fellow heirs, members of the same body, and sharers in the promise in Christ Jesus through the Gospel (Eph 3:3-6).

---

[182] The *Gospel according to Luke,* which was primarily addressed to the Gentiles, is in a canonical sense, the Gospel of the Apostle Paul.

[183] Obviously, this same revelation Paul felt was given to his fellow apostles and "prophets," i.e., Peter and John. See 2 Pet 3:9; 1 John 2:1, 2; 3:8; 4:14.

Notice the expression "holy apostles and prophets." These are not two separate categories, but in reality a reference to the dual role that the apostles had, i.e., that they were both apostles and prophets.[184] Paul was claiming the title of both apostle and prophet. He further stated

> I became its [the church's] servant according to God's commission that was given to me for you, to make the word of God FULLY KNOWN, the MYSTERY that has been hidden throughout the ages and generations but has now been REVEALED to his saints. To them God chose to make known how great among the Gentiles are the riches of the glory of the MYSTERY, which is Christ in you, the hope in glory (Col 1:25-7).

When Paul uses the expression that the word of God was fully made known, he was actually stating that he was used "to complete the word (message)." The Greek phrase is "πληρῶσαι τόν λόγον." Paul is actually echoing back to the words of Jesus who said that he came not to abolish the "Law" (the writings of Moses), nor the "prophets" (all the other writings in the Hebrew canon), but he came to "fulfill" – πληρῶσαι – "to complete" the written revelation of God (Matt 5:17). This is why the Apostle Paul could confidently say

> we also constantly give thanks to God for this, that when you received the word of God that you heard from us, you accepted it not as a human word but as what it really is, God's word (1 Thess 2:13).

> Now we have received not the spirit of the world, but the Spirit that is from God, so that we may understand the gifts bestowed on us by God. And we speak of these things in words not taught by human wisdom but taught by the Spirit, interpreting spiritual things to those who are spiritual (1 Cor 2:12-13).

There should be no mistake that the Apostles Paul, Peter, and John recognized that the spirit of prophecy had not only been restored, but that they only had the authority to create a New Testament of divinely inspired literature, and no one else in the later church had such authority. Jesus told his disciples

> I have yet many things to tell you, but you are not able to bear [them] NOW. But when the Spirit of Truth has come, it will guide you in ALL THE TRUTH, for it will not speak

[184] In Paul's list of leadership roles in the Church found in 1 Cor 12:28-30, the office of apostle ranks first, and that of prophet falls squarely behind in second place.

> of itself but what things it will hear and will declare to you the things that are to come (John 16:12-13, translation the authors).

What did Jesus mean when he said that the Spirit would guide his disciples into "all the truth" concerning "things that are to come?" This, in a sense, is a prophecy about the revelation that would be given the Apostle John, the concluding message of the New Testament canon, which is wholly about "things to come" (Rev 1:1). Jesus in fact prophesied to his disciples that they would be recipients of further divine revelation that he could not divulge to them at that time. This, in affect, was a foretelling that the apostles themselves would become prophets by virtue of the gift of divine revelation. Again, Jesus said

> but the Advocate, the Holy Spirit, whom the Father will send in my name, will teach you everything, and remind you of all that I have said to you (John 14:26).

Not only would the Holy Spirit reveal things about the future, but it would help the apostles recall the events of Jesus' life so that they could accurately produce a written gospel that contained the essential message of Jesus.[185] That prophecy has been fulfilled in a completed canon of New Testament literature that is with us to this very day.

THE BINDING AUTHORITY OF PETER

OF THE TWELVE DISCIPLES OF JESUS, PETER, JOHN, and his brother James, were three who certainly formed an inner core. Indeed, as we have mentioned above, they were given a special revelation in witnessing the Transfiguration. And out of this core, Peter decidedly stands out as pre-eminent and the leader of the apostles. It is thus important to understand some pertinent facts concerning Peter's authority as a leading apostle and his authority in formulating a canon of the precious words of the New Testament.

Peter is mentioned in the New Testament over 150 times, more than any other Disciple of Jesus. He walked on water to meet Jesus (Matt 14:28-

[185] Some authors have speculated that John's Gospel was written first because the author appears to have so many details that are fresh in his mind. Yet, the answer is not in surmising an early date of writing, but a fulfillment of John 14:26.

33). He was the first of the disciples to come to the realization that Jesus was indeed: "The Messiah, the Son of the Living God" (Matt 16:19). Peter is the one who recognized just who Jesus was and he tells Jesus: "You have the words of eternal life" (John 6:69). Peter was first to enter into the empty tomb, even ahead of John who was with him (Mark 16:7). And it was Peter whom Jesus first appeared to after the resurrection (1 Cor 15:5).

But most importantly, Jesus specifically singled Peter out for a definite purpose when he conferred upon Peter the "keys of the kingdom of heaven" (Matt 16:19). Notice carefully that Jesus told Peter at this time that "whatever you bind on earth will be bound in heaven, whatever you loose on earth will be loosed in heaven."

That Peter was given the authority to "bind" is a significant fact in understanding a very important principle in the process of canonization. In this regard, it is significant that all of the Old Testament books (except those within the *Megilloth*) end with the three letters "HZK" which has been interpreted to mean "to bind firmly together," "to be made firm," "to be confirmed," or "to be bound fast."[186] This appears to be an official stamp of "canonization" at the end of these books. At the end of the *Book of Kings* we read the following words: "Be bound, and we will bind."[187] In the last book of the Hebrew canon, *Second Chronicles*, it ends with "Be bound. So we will bind. The Lawgiver is not straightened (or powerless)."[188] The implication is that the lawgiver, God, is not powerless to complete his word to humankind.

It is in this context that we should note a very significant prophecy that Isaiah gave concerning the Messiah in which he said that the Messiah would be a "stone of stumbling, and a rock of offense" for Israel (Isa 8:14). Next, the prophecy states that the testimony of the Messiah would be the work of his disciples in the following terms:

> BIND UP the testimony, seal the Law AMONG MY DISCIPLES (Isa 8:14).

What a truly significant statement! Both Peter and Paul had referred to this very same passage concerning Jesus as fulfilling this prophecy with respect to the Jews' rejection of Christ (1 Pet 2:6-8; Rom 9:33). They were, then, totally aware of the context of this passage. Therefore, it was their

---

[186] *Gesenius' Hebrew and Chaldee Lexicon to the Old Testament Scriptures,* tr. Samuel Prideaux Tregelles (Grand Rapids: Eerdmans, 1967), 269-70; Francis Brown, Samuel Rolles Driver and Charles A. Briggs, *Hebrew and English Lexicon* (Boston: Houghton Mifflin, 1906, repr. Peabody, Mass.: Hendrickson, 2001), 304.

[187] *The Twenty-Four Books of the Holy Scriptures According to the Masoretic Text,* tr. and rev., Alexander Harkavy (New York: Hebrew Publishing Co., 1916), 1:660.

[188] Ibid., 2:1384.

responsibilities as disciples of Jesus to "bind up" their testimony concerning Jesus as the Messiah. And in this light we can see why Peter, in his final days, felt that it was he (and John) who were the only ones left who had seen the Transfiguration vision, and thus had the spirit of prophecy more fully confirmed than anyone had ever before. Only Jesus' apostles could "bind up" the testimony of Jesus. Such a startling testimony should have been noticed by canon scholars long ago.

Scholars may criticize the fact that Jesus left no writings of his own, but consider the following: the authority to canonize the words and deeds of Jesus rested squarely on the shoulders of Peter, Paul, and John. Why? Because they were now in the same position as the prophets of the Old Testament Scriptures and the work of Ezra the Scribe. They now were the very ones who had the authority to "bind up the Testimony" – indeed, to "canonize," as it were, the words of the New Covenant and seal them up for the future of the church. And it is because of their efforts that we have statements recorded by Jesus himself that say

> heaven and earth will pass away, but my words will not pass away (Matt 24:35).

Jesus' apostles were all Jews with a very Jewish perspective on the importance of their work in the light of the Hebrew Scriptures. The later Gentile church would never have had this kind of perspective incumbent upon them. The implications of the task of the apostles far exceeds any discussion today in works dealing with how the New Testament canon was developed.

The Apostle Paul also recognized the fact that he had to bind up his testimony for the future church, since his work among Gentiles gave him the kind of insight that was needed for a future church that was increasingly becoming Gentile in nature. This is why Paul requested Peter to come to Rome and give his final stamp of approval of his life's works. Peter came to Rome and gave no greater stamp of approval to Paul's writings than to classify them as "Scripture."

When Jesus told Peter that he was given binding authority (Matt 16:19; 18:16), he was giving Peter the authority to fulfill the prophesy of Isaiah 8. And from our perspective, Jesus did in fact guarantee that his words, and the words of his disciples, would be bound up for the future church. The authority of Peter came from Jesus himself, the "prophet like Moses," who was confirmed as the Messiah by the Transfiguration event. And there should be no question that the remaining witnesses to the Transfiguration vision were the ones who were more fully confirmed to provide the church with the written testimony of the powerful message of the gospel.

SECOND PETER AND CANONIZATION

PETER'S SECOND EPISTLE WAS WRITTEN SO THAT we could understand the significance of his important canonizing work. The entire second chapter is devoted to a warning about "false prophets" – those who do not have the spirit of prophesy "who will secretly bring in destructive opinions" (2 Pet 2:1).[189]

Peter knew that the spirit of prophecy had been restored and was a gift that was given to the apostles. Yet, he could see a disturbing element arising in his day with many who claimed to be prophets, but in fact were not. It is because of this fact that Peter knew that he had to put together legitimate writings of the apostles so that the future church could distinguish the truth from the false writings that were beginning to crop up. In chapter three of Second Peter, Peter says

> this is now, beloved, the second letter I am writing to you; in them I am trying to arouse your sincere intention by reminding you that you should remember the words spoken in the past by the holy prophets, and the commandment of the Lord and saviour spoken through your apostle (2 Pet 3:1-2).

How can future generations remember the words "spoken" by the holy prophets, and the Lord through the apostles, if first, they are not written down and secondly, they are not bound together in an official way that is universally recognized as the authoritative body of literature from the apostle's of Jesus? And notice here, that Peter puts the commandments of the "Lord and saviour" on the same footing as the prophets that should be remembered. Unless these words were to be codified, latter generations certainly could never be able to remember them.

Peter then talks about the scoffers who say "where is the promise of his coming?" (2 Pet 3:4). The future fulfillment of all the prophecies concerning the Messiah hinge on the fact that Jesus will return to this earth and fulfill them as he said he would. Since it was now obvious to Peter and Paul that the return of Jesus would now be way in the future, Peter had to comment on this, giving us the clue concerning a thousand years being like a prophetic day, showing us that it would be hundreds of

[189] Again, we have to legitimately ask, would some unknown later church cleric forging Second Peter be so bold as to warn us about imposters, knowing that he is an impostor that the church should watch out for? Does this in any way make sense? In order for this reasoning to work, we would have to believe that we are dealing here with religious frauds who not only had no scruples whatsoever, but defiantly so.

years before Christ returned to this earth. He admonished that we should "regard the patience of our Lord as salvation" (2 Pet 3:15).

Thus, Peter could now see the plan of God as a salvation process that would include millions more than those of just his day. With the realization that the church would have to await at least another two millennia before Jesus returned and there being already a growing apostasy, it would have amounted to a dereliction of duty of the highest order for Peter not to have "bound" together the testimonies of the eyewitnesses to the supernatural and miraculous events that point to Jesus as the fulfillment of the messianic prophecies! That was the ultimate commission that Jesus confirmed on Peter. It was to "bind." Bind what? To bind up the apostolic literature from the hands of those commissioned by Jesus to spread the words of Jesus and his appointed disciples.

Finally, Peter concludes his Second Epistle by canonizing all of Paul's letters. He tells us that Paul wrote with "wisdom" and that his collection of "all his letters" were on the same par as other "Scripture."

> So also our brother Paul wrote to you according to the *wisdom* given him, speaking of this as he does in *all* his letters (2 Pet 3:15).

When Peter says "all his [Paul's] letters" it is obvious that he is referring to the complete set of Paul's writings as we have it to this very day, since we know that Paul wrote other letters that are not included in the canon. If there were other Epistles, and Peter now calls the canonized collection of 14 Epistles "all his letters," then it is obvious that Paul delivered to Peter only those letters that Paul personally singled out and wanted to transmit to the church of the future. And Peter goes on to say that

> there are some things in them [Paul's epistles] hard to understand [specifically referring to Paul's revelation of the "Mystery"], which the ignorant and unstable twist to their own destruction, as they do the other scriptures (v. 15).

"Other Scriptures?" What an amazing testimony! Here we have Peter's own declaration that he considered all of Paul's letters (viz., the very same "Pauline Corpus" as we have today) as now being in the status of "Scripture" and therefore already as being the first body of literature to be canonized, for that is exactly what the term "Scripture" implies.

The importance of Peter's Second Epistle is an amazing testimony that Peter has now given Paul's works, his theology, and all of his brilliant theological insight the stamp of approval that in effect canonized his writings. Thus, the initial stages of the New Testament canon were already coming together and being "bound" together by Peter in Rome in the year of 67 C.E.

When Peter penned these words, the Apostle Paul had already been martyred, but his works were now safe in the hands of Peter, Mark, Luke, Timothy, Titus, Silvanus, Clement, and the other faithful believers who were there with Peter in Rome. We can only imagine that these faithful ministers were busy making new copies of these writings to be delivered to the great library of Caesarea and then, later on to Alexandria, where they would be safe-guarded from later church apostates. Once these copies were completed, all existing copies of the original autographs had to be destroyed.[190]

Peter himself knew that while he was in Rome his time was short, and that he had further work to do to secure his and other writings for the future church. It is time that we look at Peter's initial canon. This we will do in the next chapter.

---

[190] The reason for this is based upon the same principle as that of the burial of the body of Moses. Moses' burial site was to be kept secret, otherwise, his tomb would have been turned into a religious shrine. Likewise, the autographs of the original books of the New Testament would later on be turned into objects of worship. This is why no autograph has ever been found, nor, indeed, will ever be. This is just one more piece of evidence that the later Church did not canonize the New Testament.

CHAPTER 16

The Martyrdom's of Paul and Peter

CHURCH TRADITION TELLS US THAT THE APOSTLES Paul and Peter were both martyred at Rome in the last days of the Roman Emperor Nero (Ignatius, *Romans* 4:3; *1 Clement* 5:2-7). Jerome, in his famous *Lives of Illustrious Men*, believed that they were both martyred together. He recorded:

> He then, in the fourteenth year of Nero on the same day with Peter, was beheaded at Rome for Christ's sake and was buried on the Via Ostiensis, in the twenty-seventh [sic][191] year after our Lord's passion (Jerome, *Vir. ill.* 5 [*NPNF*^{2} 3.363]).

The *Liber Pontificalis* also repeats the idea that both apostles were martyred together:

> After making this arrangement he [Peter] was crowned with martyrdom along with Paul in the 38th year after the Lord suffered.[192]

From these passages we see that the early belief was that Peter and Paul not only died in martyrdom together, but that they died at the end of Nero's reign, either in 67 or 68 C.E.[193] However, the early church

[191] Obviously, this text should read "thirty-seventh year" if Paul was martyred the same year as Peter, who Jerome says died in the fourteenth year of Nero, i.e., 67/68 C.E. (Jerome, *Vir. ill.* 1 (*NPNF*^{2} 3:361).

[192] Raymond Davis, tr., *The Book of Pontiffs (Liber Pontificalis)* (Liverpool: Liverpool University Press, 1989), 2. Note that we maintain that this statement is further evidence that the early church believed that the crucifixion of Jesus occurred in 30 C.E., since, if it occurred in 33 C.E., as some contend, then 38 years later hence would place Peter and Paul's martyrdom beyond the time of Nero.

[193] Jerome also stated that Seneca "was put to death by Nero two years before Peter and Paul were crowned with martyrdom" (*Vir. ill.* 12, [*NPNF*^{2} 3:365]). Jack Finegan, *Handbook*, 388, comments: "Since Seneca, the very well-known philosopher and statesman, died in A.D. 65 (*EB* 1987, 10, 632), this means that the two apostles, dying two years later, died in A.D. 67 (and the Chronicle could mean 67/68 rather than 68/69)."

Historian, Eusebius, believed that Paul was martyred in 67 C.E. and that Peter was martyred in 68 C.E. Expounding on this fact, Daniel Wm O'Connor writes:

> Eusebius, in the Armenian version of the Chronicle together with the *Agapio*, states that the death of Paul occurred in the thirteenth year of Nero (between October 3, A.D. 66, and October 12, A.D. 67) and that of Peter in the fourteenth year of Nero (A.D. 67-68). ...Clement of Rome places the martyrdom of Paul ἐπὶ τῶν ἡγουμένων [before the rulers] (A.D. 67), during the which year Nero was in Greece and had left the government of Rome in the hands of Helius and the Praetorian Guards, headed by Tigellinus.[194]

From this evidence we can see that Paul and Peter did not die on the same day, as we will further show as we move along. However, much of modern scholarship prefers to believe that they did indeed die together, but that they died earlier than the traditional dates, placing them soon after the Fire of Rome in 64 C.E., under a general persecution by Nero against Christians in around the year of 65 C.E. Bo Reike is one such scholar who has promoted such an idea:

> Peter and Paul were both active at Rome, where they died as martyrs under Nero. Their martyrdom can be associated with the persecution of the Christians in Rome ordered by the Emperor in 65. ...Peter finally labored and died at Rome together with Paul.[195]

But did Peter and Paul really die on the same day? If so, why was Paul beheaded and Peter crucified? And why would Peter make reference to Paul as if he were already deceased when he wrote Second Peter? The answer presents a different scenario than what many scholars would have us believe.

Peter, along with the other Jerusalem-based apostles, was still in Judea at Pentecost of 66 C.E. It is likely that Peter, along with Mark, fled to Pella, but then left for Rome in the summer of 66 C.E. when the church had moved on from Pella. The Apostle Paul had requested Mark to go to Jerusalem to get Peter to come to Rome to help him with his important work of canonizing their writings for the future church. But when the Apostle Paul urgently wrote (from his Roman imprisonment) to Timothy in the autumn of 66 C.E., there is no mention of Peter being there in

---

[194] Daniel Wm O'Connor, *Peter in Rome* (New York: Columbia University Press, 1969), 57.

[195] Bo Reike, *The New Testament Era* (Philadelphia: Fortress, 1981), 218, 223.

Rome as yet.

Paul is insistent for Timothy to come to Rome soon because the sailing season was drawing to a close once the Pleiades set around November 11.[196] Paul wrote to Timothy in these words: "Do your best to come before winter" (2 Tim 4:21). The Greek literally reads: "Make haste before winter to come..."[197] Paul said that Luke, the author of Acts and the Gospel which bears his name, was with him there at Rome and that he wanted Timothy to "get Mark and bring him with you, for he is useful in my ministry" (2 Tim 4:11).

Mark was Peter's secretary (Eusebius, *Hist. eccl.* 6.14.6) and the one who wrote the Gospel that also bears his name. Summoning Peter's secretary for a useful service (διακονίαν) was Paul's tasteful way of inviting Peter to come to Rome with Mark if he so chose. Paul realized that if Peter came to Rome, it would seal Peter's fate, and he did not want Peter to come there and risk his life.[198] But he did wish Peter to send Mark with copies of special writings, possibly Matthew's Gospel and the Epistle of Jesus' brother, James.

Peter knew exactly what Paul had in mind with his request for Mark and what "service" that Paul was embarking upon. Think of it, with Peter, Paul, Mark and Luke together, along with the evangelists Timothy and Silvanus, all at Rome at the same time, we have virtually the writers of 70% of the New Testament material together for nothing less than a summit on the canonization of their works for the future church. Here is the real first convention on canonization![199]

This adventure of Peter and Mark traveling to Rome was the beginning of the greatest literary effort in ancient times! Peter would also bring with him a copy of the two most respected documents within the Jerusalem community – Matthew's Gospel and the Epistle of James.[200] Peter and Paul would thus see to it that the first compilation of authoritative church documents would be bound together for the survival of the future church.

But, as we pointed out, Peter knew that if he went to Rome he would

---

[196] So Pliny, *Natural History*, 2.47. See on this Jack Finegan, *Handbook of Biblical Chronology* (Peabody, Mass.: Hendrickson Publishers, 1998), 400.

[197] See Robert K. Brown and Philip W. Comfort, *The New Greek-English Interlinear New Testament* (Wheaton, Ill., Tyndale: 1990), 745.

[198] Unlike Paul, who was a Roman citizen, Peter was not. Therefore, he did not have the same guarantees as Paul for a trial.

[199] Before anyone criticizes this view as lacking evidence, bear in mind that no canon historian can produce any evidence that any post apostolic summit was ever held on canonization until the end of the fourth century! Scholars look vainly for any such summit in post apostolic times only because of their disillusioned theories that place many of the New Testament books in the second century. But such nonsensical theories should, in reality, find no legitimate place in any disciplined biblical scholarship.

be facing capture and imprisonment himself. But he had no other choice. He had to go and help Paul with this monumental task. And If Peter and Paul were to be martyred soon, they had to act quickly so that Mark and Luke could finish the job of editing the material for canonization and then delivering it to the Apostle John, who had relocated in Ephesus.[201]

PETER CONFRONTS SIMON MAGUS

THERE ARE TRADITIONS THAT SAY THAT THE Apostle Peter needed to go to Rome in order to counter the spreading ministry of the arch heretic Simon Magus. Hippolytus wrote that Simon Magus,

> journeying as far as Rome, he came in conflict with the apostles. Peter offered repeated opposition to him, for Simon was deceiving many by his sorceries (Hippolytus, *Haer.* 15 [*ANF* 5.81]).

The Apocryphal book, *The Acts of the Holy Apostles Peter and Paul,* is an interesting document that preserves a tradition that Peter, Paul and Simon Magus also stood before Nero. In this work we read:

> Then Simon, having gone in to Nero, said: Hear, O good emperor: I am the son of God come down from heaven. Until now I have endured Peter only calling himself an apostle; but now he has doubled the evil: for Paul also himself teaches the same things, and having his mind turned against me, is said to preach along with him; in reference to whom, if thou shalt not contrive their destruction, it is very plain that thy kingdom cannot stand.[202]

---

[200] We believe, consistent with ancient testimony, that Matthew was written to the Jews during the time when James was leader of the Jerusalem church. This being the case, the *Gospel of Matthew* represents James' sanctioned gospel account. In this respect we should consider the *Gospel of Matthew* as the representative Gospel of the Apostle James, just as we do with Mark's Gospel as really being the official Gospel of Peter and Luke's Gospel as being the official Gospel of Paul.

[201] The tradition that Peter and Paul confronted "the man of sin" — Simon Magus — is significant in the overall story of the canon. Why? Because it brings up the subject of early heresy that we will look at fully in the next chapter.

[202] *ANF* 8:480. This work also places the death of Peter and Paul at the same time, on the "29th of the month of June" (ibid., 485).

We next read:

> Then Nero, filled with concern, ordered to bring them speedily before him. And on the following day Simon the magian, and Peter and Paul the apostles of Christ, having come in to Nero, Simon said: These are the disciples of the Nazarene.[203]

One thing that is significant about this reference is the fact that if it is in any way recalling a first century tradition, then it shows us that the Apostles Peter and Paul were together in Rome at this time and standing before Nero. If this is so, then they were standing before Nero prior to the time when Nero had left for Greece in early October of 66 C.E.

Therefore, if this account is in anyway accurate, then we would expect Peter to have arrived in Rome around September of 66 C.E., which makes perfect sense if he left Judea sometime after Pentecost when the rest of the church in Jerusalem had fled from Jerusalem to the area of Pella. Consequently, Paul's letter to Timothy was most likely written sometime before Peter arrived in Rome, in the summer of 66 C.E., probably in July, in order for the appropriate time travel to have occurred.

WAS PETER EVER IN ROME

THE TRADITIONS THAT PLACE THE APOSTLE Peter in Rome are too strong and universal to be summarily dismissed. Indeed, Gaius, Irenaeus, Clement, Tertullian, Origen, and later church Fathers all contribute to the sentiment that Peter died in Rome. Nevertheless, there are many who, rejecting the idea that Peter was ever a bishop of Rome, go to the extreme of denying that Peter was ever in Rome in the first place. George Salmon, a critic of the Catholic faith, however admits:

> Some Protestant controversialists have asserted that Peter was never in Rome. ...I think the historical probability is that he was. ...Protestant champions had undertaken the impossible task of proving the negative, that Peter was never in Rome. They might as well have undertaken to prove out of the Bible that St. Bartholomew never preached in Pekin. ...For myself, I am willing, in absence of any opposing tradition, to accept the current account that Peter

[203] Ibid.

suffered martyrdom at Rome. If Rome, which early laid claim to have witnessed that martyrdom, were not the scene of it, where then did it take place? Any city would be glad to claim such a connection with the name of the Apostle, and none but Rome made the claim. ...If this evidence for Peter's martyrdom be not be deemed sufficient, there are few things in the history of the early Church which it will be possible to demonstrate.[204]

Jaroslav Pelikan points out some interesting facts also in this regard:

The martyrdom of both Peter and Paul in Rome. ...has often been questioned by Protestant critics, some of whom have contended that Peter was never in Rome. But the archaeological researches of the Protestant Historian Hans Lietzmann, supplemented by the library study of the Protestant exegete Oscar Cullman, have made it extremely difficult to deny the tradition of Peter's death in Rome under the emperor Nero. The account of Paul's martyrdom in Rome, which is supported by much of the same evidence, has not called forth similar skepticism.[205]

Oscar Cullman's assessment is as follows:

It is sufficient to let us include the martyrdom of Peter in Rome in our final historical picture of the early Church, as a matter of fact which is relatively though not absolutely assured. We accept it, however facts of antiquity that are universally accepted as historical. Were we to demand for all facts of ancient history a greater degree of probability, we should have to strike from our history books a large portion of their contents.[206]

Eusebius preserves a fragment from Gaius (ca. 198) on the tradition that both Peter and Paul were killed in Rome:

It is, therefore, recorded that Paul was beheaded in Rome itself, and that Peter likewise was crucified under Nero. This account of Peter and Paul is substantiated by the fact that their names are preserved in the cemeteries of that place even to the present day. It is confirmed likewise by Caius, a member of the church, who arose under Zephyrinus, bishop of Rome. He, in a published disputation with Proclus, the leader of the Phrygian heresy, speaks as follows concerning the places where the sacred corpses of

[204] George Salmon, *Infallibility of the Church* (Grand Rapids: Baker, 1959), 348-9.
[205] Jaroslav Pelikan, *The Riddle of Catholicism* (New York: Abingdon, 1959), 36.
[206] Oscar Cullman, *Peter, Disciple, Apostle, Martyr* (London: SCM, 1962), 114.

> the aforesaid apostles are laid: "But I can show the trophies of the apostles. For if you will go to the Vatican or to the Ostian way, you will find the trophies of those who laid the foundations of this church" (Eusebius *Hist. eccl.* 2.25.5-7 [*NPNF*[2],1:129-130]).

We could go on with many similar quotes, but for our purposes here, we need not make the point by overstating the evidence. There will be more evidence presented in Appendix 2. However, for now, we need to get back on track of our overall story and look at how the initial canon of the New Testament came about. This we will do in the next chapter.

CHAPTER 17

The Initial New Testament Canon

THE NEW TESTAMENT, AS IT HAS COME DOWN to us, is assembled in a very orderly and precise manner. How did it get this way? The gradual acceptance theory cannot account for the fact that the New Testament was canonized in a structured organization from a very early date, which certainly indicates that it was a matter of premeditated design and purpose – certainly not a haphazard collection of writings that came together slowly over a great span of time, as modern day scholars presently conceive it.

It is this structured canon that defies theories of a slow progression of development.[207] Indeed, the structure of the canon is in itself testimony that it is a compilation of a plan and a design for the purpose of progressive teaching. What this shows us is that the New Testament virtually was assembled all at once and at a very early date.

THE DESIGN OF PAUL'S EPISTLES

PRIOR TO HIS DEATH, THE APOSTLE PAUL PLACED his letters into a pre-conceived order that was not chronological.[208] This order shows us that it was Paul himself (and not some post apostolic editor), who had a definite plan in mind in this arrangement. And this we will demonstrate within this chapter. The reader needs to carefully read this chapter concerning this fact in order to gain a definite appreciation for this.

[207] Harry Y. Gamble, "Canon: New Testament," in *The Anchor Bible Dictionary*, David Noel Freedman, ed., (New York: Doubleday, 1992), 1:853, notes that "The NT canon is not so much a collection of individual documents as it is a collection of collections: its major components are a collection of Gospels, a collection of letters of Paul, a collection of 'catholic Epistles.'"

Ernest L. Martin, a leading pioneer in championing the thesis that we are here expounding upon, noted the following:

> Paul's fourteen epistles are arranged in three self-evident sections. The first Section consists of nine epistles written to seven church congregations: (1) Romans, (2) Corinthians, (3) Galatians, (4) Ephesians, (5) Philippians, (6) Colossians, (7) Thessalonians. The Second Section is composed of one general letter to all Christians – the Book of Hebrews. The Third Section is that called in modern circles the Pastoral Epistles – Paul's private letters to individual pastors: Timothy, Titus and Philemon.[209]

Some have criticized the order of the Pauline Epistles as being haphazard because of the fact that they don't fall into a chronological order. But the fact that they are not assembled into a chronological scheme points, not to disorder, but rather to another standard that is apparent if we look more closely.

First of all, we note that Paul wrote to seven different congregations. This fact has been observed down through the ages as being significant in itself. F. F. Bruce writes:

> The analogy between Paul's seven churches and John's is pointed out by Cyprian [Exhortation for Martyrdom, 11] and Victorinus of Pettau [On the Apocalypse, 1.7, on Rev. 1:20].[210]

Bruce M. Metzger also states in this regard:

---

[208] It would seem that anyone other than Paul would have strived to organize his letters most logically in chronological order. However, there appears to be some other reasons for the order of Paul's epistles. One online source (http://www.christiananswers.net/dictionary/epistles.html) explains: "Paul's Epistles, fourteen in number, including Hebrews. These are not arranged in the New Testament in chronological order, but rather according to the rank of the cities or places to which they were sent. Who arranged them after this manner is unknown." Another source (http://www.winternet.com/~swezeyt/bible/swezauth.htm) states: "Paul's Epistles appear in the Bible in order of diminishing length within two groups - letters to churches and letters to individuals (followed by Hebrews)." Still, another source (http://www.bereanworkman.com/books/rom_phile/order.htm) gives the following insightful explanation as to the order: "Order of Paul's Epistles: (2 Timothy 3:16 KJV) 'All scripture is given by inspiration of God, and is profitable for doctrine, for reproof, for correction, for instruction in righteousness' ...Now look at the how Paul's Epistles are placed in the Bible: Romans — doctrine; 1 and 2 Corinthians — reproof; Galatians — correction; Ephesians — doctrine; Philippians — reproof; Colossians — correction; 1 and 2 Thessalonians — doctrine; 1 and 2 Timothy — instruction; Titus and Philemon — instruction."

[209] Ernest L. Martin, "Design and Development of the Holy Scripture" (Ph.D. diss., Ambassador College Graduate School of Theology, 1965, 1971), 394.

[210] F. F. Bruce, *The Canon of Scripture* (Downers Grove, Ill.: InterVarsity Press, 1988), 164, n. 15.

> Number-symbolism found its earliest literary expression in the Muratorian Canon with the observation [lines 49-50] that Paul, like John in Revelation ii-iii, had written to seven churches, and thus to the whole Church. This point reappears in the writings of Cyprian, Victorinus of Pettau, and later authors.[211]

Most scholars, of course, reject the idea that it was Paul who followed John's precedent, since they feel that the *Book of Revelation* was not composed until the end of the first century.[212] But, as we have shown in appendix 3, John initially composed this work in the time of Nero, in the mid-50's C.E., and thus, this would be in agreement with these ancient commentators.

The *Muratorian Fragment* states:

> The blessed apostle Paul himself, following the example of his *predecessor* John, writes by name to only seven churches... It is true that he writes once more to the Corinthians and to the Thessalonians for the sake of admonition, yet it is clearly recognizable that there is one church spread throughout the whole extent of the earth. For John also in the Apocalypse, though he writes to seven churches, nevertheless speaks to all.[213]

Victorinus of Pettau, writing around 290 C.E., likewise comments:

> That in the whole world are Seven Churches; and that those churches called seven are one general church as Paul has taught; and that he might keep to it, he did not exceed the number of Seven Churches, but wrote to the Romans, to the Corinthians, to the Galatians, to the Ephesians, to the Philippians, to the Colossians, to the Thessalonians. Afterwards, he wrote to particular persons, that he might not exceed the measure of Seven Churches: and contracting his doctrine into a little compass, he says to Timothy: "That thou mayest know how thou oughtest to behave

---

[211] Bruce M. Metzger, *The Canon of the New Testament* (Oxford: Clarendon Press, 1992), 264.

[212] F. F. Bruce, *Canon*, 164, writes: "This making Paul follow the precedent of John is chronologically preposterous." On the other hand, Krister Stendahl, "The Apocalypse of John and the Epistles of Paul in the Muratorian Fragment," in William Klassen and Grayden F. Snyder, eds., *Current Issues in New Testament Interpretation: Essays in Honor of Otto A. Piper* (New York: Harper & Brothers, 1962), suggests that it was not Paul who used John's precedent, but some unknown second century compiler of Paul's letters who was the one who depended on the canonicity of John's Apocalypse, and therefore, is the one responsible for this tradition. However, once we date the *Revelation* to the fifties C.E., then all the problems seemingly disappear.

[213] Quoted from Metzger, *Canon*, 210-211.

thyself in the Church of the living God."[214]

Understanding that the Apostle John wrote the initial draft of the *Book of Revelation* before Paul compiled his corpus is the vital key to understanding that Paul did in fact follow the precedent set forth in John's Apocalypse, and not vice-versa!

Nevertheless, it was the Apostle Paul who was the pacesetter in the first steps in canonizing the New Testament. He was the first to foresee that a collection of literature was needed for a future church and he was the first to collect his own writings, edit them, and place them in a particular order for the very purpose of scriptural canonization.

Paul was the first to recognize that the coming apostasy made it necessary to bind up the testimony of the disciples of Christ, just as was foretold in Isaiah (Isa 8:14), for the future church. Paul's canon has come to be known in today's modern parlance as the *Pauline Corpus*.[215]

The fact that Paul's letters were placed in a particular order shows us that they were grouped and edited as a collection, and not just assembled together in some agonizingly slow, three century acceptance process. Scholars may criticize this proposition all they want, but the fact of the matter is that until they have hard evidence to the contrary, they have no case. Common sense should tell us that the gradual acceptance theory breaks down when we recognize the fact that Paul's letters were a corpus very early.

---

[214] Quoted from Nathaniel Lardner, *The Credibility of the Gospel History* (London: William Bell, 1838), 3:177.

[215] Brevard S. Childs, *The New Testament as Canon: An Introduction* (Valley Forge, Penn.: Trinity Press, 1994), 422, writes: "During most of the history of the early church the letters of Paul were transmitted, not in isolation from each other, but within a collection. The earliest textual witnesses of his letters already reflect the form of a corpus." Indeed, when Peter describes Paul's writings as "all his letters" (2 Pet 3:15), this is not to be taken as an indication that Second Peter was written long after Paul's letters had gradually come together as a corpus, but rather, that Paul's corpus was complete when the Apostle Peter wrote in 67 C.E. In other words, here we have startling verification that the Apostle Paul is the very one who had canonized his own writings just prior to his martyrdom in Rome!

HEBREWS — KEY TO THE ORDER OF PAUL'S EPISTLES

THE ORDER OF THE PAULINE EPISTLES WAS designed to lead a reader through a progression of doctrinal teaching. Modern theories on how the letters of Paul were assembled seem to be completely oblivious of this fact.

Also, we should note that as a body of literature, the *Pauline Corpus* contained exactly 14 Epistles, *including* the letter to the "Hebrews." This fact is not only significant in showing us that it has the stamp of completeness placed upon it (2 x 7),[216] but that the letter to the Hebrews was certainly to be included among the letters of Paul.[217]

We should realize that the number seven stands out in obvious symbology in the Hebrew canon. It is apparent that the apostles were capitalizing on the significance of the number seven to likewise give their words a stamp of authority and completeness in a closed collection of apostolic writings.[218]

The post apostolic, Gentile church of the second century and beyond would never have arranged the Epistles of Paul in the manner that they have come down to us in the earliest manuscript tradition. Indeed, we should make no mistake in understanding that the anti-semitic bias that was dominant in the second century would pretty much eliminate the *Epistle to the Hebrews* from any post first century canon. To think that an unsigned Epistle addressed to "Hebrews" would ever have been

---

[216] Both Testaments place great importance on the number seven. In Hebrew, the word is *shevah* and comes from the root *savah,* to be full or satisfied. Hence when God rested on the seventh day, creation was full, complete and perfect. The word *shavath* was therefore applied to that day. Even in nature, seven completes the colors of the spectrum, rainbow, and even the notes of the musical scale. Abraham's blessing was sevenfold (Gen 12:2, 3). Likewise was the Covenant with Israel (Exod 6:6-8). In the New Testament, the use of the number seven, especially in the *Book of Revelation,* is certainly deliberate and by a conscious design (for more on the significance of the number seven in Scripture, see E. W. Bullinger, *Number in Scripture* [Grand Rapids: Kregel, 1997], 167-95).

[217] The earliest manuscript tradition has the *Epistle to the Hebrews* placed well within the Pauline Corpus, and coming right after *Second Thessalonians.* "In codex Vaticanus and codex Sinaiticus, along with seven later uncial manuscripts and about sixty minuscules, Hebrews stands between 2 Thessalonians and before 1 Timothy (that is, it follows the Epistles to the churches and precedes those to individuals)," Metzger, *Canon,* 298.

[218] Metzger, *Canon,* 201, in referring to the author of the Muratorian canon, states: "The Epistles that Paul sent to specific, local congregations are, nevertheless, intended for the church universal, he argues, inasmuch as Paul wrote to seven such churches. Here the hidden presupposition rests upon the mystical meaning conveyed by the numeral seven, implying completeness and totality."

included among the collection attributed to the apostle to the Gentiles, in the light of its contended authenticity, is to ignore the gravity of this issue.[219] This fact alone points out that *Hebrews* was not placed within the canon by the post-apostolic church, but by none other than by the Apostle Paul himself.[220]

Whether the Apostle Paul actually composed the letter of Hebrews or not is not as important as to understand that whoever the dominant author of the Epistle was, it is obvious that there are features within the Epistle that stand out as being personal editorial notes of the Apostle Paul himself.[221] One significant example is chapter 6, verses 1 through 12. Who are these verses being addressed to? The general title of the Epistle is "To the Hebrews." Specifically, it is written to those still in the Jerusalem church, i.e., Peter, John, Jude and to all those who were still in Jerusalem awaiting the fulfillment of the prophetic revelation that was given to the Apostle John in the mid 50's.

"HEBREWS" AND PAUL'S MESSAGE

NOW UNDERSTAND HOW PAUL PLACED HIS writings together. Many have completely overlooked the importance of Hebrews, the sixth chapter in this regard.

Beginning in the sixth chapter of the *Book of Hebrews* are listed seven basic doctrines of the church. These doctrines reflect the very order of the nine Epistles to seven churches that immediately precede the *Letter to the Hebrews.* Right after enumerating these doctrines, Paul states that "we will do this if God permits" (Heb 6:3). What is it that "we will do" if God permits? We are to go on from the elemental things concerning Christ to

[219] If the *Epistle to the Hebrews* was omitted from Marcion's canon, the Muratorian canon, and disputed by later church fathers, we can then be sure that it would never have made it into any canon of the post-apostolic age had the bishops of Rome anything to say about it.

[220] Donald Guthrie, *New Testament Introduction* (Downers Grove: InterVarsity Press, 1990), 673-4, notes: "In [Hebrews] 2:3 it is evident that the author had received his Christian instruction directly from those who had heard the Lord, whereas Paul was particularly insistent that he was brought into salvation by a supernatural revelation (cf. Gal. 1:12)." However, even though the Apostle Paul appears not to be the author of the *Epistle to the Hebrews,* this Epistle does reflect Pauline theology, as we shall in this chapter point out.

[221] It is obvious that Heb 13:22-25 is a salutation in the style of Paul and was appended for canonization purposes. We maintain that it was Paul himself who added this greeting while assembling and editing his writings for the purpose of canonization. In fact, the entire 13th chapter appears to be words of Paul.

the teachings that lead to spiritual maturity (v. 1). Paul intended that his writings do that very thing, "if God permits?" Paul needed Peter to come to him in the Mamertine Prison in Rome to help him accomplish this fact.

The *Epistle to the Hebrews* itself, therefore, provides us the very key to correctly understanding how the Epistles of Paul were arranged. Notice the significant statement in *Hebrews*, the sixth chapter, where we read the following amazing statement:

> Therefore let us go on toward PERFECTION, leaving behind the basic teaching about Christ, and not laying again the foundation; REPENTANCE from dead works and FAITH toward God, instruction about BAPTISMS, LAYING ON OF HANDS, RESURRECTION of the dead, and ETERNAL JUDGEMENT. And we will do this if God permits (Heb 6:1-3).

If one reads these verses carefully, it becomes obvious that these very basic doctrines are listed in a progression that clearly lays out the plan of God in the perfecting process of the ones that are called out in this present evil age. If we recognize that "perfection" is the goal of the six doctrines that are listed after its mention, then "perfection" itself is part and parcel with the plan of God and is likewise a doctrine to be included in the list which must stand at the end of the list. Therefore, what we have here are seven basic doctrines of the plan of God, which are laid out in the following order:

1. Repentance;
2. Faith;
3. Baptisms;
4. Laying on of hands (the work of God's Holy Spirit);
5. Resurrection of the dead;
6. Eternal Judgment;
7. Perfection.

The author of at least this section of the Epistle could be none other than the Apostle Paul himself, for the list follows, in perfect order, the plan of God for his church as taught by Paul throughout his Epistles.

1. Repentance of a sinful life;
2. Expression of faith in God and his Son;
3. Baptizing for the remission of sins;
4. After this, the laying on of hands upon the individual for the reception of the Holy Spirit;
5. Growth in spiritual maturity during this lifetime, awaiting the resurrection of the dead;
6. Judgment, now on those being called out in this present evil age

and those who are called out in a future age of the rest of the world that will be resurrected at the time of the end;

7. Perfection is achieved when we are changed from mortal to immortality.

Now, if we overlay this seven doctrine template to the arrangement of Paul's letters, as they have come down to us, we shall find that there is an excellent correlation.

The first letter in the Pauline Corpus is the Epistle to the Romans, wherein Paul begins in the opening two chapters with a discussion about turning from sin and that "God's kindness is meant to lead you to REPENTANCE" (Rom 2:4). How significant that this is the first doctrine of Hebrews 6 and the *Book of Romans* is the first Epistle of Paul's letters.

Chapters 3, 4 and 5 of Romans next discusses the doctrine of faith. Notice what Paul says at the conclusion of this section:

> Therefore, since we are justified by FAITH, we have peace with God through our Lord Jesus Christ, through whom we have obtained access to this grace in which we stand; and we boast in our hope [faith] of sharing the glory of God (Rom 5:1-2).

On the heels of this, Paul launches into a discussion about baptism in chapter 6 of Romans: "Do you not know that all of us who have been baptized into his death?" (Rom 6:3).

Then, chapters 7 and 8 discusses the work of the Holy Spirit. Indeed, Romans chapter eight, can be considered as being the Holy Spirit chapter in the New Testament revelation:

> But you are not in the flesh; you are in the SPIRIT, since the SPIRIT of God dwells in you. Anyone who does not have the SPIRIT of Christ does not belong to him. But if Christ is in you, though the body is dead because of sin, the SPIRIT is life because of righteousness. If the SPIRIT of him who raised Jesus from the dead dwells in you, he who raised Christ from the dead will give life to your mortal bodies also through his SPIRIT that dwells in you (Rom 8:9-11).

Right within the context of these words we can see the progression from the sinful flesh, the work of the Spirit, to a resurrected spirit being. There is a definite progression here in the program that is in the direction as laid out in *Hebrews* 6:1.

Chapters 9, 10 and 11 of Romans goes into a discussion about the future blessing of "Israel," and the Gentile nations as well by a future resurrection and judgment: "And so all Israel will be saved, ...For God has imprisoned all in disobedience so that he may be merciful to all" (Rom 11;26, 32).

The order in which Paul discusses these principles is in the exact same order laid out in the *Epistle to the Hebrews*, chapter 6. What we are witnessing here is not the work of happenstance, nor caprice, but an intentional spiritual teaching. It not only demonstrates that this is the logical order in which to explain the plan of God, but that the *Epistle of Hebrews*, far from being a production of some unknown author other than Paul, is in fact the work of Paul's unique perspective, tying this *Letter to the Hebrews* to Paul's previous letters. Indeed, it locks in the entire *Pauline Corpus*, including *Hebrews*, as that of being the work of the Apostle Paul (whether Paul actually wrote the Epistle himself or not).

Following after the *Epistle to the Romans,* the next Epistle in the *Pauline Corpus* is *First Corinthians.* It is here wherein the doctrine of the laying on of hands is expounded upon in the context of the gifts and fruits of the Holy Spirit. The Epistle concludes with an all encompassing discussion of the resurrection and judgment. Paul recognized that he was still giving basic instruction about the "first principles," for he writes here that he speaks to the Corinthians as "infants in Christ" and that he had to spoon feed them with "milk" and not "solid food" (1 Cor 3:1-2, see also 1 Cor 14:20).

Next in the Pauline corpus comes the *Epistle to the Galatians.* This Epistle gives more progressive instruction, but it must be admitted that it is still in the basic areas of "first principles." It builds upon what Paul has already taught, but even the Galatians were reprimanded by Paul for returning to the "schoolmaster" (Gal 3:24) and were reverting to being children again (Gal 4:1-6). Ernest L. Martin again gives us some insightful observations:

> Notice the progression of teaching within the epistles of these first three churches of Paul. He had never seen the Romans and presented them with the ABC's of Christian doctrines. The Corinthians had learned a little more having had Paul in their midst for 18 months. The Galatians had been given even more teaching with four or five years of instruction – but all three groups were still children in the faith.[222]

When we move on to the *Epistles of Ephesians, Philippians* and *Colossians,* we graduate to a higher level of instruction. It is here that Paul introduces "the Mystery," as Paul calls it, and relates that God's spiritual gifts were given "for the perfecting [maturing] of the saints" (Eph 4:12; see

[222] Ernest L. Martin, *Restoring,* 370.

also Col 1:25, 26). Absent from these Epistles is any discussion about repentance, faith, baptisms, the Holy Spirit, or even the resurrection or judgment.

Finally, the two letters to the *Thessalonians* deal with the return of Christ, when the resurrected saints will receive their reward at the end of this age and achieve spiritual perfection. This completes the letters to the seven churches.

Following the letters to the seven churches, we have a general Epistle which concerns "the world to come, about which we are speaking" (Heb 2:5). The section from *Hebrews* 3:7 to 4:12 discusses the Sabbath rest to the people of God and reflects the millennial period, the New Jerusalem (11:16), and therefore must progressively come after the theme brought out in *Thessalonians* because it discusses events that are beyond the Parousia.

Next in order comes the Pastoral Epistles. The two letters to Timothy stand first, for Timothy was Paul's closest companion and was half Jewish, and these letters are the largest of the Pastorals. Next in order stands the letter to Titus, another evangelist, but a Gentile. And finally, comes the smallest pastoral letter, Philemon, a private Christian, who likewise was most likely a Gentile (following the principle, to the Jew first). Thus, the order of Paul's Epistles follows a definite plan and design of the plan of God as laid out in the seven doctrines to perfection in Hebrews, chapter six.

THE ORDER OF THE GOSPELS

THE *GOSPEL OF LUKE* AND *ACTS OF THE APOSTLES* were composed under Paul's direction and should be considered in reality the testimony of the Apostle Paul. The Muratorian Fragment confirms this conclusion:

> The third book of the Gospel, that according to Luke, was compiled in his own name on Paul's authority by Luke the physician, when after Christ's ascension Paul had taken him to be with him like a legal expert. Yet neither did he see the Lord in the flesh; and he too, as he was able to ascertain events, begins his story from the birth of John.[223]

The testimony of the Apostle Peter is expressed in *The Gospel of Mark,* composed in Rome most likely after Peter's first visit to Rome in

42 C.E., and then redacted by Peter himself in Rome in 67 C.E.

First, the Apostle Paul, and later (after Paul's death), Peter took the initial steps in editing and "canonizing" their important literary works that proclaimed the life of Jesus and the message of the gospel.

In Peter's initial canon, he assembled the three Gospel accounts of first Matthew, then Mark, and then Luke in that order. This represented the threefold gospel testimony of the Apostles of James, Peter, and Paul, written by their amanuenses respectively, and set in place according to their rank.

The *Gospel of Matthew* had been early circulated among the Jews in Judea in the Hebrew language under the leading Apostle of the time, James, the brother of Jesus, and now needed to be translated into Greek for posterity.[224] The *Gospel of Matthew*, for all intent and purposes, represented the gospel of the leading apostle of the early church, James. This Gospel, because of James' rank, would stand first in the canon, and by the same token, the *Epistle of James* would stand first among all of the Epistles.[225]

Luke's two part testimony of the *Gospel* and then the *Acts of the Apostles* was followed by the *Epistles of James*, Peter's two *Epistles*, followed by the 14 Epistles of Paul. Thus, Peter arranged the Gospels and the Epistles in the same order of rank: James, Peter, and Paul.

The *Gospel of John*, the Epistles of *First*, *Second*, and *Third John*, along with *Jude* were most likely not written yet. The *Book of Revelation* apparently was excluded by Peter. But it would be up to John to either add his testimony to the canon or leave it as Peter and Paul had completed it. After all, in Peter's eyes, the canon that he and Paul had put together could be considered sufficient enough for the instruction of the future church.

The number of books was 21. It already had the stamp of

---

[223] Quoted from James Stevenson, *A New Eusebius* (London, SPCK, 1993), 123. Stevenson's comment on the phrase "legal expert" is worth noting: "*to be with him like a legal expert* (*ut iuris studiosum*): the Latin is usually take to mean 'a student of law'. (Westcott, *Canon of NT*, p. 534, n. 3, believing in a Greek original, regard the words *ut iuris* as corrupt: Souter, *Text and Canon of the NT*, p. 208, prints, with a query, a conjecture 'adiutorim', helper). 'The description of *iuris studiosus* does not only apply to somebody who is being trained in the law, but also to a legal expert who acts on behalf of a Roman official, provincial governor or the like ...Such an *adsessor* or *iuris studiosus* issued an *edictum, decretum* or *epistula* either in the name of the Roman official to whom he was attached, or else *su nomine ex opinione* of his superior.' (Erhardt, *The Gospels in the Muratorian Fragment*, Ostkirchliche Studien, II.2, 1953, p. 125.) Thus St Luke's Gospel was written on Paul's authority (ibid. 124)."

[224] Greek had become the *lingua franca* of the day and was chosen to be the vehicle of expression for the Christian canon.

[225] The earliest manuscripts show this correct order. This is significant because it shows that rank and authority did play a role in the decision of how the books in the canon would be arranged.

completeness. Was there anything that John could do to add to this canon, and thus tamper with its already apparent mark of completion? Was the testimony of the Apostle John even required? And in the light of his failed prophecy should he even be considered in contributing to the canon of literature for the church?

Nevertheless, Peter must have realized that John, like Peter, was the final witness to the Transfiguration vision. He also realized that Jesus told his disciples that they would be recipients of later revelation:

> I have yet many things to tell you, but you are not able to bear [them] now. But when the Spirit of Truth has come, it will guide you in ALL THE TRUTH, for it will not speak of itself but what things it will hear and will declare to you the things that are to come" (John 16:12-13, translation the authors).

Therefore, Peter had to deliver the canon as it stood to John for the safe-guarding of its transmission to the future church. John Mark's ministry that Paul initially set him on would find him delivering Peter and Paul's canon to John, who had by this time settled in the city of Ephesus.

The Apostle Peter made sure that after his death the preliminary canon that he and the Apostle Paul assembled would be sent to John, most likely by John Mark, in his completion of the task or "ministry" that was set out for him (2 Tim 4:9-13). John had now moved to the city of Ephesus in Asia Minor to administer to the faithful Jewish Christians who had fled to this area, with his faithful entourage. It would now be the responsibility for John to add his necessary eyewitness contributions and complete a finalized canon for the church.

Once John had received Peter and Paul's canon, John could now see the inspiration of Paul's final revelation and how Peter had put his stamp of approval on Paul's writings as being Scripture. He could see the threefold gospel testimony of James, Peter and Paul, including the works of Paul embodied in the Acts of Luke, as well as the Epistles of James, Peter, and Paul.

The mantel for completing the canon was now to fall on the shoulders of the Apostle John and his "Elders" – the "Johannine Circle" as Oscar Cullman calls them[226] – for putting the finishing touches on the canon. This we will explore in the next chapter.

---

[226] Oscar Cullman, *The Johannine Circle* (London: SCM, 1976).

CHAPTER 18

The Apostle John and the Canon

MANY TODAY, INCLUDING A NUMBER OF scholars, believe that the New Testament canon is the product of the Roman Catholic Church. To disagree with this belief is to invite laughter and ridicule. But if the Roman Catholic Church did produce the canon, aren't proponents of this view obliged to offer substantiating evidence for its support? The only thing that we have is that by the end of the fourth century, the church of Rome finally acknowledged and published a table of contents to the existing canon that already was in existence from the first century.[227]

We must realize, however, as we have said before, that if any of the bishops of Rome ever had a hand in selecting the books of the New Testament canon in the second, third, or especially the fourth centuries, the canon would certainly never have come down to us in the form that it has, nor would certain books even have been included in it that are there today.

Indeed, we can be sure the other books would have been introduced and placed in prominent positions within the canon that aren't there today. To be sure, the *Epistle of Clement* of Rome would have been included, for he is held in the greatest of esteem by the early church fathers. Even today, many are baffled over the fact that Clement's Epistle is not situated within the Holy Bible of the Catholic Church. To think that the Roman bishops after Clement, if they ever had any say in the matter, would have left out Clement's Epistle, is totally preposterous.[228] Immediately, with this realization, we are confronted with a fact that tugs

[227] Scholars, of course, see this as proof that the canon did not come into existence until the mid-fourth century.

[228] In the year of 1628, when the Patriarch of Constantinople, Cyril Lucas, delivered to King James I the Codex Alexandrinus, it also contained 1 Clement and the Ignatian Epistles. The esteem that these documents still commanded within the Eastern Church should be noted as evidence of their near canonical status in the eyes of the church. A "Catholic Church" canon would simply never have left these documents out of any canon that such church would have produced.

at our sensibilities in trying to understand why this is the case.

We must not forget that the church in the second century was moving away from Judaism and Jewish concepts. Yet the earliest manuscript order placed into the primary position in the canon that of Matthew's Hebrew Gospel in the first position, as well as the Epistle of the Jewish apostle, James, first in order of the Epistles. Such an arrangement would be totally out of the question if later Roman officials had any say whatsoever in drawing up a canon for the Catholic church.

The canon, as we have it in the order found in Codex Vaticanus (and Athanasius' list), reflects an arrangement and a selection of material that is something that would have been done in the first century by the Jewish apostles who still looked upon James as the leading apostle of the Jerusalem church, even after James' martyrdom. But never would this have occurred in the second century or beyond in the minds of the Gentile leaders of the post apostolic church.

We repeat for emphasis, the esteemed letter of the Roman Bishop Clement, known as *First Clement,* must be understood as a canonical document if the Roman church had formed the canon. No Roman church sanctioned canon would have ever left this Epistle out. From this fact alone we can dismiss any theories that attempt to construct a New Testament canon in the second, third, and fourth centuries. It is frankly utter nonsense to even entertain such a theory!

Furthermore, it is not inconceivable that the letter of *First Clement* would have stood in a primary position right after the letters of Paul. This fact alone points away from a Catholic canon and should have flagged scholars that any theory of Rome developing the New Testament canon was, and is, entirely false! We therefore maintain that the New Testament canon was in place within the lifetime of the last Apostle, John, by the end of the first century. And it was John and his "elders" that finalized John's writings and combined them with the completed canon of Peter.

We can also be sure that if the Roman church authorities, after the turn of the first century, had any say in the matter of canonization, then also to be included would have been the seven *Epistles of Ignatius,*[229] the *Epistle of Barnabas*, the *Shepherd of Hermas,*[230] the *Gospel of Thomas*,

[229] Ignatius was so highly thought of in the second century church that legends grew around him that he was the child whom Jesus set in the midst of the disciples (Mark 10:35-37) and a student of Peter, John and Paul. Polycarp, Bishop of Smyrna, gathered the Epistles of Ignatius after his martyrdom in Rome for posterity in the church. See Walter H. Wagner, *After the Apostles* (Minneapolis: Fortress, 1994), 260.

[230] The *Muratorian Canon* identifies Hermas as a brother of Pius I, Bishop of Rome ca. 140-55 C.E. An interesting discussion of this work is to be found in Robin Lane Fox, *Pagans and Christians* (San Francisco: Harper & Row, 1986), 381-90. If this is so, would a canon decided by Roman clerics of the second century not have included this document?

the *Didache*, the *Apostolic Constitutions*, (where would the list end?) to name a few – much of this material would have been included in a canon that the bishops of Rome would have produced.[231]

BACKDROP TO JOHN'S FINAL WORKS

THE JERUSALEM CHURCH WAS FORCED TO FLEE before the Roman war sometime before the year of 67 C.E. to an area north of Jerusalem, called Pella, along the Jordan River. Jesus in fact predicted that the church would flee to the mountains just before his return (Matt 24:16). The fact that the prophecy of Jesus returning before this time had failed to occur was a very bitter pill to swallow. And in the period after the war from 70 to 85 C.E., many Jewish Christians simply abandoned the faith altogether. The future of the Christian community in Jerusalem was loosing its direction. On top of this, around 85 C.E., the Jewish religious authorities even placed a ban on any Jews from attending Synagogue, who believed in Jesus.[232]

Meanwhile in Rome, Paul had been martyred in January of 67 C.E. and Peter martyred the next year, in February of 68 C.E. In Jerusalem at this time, the church was completely gone. The Roman armies were now strangling the Jewish resistants in Jerusalem. The Apostles John and Jude had migrated out of the Jerusalem area with the fleeing church northwards, into Asia Minor. These faithful "Nazarene" brethren may have still stood by John and firmly believed that his apocalyptic vision would come to pass, just as he had faithfully recorded in the first edition of *The Revelation.* But after Jerusalem fell, with Peter and Paul now being

[231] Scholars need to stop and realize this ever so important point. The canon would never have taken the shape that it has come down to us if indeed the Roman Catholic Church ever once had to decide upon its contents. This fact cannot be emphasized enough. Indeed, it has always remained a puzzle to scholars down through the centuries as to why these works would not have made it into the New Testament canon. This is because they all have been laboring under the complete misconception that the church bishops of Rome were the final authority in all religious decisions from the time of Peter and Paul and onward. That the church of Rome was early a leader in religious matters is not contested, but in the case of canon history, this assumption has had disastrous consequences in trying to understand the background to the development of the New Testament canon. The final canon that has come down to us clearly has the stamp of the Apostles Peter, Paul, and John on it and not some unknown clerics in the latter church.

[232] F. F. Bruce, *New Testament History*, (New York: Doubleday, 1971), 385-6. For a discussion of the *BirKat ha-mînîm*, see Ray A. Pritz, *Nazarene Jewish Christianity: From the End of the New Testament Period until its Disappearance in the Fourth Century* (Jerusalem: Magness Press, 1995), 103-7.

dead, and with the apparent dismal failure of the prophecy of Christ's return, as depicted in "*The Revelation,*" John was forced to witness not only a rejection of his prophecy by many of the Jerusalem Church, but even a definite falling away by many who had witnessed first hand the collapse of the Jewish hope.

If John's prophetic message was in error, then his inspiration and authority in the church may now have even became suspect. And this is exactly what we see expressed in John's third Epistle – a Gentile minister by the name of Diotrephes within the church flatly rejecting John's authority (3 John 1:9).

The question that many had now was, did John really have such a vision from Christ or had he dreamed the whole thing up? The answer, of course, was that the prophecy of John [and, indeed, that of Jesus] did not fail – it just was not the right time for the prophecy to occur. Peter even had to combat this distrust in the Apocalypse of John by writing:

> One day with the Lord is as a thousand years, and a thousand years as one day. The Lord is not slack concerning his promise, as some men count slackness... but the Day of the Lord will come as a thief in the night; in which the heavens will pass away with a great noise (2 Pet 3:8-10).

The Apostles Peter and Paul, in their final days, could now see that the timing was not right for the "Day of the Lord" in their generation and therefore they were now moved by another imperative that preserved the written message for the future of the church. We have to place ourselves back in time and put ourselves in the place of Peter and Paul. What was uppermost in the minds of Peter and Paul in their last days in Rome was to provide a body of Christian Scripture for future generations after they were gone. Their statements in their last letters clearly indicated that this is not just speculation, but actual fact.

As long as it was believed that Jesus would return in their lifetime, there never was any motivation for any of the apostles to think along these lines. Now, it was essential to create a Christian canon by the apostles, and no one else! It was now necessary that they take action and move fast while they had the opportunity.

When Peter sent John Mark to John (who was now in Ephesus) with the initial canon that he and Paul had put together, it may have only included 21 books (3 X 7). This had a mark of completeness in its own right. These would have been:

1. Matthew (James)
2. Mark (Peter)
3. Luke (Paul)

4. Acts
5. Epistle of James
6. First Peter
7. Second Peter
8. Romans
9. First Corinthians
10. Second Corinthians
11. Galatians
12. Ephesians
13. Philippians
14. Colossians
15. First Thessalonians
16. Second Thessalonians
17. Hebrews
18. First Timothy
19. Second Timothy
20. Titus
21. Philemon.

What is missing out of this list is the writings of John and the Epistle of Jude. The only writing that John had made up to that time was the *Apocalypse*. But Peter, it would seem, could not include it within the canon, due to its seeming failure. Nevertheless, Peter knew that the Apostle John was the last remaining eyewitness to the Transfiguration, and that John, if he wished, could supply his own testimony of some sort. Yet, there was this nagging issue that John's credibility had been so damaged, that John could just as well have left the 21 book canon as it stood.

Jude may have been with John at the time, and John, realizing that Jude had written a tiny Epistle to the scattered Jerusalem brethren that confirmed Peter's predictions in his second Epistle, may have decided to include that letter in Peter's canon to round out the number of books to 22, exactly the same number of books found within the Hebrew canon (Eusebius, *Hist. eccl.* 4.26.14). This last touch may have been all that John intended to do to. It has all the earmarks of John's Jewish heritage that the New Testament canon should mimic that of the Hebrew canon in its numbering of books.

But, as we will soon see, the companions of John, as well as the Apostles Philip and Andrew, and possibly Jude, encouraged John to write a Gospel. And to bolster John's credibility they added their own comments in the famous "we" sections that verified what John wrote was indeed true.

JOHN'S AUTHORITY TO CANONIZE

JOHN WAS NOT ONLY AN APOSTLE, BUT HIS extraordinary vision declared him to be a prophet on the same rank as the Old Testament prophets. Indeed, when Peter said that "we have the prophetic message more firmly confirmed" (2 Pet 1:19), that confirmation was the direct result of the visionary experience that James, Peter, and John witnessed on the mount of Transfiguration. So, in this context, the "we" that Peter referred to could only point to himself and John, the last two remaining apostles that saw that vision. And after the death of Peter, John was the only apostle and prophet left in the church that had seen this vision. By this visionary experience, John was given even a "more fully confirmed" prophetic authority than the very prophets of old. This is indeed the entire thrust of what Peter informs us – there should be absolutely no confusion about this.

Even though John may have lost some credibility among a church that was swiftly falling into apostasy, there was no one else who had the authority to finalize the New Testament canon of Scripture, pure and simple.

We need to also realize John's other qualification in this regard. John was from of a priestly family,[233] and a cousin of Jesus.[234] He therefore had the priestly authority to finalize a New Testament canon. The bishops of Rome of the succeeding centuries never even came close to having such authority to canonize Scripture. Scholars who think that the Christian canon was the product of the bishops of Rome are entirely off base on this account alone.

A decade or so after the completion of the canon, as we have come to call it, we see Ignatius and Polycarp quoting from all over the New Testament writings, as if they had a copy of all the books in front of them. Ignatius even refers to them as the "archives" or "charters" of the church.[235] What archives was Ignatius talking about? He was referring to

---

[233] That John had become a member of the sacrificing priesthood and was accorded the priestly privileges as wearing a mitre – the sacredotal plate – is recorded by Polycrates in Eusebius, *Hist. eccl.* 3:31.3 and 5:24.3.

[234] See the *Fragments of Papias,* no. 10 (*ANF* 1:155). For an interesting discussion on this, see John A. T. Robinson, *The Priority of John* (London: SCM Press Ltd., 1985), 119-22.

[235] Ignatius, *Epistle to the Philadelphians,* 8:2, LCL, as cited in Lee M. McDonald, *The Formation of the Christian Biblical Canon* (Peabody, Mass.: Hendrickson, 1995), 146. Scholars, of course, have assumed that Ignatius was only referring to the Old Testament Scriptures, e.g., Bruce M. Metzger, *The Canon of the New Testament,* (Oxford: Clarendon Press, 1987), 48, since they wrongly believe that there was no such thing as New Testament Scripture so early.

official repositories in the leading libraries of Jerusalem, Caesarea, and Alexandria. It was the genius of the apostles to place their writings in the safe custody of these great libraries for their protection, the copying and the archiving of the New Testament canon, rather than to leave the posterity of the canon in the custody of latter church bishops.[236]

Why Did the Roman Bishops Reject John?

WHY DID THE CHURCH OF ROME, SPECIFICALLY Clement, reject the authority of John? Clement was ordained by Peter shortly after the death of Linus in the year of 67 C.E. Clement may have shared some of the suspicions that Peter and Paul both had concerning John's failed prophecy.

After Peter was martyred in February of 68 C.E., the church of Rome witnessed many of the Jewish heritage in the church turn away from apocalyptic Christianity. The days when John had written that it was prestigious to be a Jew were long over (Rev 2:10). And in the succeeding years, all that we know is that the Western church began moving away from Jewish Christianity, to a Gentile Christianity, in form, liturgy, and just about everything. But what other reasons would the Gentile bishops of Rome have against John?

We should remember that John was one of the "sons of thunder," a name that Jesus bestowed on John, the son of Zebedee, and his brother James (Mark 3:16-17). Could this nickname of "Thunder" have reflected a brash temperament that many interpreted as being headstrong, intolerant and abrasive in personality? Could John's personality have been a turn off to many who could not abide his headstrong nature? We can only speculate. But we do know that John and the rest of the Jewish Apostles that remained in Jerusalem, until they had to flee, may have looked at the

---

[236] Indeed, the apostles warned that the later bishops of the church would fall into apostasy, and therefore, the last place for the safeguarding of the New Testament canon would be in the hands of future apostate church leaders, believe it or not! The bits and scraps of papyri that scholars have been able to find today are copies made from the master copies within these libraries. Had the great library of Caesarea not had the entire New Testament in the time of Eusebius, when he produced the 50 Bibles for Constantine, the New Testament could have been lost due to the many church persecutions and book burnings that destroyed local church copies. By placing the canon within the repositories of these great Libraries, however, the New Testament writings were classed as historical literature rather than cultic propaganda, and thus, escaped the destructive forces that sought to eliminate the inspired books of the church.

Apostle Paul with suspicion because Paul's teachings moved away from Judaism and the Law and emphasized "grace."

Even Peter initially may have had some doubts about Paul's ministry. The death of James, however, in 62 C.E., may have been the turning point in Peter's thinking. That unexpected event was what jolted Peter (and many others in the Jerusalem church) that events were not turning out for John's prophecy to occur within their lifetime. Peter is said to have gone to Antioch and established a church with an overseer[237] – the same practice that Paul was engaging in with Titus, Timothy and Linus in Rome. Then when Peter finally went to Rome with John Mark and saw Paul personally and read Paul's Epistles, he could now understand the inspiration and special gift of the Apostle to the Gentiles.

The later bishops of Rome certainly identified with the Apostle Paul, and since Peter had come to Rome to endorse Paul's teachings by including them in an official church canon, then Peter was also accepted by the Gentile church of Rome. But John may still have been antagonistic toward the anti-law direction taken by Paul and the Gentile Roman church.

When John arrived in Ephesus he witnessed the fact that Clement, the bishop of Rome, had sent an Epistle of admonishment to the congregation in the city of Corinth. In this Epistle, there is no mention of the Apostle John, nor any appeal to his authority. If John was in Ephesus, would not Corinth fall under John's purview? Indeed, even if John was not in Ephesus by the time Clement wrote his Epistle, the lack of mentioning him appears to be a rebuff of John's authority.

Was there another factor about John that may have caused Clement of Rome to reject him? John administered to the Jewish Christians predominantly in Asia and his apparent hostility to Gentiles was, no doubt, another bone of contention with the Gentile bishops of Rome in their attitude with John.

John appears to have expressed a disdain for Gentile Christians in his statement to Gaius that he should not take any money from the Gentile (ἐθνικῶν) Christians (3 John 1:7)?[238] Could Diotrephes have been a Gentile minister and was insulted by John's refusal to take support from the Gentiles in the church and therefore Diotrephes in turn rebuffed John, setting a precedent that continued among the Gentile bishops in the church?

---

[237] Jerome, *Vir. ill.* 1 (*NPNF*[2] 3:361).; Raymond Davis, *The Book of Pontiffs* (Liber pontificalis) (Liverpool: Liverpool University Press, 1989), 1-2.

[238] It is obvious that in this context John is referring to Gentile Christians and not outsiders of the church, as many modern translations imply, e.g., "non-believers" in the *NRSV*. Why would non-believers offer their support to a Christian cause?

One thing is for sure. In the Letter that Clement writes to the Corinthian congregation while John was still alive, not one mention of John is made, nor to any of his writings. And this can only be interpreted as a complete slap in the face to the Apostle John. But there is more worth considering. Was the Apostle John the source of inspiration of early church heretics?

JOHN AND THE HERETICS

THERE IS ANOTHER POINT TO CONSIDER ABOUT John, which if true, could explain why John was held in suspicion by Western clerics of the church. There is a tradition that is contained in Fortunatian's fourth-century Latin preface to the Fourth Gospel that the amanuensis of John was actually Marcion, who latter became the heretic that so many of the early church fathers wrote against. This preface states:

> The Gospel of John was revealed and given the churches by John whilst he was still alive in his body, as Papias, called the Hierapolitan, the beloved disciple of John, has reported in his five books of "Exegetics." But (he who) wrote down the Gospel, John dictating correctly the true (evangel), (was) Marcion the heretic. Having been disapproved by him for holding contrary views, he was expelled by John. He had, however, brought him writings, or letters, from the brethren who were in Pontus.[239]

Was it the fact that Marcion's close relationship with John in his earlier years gave discredit to John and his teachings later on? Even though John is reported to have expelled Marcion, the question that naturally would arise is: were Marcion's heretical ideas somehow derived from the Apostle John's? Could this be another factor that weighed upon Clement's and succeeding Roman bishops' thinking? Indeed, another infamous heretic at that time, Cerinthus, also had contact with the Apostle John, at least in the legendary accounts that have come down to us. Eusebius quotes Dionysius of Alexandria, bishop of Alexandria (ca. 247-64 C.E.) that this Cerinthus reportedly was latter claimed to be the true author of the *Book of Revelation*:

---

[239] Quoted from Robert Eisler, *The Enigma of the Fourth Gospel* (London: Methuen, 1938), 208-11, quoted from Norman Walker, "The Reckoning of Hours in the Fourth Gospel," in *Novum Testamentum* 4 (1960): 73.

> Some of our predecessors [Bishops of Alexandria] rejected the book [of Revelation] and pulled it entirely to pieces, criticizing it chapter by chapter, pronouncing it unintelligible and illogical and the title false. They say it is not John's and is not a revelation at all, since it is heavily veiled by its thick curtain of incomprehensibility: so far from being one of the apostles, the author of the book was not even one of the saints, or a member of the Church, but Cerinthus, the founder of the sect called Cerinthian after him, who wished to attach a name commanding respect to his own creation (Eusebius, *Hist. eccl.* 7:25.1).

If the *Book of Revelation* was held in suspicion by many in the early church, and some even attributed the authorship to the heretic Cerinthus, and not John, then could it be that the bishops of the West looked suspiciously at John as producing heretics by his different gospel message and his mystical *Book of Revelation*? Is this another reason why the bishops of Rome wished to distance themselves from this controversial apostle? Whatever the case, we can again see that it was John himself who wished to have nothing to do with this heretic Cerinthus, as shown in this following story:

> John, the disciple of the Lord, going to bathe at Ephesus, and perceiving Cerinthus within, rushed out of the bath-house without bathing, exclaiming, 'Let us fly, lest even the bath-house fall down, because Cerinthus, the enemy of truth, is within'. And Polycarp himself replied to Marcion, who met him on one occasion, and said, 'Do you recognize me.' 'I do recognize you, the first-born of Satan.' Such was the caution which the apostles and their disciples used against holding even a verbal communication with any corrupters of the truth (Irenaeus, *Haer.* 3:3:4 [*ANF* 1:416]).

John, as well as his disciple, Polycarp, are memorialized as being combatants to Marcion and Cerinthus, but the Roman bishops may have not fully appreciated the extant of their relationship and therefore looked on John's teachings as spawning heresy, even though John is said to have expelled Marcion and Cerinthus. Indeed, Jerome even tells us that one of the reasons John wrote his Gospel was specifically to counter the teachings of Cerinthus:

> John, the apostle whom Jesus most loved, the son of Zebedee and brother of James, the apostle whom Herod, after our Lord's passion, beheaded, most recently of all the evangelists wrote a *Gospel*, at the requests of the bishops of Asia, against Cerinthus and other heretics (Jerome, *Vir. ill.* 9 [*NPNF*[2] 3:364]).

Since the heretics Marcion and Cerinthus are reported to have been in contact with the Apostle John, it may be that John's authority became diminished in the eyes of those who followed in the footsteps of the Apostles Peter and Paul, whose pro-Gentile philosophy was more in keeping with the church, that was, in the second century, becoming more and more Gentile in make up.

Also, John may have had another shadow of suspicion cast over him. The apostle, who predicted Jesus as a returning Jewish Messiah, waving a sword on a horse with blood up to the horse's bridles, was no longer considered a viable message for the Christian church. That message failed and it might be better if the *Book of Revelation* be put away and not mentioned at all. It was a "Jewish" Apocalypse and its message was cryptic and subject to much interpretation.

The Roman church authorities could only look at such Jewish apocalyptic writing as something of a revolutionary provocation for Jewish Messianic Zealots to re-emerge again on the scene, with ideas of overthrowing Rome. There is simply no way that any bishop of Rome would have ever placed the *Book of Revelation* in a canon for the New Testament church. Even to this very day, Catholic parishioners are advised by their priests not to read *Revelation* due to its confusing message.

The messages of Peter and Paul, on the other hand, certainly seemed more appropriate for the future of Christianity. Yet, the Roman bishops must have realized, on the testimony of Peter's second Epistle, that they did not have the authority to canonize Scripture. And what is remarkable is that no bishop of Rome ever crossed that line! But what they did do was to try to ignore John while he was alive and for some time afterward, and ignore him they did. This can definitely be seen in the *Epistle of Clement* to the Corinthians. It was written while John was still alive and with a deliberate refusal to acknowledge the Apostle John in any way, as we have already noted.

John's Addition to the Canon

We know that just before the fall of Jerusalem, John had moved to Ephesus in Asia Minor, bringing with him the mother of Jesus and a faithful entourage. Peter and Paul were now dead. What would happen to the canon that they had prepared? It was now up to the final leading apostle to make sure that it would stand the test of time. While John was in Ephesus, John Mark, Peter's personal secretary, completed his "profitable ministry" in delivering a copy of Paul's and Peter's canon to John in most likely the very same letter case that Paul had John Mark carry the scrolls and Parchments to him at Rome.[240]

John may have already been working on an early draft of his Gospel before the destruction of the temple, as certain passages indicate, but now he was urged by his friends and fellow eyewitnesses that were with him to finish the task and add it to the canon of Peter and Paul. Eusebius wrote:

> But last of all, John, perceiving that the observable facts had been made plain in the gospel [written by Matthew, Mark and Luke], being urged by his friends, and inspired by the Spirit, composed a spiritual Gospel (Eusebius, *Hist. eccl.* 6:14:7).

The *Muratorian Fragment* also states:

> The fourth Gospel is by John, [one] of the disciples. To his fellow disciples and bishops, who had been urging him [to write], he said, "Fast with me from today for three days, and what will be revealed to each one let us tell it to one another." In the same night it was revealed to Andrew, [one] of the apostles that John should write down all things in his own name while all of them should review it.[241]

The *Gospel according to John* was thus a collective effort of John, Andrew, Phillip, and those remnants of the 500 witnesses that were still alive in 54 C.E. that Paul referred to (1 Cor 15:6). This explains the "we sections" in the Gospel and John's Epistle:

> This is the disciple [John] who bears witness about these things – *and WE know that the witness he gives is true (John 21:24).*

The "we" who knew that John's witness was "true," knew so because they too were witnesses to the events reported by John. The *Gospel of John* was corroborated by additional eyewitness testimony that what John said was indeed true. Why would such statements be necessary if John's testimony had not been called into question? John's authority had been challenged. The "we" sections are also seen in 3 John and even in this tiny Epistle the "witnesses" back up what John writes by adding:

> WE also are bearing witness, and you know that the witness

---

[240] 2 Tim 4:13 is not speaking of a "cloak," but a letter case to carry the parchments that Paul is referring to.

[241] Cited from Metzger, *Canon*, 306.

WE give is true (3 John 1:12).

If John's witness was called into question, the testimony of his other eyewitnesses to Jesus were now called upon to back him up.[242] These witnesses and helpers of John in his writings were no doubt the "Elders" mentioned by Papias (ca. 110 C.E.), who is said not only to be a hearer of John but the real one (not Marcion) who wrote the *Gospel of John*, as John had dictated.

> For the last of these, John, surnamed "the Son of Thunder," when he was a very old man ...and about the time when terrible heresies had cropped up, dictated the Gospel to his own disciple, the virtuous Papias of Hierapolis, to complete the message of those before him who had preached to the peoples of the whole world.[243]

Irenaeus refers to the teaching and the tradition of these "elders" in his writings as if they constituted an authoritative body, as in:

> The age of thirty years is the prime of a young man's ability, ...This was our Lord's age when he taught, inasmuch as the Gospel and all the *Elders* who lived with John, the Lord's disciple, in Asia testify that John delivered this tradition to them. For he remained with them until the time of Trajan. And some of them saw not only John, but other apostles as well, and heard this same account from them and testify concerning the previously mentioned account (Irenaeus, *Haer.* 2:22:5 [*ANF* 1:391-2], also see 5:5:1; 5:30:1; 5:33:3; and 5:36:1-2).

John completed his Gospel and included many statements made by the other eyewitnesses to the events. This certainly explains the patch work nature of the Gospel. It was up to John now to include this Gospel in the canon of Peter and Paul.

John also included his three Epistles to the canon at that time. However, the *Book of Revelation* still was probably not going to be a part of the canon. But then, a quarter century later, tradition has it that John was exiled to the very island that had been the stage of his initial vision. It is there that the vision was reaffirmed and at last, John was vindicated. He updated that work with some new comments, especially his closing remarks, that sealed the canon shut until the time of the return of Jesus (Rev 22:18-21). This we will look at now in the next chapter.

---

[242] See also John 1:14; 1 John 1:1-4; 4:14.

[243] *The Fragments of Papias* in *The Apostolic Fathers, trans.* J. B. Lightfoot and J. R. Harmer, (2d ed. Grand Rapids: Baker Books, 1989), 324.

CHAPTER 19

The Final Canon of John

THE NEW TESTAMENT CANON SURELY SHOWS THE hand of John in its final arrangement. In the Epistles section we can see that they were arranged according to rank, James first, then Peter, then John, then Jude and finally the Epistle's of Paul.[244] The first three names are the very same names and order that the Apostle Paul referred to as being the "Pillar Apostles" (Gal 2:9) – James, Peter, and John.

When we look at the arrangement of the Gospels, there is a curious thing that stands out. In the initial canon of Peter, the three-fold Gospel testimony is arranged in this exact same order of rank, Matthew (James), Mark (Peter) and Luke (Paul). If John's Gospel was to be added, then its rightful place according to the rank of the "Pillar Apostles" would seem most likely to be right after the *Gospel of Mark*. But that would break up the "Synoptic" testimony because John's Gospel was different. But to place it after Luke would break up Luke's two part testimony of part one: Jesus' ministry and part two: the *Acts of the Apostles.*

Where would John place his Gospel? It is obvious that if anyone other than John would have made that decision, then the *Gospel of John* would have been placed after Mark's because who would have not placed John's Gospel according to rank, right after Peter (Mark's Gospel)? Furthermore, who would have dared to separate Luke's two-part testimony other than someone who had the authority to do so? Indeed, the rightful place would have been after the *Gospel of Mark*, thus representing the threefold testimony of these "Pillar Apostles" in the order of their rank: James [Matthew], Peter [Mark], and John.

No one other than John himself could have decided to divide Luke's two part work and wedge his Gospel right in between. Who could have or would have done such a thing if not someone with more authority than the Apostle Paul? It could be none other than the Apostle John himself!

[244] This was the original manuscript order of the Epistles, as is testified in numerous sources. For a list of these sources see Ernest L. Martin, *Restoring*, 11-17.

Again, the gospel arrangement clearly has the mark of John in its ordering.

The canon that John received from Peter and Paul had exactly 21 books. John may have initially only intended to add Jude's Epistle to come up with the very same number of books that made up the original Hebrew canon.[245] John complemented this with 5 books of his own which brought the total to 27 books for the New Testament and 22 for the Old Testament – thus a total of 49 books (7 X 7). Seven signifies the number of completion and seven times seven has the very mark of a completed testimony for the entire revelation of God. Even in this fact we see the final seal of a closed canon.

The Tripartite division of the Old Testament – the Law, the Prophets and the Writings – was now added to by the four part division of the New Testament – the Gospels, the Acts, the Epistles and the Revelation. This now made up a Bible of seven grand divisions. And this seven-fold significance also reveals a completeness that cannot be tampered with. No Gentile bishop of Rome would have so ingeniously organized and designed such a Jewish type of canon other than someone who had come from a priestly background, such as John.

The prodigious effort of John and his elders was to take the books that Peter had sent to John and recopy them into Greek within a codex format and then place them in the major library of Caesarea, then later in Alexandria and Antioch, and so on. The apostles were well aware that the Jerusalem area is where the Word of God was to go forth (Isa 2:3) – not Alexandria or Rome. Therefore, the authoritative area from which the word of God would initially reside until copies could be made to the

---

[245] The Hebrew canon originally numbered 22 books, but today numbers 24 books. This is due to dividing Joshua-Judges and Ezra-Nehemiah into two books, not because two additional books were added to the original canon of Ezra. The Rabbis certainly could see that their 22 books joined with the 27 books of the New Testament added up to 49, a number that certainly was uncomfortable to say the least. Thus, by dividing Joshua-Judges and Ezra-Nehemiah into two books they were able to foil the significance a complete revelation (49) into a totally meaningless number of 51 books. But since the number 22 was significant in that it represented the number of letters in the sacred alphabet of Jacob's tongue (Jubilees 2:23-24), then how could the Jews change from 22 books to 24? Ernest L. Martin ("Design and Development of the Holy Scripture" [Ph.D. diss., Ambassador College Graduate School of Theology, 1965, 1971], 43-4), answers: "The excuses some Jews finally gave for making their unauthorized change are almost amusing. They would never once mention the obvious reason. What was their major excuse? It is given by Sixtus Serensis (*Bibliotheca Sancta ex Praecipuis Catholicae Ecclesiae Auctoribus Collecta*, 1.1 [Naples: 1742], p. 2). He admitted that the original number was twenty-two books in agreement with the twenty-two letters of the Hebrew alphabet. But since there was only one *yodh* among the twenty-two letters, and because the Jews started a peculiar habit of writing the unpronounceable name of *YHVH* with three *yodhs*, it was necessary, Sixtus tells us, to re-number the Old Testament books by the addition of the two extra *yodhs*."

other major libraries and church areas would be the greater Jerusalem area – not Rome nor Alexandria.

The city of Jerusalem suffered destruction by the Romans in the years of 66-73 C.E. and in the Bar Kochba revolt of 132-5 C.E. However, should we think that the precious documents of the apostles would be deposited in a library that was to be destroyed? Should not there be some divine providence in the protection of these documents? Eusebius tells us, when writing about the scholar Origen (185-234):

> There flourished many learned men in the Church at that time, whose letters to each other have been preserved and are easily accessible. They have been kept until our time in the library at Aelia,[246] which was established by Alexander, who at that time presided over that Church. We have been able to gather from that library material for out present work (Eusebius, *Hist. eccl.* 6.20.1).

Based upon this testimony, we therefore believe that the Libraries at Jerusalem and Caesarea survived the ravages of the wars with the Romans. And it was to these Libraries (and later on, the great library at Alexandria) that later church scholars would go to in order to study the authoritative texts of New Testament. Caesarea is where Origen, Pamphilus and Eusebius worked. It is from this Library that Eusebius made the 50 Copies of the Bible for Emperor Constantine, which no doubt is evidenced in the great uncial manuscripts called the codex Vaticanus and Sinaiticus.[247]

Again, we must emphasize the fact that had the bishops of Rome ever had any authority in canonizing the New Testament it would have looked far different than it does today. Certainly, they never would have included the *Book of Revelation* in it, nor would they have ever had included the third Epistle of John. However, they certainly would have included the letter of the esteemed bishop of Rome, Clement to the church in Corinth. But the area of Rome, which Peter figuratively called "Babylon" (1 Pet 5:13), would not be the area from where the word of God would go forth (Isa 2:3). In other words, Rome, nor Egypt for that matter, simply cannot be the place to be looking for the origin of the canon.[248]

The silence with which the Roman church officials had concerning

---

[246] The city of Aelia Capitolina was the name that Hadrian gave to the city of Jerusalem after the Bar Kochba revolt in 135 C.E.

[247] Scholars have labeled the text type of these manuscripts as being Alexandrian. This is apparently due to the influence of Origin, who came from Alexandria. The reality is, however, that the text type witnessed in ℵ and B would better be classified as the true Caesarean text types. See appendix 10 for more discussion on this.

[248] This is a fact that many canon scholars seem to be oblivious to, but nevertheless needs to be a primary focus of consideration.

the canon during the second century only reflects the precedent of Clement and the reticence of later Roman bishops to accept John's authority. However, there is no basis for believing that there was no canon in place at that time. It only shows us that the church of Rome at this time still did not acknowledge John's authority. It wasn't until the fourth century that the church of Rome finally accepted John's writings, since at that time the church was trying to fight Arianism and John's message was now beginning to be interpreted in ways that seemed to support the Trinitarian idea of a pre-existent Jesus as a divine being in a Triune God-head.

Indeed, it wasn't until some three hundred years after Peter and John's canon – in 397 C.E. – did the Roman Catholic Church officially endorse the Canon of Peter and John.[249] So much for any idea that the Church of Rome produced the canon of the New Testament. Indeed, it took the Roman Catholic Church some three centuries to finally give its seal of approval to the canon of John. And even in accepting this they had to admit that this canon was not theirs, but that which "we have received from our fathers to be read in church."[250]

But, by then, even though they dared not take away any of the books of the canon, they felt compelled to rearrange it. They pushed the Epistles of James, Peter, John and Jude, (the Jewish apostles) to the back, behind those of the Apostle Paul (the Apostle to the Gentiles). Now the first Epistle after the *Book of Acts* was Paul's Epistle to the church of Rome. Certainly, this is an arrangement that could be seen to better suit the tastes of the Roman Catholic Church. Such an arrangement places the Apostle Paul, the apostle to the Gentiles, as the leading apostle, and the church of Rome as the leading church.

And further, the *Epistle to the Hebrews* was dislodged from occurring after *Second Thessalonians*, and pushed all the way back, to the end of Paul's Epistles, and just before the *Epistle of James*. This arrangement placed the *Epistle to the Hebrews* next to the Jewish Apostle James. By doing this, it distanced Paul's general Epistle to the Jewish brethren in Jerusalem from within the core of his corpus, and put it on the fringe of of Paul's Epistles. *Hebrews* now held last place, right on the edge of being booted out of the Pauline corpus altogether. Such tampering is not only blatantly apparent – it even went against the official order of books within the canon of the New Testament as recorded by Athanasius.

Thus, John may have had his way in deciding what books belonged to the canon, but Rome finally achieved an arrangement of the canon that

---

[249] At the third Synod of Carthage, in 397.

[250] Metzger, *Canon*, 315.

clearly was a Roman Catholic arrangement in every sense. What this shows us is that had the church of Rome really created the canon, they would have certainly produced one that exalted the church of Rome. This means that the Epistle of Clement would never have been left out of the canon. Obviously, however, John rebuffed the bishop of Rome (Clement) by not including the Epistle that rebuffed his authority. And Rome obviously knew down through the centuries that it could never reverse Peter and John's ultimate decision of what the canon should be.

Also, although the Roman bishops dared not add apocryphal books to the New Testament, they had no compunction about adding Old Testament apocryphal books and following the Greek Septuagint arrangement. Thus, in the end, the church of Rome sanctioned a Bible that was a jumbled up mess that had no order, no symmetry, nor significant number. Indeed, by taking the Septuagint 39 books and adding the 27 books of the New Testament they came up with the embarrassing number of 66 books. Therefore, in order to get away from this stamp of "man's number," the Roman authorities simply added eleven apocryphal books to the Old Testament to give them 77 books. Thus, the Roman Catholic Church now had a Bible that finally smacked of a complete Bible that they could boast had more revelation than any other Bible and had the appearance of completeness as well.[251]

Papias, in his second book, tells us that John was martyred, shortly after his second vision of the *Revelation* by the Jews. And right on the heels of John's death there were numerous works being circulated bearing the names of apostles, but to no avail. The canon was complete and archived in the great Library of Caesarea. No one dared tamper with the canon that John had established – not even the later bishops of Rome. It was no longer a matter of whether other works were genuine writings of the apostles, or not and whether they should be included in the canon. Even if such works were found to be the genuine works of other apostles, they could not be introduced into the official canon that the Apostle John left behind and closed. The canon was indeed closed by John – is closed to this day – and shall remain closed until the time of the end, despite fortuitous efforts which wish to add to the canon today.

The magnitude of the problem between the Apostle John's authority and the bishops of Rome at the end of the first century and into the second century is a key in canon history that is lost among modern day

[251] Obviously, if the Roman church authorities had no compunction about adding books to the Old Testament, and reshuffling the order in the New Testament, they would have certainly added *First Clement* to the New Testament if they thought that they could get away with it. But the New Testament was early on already wide spread and closed, and every bishop of Rome since Clement knew that.

scholarship. It would not be until after the death of John and the collapse of the Jerusalem church that Rome could even think of moving away from Jewish practices that were the tradition of John and other Jewish apostles. But after the second Jewish revolt in 135 C.E., Rome could now assert itself in matters of church liturgy, as witnessed in the Quartodeciman controversy, but there is no evidence that it asserted itself in the area of the canon.

The post apostolic atmosphere of the Western church obviously was to divorce itself from anything Jewish. But not all the churches of the East, in Asia Minor, were in agreement with this move. It is this difference that caused a debate about Passover that grew into a severe controversy. The tradition of John had no affect whatsoever in changing Rome's policy on the matter, much to the utter dismay and unbelief of the bishops of Asia. The only obstacle to the supremacy of Rome was the remaining loyal followers of John in the Asian churches. The struggle thus became a struggle of authority between the seats of Ephesus and Rome. To better understand this controversy, we need to look at it further. This we will now do in the next chapter.

CHAPTER 20

Background to the Post-Apostolic Church

A CENTURY AFTER THE FLEDGLING CHURCH that the apostles left behind, it began to be severely divided over an issue that turned out to become a major controversy. And now, without guidance of apostolic authority, the parties involved appealed to the tradition of those apostles that they believed supported their case.

Before looking at the controversy itself, it is first necessary to understand the background in which this controversy developed by looking at the major players in this drama. The Apostle John is very important to this story. He is said to have lived to nearly the end of the first century. He was the last of the remaining twelve apostle's of Jesus. Mystery surrounds this apostle, as we have pointed out, but since John outlived Peter and Paul by about three decades, his tradition was still within the memories of some of the second century bishops in the Asian churches.

Two disciples of the Apostle John that should be looked at were the bishop of Antioch, Ignatius (ca. 35-110 C.E.) and the bishop of Smyrna, Polycarp (ca. 69-156 C.E.). The relationship of Ignatius to Polycarp and John is given in the treatise, *the Martyrdom of Ignatius:*

> And after a great deal of suffering he (Ignatius) came to Smyrna, where he disembarked with great joy, and hastened to see the holy Polycarp, [formerly] his fellow-disciple, and [now] bishop of Smyrna. For they had both, in old times, been disciples of St. John the Apostle (*The Martyrdom of Ignatius* in *ANF* 1:130).

What is interesting in this citation is that both Ignatius and Polycarp were disciples of the Apostle John, yet we learn that Ignatius seems to have aligned himself with the traditions of Peter and Paul, whereas Polycarp remained a follower of the Apostle John. These two individuals who emerged early in the second century seem to reflect the overall differences between the church at Rome and the churches of Asia, with its seat in Ephesus. Whereas the churches of the West (Rome) tended to follow the so-called apostles to the Gentiles, Peter and Paul, the churches of Asia followed the tradition of John and the so-called "Jewish apostles."

The Western churches were moving away from Jewish religious customs, whereas the churches of the East still clung to them, such as the observance of the weekly Sabbath and Passover and Pentecost. It is in this respect that we can see Ignatius preaching a separation from these "Jewish" customs and Polycarp still defending the traditions that he received from John, who was considered a "Jewish" apostle.

In the last year of Ignatius' life, a decade after the death of the Apostle John, he was received by the Bishop Polycarp in Smyrna on his escorted route by ten Roman guards to be taken to Rome to be martyred. From Smyrna, just before he was taken to Rome and thrown to lions at the Colosseum, Ignatius wrote Epistles to Ephesus, Magnesia and Tralles. These letters are insightful because, in one instance, Ignatius talks about a new kind of Sabbath observance, unlike that of the Jews, and emphasizes the "eighth day" – the Lord's Day, as the new Christian Sabbath. Here we have a disciple of John moving away from a decidedly Jewish institution. To the Magnesians we hear this echoed in the following:

> Let us therefore no longer keep the Sabbath after the Jewish manner, ... But let every one of you keep the Sabbath after a spiritual manner, rejoicing in meditation on the law, ... And after the observance of the Sabbath, let every friend of Christ keep the Lord's Day as a festival, the resurrection-day, the queen and chief of all the days [of the week]. Looking forward to this, the prophet declared, "to the end, for the eighth day," [Ps. 6:12] on which our life both sprang up again, and the victory over death was obtained in Christ. ... Lay aside, therefore the evil, the old leaven (I Cor. 5:7), and be ye changed into the new leaven of grace. Abide in Christ, that the stranger [Jews in this context] may not have dominion over you. It is absurd to speak of Jesus Christ with the tongue, and to cherish in the mind a Judaism which has now come to an end. For where there is Christianity there cannot be Judaism (Ignatius, *Epistle to the Magnesians, ANF* 1:63).

Ignatius' tone, a decade after the last apostle, John, is to move away from Judaism. Although Ignatius may have been a disciple of the Apostle John, he seems to be more infatuated with the Roman bishops of his day. He had a special esteem for the Roman Bishop Clement, who was the successor of Paul and Peter, as he wrote to a Mary of Neapolis:

> Now it occurs to me to mention, that the report is true which I heard of thee whilst thou wast at Rome with the blessed father Linus, whom the deservedly blessed Clement, a hearer of Peter and Paul, has now succeeded (*The Epistle of Ignatius to Mary at Neapolis,* ibid., 1:122).[252]

It is interesting that in the writings of Ignatius he makes no similar statement concerning the Apostle John, even though tradition tells us that he was a disciple of John. It is therefore hard to believe that one who had seen and heard the Apostle John cannot pass on anything of note about John. Ignatius does not seem to want to identify with John, even though he supposedly had, in his younger years, met with and seen the Apostle John and Mary, the mother of Jesus. Ignatius is even said to have written two Epistles to John and one to Mary, the mother of Jesus. And curiously, Mary is reported to have written back to Ignatius. Although this correspondence has been dismissed as total fiction by critical scholarship, there does not seem anything within these letters that would deem them impossible.

The fact that Ignatius was born around the time that Jesus died, makes it quite possible chronologically that he could have met the mother of Jesus. In any case, these letters, whether genuine or not, may reflect back to the tradition that Ignatius did in fact have early contact with John and Mary.

The curious thing about Mary's letter is that she admonishes Ignatius that John's teachings are true and that Ignatius should believe in them:

> The things which thou has heard and learned from John concerning Jesus are true. Believe them, cling to them, and hold fast the profession of that Christianity which thou hast embraced, and conform thy habits and life to the profession. Now I will come in company with John to visit thee, and those that are with thee. Stand fast in the faith, and show thyself a man; nor let the fierceness of persecution move thee, but let thy spirit be strong and rejoice in God thy Saviour. Amen (ibid., 1:126).

The things that Ignatius learned from John were seemingly authenticated by the mother of Jesus. It almost sounds as if John's message was called into question and Mary, the mother of Jesus, must write to tell Ignatius to "hold fast" to what John taught. Could there have been some suspicion already in the minds of some concerning John's

[252] It would appear from this Epistle that it was written not long after Clement succeeded Linus in 67 C.E. Do notice that according to this testimony, Clement directly succeeds Linus, which is exactly what the *Liber Pontificalis* also reports, but is against what the present day Catholic Church accepts as official. For details, see appendix 4.

different gospel message than that of Matthew, Mark and Luke?

It is most instructive to understand that John, in the beginning of the second century, was not looked upon with all that much esteem. His writings were even looked upon with some suspicion and he constantly had to have others testify that what he wrote was true.

To the Philadelphians, Ignatius had written that they should have one Eucharist. This was written several decades before there were any differences among the churches regarding the taking of the Eucharistic emblems or when they should be taken:

> Wherefore I write boldly to your love, which is worthy of God, and exhort you to have but one faith, and one [kind of] preaching, and one Eucharist. For there is one flesh of the Lord Jesus Christ; and His blood which was shed for us is one; one loaf also is broken to all [the communicants], and one cup is distributed among them all (ibid., 1:83).

Ignatius says that the church should have *one* Eucharist and that the focus was to be on Jesus. Is there a hint here that already there were more than one type of Eucharist being celebrated and Ignatius is calling for a unified method within the church?

The church at Rome was founded by the Apostles Peter and Paul. It is significant that Rome showed no allegiance to the Apostle John in the time of the early church fathers, but only to Peter and Paul. This is so significant to the story that it is necessary to understand the history of this time before moving on.

Irenaeus demonstrates the succession of bishops in the church of Rome from the apostles:

> The blessed apostles (Peter and Paul), then, having founded and built up the Church, committed into the hands of Linus the episcopate. Of this Linus, Paul makes mention in the Epistles to Timothy (II Tim. 4:10). To him succeeded Anacletus; and after him, in the third place from the apostles, Clement was allotted the bishopric. This man, as he had seen the blessed apostles, and had been conversant with them, might be said to have the preaching of the apostles still echoing [in his ears], and their traditions before his eyes (Irenaeus, *Haer.* 3.3.3 [*ANF* 1:416]).

It is indeed striking that Ignatius could be said to still have had the words of the Apostle John echoing in his ears, just as Clement had the preaching of Peter and Paul in his ears, and yet Ignatius never once passed on to his readers a single quote from the Apostle John.[253] Eusebius identified Clement as being the person in the Apostle Paul's letter to the

Philippians (Phil 4:3, quoted by Eusebius, *Hist. eccl.* 3.4.10). And, as we have seen, Ignatius had the highest regard for this Roman bishop, Clement. Irenaeus continues in his list of Roman bishops and then tells us the significance of their authority.

> Evaristus succeeded Clement, and he was succeeded by Sixtus, the sixth from the apostles. After him came Telephorus, who was gloriously martyred, then Hyginus, after him Pius, and then after him Anicetus was appointed. Anicetus was succeeded by Soter and Eleutherius, who is the twelfth from the apostles and now holds the inheritance of the episcopate. In this order, and by this succession, the ecclesiastical tradition from the apostles and the preaching of the truth have come down to us. And this is the most abundant proof that there is one and the same vivifying faith, which has been preserved in the Church from the apostles until now, and handed down in truth (Irenaeus, *Haer.* 3.3.3 [*ANF* 1:416]).

Irenaeus hammers home the idea that the tradition of the bishops of Rome is where "the truth" had "come down to us." Indeed, after making this striking claim, he later says that even if there were no apostolic writings, then this church tradition from Rome should be the over riding guide in determining the truth.

> For how should it be if the apostles themselves had not left us writings? Would it not be necessary in that case to follow the course of the tradition which they handed down to those to whom they handed over the leadership of the churches? (Irenaeus, *Haer.* 3.4.1 [*ANF* 1:417]).[254]

From such a statement we learn at least two important things: 1) The apostles had already left writings in the form of an authoritative canon for instruction for the future church, and 2) In the case where the apostles left no direct instruction on a given matter, then the succession of leadership within the church of Rome was a sufficient replacement.

There is, however, only one problem in this. By the end of the first century there were at least three areas of authority that had emerged, not just Rome. There was the church in Jerusalem, following the bishops of the family of Jesus, the church of Ephesus where the Apostle John had

[253] Some scholars have wondered if Ignatius was even familiar with the writings of John, e.g., W. J. Burghardt, "Did Saint Ignatius of Antioch know the Fourth Gospel?" *Theological Studies* 1 (1940): 1-26 and 130-56. However, Bruce M. Metzger, *The Canon of the New Testament* (Oxford: Oxford University Press, 1992), 46-9, sees a number of allusions to John's Gospel in Ignatius' writings.

[254] Ibid., 3.4.1., 1:417.

settled to administer to Jewish Christians who had fled Palestine to the area of Asia Minor, and finally the church at Rome.[255]

But by the end of the second century, it appears by these testimonies, that the church of Rome was given the eminence by the time of Irenaeus, and the churches of Jerusalem and Ephesus were dismissed without any comment. And with this being said, we now can see right during John's lifetime how his authority was ignored, as well as the bishops of Jerusalem. To see just how much influence Rome had over the other seats of authority in the middle of the second century, we now look in depth at the great Quartodeciman Controversy in the next chapter.

[255] Antioch and Alexandria were other major church areas later on, but at the turn of the second century they were not seats of authority as they would turn out to be in the third and fourth centuries.

CHAPTER 21

The Controversy that Divided the Church

IN THE MIDDLE OF THE SECOND CENTURY OF THE common era a major controversy erupted in the church that shook it to its very foundation.[256] Indeed, this controversy represented a virtual showdown between the legacy of John in Ephesus pitted against the legacy of Peter and Paul in Rome. The early church historian Eusebius gives us his version of the controversy:

> It was at that stage that a controversy of great significance took place, because all the Asian dioceses thought that in accordance with ancient tradition they ought to observe the fourteenth day of the lunar month as the beginning of the Paschal festival – the day on which the Jews had been commanded to sacrifice the lamb (Nisan 14), on that day, no matter which day of the week it might be, they must without fail bring the fast to an end. But nowhere else in the world was it customary to arrange their celebrations in that way: in accordance with apostolic tradition, they preserved the view which still prevails, that it was improper to end the fast on any day other than that of our Saviour's resurrection. So synods and conferences of bishops were convened, and without a dissentient voice, drew up a decree of the Church, in the form of letters addressed to Christians everywhere, that never on any day other than the Lord's Day should the mystery of the Lord's resurrection from the dead be celebrated, and that on that day alone we should observe the end of the Paschal fast (Eusebius, *Hist. eccl.* 5:23:1-2).

This quotation is very revealing. The Asian dioceses of Laodicea and

[256] The controversy actually went on for centuries and in one sense it is still among us to this very day. It may have been quieted from time to time, but it never truly died out. For more on this, see Paul R. Finch, *The Passover Papers* (Palm Bay, Fla.: Sunrise Publications, 1998).

Ephesus observed Nisan 14 based on "ancient tradition" – presumably the "ancient tradition" of the Jews, as well as that of John, the Apostle. These churches were the last hold-outs to this "ancient tradition" because Eusebius goes on to say that even the Palestinian bishops of Jerusalem, Narcissus, and the bishop of Caesarea, Theophilus (Gentile bishops!), had switched to the new ruling of the church of Rome and, therefore, no longer followed the custom of the Eastern "ancient tradition." In other words, they abandoned the practice of keeping a "Christian Passover" in favor of the new custom of celebrating the Eucharist weekly on the day of Christ's resurrection – Sunday.[257]

This new practice was also adopted in Corinth, in Asia Minor, Pontus, Gaul, Osrhöene (in Mesopotamia) – "nowhere else in the world" was Nisan 14 observed. And the church of Rome also based their practice on supposedly "apostolic tradition." The churches of Ephesus and Laodicea were surrounded like a western caravan of Indian war parties. Yet, they appear to be the last hold-outs to the tradition of the Apostle John.

The Asian churches consisted of the last remnants of those who fled from Jerusalem before the war with Rome from 66-70 C.E. They were disparagingly classified as "Quartodecimans" because, in their belief, they were to celebrate the Christian Passover once a year on the 14th of the Hebrew calendar, following the practice of Jewish tradition. These faithful observers of Passover were the last remnants of the Nazarene faction within the church.[258] Later church bishops further denigrated these

---

[257] There are modern day Sabbath keeping followers of Jewish style Christianity that maintain that Jesus was not resurrected on Sunday morning at day break, but rather at sunset of the previous evening, which would be on the Sabbath based on E. W. Bullinger's literal reading of Matthew 12:41. This supposedly demands that Jesus was buried on Wednesday sunset and arose exactly three days and three nights (72 hours) later. See E. W. Bullinger, Appendix 144, "The 'Three Days' and 'Three Nights' of Matt. 12.40," *The Companion Bible* (London: Samuel Bagster & Sons, 1969), 170. This issue has been thoroughly answered in Paul R. Finch, *The Passover Papers* (Palm Bay, Fla.: Sunrise Publications, 1998), 223-51, and by the same author, "Der Tag der Kreuzigung Christi – Freitag oder Mittwoch?," 1995, Online at http://www.wcg.org/de/artikel/crucifix.pdf.

[258] Remember that the term "Nazarene" was derived from Matt 2:23. Later, the Apostle Paul was accused of being a ring leader of the "heresy" of the *Nazoraioi* (Acts 24:5, which, by the way, Paul does not disclaim). The *Book of Acts* tells us that the followers of Jesus were also called Christians (Acts 11:26), which in the context that it was given, implies a derogatory epithet. Interestingly enough, these two terms had later overtones in which the Gentile church of Rome preferred the term of "Christian," while the church of Jerusalem and later Ephesus preferred "Nazarene." The first century lists of heretic groups never mention the Nazarenes as a group that was to be condemned, but later on, as we note above, the remnants in Epiphanius' day were marked out as heretics. Stephen Goranson, "Nazarenes," *The Anchor Bible Dictionary*, David Noel Freedman, ed., [New York: Doubleday, 1992], 4:1049-50, notes: "To define Nazarene, one must take into account the time, place, language, and religious perspective of the speaker, as well as the meanings of other available religious group names."

loyalists to their Hebrew heritage as being of a Christian sect known as the Nazarenes. Epiphanius describes them in the following terms:

> The sect [of the Nazarenes] originated after the flight from Jerusalem, when the disciples were living in Pella, having left the city according to Christ's word and migrated to the mountains because of its imminent siege. Therefore in this manner it arose when those of whom we spoke were living in Perea. From there the heresy of the Nazarenes first began (Epiphanius, *Pan.* 29,7 [PG 42:402]).

Notice that Epiphanius identifies the Nazarenes now as heretics. Yet, what was it that classed them as heretics? Let Epiphanius explain it in his own words:

> The Nazarenes do not differ in any essential thing from them [the Jews!], since they practice the custom and doctrines prescribed by the Jewish law, except that they believe in Christ. They believe in the resurrection of the dead and that the universe was created by God [not Jesus!]. They preach that GOD IS ONE [non-Trinitarian/Binitarian] and that Jesus Christ is his Son. They are very learned in the Hebrew language. They read the law ... Therefore they differ both from the Jews and from the Christians; from the former, because they believe in Christ; from the true Christians because they fulfill till now Jewish rites as the circumcision, the Sabbath and others (ibid.).

One has to ask, what is heretically wrong with this description of the Nazarenes, other than that they still observed Jewish rites and Holy Days? If these be heretics, then this would also make Jesus a heretic, based upon these charges. But in the time that Epiphanius wrote, the church of Rome had moved totally away from "Jewish Christianity." Notice that the Nazarenes also believed in "One God" and that Jesus was his Son, certainly not in any Trinitarian concept that was being adopted by the Roman and Alexandrian churches, which were predominantly Gentile in makeup. In other words, the Nazarenes withstood the pressures of the church of Rome to remain faithful to the beliefs that Jesus himself subscribed to. And in the third and fourth centuries they were now being called heretics.

Back in the second century, the church of Rome took the lead in actually attempting to disfellowship the churches of Ephesus and Laodicea of the Nazarenean persuasion for not following what Rome had decided to be the official liturgy of the now official Catholic Church of Rome.

But we need to ask, what was the apostolic tradition that the Western churches based their practices on? Eusebius gives us no explanation.

Could it be that there was none? Indeed, another early church historian, Sozomen, points out the problem:

> Moreover the Quartodecimans affirm that the observance of the fourteenth day was delivered to them by the apostle John: while the Romans and those in the Western parts assure us that their usage originated with the Apostles Peter and Paul. Neither of these parties however can produce any written testimony in confirmation of what they assert (Sozomen, *Hist. eccl.* 5:22, [*NPNF*[2] 2:131]).

Here we see that both parties claimed apostolic tradition as the basis for their practice. The Quartodecimans (Nazarenes) claimed the Apostle John as their champion, whereas the Western churches claimed the Apostles Peter and Paul for their practice. John's authority in this matter was pitted against that of the Apostles Peter and Paul. But the early church historian, Sozomen, here finds no written confirmation of what these two parties asserted concerning the apostolic authority of their position. Yet, herein lies the very heart of the problem. John outlived the Apostles Peter and Paul by some thirty years. His practices were still within the memory of many of the leading Quartodecimans. Indeed, if the Eastern churches were by and large Quartodecimans, it was because of the influence of the Apostle John, who, by the way, could be said to be a Quartodeciman, if not a "Nazarene," himself.

The Eastern churches, therefore, had ostensibly the stronger case, as far as apostolic authority was concerned. But that had seemingly no apparent weight in the matter. The Roman church would no doubt have liked to have had written authority for their position, but they had none. And even the early church historians, such as Sozomen, could not find a scrap of written evidence that backed up the claims of either side.

The Eastern churches in Asia Minor maintained that a yearly Passover service was the tradition of the Apostle John. And this tradition was transmitted by a disciple of John, whose name was Polycarp (Irenaeus, *Haer.* 3.3.3 [*ANF* 1:416]). Polycarp was martyred around 155 or 156 C.E. He claimed to have served Christ for 86 years, and therefore could have been a centenarian at the time of his death and a definite contemporary of John in his youth (Eusebius, *Hist. eccl.* 4:23, 120).

Unlike many of his contemporaries, Polycarp stands out as one who held fast to the traditions taught by the Apostle John. One of these traditions was the yearly celebration of the Eucharist memorial on Nisan 14. In the last years of his life (ca. 154 C.E.) Polycarp journeyed to Rome (possibly accompanied by Irenaeus) to persuade the Roman bishop, Anicetus, that the yearly memorial of Nisan 14 was the tradition of the Apostle John, which he received, and therefore must continue in practice.

Polycarp must have naïvely believed that his own prestige and testimony as a disciple of the Apostle John in this matter should have persuaded the Roman bishop to change accordingly. Yet, the influence of the Apostle John seems to have had virtually no effect in the matter. This again emphasizes a strange phenomenon concerning the prestige of John and his authority. If during John's own time there were ministers not recognizing his authority, as we have seen in 3 John 1:9, then it is no wonder that John's influence would not be enough to sway the Roman bishop Anicetus in this matter some six decades after John's death.

Not only did the Roman Bishop Anicetus not budge from his position, he switched the tables on Polycarp and seized the opportunity to try to convince Polycarp to change his practice. Much to Polycarp's disappointment, his whole purpose for this one-on-one visit failed to convince Anicetus and the Western bishops to change their own tradition. Polycarp and Anicetus parted in a virtual standoff, but at least, at this period of time, they left on a friendly basis and in respect for each other's position.

The thing to notice is that what we are witnessing here is a struggle between the authority of the church of Rome versus that of Ephesus, the seat of the Asian churches, and the traditional home of the Apostle John for some 30 years. Which tradition was to stand and whose authority would finally be accepted as the one voice of the entire Catholic Church? The winner was Rome, of course. This precedent of the Roman bishop to rebuff the authority of the Apostle John was a major defeat of the Quartodecimans that only ended up solidifying the Roman position hence forward.

A few decades later the dispute between the East and the West was not as gracious. The Quartodeciman problem resurfaced and became once again a hotly contested issue. This time the Roman Bishop Victor attempted to excommunicate whole churches in Asia who did not follow the practice of the Western churches and the decree that they had issued.

The Western bishop Irenaeus from Lyons, France (Gaul), supported "the view that only on the Lord's Day might the mystery of the Lord's resurrection be celebrated," which was a position supporting the practice of the Roman Church (Eusebius, *Hist. eccl.* 5:24:9-11). Nevertheless, even Irenaeus could not support Victor in his wholesale decision to banish the churches of Asia over this dispute.

Irenaeus, like many other bishops with him, felt that Victor had gone too far and urged Victor, in a letter, to come to his senses and not ostracize entire churches because of this matter. Irenaeus wrote a letter back to the Roman bishop Victor concerning this, preserved by Eusebius, and it is here where we are informed of the earlier Polycarp incident.

Irenaeus writes the following:

> The dispute is not only about the day, but also about the actual character of the fast. Some think that they ought to fast for one day, some for two, others for still more; some make their 'day' last forty hours on end. Such variation in the observance did not originate in our own day, but very much earlier, in the time of our forefathers, who – apparently disregarding strict accuracy – in their naïve simplicity kept up a practice which they fixed for the time to come. In spite of that, they all lived in peace with one another, and so do we: the divergency in the fast emphasizes the unamity of our faith. ... Among these were the presbyters before Soter, who were in charge of the church of (Rome) which you are the present leader (Victor) – I mean Anicetus, Pius, Hyginus, Telesphorus, and Xystus. They did not keep it (Nisan 14) themselves or allow those under their wing to do so. But in spite of their not keeping it (Nisan 14), they lived in peace with those who came to them from the dioceses in which it was kept, though to keep it was more objectionable to those who did not. Never was this made a ground for repulsing anyone, but the presbyters before you, even though they did not keep it, used to send the Eucharist to Christians from dioceses which did.
>
> And when Blessed Polycarp paid a visit to Rome in Anicetus' time, though they had minor differences on other matters too, they at once made peace, having no desire to quarrel on this point. Anicetus could not persuade Polycarp not to keep the day, since he had always kept it with John the disciple of our Lord and the other apostles with whom he had been familiar; nor did Polycarp persuade Anicetus to keep it: Anicetus said that he must stick to the practice of the presbyters before him. Though the position was such, they remained in communion with each other, and in church Anicetus made way for Polycarp to celebrate the Eucharist – out of respect, obviously. They parted company in peace, and the whole Church was at peace, both those who kept the day and those who did not (Eusebius, *Hist. eccl.* 5:24:12-17).

Irenaeus admits that the "forefathers" of the bishops of Rome only went back as far as Xystus (Sixtus I). Obviously, Xystus was responsible for the new tradition of the Sunday Eucharist. Also, we see that Xystus "apparently disregarding strict accuracy – in their naïve simplicity kept up a practice which they fixed for the time to come." Thus, it was not apostolic tradition that the church of Rome had derived their practice, but rather a tradition that only went back some 50 years before Victor, to the time of the Roman bishop Xystus.

Eusebius tells us that Xystus was bishop for ten years, from the third year of Hadrian to Hadrian's year twelve (119-128 C.E., Eusebius, *Hist. eccl.* 4:4:1; 4:5:5). Irenaeus lists Xystus as being the sixth bishop from the Apostles Peter and Paul (Irenaeus, *Haer.* 3:3:4 [*ANF* 1:416]).

It was at this very time, during the reign of the Emperor Hadrian, that anti-semitism became acute in the Roman Empire. It finally ended in the Bar Kochba blood bath in the Province of Judea in 135 C.E. It was also during this period of time that the pagan Romans could hardly distinguish Christians from the Jews in practice. They generally considered Christians as a Jewish sect rather than a distinct religion in its own right. Such a situation brought undo persecution to Christians.

It is believed that during the time of the Roman Emperors, Domitian (81-96 C.E.) and Trajan (98-117 C.E.), many Christians were persecuted and executed. For the bishop of Rome to be following Jewish religious practices during such an uneasy period of time must have certainly had an influence on those bishops at the seat of Roman power to move away from Jewish practices and evolve its own distinct identity.

Xystus is recorded as having united the Roman church with the colony of Asiatic Greek Christian residents within the capital city.[259] The fact that Xystus was credited for such diplomacy may reveal his ability and skill to lead the church of Rome during this dangerous time. Indeed, political expediency must have been the motivation for Xystus to dare make a change in the Paschal observance for the church. If Xystus disregarded "strict accuracy" concerning the Paschal Feast, it was for the benefit of establishing a new church liturgy that was more in keeping with a commemoration of the founder of the Christian faith and less offending to the Roman authorities. Indeed, as time moved on, the church of Rome was saying by its evolving liturgy that it would rather have Jesus than Moses. The Gentile bishops of Rome were trying to move away from Judaism, while many in the Eastern churches in Asia were trying to cling to the old traditions of the Jewish apostles, and especially that of John.

There were other factors that caused, indeed, forced the church of Rome to move away from anything that seemed to identify Christianity in the eyes of the Roman emperors as a sectarian faction of Judaism. This was especially true in the time of Hadrian (117-38 C.E.), who was the Emperor during the second Jewish revolt of 135 C.E.

It was right after this time that the Quartodeciman Controversy erupted in Asia Minor. Xystus had no choice but to change the direction

---

[259] Nicholas Cheetham, *A History of the Popes* (New York: Dorset, 1992), 10.

of the church of Rome from Judaism to that which had no appearance with anything Judaic.[260] Obviously, Xystus felt that he had to abandon the tradition of the church up to that time in favor of a more neutral observance that had no dependence on Judaism. So, in reality, there was no apostolic tradition that the Roman church bishops could definitely appeal to, only to the "forefathers," i.e., the bishops who preceded Victor down to Xystus, that maintained this position. Samuele Bacchiocchi notes:

> Bishop Sixtus (ca. A.D. 116-ca. 126) ...administered the Church of Rome right at the time of Emperor Hadrian (A.D. 117-138) who ... adopted a policy of radical repression of Jewish rites and customs. These repressive measures would encourage Christians to substitute for customs regarded as Jewish, new ones. ...It was also at that historical moment that, according to Epiphanius, the Easter-controversy arose.[261]

It is around this time also that new literature was beginning to be circulated that bore apostle's names, but were obviously written at this time, in order to strengthen the Roman position. The so-called *Epistle of Barnabas* was written around the time of Xystus. In that Epistle we see another move away from Judaism, where Sunday is now beginning to be emphasized in favor of the Jewish Sabbath. Here we see 'Barnabas' quoting Isaiah 1:13 in explaining that the Sabbaths are no longer essential to Christians, but rather the day in which Jesus was resurrected had more significance.

Finally, the author of *Barnabas* says:

> "I cannot bear your new moons and sabbath" [quoting Isa 1:13]. You see what he means: it is not the present sabbaths that are acceptable to me, but the one that I have made; on that Sabbath, after I have set everything at rest, I will create the beginning of an eighth day, which is the beginning of another world. This is why we spend the eighth day in celebration, the day on which Jesus both arose from the dead and, after appearing again, ascended into heaven.[262]

Could this be the apostolic tradition that the Western churches could now appeal? Barnabas was an apostle and a companion to the Apostle

---

260 "The controversy arose after the time of the exodus of the bishops of the circumcision [from Jerusalem in 135 C.E.] and it has continued until our time," Epiphanius, *Pan.* 70:9 [PG 42:355-56].

261 Samuele Bacchiocchi, *From Sabbath to Sunday* (Rome: The Pontifical Gregorian University Press, 1977), 200.

Paul. If this letter was beginning to be circulated around the time of Xystus, claiming the authority of the Apostle Barnabas, then what we would have here is one of the first writings that presumably bears apostolic authority, which promotes the observance of Sunday instead of the Jewish Sabbath. The position of the Western bishops was therefore in motion to move away from Jewish practices of observing Sabbaths and Feasts.

By the time of the Roman bishop of Rome, Victor (189-99 C.E.), the Roman practice was pronounced the only acceptable method allowable, which only brought matters to a head.[263] What was it that so infuriated the Roman Bishop Victor that he wished to cut off the churches of Asia? It was a Quartodeciman bishop of Ephesus, the former seat of the Apostle John's authority and legacy, by the name of Polycrates, who defied the decision of the Synods and even dared to rebuke the Roman Bishop Victor in a most stern manner.

The showdown between Ephesus and Rome had finally arrived. Ephesus, the seat of John's authority, was now represented by the bishop Polycrates. He was now directly facing off with Victor, the bishop of Rome. Notice this amazing letter from Polycrates to the Roman church, which spells out the Asian position, backed up by real Apostolic authority that he could cite as proof of his premise:

> We for our part keep the day [Nisan 14 Passover] scrupulously, without addition or subtraction. For in Asia great luminaries sleep who shall rise again on the day of the Lord's advent, when He is coming with glory from heaven and shall search out all His saints – such as Philip, one of the twelve apostles, who sleeps in Hierapolis with

---

[262] *The Epistle of Barnabas,* 15:8-9 in *The Apostolic Fathers,* trans. J. B. Lightfoot and J. R. Harmer, 2d ed. (Grand Rapids: Baker, 1989), 183. The term "eighth day" is interesting because in a seven day weekly cycle there is no such thing as an eighth day. Yet, Barnabas himself seems to be introducing a new significance to the eighth day in the overall plan of God. Notice: "He [God] speaks of the Sabbath at the beginning of the creation: 'And God made the works of his hands in six days, and finished on the seventh day, and rested on it, and sanctified it' [Gen 2:2-3]. Observe, children, what "he finished in six days" means. It means this: that in six thousand years the Lord will bring everything to an end, for with him a day signifies a thousand years. And he himself bears me witness when he says, 'Behold, the day of the Lord will be as a thousand years' [2 Pet 3:8]. Therefore, children, in six days – that is, in six thousand years – everything will be brought to an end. 'And he rested on the seventh day.' This means: when his Son comes, he will destroy the time of the lawless one and will judge the ungodly and will change the sun and the moon and the stars, and then he will truly rest on the seventh day" (*Barnabas,* 13).

[263] Victor himself is said to have written a work on the Paschal Feast, but this too has been lost: "Victor, thirteenth bishop of Rome, wrote, *On the Paschal Controversy* and some other small works. He ruled the church for ten years in the reign of the Emperor Severus," so states Jerome, *Vir. ill.* 34 (*NPNF*[2] 3:370).

> two of his daughters, who remained unmarried to the end of their days, while his other daughter lived in the Holy Spirit and rests in Ephesus. Again there is John, who leant back on the Lord's breast, and who became a priest wearing the mitre, a martyr, and a teacher, he too sleeps in Ephesus. Then in Smyrna there is Polycarp, bishop and martyr; and Thraseas, the bishop and martyr from Eumenia, who also sleeps in Laodicea, or blessed Papirius, or Melito the eunuch, who lived entirely in the Holy Spirit, and who lies in Sardis waiting for the visitation from heaven when he shall rise from the dead. All of these kept the fourteenth day of the month as the beginning of the Paschal festival, in accordance with the Gospel [apparently appealing to the Gospel of John], not deviating in the least but following the rule of Faith. Last of all I too, Polycrates, the least of you all, act according to the tradition of my family, some members of which I have actually followed; for seven of them were bishops and I am the eighth, and my family have always kept the day when the people put away the leaven. So I, my friends, after spending sixty-five years in the Lord's service and conversing with Christians from all parts of the world, and going carefully through all Holy Scripture, am not scared of threats. Better people than I have said: 'We must obey God rather than men' (Eusebius, *Hist. eccl.* 5:24:2-7).

Wow! What a powerful indictment against the bishop of Rome. Polycrates stands on the authority of the Apostles John, Phillip, and other leading Asiatic bishops. His courageous words end with a Scriptural quotation of the Apostle Peter in Acts 5:29. This, no doubt, was a biting remark to the bishop of Rome who claimed to be a successor of the Apostle Peter, but who could produce no apostolic authority for his own position, other than obedience to the bishop Xystus and his successors.

Once again, John's authority is called upon to settle the matter and once again the bishop of Rome ignores John's authority. It is as if the Apostle John had absolutely no weight at all in changing the policy of the Roman bishops. And yet, the bishop of Rome is only following the lead of his predecessors right on back to the time of Clement, the second bishop of Rome that spurned the authority of John, as well as Diotrephes, who cast out John's ministers from the church (3 John 1:9).

The bishops of Rome rested on their succession from the Apostles Peter and Paul. They not only paid no attention to Ephesus, the seat of John's authority, but refused to acknowledge John's authority in settling a matter of dispute. Rome was flexing its muscles of authority and winning. Even though Ephesus and Rome were at a standoff, Rome could reject the authority of John's heritage and get away with it.

The showdown of Polycrates and Victor, just like in the days of Polycarp and Anicetus, was a draw. Anatolius of Alexandria (d. ca. 268 C.E.), goes on to explain that neither side at this time would fold under the weight of each others supposed authority:

> Following their example up to the present time all the bishops of Asia – as themselves also receiving the rule from an unimpeachable authority, to wit, the evangelist John,[264] who leant on the Lord's breast, and drank in instructions spiritual without doubt – were the way of celebrating the Paschal feast, without question, every year, whenever the fourteenth day of the moon had come, and the lamb was sacrificed by the Jews after the equinox was past; not acquiescing, so far as regards this matter, with the authority of some, namely the successors of Peter and Paul, who have taught all the churches in which they sowed the spiritual seeds of the Gospel, that the solemn festival of the resurrection of the Lord can be celebrated only on the Lord's day. Whence also a certain contention broke out between the successors of these, namely, Victor, at the time bishop of the city of Rome and Polycrates, who then appeared to hold the primacy among the bishops of Asia, and this contention was adjusted most rightfully by Irenaeus, at the time President of a part of Gaul, so that both parties kept by their own order, and did not decline from the original custom of antiquity. The one party [the Quartodeciman] indeed kept the paschal day on the fourteenth day of the first month, according to the Gospel [of John], as they thought adding nothing of an extraneous kind, but keeping through all things the rule of faith and the other party [the Sunday proponents], passing the day of the Lord's passion as one replete with sadness and grief, hold that it should not be lawful to celebrate the Lord's mystery of the Passover at any other time but on the Lord's day, on which the resurrection of the Lord from death took place and on which rose also for us the cause of everlasting joy.[265]

Anatolius of Alexandria put his finger exactly on the problem by showing that the Pascal Controversy really boiled down to a showdown between the church of Rome (who felt that their authority was derived directly from Peter and Paul) – and the authority of Ephesus (who rested in the fact that their authority was derived from the Apostle John). It is as if Rome needed an excuse to flex its muscles against the last remnants of

---

[264] Notice here that the "Evangelist John" is none other than the Apostle John by way of the description that he leaned on the Lord's breast.

[265] *The Paschal Canon of Anatolius of Alexandria,* 10, in *ANF,* 6:148-9.

Jewish Christianity within the church in order to achieve its preeminence.

The significant point for us to consider here is that, although Rome pitted Peter and Paul against John in matters of liturgy, Rome knew too well that the canon of Scripture that John left behind had the endorsement of Peter and Paul, as well as John. They therefore did not meddle with it, other than to push the Jewish Epistles (general or Catholic Epistles) back behind the Epistles of Paul (apostle to the Gentiles), producing an arrangement that put the Epistle to Rome as the first Epistle right after the *Book of Acts.*

Canon scholars need to get a real appreciation of this important struggle between the power seats of Ephesus and Rome in the second century. Once such an appreciation is realized, then we are forced to conclude that there is simply no way that the church of Rome, after the second century, would ever have shaped the canon as it now stands, leaving out Clement, Barnabas, Ignatius, and a host of other material that would have supported their authority over the legacy of John.

Unfortunately, modern day post apostolic canonization theories are totally bereft of any idea of the struggle between John's tradition and that of Rome. And since the canon was archived within the great libraries of Caesarea and Alexandria long before the Quartodeciman struggle began, there was simply nothing that the "Church" of Rome could do to change it, other than reorder certain books later on.

Thus, the Quartodeciman Controversy is very important to the story because it informs us of the struggle that went on between Rome and Ephesus, and how eventually the authority of Rome triumphed. The Quartodecimans continued within the church for quite some time, but the final blow came at the Council of Nicea in 325, where it was finally established that Easter would replace the traditional Jewish Passover observance.

The road to Nicea was a hard and difficult one, but that story lies beyond the scope of this book and, unfortunately, will have to await a future volume. For now, our story will have to end here.

CHAPTER 22

Conclusion

THE GREATEST POST ACTS ENDEAVOR OF THE apostles was the solidifying and canonizing efforts of Paul, Peter and John. These three men could be said to be the real canonizers of the New Testament. Each had a major share in the enterprise, and it is clearly evident if we look at the internal evidence as the primary source of our thesis. It is they, with the help of John Mark, Luke, Timothy, Apollos, Silvanus, the Apostle John's "elders," the Apostle Andrew, Philip and maybe countless others of the apostolic era that helped in the effort to establish a "New Testament" body of literature for those that would be called to the faith in future eras of the church. But in the final analysis, it was the Apostles Peter and John who gave us the canon of the New Testament.

The three-fold testimony of the New Testament resounds in one very important fact that no one can deny:

> Heaven and earth shall pass away, by MY words shall NOT pass away (Matt 24:35; Mark 13:31; Luke 21:33)!

And guess what? These words, plus the entire gospel message, still exists to this very day! The words that have been carefully documented by the early apostles of Jesus have not passed away. And they still find fulfillment in the fact that they are in every corner of the world in every language today.

The Apostle Peter was inspired to write: "The word of the Lord endures forever" (1 Pet 1:25). And it is because of Peter's diligent efforts, as well as that of the Apostle Paul's and John's, that the gospel message is here with us to this very day.

But most significantly to the entire subject of canonization is the understanding of the importance of the *Book of Revelation* as being the final "Word" on the entire subject. The *Book of Genesis* introduces us to the revelation of God, and significantly, the *Book of Revelation* closes that revelation in a most complimentary way. In this respect, the expression "the alpha and the omega" not only represents the central figure of the entire word of God, but implies that the *Book of Genesis* is the alpha book and the *Book of Revelation* is indeed the omega book of the entire revelation of God.

The *Book of Genesis* introduces God's creative work in the introduction of the human race into the universe. And at the end of the *Book of Revelation* we see the conclusion of the plan of God in the Great White Throne Judgment. It is here we read:

> And I saw the dead, great and small, standing before the throne, and BOOKS were opened. Also another BOOK was opened, the BOOK OF LIFE. And the dead were judged according to their works, as recorded in the BOOKS. And the sea gave up the dead that were in them, and all were judged according to what they had done. Then Death and Hades were thrown into the lake of fire. This is the second death, the lake of fire; and anyone whose name was not found written in the BOOK OF LIFE was thrown into the lake of fire (Rev 20:12-15).

This is a prophecy of the great resurrection of the dead wherein a judgment process begins. The prophecy makes it clear that it is by means of books and the "book of life" that people will be judged – indeed, "by the things written in THE BOOKS [τοῖς βιβλίοις]" (v. 12). It is significant that John uses the definite article to describe "the books." The implication is THE complete set of books that are now contained within the entire two testament Bible.[266]

It is also clear that the Apostle John had in mind in the *Book of Revelation* the entire canon of Scripture that he had finalized, for he had already made it clear in his Gospel that

> the one who rejects me and does not receive my word has a judge; on the last day the word that I have spoken will serve as judge, for I have not spoken on my own, but the Father who sent me has himself given me a commandment about what to say and what to speak. And I know that his commandment is eternal life. What I speak, therefore, I speak just as the Father has told me (John 13:48-50).

How could the words of Jesus judge anyone if they were not recorded

[266] Daniel 7:9-10 gives a similar scene of judgment where the "Ancient one took his throne ...the court sat in judgment, and [the] books were opened." Translators have supplied a definite article before "books" that is not in the original Aramaic. In other words, in Daniel's time there was not yet a complete and definite set of books in existence for judgment. John, however, could now refer to a definite set of books with his final contribution of the *Book of Revelation.*

in an official way? John obviously understood his role in canonizing the words of Jesus for the future church, especially so with his final words on the subject:

> And the one who was seated on the throne said, "See, I am making all things new." and he said, "Write this, for these words are trustworthy and true." Then he said to me, "It is done! I am the Alpha and the Omega, the beginning and the end" (Rev 21:5-6).

The word of God has been brought to a conclusion. John's final words show us just that:

> I warn everyone who hears the words of the prophecy of this book: if anyone adds to them, God will add to that person the plagues described in this book; if anyone takes away from the words of the book of this prophecy, God will take away that person's share in the TREE OF LIFE and in the holy city, which are described in this book (Rev 22:18-19).

Thus, the Tree of Life that was introduced in the *Book of Genesis* is tied to the final words of the completed canon of Scripture. It is in this light that we must understand that the apostles knew very well that their testimony would be corrupted and lost if they did not cast in concrete what they had so strongly proclaimed. The Apostle Paul wrote to the church at Thessalonia: "Be not soon shaken in mind, or be troubled, neither by spirit, nor by word, NOR BY LETTER AS FROM US ... Let no man deceive you by ANY MEANS" (2 Thess 2:2-3).

Today, scholars tell us the pseudonymous writers after the apostles had written letters "as from us." Paul's warning to believers is "let no man deceive you by ANY MEANS." Could the "means" which Paul is referring to be what we see in writings that abound in some scholarly circles today?

The instruction to the followers of Jesus in every age is to be not deceived by pseudonymity. We should listen to these stern words, for they come from an apostle of Christ! The utter sense of urgency on the part of the apostles, which is expressed in statements like these, is a real criterion of authenticity that is enough to dismiss the entire idea of pseudonymity. The apostles feared the worst in the apostacizing forces that were even then at large.[267]

---

[267] The *Epistle of Barnabas* appears to be the first apostolic hoax written in the name of an original apostle of the first century. Whether or not it contained genuine material from the Apostle Barnabas is irrelevant, since it was not included in the canon of Paul, Peter, or John, and is therefore uncanonical, as it should ever remain.

The gradual acceptance theory of how the New Testament came to be, maintained by most of modern day scholarship, is an exercise in futility. We therefore maintain the following premise. The subject of canonization should be considered an issue that is totally black and white. In other words, if the gradual acceptance theory be true, then the message of the New Testament should indeed be considered a total myth. There are no in-between gray areas. Gradual acceptance theories only ultimately lead to Burton Mack/Robert Funk scenarios. There is no middle ground.

It is because conservative biblical scholars have flirted with the ridiculous idea of first pseudonymity and then the gradual acceptance theory, that they are the real ones responsible for allowing modern day agnostic atheists to take over and dominate the thinking on the subject. The end result is that the entire subject has disintegrated into theories of nonsense. Indeed, canon scholarship represents *the* very worst area of biblical scholarship that exists today. It is filled with unsubstantiated guess work from beginning to end that is entirely amiss with the overall message of the inspired works within the canon.

Modern day Gnosticism is not the direction to find the truth. The Apostle Paul sternly and vehemently warned:

> Guard what has been entrusted to you. Avoid the profane chatter and contradictions of what is falsely called knowledge [gnosis] (1 Tim 6:20).

New Testament scholars of today, under the guise of being critical, have let down their guard. The true Jesus myth-makers are the so-called "Jesus Scholars" of today. Indeed, the latest bunch of "Jesus" scholars make no bones about their belief in the fact that the New Testament is the chief obstacle to being able to see the real Jesus of history. What kind of nonsense is this? Is the real Jesus of history to be found in the writings of modern day agnostics? The ax that they grind is to destroy the very body of literature that was produced to perpetuate and proclaim the work of the eternal God through the testament of his original disciples and apostles.

This new fringe element of modern day scholarship is getting all the sensational publicity in the media today, but fails to understand, appreciate, and recognize the form, the breath, and the life of the very soul of the New Testament. They, frankly, haven't the slightest clue as to what they are up against.

The New Testament canon resounds with a message of the earliest Nazarene Jewish followers of Jesus. That their vision has been blurred and obscured by a later Gentile Christian legacy of Rome and Alexandria is exactly what the apostles had feared and predicted would happen. Yet scholars look to these areas for the answers concerning canon development. And because they have falsely viewed the New Testament as a post apostolic production, then it is easy to see the reason why they are off chasing rainbows in the second, third, and fourth centuries. The entire enterprise is fortuitous simply because their endeavor has produced nothing but pure speculation. It is the greatest example of the Emperor's New Cloths scenario that exists today in biblical scholarship. Many scholars are guilty of seeing something that does not exist. Let those who have not been so indoctrinated stand up and be counted. Like the Emperor, the entire gradual acceptance theory is totally devoid of any fabric of truth.

There never was any post apostolic canonizing endeavor, pure and simple. Scholars can't find evidence for such an activity – no discussions, no meetings, no councils, no writings of an official nature – there is absolutely nothing.

> The striking fact that the early Councils had nothing whatever to do with forming the canon of the New Testament, has been so emphasized by a number of writers that one is astonished that it is not more widely known.[268]

Again, we read:

> It is a remarkable fact that we have no early interference of Church authority in the making of a Canon; no Council discussed the subject; no formal decisions were made. The Canon seems to have shaped itself; and if, when we come further on, you are disposed to complain of this because of the vagueness of the testimony of antiquity to one or two disputed books, let us remember that this non-interference of authority is a valuable topic of evidence to the genuineness of our Gospels; for it thus appears that it was owing to no adventitious authority, but by their own weight, that they crushed all rivals out of existence. Whence could they have had this weight except from its being known that the framers of these Gospels were men of superior authority to the others, or with access to fuller information?[269]

It is an amazing testimony to the canon that when we come to the second century we find the "Church Fathers" quoting from all over the New Testament as if it already existed as a completed canon. The reason

---

[268] John Urquhart, *The Bible: Its Structure and Purpose.* (New York: Gospel Publishing House, 1904), 1:37.

[269] George Salmon, *A Historical Introduction to the Study of the Books of the New Testament,* (New York: E & JB Young & Co., 1889), 144.

is obvious for those who have eyes to see. The canon was already established and secure in the great Caesarean Library. It is from the protection of that archive that copies were distributed to local congregations and other libraries.[270]

The word of God was to emanate from Israel, and it did (Isa 2:3). Neither Rome, nor Alexandria, can claim being the originators of the New Testament canon.

Hopefully, a new generation of scholarship will emerge that will to correctly evaluate the internal evidence and come to correct conclusions about the canon. In this regard it is refreshing to see that in some circles of scholarship they are coming to grips with the totality of a completed New Testament in the earliest stages of transmission. Note Everett Ferguson's discussion of the insightful work of David Trobisch:[271]

> Instead of taking the usual history of theology approach of tracing the development [of the Canon] by examining literary sources, Trobisch argues that the proper approach is to examine the history of the Christian Bible as a book. The four oldest manuscripts of the New Testament – Sinaiticus, Vaticanus, Alexandrinus, and Ephraemi Rescriptus – are from the fourth and fifth centuries. Each manuscript is independent of the others, but their agreement in extent and order of contents means we must assume a common archetype. The external identifying characteristics of the witnesses to the text of the christian Bible – the types of abbreviation of the *nomina sacra*, use of the codex, a common pattern of names for the individual books ("Gospel according to ..."; "General Epistle of ..."; "Epistle of Paul to

[270] Scholars somehow have the idea that the scattered local congregations were the sole repositories of what later became the canon of the New Testament. But if this were true, then we could expect that all kinds of corruptions would have infiltrated the text of the New Testament. And Bart Ehrman (*The Orthodox Corruption of Scripture* [London: Oxford University Press, 1993]) has shown us that this was the case with later editions that were obviously tampered with for doctrinal reasons. Unfortunately for his thesis, however, is that it leaves the impression that there is no recourse for determining the true text. But the answer lies in the fact that Caesarean Library maintained accurate copies of the original text. And this is why it is important to understand that the codex Vaticanus, which apparently was one of the 50 Bibles that the Emperor Constantine had underwritten, was produced in that great Library. The genius of the apostles was to safe-guard the New Testament books away from the bickering congregations that the apostles themselves could see were falling into apostasy. Indeed, the Vaticanus may very well represent one of the purest forms of text to judge all others by that exists today, since it was produced from the great Caesarean Library where the elders of John had deposited the original text. This will be dealt with in appendix 10.

[271] David Trobisch, *Die Endredaktion des Neuen Testaments: Eine Untersuchung zur Entstehung der christlichen Bibel* (Freiburg: Unversitätsverlag: Göttingen: Vandenhoech & Ruprecht, 1996) and the English volume, idem, *The First Edition of the New Testament* (Oxford: Oxford University Press, 2000).

> ..."), and a uniform name for the two parts of the whole collection ("New Testament" and "Old Testament") – all go back to the earliest stage of transmission. They show the work of a single redactor who produced the canonical edition of the New Testament as part of a total Christian scripture.[272]

Modern day New Testament scholarship comes ever so close, but still can't see the testimony of the internal evidence. And until they do and throw off pseudonymity and gradual acceptance theories, they never will be able to produce a credible history of the canon that accurately portrays the actual events of the last days of the apostles.

The New Testament canon simply cannot be a part of the second century and beyond. The apostles warned of the coming apostasy that would follow them. To combat this, they canonized their writings and placed them in the guardianship of the great library at Caesarea in Palestine. But what do scholars do? They look to the post-apostolic church for clues about the canon. Their entire methodology is doomed from the start. They have fallen right into the hands of the greatest of all deceptions in literary history.

For example, when scholars bring Marcion to the forefront of the discussion and see him as part of the long process of gradual acceptance, they have derailed their entire ability to see the truth. Marcion's confusion and prejudice of what should be in the New Testament and what should not has not the slightest bearing on the reality that the New Testament canonization. It was already complete by his time.

We also must not forget the fact that if the church of the West, i.e., Rome and Alexandria, ever for one moment had a hand in forming a "New Testament," as we have herein maintained, we can be assured that it most certainly never, *never*, NEVER! – would have come down to us with the books now contained therein – and scholars should no better than to have missed such an obvious fact! It is an entirely ridiculous notion that the New Testament is a post apostolic creation for all the reasons that we have brought out within this volume, not the least of which is this one fact alone.

To be sure, if the post-apostolic church ever had a hand in producing a New Testament, we must realize that it could never have carried the

---

[272] Everett Ferguson, "Factors Leading to the Selection and Closure of the New Testament Canon: A Survey of Some Recent Studies" in *The Canon Debate: On the Origins and Formation of the Bible* (ed. Lee Martin McDonald and James A. Sanders, Peabody, Mass.: Hendrickson, 2002), 311. Ferguson, ibid., also notes that Trobisch "does not venture a specific place, person or circle where this edition originated." The reason, of course, is that even Trobisch is guilty of looking into the second century for such evidence, but, alas, there is no evidence that any canonizing activity ever took place during that time or later.

weight and authority of being of the "Word of God" – nor even the authority of the apostles. And given what we now know about the warnings of future heresies by the apostles that were to come within the church, a post-apostolic New Testament would have only left us with a heretical sham that would be worthless for deciding true doctrine for the period of the church *Beyond Acts*. It is therefore no surprise that the conclusion of the new Jesus scholars, who have muscled in on the New Testament scholarship scene like gang busters – with their "destructive opinions" (2 Pet 2:1) – have entirely no regard to the sanctity of canonized Scripture.

Canon scholars would do well in recalling the words of the great Roman Catholic Church leader, Augustine, who wrote:

> Distinguished from the books of later authors is the excellence of the canonical authority of the Old and New Testaments; which, having been ESTABLISHED IN THE TIME OF THE APOSTLES, hath through the succession of overseers and propagators of churches been set as it were in a lofty tribunal, demanding the obedience of every faithful and pious understanding (Augustine, *Faust.* 11.5 [*PL* 42:249]).

The authority of the New Testament hangs in the balance of our thesis. It stands or falls on whether the apostles themselves canonized their writings or not! This premise alone demands that the decision of what was to be included within the New Testament was not left to chance, nor to later bickering church clerics who themselves were confused over the authorship and validity of various New Testament books.

If our premise is wrong, then the New Testament writings are indeed mere myths, just as the Jesus Seminar scholars maintain. This is why, in one sense, the subject of canonization is the most important biblical topic of all. Indeed, it is entirely worthless to discuss anything else within the entire Bible if the basis for the discussion is in itself found to be in reality mythology. The horse must be made to be put before the cart. The authority of the entire Bible stands or falls on what we have brought out in this volume.

In the words of the great canonizer, the Apostle Peter, we are reassured that we have the message that was intended to be handed down to the end of this time period in the plan of God:

> For we did not follow cleverly devised myths when we made known to you the power and coming of our Lord Jesus Christ, but we had been eyewitnesses of the his majesty. ...So we have the prophetic message more fully confirmed. You will do well to be attentive to this as to a lamp shining in a dark place, until the day dawns and the

morning star rises in your hearts (2 Pet 1:16, 19).

A line has now been drawn in the sand that merits the attention of all those seeking the truth in this matter. The case that we have presented for the true history of the New Testament canon is as solid as any emanating from esteemed scholars in higher institutions of learning around the world. Their guess work and anti-spiritual bias cannot take away from the fact that the Bible is a phenomenon like no other literary production in all of human history. They are perplexed by its audacity to be the Word of God. They are dumbfounded by its ubiquitous presence. It has survived despite "destructive opinions," persecutions, and book burnings that have sought to extinguish its existence. And how did it all came about? The answer can only be in the scenario that we have herein submitted. Anything short of that renders the entire story as ALL myth.

APPENDIX 1

Who Wrote Second Peter?

MODERN DAY SCHOLARSHIP IS VIRTUALLY united in rejecting the idea that the Apostle Peter wrote the Epistle known as Second Peter. Indeed, we can be fairly certain that all critical scholarship entirely rejects the idea of Petrine authorship.[273]

On the other hand, the autobiographical internal evidence (2 Pet 1:13, 14, 16-18; 3:1) puts the conservative and faithful believer of the inerrancy of Scripture in an uneasy predicament. Unfortunately, inerrist apologetics have only been seen as damage control that has done little to reverse the tide of critical thinking on this matter. Nevertheless, it is important for the reader to realize just what is at stake here. Indeed, the importance of this matter cannot be thought of as some minor point of interest. The reality is that the very inspiration and authority of the entire Bible stands or falls on this one point alone!

The question that we pointedly ask, therefore, is this: do these biblical critics really have proof that the Apostle Peter did not write the Second Epistle bearing his own name? The answer is no![274] Smoking guns and negative evidence do not represent solid proof of their assertions. At the outset, we must first consider a significant point that should make us take this matter more seriously:

> The epistle specifically claims to be the work of Simon Peter (1:1). The writer represents himself as having been present at the Transfiguration of Christ (1:16-18); and of having been warned by Christ of his impending death (1:14). This means that the Epistle is a genuine writing of

[273] W. G. Kümmel, *Introduction to the New Testament* (Nashville: Abingdon, 1986), 43-4, presents all the classic arguments that force critical scholars to recognize Second Peter as a pseudigraph and written as much as a century after the Apostle Peter lived. His argument can be viewed online at: http://www.earlychristianwritings.com/2peter.html. For a detailed alternative discussion, see http://www.christian-thinktank.com/ynotpeter1.html.

[274] This has been adequately demonstrated in E. M. B. Green, *2 Peter Reconsidered* (London: Tyndale, 1960), of which some of the poignant points are reiterated here.

> Peter, or that it was the work of some one who professed himself to be Peter. ...Some modern critics regard it as a pseudonymous work of the late second century, written by some unknown person who assumed Peter's name, a hundred years after Peter's death. To the average mind this would be just plain common forgery, an offense against civil and moral law and ordinary decency. The critics, however, over and over aver that there is nothing at all unethical in thus counterfeiting another's name.[275]

If scholars find that pseudonymity is not at all unethical with letters in the name of apostles, who, by the way, condemned false apostles in the strongest of language, then we can only assume, like they do, that the New Testament is nothing more than ancient literature on the same level as Plato and Homer. This makes the entire matter quite simple in coming to a resolution. Either the New Testament can speak on its own behalf in the strongest of terms against pseudonymity, or we do indeed have a collection of myths, just as is claimed in some circles of New Testament scholarship. There is simply no middle ground to stand on whatsoever. Let us see the reasons why.

Both Epistle's of Peter record that they came from "Simon Peter." Yet, we are told to believe that some imposter a century later wrote this Epistle – a deliberate lie! – and then signed his name as the Apostle Peter. Would the Christian church then accept this Epistle as Peter's, long after Peter was dead, in the light of the Apostle Paul's scathing denunciation of "false apostles... disguising themselves as apostles of Christ" (1 Cor 11:13)?[276]

Also consider the fact that the writer of Second Peter speaks of the Transfiguration as an eyewitness, he reflects upon the prophecy of his own death, and talks about bringing into remembrance in the future concerning the promises. Would a second century pseudepigrapher be concerned with such first century topics?[277] Not logically. But it would be very natural for Peter himself to write about such things.

Furthermore, scholars are simply wrong in telling you that

[275] Henry H. Halley, *Halley's Bible Handbook* (Grand Rapids: Zondervan, 1965), 666.

[276] The logistics of forgery are just too overwhelming to be seriously entertained. First of all, how would a forgerer bring their forgery to the attention of church authorities? Would they say, "Hey, look what we discovered shuffled among all these old manuscripts? It's a genuine Epistle of Peter that no one ever knew about before." Could anyone think that they could get away with such a trick? In what city would the place of discovery occur? What kind of material was the hoax written on? What kind of handwriting was it written in? Who could even verify its authenticity? Why did not second century clerics write about such a sensational discovery? On and on go the questions that one would have to be prepared to answer in order to make the theory of pseudepigraphy stick with not only Second Peter, but all of the apostolic works that are claimed to be pseudonymous. Nevertheless, scholars seem to be undaunted in their blind faith in such an amazing and desperate supposition.

pseudepigraphy was an accepted practice concerning New Testament books. It most certainly was not! What post apostolic impostor would write about "cleverly devised myths' (2 Pet 1:16)? A pseudonym must "cleverly disguise" his forgery, knowing all along that his work is a total "myth." This alone would amount to the most dastardly assault on a persons trust in such a document imaginable. What pseudonym, knowing that he is lying, would dare write about "false prophets also arose among the people, just as there will be false teachers among you" (2 Pet 2:1)?[278]

Again, the Apostle Paul had this to say to the Thessalonians:

> You know, we had courage in our God to declare to you the gospel of God in spite of great opposition. For our appeal does not spring from deceit or impure motives or trickery, but just as we have been approved by God to be entrusted with the message of the gospel, even so we speak (1 Thess 2:2-4, see also 2 Thess 2:2).

Impostors know that they have not been approved by God to be entrusted with the message of the gospel as though they were speaking for the apostles. The internal evidence of the New Testament itself must be the first consideration on the subject.

The entire case of the gradual acceptance theory of how the New Testament came to be stands or falls with the belief in pseudonymity. But it is obvious that critics who propose pseudonymity brush off such strongly worded New Testament safe-guards that decry such a practice. Be

[277] C. Biggs, *The Epistle of St. Peter and St. Jude,* International Critical Commentary (1901), 233 remarks: "The pseudonymous writer of the early church, from the nature of things, were never either intelligent or critical. They did not attempt to qualify themselves for their task by an accurate study of the past; indeed, it would not have been possible for them to do so. There is hardly an instance of a really good pseudo-antique except the Platonic Letters, the work of an otiose scholar, who had thoroughly studied his exemplar, and could reproduce his style and circumstances to a nicety. But what was difficult for an Athenian professor with a library at his command, was quite beyond the capabilities of an uneducated Christian. Such a man does not comprehend even the simplest rules of the forger's art. We may apply to him the words of Persius 'Digitum exsere, peccas.'" Nevertheless, some scholars of today, unable to satisfactorily address the real issues surrounding the development of the New Testament, can only pass on shallow reasoning without the substance of real proof: "Even after one grows accustomed to the creative borrowing, pseudonymous attribution, and the putting of words into the mouths of fictional characters typical of Greco-Roman literary practice, 2 Peter catches one's attention," Burton L. Mack, *Who Wrote the New Testament?: The Making of the Christian Myth* (San Francisco: HaperSanFrancisco, 1989), 211.

[278] Instead of seeing statements like these as built in safeguards, Bart Ehrman (*The Orthodox Corruption of Scripture* [London: Oxford University Press, 1993]), 23, turns the tables around and notes that "the frequent occurrence of forgery in this period does not suggest a basic tolerance of the practice. In actuality, it was widely and strongly condemned, sometimes even within the documents that are themselves patently forged. This latter ploy serves, of course, to throw the scent off one's own deceit."

that as it may, faithful believers should reassure themselves with such strong statements in order to realign their thinking with what the Bible itself teaches us on the subject of canonization! We must stay within the guidelines that the Bible itself imposes or we will end up in the hopeless dead end where scholars have driven themselves.[279]

What many scholars want us to believe is that later church authorities knowingly added documents to the canon of divine literature which everyone else knew at that time was a total fake. This alone puts undo strain on the credibility of the entire theory. We, therefore, must maintain that if critical scholars see no problem in believing this to be the case, critical believers in the veracity of the Word of God most certainly should! Indeed, if we are to believe that outright liars wrote many of the books within the New Testament, then we should not be expected to have any confidence in the veracity of its content whatsoever. The subject is just that important and must be confronted head on by all who have spiritual eyes to see the truth!

THE FORGERER THAT GOT CAUGHT

THERE IS A EXAMPLE OF A SECOND CENTURY minister in Asia minor who was defrocked and kicked out of the ministry for writing in the name of the Apostle Paul. The document is known as the *Acts of Paul and Thecla*, and Tertullian writing around 198-200 stated that

> if those who read the writing that falsely bears the name of Paul adduce the example of Thecla to maintain the right of women to teach and to baptize, let them know that the presbyter in Asia who produced this document, as if he could of himself add anything to the prestige of Paul, was removed from his office after he had been convicted and had confessed that he did it out of love for Paul (Tertullian, *De batismo* 17).[280]

[279] The New Testament is literature that stands miles apart from the pagan philosophers of the ancient world. Using the same criteria to judge the New Testament as those documents is therefore an exercise that ignores the strongly worded testimony of its writers and is a procedure that should be condemned because of its blatant disregard to the internal evidence.

[280] Quoted from Edgar Hennecke, *New Testament Apocrypha.* Wilhelm Schneemelcher, ed., (Philadelphia: Westminster Press, 1963), 2:323.

Now we have to ask: if pseudonymity was punished within the church in the second century for claiming apostolic authorship, where do scholars of today get off in claiming that pseudonymity was an accepted practice in the church at this time? It was not! And, as we see above, discovered forgerers were punished and kicked out of the church for attempting to get away with such an act of forgery.

Oskar Skarsaune comments in this regard:

> It should be evident that the rather arrogant assumption prevalent in much modern scholarship – namely, that ecclesiastical authorities in the second and third centuries, when the New Testament Canon was shaped, were extremely naive and credulous – is quite simply a mistake.[281]

SECRETARIES ARE NOT PSEUDONYMS

THE AUTHOR OF SECOND PETER TELLS US PLAINLY that he is the one who wrote the first Epistle (2 Pet 3:1). Yet, the First Epistle of Peter states that it was literally written by an amanuensis by the name of Silvanus (1 Pet 4:12). Therefore, if Peter dictated his First Epistle to Silvanus (which most scholars do accept as Petrine authorship), then the actual writing style of First Peter is that of Silvanus and not of Peter. Thus, if Peter did write Second Peter (or another amanuensis) then differences in writing style are worthless as a criterion to reject Petrine authorship.

Indeed, the use of amanuenses by Paul and Peter is a long established fact. Critical scholars, thus, should know better than to use an argument about differences in writing style to prove a point of authorship other than the apostles, since they themselves know fully well that ancient writers regularly employed amanuenses.

> The activity of secretaries is elsewhere intimated in the NT, especially in the letters of Paul. It was apparently Paul's

---

[281] Oskar Skarsaune, *In the Shadow of the Temple: Jewish Influences on Early Christianity.* (Downers Grove, Ill.: InterVarsity Press, 2002), 297. Skarsaune further comments: "It is often assumed in present scholarship that all people in antiquity were extremely naive in questions of authorship and literary forgery, and, more specifically, that our moral condemnation of pseudonymity (one author borrowing a more famous author's name for his own product) was utterly foreign to them. Nothing could be further from the truth" (ibid., fn. 43). For a recent discussion on the matter, see Robert M. Grant, *Heresy and Criticism: The Search for Authenticity in Early Christian Literature* (Louisville: Westminster, 1993), 15-32.

> custom to dictate his letters to a secretary. The 'oral style' of the letters is only one indication of this. In Rom 16:22, one Tertius expressly designates himself as the transcriber of the letter. Paul's practice in other letters of adding greetings (1 Cor 16:21, 2 Thess 3:17, Col 4:18), an asseveration (Phlm 19), and a summary statement (Gal 6:11-18) in his own handwriting implies that the letters themselves were written at the hands of amanuenses who transcribed at Paul's dictation. Indeed, 2 Thess 3:17 claims that Paul's appended greeting, written in his own hand, was a "sign" or "mark" employed in each of his letters. This practice suggests that these letters were normally in the handwriting of a secretary. A similar use of an amanuensis is also indicated by 1 Pet 5:12. In dictating his letters to a secretary, Paul was following a well-established practice in antiquity. Many papyrus letters preserved from the period were written in the hand of a secretary, with the final greeting or other closing matter written in the hand of the sender. In addition, classical literature often attests the use of a secretary. Cicero, a prolific letter writer, often dictated letters to his secretary, Tiro, and frequently alluded to this practice. Plutarch mentions it for Caesar (*Vit. Caes.* 17.3), Pliny the Younger mentions it for his uncle (*Ep.* 3.5, 9.36), and Quintilian objects to its widespread use (*Inst.* 10,3,19).[282]

Certainly, differences in writing style must be shelved as an argument against Petrine authorship. Peter may have given Silvanus, in his first Epistle, a great deal of latitude in wording style, knowing that his audience was widely spread out and he needed the literary polish that would have been needed for just such a case.[283]

The thematic differences between First and Second Peter are also not reasons to decry different authorship. Indeed, it is a matter of what we are trying to bring out in this book. As we have already brought out, the circumstances had greatly changed in the interval between these two writings.

---

[282] Harry Y. Gamble, "Amanuensis" in *The Anchor Bible Dictionary,* David Noel Freedman, ed., (New York: Doubleday, 1992), 1:172.

[283] Ralph P. Martin and Peter Davids, eds., *Dictionary of the Later New Testament and its Development.* (Downers Grove: InterVarsity Press, 1997), 916, writes: "If 1 Peter is, as it appears to be, an encyclical on behalf of the church at Rome to a wide circle of churches on the frontiers of the Roman Empire in five provinces of Asia Minor, then the author would likely have had scribal help with vocabulary and style, and his helpers would likely have remained anonymous."

FROM FIRST PETER TO SECOND PETER

IN PETER'S FIRST EPISTLE, PETER IS WRITING FROM Jerusalem in the summer of 65 C.E. There, he still had a strong conviction that the return of Jesus would be in his lifetime. It is there that Peter informs his readers that these are "the last times" (1 Pet 1:20) and that "the end of all things is at hand" (1 Pet 4:7). He speaks of "the fiery trial which is to try you" (1 Pet 1:12) and that "the time is come that judgement must begin at the house of God" (v. 17). Peter must be referring to the great persecution that was happening in Jerusalem, and he felt that the predictions of Jesus were about to transpire. He is writing to the refugees from the Jerusalem church who now had left Jerusalem and were being scattered into the upper regions of Asia Minor.

Obviously, Peter must have felt that the end-time was still imminent when he wrote his First Epistle. But when we come to Peter's Second Epistle we see a very different Peter than what we saw back in his First Epistle. It is because of this difference in style and message, that many scholars assume that the writer of the second Epistle was a different person altogether. This Peter, unlike the Peter in the First Epistle, now refers to "the last days" as being far into the future. This is in sharp contrast to the Peter we read back in the First Epistle who was talking about the last time and the end of all things being at hand. Peter was now living in a time when people were complaining that Christ had delayed his coming. Some also were starting to say "where is the promise of his coming?" (2 Pet 3:4).

Despite these differences, however, we should not be so swift in jumping to the conclusion that this is a different person than the author of the First Epistle. Second Peter was now written from Rome. When Peter joined up with the Apostle Paul in Rome in the summer of 66 C.E., it is obvious that Paul had a definite effect on Peter's outlook, theologically and apocalyptically. It is also apparent that Paul, who now was convinced that the Parousia was far into the future, was able to change Peter's mind entirely on the subject of the Lord's intervention in world affairs during their generation. Now it was apparent to Peter, as well as Paul, that Jesus would return far into the future. Upon this realization, Peter, like Paul, now understood the importance of "binding" the testimony of Jesus' disciples for the future church down through the ages.

Peter, and his entourage, had just fled from Jerusalem with the enclosing Roman armies. It was now obvious to both Peter and Paul that a "this generation" fulfillment of end-time prophecy was a generation far into the future. In other words, both Peter and Paul made a complete turn-about from their earlier prophetic views. This is why Peter now has come to the conclusion that a day with God is like a thousand years in prophecy (2 Pet 3:8) and that God is not slack in his promises (v. 9). Peter changed his mind on prophetic matters due to the circumstances that he and Paul were witnessing in Jerusalem and within the Roman Empire.[284]

In First Peter, Peter was addressing the Jerusalem church which was beginning a mass exodus out of Judea, fleeing, not as Jesus said "to the mountains" nearby, but first to the northern plains of Pella, and then on to the northern areas of Asia Minor, which Peter wrote to as being the area where the "exiles of the Dispersion in Pontus, Galatia, Cappadocia, Asia, and Bithynia" (1 Pet 1:1) now were. These people were experiencing "various trials" (1 Pet 1:6), and were being tested "by fire" (v. 7). They were admonished to "live in reverent fear during the time of your exile" (v. 17), yet Peter, at the time of his writing this Epistle, was still of the belief that they were living "at the end of the ages" (v. 20).

Peter further admonished the readers of his First Epistle:

> For the Lord's sake accept the authority of every human institution, whether of the emperor as supreme, or of governors, as sent by him to punish those who do wrong and to praise those who do right. ...Honor the emperor (1 Pet 2:13-14, 17).

Obviously, we see a situation here where many back in Judea were beginning to rebel and join forces with the Jewish rebels who wanted to overthrow Rome at this time. Peter was warning his audience not to take part in this futile cause but rather even "honor" Emperor Nero, of all things?[285] Nevertheless, Peter, still expressed the opinion that "the end of all things is near" (1 Pet 4:7) and that "the time has come for judgment to begin with the household of God" (v. 17).

Finally, Peter writes from Jerusalem, "Your sister church in Babylon, chosen together with you, sends you greetings; and so does my son Mark" (1 Pet 5:13). Who is this sister church referred to as Babylon? It is not the church from where Peter is writing, as so many assume. Peter is writing from Jerusalem to the now scattered Jerusalem brethren in Asia Minor. It is also not a church in the literal city of Babylon in Mesopotamia. Why?

---

[284] We should ask, is it possible for Peter to change his mind so dramatically within a year's time frame? Of course it is. It is exactly what we should expect Peter to do in light of the events that he was witnessing in Jerusalem and Rome, as well as gaining the insight now of the Apostle Paul.

[285] Right at the very time that Nero was launching a persecution against Christians in Rome in the year of 65 C.E., Peter was here advising Christians that they should be honoring him. What an amazing piece of instruction!

The clue is the presence of John Mark. Because the fact that Mark was with Peter at this time gives us the key to the identity of this sister church that Peter describes as Babylon.

The Apostle Paul, who was at Rome, had requested Mark to go to Jerusalem for a definite "service" (2 Tim 4:11). The service that Mark provided was to go to Peter in Jerusalem and request his presence at Rome to help Paul with creating a body of literature for the future church. The Apostle Paul knew at this time that the end-time prophecies were for the future. Peter at this time may still have not had this same persuasion as Paul in these prophetic matters.

Commentators are correct in identifying "Babylon" as a euphemism for Rome, but they are wrong in thinking that it was Peter that was sending the greetings from the place that he is writing. A careful reading shows us that Peter was passing on the greetings of John Mark, and from the "sister church" where John Mark had just come from. Rome was where the apostle Paul was at this time. Peter is sending greetings from Mark and Paul and from the sister Church, which Peter euphemistically referred to as "Babylon." Peter was obviously still following the precedent that the Apostle John had previously used in his *Revelation* in referring to Rome as Babylon (Rev 14:8; 16:19; 17:5; 18:2, 10, 21).[286] It is an established fact that many of the early apostles believed that Rome was a reincarnation of the ancient sinful city of Babylon.[287]

We now come back to Peter's Second Epistle. Peter, when writing this Epistle, is obviously in Rome, although he is writing to the very same exiles of the Jerusalem church as he did in his first Epistle. One thing is now obvious. By the time that Peter wrote this Second Epistle, it is apparent that he had now read all of Paul's letters (2 Pet 3:15-16). The impact of Paul's letters on Peter certainly influenced his outlook to the degree that it had a definite effect on his message in this Second Epistle. Indeed, the fact that Peter mentions "all his [Paul's] letters" (2 Pet 3:16), with reference to Paul in the past, indicates that Peter had the entire collection of Paul's letters in his presence and they were now bound in a collection that has come down to us as the fourteen Epistles of the Pauline corpus.

Paul had assembled and edited all of his letters and presented them to Peter to be included in a body of literature that Peter referred to when he said that he would "keep on reminding" the future Church of God (2 Pet 2:12). Paul knew that he, himself, did not have the authority to

---

[286] This is another indication that the *Revelation* of John was written earlier than 65 C.E.

[287] See Oscar Cullman, *Peter: Disciple, Apostle, Martyr* (2d ed.: Philadelphia: Westminster, 1962), 84 and Carsten Peter Thiede, "Babylon, der andere Ort: Annermerkungen zu 1 Petr 5, 13 und Apg 12, 7", *Biblica* 67 (1986): 532-8.

accomplish this task. He needed the chief apostle of the Church of God to endorse this effort. Indeed, if Peter did not place his stamp of approval on Paul's writings, none of them would have been included in any authoritative New Testament, whether one wishes to believe such a fact, or not, makes no difference, that is the absolute fact of the matter![288]

In short, the collective writings of Paul were thus canonized by the chief apostle, Peter. The fiction that some unknown clerics in post-apostolic times did this is a fabrication that should never be seriously entertained by anyone who has any sense that Paul's writings represent the word of God.

SECOND PETER — EARLIEST QUOTED BOOK

CRITICS ARE SO QUICK TO POINT OUT THAT NO one in the second century ever quoted Second Peter. Really? Well, let us here consider the following. Clement, the bishop of Rome, writing most probably in the year of 69 C.E.,[289] makes the very same allusion to the Lord delaying his coming as do we read in the Epistle of Second Peter 3:4:

> Let this SCRIPTURE be far from us where he says, "Wretched are the double-minded, those who doubt in their soul and say, 'We heard these things even in the days of our fathers,[290] and look, we have grown old, and none of these things have happened to us" (1 Clem 23:3).[291]

---

[288] In the very letter that Paul recounts his touchy visit to Jerusalem with the three leading apostles, James, Peter, and John, he mentions that he went to Jerusalem in response to a revelation to lay before them his gospel message to the Gentiles, "in order to make sure that I was not running or had not run, in vain" (Gal 2:12). In other words, if Paul did not have the approbation of these "pillar" apostles, then his work was, in his own words, entirely in vain. Since this is the principle that guided the Apostle Paul then, it is this same principle that Paul believed in that guides us in our opinion here.

[289] Clement's reign as bishop of Rome should be correctly dated from 68-79 C.E., as we bring out in appendix 4. Clement, whose *Epistle to the Corinthians* should be rightly dated to the year of 69 C.E. (not the other way around), was ordained by Peter himself and assumed the bishopric of Rome in 67 C.E., while Peter was still alive! First Clement, therefore, was probably written shortly after Peter's martyrdom, maybe as early as 68 or 69 C.E. at the latest.

[290] Scholars wish to believe that the reference to "fathers" in this context indicates the church fathers of the second century. Therefore, a second century dating is demanded. Such is the kind of overwhelming evidence that is put forth as overthrowing Petrine authorship. It is significant also to note here that Clement's reference to Peter's Epistle as already being in the status of "Scripture" is ignored by most scholarly works on the subject.

Clement's obvious reference to Second Peter in reality is the earliest attestation that Second Peter was already considered Scripture by the year of 69 C.E.[292]

J. R. Michaels offers some other points to consider:

> As a testament, 2 Peter speaks clearly of the apostle's approaching death. Early tradition states almost unanimously that Peter died as a martyr... It is remarkable that a second-century tract pretending to be Peter's testament would omit any reference to his glorious martyrdom. Such reticence is more what we would expect if Peter were himself the author. ...In general 2 Peter is free of the legendary and apocalyptic details that characterize the apocryphal Petrine literature. In this respect at least, 2 Peter is more like 1 Peter than like any other writing that bears the Apostle's name.[293]

Donald Guthrie, in discussing some remarks about Second Peter by the early church, makes the following comment:

> It will be convenient to regard Origen as the pivotal Christian Father in this discussion, because reviews of the evidence so often commence with the statement that the epistle was not certainly known until his time and the authenticity becomes immediately suspect, especially as he also mentions doubts held by some about it. He uses the epistle at least six times in citations and shows little hesitation in regarding it as canonical... Some suggestion of doubt on Origen's part might be inferred from Eusebius' statement (*HE* 6.25) that he held Peter to have left one acknowledged epistle and 'perhaps also a second, for it is disputed'. But Origen mentions no explanation from the doubts which were apparently current among some Christians, neither does he give any indication of the extent or location of these doubts. It is a fair assumption, therefore, that Origen saw no reason to treat these doubts as serious, and this would mean to imply that in his time the epistle was widely regarded as canonical.[294]

---

[291] Quoted from *The Apostolic Fathers,* trans. J. B. Lightfoot and J. R. Harmer, (2d ed. Grand Rapids: Baker Books, 1989), 42.

[292] Another allusion to Second Peter in Clement is the use of the phrase "magnificent and glorious will" (1 Clem 9:1) to that of the Majestic Glory in 2 Pet 1:17. Also, Clement's reference to Noah, who preached repentance (1 Clem 6:7; 9:4) answers directly to 2 Pet 2:5: "Noah, a preacher of righteousness." We should also not forget that Jude quoted Second Peter virtually verbatim. Of the 25 verses in Jude, 19 are direct quotes from Second Peter.

[293] J. R. Michaels, "Peter, Second Epistle of" in *The International Standard Bible Encyclopedia* (Grand Rapids: Eerdmans, 1979), 3:817.

Recapping much of what we have brought out in this chapter, let us consider the following. At the time that Peter wrote his First Epistle in the early summer of 65 C.E., Peter was most likely in Jerusalem. The salutation at the end of First Peter mentions the fact that Mark was now there with Peter in Jerusalem. Mark had just arrived from Rome on a mission or "service" from the Apostle Paul to request Peter to come to Rome for the very purpose of helping Paul put together a New Testament canon. Peter sends greetings to the scattered Jerusalem faithful who were now relocated in areas of upper Asia Minor. He sends greetings from their sister church in Babylon (Rome) where Mark had just come from and Mark, in turn, also sends greetings to those whom he was familiar with that had left Jerusalem (1 Pet 5:13).

When Peter writes his second Epistle, it is two years later. The circumstances have now changed so dramatically that scholars cannot believe that this is the same Peter that could possibly have written the first Epistle, despite the fact that Peter specifically says that this is the second Epistle to the same brethren. Peter was now in Rome. Upon coming to Rome Peter met with the Apostle Paul and there Peter had a chance to personally talk to Paul about his literary endeavor, his new revelation of the "mystery," and the meaning of how the prophetic events were shaping up. Peter then read all of Paul's letters that Paul edited and bound into a collection, including Ephesians and Colossians which talked about the "mystery" and the Epistle to the Galatians, which talked about Paul and Peter's disagreements. It is obvious that Peter now had abandoned the idea that Jesus would return in his lifetime, based upon Paul's accurate interpretation of the political facts and in the light of how the prophecies were (or were not) shaping up.

It now was imperative for Peter to inform the scattered Jerusalem brethren (which, by the way, most likely included John, Jude and possibly Phillip) that he had the authority to bind up the testimony of the disciples. Peter needed the disciples to know that Paul, whose beliefs were held in some skepticism by the Jerusalem church, was now totally accepted by the leading apostle, Peter. And what we have is the fact that Peter endorsed Paul's writings, but in so doing he noted that unstable people wrestled with Paul's writings because some of the things that Paul wrote about concerning the new "mystery" revelation in Ephesians and Colossians were hard to understand. Nevertheless, Peter was going to see to it that Paul's works were the authoritative writings of the future New Testament and would be ready for recall from then on.

---

[294] Donald Guthrie, *New Testament Introduction* (Downers Grove: InterVarsity Press, 1990), 806.

Now, back to the question, who wrote Second Peter? It is our firm belief that it could be none other than the Apostle Peter himself. This is so abundantly clear if we put on our spiritual eye glasses, so to speak, and read Second Peter with renewed vision. When we thus do, we can now see Second Peter in a new light. Indeed, rather than being some worthless forgery on the verge of being kicked out of the New Testament canon, Second Peter stands as the most important document on the subject of New Testament canonization that exists anywhere in ancient literature!

APPENDIX 2

The Chronology of Acts and Beyond

THIS APPENDIX PROVIDES NEW INSIGHT INTO THE controversial subject of New Testament Chronology. If we didn't have something new to bring to the discussion, then we could just as well have adopted any number of popular chronologies that are presented in most Bible dictionaries. The problem, however, with that approach is that these chronologies, to put it bluntly, are *all* wrong! Indeed, our story cannot be correctly told until we straighten out the error that prevents us to see the true historical picture in the period of main interest to us here – the time of *Beyond Acts.*[295]

THE RESURRECTION AND BEYOND

THERE ARE TWO LEADING CONTENDER DATES for Passion week: 30 C.E. and 33 C.E.[296] The reason why these two dates are separated by three years apart owes to the astronomical requirement of

[295] The present author readily admits that not every detail of New Testament chronology has been worked out to the degree of satisfaction that we all would desire. However, a future volume will address the many other unsolved riddles. Any suggestions by readers will be appreciated.

[296] The 33 C.E. date is maintained, as of late, by Jack Finegan, *Handbook,* 362, who believes that the vacillation of Pilate during the trial of Jesus would not be possible while the anti-Semitic Sejanus, head of the Praetorian Guard, was still the real power in Rome. Sejanus was deposed in 31 C.E., followed by Vitellius, who instructed his provincial governors to treat the Jews with more consideration, thus the temperament of Pilate would better reflect this atmosphere. For a full discussion of this, see Gary DeLashmutt, "Sejanus and the Chronology of Christ's death," online at: http://www.xenos.org/essays/sejanus.htm. Other leading proponents of the 33 C.E. date are: Harold W. Hoehner, *Chronological Aspects of the Life of Christ* (Grand Rapids: Zondervan, 1977),; Paul L. Maier, in Jerry Vardaman, ed., *Chronos, Kairos, Christos II: Chronological, Nativity and Religious Studies in Memory of Ray Summers* (Macon, Ga.: Mercer University Press, 1998), 281-319.

having the day of the crucifixion fall on a Friday in a year when Passover fell on the Sabbath.[297] Harold Hoehner champions the date of 33 C.E., but it is apparent from Hoehner's work that his motivation for accepting this date appears to be based on his theory of interpreting the seventy weeks prophecy of Daniel.[298]

The year of 33 C.E. is also the year that the Roman Catholic Church officially endorses. However, from the internal data given in Acts, the squeeze that 33 C.E. imposes on the data makes it a date that is impossible to work with.

We, therefore, place the date of the crucifixion/resurrection of Jesus to the year of 30 C.E., along with the majority opinion of noted specialists in the field.[299] Indeed, one scholar, Professor A. T. Olmstead, vigorously expressed his confidence in this date in the following words:

> No longer is doubt permissible as to the date of the crucifixion. Friday, April 7, AD 30 is established as firmly as any date in ancient history; in fact, few dates in Greek and Roman history before the adoption of the Julian calendar are as sure.[300]

The date of 30 C.E. accords well with the overall scheme of the New Testament, which can be divided into two chunks. A twelve-year period from the time of the resurrection to the time when Peter, and the rest of the apostles, set out to evangelize the world.[301] The second period represents 25 years from this time when Peter first arrived in Rome to the

---

[297] There are some who place the crucifixion on a Wednesday (or even on Thursday) which find support for 31 C.E. For discussion on this, see Harold W. Hoehner, *Chronological Aspects of the Life of Christ* (Grand Rapids: Zondervan, 1977), 65-71 and Paul R. Finch, *The Passover Papers* (Palm Bay, Fla.: Sunrise Publications, 1998), 213-251.

[298] Hoehner, *Chronological Aspects,* 115-140. The present writer finds the entire line of reasoning a remarkable example of fundamentalist ingenuity. For example, on page 138 we encounter the following amazing supposition: "Using the 360-day year the calculation would be as follows. Multiplying the sixty-nine weeks by seven years for each week by 360 days gives a total of 173,880 days. The difference between 444 C.E. and A.D. 33, then, is 476 solar years. By multiplying 476 by 365.24219879 or by 365 days, 5 hours, 48 minutes, 45.975 seconds, one comes to 173,855.28662404 days or 173,855 days, 6 hours, 52 minutes, 44 seconds. This leaves only 25 days to be accounted for between 444 B.C.E. and A.D. 33. By adding the 25 days to March 5 (of 444 B.C.), one comes to March 30 (of A.D. 33) which was Nisan 10 in A.D. 33. This is the triumphal entry of Jesus into Jerusalem." Either this explanation is an example of amazing insight into this prophecy (which many people believe it truly is) or it demonstrates how one can prove just about anything if one is clever enough.

[299] Raymond Brown, *The Death of the Messiah* (New York: Doubleday, 1994), 2:1374-1375, cites the German scholar Josef Blinzler having catalogued the opinions of about 100 scholars, with 53 opting for 30 C.E., 24 choosing 33 C.E., and between one to three choosing the other years from 26-36 C.E.

[300] A. T. Olmstead, "The Chronology of Jesus' Life," *Anglican Theological Review* 24 (1942): 6.

time when he is finally martyred in that city (42-67/68 C.E.).

The Church Father, Jerome (ca. 135-420), preserved in his work Concerning Illustrious Men:

> Simon Peter ...after his bishopric at Antioch and his preaching to the dispersed of the circumcision who believed, in Pontus, Galatia, Cappadocia, Asia and Bithynia, in the second year of emperor Claudius, went to Rome to expel Simon Magus and occupied there the sacredotal seat for twenty-five years until the last year of Nero, that is, the fourteenth (*De vil. ill.* 1).

Although the Catholic Fathers sought to present the view that Peter's stay in Rome was a continuous 25 year period (in order to justify the papal notion of the "See of Rome"), the data for Peter's two journeys to Rome appears to coincide with Eusebius.[302] From the data contained in Eusebius's Chronicle (using the preferred text of Jerome's Latin version) we see that Eusebius places the coming of Peter to Rome in the second year of Claudius (42 C.E.).[303] This date accords well with the fact that it was in the year of 41 C.E. that Herod Agrippa had Peter arrested, where upon his release he went to first Antioch, then on to Asia Minor, and then to the city of Corinth, before finally arriving at Rome in the year of 42 C.E.

The date of 42 C.E. is also significant in that in Rome a change of government went from Caligula to Claudius the year before, who confirmed the Province of Judea upon Herod Agrippa I. The newly appointed Herod wished to attain the esteem of the popular Pharisees, so during the Feast of Unleavened Bread in the spring of 41 C.E., he first had the Apostle James, the brother of John, rounded up and slain by the sword, apparently without even a trial (Acts 12:1-2). Agrippa next had Peter arrested at the same time, but Peter was only able to escape with angelic intervention, which cost the sentinels of Peter's cell their lives

---

301 Claudius Apolinarius (fl. 170-80), bishop of Hierapolis, is first to record the twelve year tradition (Eusebius, *Hist. eccl.* 5.18.13): "He speaks, moreover, of a tradition that the Saviour commanded his apostles not to depart from Jerusalem for twelve years." The *Acts of Peter,* 2:5, written also around this time, stated: "But as they mourned and fasted, God was already preparing Peter for what was to come, now that the twelve years in Jerusalem which the Lord Christ had enjoined on him were completed" (Edgar Hennecke and Wilhelm Schneemelcher, *New Testament Apocrypha* [Philadelphia: Westminster Press, 1965], 2:284). Finally, Clement of Alexandria (ca. 150-215), in his *Stromata* 6.5.43: "If now any one of Israel wishes to repent and through my name to believe in God, his sins will be forgiven him. And after 12 years go ye out into the world that no one may say, 'We have not heard [it]' "(Hennecke, *Apocrypha,* 2:101).

302 Finegan, *Handbook,* 384-85.

303 Finegan, *Handbook,* 379-80.

(Acts 12:3-11; 18-19), demonstrating the seriousness of Herod's aggression.[304]

After a brief stay at the home of John Mark's mother, where the church had been congregating in secret (Acts 12:12-17), Peter leaves the Jerusalem area "for another place" (v. 17) that is not named.[305] However, this may be when Peter goes first to Antioch, through upper Asia Minor, and into Rome, where he contended with Simon Magus.[306]

Peter's stay in Rome was only passing, and we find him again at the Jerusalem Conference (Acts 15:7) shortly after, most likely after the death of Herod Agrippa in 44 C.E.[307]

THE OUTLINE OF ACTS

IT IS ESSENTIAL TO GET THE CORRECT DATING sequence in the *Book of Acts* because it has an overall bearing on the true story that we are herein presenting. Needless to say, if the Apostle Paul met his death at the completion of the *Book of Acts*, as a some scholars maintain,[308] then the entire story really comes to an end there. However, this view is not what history and the Bible declare. The story does not end there, and once we come to understand this, then a flood of information will shed new light on the mission of Paul (and Peter) after the *Book of Acts* concludes.

There have been many erudite studies on the chronology of the New

304 Not since the Saulian Persecution was there such a crack down on the apostles' activity in Jerusalem. This may have been the impetus for the apostles to leave the Jerusalem area (for the time being) to spread the word to the remote regions of the Empire. It is most likely then, that the testimony of Matthew was the officially endorsed Gospel by James, the brother of Jesus and the leading apostles for this evangelizing activity. The twelve years, therefore, would be counted inclusively, as supported by S. Dockx, "Chronologie zum Leben des heiligen Petrus" in Carsten Peter Thiede, ed., *Simon Peter: From Galilee to Rome* (Exeter: Paternoster, 1986), 90.

305 Carsten Peter Thiede, "Babylon, der andere Ort: Annermerkungen zu 1 Petr 5, 13 und Apg 12, 7' *Biblica* 67 (1986): 532-8, discusses the reasons to identify the other place with Rome.

306 Tradition has it that Peter, from Rome, went on to Britain at this time. See George F. Jowett, *The Drama of the Lost Disciples* (London: Covenant Publishing Co., 1961), 174-5.

307 Dockx, "Petrus," 86, 94, places the date of Herod Agrippa on March 10, 44 C.E.

308 So Loveday C. A. Alexander, "Chronology," *Dictionary of Paul and His Letters* (Downers Grove, Ill.: Inter Varsity Press, 1993). Rainer Riesner, *Paul's Early Period*, 26-7, also cites the recent works that support the 62 C.E. date: M. A. Hubaut, *Paul de Tarse.: Bibliothèque d'Histoire du Chistianisme* 18 (Paris, 1989), 29-57; Jürgen Becker, *Paulus: Der Apostle der Völker* (Tübingen, 1989), 17-33 (Eng. trans., *Paul: Apostle to the Gentiles* [Louisville, 1993]).; E. Dassmann, *Kirchengeschichte* I (Stuttgart, 1991), 6 (Chronological Table), 48-52.

Testament and the Apostle Paul.[309] Most of these studies, however, as scholarly as they may appear to be to the average lay person, are flawed in some of their reasonings on a number of significant points, as we shall herein show. Therefore, their final conclusions in the matter of chronology must be discarded in favor of some new evidence provided herein.

The study of the chronological aspects of the life of Paul are interesting and even exciting to the overall story flow. A clear understanding of the chronology crystallizes the events into a correct perspective that overthrows many of the critical views of the New Testament era and even the authorship of the books within the New Testament itself.

There are two significant datum points that we need to first consider. These are Paul's appearance before the Roman Proconsul Gallio in the Province of Achaia, with its seat in Corinth, mentioned in Acts 18:12. Secondly, Paul's appearances before Felix and Porcius Festus, the Procurators of Palestine, mentioned in Acts 21:39 and 24:27.

PAUL BEFORE GALLIO

IN ACTS 18:12 WE READ THAT JEWISH OFFICIALS in Corinth brought Paul before the proconsul Gallio. Most scholars believe that this occurred immediately after Gallio assumed his new post.[310] The interesting thing about Proconsuls is that they regularly held office for only a period of one year.[311] Also, Emperor Claudius had established that proconsuls were to set out for their assigned duty before the fifteenth day of April (Dio Cassius, *Roman History*, 60.11.6).[312]

The one year that Gallio held office has been established by an inscription found just across the bay from Corinth in the city of Delphi. In this inscription it mentions Gallio in his official capacity and also the

---

[309] For example, George Ogg, *The Chronology of the Life of Paul* (London: Epworth Press, 1968); Robert Jewett, *A Chronology of Paul's Life* (Philadelphia: Fortress Press, 1979); Jack Finegan, *Handbook of Biblical Chronology*, "The New Testament" (Peabody, Mass.: Hendrickson Publishers, 1998), 270-402; Rainer Riesner, *Paul's Early Period: Chronology, Mission Strategy, Theology* (Grand Rapids: Eerdmans, 1998); Jerome Murphy-O'Connor, *Paul: A Critical Life* (Oxford: Clarendon Press, 1996), 1-31; Colin J. Hemer, *The Book of Acts in the Setting of Hellenistic History* (Winona Lake, Ind.: Eisenbrauns, 1990). For further studies, see the many references cited in these works.

[310] Finegan, *Handbook*, 393.

[311] Finegan, *Handbook*, 191.

fact that the Roman Emperor Claudius at this time received his 26th Imperial Acclamation. We learn that the 26th Imperial Acclamation is tied to what is called the 12th Tribuncian Power in another inscription, known as the Carian inscription.[313] This has been dated to the year of 52 C.E. Jack Finegan informs us that

> the tribuncian power of Claudius was reckoned from Jan 25, A.D. 41, and renewed annually, therefore his *tribunicia potestate XII* corresponded to Jan 25, A.D. 52, to Jan 24, A.D. 53.[314]

The period of Gallio's administration can even be narrowed down further by recognizing the fact that before August 1, 52 C.E., the Roman Emperor Claudius received his 27th Imperial Acclamation.[315] Therefore, the Delphi inscription must be dated between January and August of 52 C.E. And if Gallio was in office between these dates, and for the first half of the year 52 C.E., then Gallio assumed office the year before, in the spring of 51 C.E.[316] Now, if Paul stood before Gallio when he was newly installed, then Paul stood before him in the spring or early summer of 51 C.E.

But could Paul have stood before Gallio later on in Gallio's year in office? The answer is no! A number of scholars have pointed out that Gallio became ill due to the damp Corinthian climate and had to return to Rome as early as October, 51 C.E. even though his term of office did not expire until the spring of 52 C.E.[317]

Thus, attempts to place the appearance of Paul before Gallio in the year of 52 C.E. are in error and such studies from this point on are at least a year too late.[318] Based upon the foregoing, however, we are forced to fix the appearance of the Apostle Paul before Gallio in July of 51 C.E.

---

[312] Jerome Murphy-O'Connor, "Paul and Gallio," *Journal of Biblical Literature* 112:2 (1993): 316, notes: "The ruling of Tiberius in 15 C.E. that provincial office holders should leave Rome by 1 June (Dio Cassius, Roman History, 57.14.5) implies that they took up their posts a month later. That time was allowed for travel is confirmed by the 42 C.E. legislation of Claudius, who moved the departure date back to 1 April only because officials tarried in Rome (Dio Cassius 60.11.3). This was too early for sea travel, and the following year he was forced to change the date to 15 April (Dio Cassius 60.16.7.3). There is no evidence of any modification of the date of assumption of office."

[313] Finegan, *Handbook*, 192.

[314] Ibid., 392.

[315] Ibid.

[316] Ibid., 393.

[317] Adolf Deissmann, *Paul: A Study in Social and Religious History* (2d ed.; London: Hodder & Stoughton, 1926), 279.

FROM GALLIO TO FELIX

LUKE'S REFERENCE TO GALLIO AS PROCONSUL of Achaia in Acts 18:12 provides us with a fixed anchor with profane history that we can now build upon for a sure chronology, forward and backwards. Just prior to this reference (Acts 18:11), Luke tells us that Paul had taught the Jews in Corinth "a year and six months." This, therefore, places Paul's arrival in Corinth at midwinter of 49/50 C.E. and his departure from there in the summer of 51 C.E.

Moving forward from July, 51 C.E., Paul stayed in Corinth "a number of days" (Acts 18:18), then moved on to Ephesus (v. 20), then he returned to Caesarea, then on to Jerusalem (for the fall Holydays?), and then on to his home in Antioch, where he "stayed for some time" (vv. 20-22). It is thus logical to see Paul back in Antioch in November of 51 C.E., where he wintered until the spring of 52 C.E.

In the spring of 52 C.E., Paul is again on the move in what is called his "third missionary journey," going from Antioch through Galatia and Phrygia (Acts 18:23), then on to Ephesus (Acts 19:1), spending three months there (v. 9), teaching in the Synagogue, which brings us to say July/August 52 C.E. After this, Paul taught for "two years" in the Hall of Tyrannus (v. 10), which moves us forward in time to the spring of 54 C.E.[319]

Paul then leaves Ephesus after the riot of Demetrius and travels through Macedonia (Acts 20:1-3), passes through Troas (Acts 20:7-12), then keeps Passover at Philippi (Acts 20:9). This brings us to April of 54 C.E. He stayed in Greece for three months (Acts 20:3), viz., December, January and February, and then returns, going first back through Macedonia again, then on to Philippi for the Days of Unleavened Bread in the spring of 55 C.E. From there, Paul sails to Troas in April of 55 C.E., where he

[318] Unfortunately, Ernest L. Martin is one scholar who not only placed Paul before Gallio in 52 C.E., but also subscribed to the fact that Paul's Caesarean imprisonment lasted two years, as well as subscribing to the cycle of Sabbatical years followed by Ben Zion Wacholder. Thus, he ends up adding a year from Gallio on, and two years after Paul's Caesarean imprisonment, which artificially makes the *Book of Acts* conclude three years later than our chronology (viz. 61 C.E. versus 58 C.E.). See his "The Chronology of New Testament Times," online: http://askelm.com/prophecy/p950102.htm.

[319] These two years and three months are referred to in Acts 20:31 as "three years" in keeping with the Jewish time reckoning principle that parts of a year represent a full year. See Finegan, *Handbook*, 78, 397. If this is the case, then one should question whether the two year reference in Acts 19:10 should equal exactly 24 months. Since Paul keeps Passover at Philippi (Acts 20:9) in the second year, and the beginning of the period started in August of 52, then we would have to conclude that the two years is more likely 19 months.

spends a week. Then, sailing to Assos, Mytelene, Chios, Samos, Miletus, and bypassing Ephesus, he hastened to be at Jerusalem for Pentecost of 55 C.E. (Acts 20:13).

From the foregoing it is obvious that Paul's visit to Jerusalem occurred in the spring of 55 C.E., and not at any time before or after. This date perfectly dovetails with the fact that this year was a Sabbatical year (54/55 C.E.) and the purpose of Paul's visit was to deliver the contribution of food that he had gathered in Macedonia for the church in Jerusalem during this austere year where no harvest was gathered.[320]

THE SEQUENCE OF SABBATICAL YEARS

THE SEQUENCE OF SABBATICAL YEARS IS IMPORTANT TO the discussion and one in which we must look at closer for our study. First of all, we should note that the Jews had a tough going in Sabbatical years.[321] It is because of this fact that every seven years the Jews of Palestine would cease agricultural pursuits in the Sabbatical years and many who did not prepare for this year (as they should have, Lev 25:18-24) were in dire straights, economically. In fact, the economy of all of Judea was brought to a virtual standstill. And it was customary for the Jews living in the Diaspora to send their relatives in Judea food and aide to help them through such years. Therefore, if we can properly understand the Sabbatical sequence of years during the first century, it will help us understand the correct dating of certain events within the New Testament. With this fact in mind, we note the pertinent remarks by Ernest L. Martin, who explains that

> when Paul and Barnabas were given the right hand of fellowship that they should go to the gentiles and the "pillar" apostles were assigned to the circumcision, the only extra requirement imposed on Paul was that he "remember

---

[320] The sequence of Sabbatical years, which we will discuss next, is a complex issue and one of the complexities is that the eighth year was even more severe than the seventh, since during the seventh year, people were to still survive off of the double portion store of the sixth year, but during the eighth year, the shortages may have become acute. Paul's contribution, therefore, was to help the people through the coming year, before they could resume harvesting.

[321] It would seem ironic that there would be poor in Palestine when the later Roman Emperor, Titus, said that Judea was proportionately more prosperous than Rome itself (cf. Josephus, *B.J.* 6.6.2 [335]; *A.J.* 5.1.21 [76-9]). But a recent famine, coupled with a land Sabbath observance, should account for the austere years in question.

> the *poor*" (Gal 2:10). The *poor* in question, as the context certainly shows, were the *poor* among the Jews in Palestine – because Paul and Barnabas would surely have considered it incumbent on them to show benevolence upon the gentiles to whom they were commissioned to preach. But why were the Jews *poor*? The answer should be evident once the sequence of Sabbatical Years is recognized. The truth is, A.D. 48 to A.D. 49 was a Sabbatical Year, and the apostle Paul had the conference with the "pillar" apostles some time in A.D. 48 – right at the start of a Sabbatical Year! There would have indeed been many "*poor*" in Palestine during the next year or so.[322]

The fact that first century Jews in Palestine did observe Sabbatical years has been generally accepted by most scholars. As for which of those years were land Sabbaths has been based on the fact that the Jerusalem temple was destroyed the year following a Sabbatical year, known as a *Shemitah.*[323] Since the temple fell in August of 70 C.E., then the year of 68/69 C.E. should be a Sabbath year, or was it? Let us look at this a little closer.

Based on the *Shemitah* (and other evidence), a sequence of Sabbatical years has been established by Benedict Zuckermann[324] and has been accepted by the majority of scholars until most recently. Now, however, this traditional sequence has been challenged by a noted professor at Hebrew Union College in Cincinnati, Ohio, Ben Zion Wacholder,[325] who maintains that the Zuckermann sequence is a year too early. For instance,

---

[322] Ernest L. Martin, "The Year of Christ's Crucifixion," *The Foundation Commentator* [a publication of the Foundation for Biblical Research, Pasadena, Calif.] 10:3 (April, 1983), 8. This article has been essentially reproduced in Ernest L. Martin, "The Sabbatical Years and Chronology," in *The Star that Astonished the World,* (Portland, Oreg.: Associates for Scriptural Knowledge, 1996), 239-59, and is now online at: http://www.askelm.com/prophecy/p950102.htm. The point that Dr. Martin is here attempting to make is that the year of 48-49 C.E. was a Sabbatical year. However, although we can accept the year of 48 C.E. as being the year of the Jerusalem Conference, it has to be admitted that there is nothing here that would pinpoint 48-49 C.E. as being a Sabbatical year, simply because the writing of Galatians surely occurred after the conference (Dr. Martin wrongly believed that *Galatians* was written before the conference) and, therefore, that the Gal 2:10 reference could refer to the Sabbatical year, the year prior to the Sabbatical year, or the year following the Sabbatical year, where shortages would most likely be really severe.

[323] This fact has been stated in the Jewish work of the second century attributed to Rabbi Yose ben Halafta, known as the *Seder 'Olam Rabbah* (30.86-97). See Jack Finegan, *Handbook,* 107, 122. Finegan finds it hard to accept that the tradition of the Shemitah would not have been preserved accurately down until the time of writing of the Seder Olam (150 C.E.), a point that we also find extremely difficult to discount.

[324] Benedict Zuckermann, *A Treatise on the Sabbatical Cycle and the Jubilee: A Contribution to the Archaeology and Chronology of the Time Anterior and Subsequent to the Captivity* (trans. A Löwy; London: Chronological Institute, 1866; repr. New York: Sepher Hermon Press, 1974).

according to the Zuckermann sequence, the year 54/55 C.E. was a Sabbatical, but according to Wacholder, it should be pushed forward a year, to the year of 55/56 C.E.

Recently, Don Blosser[326] has defended the Zuckermann sequence, although not without being challenged by Wacholder.[327] Wacholder's final argument boils down to a Dead Sea Scroll note of indebtedness that was dated as a year of release and to the second year of Nero 54/55 C.E. Jack Finegan has carefully analyzed this objection and found that it is a clear case of antedating, thus, should be dated to Nero's first year and not his second.[328] This being the case, the Wacholder sequence appears to be indefensible, and the Zuckermann sequence remains vindicated. This sequence, interestingly enough, coincides beautifully with the chronology that we have thus far established.

Therefore, the Sabbatical sequence of years that we will be following in this study is that proposed by Benedict Zuckermann. Following this sequence, it is apparent that the year beginning in the autumn of 47 C.E. and ending in the autumn 48 C.E. was also a Sabbatical year. Therefore, the Jerusalem conference of Acts 15 was held during the Sabbatical year of 48 C.E., and most likely on the Day of Pentecost.

Now, in the *Epistle to the Galatians*, the Apostle Paul mentions that he went to Jerusalem twice to discuss doctrinal issues with the "Pillar" apostles. One such visit was three years after his conversion and then another fourteen years after his conversion.[329] Paul told the Galatians that he, Barnabas, and Titus had gone by revelation to the apostles in Jerusalem to discuss their special commissions of preaching to the Gentiles. This later visit most likely occurred in the year of the Jerusalem Council in 48 C.E. Fourteen years before this Council meeting Paul was struck down on the road to Damascus and converted. This leads us back to 35 C.E. for the conversion of Paul (counting inclusively after the Jewish manner).

---

[325] See Ben Zion Wacholder, "The Calendar of Sabbatical Cycles During the Second Temple and the Early Rabbinic Period," *Hebrew Union College Annual* 44 (1973): 153-96; "The Timing of Messianic Movements and the Calendar of Sabbatical Cycles," *Hebrew Union College Annual* 46 (1975): 201-18. Also see *The Interpreter's Dictionary of the Bible*, Suppl. vol., 762-3. Wacholder's cycle is a year later than that of Zuckermann's.

[326] Don Blosser, "The Sabbath Year Cycle in Josephus" *Hebrew Union College Annual* 52 (1981): 129-39.

[327] Ben Zion Wacholder, "The Calendar of Sabbath Years During the Second Temple Era: A Response" *Hebrew Union College Annual* 54 (1983): 123-33.

[328] Finegan, *Handbook*, 124. Finegan goes on to establish that the contracts found at Murabbáat also establish the Zuckermann sequence (ibid., 124-6). This is further supported by E. Jerry Vardaman, "Progress in the Study of the Sabbatical/Jubilee Cycle since Sloan" in Jerry Vardaman, ed., *Chronos, Kairos, Christos II: Chronological, Nativity and Religious Studies in Memory of Ray Summers* (Macon, Ga.: Mercer University Press, 1998), 281-319.

THE DAILY ACCOUNT BETWEEN FELIX AND FESTUS

BASED UPON THE DATES THAT WE HAVE established above, Paul arrived in Jerusalem in the Sabbatical year of 55 C.E., the day before Pentecost (May 19th), and that "the next day" (Acts 21:17-18), Paul met with James, Peter and John (the pillar apostles) at an assembly of all the elders, which seems most likely to be on the day of Pentecost itself (May 20th, 55 C.E.). It is on this day that the Apostle James then demands of Paul that he go through a seven day period of purification (Acts 21:26-7), which began on the "next day" after Pentecost (v. 26), thus running from May 21st to May 27th. On the next day, May 28th, Paul is arrested (Acts 21:33). The "next day" (Acts 22:30), May 29th, Paul is brought before the Sanhedrin. On the next morning (May 30th), over 40 Jews take an oath not to eat nor drink until Paul is executed (Acts 23:12-15).[330]

Paul's nephew[331] then tips off the Roman Tribune concerning this

---

[329] Gal 1:18; 2:1. The question of whether the 3 and 14 year periods are to be reckoned consecutively or whether the 3 years is to be included within the 14 years is addressed by Jewett, *Chronology*, 52-4, who concludes that the grammar only allows consecutive reckoning. Reisner, however, *Early Period*, 319, states that "grammatically, both [positions] are possible." Jack Finegan, *Handbook*, 395, nevertheless, concludes that "The sequence of his references [makes] it likely that in both cases he [Paul] is counting from the most decisive point of his conversion. In the latter case, 'after fourteen years' Paul reported to 'those ... of repute' at Jerusalem on his preaching among the Gentiles and received their approval (Gal 2:2, 9), which is almost unmistakably a description of what happened at the Jerusalem conference, where Paul told of his work and the 'apostles and elders' (Acts 15:6, 22) approved his mission." If the 3 and 14 years are to be taken consecutively, this would lead back to 31/32 C.E. for the conversion of Paul, which is only a year or so after the crucifixion and which seems hardly enough time for a flourishing community of Christians to be in existence in Damascus. The simple reading of "then after three years" and "then after fourteen years" certainly hales back to a common starting point. Thus, we believe that the 3/14 years are inclusive and that it leads back to a date of 35 C.E. for Paul's conversion. We note also that Paul must have visited Jerusalem at other times, but apparently not with the express purpose of discussing doctrine and the relevance of his special commission, which is what he is pointing out in the letter to the Galatians. Indeed, one such other visit is recorded in Acts 11:28-30, which S. Dockx, *Chronologie*, 263, places in 44 C.E.

[330] The fact that this oath is mentioned is interesting in the context of the story flow here that would never have any resolution if Paul were thrown into prison and left there for a period of two years.

[331] Paul receives help from a family relative (who is otherwise unknown to us), but the thing that is interesting is that we get no indication that any of the church leadership had come to Paul's assistance in this matter. Should we gather that the "pillar" apostles distanced themselves from Paul to the point that they abandoned him altogether in this situation?

conspiracy against Paul (Acts 23:16), so the Tribune orders a centurion, Claudius Lysias, to take Paul that very night, at 9:00 PM, and leave for the city of Antipatris and from there, the following day (May 31st), head out for the city of Caesarea. Five days later (June 5th), the High Priest Ananias, along with the other elders, and his lawyer, Tertulus, arrive in Caesarea for the trial (Acts 24:1). It is on this day, by our calculation, June 5th, 55 C.E., that Paul is put on trial before Felix, wherein he salutes the fact that Felix had been "for many years a judge over this nation" (Acts 24:10). Felix defers judgement on the case until the tribune Lysias comes to Caesarea (Acts 24:22). Several days later (mid-June), Felix and his wife Drusila, have a private audience with Paul. This may have occurred on June 9th or June 10th.

We next are told that Felix was hoping that Paul could buy his way out of his predicament, and would send for him very often over the course of the next couple of weeks (Acts 24:26). By this time, it was getting very close to July 1, the time when new Procurators are installed into office. Further, if Felix knew that Festus was already on his way to replace him, it would be quite understandable that Felix would just leave the matter for Festus to deal with. And interestingly enough, we are told in Acts 24:27b that very fact – that Felix "wanted to grant the Jews a favor, [so] Felix left Paul in prison [until Festus arrived]." In other words, Felix decided to just ignore Paul's plight for the time being, choosing to grant the Jews one last favor (leaving Paul in prison), which had the effect of enhancing his outgoing administration in the eyes of the Jews.[332] The interesting thing about this entire account here is that it is virtually a daily chronicle of events from the beginning of Paul's arrest to his appearance before the next Procurator, Festus.

PAUL BEFORE FESTUS

PAUL'S APPEARANCE BEFORE FESTUS HAS found a wide range of dates among scholars: "from 55 C.E. to 61 C.E."[333] The earliest opinion was expressed by Eusebius, that Festus succeeded Felix

[332] To believe that Felix had the authority to incarcerate Paul for two years for no good reason while Paul was on an appeal to Caesar is not reasonable.

[333] Joel B. Green, "Festus, Porcius" in *The Anchor Bible Dictionary,* David Noel Freedman, ed., [New York: Doubleday, 1992], 2:795. Green's appraisal of the data is disappointedly not up to date, indeed, it is virtually a rehash of every point brought out in R. Jewett's (*op. cit.*) 1979 treatment.

in 55 C.E.[334] The early Catholic scholars, Dionysius Petavius and later on, Cardinal Baronius, placed the succession of Felix to Festus in 55/56 C.E.[335]

A number of modern New Testament scholars are beginning to lower the previously preferred high dates (57 C.E. - 61 C.E.) to be either in 55 C.E. or 56 C.E.,[336] yet there are some scholar's who prefer 59 C.E.[337]

Jerome, it should be pointed out, stated early on the following:

> And because a full account of his life is given in the Acts of the Apostles, I only say this, that the twenty-fifth year after our Lord's passion, that is the second of Nero, at the time when Festus Procurator of Judea succeeded Felix, he was sent bound to Rome, and remaining for two years in free custody, disputed daily with the Jews concerning the advent of Christ. It ought to be said that at the first defence, the power of Nero having not yet been confirmed, nor his wickedness broken forth to such a degree as the histories relate concerning him, Paul was dismissed by Nero, that the gospel of Christ might be preached also in the West (Jerome, *Vir. ill.* 5 [*NPNF*[2] 3.36]).

This passage is insightful for the simple reason that it not only places the exchange of Felix and Festus in the second year of Nero (55 C.E.), but also states that the second year of Nero was the 25th year of the Lord's passion (30 C.E.). These dates are in exact agreement with what we believe to be the true chronology.

Now, if it is assumed that Festus was indeed installed on July 1, 55 C.E., two years to the day from when Felix was installed on July 1, 53 C.E., then we have an account that makes perfect sense. And this is exactly what

---

[334] According to Jerome's Latin version of the *Chronicle.* In it, over against the year 2072 from Abraham, the second year of Nero (55 C.E.), and the 12th year of Agrippa II, there is entered the note: "Festus succeeds Felix, before whom and in the presence of king Agrippa the Apostle Paul expounds the doctrine of his own religion and is sent as a prisoner to Rome" (Alfred Schoene, *Eusebi Chronicorum* [Berlin, 1875], 2.155 and Rudolf Helm [ed.], *Die Chronik des Hieronymus, Eusebius Werke* [Berlin: Akademie-Verlag, 1956], 7:182. The Armenian version of the Chronicle, however, lists this same event in the year of 2070 from Abraham, the 14th year of Claudius, the 10th year of Agrippa II (54 C.E.). This unexplained anomaly is confounded further by Eusebius' *History of the Church,* wherein he there says that Festus was sent to succeed Felix by Nero, not Claudius (*Hist. eccl.* 2.12.1). Josephus also supports the fact that Festus was sent by Nero (*A.J.* 20.8.9 [182]). George Ogg (op. cit.), 151-155, discusses this knotty problem for those who wish to delve into this further in depth.

[335] Ogg, *Chronology,* 147.

[336] Jack Finegan, *Handbook,* 397; For a good updated summary of scholarly opinion, see Rainer Riesner, *Paul's Early Period: Chronology, Mission Strategy, Theology* (Grand Rapids: Eerdmans, 1998), 3-28.

[337] Jewett, *Chronology,* 44; G. B. Caird, "Chronology of the New Testament" in *Interpreter's Dictionary of the Bible* (Nashville, 1961), 1:604f; R. Rainer, *Paul's Early Period,* 223-4.

Luke is telling us: "After two years had passed, Felix was succeeded by Porcius Festus; and since he wanted to grant the Jews a favor, Felix left Paul in prison" (Acts 24:27).

There is nothing here about Paul being in prison for a period of two years, despite vigorous scholarly opinion to the contrary. Indeed, the two year imprisonment at Caesarea is almost unanimously accepted by all scholars, with hardly any in-depth discussion concerning its validity. A serious student of history, however, should inquire why? Scholarly opinion on the matter is most baffling, since there is really no evidence for such a conclusion at all. Indeed, those scholar's who, for whatever reason, prefer the two year Caesarean imprisonment, usually dismiss those who reject it with condescending words, as if it is not even worthy of discussion. Robert Jewett stated that

> it has also been suggested that the 'two years' in Acts 24:27 referred to the period Felix held office, rather than to the period of Paul's incarceration. But I would concur with Weiss' reasoning that Acts 24:27 would not refer to the length of Felix's administration unless its beginning had been specifically mentioned in Acts. The topic of Acts, after all, is Paul's imprisonment rather than the history of Roman provincial administration.[338]

First of all, the beginning of all Procurator's administrations was July 1, and therefore we certainly do know the beginning of Felix's administration, viz., July 1, 53 C.E. Secondly, Weiss' reasoning makes no sense, however, since we don't know the beginning of Paul's incarceration. What kind of an objection is that?

Rainer Riesner also chimes in with:

> A consideration of Acts 24:10 already makes highly improbable any interpretation of διετία as referring to the duration of Felix's term of office. Moreover, Luke nowhere exhibits any interest in the duration of any particular procurator's term of office, but does indeed exhibit such interest with regard to the duration of Paul's imprisonment (Acts 28:30).[339]

Dale Moody is also of the persuasion that the two years of Acts 24:27 refers to Paul's imprisonment:

> The *dietia* is the last of a series of time references to Paul's imprisonment, and there is no evident concern about the

[338] Robert Jewett, *Chronology*, 43.

[339] Rainer Riesner, *Paul' Early Period*, 224.

> length of Felix's term. Note the phrases: "put them off" (24:22), "when I have opportunity" (24:25), "sent for him often" (24:26), and "when two years had elapsed" (24:27). It would be strange indeed if the last reference suddenly became interested in how long Felix was procurator.[340]

None of these objections, however, are facts that overthrow the story flow of Acts. Indeed, what we are witnessing here is a breakdown of critical scholarship in favor of gratuitous reasoning that seeks to arbitrarily lengthen Pauline chronology to fit a preconceived notion that Paul never went on a western campaign and therefore, must stretch out the story of Acts to fill the gap, and nothing more. The fact of the matter is that none of these scholarly opinions represent persuasive evidence for establishing a two year silence amidst the day-by-day story flow of Acts in this period. We maintain that the internal evidence clearly contradicts such a theory.

Indeed, it would be a serious misinterpretation to believe that Paul was left in prison for a period of up to two years, and then when the two years were up, Luke now supposedly swings back in gear, telling us that Felix decides to leave Paul in prison as a favor for the Jews. What? Did not Paul just remain in prison for two whole years? If he did, what would Luke be trying to convey to us if he were saying that Felix decided to leave Paul in prison after that fact?

If Paul had already been left in prison for two years, it makes no sense that now Felix had made a decision to leave Paul in prison for some additional unspecified time. The two year Caesarean imprisonment theory only adds confusion to Luke's day-by-day narrative, since it does not fit the circumstances of what Luke is writing about.

The anomaly is resolved simply by saying farewell to a theory that needs to be scrapped altogether. A more insightful interpretation of this passage is found in S. Dockx's following appraisal:

> We can certainly read 'Two years (implying the tenure of Felix) having passed, Felix was succeeded by Porcius Festus,' but not 'two years (implying the imprisonment of Paul) having passed, Felix was succeeded by Porcius Festus.' In the first case, there is only a single subject of this sentence (one understood and one expressed). It is Felix that accomplishes the end of his jurisdiction, and receives Festus as successor. In the second case, there are two subjects: Paul completes a two year imprisonment, precisely at the moment

---

[340] Dale Moody, "A New Chronology for the Life and Letters of Paul" in Jerry Vardaman and Edwin Yamauchi, eds., *Chronos, Kairos, Christos: Nativity and Chronological Studies Presented to Jack Finegan* (Winona Lake, Ind.: Eisenbrauns, 1989), 225.

when Felix receives Festus as his successor.[341]

The context in Acts 23 through 25 knows of no two-year gap in Luke's daily chronicle. Indeed, up to this point in the story, Luke carefully gives us a virtual day by day account of Paul's activities, as we have carefully documented. Are we to believe that now, all of a sudden, Luke goes blank on us for a period of two full years, only to pick up his daily account in Acts 25:1 as if nothing had happened in between? What was Paul doing during all of this time[342] and what were the conspiring Jews doing who had taken an oath not to eat nor drink again before they had killed Paul? They reappear after the arrival of Festus (Acts 25:24) as if no long period had transpired in between.

Taking the entire context as a whole, the flow of events is continuous from Felix to Festus, from around June 10th to July 4th in the year 55 C.E. All of this makes perfect sense if we are talking about a four to five week transitional period, but makes no sense at all if we artificially interject a two year vacuum in the middle of the story and, indeed, into the life of the Apostle Paul.

We have carefully followed the chronological references in Acts from the Gallio incident in the summer of 51 C.E. to the placing of Paul standing before Felix in the spring of 55 C.E. And this is the exact time that Eusebius and Jerome tell us when Paul stood before Festus. If we had no other information, we would have to conclude that Felix's replacement by Festus would also have had to have occurred at this very time. Yet scholars seem bent on throwing out this evidence in favor of a chronology that is artificially stretched out. The point is just too important to simply ignore. Let us therefore take a closer look at the so-called scholarly arguments against our low chronology.

Objections Answered

Supposedly, PAUL'S STATEMENT TO FELIX,

[341] S. Dockx, "Chonologie de la Vie de Saint Paul, Depuis sa Conversion jusqu'a son sejour a Rome," 13 *Vetus Testamentum*: 288 (translation the author's).

[342] Jerry Vardaman, "A Chronology of Paul's Life," *Biblical Illustrator* (Winter, 1991): 70, believes: "While Paul was at Caesarea, he carried on a furious correspondence, leading Festus to say that his 'many writings were turning him mad' (a better translation of Acts 26:24, rather than 'your great learning is turning you mad'). Thus, it is probable that most of Paul's imprisonment letters were written from Caesarea, and not from Rome." This deduction, of course, is totally erroneous, as we demonstrate elsewhere in this book.

that he had administered justice in Judaea "many years" (Acts 24:10) proves that the "two years" of Acts 24:27 does not apply to Felix and should rather be applied to Paul's imprisonment in Caesarea. We should note, however, that the Roman historian Tacitus (*Annals* 12.54.3) tells us that at this time Judea was divided under the joint rule of Felix and Ventidius Cumanus, the former ruling over Samaria and the later over the Galileans.[343] F. F. Bruce points out in this regard:

> Tacitus's statement might be explained if Felix, before becoming procurator of Judaea, held a subsidiary post under Cumanus, with special responsibility for Samaria. ...When Tacitus, dealing with the events of A.D. 52, says that Felix had been set over Judaea for a long time now (Tacitus, *Annals* 12.54.1), this can only be explained if Felix held a subordinate office in the province since early in Cumanus's governorship. But one may wonder if Tacitus's sources misled him. He further says that Felix was one of the judges appointed by Ummidius Quadratus, legate of Syria, to help Claudius in reaching a decision in a quarrel between Judaeans and Samaritans (Ibid., 12.54.7).[344]

The statements of Tacitus simply cannot be rejected out of hand.[345] But even if it is, we must ask, is this "many years" statement of Paul in Acts 24:27 to be understood in strict chronological terms, or should we not see in it, as it is used here, a kind of oratorical flattery that is typical of the style that Roman administrators are used to? Indeed, at face value, the "many years" point seems a little too desperate to be taken as serious evidence against what we are here proposing. Surely, Felix had other administrative experiences before he came to Judea, so the entire objection is certainly a weak one.

Moreover, let us not forget that a term which extends from July 1, 53 C.E. to the end of June, 55 C.E. is reckoned as 3 years according to ancient Jewish time reckoning practice, i.e., any portion of the first year is counted as a whole year. Since the Jewish year began in the autumn, Felix's first year would be from July 1, 53 C.E. to autumn of 53 C.E. His second year would go from autumn of 53 C.E. to autumn of 54 C.E. And his third year

---

[343] It should be noted that Josephus knows of no such joint rule, only that Cumanus preceded Felix. Therefore, it has been suggested that Tacitus may not have gotten his facts straight. However, we cannot rule out that he may also be reflecting a tradition of some sort that Felix was involved in some capacity while Cumanus was still procurator proper.

[344] F. F. Bruce, "Chronological Questions in the Acts of the Apostles" *Bulletin of the John Rylands University Library of Manchester* 68 (1986): 285-6.

[345] Ernst Haenchen, *The Acts of the Apostles* (Philadelphia: Westminster, 1971), 70, nevertheless colors the issue by saying that "Tacitus' version of these events is well nigh worthless."

would go from autumn of 54 C.E. to end of June, 55 C.E. Thus, Paul, without any exaggeration, could say that Felix had ruled in Judea for several or "many" years.

Also, there is the fall of Pallas, the brother of Felix, to consider. We are told that Felix was saved from disgrace or censure due to the intervening efforts of his influential brother, Pallas (Josephus, *A.J.* 20.8.9 [182]). Yet, Pallas himself lost his office as financial secretary to the Emperor in the later part of the year 55 C.E. As a result, his influence to save his brother Felix from censure could hardly have occurred after 55 C.E.[346] A close reading of Josephus shows us that Pallas' intervention came "at that time" when he was *still* in the "highest" of honor with Nero:

> And he (Felix) had certainly been brought to punishment, unless Nero had yielded to the importunate solicitations of his brother Pallas, who *at that time* had in the *greatest honor* by him (Josephus, *A.J.* 208.9 [182]).

Scholars who toss this evidence aside are neglecting the careful wording of Josephus. After the year of 55 C.E., Pallas may still have maintained some of his influence, but he certainly would not be in the "greatest honor" with Nero "at that time." Yet, if Felix was relieved of his duty in July of 55 C.E., he could have arrived back in Rome toward the end of August, in plenty of time for his brother Pallas to throw his utmost political weight and influence around to save his brother, Felix, before the end of 55 C.E.[347] Therefore, Felix had to have been relieved in July of 55 C.E., which places Paul before Felix in the spring of 55 C.E.[348]

Another fact to be considered is the numismatic evidence. Rainer

[346] Nevertheless, this is not seen as an obstacle to Jewett, *Chronology*, 42-3, who maintains that Pallas was still influential, since he still maintained vast wealth (Nero reportedly killed Pallas in 62 C.E. out of greed for his 400 million sestarces). Riesner, *Paul's Early Period*, 221, threw in his support for Jewett's argument, which, apparently, has become the apologetic *de jour* on this matter. L. C. A. Alexander, "Chronology," *Dictionary of Paul*, 120, states: "The activities which Josephus assigns to Felix's procuratorship (including the Egyptian agitator of Acts 21:38 and Josephus *J.W.* 2.13.5 § 261) seem to require that he was in office several years under Nero (Josephus *J.W.* 2.13.1-7 §§ 250-70), that is after October 54." The reader should consult Josephus themselves here, for we find that there is nothing in the passage of Josephus to justify a lengthy term of Felix under Nero.

[347] Rainer Riesner, *Paul's Early Period*, 222, maintains that: "The dismissal [of Pallas] must have taken place already before the birthday of Britannicus on 13 February A.D. 55 (cf. Tacitus, Ann. xiii.15.1)." However, the correct date for Britannicus' 14th birthday should be 13 February 56 C.E. Britannicus was not born on the 20th day of the *Imperium Claudii* (Feb. 13, 41 C.E.), but on the 20th day of the second year of Claudius (Feb. 13, 42). This fact has long been noted by Ernst Haenchen, *Die Apostelgeschichte* (Göttingen: Vandenhoeck & Ruprecht, 1961, 13th ed.), 63, n. 3. This same mistake is repeated by Colin J. Hemer, *The Book of Acts in the Setting of Hellenistic History* (Winona Lake, Ind.: Eisenbrauns, 1990), 171. Once scholars get their facts straight then they can move on to a genuine solution of the data that makes good sense.

Riesner notes: "The last coins unquestionably dating from Felix's term of office can be dated to the first year of Nero (A.D. 54/55)."[349] It was not until the 5th year of Nero (58/59 C.E.) before a noticeably new number of coins were struck. It is believed by Riesner (and others) that the introduction of new coins at this time represents the change in procuratorships. But the very fact that the last coins dating from Felix's reign are dated to 55 C.E., appears to be significant. If Felix struck coins in 55 C.E., Festus may have waited until the year of 58/59 C.E. before striking any new mintage. So, we really have no solid proof one way or the other with this line of reasoning.

Now among certain scholars there is (supposedly) new evidence that Festus reckoned his term from 56 C.E. Jack Finegan relates in this regard:

> Dates proposed for the succession of Festus to Felix run ...from A.D. 55 (Knox, p. 66) to 60 (Armstrong, ISBE [1929], I, 649). According to new "micrographic" evidence discovered by J. Vardaman, however, the date can be fixed in A. D. 56. On a coin of Nero's fifth year are the names of the consuls of the year 58 and the notation that this was the third year of Festus. Therefore the first year of Festus was 56.[350]

This new evidence presented by Jerry Vardaman apparently now has the recognition of establishing the date of Festus' arrival in Caesarea and it appears to have been just as Eusebius has stated all along. In reference to this, Dale Moody noted the following:

> If J. Vardaman (personal communication) is correct that the Festus coin of A.D. 58 reads "in the fifth year of Nero" and "the third year of Marcus Porcius Festus," the issue is settled in favor of A. D. 56 and Eusebius is vindicated.[351]

But is Eusebius really vindicated by this new evidence? Eusebius said that Festus came to office in Nero's second year. That would place Festus in office in the year of 55 C.E., which is in exact agreement with what we

---

[348] This is not only good history, but it doesn't sacrifice good history at the expense of gratuitous reasoning.

[349] Rainer Riesner, *Early Period*, 223.

[350] Jack Finegan, *The International Standard Bible Encyclopedia*, article "Chronology of the New Testament" (Grand Rapids: Eerdmans, 1979), 1:691. See also Jack Finegan, *The Archaeology of the New Testament: Mediterranean World of the Early Christian Apostles* (Boulder: Westview Press, 1981), 5, 14 and Jerry Vardaman, "A Chronology of Paul's Life," *Biblical Illustrator* (Winter, 1991), 66-70.

[351] Dale Moody, "A New Chronology for the Life and Letters of Paul" in Jerry Vardaman and Edwin Yamauchi, eds., *Chronos, Kairos, Christos: Nativity and Chronological Studies Presented to Jack Finegan* (Winona Lake, Ind.: Eisenbrauns, 1989), 226.

have maintained. But if year 3 of Festus, as Jack Finegan notes,[352] is the same as year 5 of Nero, then year 1 of Festus is the same as year 3 of Nero, not year 2, as Eusebius stated! So, we must ask, how is Eusebius vindicated by this new "micrographic" evidence?

One must also ask, are the years mentioned here actual years of Nero, or calendar years? And which calendar years should we use? The Roman Calendar or the Jewish Calendar or the Syro-Macedonian Calendar? If actual years are counted, then the first year of Nero extends from Oct 13, 54 C.E. to Oct 12, 55 C.E. But if reckoned according to the Roman Calendar, Nero's first year would be from Oct 13, 54 C.E. to Dec 31, 54 C.E., and his second calendar year would be from Jan 1, 55 C.E. to Dec 31, 55 C.E. Reckoning in this manner, Festus would assume his duties in Nero's second calendar year, which is still one year earlier than this new coin information given by Vardaman. Until Vardaman's evidence can be substantiated, however, we must move forward on this point, accepting the date of 55 C.E. as the year that Paul stood before Felix. Our chronology, in fact, is truly in accordance with that of Eusebius and Jerry Vardaman's is the one that is out of sync.

The Final Years of the Apostle Paul

AS SOON AS FESTUS BECAME PROCURATOR, Paul made his appeal to Caesar. Once having done that, Paul, a Roman citizen, could now go before the Emperor himself and appeal his case. The *Book of Acts* tells us that he did that very thing. He left for Rome in the fall of 55 C.E. on his famous "shipwreck" journey, wherein he wintered on the Isle of Malta before finally arriving at Rome in the spring of 56 C.E. Then the *Book of Acts* tells us that Paul spent two years under house arrest in Rome, and therefore the ending of the story in the *Book of Acts* occurs in the summer of 58 C.E. and not anytime later.

Tradition tells us that Paul, upon his release from prison, did fulfill his desire to go on a western campaign.[353] Such a vast journey, wherein

[352] Jack Finegan, *Handbook*, 399.

[353] We believe that Paul wanted to go to Britain to see first hand if anti-Roman forces there would bring the mighty Roman Empire down. Paul must have wanted to return to the churches of Asia Minor in the crucial year of 63 C.E., with the knowledge, one way or the other, if the prophecies of Rome's fall would occur at that time. With the failure of the Boadicean uprising, and Parthia offering terms of peace, it was now all too apparent to Paul that the time of the end was not on the near horizon.

Clement of Rome tells us that Paul "taught righteousness to the WHOLE WORLD, having travelled to the LIMITS of the west" (1 Clem 5:7), may have taken upwards of fives years of Paul's life, an endeavor that we know virtually nothing about. It is not until Paul returns to Asia that the story picks up again, but not in the *Book of Acts*, but only in Paul's later Epistles (Pastorals, *Ephesians*, *Colossians* and *Philemon*).[354]

THE CHRONOLOGY OF BEYOND ACTS

WHEN PAUL RETURNED FROM HIS TRIP FROM the west, it appears that he first went to the Island of Crete with Titus, and then on to Nicopolis in western Greece, probably in the spring or summer of 63 C.E. He wintered in Nicopolis and in the following spring moved on to Macedonia.

After writing the Epistle of *First Timothy* in the spring of 64 C.E., in Macedonia, Paul returned to Ephesus in late summer of 64 C.E. to visit Timothy (1 Tim 1:3). It was there, in the city of Ephesus, that the Apostle Paul was again taken into custody in his sixth major imprisonment.[355] It is this Ephesian imprisonment where Paul writes the Prison Epistles of *Colossians*, *Philemon*, and *Ephesians*.[356] We thus place the writing of these Epistles in 64/65 C.E. Paul was probably released from bonds the following spring of 65 C.E. and then went to Laodicea and Colossae. He then continued his journey into Galatia, specifically Antioch, Iconium, and Lystra, where he encountered stiff opposition and persecution.

After Paul's stay in Galatia, Paul then journeyed to Corinth, then to

---

[354] The vacuum of biblical information for this time period appears to this writer to be deliberate due to the lack of an "amen" at the end of the *Book of Acts*. Only outside sources tell us of Paul's activity of *Beyond Acts*.

[355] Hemer, *Book of Acts*, 272, objects to an Ephesian imprisonment for the following reasons: "The difficulty with Ephesus is that of positing, not an imprisonment as such, but the exceptional, prolonged captivity situation. Imprisonment was commonly used either for the overnight lock-up of a trouble-maker (*coercitio*, cf. Acts 16:23, 35, at Philippi), or for those awaiting trial or execution. Only in exceptional or irregular circumstances might one expect a prolonged captivity pending trial, as at Caesarea and Rome. Both were apparently forms of open arrest imposed by Roman authority, where the victim or his friends, not the state, bore the costs of his support. If at Ephesus Paul had fallen foul of civic authorities, they are unlikely to have had the occasion or facility to hold a prisoner for long. Exile, not imprisonment, was the likely penal sentence, and that would be the prerogative of the Roman governor." Isn't it interesting that scholars have no problem letting Paul sit in prison in Caesarea for two years and not bring up this objection, but jump forward with it to argue against an Ephesian imprisonment? Hopefully, a new generation of scholars will see the obvious, and then some refreshing analyses will appear to paint a picture that finally makes sense.

Malta (2 Tim 4:20), and then finally to Rome, arriving there around the autumn of 65 C.E. It is there, and at this time, that Paul wrote his second letter to Timothy, asking him to come to Rome with John Mark before the winter of 65/66 C.E. set in. Then, in the spring of 66 C.E. Paul sends John Mark back to Jerusalem to get Peter to come to Rome. This is when Peter writes his Epistle of *Second Timothy.*

It was sometime in the autumn of 66 C.E. that Paul was eventually re-incarcerated at Rome, where tradition tells us that he finally met his execution in early 67 C.E.

THE DATE OF PAUL'S MARTYRDOM

CLEMENT OF ROME, WRITING SOON AFTER PETER and Paul had been martyred, stated that the Apostle Paul gave his final testimony, not before Nero, but before "the rulers" (1 Clem 5:7). This would indicate that Paul's testimony for his own defence occurred after the general persecution of 65 C.E., when Nero was absent from Rome and in Greece, a fact that places Paul's demise somewhere between October 66 C.E. and June of 68 C.E. These "rulers" were acting on Nero's behalf while Nero was absent from Rome. Arthur Stapylton Barnes informs us that:

> Either the phrase ["under the rulers"] has no meaning at all or it must mean that the martyrdom [of Paul] took place during the time that Nero was absent from the city, and that sentence was pronounced not by the Emperor in person but by the *Praefecti* whom he had left in charge. It is noteworthy too that several of the apocryphal 'Acts' represents the Apostles as condemned not by the Emperor but by the Praefects.[357]

---

[356] Most scholars add *Philippians* to this list, but, although *Philippians* is a Prison Epistle, it belongs to Paul's first Roman imprisonment. Scholars have not yet recognized an Ephesian imprisonment after Paul's Roman imprisonment. The scholar George S. Duncan, (*St. Paul's Ephesian Ministry* [London: Hodder and Stoughton, 1929]), although recognizing an Ephesian imprisonment, unfortunately placed it within the time period of *Acts,* which is impossible. Therefore, his theory never really gained any acceptance. Needless to say, however, is the fact that the post-Acts Ephesian imprisonment is just another vital key to understanding the period of *Beyond Acts* that we here have at last provided for an accurate picture of New Testament history.

[357] Arthur Stapylton Barnes, *The Martyrdom of St. Peter and St. Paul* (New York: Oxford University Press, 1933), 71.

With this in mind, it appears that the date of the death of the Apostle Paul would fall during the time when Nero was still in Greece, and that would be after the general persecution of 65 C.E.[358] The most likely date for the death of the Apostle Paul is preserved in a document called the *Depositio Martyrum.*[359] Daniel Wm. O'Connor, in his thoroughly researched book on the subject of Peter in Rome, agrees with this conclusion:

> January 25 commemorated the death and burial of Paul in the Via Ostia. The word "conversio" was added to the notice of January 25 since this is the most spectacular event in the life of Paul.[360]

This date makes excellent sense, since it falls well within the time frame that Nero was away in Greece. Therefore, we submit, on the evidence of the *Depositio Martyrum,* that the martyrdom of the Apostle Paul occurred on January 25, in the year of 67 C.E.

THE DATE OF PETER'S MARTYRDOM

THERE ARE TWO IMPORTANT REFERENCES IN the *Depositio Martyrum* that we need to analyze in order to come to conclusion on the date of Peter's death. The date of February 22 is found in the *Depositio Martyrum* of the *Chronographer of the Year 354,* where the following item occurs:

> Mense Februario: VIII Kal. Martias. Natale Petri de Cathedra.[361]

---

[358] Jerome, (*Vir. ill.* 12, [*NPNF*^{2} 3:365]), informs us that the philosopher Seneca died two years before the apostles, which we learn from Tacitus (*Ann.* 15:48) occurred in 65 C.E. This alone would therefore place Peter and Paul's death in 67 C.E., according to the testimony of Jerome.

[359] The *Depositio Martyrum* is a section of a larger opus entitled the *Chronographer of the Year 354,* an anonymous work which may have arisen at the time indicated by the title. It is preserved in T. Mommsen's *Chronica minora* (3 vols.; Monumenta Germaniae historica, 9, 11, 13; Berlin: Weidmann, 1892-1898). Fortunately, professor Barnes has reproduced this text in its entirety in his *Martyrdom,* 120-21.

[360] Daniel Wm. O'Connor, *Peter in Rome: The Literary, Liturgical, and Archeological Evidence* (New York: Columbia University Press, 1969), 49.

[361] Barnes, *Martyrdom,* 120. This translates as: "Month [of] February: Eighth [day before the] kalends [or the first day of] March. Natal [day] of the Chair of Peter."

This corresponds to a date of February 22.[362] What did this date signify? Jérôme Carcopino believed that this date referred to the transfer or translation of Peter and Paul's bones in the year of 258,[363] but Jocelyn Toynbee counters that

> *natale*, means, not 'translation', but 'birthday', in a funerary Christian context "heavenly birthday," or 'martyrdom'; and it could only refer to a burial that took place at the time of death, or to the first solemn burial after death; it could not be used of a re-interment after an interval of nearly two-hundred years.[364]

As for the meaning of "cathedra," Daniel Wm. O'Connor offers the following:

> The word "cathedra" in the notice of the *Depositio Martyrum* may hold the key to the early character of the festival. The meaning of cathedra in Latin is "chair." On occasion it may mean also "locale," or "center of operations." In the mid-third century, however, when this festival was instituted, Latin had not yet been introduced generally into formal Church usage. It is therefore necessary to remember that the Greek "καθέδρα" may suggest a "place of rest."[365]

Based upon these scholarly assessments, therefore, the notice in the *Depositio Martyrum*, which literally translates to: "The natal day of the Chair of Peter" should be corrected to read: "The martyrdom [*natale*} and burial [Greek: *cathedra*] of Peter." This being the case, then this evidence points to February 22 for the death and burial of the Apostle Peter.

We are supported in this position with the careful insight of specialists in this field of research, such as, Daniel Wm. O'Connor, who summarizes the excellent positions of noted scholars, Jocelyn Toynbee and Henry Chadwick:

> A recent attempt at a solution to this problem was made by Toynbee, who explains that upon the authority of Henry Chadwick,[366] she is now of the opinion that February 22 commemorates the date of the death and burial of Peter at

[362] Finegan, *Handbook*, 383.

[363] Jérôme Carcopino, *De Pythagore aux Apôtres: Etudes sur la conversion du monde romain* (Paris, Flammarion, 1956), 265: "Il n'y a point de doute que lors de son institution première, elle n'ait été destinée à commémorer la translation de 258 à Catacumbas."

[364] Jocelyn M. C. Toynbee, review of *De Pythagore aux Apôtres*," by Jérôme Carcopino, *Gnomon* 29 (1957): 266.

[365] Daniel Wm. O'Connor, *Peter*, 42-3. O'Connor seems to have struck on something worth considering, i.e., that "cathedra" was not the Latin "chair," but the Greek "place of rest."

> the Vatican according to an alternative tradition that the deaths and burials of Peter and Paul took place on different days and in different years. The word 'cathedra' in the familiar notice of the *Depositio Martyrum* was added later to mark him out as the founder of the line of popes.[367]

Thus, we would have to place the death's of Paul and Peter on January 25th, 67 C.E. and February 22nd, 68 C.E., respectively, except for the fact that, concerning Peter's death, there is another date to consider. The other date that we have to consider in dating Peter's death is the one that is officially accepted by the Catholic Church and many noted scholars – i.e., June 29th. It also is derived from the *Depositio Martyrum.* Let us now investigate whether this date holds any credibility to the belief that Peter died on this date.

Did Peter Die on June 29?

The *Depositio Martyrum* mentions this second date in relation to both Peter and Paul:

> Mense Iunio: III Kal. Iul. Petri in Catacumbas et Pauli in Ostiense, Tusco et Basso Cons.[368]

The thing to notice about this entry is that the consulships of Tuscus and Bassus referenced herein are in the year of 258 C.E. and not, as we would expect, in a year in the late 60's C.E.[369] Why would this entry reference a year in the third century, if such a reference had anything at all to do with the martyrdom of Peter and Paul in the first century? The *Liber Pontificalis* may provide the solution to the problem with some additional insight as to what was going in the middle of the third century:

---

[366] Henry Chadwick, "St. Peter and St. Paul in Rome: The Problem of the Memoria Apostolorum ad Catacumbas," *Journal of Theological Studies*, New Series, 8 (1957): 31-52.

[367] Daniel Wm. O'Connor, *Peter*, 49.

[368] Barnes, *Martyrdom*, 121. This translates as "June 29. Peter in the catacombs, and Paul on the Via Ostiensis in the consulship of Tuscus and Bassus."

[369] The French scholar, Paul Monceaux, "L'Apostolat de Saint Pierre à Rome à propos d'un Livre récent," *Revue d'histoire et de Littérature religieuses*, n. s., 15 (1910): 235, believed that the scribe who wrote "Bassus and Tuscus," councils in the year of 258, mis-copied his source, which originally read, "Bassus and Crassus," who were councils in 64 C.E. But are we to believe that there just so happened to be councils in the year of 258 that coincidently had exactly the same names as a scribal error? What are the chances of that happening?

> In his time (Pope Cornelius, 251-253), at the request of a certain lady Lucina, he took up the bodies of the apostles Saints Peter and Paul from the catacombs at night; in fact first of all the blessed Lucina took the body of St. Paul and put it on her estate on the Via Ostiensis close to the place where he was beheaded; the blessed bishop Cornelius took the body of St. Peter and put it close to the place where he was crucified, among the bodies of the holy bishops at the temple of Apollo on the Mons Aureus, on the Vatican at Nero's palace, on 29 June.[370]

The ominous date of June 29 appears in this reference as a date for the transference for the bodies of Peter and Paul in the third century.[371] Indeed, there exists no evidence that this date is to be taken as the actual date of Peter and Paul's martyrdom, but rather the date of their bodies being reburied in the catacombs.[372] A. S. Barnes helps us understand one thing that is an important clue in figuring this out:

> It is a characteristic survival of pagan ideas about the relative importance of death and burial, that it was the burial and not the martyrdom that was commemorated, even in cases in which the two events were widely separated.[373]

---

[370] Davies, *Liber Pontificalis*, 9.

[371] Barnes, *Martyrdom*, 89-90, believes that this story really belongs to the first century. He states that: "It is one of the few points on which all critics are unanimous that this statement does not belong to the time of Cornelius at all, but that it has been misplaced and should be put elsewhere. ...All that need be done is to leave out the title of the Pope, doubtless supplied to fit it for being placed in the story of his life, and also the mention of the graves of the other bishops, which graves only came into existence later. The Cornelius will be seen to be very probably Cornelius Pudens, the owner perhaps of the place then known as *ad Catacumbas*, and the difficulty of imagining a second Lucina besides the one who traditionally originally buried St. Paul is done away with."

[372] From an altogether different source, we are told that in the time of Pope Vitallian, the year being 656 C.E., the bodies of Peter and Paul, along with other saints, were sent to King Oswy of Britain: "Vitallian, bishop and servant of the servants of God, to the most excellent lord, our son, Oswy, king of the Saxons: ...We have ordered blessed gifts from the saints, that is, relics of the blessed Apostles Peter and Paul and of the holy martyrs Laurence, John, and Paul, and Gregory, and Pancras to be delivered to the bearers of these letters of yours, all indeed to be taken to your excellency." The Venerable Bede, *The Ecclesiastical History of the English People* (3:29), ed. James Campell, (New York: Washington Square Press, 1968), 172, 174. John D. Keyser, "1st Century Britain and the Gospel of Christ," n.p. [cited July 20, 2002], online: http://hope-of-israel.org/1stcent.htm), stated that he "was personally told by the librarian of Canterbury Cathedral that the church inventories record the arrival of the remains of Peter and Paul to the church's safekeeping shortly after Pope Vitalian sent them to Britain. Unfortunately, though, it is believed the remains were lost, or record of their location lost, in the aftermath of the Cromwellian Rebellion." Thus, it would seem that the Catholic Church in the seventh century was not all that interested in the relics of the founders of their church and that the modern quest to find the tomb of Peter in Rome and his body only have reaffirmed that they are no longer buried on the Vatican.

[373] Barnes, *Martyrdom*, 118.

From this it appears that the dates given in the martyrologies are to be considered the days on which a body was buried, rather than the memorial of the person's death. It could be that these dates were one in the same, but in the year 258, it obviously applied to a reburial of some sort.[374] If this is so, then the June 29th date, which speaks about the catacombs (in reference to Peter) and the Ostian Way (in reference to Paul) is a commemoration of Peter and Paul's burial [or better yet, their reburial], and certainly not to their martyrdom's back in the first century!

The fact that both the Apostles Peter and Paul are remembered on the same day would fit the idea of a reburial far better than the dates of martyrdom because, as we have noted, Peter survived Paul and wrote about him as already deceased (2 Pet 3:15). Indeed, the reference to the consularships of M. Mummius Tuscus and Pomponius Bassus points away from the first century because they were consuls in the year of 258 C.E. and not in year of 67 C.E., nor 68 C.E. Obviously, Peter and Paul were reburied on June 29, 258 C.E. rather than being martyred on June 29, 67 C.E.[375]

Friedrich Gontard is also in agreement with our assessment, that June 29th, which commemorates some event concerning Peter and Paul, had something to do with the year of 258, and not with the dates of the martyrdoms of Peter and Paul:

> The Roman Catholic Church celebrates the feast of SS. Peter and Paul on 29th June, a date based on the tradition of the year 258. During the persecution under the Emperor Valerian (253-60) Pope Sixtus II (257-8) is said to have transferred the bones of the two Apostles to an underground burial-place on the Via Appia, *ad catacumbas*. The day of the transference is given as 29th June, and this is the day that is now celebrated, after gradually becoming accepted as the date of the martyrdom.[376]

A. S. Barnes also quotes a Dr. von Gerkan, the Secretary of the German Archaeological Institute at Rome, as stating:

---

[374] Scholars refer to the reburial explanation as "The Translation Theory," which is discussed at length in O'Connor, *Peter*, 126-134.

[375] Jack Finegan, *Handbook*, 383-4, who excepts the date of June 29th as the day of both Peter and Paul's martyrdom on the one hand, ironically contradicts himself with the following remark: "The year 258 was the year in which Valerian's brief but violent persecution of the Christians took place. It may be that at that time the remains of Peter and Paul, or some portions thereof, were temporarily transferred to this place for safe-keeping." Despite this insight, Finegan still believes in the June 29th, 67 C.E. as the most probable date for the deaths of Peter and Paul: "Peter and Paul suffered martyrdom, June 29th, 67" (ibid., 389).

[376] Friedrich Gontard, *The Chair of Peter: A History of the Papacy* (New York: Holt, Rinehart & Winston, 1964), 63.

> The bodies of the Apostles were brought to the place called *ad Catacumbas* on June 29th in the year 258, in fear of desecration by the Roman authorities. June 29th is the date of the translation, not of the martyrdom.[377]

Another tradition has it that June 29th is indeed the correct date of death for both the apostles, but that they died exactly a year apart. As for this intriguing theory, A. S. Barnes again comments:

> St. Peter himself, though he survived the great day of A.D. 64, according to all tradition perished in the later days of this same persecution. The date assigned for his martyrdom, as also for that of St. Paul, is 29th June, and the prevailing opinion is that the two apostles suffered, not only on the same day of the month, but in the same year. Some early writers, however, among whom may be noted Prudentius and St. Augustine, say that St. Peter suffered exactly a year later than his fellow apostle (Prud., *De Mart.*; Aug., *Serm.*, 296-97.; Arator, ii., p. 700). So strange a coincidence is in itself very unlikely, and the explanation of the existence of this tradition [June 29] is given us by a council at Rome in the time of Gelasius [492-496], which asserted that the two apostles suffered at Rome at the same time, *uno tempore uno eodemque die*, (Labbe, *Concilia*) "and not otherwise as the heretics were wont to say".[378]

Many believe, including the early church Father Jerome, that the Apostle Peter was martyred on the same day as that of the Apostle Paul, which the *Acts of Peter and Paul* places on June 29th.[379] But such a conclusion flies in the face of the internal evidence. As we have stated above, Peter was alive when he speaks of Paul in the past tense as being already dead (2 Pet 3:15). James Hardy Ropes, agrees, noting that:

> As to the date of Peter's death, it may be added that if II Peter is genuine, Peter would seem to have survived Paul, and to have written, after the later's death, a letter to gentile Christians in the provinces of Asia Minor.[380]

Henry Chadwick makes the following observation in this regard:

---

[377] A. S. Barnes, *Martyrdom*, 86.

[378] A. S. Barnes, *St. Peter in Rome* (London: Swan Sonnenschein & Co., 1900), 92-3.

[379] *ANF* 8:485. A. S. Barnes, *Martyrdom*, 71, is one scholar who accepts the date of June 29th for both apostles, Peter and Paul: "Roman tradition might easily have failed to retain with certainty whether it was in 66 or in 67 that the double martyrdom took place. It was on 29 June; that was certain." Jack Finegan, *Handbook*, 401, unfortunately also accepts the idea that Peter and Paul were both martyred on June 29, 67 C.E.

[380] James Hardy Ropes, *The Apostolic Age in the Light of Modern Criticism* (New York; Charles Scribner's Sons, 1912), 217.

> If at the last the ultimate question is to be raised concerning historical events, probability is no doubt overwhelming in favour of the view that the apostles died on different days. The notion that they died on one and the some day would naturally catch the imagination as far more dramatic, though it is interesting to observe that there was also current the same date a year apart – a view which would have the advantage of involving no liturgical complications. In the second-century *Acta Petri* and *Acta Pauli* it is simply taken for granted that the apostles died at different times.[381]

It is therefore impossible to accept the date of June 29th as the date of Peter's death, if for no other reason than it maintains that Paul also died on the same date, which, we believe is totally against the internal evidence.

Another point to consider is this. Around the year of 500, Pope Gelasius (who believed that pronouncements from the Chair of Peter were infallible), declared that it was forbidden to teach the idea that Paul ever sojourned in Spain and also that Peter and Paul had died at separate times. Arthur Stapylton Barnes notes, concerning this:

> Both Prudentius (Prudentius, *De Matyribus*, hymn xii) and St. Augustine of Hippo (St. Augustine, *Sermons*, 296-7) were misled ... and the idea [that both Peter and Paul did not die on the same day, June 29th, in the same year] was formally repudiated, as being due to heretical misrepresentation by a Roman Council under St. Gelasius about A.D. 500.[382]

Thus, the only real authority for the date of June 29th (which Barnes himself had defended so vehemently), rests upon a decree by the Catholic Pope, Gelasius, in order to counteract what he felt were heretical opinions to the contrary.

If Peter was executed a year later than Paul, and Paul was beheaded on January 25, 67 C.E., as we have shown above, then Peter met his death a year later, in the same time-frame as January, 68 C.E. And the date of February 22, 68 C.E. fits this requirement. Indeed, June 29th fails because Nero had already committed suicide on June 9th, 68 C.E. and we would not have Peter dying during the reign of Nero.

Therefore, on the basis of the *Depositio Martyrum*, it would appear that Peter did die about a year later than Paul, which we can now place as February 22, 68 C.E.

---

[381] Henry Chadwick, "St. Peter and St. Paul in Rome: the Problem of the Memoria Apostolorum ad Catacumbus" *Journal of Theological Studies*, n.s., 8 (1957):31-52.

[382] Barnes, *Martyrdom*, 70.

LINUS — ANOTHER CHRONOLOGICAL KEY

WE HAVE AN EXCELLENT CLUE TO THE CORRECTNESS of the chronology that we have presented herein in the fact that Linus was bishop of Rome from 56 C.E. to 67 C.E. This fact is stated in the *Liber Pontificalis*:

> Linus... was bishop in the time of Nero from the consulship of Saturninus and Scipio [56 C.E.] to that of Capito and Rufus [67 C.E.].[383]

It is the very year of 56 C.E. that we have placed Paul arriving in Rome. Now, if Linus was ordained in Rome in that year, who was there to ordain him to the office of bishop? The *Apostolic Constitutions* tells us that it was indeed the Apostle Paul who is the one credited for this ordination:

> Now concerning those bishops which have been ordained in our lifetime, we let you know that they are these: ... Of the church of Rome, Linus the son of Claudia was the first, ordained by Paul; and Clemens, after Linus' death, the second, ordained by me Peter (*Constitutions of the Holy Apostles* 7:46 [*ANF* 7:477-8]).[384]

But how could the Apostle Paul ordain Linus in Rome in the year of 56 C.E. if Paul did not arrive in Rome until 57 C.E., 58 C.E., 59 C.E., or even 60 C.E., as many scholars believe? We maintain that our chronology is the only one that fits the above criterion, when all the facts are considered together.

Placing Paul's arrival in Rome in 56 C.E. is the only way to accommodate the fact that Paul ordained Linus as bishop in that year, and that he died there 11 years thereafter, in the year of 67 C.E. The reason scholars seek to place Paul's arrival in Rome later is that they do not know how to fill an eleven year gap with the events of his life. It is our position, however, that Paul left Rome after his two year incarceration and journeyed to Britain and most likely back through Gaul during the years from 58 C.E. to 63 C.E.

---

[383] Raymond Davis, tr., *The Book of Pontiffs (Liber Pontificalis)* (Liverpool: Liverpool University Press, 1989)., 2.

[384] The idea that Linus was the second Pope following Peter is historically wrong. And if Paul did ordain Linus, then this would make Paul surviving Peter, which is contrary to the evidence of the *Liber Pontificalis*.

The idea that the death of Paul occurred in 61 C.E. or 62 C.E., at the time that many scholars believe that the *Book of Acts* comes to a conclusion, cuts Paul (and Peter) off right at the time that they were to complete the most important literary endeavor of their careers. Indeed, once scholars have cut off the final years of Peter and Paul, they seem to be free to place the canonization of the New Testament in the hands of later church clerics. And such a theory appears to be sustained in part by a chronology that is pure fiction. Then scholars take that fiction and use it to form their views on canon history, which is a total mess. So, can we now understand why the subject of chronology is of such extreme importance in understanding the true history of *Beyond Acts?*

SIGNIFICANT DATES OF THE FIRST CENTURY

3 B.C.E., summer	750th Anniversary of Rome, Silver Jubilee of Caesar Augustus, and the "registration" (Luke 2:1-2, no mention that this was for taxation purposes) of the "pledge of Allegiance" (Josephus, *A.J.* 17.2.4 [41-45]) by "procurator" Quirinius (Justin, *1 Apol.* 34) for Augustus' upcoming *Pater Patriae* celebration the next year.
3 B.C.E., summer	Joseph and Mary leave Nazareth to go to Bethlehem for oath of allegiance registration.
3 B.C.E., Sept 11	Jesus born in Bethlehem on Day of Trumpets.
3 B.C.E., Sept 18	Jesus circumcised.
3 B.C.E., Oct 10	Jesus dedicated in the temple.
3 B.C.E., Oct	Joseph, Mary, and Jesus return to Nazareth (Luke 2:39).
2 B.C.E., Feb 5	Caesar Augustus receives Father of the Country recognition. He states "while I was administering my thirteenth consulship the senate and the equestrian order and *THE ENTIRE ROMAN PEOPLE* gave me the title Father of my Country" (*Res Gestae* 2.8). The signatures of the entire Roman people were taken at the enrollment of Quirinius (Luke 2:1-2).
2 B.C.E., summer	Varus becomes governor of Syria for second time.
2 B.C.E., Dec 5	Youth tears down eagle from east entrance of temple.
2 B.C.E., Dec 25	Joseph, Mary, and Jesus return to Bethlehem for Feast of Dedication (Hanukkah). Magi delegation from Parthian Kingdom visit first Herod in Jerusalem, then Jesus in Bethlehem and bestow expensive gifts to the new born King of the Jews. Jesus is a 14 month toddler at this time and they are in a house – not a manger nor an Inn. Joseph, Mary, and Jesus go to Egypt to Escape Herod.
1 B.C.E., Jan	Herod slays male children of Jerusalem up to 2 years old
1 B.C.E., Jan 28	Herod the Great dies.
1 B.C.E., Jan 10	Total Eclipse of the sun associated with Herod's death.
1 B.C.E., Passover	3000 Jewish worshippers lose lives at temple.
1 B.C.E., summer	The *War of Varus* in Galilee, Judea, and Idumea.
2 C.E.	Tiberius returns to Rome from Rhodes.

4	Gaius Caesar dies. Tiberius is adopted by Augustus and returns to Germany to suppress revolts in Panonia and Dalmatia until 9 C.E.
6	Quirinius becomes legate of Syria-Cilicia.
6	Herod Archelaus, Ethnarch of Judea, deposed by Augustus and is exiled to Gaul. Direct Roman rule of Judea begins. Even the Pharisees preferred this to the rule of a Herod. Caesarea (on the Mediterranean) becomes Rome's capital city for the province of Judea, Samaria, and Idumea.
6	Quirinius conducts Roman Census for taxation purposes
6	Coponius becomes Roman Procurator of Judea.
6	Quirinius appoints Annas ben Seth as high priest, succeeding Joazar.
6	Development of Jewish resistance begins with a tax revolt against Rome by Judas of Gamala and Zadok, the Pharisee (Acts 5:37, Josephus, *A.J.* 20.5.2 [102]; 18.1.1 [4-10]; *B.J.* 2.8.1 [118]).
9	Marcus Ambibulus becomes Roman Procurator of Judea, replacing Coponius.
9	Jesus, age 12, at Jerusalem temple, astounds Jewish Sages, including most likely Hillel and Shammai.
10	Hillel, President of the Sanhedrin, Great Jewish Scholar, Religious teacher, and founder of the Sect of Pharisees, dies. Interestingly, Josephus, the noted first century Jewish historian, never mentions him. His son Simon succeeds the leadership of the Pharisees.
12	Birth of Gaius Caesar (Caligula).
12	Annus Rufus becomes Roman Procurator of Judea, replacing Marcus Ambibulus.
14, Aug 19	Roman Emperor Augustus Caesar, dies.
14	Tiberius becomes second Emperor of Rome.
14, Sept 17	Roman Senate decrees Augustus Caesar a "god."
15	Valerius Gratus becomes Roman Procurator of Judaea, succeeding Annus Rufus.
15	Gratus deposes Annas as High Priest and appoints Ishmael.
16	Gratus deposes Ishmael as High Priest and appoints Eleazar.

17	Gratus deposes Eleazar as High Priest and appoints Simon
17	Devastating earthquake destroys Ephesus.
18	Gratus deposes Simon as High Priest and appoints Joseph Caiaphas, son-in-law to Annas. Annas still holds real power and influence (cf. Luke 2:23, Acts 4:6).
19	Expulsion of the Jews from Rome. 4000 Jewish freemen forced to conduct military expedition to Sardinia.
21	Quirinius dies.
25	Saul, future persecutor of the church and then leading apostle of the church, studies "at the feet of Gamaliel" (Acts 22:3).
26	Pontius Pilate becomes Procurator of Judaea, succeeding Valerius Gratus.
26	Beginning of a Sabbatical year.
26	John the Baptist begins ministry.
27	Emperor Tiberius retires to island of Capri leaving control of Rome to Praetorian Prefect Lucius Aelius Sejanus.
27, autumn	Jesus is baptized by John the Baptist and begins his ministry.
27, autumn	End of a Sabbatical year.
28	John the Baptist is imprisoned and beheaded by Herod Antipas (son of Herod the Great), Tetrarch of Galilee.
30, Apr 7	Jesus crucified, Nisan 14.
30, Apr 7	Joseph of Arimathea petitions Pontius Pilate for the body of Jesus to be buried in his own tomb.
30, Apr 9	Jesus resurrected, Nisan 16.
30, June	Pentecost, ascension of Jesus.
30, June	Pentecost, outpouring of Holy Spirit. New Testament Church of God begins.
31	Tiberius becomes convinced of Praetorian Prefect Sejanus' treason and has him executed. Sejanus is replaced by Vitellus.
32	Gamaliel warns Sanhedrin about resisting the work of God (Acts 5:34).
32	Shortage of grain in Rome leads to public protests.

33	Calling of the seven evangelists, Stephen, Philip, Prochorus, Nicanor, Timon, Parmenas, Nicolas of Antioch (Acts 6:5).
34	A great number of the Priesthood become followers of the faith (Acts 6:7).
34	Stephen disputes with some of the synagogues of the Libertines, Cyrenians, Alexandrians, Cilicians, and Asians (Acts 6:9).
34	Philip, Ethnarch of Ituraea, dies. His province becomes part of Syria.
35, spring	Stephen stoned to death at the feet of Saul (Acts 7:58).
35, summer	Philip the evangelist goes to Samaria to preach the Gospel and there meets Simon Magus, who had a long history there of sorcery (Acts 8:5-11).
35, summer	Saulian persecution begins in earnest against the "Way" (Acts 9:2). Closest friends and relatives of Jesus forced to flee. Banished in a boat without oars to the Mediterranean are Joseph of Arimathea, Lazarus, Nicodemus, Mary, mother of Jesus, Mary Magdalene and others. They finally land on the shores of Gaul and migrate to Britain.
35, summer	Conversion of Saul on the road to Damascus, Syria, 14 years before going to Jerusalem [Conference] (Gal 2:1). Saul then leaves for Arabia for a 3 year period (Gal 1:15-18).
36	High Priest Caiaphas deposed, replaced by Jonathan.
36	Philip baptizes Simon Magus and Simon works with Philip among the Samaritans (Acts 8:13).
36	Samaritans complain about Pontius Pilate's brutal severity and he is ordered to return to Rome.
36	Artabanus, King of Parthia, makes peace with Rome.
36	Apostles at Jerusalem send Peter and John to Samaria.
36	Simon Magus attempts to bribe Peter for power of Holy Spirit.
36	Apostles preach to many cities in Samaria.
36	Imprisonment of Herod Agrippa I.
37, Mar 16	Emperor Tiberius dies.
37, Mar 18	Gaius Caesar (Caligula), age 25, becomes third Roman Emperor.

37	Marcellus becomes Procurator of Judaea, succeeding Pontius Pilate.
37	Pontius Pilate is exiled to Vienne, Gaul.
37	Philip preaches in Gaza (Acts 8:26) and baptizes first Gentile, the Ethiopian eunuch. He then goes to Azotus and finally ends up in Caesarea (Acts 8:26-40).
37	Caligula releases Herod Agrippa from prison. He is restored to power as tetrarch of Judea, upper Galilee, Abilene, and parts of Lebanon, thus ending Roman direct rule, and re-establishing Jewish self-rule in these regions. Roman Procurator Marcellus is then recalled to Rome.
37, summer	King Aretas of Nabatabea (Petra), a client King of Rome is given some jurisdiction over Damascus around this time.
37, summer	Saul appears before the ethnarch Aretas (2 Cor 11:33), then escapes Damascus through a window in a basket (3 years after his conversion, Gal 1:18).
37, summer	Saul arrives in Jerusalem for the first time since his conversion. Apostles were afraid of Saul and disbelieved that he could be a disciple of Jesus (Acts 9:26). Barnabas vouchsafes Saul's preaching in Damascus before the "pillar" Apostles, James, Peter, and John (Acts 9:37). Saul then stays with Peter for 15 days (Gal 1:18). Saul sees no other Apostles at this time, except the Apostle James, the Lord's brother (Gal 1:18-19).
37	Tradition places Joseph of Arimathea and his entourage (including Mary, mother of Jesus) as arriving in Britain at this time.
37, autumn	Saul leaves Jerusalem, goes to Caesarea, then Tarsus (Acts 9:30).
37, Dec	Birth of Nero, future emperor of Rome.
38	Anti-Jewish riot in Alexandria.
38	British Prince Adminius rebels against British King Cybeline.
38	Churches in Judea, Galilee, and Samaria enjoy a period of peace (Acts 9:31).
38	Saul is still unknown by face to the churches in Judea (Gal 1:22).
38	Peter passing through all quarters comes to Lydda and heals Aeneas (Acts 9:32).

38	Peter goes to Joppa where he raises Dorcas from the dead (Acts 9:39).
38	Peter stays in Joppa by the sea in the home of Simon the tanner for many days, until he is sent for by the apostles to return to Jerusalem (Acts 9:43; 10:5). Interestingly, a Gentile from Caesarea by the name of Cornelius, a centurion of the Italian cohort (body-guards to Vitellius?), sends his delegates to request Peter's presence in Caesarea (Acts 10:9).
38	Peter's vision prepares him to receive Cornelius and his Gentile companions at Caesarea (Acts 10:26). Cornelius, and his family are baptized.
38	Peter returns to Jerusalem to defend his actions before the Jewish believers (Acts 11:1-11:18).
39	Banishment of Agrippina and her son Nero by Caligula.
39	Herod Antipas, murderer of John the Baptist, exiled to the Pyrenees in Gaul by Caligula for alliance with Parthians.
39	Aretas IV, Ethnarch of Nabatabea, dies (Acts 9:23-5; 2 Cor 11:32) and is succeeded by Malichus II.
39	Emperor Caligula leads the Roman army to the Rhine, then diverts it to the coast of Gaul with intentions of invading Britain. He then cancels plans to invade Britain.
40	Jews in Jamnia destroy an altar erected by pagan Greek minority.
40	Caligula orders statue of himself to be set up in the temple at Jerusalem.
40	Philo of Alexandria leads an embassy of Jews from Alexandria to Emperor Caligula in Rome. The Jews of Alexandria then become the subject of a Roman pogrom, which Philo and his companions hoped to end. Caligula, however, cut Philo off as he spoke. Philo later told his fellow ambassadors that God would punish Caligula.
40	Jerusalem Church sends Barnabas to Antioch (Acts 11:22).
40	Barnabas leaves Antioch and goes to Tarsus to seek out Saul (Acts 11:25).
40	Saul and Barnabas return together to Antioch, and remain there for a period of a year. It was then and there that the new term "Christian" (derogatory?) was invented by the

	Antiocenes and applied to the followers of the Way (Acts 11:26).
40	Prophets from Jerusalem go to Antioch. One of them, Agabas, predicts a severe famine (Acts 11:28).
40	Publius Petronius becomes legate of Syria, succeeding Vitellius.
40	Matthew writes his Gospel in preparation for worldwide evangelistic campaign. It is the Gospel endorsed by James, the brother of Jesus. James writes his Epistle as a cover letter to Matthew's Gospel specifically addressed to the "twelve tribes" of Israel.
40	British prince Aminius, son of Cunobelinus, flees to Rome. Caligula confirms him as King of Britain.
40, autumn	Beginning of Sabbatical year.
41, Jan 24	Roman Emperor Caligula murdered by soldiers of the Praetorian guard.
41, Jan 25	Tiberius Claudius Drusus (Claudius) becomes fourth Emperor of Rome.
41	Claudius restores Herod Agrippa I as King of the Jews, thus restoring Jewish self-rule. This Herod is the son of Herod Antipas who killed John the Baptist (Mark 6:14-29) and mocked Christ (Luke 23:7-12).
41	Birth of Claudius Tiberius Germanicus, son of Emperor Claudius and his third wife Messallina.
41, Feb 8	Herod Agrippa I sails from Rome to Caesarea.
41, Mar	Herod Agrippa enters city of Jerusalem triumphantly as King and Savior of the Jews. He immediately initiates a pogrom against the disciples.
41, Mar	James, son of Zebedee and the brother of the Apostle John, is rounded up and beheaded by Herod Agrippa during the days of unleavened bread (Acts 12:1-2).
41, Apr	Herod Agrippa imprisons Peter during days of Unleavened Bread (Acts 12:3). Peter is delivered out of prison by an angel and stays a while at the home of Mary, mother of John Mark (Acts 12:3-11).
41, Apr	Herod Agrippa, realizing that he was robbed of his chance to publicly execute Peter, has all of the prison guards executed (Acts 12:18-19).

41, May	Peter leaves Jerusalem for "another place" (Acts 12:17). The text of *Acts* here was most likely edited by Peter later on to read "another place" in order to hide the fact that Peter went to Antioch (where he ordains Euodius as bishop), then Rome, and finally Britain.
41	During year in Antioch, Saul and Barnabas amass a collection of food relief for the people in Judea during a Sabbatical year (Acts 11:27-30; *A.J.* 20:49-55). This is Saul's second trip to Jerusalem, which is unmentioned later on in the letter to the Galatians.
42	Peter leaves Antioch, then goes to Rome with John Mark.
42	Roman senator Rufus Pudens Pudentius receives the Apostle Peter into his home located on Via Urbana, the *Palatium Britannicum*, on the Viminal Hill (one of the "Seven Hills of Rome." The Viminal is a smaller ridge between the Quirinal Hill and the Esquiline Hill). Rufus was baptized by Peter at this time and he is the Rufus mentioned by Paul in Romans 16:13 and Pudens of 2 Timothy 4:21.
42	Peter leaves Rome for Britain and he is there during the coming Roman invasion.
42	Jerusalem apostles spread out on a worldwide evangelistic campaign, 12 years after church established.
42	John Mark remains in Rome, while Peter goes on to Britain. Mark is urged by the small Roman congregation to write a gospel account according to what Peter had preached there in Rome. Mark writes his Gospel there in Rome, then returns to Jerusalem.
43	Rome invades south-east Britain under Aulus Plautius. Romans defeat Caractacus (Caradoc) and Togodumnus decisively at Medway and declare southern Britain as the Roman Province of Britannia. Claudius visits Britain briefly, receives submission of many local chieftains, then returns to Rome.
43	Beginning of the expedition of Saul and Barnabas through Antioch, Cyprus, Pamphilia, and southern Galatia (Acts 13-14). John Mark accompanies them. They sail from Seleucia to Cyprus (Acts 13:4-5).
44, Mar 10	Herod Agrippa I, King of Judaea and Samaria, wearing a brilliant silver robe that sparkled in the sun, is called a god by the people of Caesarea, and is immediately consumed

	by stomach pains. 5 days later, at age 44, he dies (cf. Acts 12:20-23; Josephus, *A.J.* 19.8.2 [343-52]).
44	Cuspus Fadus becomes Procurator of Judea, succeeding the death of Herod Agrippa I. Roman rule is again restored in Judea.
44	Saul before Cypriot proconsul Lucius Sergius Paulus (Acts 13:7). Interestingly, Paul's name is now "Paulus."
44	"Then Saul, (who also is called Paul)" rebukes Elymas the magician (Acts 13:9).
44	Paul goes to Paphos, then to Perga in Pamphylia. John Mark returns to Jerusalem (Acts 13:13). Mark's return did not set well with Paul, who later viewed his return as a desertion and a reason not to take him along on the second of Paul's apostolic campaigns (Acts 15:38-39).
44	Many Jews and proselytes follow Paul and Barnabas at Antioch in Pisidia (Acts 13:43).
44	Paul and Barnabas go on to Iconium (Acts 13:50).
44, summer	Second Roman campaign in Britain. Claudius returns to Rome for his British triumph. Roman senate votes to give Emperor Claudius son's name, the prince Claudius Tiberius Germanicus, the additional title of Brittanicus in honor of the conquest of Britain.
44	Peter returns to Jerusalem from Britain with Mary, mother of Jesus. Apostle John hereafter becomes guardian of Mary (John 19:27).
45	Vardanes I, king of Parthia, dies and is succeeded by his brother Gotarzes II.
45	Paul and Barnabas remain at Iconium for a long time (Acts 14:3).
45	At Lycaonia, Paul is called Mercury and Barnabas, Jupiter (Acts 14:3).
45	Paul is stoned in Iconium (Acts 14:19; 2 Tim 3:11; 2 Cor 11:25).
45	Paul and Barnabas go to Derbe, then to Lystra, and return to Iconium and Antioch of Pisidia (Acts 14:20). They spend most of the year ordaining elders "in every city."
46	Tiberius Julius Alexander becomes Procurator in Judea, succeeding Cuspus Faddus.
46	Thrace made Roman province.

46	Herod of Chalcis appoints Joseph, son of Kami, as high Priest (*J.A.* 20.16; 20.103).
46	Paul and Barnabas set sail from Attalia to Antioch and remained for some time there (Acts 14:24-28).
47	Plautius, conqueror of Britain, is recalled to Rome and marries Gladys, sister of Silurian opponent, Caractacus (Tacitus, *Annals* 13:32). Her name is later changed to Pomponia.
47	800th anniversary of Rome. Claudius holds secular games to mark anniversary.
47	Herod of Chalcis appoints Ananias, son of Nedebaeus, as high Priest (*J.A.* 20.5.2 [103]).
47	James and Simon, rebel sons of Judas of Gamala, are crucified.
47	Ostorius Scapula appointed first Roman governor of Britain.
47	Peter and other Jewish Christians from Jerusalem come to Antioch causing dissension about Gentile men in the church having to be circumcised (Acts 15:1-2). Paul stands up to Peter (Gal 2:11). Barnabas sides with Peter (Gal 2:12-13).
47	It was decided that Paul and Barnabas were to go to Jerusalem to bring the matter before a council of apostles and elders (Acts 15:2).
47, autumn	Beginning of Sabbatical year.
48, early spring	Paul, Barnabas, and Titus (a Greek) arrive in Jerusalem to attend the first council within the church (Acts 15:4). This occurred 14 years after Paul's conversion (Gal 2:1) and is his third recorded visit to Jerusalem.
48, Passover	The **Council of Jerusalem** held (Acts 15). James, Peter, and John are the pillar apostles deliberating (Gal 2:9). James renders the decision "not to trouble the Gentiles who are turning to God" (Acts 15:19).
48, spring	The Jerusalem church sends Paul and Barnabas back to Antioch, with Silas (Sylvanus) and Judas Barsabas, along with a letter to the Antioch church that the only requirements that Gentiles are to observe is to 1) abstain from meat sacrificed to idols; 2) do not drink blood, nor eat

	anything that has been strangled; 3) avoid fornication (Acts 15:23-29).
48	Ventidius Cumanus becomes Roman Procurator of Judea, succeeding Tiberius Julius Alexander.
48	Claudius invests the 21 year old Herod Agrippa II, son of Agrippa I, who died in 44 C.E., with the office of superintendent of the temple of Jerusalem.
48, summer	Paul and Barnabas decide on a second campaign to revisit the churches of Asia (Acts 15:36). Paul does not want to take Mark with them, Barnabas disagrees (Acts 15:37). Barnabas decides to go separately from Paul, taking John Mark with him to Cyprus (Acts 15:39). Paul chooses Silas to go with him to Syria and Cilicia (Acts 15:40-41).
48, summer	Paul goes to Derbe and Lystra and recruits Timothy (Acts 16:1). As Paul goes through the cities of Phrygia and Galatia, he delivers the message of the Council of Jerusalem (Acts 16:4). They are prevented to go to Asia by the Holy Spirit. They bypass Mysia and go to Troas where the vision of Macedonia beckons them (Acts 16:6-10).
48, autumn	End of Sabbatical year.
49, spring	Paul sets sail from Troas to Samothrace, then Neapolis, then Philippi, where they stay for "some days" (Acts 16:11-12). He spends Pentecost in Philippi (1 Thess 2:2). Luke may be with them since this the beginning of the "we" sections in Acts.
49	At Philippi Paul performs an exorcism (Acts 16:13-40) which lands him and Silas in jail. Their chains are loosened and doors are opened by an earthquake, they chose not to escape the prison. This is **Paul's first imprisonment**. Officials release them due to the fact that they are Roman citizens.
49, summer	Paul and Silas come to Thessalonica (Acts 17:1). Paul argues with the Jews in a synagogue three Sabbaths in a row from the scriptures (Acts 17:2-3). Thessalonians attack Jason's house, where Paul had stayed (Acts 17:4-9).
49, summer	Paul and Silas sent to Berea by night (Acts 17:10). Thessalonians follow Paul to Berea (Acts 17:13). Paul sent to Athens and Silas and Timothy remain in Berea (Acts 17:14; 1 Thess 3:1).

49, summer	Paul requests Silas and Timothy to join up with him in Athens (Acts 17:15). In the meantime, Paul preaches to the philosophers (Acts 17:16-34).
49	Execution of Empress Messallina, wife of Claudius. Claudius then marries Agrippina.
49	Claudius expels Jewish Septuagint missionaries from Rome because of riots instigated by their leader, Chrestus (Suetonius, *Claudius*, 25). This occurred in the 9th year of Claudius (Orosius, *Adv. Pag.* 7.6.15).
49	Roman philosopher, Seneca, is recalled from Corsica and is appointed tutor to Nero.
49	The Romans begin to exploit the Mendip Tin mines in Britain, the legendary source of wealth of Joseph of Arimathea. The British tribe known as the Iceni were then cut off from their source of wealth. The Iceni were thus obliged to borrow money. Seneca advances a huge sum of money to Prasutagus, the King of the Iceni, on the security of their public buildings. Upon the death of Prasutagus, Seneca called in the loan. This was the prelude to the Boudiccan war in 62.
49, autumn	Paul leaves Athens for Corinth (Acts 18:1).
49, Nov	Paul arrives at Corinth, where he stays for a year and a half (Acts 18:1).
49, Nov	Aquila, a Jew originally from Pontus, and his wife Priscilla arrive at Corinth after being exiled from Rome (Acts 18:1-2).
49, Dec	Silas and Timothy rejoin Paul at Corinth (Acts 18:5).
50, Jan	Paul sends Timothy to the Thessalonians (1 Thess 3:1-2).
50, early spring	Paul's *Epistle to the Galatians* written from Corinth before Passover.
50, Passover	A Roman soldier exposes his genitals to Passover celebrants in Jerusalem and antagonizes a riot thereby. Some 10-20,000 celebrants end up dead.
50, spring	Timothy returns to Corinth, bringing good news about the Thessalonians (1 Thess 3:6).
50, late spring	Paul writes *First Thessalonians* from Corinth.
50	A Roman soldier destroys a Torah scroll. Jews complain to Cumanus. Soldier is beheaded.

50	Claudius adopts Lucius Dominitius (Nero) as his son, which effectively excludes his own real son, Britannicus, from succession.
50	Paul, Timothy, and Silas preach to the Corinthians (2 Cor 1:19). Crispus, leader of the Synagogue, his household, Justus, Gaius, and many other believers are baptized (Acts 18:8). Paul later remarks that only Crispus, Gaius, and the household of Stephanus, were baptized by him (1 Cor 1:14-16).
50	Roman city of Londinium in Britain is founded on the banks of the Thames river.
50, summer	Paul writes *Second Thessalonians* from Corinth.
51, June	Roman Proconsul Gallio arrives in Corinth.
51, July	Paul brought before Gallio at completion of 18 month stay in Corinth (Acts 18:11-17). This is **Paul's second imprisonment**. Sosthenes, chief ruler of the synagogue, is beaten. Gallio ignores disturbance.
51, July	Paul departs Corinth and sets sail for Ephesus with Priscilla and Aquila (Acts 18:18-21). At Cenchrea, Paul takes a vow, then shaves his head. He stays in Ephesus for a while, then sails back to Caesarea.
51, autumn	Paul goes to Jerusalem for possibly the fall Holydays (Acts 18:22). This is Paul's fourth recorded visit to Jerusalem. He then goes back to Antioch, where he spends "some time" which possibly means that he wintered there until next spring.
51	Burrus becomes Praetorian Prefect.
51	Famine in Rome.
51	British King Caractacus of Siluria, seeking refuge with the Queen of the Brigantes, Cartimandua, is betrayed, captured, and sent to Rome. Because of his noble fame and dignified demeanor, he and his family are allowed to freely reside as British war captives in Rome.
52, spring	Paul leaves Antioch to go on his third evangelizing campaign. He goes to Galatia and Phrygia (Acts 18:23).
52, spring	Alexandrian Jew Apollos, comes to Ephesus, is baptized by Priscilla and Aquila, then goes to Corinth (Acts 18:24-28; 19:1).

52, May	Paul arrives at Ephesus. He stays there for a period of 3 months (Acts 19:8) and 2 years (Acts 19:9-10).
52, Aug	Paul completes three month preaching in an Ephesian Synagogue (Acts 19:8), then teaches in the Hall of Tyrannus for two years (Acts 19:10). During this time Paul performs miracles, magicians burn their books, Paul fights beasts [literal or figurative?] (1 Cor 15:32).
52, autumn	Paul sends Titus to Corinth, Timothy and Erastus to Macedonia (Acts 19:22).
52, autumn	Paul is apprehended by a mob at Ephesus initiated by Demetrius the Silversmith This is **Paul's third imprisonment** (Acts 19:371 cf. 2 Cor 11:23; Rom 16:7).
53, March	Paul writes *First Corinthians* in Ephesus before Passover (1 Cor 4:6-8). He therein mentions the influence of Apollos and Cephas before him (1 Cor 1:12, 16:12). He also mentions that other apostles, and Cephas, travel with their "wife" also (1 Cor 9:5). He refers to Barnabas and himself as workaholics (1 Cor 9:6).
53, March	Paul sends Timothy from Ephesus to Corinth before Passover (1 Cor 5:17).
53, Apr	Paul receives Timothy back at Ephesus after Passover (1 Cor 4:17).
53, May	Paul stays in Ephesus until Pentecost (1 Cor 16:8).
53, July 1	Marcus Antonius Felix becomes Procurator of Judaea, succeeding Cumanus.
53, summer	Stephanus, Fortunatus, and Achaicus (Gaius?) come to Ephesus from Corinth to see Paul (1 Cor 16:17). Sosthenes also with Paul (1 Cor 1:1).
53	Nero marries his step-sister, Claudius' daughter Octavia.
53	Roman senator Rufus Pudens Pudentius, a Christian who had been baptized by Peter in 42 C.E., marries Gladys, daughter of British King Caractacus and brother of Linus, future bishop of Rome.[385]
53, Sept 18	Trajan, future emperor of Rome, born.
54, March	Paul leaves Ephesus after the riot of Demetrius and travels through Macedonia (Acts 20:1-3), passes through Troas (Acts 20:7-12), keeps Passover at Philippi (Acts 20:9).
54	Agrippina, with the help of the Prefect of the Praetorian Guard, Burrus, assured herself the title of Augusta.

54	British King Caractacus dies in Rome.
54, autumn	Paul in Greece (Acts 20:1-3), stays there for 3 months, meets Titus and writes *Second Corinthians.* where he writes that he will come to Corinth a third time (2 Cor 13:1).
54, autumn	Beginning of Sabbatical Year.
54, autumn	Paul, at the end of his three month stay in Corinth, writes *Epistle to the Romans* (Acts 20:2-3).
54, Oct 13	Emperor Claudius is murdered. Having now secured the throne for her son, Agrippina poisons her husband with a plate of mushrooms, thus elevating her seventeen year old son, Nero, to the throne as the fifth Emperor of Rome.
55, Apr	Luke and others sail to Assos, but Paul travels by land. There they rejoin and sail to the island of Mytelene (Lesbos), then to Chios, Samos, and Miletus (Acts 20:13-16). Paul by-passes Ephesus, but had previously summoned the Ephesian elders to meet him in Miletus, where he delivers a farewell address (Acts 20:18-35). The two years and three months that he stayed in Ephesus is here referred to by Paul as being "three years" (Acts 20:31), another confirmation of inclusive reckoning in biblical time references.
55, May	Paul and company sail for Cos, Rhodes, Patara and land in Tyre (Acts 21:1-3). They look up disciples and stay seven days there who tell Paul not to go to Jerusalem (vv. 4-6). They set sail from Tyre to Ptolemais, then travel to Caesarea where they stay at the home of Philip the evangelist (vv. 7-10). There, the prophet Agabus foretells Paul's incarceration in Jerusalem (vv. 8-14). They go to Jerusalem and stay at the home of Mnason.

[385] Upon their marriage Gladys adopts the Roman name of Claudia in compliment to Emperor Claudius, who had treated the British royal family in Rome with dignity and respect. Their children are Timotheus, Novatus (martyred 137), Pudentiana (martyred 107), and Praxedes. The home of Pudens became known as the Palatium Britannicum, and later as the Hospitium Apostolorum, and finally, the Titulus – which probably served as the only church building in Rome until the time of Constantine. This house is most likely the home where Paul was kept under house arrest for two years (56-58 C.E.). Its baths were named after Timothy and Novatus, two of the children of Rufus and Claudia. It later became the place where Praxedes hid martyrs, then a hospice for pilgrims from the East, and under bishop Evaristus (100-109 C.E.), a church. It then was called Pastor's (probably after Pastor Hermas, who wrote to them). Baronius says that Timotheus was a disciple of Peter and Paul (Baronius, 2.56.47). Pastor Hermas says that all four children, Timotheus, Novatus, Praxedes and Pudentiana, were instructed by preaching of the Apostles (Baronius, 2.8-148). In the second century the Basilica of St. Pudentiana was built over the house.

55, spring	Alexandrian Jew known as the "Egyptian" attempts to take Jerusalem with some 4000 followers, but is defeated by Felix.
55, May 19	Paul arrives in Jerusalem, the day before Pentecost.
55, May 20	Paul meets with James, Peter, and John (the pillar apostles) at an assembly of all the elders, on the day of Pentecost. James requires Paul to go through a seven day purification ritual (Acts 21:26-7).
55, May 21-27	Paul begins his purification.
55, May 28	Paul is arrested in Jerusalem (Acts 21:28-33). This is **Paul's fourth imprisonment**.
55, May 29	Paul before Sanhedrin (Acts 22:30). Over 40 Jews take an oath not to eat nor drink until Paul is executed (Acts 23:12-15).
55, May 30	Paul taken to Antipatris, then to Ceasarea (Acts 23:16).
55, June 4	High Priest Ananias arrives in Caesarea (Acts 24:1).
55, June 9	Felix and his Jewish wife, Drusila, have private audience with Paul (Acts 24:24).
55, July 1	Porcius Festus arrives in Caesarea, replacing Felix as Procurator of Judaea.
55, July 4	Paul appears before Festus and appeals his case to Caesar.
55, summer	Felix arrives back in Rome.
55, autumn	End of Sabbatical Year in Judea.
55, Oct	Paul, under custody, begins voyage to Rome after Day of Atonement.
55, Nov	Paul and Luke ship-wrecked on the isle of Malta, where they winter (Acts 28:11).
56, late winter	Nero has Britannicus, son of Claudius, a pretender to the throne, poisoned. Titus, Nero's friend and later Emperor, drinks from same beverage and nearly dies as well.
56, Apr	Paul arrives in Rome, spends two years in house arrest (Acts 28:30). This is **Paul's fifth imprisonment**. There he preaches before kings, fulfilling his second commission (Acts 9:15). The kings that he specifically witnesses to are the British war captives in Rome.
56	Apostle John, in Jerusalem, initially receives a vision of the *Revelation* of the end times. It is addressed to seven churches in Asia.

56	Paul ordains the British Prince Linus, son of British war captive King Caractacus, as first Bishop at Rome.
57	Pomponia, British wife of Plautius, is accused of superstitious beliefs (Christian?) but is exonerated (Tacitus, *Annals*, 13:32).
58, Apr	Paul released from Roman prison.
58	Paul baptizes the British arch-druid, Bran, father of Caractacus.
58, spring	*Book of Acts* ends. The period of "***Beyond Acts***" begins.
58, June	Paul departs from Rome and goes possibly to Spain (no record of such), but most definitely to Britain (numerous traditions testify to such).
58	Rome renews hostilities with Parthia. Vardanes II is defeated, executed, and replaced by Vologases I.
59	Nero murders his mother, Agrippina.
60	Iccenian British king, Prasatugas, dies. Romans seize his property. His wife, Queen Boudica, and his daughters are raped.
61	Queen Boudica amasses an army of 100,000 troops to revolt against Rome. She burns the city of Londinium, center of Roman pride and imperial dominance, to the ground.
61	Laodicea suffers Earthquake (Tacitus, *Ann* 14.27).
61, autumn	Beginning of a Sabbatical year.
62, spring	Festus dies in office, causing a vacuum in Roman rule in Judea. Jewish leaders seize this opportunity and plan a public debate with James, brother of Jesus.
62, Passover	James the "Just," half brother of Jesus, is thrown off the pinnacle of the temple and bludgeoned to death with a soap makers club (Eusebius, *Hist. eccl.* 2.23).
62, summer	Luceius Albinus becomes Procurator of Judea, succeeding Festus. He drives the Sicarii out of Jerusalem.
62, summer	Soon after James' death, Apostles were driven out of Jerusalem (Eusebius, *Hist. eccl.* 3.5).
62	Agrippa II replaces High Priest Ananus with Jesus son of Damneus (Josephus, *A.J.* 20.9.1 [203], *B.J.* 6.2.2 [114]).
62, summer	First wave of Christians begin to disperse to other parts of the Empire (Eusebius, *Hist eccl.* 3.1).

62	Tradition has it that Bartholomew was martyred in Kalyana, a city state on the west coast of India, near modern-day Bombay. Bartholomew was skinned alive and crucified.
62	Joshua ben Ananias pronounces prophetic dirge against Jerusalem and temple (Josephus, *B.J.* 6.5.3 [300-9]).
62	Suetonius Paulinus is sent to Britain with 10,000 troops to squash Boudiccan rebellion. She takes poison rather than being taken as captive.
62	Death of Pallas, brother of Festus.
62	Nero kills his wife, Octavia, and marries Poppaea Sabina, a proselyte to Judaism.
62	Afranius Burrus, the Praetorian Prefect, is murdered by Poppaea Sabina.
62, autumn	End of Sabbatical year.
63, Feb. 5	Mount Vesuvius erupts, causing great earthquake.
63, summer	Paul returns from Spain and Britain, goes to Crete.
63	Under the rule of Procurator Albinus, "the seeds of coming destruction were being sown in the city" (Josephus, *B.J.* 2.14.1 [276]).
63, autumn	Paul stays at Nicopolis for winter and writes to *Epistle of Titus.*
64, spring	Gessius Florus becomes Roman Procurator in Judaea, succeeding Albinus.
64, spring	Paul goes to Ephesus to see Timothy (1 Tim 1:3).
64, summer	Paul writes *First Timothy* from Macedonia requesting John Mark to perform a "useful service".
64, summer	Temple in Jerusalem completed.
64, summer	Paul returns to Ephesus and is imprisoned there (sixth imprisonment). This is **Paul's sixth imprisonment**.
64	Paul receives his "revelation" of the "Mystery," which completely changes his outlook in the plan of God.
64	Paul writes *Colossians, Philemon*, and *Ephesians* from an Ephesian prison to explain his revelation of the "Mystery."
64, summer	Peter writes *Epistle of First Peter* from Jerusalem to "alien residents" in Asia Minor. He sends greetings from John

	Mark, who just arrived from Rome, and the sister church at Rome, referred to as "Babylon."
64, July 19	Fire at Rome – blamed on the Christians.
64	Beginning of Christian persecution.
64	Mass exodus of Jews and Christians out of Judaea to other parts of Empire (Josephus, *B.J.* 2.14.2 [279]).
65, spring	Paul released from prison in Ephesus, goes to Antioch, Iconium, and Lystra (2 Tim 4:20). At Antioch Paul ordains Ignatius as bishop, succeeding Euodius.
65, summer	Paul receives stiff opposition and persecution in Galatia.
65	Nero kicks his pregnant wife, Poppaea, to death because she complained that he came home too late from the circus.
65	Matthias becomes high priest.
65	Seneca and Lucan commit suicide.
65	Rome is inflicted with epidemic.
65	Agrippa returns from Alexandria to Jerusalem. He delivers a speech to dissuade a revolt against Rome, but to no avail.
66, summer	Last remnants of "Nazarenes" flee Jerusalem to Pella (Eusebius, *Hist eccl.* 3.5). **This is Paul's seventh imprisonement.**
66	Paul arrested in Rome. *Second Timothy* written from Mamertine prison.
66	Tiridates of Armenia goes to Rome to receive throne of Parthia.
66	Nero marries Statilia Messalina and travels to Greece to enter Olympic games.
66	Paul in prison at Rome, edits his epistles for posterity.
66	A riot is provoked in Caesarea because of an upturned chamber pot in front of a Synagogue, defiling holy ground. Greek citizens bribe Florus not to interfere. This incident escalates into a revolt. Vespasian appointed commander in Palestine to put down revolt.
66	Tradition has Thaddeus, who was in possession of the lance which pierced Jesus' side, establishing churches in Armenia.
66, summer	Peter leaves Jerusalem via Corinth to Rome to see Paul.

66, autumn	Peter arrives in Rome and visits Paul in the Mamertine prison. Paul delivers to Peter his 14 letter collection for the preservation for the future of the church.
67, Jan 18	Paul is released from his (seventh) imprisonment in Rome, but is beheaded on the road from Rome to Ostia.
67	Linus, first bishop of Rome, is martyred, maybe at the same time as the Apostle Paul. Peter then ordains Clement (67-79 C.E.) as the second bishop of the Church at Rome.
67, summer	Peter writes his *Epistle of Second Peter*, explaining his intention to leave a body of apostolic writings for the future church.
67	Nero enters several Olympic contests, accompanied by 5000 bodyguards, and takes all the events.
67	Vespasian begins conquering Galilee and Judea. Romans win a naval battle on Sea of Galilee. 37,000 captured Jewish prisoners are sold as slaves in a stadium in Caesarea.
67	The Galilean general, Joseph ben Mattathias, surrenders to the Romans at Jotapata.
67	Jude writes his Epistle saying that what Peter had predicted was then happening.
68, Feb 22	A year after Paul's death, Peter also martyred in Rome, crucified upside down.
68, spring	Praetorian Guard recognize Servius Sulpicius as imperator. Roman senate declares Nero a public enemy.
68, June 9	Nero flees his villa outside of Rome – the House of Freedom – and is pursued by the Praetorian Guard, who surround him, leaving no choice but suicide. His dying words are reportedly: "what an artist I perish." Thus ends the Julio/Claudian dynasty. Galba is named Emperor by Senate.
68	The church in Alexandria, Egypt, is founded by John Mark, the disciple of Peter.
69	Clement, bishop of Rome, writes a letter to the Corinthian congregation. He states that attention to the dispute at Corinth had been delayed by "sudden and repeated misfortunes and hindrances which have befallen us" (1:1). He also writes: "Not in every place, brethren, ARE the daily sacrifices offered, or the peace-offerings, or the sin-offerings and the trespass-offerings, but in Jerusalem only"

	(41:2). Obviously, the temple is still in operation. The Corinthians had deposed its old clergy and replaced them with new men. Clement, acting in near apostolic authority, asks that they retain the former clergy on the grounds that these stood in due succession from the apostles, thus establishing the primacy of the apostolic succession.
69	Birth of Polycarp, bishop of Smyrna (d. 155). Irenaeus stated that Polycarp had known St. John at Ephesus.
69, Jan 15	Galba assassinated by Otho. Civil war breaks out as Otho and Vitellius seek throne.
69, Apr 16	Otho, defeated by Vitellius, commits suicide.
69, July 1	Vitellius enters Rome to take the throne. On same day, Roman army in Egypt declares Vespasian emperor.
69	According to tradition, the Apostle Andrew was crucified in Patrae, on the Peloponnesus peninsula.
69, Dec 20	Senate confirms Titus Flavius Vespasianus (Vespasian) and on the same day Vitellius' own troops drag his murdered body through the streets of Rome.
70, spring	Titus lays siege to Jerusalem.
70, summer	Rabbi Jochanan ben Zacchai is smuggled out of Jerusalem.
70, August	On the same day that the ancient Babylonian king Nebuchadnezzar destroyed the first temple (Tisha B'Av, 587 B.C.E.), Titus razes the temple of Herod.
70, Sept 7	After a 139 day siege on Jerusalem, Titus takes out last defenders of upper city of Jerusalem. 97,000 Jews are slain.
70, autumn	The temple is torn apart, stone by stone, by Roman soldiers, to extract melted gold, fulfilling the words of Jesus 40 years previously that not one temple stone would be left upon another (Matt 24:2).
70	After the fall of Jerusalem, Rabbi Jochanan ben Zacchai founds a rabbinical school in Jamnia (Javneh). He is the guiding force to reconstruct a new kind of Judaism that is not centered around temple worship. Some temple rituals are retained outside the temple precincts, such as the blowing of the shofar on Rosh ha-shanah and the carrying of the lulav (palm branches) on Sukkoth (Feast of Tabernacles).

71	Jerusalem becomes the barracks for the Roman 10th Legion. Remaining Jews became slaves to the Roman army.
71	Rome imposes a tax on all Jews throughout the empire to support the temple of Jupiter Capitolina in Rome, the god who defeated the god of the Jews, Yahweh.
71, Mar. 20	Total solar eclipse in middle East.
71	Many christians who fled to Pella, return and build church on the Mount of Olives.
71	Returning to Rome in Triumph, Titus appoints Lucilius Bassus to defeat the remaining Jewish rebel fortresses at Herodian and Masada.
71	Joseph ben Mattathias, captured Galilean general, becomes a patron of the Flavian rulers in Rome, changing his name to the Roman name of Flavius Josephus. He publishes his account of *Jewish Wars* from the time of the Maccabean revolt to the recent Jewish war with Rome. Josephus had been a leader of troops against the Romans in Galilee during the war (66-70). When captured, he predicted that Vespasian would become emperor, a move that saved his life. Josephus wrote a history of the war, and because of the favoritism he received from the Roman emperors, was detested by his fellow Jews as a traitor.
72	Tradition has it that Thomas was stabbed to death by Brahman priests in Mylapore, India.
72	Roman general Bassus dies following his capture of the Herodion and Machaerus. Next, Flavius Silva is appointed to go in and wrap-up resistance at the final Jewish resistant holdout, Masada.
73	Romans, in a sweep up operation, eliminate resistance in Dead Sea outposts, such as Qumran. The Qumran community, anticipating this, hide their valuable sacred library in caves, not to be discovered until 1947.
73	Last remnant of resistance assembles at the fortress on top of Mount Masada under the leadership of Galilean rebel, Eleazar ben Yair.
73	Romans begin siege of Masada.
74	When the Romans finally assemble a ramp which allows them to break into the fortress, they find the defenders all

	dead, having taken their lives rather than face Roman captivity or slaughter.
74	A Syrian jail prisoner, Mara Bar Serapion, writes to his son, Serapion, mentioning the "wise king" that was executed by the Jews some time in the recent past.
75, June	A triumphal procession in Rome exhibits sacred temple objects from Jerusalem.
76, Jan 24	Hadrian, future Roman emperor, is born.
77	Pliny the Elder completes his *Natural History* in 37 books.
77	The second Roman bishop, Clement, dies and is succeeded by Cletus.
78	Roman historian Tacitus marries his own daughter.
79	According to tradition, Jude and Simon were torn apart by a Persian mob after this date. Simon had joined forces with Jude after a trip to Britain. Jude had been in Armenia.
79, June 23	Roman Emperor Vespasian dies of diarrhea and is succeeded by his son, the victor of Judea, Titus Flavius Vespasianus (Titus).
79, Aug 24	Mt. Vesuvius again erupts, this time submerging the cities of Pompey, Stabiae, and Herculaneum in lava, claiming Pliny the Elder as a victim. Pliny the Younger survives and writes an eyewitness account to Tacitus. Titus does what he can to repair the damage.
79	Fire in Rome.
80	The Colosseum, which was begun during the reign of Vespasian, is completed by his son Titus. It seats 87,000 people. It is named for a colossal statue of Nero.
81, Sept 13	Emperor Titus dies and is succeeded by his brother, Titus Flavius Domitianus (Domitian).
81	Arch of Titus completed in Circus Maximus in Rome. It depicts plunder of the Jewish temple.
83	The third Roman bishop, Cletus, dies and is succeeded by Anaclitus.
85	Rome finally completes conquest of Britain.
85	Jews adopt an anathema against all "Nazarenes" in their Synagogue liturgy.

89	Domitian has astrologers and philosophers expelled from Rome.
90	The Jewish Synod of Jamnia reaffirms the 22 book Hebrew Canon (TaNaK) of Ezra.
90	According to tradition, Philip was crucified upside down (like Peter) in Hierapolis, Asia Minor.
90	According to Hippolytus, Matthew died a natural death, in Hierees, Persia.
93	Alleged persecution (doubtful) of Christians under Domitian.
95	Flavius Josephus publishes his *Antiquities of the Jews.* Book 18 refers to Jesus Christ. Scholars believe the statement was tampered with by Christians at a later date because it refers to Christ as divine.
95	The fourth Roman bishop, Anaclitus, dies and is succeeded by Evaristus.
95	Domitian executes his cousin Flavius Clemens for practicing Judaism.
96	The Apostle John banished to the Greek Island of Patmos, off the coast from Ephesus. He there receives a renewal of the Apocalyptic vision that he received in the 50's.
96, Sept 18	Domitian is executed by the Senate and is replaced by Senator Marcus Cocceius Nerva. Domitian's name and statues are obliterated. Thus ends the Flavian dynasty.
97	The Apostle John finalizes the New Testament canon. The Elders of John commit the canon to the archives at the Libraries at Jerusalem and Caesarea for protection and future dissemination. A few years later, Ignatius refers to these "archives" (Ignatius, *Epistle to the Philadelphians,* 8:2).
98, Jan	Roman Emperor Nerva dies of a stroke. Marcus Ulpius Traianus (Trajan), son of Nerva, becomes emperor.
100	The Apostle John is martyred. The apostolic era comes to an end.

APPENDIX 3

When Was the Book of Revelation Written?

THE INTERNAL EVIDENCE OF THE *BOOK OF Revelation* shows us that it is mainly a product of the pre-63 C.E. environment.[386] However, the earliest testimony places the writing of the *Book of Revelation* in the time of the Roman Emperor Domitian (81-96 C.E.). Irenaeus, at the end of the second century referred to John's vision as being

> seen no such long time ago, but almost in our own generation, at the end of the reign of Domitian (Irenaeus, *Haer.* 5.30.3 [*ANF* 1:416]. See also Eusebius, *Hist. eccl.* 3.18.3; 5.8.6).[387]

Unlike the other books of the New Testament, where we have no direct testimony as to when they were written, the *Book of Revelation* stands out as one that scholars feel confident about in its dating, for no other reason than just this reference by Irenaeus.[388] Indeed, it is because of this reference that scholars have been virtually united in accepting a date of around 95 C.E. for the compilation of the *Apocalypse.* But scholars, in their over eagerness to have a book of the New Testament dated years after the fall of Jerusalem in 70 C.E., have taken a blind eyed

[386] Based on the internal evidence, some scholars, such as John A. T. Robinson, were led to believe that all of the books of the New Testament, including the *Book of Revelation,* were written before Jerusalem fell in 70 C.E. See his *Redating the New Testament* (Philadelphia: Westminster, 1976), 221-53. Also, Albert A. Bell, Jr., "The date of John's Apocalypse: The Evidence of Some Roman Historians Reconsidered" *New Testament Studies* 10 (1977-78): 93-102. For a thorough treatment on the subject, see Kenneth L. Gentry, Jr., *Before Jerusalem Fell: Dating the Book of Revelation* (Tyler, Tex.: Institute for Christian Economics, 1989).

[387] Further, Melito of Sardis, *History,* 4.26:9, also bears similar witness to this.

[388] Irenaeus, in fact, may not be all that reliable a witness to historical accuracy, as noted by his inaccurate sequence of the first bishops of Rome (as brought out in appendix 4) and his confusion of the Apostle James with James, the brother of Jesus (Irenaeus, *Haer.* 3.12.14 [*ANF* 1:435]).

approach to the internal evidence at the expense of good critical judgement. Some of the arguments in which a late writing is sustained are not only weak, but even somewhat comical. Albert A. Bell, Jr. notes:

> Just how deeply ingrained this idea has become [a dating in the reign of Domitian] is evident when Caird can say, 'Clearly the only wise procedure is to start with the hypothesis that the date of writing was *c.* A.D. 95 and see where it leads us'[389] Not surprisingly, it leads him to the conclusion that the book was written under Domitian.[390]

However, the answer to the entire problem is in fact simple. The initial vision and compilation occurred during the time of Nero, but the final redaction occurred during the time of Domitian. Arthur Cushman McGiffert long ago offered this solution:

> Unanimous tradition, beginning with Irenaeus assigns the banishment of John and the apocalyptic visions to the reign of Domitian. This was formerly the common opinion, and is still held by some respectable writers, but strong internal evidence has driven most modern scholars to the conclusion that the Apocalypse must have been written before the destruction of Jerusalem... The case thus stood for years, until in 1886 Vischer published his pamphlet *Die Offenbarung des Johannes, eine jüdisch Apocalypse in Christlicher Bearbeitung* (Gebhardt and Harnack's *Texte und Untersuchungen,* Band II. Heft. 3), which if his theory were true, would reconcile external and internal evidence in a most satisfactory manner, throwing the original into the reign of Nero's successor, and the Christian recension into the reign of Domitian. Compare especially Harnack's appendix to Vischer's pamphlet.[391]

Armed with this approach we can thus see that the reference to a writing during the time of Domitian could refer to a second vision about 40 years after the first one, at which time John completed his final testimony. And the internal evidence of the book itself supports this view.

---

[389] George B. Caird, *The Revelation of St. John the Divine* (New York: Harper & Row, 1966), 6.

[390] Albert A. Bell, Jr., "The date of John's Apocalypse: The Evidence of Some Roman Historians Reconsidered" *New Testament Studies* 10 (1977-78): 93-4. Bell also notes that the whole idea of a Domitian persecution rests itself on shaky ground.

[391] Arthur Cushman McGiffert, *Nicene and Post-Nicene Fathers,* second series, ed. Philip Schaff and Henry Wace (Peabody, Mass., Hendrickson, 1995), 1:148, in a footnote to the *Church History of Eusebius,* 3.18.1. Thus, the double recension theory is not new at all, and should be dusted off and re-introduced for the merits of its convincing explanation of the entire *Revelation* enigma.

Notice that John was told that he would be given the information from the "little scroll" once and then "again" (Rev 10:11). It thus would appear that the *Book of Revelation* came as a result of two separate visions, spaced some 40 years apart. The initial revelation came to John in the time of Nero. The second in the time of Domitian.

Also note that John had initially been told by an angel to eat a scroll and it would be sweet to the mouth but bitter to the stomach (Rev 10:8-10). This may be a reflection of the *Book of Revelation* itself. The initial testimony of the imminent return of Jesus was sweet testimony to the early faithful. However, the failure of these prophecies to occur in the lifetime of the first generation Christians was indeed a bitter pill to swallow that gave a deep ache to their stomachs. But right on the heels of this, the angel tells John that

> you must prophesy AGAIN about many peoples and nations and languages and kings (Rev 10:11).

Notice the significant words "prophesy again." Could this be referring to a second vision after having to eat the scroll that caused so much stomach pain? John is about to explain the seventh seal in chapter 11. But then, right on the heels of this chapter, there are introduced chapters 12, 13 and 14 that appear to be insets that are unrelated to this explanation. Then in chapter 15 the explanation resumes. These insets appear to be revelations given to John a second time while he was literally exiled on the Isle of Patmos in 96 C.E.

Ernest L. Martin also makes a further interesting observation about Jesus telling Peter that he would die an old man by martyrdom (John 21:18, 19), but that John would remain alive "until I come" (John 21:22, 23).[392] Would this mean that John would remain alive until the second coming of Christ? No, because Jesus had earlier prophesied that John and his brother James would both undergo martyrdom (Matt 20:23). John's brother James was killed by Agrippa the First (Acts 12:2) and we have testimony that John was martyred also in his later years (Tertullian, *Praescr.* 18). Jesus made a similar statement on another occasion:

> For the Son of man shall come in the glory of his Father with his angels; and then he shall reward every man for his works. Verily I say unto you, There be some standing here, which shall not taste of death, till they see the Son of man coming in his kingdom (Matt 16:27, 28).

Six days later, after this prophecy, James, Peter, and John witnessed

---

[392] Ernest L. Martin, *Restoring,* 327-30.

Jesus glorified in vision on the Mount of Transfiguration (Matt 17:1-9). In other words, in less than a week this prophecy was fulfilled. We are told in the *Book of Revelation* four times that John was taken in spirit (which is another way of saying in "vision") into a future period of time and location to see the prophesied end-time events (Rev 1:10; 4:1, 2; 17:3; 21:10).

When John received his first vision, and wrote the things that he saw he said that he was on the Isle of Patmos. Yet, if he were writing in the mid-fifties C.E., he was most probably still physically located in the city of Jerusalem. However, the text says that John "came to be in the Spirit in (not on) the Lord's Day" (Rev 1:10). He was transported in vision INTO the prophesied period known in the Old Testament as the "Day of the Lord." Even his "seeing" the visions on the Isle of Patmos had a visionary aspect to them because, again, the text says: "I *came to be* in the isle called Patmos."

It was a spiritual or visionary experience that took John to Patmos in exactly the very same sense that Ezekiel was taken from Babylon to Jerusalem in vision (cf. Ezek 1:1-3, 8:1-4). Since we have testimony that John was in fact exiled to the Isle of Patmos in the mid-nineties of the first century, his initial vision may have prophetically looked forward to that time and place when John would literally be there to receive his final vision.

Tradition tells us that John was exiled in the days of the Emperor Domitian (81-96 C.E.) to a penal colony on the Island of Patmos, off the coast of Ephesus.[393] Why was John exiled to this particular Island? We don't know, but curiously, this is exactly the very Island that John was taken in vision some 40 years previously to receive his initial vision of the end time.

In what appears to be an ironic twist of fate, John was in his later life literally exiled to the very island that had been the stage of his visionary apocalypse some 40 years before. He received a second vision on the Isle of Patmos around 96 C.E. This is why his first vision carried him to this remote Island. It was itself a prophecy about what would happen to John. And it was a reaffirmation of his initial vision in the 50's.

Indeed, now John knew what Jesus had meant when Jesus prophesied that Peter would be martyred an old man, but John would remain until Christ would come again (John 21:15-23). John may have believed with others, just as these verses indicate, that John would remain alive until the

---

[393] These traditions are recorded in the manuscript codex number 188 in the library of the Patmos Monastery entitled: "Peregrinations of St. John the Divine and his disciple Prochorus, written by the later in testimony" and related in Archimandrite Theodoritos Bournis, *"I Was in the Isle of Patmos ..."* (Athens: Alex. Matsoukis, 1992).

second coming of the Lord. That is why he and many others had initially felt that the second coming would have occurred by the year of 67 C.E. John indeed did remain alive after Peter's martyrdom to see Jesus coming again, and with this confirmation John knew that he had the authority to finalize the canon and close it with words that seals it to this day (Rev 21:18-22). One century after the miraculous birth of the Messiah, the story of that miracle was confirmed, canonized, and sealed for the future of the New Testament church.

But the question that begs an answer is why would this vision be given the church in the time of Nero if it were not for that time? Indeed, did not this prophecy contribute to the idea that Jesus was going to return within the generation that succeeded his resurrection? Let us try to understand.

The entire *Book of Revelation* is made up of symbolic and allegorical language, which we must be careful with in what we take as literal. When Christ says throughout the *Book of Revelation* that his return from heaven is to occur quickly, those statements have to be interpreted within a time frame that is near the "Day of the Lord," which is the period of time that John was projected "into." It is the same with the Olivet Prophecy that Jesus gave concerning the end time recorded in Matthew 24, Luke 21, and Mark 13. There was a first century application, but concerning the events surrounding Christ's return to this earth, those events were to be yet future.

But again, why would Jesus seemingly mislead his own disciples into believing that he would return during their lifetime? If we look at the growth of the church in the period of Acts we see that the early church grew by the thousands. Indeed, all "Adventist" type movements, where the feeling and the hope of Christ's return is imminent, experience a rapid growth and a zeal and enthusiasm that is exciting and motivating. But those who believe that Christ's return (or the coming of the Messiah) is to be yet far into the future and that they will not soon be delivered from the bondage of this "present evil world" usually become lackadaisical or lose interest in prophecy altogether. Therefore, the writings of the New Testament, mostly written before the destruction of the temple in 70 C.E. have captured the zeal of these early writings for the future church. The net result is that the writings of the New Testament are up to date and vibrant with the same zeal in every age.

Jesus never gave a date for his return. But for those who read his words in whatever age they live in, Christ could indeed come "quickly." This is the kind of testimony that the apostles finally were inspired to see was the way the message was to be brought forth in every age. It is up to date, and written with the excitement of those who actually felt the fervent belief of Jesus returning within their generation. And this is the kind of vibrant and exciting message that readers are left with, within the pages of the New Testament canon.

The first revelation that John received in the late fifties came into disrepute after 70 C.E. because many now saw it as a dismal failure. But John, the last of the living apostles, was given the vision a second time, obviously to reassure him and the church that the prophecies were indeed true, but that they were intended to take place in a future age. Thus, the truthfulness of these prophecies was confirmed by the testimony of two witnesses, as it were. This, in fact, is a biblical principle. A minimum of two witnesses is required for establishing the truthfulness of one's testimony. Even Jesus himself referred to this principle in Matthew 18:16 and John 5:31-5.[394]

After the decade of the sixties in the first century, with the fall of Jerusalem and the destruction of the temple now past, and the failure of Jesus to return at that time, the *Book of Revelation* must have been seen as a dismal failure. But we should legitimately ask, if that is the case, then how could such a prophetic failure be included into the canon of Scripture? John himself may have at first not intended it to be included in the canon. It is for this reason, therefore, that John received his second vision at the end of his life in order to re-verify the fact that the prophecies contained in that book were for a future, "end-time" generation. It was at the time of John's second vision that he would have added the very strongly worded final chapter to that work.

THE BOOK OF REVELATION AND THE CANON

THE CHURCH OF JERUSALEM WAS FORCED TO flee in the summer of 66 C.E. The Apostle Peter was still alive and there at

[394] In the Old Testament there is also precedent for this kind of repetition, especially in reference to dreams and visions. The dream that God gave to Pharaoh that Joseph interpreted was given to him twice (Gen 41:5). In verse 32 it says: "And the doubling of Pharaoh's dream means that the thing is fixed by God, and God will shortly bring it about." Joseph also was given two dream revelations (Gen 37:7, 9). Job stated: "For God speaks in one way, and in two, though people do not perceive it. In a dream, in a vision of the night." (Job 33:14, 15). David said "Once God has spoken; TWICE have I heard this; that power belongs to God" (Ps 62:11). Nebuchadnezzar was given a dream about prophetic events of the future which was revealed to Daniel a second time (Dan 2). Daniel himself received his vision first and the interpretation was given by Gabriel 21 days later (Dan 10). Many of the Old Testament prophets had a series of visions like Isaiah, in which some of the information was repeated in successive visions.

Jerusalem before they fled. The prophecy, as they understood it, failed. Peter then went to Rome on an urgent mission to the Apostle Paul because he knew that he had the responsibility and authority, as Jesus brought out in this context, to "feed my sheep" (John 21:15, 16, 17). Paul had asked Timothy in 65 C.E. to get the services of Peter's secretary, John Mark, and to gather the manuscripts together for a specific "Ministry" (2 Tim 4:11-13).

Peter may have held out with John in Jerusalem as long as it was safe, believing in the soon coming Parousia. But after the death of James, the brother of Jesus, then Peter's doubts began and eventually he could see what Paul had already concluded some time before was exactly right – that the time of the end was not then, but much further into the future. And a future church needed overseers and an authoritative body of literature by the apostles in the face of the future persecutions and apostasy.

With the realization that the return of Jesus was now far into the future, the Apostles Paul, Peter, and John switched gears and changed their entire focus, direction, and motivation. Anyone else in their positions would no doubt have done exactly the same thing. This is why it is important (in order to truly understand the events *Beyond Acts*) to put ourselves in the sandals of the apostles. Once we have the ability to do just that, then we begin to see things as the apostles saw them, and we can reconstruct the history of the times correctly, rather than assume that after the *Book of Acts* ends, the apostles blithely just went along as business as usual.

The miraculous events that occurred in the spring of 66 C.E. in Jerusalem were the turning point for Peter, no doubt. Peter then knew that he had to go to Rome and meet with Paul, before Paul himself was martyred, and complete the task that Paul had begun. When Peter does meet up with Paul in the fall of 66 C.E., it was to be for only a few short months, for Paul was martyred in January of 67 C.E. Peter, the leading apostle at that time, then takes up the task of editing and completing his contribution to the canon to what Paul had begun.

After having read "*all*" of Paul's Epistles (2 Pet 3:16), Peter then composes his last Epistle which is very different in tone than his previous one. One can see the effect that Paul's Epistles had on Peter, even though Peter himself said that Paul had written some things hard to understand that the spiritually unstable will wrestle with to their own destruction.

After Peter finishes his contribution to the canon he dispatches John Mark to deliver the precious carrying case of literature to the Apostle John, who is now in Asia Minor. Peter was then martyred in February of 68 C.E. Once John received Peter's canon, John himself could now see that the time of the Prophecy was not for a long time hence. However, the question remained, would John remain alive until the end? No, but he would remain alive until Jesus came again in a second vision just like the first one he had a decade or so before. But it would be nearly another 30 years before that would happen. And it did happen around the year of 96 C.E.

The Roman authorities, who may have considered the author of a Jewish Apocalypse as a threat to the state, may also have believed that the perfect punishment for John would be to banish him to the very island that he supposedly first received his controversial vision. It would be as if the Roman authorities were rubbing John's nose in his own embarrassing prophesy failure. It was the final insult. Yet, the Romans may have been only pawns in the bigger picture.

So now we can see that after the time that the *Revelation* was first given back in Jerusalem prior to the Jewish War, the *Book of Revelation*, as we have said, fell into disrepute. It became a stumbling block to many and even caused John to loose much of his own credibility – so much so that he had to be constantly backed up by additional eyewitnesses, including the mother of Jesus[395] and fellow apostles as to the truth of whatever he wrote. Diotrephes (and possibly Clement of Rome by way of rebuffing him) even went so far as to reject John's authority.

But now, with John's second vision on the Isle of Patmos, in the end of the first century, the doubts about John's *Revelation* were dispelled (at least to John and his circle) and the truth of its message was thus reaffirmed. Indeed, John now had the bold confidence to include the *Book of Revelation* as the final book within the New Testament canon for the future church. John's testimony became the pinnacle to the final testimony of the apostles' of Jesus. Indeed, his work capped off the entire revelation of God of both Testaments.

When John finalized his message, after his second vision, his confidence was now so strong in his prophecy that he adds the final remarks to this book and to the entire canon:

> I warn everyone who hears the words of the prophecy of this book; if anyone adds to them, God will add to that person the plagues described in this book; if anyone takes away from the words of the book of this prophecy, God will take away that person's share in the tree of life and in the holy city, which are described in this book (Rev 22:18-21).

---

395 *The Epistle of Ignatius to Mary at Neapolis,* in *Ante-Nicene Fathers,* ed. Alexander Roberts and James Donaldson (Peabody, Mass.: Hendrickson, 1995), 1:126.

Just look at the power and authority of such strong wording! These are indeed the words of authority. These are the words of a canonizer. These are the words of a "son of Thunder" apostle of Jesus who is now able to speak in bold confidence. There can be no doubt that these words were designed to counter any tampering with the message of this now forever closed canon. And, the New Testament canon has remained basically in tact to this very day, albeit some corruptions have been attempted, but have been identified by scholars.[396]

It is with these words the Apostle John closes the canon of New Testament Scripture. John himself admitted that

> there are many other things that Jesus did; if every one of them were written down, I suppose that; the world itself could not contain the books that would be written (John 21:25).

This is another way of saying that the many other Gospels that were being circulated, even by other apostles, may in fact be insightful, but they were not selected by Peter and John to be a part of the official canon of the church, and that is that! Thus, the New Testament canon was closed around the year of 96 C.E. and it has been closed ever since, as indeed, it should remain.

The stern warning at the end of the *Book of Revelation* was addressed to all those who questioned the authority of John, especially in the matter of canonization. The primary work that had become the reason for John's rejection – the *Book of Revelation* – had now become the pinnacle of his inspiration. It perfectly compliments the *Book of Genesis* and it seals the Revelation of God to all of mankind.

---

[396] See, for example, Bart D. Ehrmann, *The Orthodox Corruption of Scripture* (London: Oxford University Press, 1993).

APPENDIX 4

Was the Apostle Peter the First Pope?

THE *LIBER PONTIFICALIS*, WRITTEN BY AN unknown author between 514 - 530 C.E., attempted to catalog a list of bishops of Rome from the Apostle Peter on down to his own time. This catalog was in part based on an earlier version, known as the *Liberian Catalog*, which was a part of a larger work known as the *Chronographer of 354*.[397] It is recognized by scholars that the *Liber Pontificalis* is an admixture of conflicting sources, and therefore difficult to interpret satisfactorily.[398]

One common feature about these two lists is that they both claim that the Apostle Peter was a presiding bishop of Rome for a period of some 25 years,[399] from 42 to 67 C.E.[400] Thereafter, Peter is supposedly followed by a bishop by the name of Linus. After Linus, the two lists disagree as to who followed whom – the *Liber Pontificalis* states that it was Cletus, followed by Clement, whereas, the *Liberian Catalog* states that it was Clement, followed by Cletus. We will now attempt to make some sense out of the data that is contained therein and other accounts, which will not only answer the question offered by the heading, but offer a new

---

397 Raymond Davis, tr., *The Book of Pontiffs (Liber Pontificalis)* (Liverpool: Liverpool University Press, 1989). Davis provides the *Liberian Catalogue* in his appendix 1, 93-6.

398 For a good discussion on all the various papal lists, see Daniel Wm O'Connor, "The Papal Lists of Hegesippus, Irenaeus, Epiphanius, Julius Africanus, and Eusebius," in *Peter in Rome* (New York: Columbia University Press, 1969), 27-35.

399 John Wenham, "The Date of Peter's Going to Rome" in *Redating Matthew, Mark & Luke* (Downers Grove, Ill.: InterVarsity Press, 1992), 146-72, gives reasons for accepting this 25 year stay of Peter in Rome. We believe, however, that the 25 year period marked Peter's initial visit in 42 C.E. and his final one in 67 C.E., rather than one continuous stay in Rome during that 25 year period.

400 In order to appreciate the kind of material we are dealing with in these two sources, we note that the *LP (Liber Pontificalis)* states that Peter came to Rome during the time of Nero, yet, on the other hand, [borrowing obviously from the *LC, Liberian Catalogue*] it states that Peter was in Rome during the reigns of Tiberius, Gaius, Claudius and Nero. Since Tiberius died in 37 C.E., the 42 C.E. date is impossible. The author of the *LP* obviously borrowed from the erroneous chronology of the *LC*, which reckoned the 25 years of Peter as being from 30 to 55 C.E.

arrangement of the first bishops of Rome that finally makes sense out of the data.

Common to both lists is the fact that Linus was indeed a bishop of Rome, but he did not succeed Peter – he is recorded as preceding him. The *Liber Pontificalis* clearly states that Peter suffered martyrdom "in the 38th year after the Lord suffered" (i.e., 68 C.E.), whereas Linus "was bishop in the time of Nero from the consulship of Saturninus and Scipio (56 C.E.) to that of Capito and Rufus (67 C.E.).[401]

Linus had been bishop of Rome for eleven years, dating back to the year 56 C.E. Now understand this amazing fact. It was in the spring of 56 C.E., by our chronology, that the Apostle Paul had just arrived in Rome for a two year house arrest before his trial. This fact, by itself, would imply that it was the Apostle Paul who was responsible for the ordination of Linus at the time of his arrival in Rome.[402] At last, we have history and tradition unitedly agreeing to give us a true picture of the past.

The eleven years accorded to Linus now make perfect sense if he held office from the time that Paul arrived in Rome in 56 C.E. until just before Peter was martyred in 68 C.E. Then, some time before Peter was martyred in Rome on February 22, 68 C.E., Peter ordains Clement as the second bishop of Rome, succeeding not himself, but rather Linus, the real first bishop of Rome. And this is exactly in agreement with the testimony that we have in the *Apostolic Constitutions*. Indeed, it is in this earlier account that we have a more believable tradition of who were the first bishops of all the various cities in the first century:

> Now concerning those bishops which have been ordained in our lifetime, we let you know that they are these: – James the bishop of Jerusalem, the brother of our Lord; upon whose death the second was Simeon the son of Cleopas; after whom the third was Judas the son of James. Of Caesarea of Palestine, the first was Zacchaeus, who was once a publican; after whom was Cornelius, and the third Theophilus. Of Antioch, Euodius, ordained by me Peter; and Ignatius by Paul. Of Alexandria, Annianus was the first, ordained by Mark the evangelist; the second Avilius by Luke, who was also an evangelist. Of the church of Rome, Linus the son of Claudia was the first, ordained by Paul; and Clemens, after Linus' death, the second, ordained by me Peter (*Constitutions of the Holy Apostles* 4:46 [*ANF* 7:477-8]).

---

[401] Ibid., 2. Notice that 38 years after the crucifixion only works with a crucifixion date of 30 C.E., and not, as a few suggest, and the majority reject, in 33 C.E.

[402] Cletus, who appears second in the list of the *Liber Pontificalis*, seems to have been correctly placed third in the list after Clement in the *Liberian Catalog*. Indeed, in the *LC*, Cletus is seemingly a misfit, squeezed in between Linus and Clement. The *Liberian Catalog* evidence certainly has the merit of alleviating this quandary.

Notice carefully that Linus is here considered to be the first bishop of Rome, then followed by the second bishop of Rome, Clement, who was ordained by the Apostle Peter. This testimony obviously reflects the earliest tradition and therefore should be preferred over the conflicting traditions of Irenaeus and Eusebius. And it is this testimony that agrees with exactly what we have seen in both in the *Liber Pontificalis* and the *Liberian Catalogue*, that Linus was bishop ten years before Peter came to Rome.

Further support of our thesis is to be found in Tertullian (ca. 160 - ca. 225), who claims to have been an actual eyewitness to the registries of the churches of Smyrna and of Rome. Tertullian recorded that:

> For this is the manner in which the apostolic churches transmit their registers: as the church of Smyrna, which records that Polycarp was placed therein by John; as also the church of Rome, which makes Clement to have been ordained in like manner by Peter (Tertullian, *Praescr.* 1:22 [*ANF* 3:258]).

Tertullian is said to have been a lawyer and was especially interested in getting his facts straight by the official records. His testimony, therefore, is extremely important in settling this matter. From this piece of evidence we can see that in the time of Tertullian, the official register of the church at Rome recorded that it was Peter who ordained Clement. And if that is so, then Clement was ordained before February 68 C.E.

We now go to the pseudo-clementine literature, where another tradition confirms that Clement himself supposedly explains that he was ordained directly by the Apostle Peter:

> But about that time, when he [Peter] was about to die, the brethren being assembled together, he suddenly seized my hand, and rose up, and said in presence of the church: "Hear me, brethren and fellow-servants. Since, as I have been taught by the Lord and Teacher Jesus Christ, whose apostle I am, the day of my death is approaching, I lay hands upon this Clement as your bishop; and to him I entrust my chair of discourse even to him who has journeyed with me from the beginning to the end" (*Epistle of Clement to James* 2 [*ANF* 8:218]).

At the end of the fourth century, Rufinus of Aquileia commented on this very passage in the following terms:

> There is a letter in which this same Clement writing to James the Lord's brother, gives an account of the death of Peter, and says that he has left him as his successor, as

> ruler and teacher of the church. ...Linus and Cletus were Bishops of the city of Rome before Clement. How then, some men ask, can Clement in his letter to James say that Peter passed over to him his position as a church-teacher. The explanation of this point, as I understand, is as follows. Linus and Cletus were, no doubt, Bishops in the city of Rome before Clement, but this was in Peter's lifetime; that is, they took charge of the episcopal work, while he discharged the duties of the apostolate (Rufinus, *Clem. Recogn. NANF* 3:564).

It is obvious that Rufinus accepts the tradition of Irenaeus in making Linus and Cletus to come before Clement, but he must admit that they actually were bishops together during Peter's lifetime. Irenaeus (ca. 130 - ca. 200) appears to be the one who started the tradition that Linus and Cletus followed Peter in succession, but even he betrays this conviction if we notice carefully what he says about Clement:

> The blessed apostles, then, having founded and built up the Church, committed into the hands of Linus the office of the episcopate. Of this Linus, Paul makes mention in the Epistle to Timothy (2 Tim 4:21). To him succeeded Anacletus; and after him, in the third place from the apostles, Clement was allotted the bishopric. This man, as he had seen the blessed apostles, and had been conversant with them, might be said to have the preaching of the apostles [of Peter and Paul] still echoing [in his ears], and their tradition before his eyes (Irenaeus, *Haer.* 3.3.3 [*ANF* 1:416]).

It would be hard to imagine that Clement would still have the message of the apostles still ringing in his ears when he assumed the office of bishop if he only attained that office a quarter century after these apostles had passed from the scene. The letter of Clement to the Corinthians exuberates with recent recollections of both Paul and Peter. Indeed, the reference to the church envoy Fortunatus in Clement (1 Clem 65:1) is obviously the very same Fortunatus who was an envoy in Paul's first letter to the Corinthians (1 Cor 16:17).[403]

Clement was a fellow worker with Paul in Rome and is mentioned by Paul in his first imprisonment at Rome (Phil 4:3), which by our dating, extended from 56 to 58 C.E. The fact that Clement was a contemporary of

---

[403] Although not impossible, we feel that this seems very unlikely that a quarter century would have passed with the same envoy (or a coincidental namesake) still carrying on the same task. Indeed, what is starring us in the face is testimony that the two are one in the same person and, therefore, *First Clement* must be lowered in date to the same generation as that of the Apostle Paul.

Paul in the late fifties makes it more likely that he was an active leader in the church during the next decade, and not some four decades later.

Also, if the Apostle John was now residing in Ephesus, even on down to the late nineties of the first century, it makes no sense that Clement would not defer the Corinthian matter to John the apostle, who was only some 300 miles away, rather than to rebuff John, and take the matter into his own hands, who was some 700 miles away.[404] This fact alone would necessitate the fact that the time of writing of *First Clement* should be lowered from 95/6 C.E. to about 69/70 C.E., just prior to the arrival of John in Ephesus.[405]

Even the entry in the *Liber Pontificalis* for Clement specifically states that Clement was bishop "in the time of Galba and Vespasian from the consulship of Trachalus and Italicus [68] to the 9th of Vespasian and that of Titus [79]."[406] Notice that Clement begins his reign in the same year as Peter dies. This perfectly coincides with exactly what we have been presenting here. And also note that if this tradition is in anyway true, then Clement was not even alive in 95 C.E. and his *Epistle to the Corinthians* could not have been written any earlier than 79 C.E.

After Clement, it appears that the *Liberian Catalog* has correctly placed Cletus as being the third bishop of Rome: "He [Cletus] was bishop in the time of Vespasian and Titus and the beginning of Domitian from 77 to 83."[407] Then follows Anaclitus (84-95), Evaristus (96-108), Alexander (109-116), and then Xystus (117-126), after which there seems to be agreement between the two lists.[408]

Now to answer our question, was Peter the first Pope? It appears that the whole purpose of the *Liber Pontificalis* was manufactured to establish just such a fact. But it is also obvious that much of the early data in this work is pure invention for this very purpose. However, one thing is certain. The first bishop of Rome was a person by the name of Linus, not the Apostle Peter at all. And from this evidence it appears that Linus was ordained by the Apostle Paul in 56 C.E. and was never the second bishop

---

404 Dr. Ernest L. Martin makes mention of this fact in his book, *Restoring the Original Bible* (Portland, Oreg., Associates for Scriptural Knowledge, 1994), 418-420, but has the chronology wrong. I had the chance to discuss this fact personally with Dr. Martin in November, 2000 at the convention for the Society of Biblical Literature in Nashville, Tennessee. After I had presented to him my chronology he said that he felt that what I suggested was right and that he would address this in a future publication. Unfortunately, Dr. Martin died in January, 2002, without having provided us with his insight on this matter.

405 John A. T. Robinson, *Redating the New Testament* (London: SCM Press, 1977), 352, dates 1 Clement at 70 C.E.

406 Davis, *Liber*, 3. Modern scholars, however, prefer to follow Eusebius, *Hist. eccl.* 3.15, 34, who dates Clement as holding office from 92-101 C.E.

407 Ibid., 93.

408 Ibid.

of Rome following Peter in 68 C.E.

The idea that Peter was in Rome as bishop for some 25 years also seems to fall apart, just on the evidence that when Paul wrote to the Romans in 54 C.E., he salutes everyone that he can think of, the longest list of salutees in all of his letters, mentioning everyone from his relatives to prominent people, yet the highest ranking apostle in the church receives not the slightest mention. This evidence, to this author, is conclusive enough to say that if Peter was in Rome at this time, then this apparent *faux pas* would represent a slight to the chief apostle that would be entirely inexplicable.[409]

We must remember that Peter, like all the apostles, was an itinerant evangelist, so to speak, not a stationary overseer or bishop of any single congregation.[410] The later Catholic Church seized upon the fact that Peter went to Rome in his final year of his life and from this fact apparently drew up a history that to them established a basis for the bishop of Rome to be the supreme bishop over all other bishops within Christendom. The church of the fourth century, therefore, drew up a scenario that suited this premise. However, we should not ignore the facts. The testimony of Eusebius (ca. 260 - ca. 340) concerning Peter was that:

> Peter seems to have preached in Pontus, Galatia and Bithynia, Cappadocia and Asia, to the Jews of the Dispersion. Finally, he came to Rome where he was crucified, head downwards at his own request (Eusebius, *Hist. eccl.* 3.1.2).

Peter worked among the Jews of the dispersion, not among the Gentiles of Rome. Indeed, we should ask the important question, what does it mean when Eusebius says that Peter "*finally* came to Rome?" It means just as the most reliable history tells us – that Peter only recently arrived in Rome in the final year of his life, pure and simple. And, although this may be exactly 25 years from Peter's first visit, there is no evidence that Peter remained in Rome throughout that 25 year period in the role of a bishop of that city.

---

[409] Although Peter may have journeyed to Rome in 42 C.E., he did not stay there as a bishop. If some of the converts that Paul addressed in his Epistle to the Romans were the result of Peter's work some twelve years earlier, then it is understandable why Paul expressed in his letter to the Romans his reluctance to build upon another man's foundation (Rom 15:20).

[410] We should also note that tradition has it that Peter ordained Euodius as the first bishop of Antioch (Eusebius, *Hist. eccl.* 3:22). If this is so, then why was not Peter considered the first bishop of Antioch and Euodius as the second bishop of Antioch? The answer is that the bishops of Antioch were not concerned with drawing up a list to establish its primacy, only Rome was.

Also, consider that if Peter was a bishop and he ordained a successor, then by that very act he would have divested his own authority as bishop to his successor. C. De Lisle Shortt observes in this regard:

> As St. Peter was an Apostle, he could not lay down his office of bishop, if he ever was such, nor could he adopt another to preside over the See of Rome with him, or to succeed him. Innocent I., bishop of Rome, condemned such actions as irregular and as never known before his time. In his epistle to the clergy and people of Constantinople he says: "We have never known these things to have been daringly attempted by our fathers, but rather to have been hindered; for no one hath any right entrusted to him to ordain another in the place of one living" (*P. Innoc. I. apud Soz.* viii. 26.).[411]

Also, note that Irenaeus stated that:

> The Roman Church was founded by the two most glorious Apostles, Peter *and* Paul (Irenaeus, *Haer.* 3.3.2 [*ANF* 1:415]).

If anything, the Apostle Paul, *the* apostle to the Gentiles, was more of an actual contributor to the establishment of the Roman church than Peter ever was. Indeed, it was Paul who ordained the first bishop of Rome in 56 C.E. – eleven years before Peter arrived in Rome before his martyrdom in 68 C.E.

Therefore, our answer to the question, "Was Peter the first Pope?" is a simple one based on the evidence. Peter was never a bishop in the first place, let alone a "Pope" in the modern sense. He was an apostle who ordained bishops in various cities, not just Rome. The idea that Peter was the first bishop of Rome was a later construction invented to establish the See of Rome as the ultimate authority over all other churches within Christianity. But such a concept was never the intention of the original apostles.

---

[411] C. De Lisle Shortt, *Who Was the First Bishop of Rome?* (Edinburgh: T&T Clark, 1935), 169.

APPENDIX 5

When Were the New Testament Books Written?

IT IS ESSENTIAL TO UNDERSTAND THAT ALL OF the New Testament books were written before the end of the first century, i.e., within the lifetime of the Apostle John.[412] Indeed, except for the *Gospel of John*, the *First Epistle of John*, and a redaction of the *Apocalypse* in the 90's C.E., we believe that all of the books were written prior to 68 C.E. In some cases, we can place the writing of Paul's letters fairly closely, based upon information given to us in the *Book of Acts*. In other cases, we have to rely on internal and external evidence, and the chronology that we have developed in Appendix 2, in order to make an educated guess.

We will not spend a lot of time here debating all the arguments, since we believe that the earliest testimony for the traditional datings must bear the greatest weight in our assessment, rather than modern theories that rest on a host of assumptions that amount to, in our opinion, a desire to place the writings as late as possible. Of course, the motive for late dating is all too transparent. The further beyond the apostles time that scholars can push the dates, the easier it is to support the notion of non-apostolic authorship.

Let us now look at the time of the writing of the New Testament books from a different perspective. It will be most illuminating.

---

[412] For some detailed scholarly assessments of this assertion, see John A. T. Robinson, *Redating the New Testament* (London: SCM Press, 1976); John Wenham, *Redating Matthew, Mark & Luke* (Downers Grove, Ill.: InterVarsity Press, 1992); and Francis David Pansini, *Our First Gospel* (Washington, D.C.: The Catholic University of America Press, 1946). For a balanced survey of the pros and cons, see Donald Guthrie, *New Testament Introduction* (Downers Grove: InterVarsity Press, 1990).

MATTHEW

THE GOSPEL OF MATTHEW HAS ATTAINED THE leading position in the New Testament canon. The prestige that this gospel account has been accorded is testimony that the primitive church held it in the highest of esteem. All of the earliest traditions place Matthew's Gospel first in canonical order, as well as in date.[413] John Wenham summarizes the position of the early church:

> Eusebius (writing probably at the very end of the third century) ... says of Matthew: 'when he was on the point of going to others he transmitted in writing in his native language the Gospel according to himself, and thus supplied by writing the lack of his own presence to those from whom he was sent' (*HE* 2.24.6). There is a suggestion here that the writing of the gospel preceded the departure of Matthew from Palestine. ...there was a widespread belief that the apostles were dispersed from Jerusalem twelve years after the crucifixion. Acts may perhaps hint that this had taken place by the time Peter was released from prison in 42, James the apostle having been killed and James the brother of the Lord having become head of the church there (Acts 12:2, 17). In his *Chronicon* Eusebius places the writing of the gospel in the third year of the reign of Caligula, that is, in 41.[414]

The logic of this appraisal is simple and satisfactory, since it fits the known internal facts. The tradition that the apostles remained in Jerusalem for a period of twelve years before embarking on a worldwide evangelistic campaign provides the key to correctly dating Matthew.[415]

---

[413] The nineteenth century German scholar, Johann Jakob Griesbach, supported Matthean priority and since he was the first to so strongly advocate this position, his theory became known as the "Griesbach hypothesis." His thesis is alive today in such works as the late William R. Farmer, *The Synoptic Problem: A Critical Analysis* (Macon, Ga.: Mercer University Press, 1981); *The Gospel of Jesus* (Philadelphia: Westminster, 1994) [his arguments can also be seen online at http://www.maplenet.net/~trowbridge/farmer.htm]; Bernard Orchard, *Matthew, Luke and Mark,* 2d ed. (Manchester, Eng.: Koinonia Press, 1977) and H. H. Stodt, *History and Criticism of the Markan Hypothesis* (trans. and ed. D. L. Niewyk, Macon, Ga.:1980). The majority of critical scholarship dominate the Marcan priority position, however. But in so doing they had to invent a previous forerunner document called "Q." This is where the web they weave becomes so entangled that they cannot pull themselves from this entire Emperor's New Clothes scenario.

[414] John Wenham, *Redating Matthew, Mark & Luke* (Downers Grove, Ill.: InterVarsity Press, 1992), 239.

[415] See Appendix 2 for details on this twelve year period.

Since Jesus died in the year of 30 C.E., then the year of 41/42 C.E. would be the year that the apostles left Jerusalem for their worldwide evangelistic campaign. The dating given by Eusebius to the year of 41 C.E. (as given above) would assume that the *Gospel of Matthew* was composed just before that time in preparation for that great mission.

Eusebius further says, in this regard:

> Matthew had begun by preaching to Hebrews; and when he made up his mind to go to others too, he committed his own gospel to writing in his native tongue, so that for those with whom he was no longer present the gap left by his departure was filled by what he wrote (Eusebius, *Hist. eccl.* 3.24.6).

Eusebius also preserves a tradition that the *Gospel of Matthew* was discovered far afield from Jerusalem, in India, indicating that this was due to the fact that Matthew's Gospel was indeed used by the apostles in their worldwide evangelistic campaign:

> At that time (ca. 185) the school for believers in Alexandria was headed by a man with a very high reputation as a scholar, by name Pantaenus...He went as far as India, where he appears to have found that Matthew's gospel had arrived before him and was in the hands of some there who had come to know Christ. Bartholomew, one of the apostles, had preached to them and had left behind Matthew's account in the actual Hebrew characters, and it was preserved till the time of Pantaenus' mission (Eusebius, *Hist. eccl.* 5.10.1-3).

The church fathers that commented on Matthew were virtually unanimous that the Gospel was originally written in the Hebrew language.[416] Modern theories that Matthew borrowed from Mark, who wrote in Greek, seem to have brushed this fact aside. Also, Matthew was one of the leading apostles of the twelve and an eyewitness to the events he writes about.

Vincent Taylor also notes that it is

---

[416] The traditions that Matthew wrote in Hebrew are Papias (*apud* Eusebius, *Hist. eccl.* 3.39.16); Irenaeus, *Haer.* 3.1.1; Origen; (*apud* Eusebius, *Hist. eccl.* 6.25.4); Eusebius, *Hist. eccl.* 3.24.6; Epiphanius, *Pan.* 30.13.1-30.22.24; Jerome, *Epist.* 20.5. See also George Howard, *The Gospel of Matthew according to a Primitive Hebrew Text* (Macon, Ga: Mercer University Press, 1988). Also, James D. Tabor, *A Hebrew Gospel of Matthew*, online at http://www.uncc.edu/jdtabor/shemtovweb.html. Donald Guthrie, *Introduction*, 47-48, also notes: "Evidence points to an unbroken tradition that Matthew wrote his Gospel in Hebrew, and advocates of any hypothesis which disagrees with this must suggest an adequate explanation of so consistent a tradition."

> improbable in the extreme that an apostle would have used as a source the work of one who was not an eyewitness of the ministry of Jesus.[417]

Today, there are all kinds of theories advanced by critical scholars in the dating of Matthew.[418] These theories have distanced themselves from the early testimony. The kind of arguments for establishing a post 70 C.E. date in the end are unconvincing. For instance, John Shelby Spong writes:

> Matthew was written in Jewish circles well before the final tearing away of Jewish Christians from their participation in synagogue worship that occurred around the year 88 C.E.[419]

So far we couldn't be more in agreement, especially when we notice the phrase "well before." But then we next read:

> That would tend to anchor the date for this gospel between 75 C.E. and 85 C.E., with the range of 80 C.E. to 82 C.E. being the best guess of most scholars.[420]

How does such reasoning anchor the dates of Matthew's writing to the early eighties? Such scholarly guess work fails to note the fact that the fall of Jerusalem in 70 C.E. was a future event in the Gospel, since the readers are warned to flee when they begin seeing the signs of the end (Matt 24:16). Also, there are a number passages that presuppose that the temple was still intact, e.g., Matt 5:23-4; 17:24-7; 23:16-22. Why wouldn't these passages have been edited out of any post Jewish War Gospel, is a question that post Jewish War advocates need to answer. Until they can offer supporting evidence, such objections can not be sustained.

We find that the earliest testimony which has Matthew writing just prior to the dispersion of apostolic missionary activity more compelling than modern second guessing to the contrary. Indeed, are scholars forgetting the fact that the early Christian movement began as a kind of Jewish off shoot, sectarian faction? Matthew's Gospel reflects this aspect of time, whereas Mark's is more oriented toward the Gentile culture?

If we date the *Gospel of Matthew* to the year of 40 C.E., then we are on territory that makes perfect sense with the known facts. And if this

---

[417] Vincent Taylor, *Gospels: A Short Introduction* (London: Epworth, 1952), 81.

[418] See summaries online at: http://www.mindspring.com/~scarlson/synopt/problem.htm; http://www.proaxis.com/~deardorj/priority.htm; http://www.centerce.org/BIBL301/SynopticProblem.htm; http://www.tjresearch.info/mksecond.htm.

[419] John Shelby Spong, *Liberating the Gospels* (New York: Harper Collins, 1996), 102.

[420] Ibid. One should ask at this point, if dates from 75-85 C.E. are "well before" 88 C.E., then isn't this author asking a little too much of his adverbs?

date be correct, then Matthew wrote during the hegemony of James the Just. And if that is the case, then Matthew could actually be seen as the authorized Gospel of James, the brother of Jesus.[421] This has to be the case, because if Matthew wrote in the early 40's, then he would have had to have had the sanction of James, the recognized leader of the Jerusalem church at this time. And from what we know of James, the *Gospel of Matthew* would certainly be one that James would indeed sanction.

Remember also that we are at a time when it was important that such written testimony carry the weight of recognized leaders within the church who had the proper credentials to make a legitimate case for authenticating Jesus' messiahship. Thus, Matthew's Gospel was first in the canon due to not only rank,[422] but as well as in time.

Also we have to realize that there is a principle that the apostles rigidly followed, which was that the gospel was to go to "the Jew first" (Rom 2:9, 10).[423] Matthew's Gospel speaks to the Jewish people first and foremost. Quotes from the Hebrew Scriptures abound in Matthew concerning the messianic prophecies that were fulfilled in the appearance of Jesus. Gentiles reading Matthew would not have had the same appreciation of this that the Jewish people (and even scattered Israelites) would have had on this feature.

Thus, our placement of the *Gospel of Matthew* is that it was written in preparation of the great evangelizing effort of the apostles that started in 41 C.E., which makes the year of 40 C.E. the best candidate for the compilation of James' authorized Gospel, which bears the name of the eyewitness reporter, the Apostle Matthew.

MARK

EUSEBIUS PLACES THE WRITING OF THE *GOSPEL of Mark* at the time that Peter went to Rome in 42 C.E. It is there that the

[421] James had Levitical heritage, as apparently did Matthew, whose surname was Levi. John Painter, *Just James: The Brother of Jesus in History and Tradition* (Minneapolis: Fortress, 1999), 260-5, brings out some striking parallels between the *Gospel of Matthew* and the *Epistle of James.*

[422] When the Apostle Paul made reference to the Jerusalem-based apostles, his order of precedence appears to be that of administrative rank: James, Cephas [Peter] and John (Gal 2:9).

[423] When Paul and Barnabas addressed the Jews in Galatia, they said: "It was necessary [a strict requirement incumbent upon them] that the word of God should be spoken first to you" (Acts 13:46).

people of Rome who heard Peter speak wanted a written testimony to what Peter had preached.

Obviously, if Peter did go to Rome armed with a copy Matthew's Hebrew Gospel, this would hardly have been any help to the Greek and Latin speakers there. Apparently, Peter preached to them the basic outline of Matthew's message, but from his own eyewitness point of view. Mark, apparently took sermon notes on Peter's discourses, then later assembled them into an account that was, in effect, a Gospel according to Peter. This occurred, apparently, after Peter had left the city of Rome.[424]

Eusebius writes:

> And so greatly did the splendor of piety illumine the minds of Peter's hearers that they were not satisfied with hearing once only, and were not content with the unwritten teaching of the divine Gospel, but with all sorts of entreaties they besought Mark, a follower of Peter, and the one whose Gospel is extant, that he would leave them a written monument of the doctrine which had been orally communicated to them. Nor did they cease until they had prevailed with the man, and had thus become the occasion of the written Gospel which bears the name of Mark. And they say that Peter, when he had learned, through a revelation of the Spirit, the zeal of the men, and that the work obtained being used in the churches. Clement in the eighth book of his Hypotyposes gives this account, and with him agrees the bishop of Hierapolis named Papias (Eusebius, *Hist. eccl.* 2.15.1).

Eusebius also gives us Papias's direct testimony, based upon the testimony of the Apostle John, who was his mentor:

> Papias gives also in his own work other accounts of the words of the Lord on the authority of Aristion who was mentioned above, and traditions as handed down by the Presbyter John. ..."This also the presbyter [John] said: Mark, having become the interpreter of Peter, wrote down accurately, though not indeed in order, whatsoever he remembered of the things said or done by Christ. For he neither heard the Lord nor followed him, but afterward, as I said, he followed Peter, who adapted his teaching to the needs of his hearers, but with no intention of giving a connected account of the Lord's discourses, so that Mark committed no error while he thus wrote some things as he remembered them. For he was careful of one thing, not to omit any of the things which he had heard, and not to

[424] This is probably the time that tradition tells us that Peter then went to Gaul and then on to Britain.

state any of them falsely" (Eusebius, *Hist. eccl.* 3.39.15).

Like Matthew, the internal evidence shows us that it was written with the anticipation of the "abomination of desolation" being set up in the temple and that the church in Jerusalem was to flee upon seeing that event (Mark 13:14). This alone places it pre-66 C.E. in time.

The dominant view among scholars, of course, (based upon a host of mind boggling assortments of textual considerations) is that first there was an unknown "sayings" document under the sobriquet of "Q" (German: *Quelle* = Source). Then there came out of this the *Gospel of Mark*, and then thirdly we have Matthew as supposedly the ultimate copy-cat. All of this, of course, is extremely hypothetical, if not totally imaginary.[425]

What we propose, based on the earliest testimony, is the following: Peter first arrived in Rome in the year of 42 C.E., with Mark by his side. Peter then moves on, leaving Mark behind in Rome. Mark then decides to write down the sayings of Peter in a gospel format, basically following Matthew's outline. This was the first draft of Mark's Gospel. We say first draft because it is most likely that it was edited later on by Peter himself when Peter returned to Rome in the fall of 66 C.E. to confer with the Apostle Paul concerning the matter of canonization. It is at this time that Peter most likely added the last verses of Mark (Mark 16:9-20). Therefore, Mark was written around the year of 43 C.E. and redacted by Peter in 67 C.E.

LUKE-ACTS

THE DATING OF THE *GOSPEL OF LUKE* IS CLOSELY tied to the dating of the *Acts of the Apostles*, which is also credited to Luke. Thus, most combine the *Gospel of Luke* with the *Acts of the Apostles*, which make up a two part volume of a single work. And since the *Acts of the Apostles* ends with the release of the Apostle Paul in the year of 58 C.E., then the *Gospel of Luke* must have been written around the same time, for Luke represents the first part of a two part manuscript: volume 1, the *Gospel of Luke* and volume 2, the *Acts of the Apostles.*

Luke begins his Gospel as follows:

---

[425] For those inclined to immerse themselves in what has become known as the "Synoptic Problem," see Donald Guthrie, *New Testament Introduction* "The Synoptic Problem" (Downers Grove: InterVarsity Press, 1990), 136-208 and online: http://www.web-therapy.com/q.htm.

> Since many have undertaken to set down an orderly account of the events that have been fulfilled among us, just as they were handed on to us by those who from the beginning were eyewitnesses and servants of the word. I too decided, after investigating everything carefully from the very first, to write an orderly account for you, most excellent Theophilus, so that you may know the truth concerning the things about which you have been instructed (Luke 1:1-4).

Likewise, the *Acts of the Apostles* begins with the following:

> In the first book, Theophilus, I wrote about all that Jesus did and taught from the beginning until the day when he was taken up to heaven, after giving instructions through the Holy Spirit to the apostles whom he had chosen (Acts 1:1).

Eusebius provides the following biographical information concerning Luke:

> Luke, by birth an Antiochene and by profession a physician, was for long periods a companion of Paul and was closely associated with the other apostles as well. So he has left us examples of the art of healing souls, which he learnt from them in two divinely inspired books, the Gospel and the Acts of the Apostles. The former, he declares, he wrote in accordance with the information he received from those who from the first had been eye-witnesses and ministers of the word, information which, he adds, he had followed in its entirety from the first. The latter he composed not this time from hearsay but from the evidence of his own eyes. It is actually suggested that Paul was in the habit of referring to Luke's Gospel whenever he said, as if writing of some Gospel of his own: "According to my gospel"[426] (Eusebius, *Hist. eccl.* 3.4.7-8).

Jerome likewise informs us:

> Luke a physician of Antioch, as his writings indicate, was not unskilled in the Greek language. An adherent of the apostle Paul, and companion of all his journeying, he wrote a *Gospel*, concerning which the same Paul says, "We send with him a brother whose praise in the gospel is among all the churches (2 Cor 8:18)" and to the Colossians "Luke the beloved physician salutes you (Col 4:14)," and to Timothy "Luke only is with me (2 Tim 4:11)." He also wrote another excellent volume to which he prefixed the title *Acts of the*

[426] Rom 2:16, 16:25; 2 Tim 2:8.

> *Apostles*, a history which extends to the second year of Paul's sojourn at Rome, that is the fourth year of Nero, from which we learn that the book was composed in that same city (Jerome, *Vir. ill.* 7 [*NPNF*² 3:363]).[427]

Thus we can see that both the *Gospel of Luke* and the *Acts of the Apostles* represent a two volume production of *Luke-Acts* which was dedicated to an individual, whom Luke calls in his first volume "most excellent [Greek, κράτιστε] Theophilus" (Luke 1:3). The phrase is one that is typically addressed to a personage of high rank in government or of royalty, equivalent to "your excellency" or "your highness."[428]

Since the name "Theophilus" means "Friend of God" or "Beloved of God," it might be just a cognomen for someone who appears to be a real person, but whose identity had to remain anonymous for political reasons, even though he was friendly to the gospel message. It is also most likely that this Theophilus was the patron who sponsored the composition.

If *Luke-Acts* was written when Paul was in Rome during his two year house arrest, then the official was most likely someone of high rank in the Roman government. Who was Theophilus? The *Anchor Bible Dictionary* lists eight candidates for the identity of this individual, none of which is the one that we propose here.[429]

Let us ask, who of high rank in the Roman government at that time might show a decided interest in the philosophical and intellectual reasonings supporting the Christian persuasion? The answer is the Roman philosopher, poet, playwright, senator and tutor of Nero, Seneca. We know that Seneca was a literary patron to the court Poets and historians.[430] He was also one of the wealthiest men in all of Rome.[431]

Jerome, in his *Lives of Illustrious Men,* included even the pagan philosopher, Seneca, with the following appraisal:

---

[427] According to Jerome's testimony, the dating of *Luke-Acts* is in the fourth year of Nero, 58 C.E., which accords exactly with the chronology that we have established in appendix 2.

[428] Luke used the same expression in three other instances to refer to the Roman governors Felix and Festus (Acts 23:26; 24:3; 26:25). It was a common literary practice to dedicate their works to distinguished personages. Josephus (37- ca. 100 C.E.) dedicated his two-part work, *Contra Apionem,* to one Epaphroditus, where he similarly addressed him as: "Epaphroditus, most excellent [κράτιστε] of men" (1:1). The second book of *Contra Apionem* began: "By means of the former volume, my most honored Epaphroditus, I have demonstrated our antiquity ..." (2:1). The similarity to Luke's dedication is a striking parallel.

[429] See Robert F. O'Toole, "Theophilus" in *The Anchor Bible Dictionary,* David Noel Freedman, ed., (New York: Doubleday, 1992), 6:511-12.

[430] Miriam T. Griffin, *Nero: The End of a Dynasty* (New Haven: Yale University Press, 1985), 84-5, 148-9.

> Lucius Annaeus Seneca of Cordova, disciple of the Stoic Sotion and uncle of Lucan the Poet, was a man of most continent life, whom I should not place in the category of saints were it not that those *Epistles of Paul to Seneca and Seneca to Paul*, which are read by many, provoke me. In these, written when he was tutor of Nero and the most powerful man of that time, he says that he would like to hold such a place among his countrymen as Paul held among Christians. He was put to death by Nero two years before Peter and Paul were crowned with martyrdom (Jerome, *Vir. ill.* 12 [*NPNF*^{2} 3.365]).

From an another ancient work entitled the *Passio sancti Pauli apostoli*, we also read:

> From the house of the emperor there came to him many who believed on the Lord Jesus Christ, and great gladness and joy increased daily among the believers. Even the emperor's tutor, recognizing the divine wisdom that was in him, became so united to him in friendship that he could scarcely refrain from conferring with him. As oral discussion was not possible, they frequently entered into mutual correspondence, and he (Seneca) enjoyed his amiability, his friendly talk and his counsel; and so very much was his teaching disseminated and loved through the working of the Holy Spirit that now he taught with express permission and was gladly heard by many. For he disputed with the philosophers of the heathen and refuted them, for which reason also very many followed his teaching. The emperor's teacher also read some of his writings in his presence over and over again and brought it about that all admired him. The senate also thought very highly of him.[432]

Whether one accepts the extant Epistles between Seneca and Paul, the idea that Paul and Seneca had crossed paths in Rome is not only believable, but certainly most likely.[433] At any rate, we place the writing of *Luke-Acts* in Rome in the year of 58 C.E.

---

[431] Griffin *Nero*, 205-6, notes: "Seneca was accused of trying to surpass the Princeps in the wealth and magnificence of his villas and gardens out of political ambition." Seneca is also blamed as the initial cause of the Boadicean War in Britain. Cassius Dio, *Roman History, Xiphilinus Excerpta*, 62, wrote: "An excuse for the war was found in the confiscation of the sums of money that Claudius had given to the foremost Britons; for these sums, as Decianus Catus, the procurator of the island, maintained, were to be paid back. This was one reason for the uprising; another was found in the fact that Seneca, in the hope of receiving a good rate of interest, had lent to the islanders 40,000,000 sesterces that they did not want, and had afterwards called in this loan all at once and had resorted to severe measures in exacting it."

[432] Quoted from Edgar Hennecke and Wilhelm Schneemelcher, *New Testament Apocrypha* (Philadelphia: Westminster Press, 1965), 2:134-5.

THE GOSPEL AND EPISTLES OF JOHN

THE DATING OF THE *GOSPEL OF JOHN* BY THE earliest testimony is that it was composed after the Synoptics. On the authority of Clement of Alexandria (ca. 190 C.E.), Eusebius records:

> Last of all, aware that the physical facts had been recorded in the [Synoptic] gospels, encouraged by his pupils and irresistibly moved by the Spirit, John wrote a spiritual gospel (Eusebius, *Hist. eccl.* 6.14.7).

Although many early authorities place the dating of John's Gospel late in the first century, we also have testimony that John's Gospel was actually a corroboration of himself, the Apostle Andrew, and other eyewitnesses to the actual events. The *Muratorian Fragment* (ca. 200 C.E.) is another early witness to this fact:

> The fourth Gospel is that of John, one of the disciples. When his fellow-disciples and bishops entreated him, he said, "Fast now with me for the space of three days, and let us recount to each other whatever may be revealed to each of us." On the same night, it was revealed to Andrew, one of the apostles, that John should narrate all things in his own name – as they called them to mind.[434]

When John composed his Gospel, Peter and Paul had already been martyred in Rome, i.e., after February of 68 C.E. John Mark had taken Peter's 22 book canon to John who was now at Ephesus. John was now the last of the three apostles alive who had witnessed the Transfiguration and therefore his final endorsement to the entire project was paramount.

The fact that the Apostle Andrew and other eyewitnesses helped compose this special gospel account lends itself to an early dating rather than a late one. And yet, it does not appear to have been written after the fall of Jerusalem in 70 C.E. J. A. T. Robinson notes in this regard:

---

[433] In letter 7 (ibid., 237) Seneca greets Paul and Theophilus, which would indicate by this that Theophilus was someone other than Seneca. It is also interesting that three of the letters (10, 13, 14) are dated to the Consulships of Lurco and Sabinus (58 C.E.), Letter 12 to that of Apronianus and Capito (59 C.E.) and letter 11 to that of Frugi and Bassus, (64 C.E.). These dates would suit the low dating that we propose, with letter 11 being written after the fire in Rome in 64 C.E., showing an absence of activity of five years, during which the Apostle Paul was absent in the far west of Europe. Once again, we have striking confirmation for the chronology of the Apostle Paul that this book alone has established.

[434] Quoted from *A Dictionary of Early Christian Beliefs*, David W. Bercot, ed., (Peabody, Mass.: Hendrickson, 1998), 382.

> Of all the writings in the New Testament, with the exception perhaps of the epistle to the Hebrews and the book of Revelation, the gospel of John is that in which we might most expect an allusion (however indirect, subtle or symbolic) to the doom of Jerusalem, if it had in fact already been accomplished. For the focus of the gospel is on the rejection by metropolitan Judaism of the one who comes to his own people (1.11) as the Christ and King and Shepherd of Israel. This coming and this rejection must inevitably mean the judgment and the supersession of the old religion, represented by the law (1.17), the water-pots of purification (2.6), the localized worship of Gerizim and Jerusalem (4.21), the sabbath (5.10-18), the manna that perishes (6.31f.), and much else. Above all it means the replacement of the temple by the person of Christ himself (2.21). Yet, for all the capacity of this evangelist for overtones and double meaning and irony, it is hard to find any reference which unquestionably reflects the events of 70.[435]

Indeed, we note that John records an unfulfilled prophecy of the Jewish leaders:

> This man [Jesus] is performing many signs. If we let him go on like this, everyone will believe in him and the Romans will come and destroy both our holy place [the temple] and our nation (John 11:47-8).[436]

We thus would place the writing of the *Gospel of John* in the year of 68 C.E., or 69 C.E. at the latest.

As to John's *First Epistle,* it also appears to be written around this same time due to the similarity of the opening remarks with his Gospel. Indeed, John's First Epistle appears to be a kind of cover letter to the Gospel, if not a commentary on it in some respects.[437]

---

[435] John A. T. Robinson, *Redating the New Testament* (Philadelphia: Westminster, 1976), 276.

[436] John also makes mention of the fact that the temple had been 46 years in construction during Jesus' ministry (2:20) and gives details of the temple's structure that readers, who were familiar with the temple, could relate to (5:2).

[437] For instance, in the Gospel, one could jump to the conclusion, as many later interpreters have, that the *Logos* was a pre-existent God-Being, but the *Epistle of First John* begins in like fashion as the Gospel, only this time the ambiguity is erased for any such conclusion, since here it is explained in more detail that the *Logos* was in fact the "Word of Life" and that "this life was revealed, and we have seen IT and testify to IT (not Him), and declare to you the ETERNAL LIFE that was with the Father [not some pre-existing God-Being] and was revealed to us" (1 John 1:2). Unfortunately, John's own commentary on his gospel message has been brushed aside by later church councils that had a different mind-set than the early Jewish apostle who wrote these words.

The *First Epistle of John* also testifies that it is a corroborative work just like *the Gospel of John* due to the same kind of "we" sections that it contains. The summary statement at the end of the Gospel also tells us that

> this is the disciple [John] who is testifying to these things and has written them, and WE know that his testimony is true (John 21:24).

Likewise, in the *First Epistle of John* it begins:

> WE declare to you what was from the beginning, what WE have heard, what WE have seen with OUR eyes, what WE have looked at and touched with OUR hands, concerning the word of life ...WE declare to you what WE have seen and heard so that you also may have fellowship with US; and truly OUR fellowship is with the Father and with his Son Jesus Christ. WE are writing these things so that OUR joy may be complete (1 John 1:1-4).

John's *Second* and *Third Epistles* have been criticized as not being that of the Apostle John, but there is no real basis for such objections. In *Second John*, he addresses his letter to the elect Lady and her children and warns "Everyone who does not abide in the teaching of Christ (the Messiah), but goes BEYOND it, does not have God" (2 John 1:9). Already, in John's time, people were going "beyond" the teaching of Christ (as the Messiah of Israel), and we are now in a period when apostasy is beginning in the development of a high Christology that is of major concern to John. In the next two centuries, the going beyond the "teaching of the Messiah" culminated in retrojecting Jesus into a divine pre-existent phenomenon – an oxymoron that defies all logic, reason, and sound biblical teaching. And of all things, John, who was so concerned about this evil trend, is the one who became the ventriloquist's dummy in supposedly expounding it.

Third John shows us that there is beginning to be a breakdown in church government, and a person by the name of Diotrephes is causing problems. And again, in this tiny Epistle we encounter the same kind of "we" sections that we have seen earlier:

> Everyone has testified favorably about Demetrius, and so has the truth itself. WE also testify for him, and you know that OUR testimony is true (3 John 1:12).

It could be that these Epistles were written some time after the Gospel, which may be in the 70's, 80's, or 90's C.E. Since John lived until the last decade of the first century, any of these dates are possible.

The *Book of Revelation* is a special case that we have already dealt with separately in appendix 3.

THE EPISTLE OF JAMES

THE *EPISTLE OF JAMES* IS SPECIFICALLY WRITTEN to the "Twelve Tribes in the Dispersion" and thus reflects the time when the twelve apostles left Jerusalem on a world wide evangelistic campaign to the scattered descendents of the lost tribes of Israel, twelve years after the resurrection. If this be the case, then this letter was written most likely when James appears to have become the recognized leader of the Jerusalem church, around the year of 40 C.E.

In the original "Canonical Edition"[438] of the New Testament, the *Epistle of James* leads the Catholic Epistle section, which immediately comes after the *Acts of the Apostles.*[439]

The *Epistle of James* contains very basic teaching, and in the belief that teaching should be progressive, no better Epistle is there than to have the most basic teaching in the entire New Testament begin the Epistles section.[440]

Also, to be noted is the fact that every New Testament book ends with an "Amen" except the *Acts of the Apostles,* the *Epistle of James,* and *3 John.* It almost seems that the *Amen* represented what we find in the Old Testament canon where each book ended with "be bound." The fact that these books lack this important canonization stamp appears to be a deliberate removal of some information that the original writer included, but was decided to be removed for reasons only known to Paul, Peter, and John.[441]

The one common thread that appears to be a link between these documents is the fact that *James* was written to the scattered tribes of Israel and immediately after the Apostle Paul is released from his Roman

---

438 I borrow this excellent term from David Trobisch, *The First Edition of the New Testament* (Oxford: Oxford University Press, 2000), 8.

439 F. H. A. Scrivener, *A Plain Introduction to the Criticism of the New Testament,* 4th ed. (London: George Bell & Sons, 1894), 1:72, "Whether copies contain the whole or a part of the sacred volume, the general order of the books is the following: Gospels, Acts, Catholic Epistles, Pauline Epistles, Apocalypse."

440 If the two short references to Jesus were omitted (1:1 and 2:1), then the entire Epistle could be said to be nothing more than an essay on pure religion in a general sense, based upon simple Old Testament values and theology. See Donald Guthrie, *Introduction,* 756.

incarceration, he travels to the far west to fulfill his final portion of his threefold commission to preach to the Gentiles, kings, and the people of Israel (Acts 9:15).

In the spirit of speculation, it would appear that the identity of the lost tribes of Israel, with many of the descendents in the British Isles, was to remain hidden to the general reader until it was to be revealed at the time of the end. Thus, the only canon expansion conceivable would be the final testimony of these two books. However, that will have to remain until a future age when all things shall be revealed (Luke 12:2). We have thus contributed to that revelation and to the unlocking of this great mystery in our pursuit of the story of *Beyond Acts.*

THE EPISTLES OF PETER

WE HAVE DEALT WITH THE PERTINENT STORY of Peter's Epistles throughout our adventure with the following conclusion. *First Peter* was written from Jerusalem in the summer of 66 C.E. and *Second Peter* was written from Rome in the summer of 67 C.E.

THE EPISTLE OF JUDE

THE *EPISTLE OF JUDE* WAS WRITTEN BY THE brother of James and Jesus, to the brethren at Rome to verify what Peter had predicted in Peter's *Second Epistle* was coming true. Thus, all ideas that Peter borrowed from Jude miss the entire thrust of what is being said

[441] The *Epistle of James,* like the *Book of Acts,* has no "amen" to conclude it. It was specifically addressed to the "twelve tribes of Israel" and it may have originally contained salutations at the end of it that would identify the locations of these peoples. There appears to have been a conscious effort by the Apostles Peter and Paul, when they edited the writings for the New Testament canon, to conceal the fact that they went to the British Isles. Indeed, this is why the *Book of Acts* breaks off just before Paul's departure to Britain and is the reason why Paul's stated intention to go to Britain, when writing to the British war captives in Rome, was edited to read "Spain" instead (Rom 15:24). There are no traditions that Paul or Peter ever went to Spain, but to the British Isles, there are many. Indeed, the whereabouts of Joseph of Arimathea, Lazarus, and others who went to Britain in the mid-thirties was most certainly also edited out of the account in Acts. The reason was to conceal the identity of the whereabouts of the Lost Tribes of Israel until the time of the end. Thus scholars and readers in general have been deliberately thrown off the track. And, to whit, the strategy worked.

in these two Epistles. Jude was therefore written from the areas of where the many of the Jerusalem church had spread itself in the upper regions of Asia Minor to confirm what Peter had warned about, and therefore, most likely in the summer of 68 C.E.[442]

ROMANS

WITHIN THE CONTEXT OF THE LETTER ITSELF, Paul states that he had not yet been to Rome (Rom 1:11, 13, 15). The Epistle, therefore, was written before his imprisonment at Rome. Also, since there is no intimation that he is in prison, it is apparent that he is free and therefore, it preceded the Caesarean imprisonment and the arrest in Jerusalem (Acts 21:33). On the other hand, the Epistle also implies that Paul had long been engaged in apostolic work and points to a comparatively late period in his career.

In the Epistle, Paul states his intention to go to Rome after first visiting Jerusalem (Rom 15:23-8). A comparison with Acts 19:21 shows this was his exact purpose during his three month residence at Corinth. He was on the point of starting for Jerusalem to bear a contribution of fruit from Macedonia and Achaia. The Corinthian letters show this contribution still in process of collection and also show the apostle on his way to Corinth, planning after his visit there to go to Jerusalem (1 Cor 16:1-5; 2 Cor 9:1-5; 13:1). From Acts 24:17, we see that Paul in fact did carry this plan out.

When Paul wrote the *Epistle to the Romans*, Timothy, Sosipater, Gaius, and Erastus were with him (Rom 16:21, 23). Of these, the first three are expressly mentioned in Acts 20:4 as having been with Paul at Corinth during his three month visit. Erastus was himself a Corinthian, and had been sent to Macedonia with Timothy from Ephesus (Acts 21:22; see also 1 Cor 16:10-11). Also, Phoebe, a deaconess who brought the Epistle to Rome, was from the Corinthian port of Cenchrea (Rome 16:1).

Romans, therefore, appears to have been written a little after the Corinthian letters, from the city of Corinth, near the end of Paul's third apostolic campaign. By our chronology, a date in the autumn of 54 C.E. would appear to be most likely for the writing of the *Epistle to the Romans.*

---

[442] See also page 120.

First Corinthians

PAUL WROTE FIRST CORINTHIANS FROM THE CITY of Ephesus (1 Cor 16:8). In the letter Paul states his intention of visiting the Corinthian church after going to Macedonia (1 Cor 16:5). This would coincide with Paul's two year stay at Ephesus recorded in Acts, the nineteenth chapter. In Acts 19:21-2 it states that after Paul's stay in Ephesus he then purposed to go to Macedonia and Achaia (the province in which Corinth was situated). Paul's stay in Corinth lasted from the spring of 53 C.E. until the summer of 55 C.E. (1 Cor 16:8).

First Corinthians 5:9 states that Paul had written to the Corinthians on a prior occasion. This means one of two things. Either we have a lost Epistle of Paul that was written prior to First Corinthians, or Second Corinthians may be first in chronological order, but not in canonical order. Another suggestion is that First Corinthians was two letters that have been fused together, which is quite possible.

From 1 Cor 7:1 we learn that the Corinthians had also written to Paul, in answer to the letter Paul had sent them. Also, it appears that Paul had received a visit from three members of the Corinthian church who were perhaps the bearers of their letter. And further, from 2 Cor 12:14 and 13:11, it would appear that Paul himself had visited Corinth before the writing of First Corinthians. All this communication suggests that *First Corinthians* was written toward the latter part of Paul's stay at Ephesus.

From 1 Cor 16:8 it appears that when Paul wrote First Corinthians, he was already planning to leave Ephesus to go to Macedonia and Achaia. His language also suggests that the Day of Pentecost was not very far off. Paul speaks of Passover and the Feast (of Unleavened Bread) as though it were about to occur (1 Cor 5:6-8). Again, in 1 Cor 11:23-34, Paul speak of the meaning of Passover. Therefore, by our chronology it appears that *First Corinthians* was written shortly before Passover in 53 C.E.

Second Corinthians

PAUL, IN THIS LETTER, STATES THAT HE INTENDS to carry out his travel plans that he announced in First Corinthians (cf. 1 Cor 16:5-9; 2 Cor 3:12; 7:5). We also see that Timothy is with Paul according to the plan indicated in First Corinthians (cf. 1 Cor 16:10, 11;

2 Cor 1:1). And we further note that Paul is ready to come to the Corinthians a third time (2 Cor 13:1). This places this letter after First Corinthians. Since we know that his intention was to winter in Corinth (Acts 20:2), and that the circumstances had sufficient time to change from those of *First Corinthians*, then it appears that this letter was written in late summer, early autumn of 54 C.E.

GALATIANS

SCHOLARS HAVE TRADITIONALLY DATED THE letter to the Galatians after Paul's visit to Jerusalem recorded in Acts 15:1-29, based on a superficial comparison of Galatians 2 and Acts 15. Now, however, there is a growing trend to move the writing of this letter to before the Jerusalem visit of Acts 15, wherein the famous Jerusalem conference occurred in the spring of 48 C.E. Indeed, some scholars believe that the controversy in Galatia is what brought the apostles to the conference table in the first place. In this regard, Ernest L. Martin notes:

> This book [Galatians] was certainly composed by the apostle Paul before the Jerusalem Council... This has to be the case because it is inconceivable that six full chapters had to be written about the non-need for gentiles to observe circumcision and the Mosaic law if Paul could simply have referred the Galatians to the official decrees concerning the matter which were ordained by the apostles, and all others, at the Jerusalem Council (Acts 15).[443]

Ben Witherington III also agrees with this assessment and he therefore identifies Galatians 2 with the Acts 11 visit, rather than the Acts 15 visit.[444] Colin J. Hemer concurs, offering the following to consider:

> A focal problem is the relation of the Jerusalem visits in Acts with those described by Paul himself in Gal. 1-2. It is commonly regarded as a decisive condemnation of Luke that the two versions cannot be reconciled, and a great deal may be built out of extrapolation from this one point. But it is possible to identify the visit of Acts 9 with that of Gal. 1, and the visit of Acts 11 with that of Gal. 2, the Council

[443] Ernest L. Martin, *Secrets of Golgotha*, 2d ed. (Portland, Oreg.: Associates for Scriptural Knowledge, 1996), 433.

[444] Ben Witherington III, *The Paul Quest* (Downers Grove, Ill.: InterVarsity Press, 1998), 314-18.

> visit of Acts 15 not being mentioned because it had not taken place by the time of the writing of Galatians. ...This view... [and] its persuasiveness is tied to the acceptance of the 'South Galatian" view of the destination of the epistle, identifying Paul's first coming to 'Galatia' (Gal. 4:13) with the narrative of his 'first journey' into one of geography and terminology, a more objective sphere in which firmer answers about usage may be obtainable.[445]

S. Dockx believes that the solution to the problem is that the visit mentioned in Acts 11:30 and 15:1-29 are actually one and the same:

> It is historically certain that the year 48 is the date of the ascent of Paul to Jerusalem and his bearing the collection for the great famine there. Acts 11:30 and Act [sic!] 15:1-29 represent then the one and same visit of Paul to Jerusalem. This correlates with the categorical affirmation of Paul that he only went up twice to Jerusalem, the first time, three years after his conversion (Gal 1:18).[446]

From our point of view, however, it appears that scholars are trying to jump through an imaginary hoop of reconciling the fact that Paul would not have left out any journeys to Jerusalem prior to Acts 15. In other words, according to Acts, the Jerusalem Council visit is Paul's third visit, but according to Galatians 2, it is his second. Solution: identify the Galatians 2 visit with the Acts 11 visit, and all the problems at once vanish. But do all the problems vanish, or are we introducing new ones that are even more problematic than the ones which this theory seeks to resolve? What makes scholars believe that Paul had to enumerate every single visit to Jerusalem in his letter to Galatians? Ernest L. Martin again notes:

> It is not to be imagined that Paul meant he only went to Jerusalem twice in that seventeen year period. Not at all. Paul may have visited the capital several times during the interval, and one such time is mentioned in Acts 11:30. In the Book of Galatians, Paul meant that he had gone to Jerusalem twice to discuss doctrine and the relevance of his special commission. In Paul's other visits over that period

---

[445] Colin J. Hemer, *The Book of Acts in the Setting of Hellenistic History* (Winona Lake, Ind.: Eisenbrauns, 1990), 247-8.

[446] S. Dockx, "The First Missionary Voyage of Paul: Historical Reality or Literary Creation of Luke?" in *Chronos, Kairos, Christos: Nativity and Chronological Studies Presented to Jack Finegan*, ed. Jerry Vardaman, et al., (Winona Lake, Ind.: Eisenbrauns, 1989), 211. The problem with this view is: what do we do with Paul's first missionary journey reported in Acts 13:4-14:27? Dockx' solution is: "This journey (Acts 13:4-14:28) is not a page of history, but a painting by Luke" (ibid., 221).

> of seventeen years (and there must have been several) the issue of doctrine and Paul's special commission must not have come up because there is nothing about it in his writings. That's why he never mentioned his other journeys to Jerusalem in the Book of Galatians.[447]

Martin is correct in observing the context of these visits is the overall deciding factor to the entire solution. H. N. Ridderbos also notes in this regard:

> Paul was concerned here [Gal. 1:16-2:1] merely to show, first, that he was independent as an apostle, and second, that he was in agreement with the apostles in Jerusalem. For this reason, he said first (Gal 1:17-24) that he did not go directly to Jerusalem after his conversion; he went there three years later for a fifteen-day period, at which time he had contact only with Peter. Thus he showed that he had received his commission and his gospel not from men, but from God. When he continued in 2:1, "Then after fourteen years I went up again to Jerusalem," his argument is not the same as in 1:17-24. He had no more need of demonstrating his independence and he was not concerned to enumerate his (few) journeys to Jerusalem. His concern, rather, is now to show how, on the matter of circumcision, he not only stood his ground in the presence of the Jerusalem leaders, but also met with their concurrence on every point. The matter that is at issue here is thus his quarrel with opponents in Galatia, and the attitude of the apostles with regard to it. It is therefore no surprise that he did not mention the collection journey of Acts 11:30, nor need this be regarded as a suppression of the truth (cf. 1:20). That journey was entirely beside the point here, having no relation to the conflict between Paul and his opponents.[448]

Another point that we observe is that scholars who accept the equation of Acts 11 = Gal 2 are forced into emphasizing the differences of the accounts at the expense of the obvious similarities of Acts 15 = Gal 2.

Ben Witherington III is one such scholar who promotes the Acts 11 = Gal 2 equation, and in so doing, notice the differences that are supposedly the clinching *coup-de-grâce* to the traditional theory:

> In Galatians it appears that the circumcision issue is raised after Paul arrives in Jerusalem, whereas in Acts 15 it has been a live issue before Paul's arrival. In Galatians Paul

---

[447] Martin, *Secrets*, 433.

[448] H. N. Ridderbos, "Galatians, Epistle to," in *The International Standard Bible Encyclopedia* (Grand Rapids: Eerdmans, 1979), 2:383.

> says he went up to Jerusalem "by" or in response to a revelation, but in Acts 15 he is clearly sent up as an emissary of a church. In Galatians Paul is quite clear that he met privately with the pillar apostles, even though some intruders invaded this private meeting. Acts 15 portrays a public or large congregational meeting. ...Paul does not mention the decree at all in Galatians, and it would have been most advantageous for him to do so if he knew of it.[449]

Such reasoning, however, is a weak defense when considering the context of what Paul is saying in his letter to the Galatians. Indeed, it is the strong similarities that, in spite of these objections (and north Galatian theories versus south Galatian theories), and a host of other issues, that have made the entire subject seem complex beyond what it needs to be.[450]

The issues to be considered are in fact simple. The entire tone of Galatians is one of reflection on the part of the Apostle Paul to something where it appears some considerable time has past, and not to some immediate circumstances. And when we consider the fact that *Galatians* and the *Epistle to the Romans* have so much in common,[451] it seems justified in placing the writing of both of these Epistles near in time.

In Galatians 2:9-10, Paul speaks of the collection for the poor as a past event. This was the first collection for the Sabbatical year of 47/48 C.E. The Jerusalem Conference occurred during this year, and so what we read in Acts 11:27-9 is the proposed relief that he would have to gather in Asia and then return in 48 C.E. for distribution. Also, notice the mention of Agabus (Acts 11:28) who predicts a soon coming famine. This, obviously, is the "revelation" that Paul went to Jerusalem as a response to (Gal 2:2).

Notice also the similarity in the fact that Paul and Barnabas both consult the Jerusalem church in Acts 15 and Galatians 2, which in both cases, they must overcome strong opposition. H. N. Ridderbos again notes that

---

[449] Ben Witherington III, *The Paul Quest* (Downers Grove, Ill.: InterVarsity Press, 1998), 317.

[450] All the literature on the subject is enough to make one's head spin. But for those who want to dig into it a little further and follow all the sources, see: R. H. Stein, "The Relationship of Galatians 2:1-10 and Acts 15:1-35: Two neglected arguments," *Journal of the Evangelical Theological Society* 17 (1974), 239-42; Donald Guthrie, *New Testament Introduction* (Downers Grove: InterVarsity Press, 1990), 452-65; Colin C. Hemer, "Acts and Galatians Reconsidered," *Themelios* n.s. 2 (1976-77): 81-8; H. Stadelmann, "Die Vorgeschichte des Galaterbriefes. Ein Testfall für die geschictliche Zuverlässigkeit des Paulus und Lukas," *Bibel und Gemeinde* 2 (1982): 153-65.

[451] Gerd Luedemann, *Paul, Apostle to the Gentiles: Studies in Chronology.* (Philadelphia: Fortress, 1984), 85.

> it is difficult to deny that Gal. 2 and Acts 15 describe the same event, although it may be that they do so in different ways and from different points of view. In both reports the same matter was at stake – namely, to what extent gentile believers must subject themselves to the law of Moses, and especially whether they should be circumcised. Both reports show Paul and the leaders of the Jerusalem church (Peter, John, and James) arriving at a common viewpoint and adopting a common policy. That the same matter should be dealt with upon two different occasions under almost the same circumstances is highly unlikely.[452]

Within the context of the letter, Paul refers to preaching to the Galatians on a former of two visits that he had made to them (4:13). This in itself shows us that the letter was written after Paul had passed through Galatia on his "second" apostolic tour.

When Paul states that he is marveled at how "soon" they have removed from the original gospel message that they had received from Paul (1:6), we have no way of knowing if this involved a previous letter (to which we no longer have) or by direct teaching.[453] In any event, we should understand that the Galatians were in some way already instructed in the decision of the Jerusalem Council and now, Paul is astonished that they are reverting back to pre-councilor Judaizing.

Paul was constantly on the move during his second apostolic journey, except for his 18 month stay at Corinth. It would seem most probable that while he remained at Corinth, he could have received reports concerning the state of the Galatian churches and thereby dispatched this letter. Paul was in Corinth by our chronology from November, 49 C.E. to June of 51 C.E. Therefore, to assign a date of around the spring of 50 C.E. allows for reports to have been received by him concerning Galatia just after the winter season, which is in compliance of how "soon" the Galatians were back sliding.

This date also seems likely based on the fact that in the 5th chapter of Galatians Paul speaks of the Christian significance of the days of Unleavened Bread. In verses 6 through 9, Paul speaks of circumcision which was always associated by the Jews with the first day of Unleavened bread. It would seem from this that Paul most likely wrote *Galatians* just before the Passover of 50 C.E.

---

[452] H. N. Ridderbos, "Galatians, Epistle to" in *The International Standard Bible Encyclopedia* (Grand Rapids: Eerdmans, 1979), 2:383.

[453] "As they went from town to town, they delivered to them for observance the decisions that had been reached by the apostles and elders who were in Jerusalem" (Acts 16:4).

PHILIPPIANS

THE EPISTLE TO THE PHILIPPIANS WAS WRITTEN when Paul was a prisoner at Rome (Phil 1:7, 13; 4:22). It was written during Paul's first imprisonment at Rome for the following reasons: 1) Paul was in custody of the Praetorian Guard (cf. Phil 1:13 with Acts 23:35), which was in Rome; 2) Paul sent greetings from the Emperor's household (Phil 4:22), which was also at Rome; 3) Paul, at the time of writing, is expecting a decision of his cause of imprisonment, which could only come from Rome (Phil 1:19, 2:24); 4) The situation that he describes in the first chapter of the Epistle (Phil 1:12-14) agrees with that mentioned in Acts 28:16, 30-31, where Paul has enough freedom to carry on correspondence and preach the gospel; 5) There also exists some tradition that the Epistle was written from Rome, which is preserved in the Marcionite Prologue.

Paul seems to have had considerable influence on the Praetorian Prefect (Acts 28:16), the Praetorian Guard (Phil 1:13), and even the very household of Caesar (Phil 4:22). It was Paul's influence on these Roman leaders which also helped his fellow Christians preach the gospel more boldly in Rome (Phil 1:14).

Paul obviously was in Rome during a time prior to when the Praetorian Prefect Tigellinus had taken control in the year of 62 C.E. Before this time, there seems to have been two rival factions in Rome. On the one side there was Poppaea, Nero's mistress, who was a Jewish proselyte and therefore would not have tolerated Paul's Christian teaching. And on the other side there was the Praetorian Prefect, Afranius Burrus, who was against the Jews and therefore, would have taken Paul's side against his Jewish accusers for political reasons, if for nothing else. In the pre-62 C.E. years, Burrus and Seneca maintained the stability of Nero's government. Things changed dramatically when Burrus died in 62 C.E., to say the least.

It was also in 62 C.E. that Poppaea married Nero. She appointed Tigellinus as the new Praetorian Prefect, who turned out to be a ruthless tyrant. The pro-Jewish faction had now won out and turned the tables around. For this reason alone, there was no way that Paul could have been still in prison while Tigillinus and Poppaea had come to power. Therefore, the situation appears to be that Paul's imprisonment was before this time. Indeed, Paul would have to have been released from his two year imprisonment prior to 62 C.E., which means that at the very latest he had to have been released sometime in 61 C.E. And by our chronology, Paul's release was in the relative time of stability, in the summer of 58 C.E. Thus, Philippians was most likely written in the spring of 58 C.E.

COLOSSIANS, EPHESIANS, AND PHILEMON

MANY SCHOLARS, WHO DATE PAUL'S imprisonment to the year of 62 C.E., believe that he also lost his life then, and thus, either have to place Paul's other "Prison Epistles" in Paul's supposedly one and only Roman imprisonment, or concede that they were written by someone else after this time. And since there is little evidence within these other Prison Epistles that indicate that they were written during the same time as that of the last verses of Acts, or the *Epistle to the Philippians*, then most scholars opt for the conclusion that these Epistles were written after Paul's death by someone within Paul's circle, and they were passed off as letters written by the Apostle Paul.

However, the internal evidence is strong that these Epistles are indeed genuine Epistle's of Paul. This has long ago been noted:

> It is clear that they were ...written from prison (Philem 1, 10, 23; Col. 4:10, 18; Eph. 3:1; 4:1; 6:20). It is evident, moreover, that the three were written at about the same time. Thus, besides the fact that all three were written when Paul was a prisoner, there were with Paul when he wrote Colossians, Timothy (1:1), Epaphras (1:7; 4:12), Aristarchus and Mark (4:10), Luke and Demas (4:14); and all these were with him when he wrote the letter to Philemon (vs. 1, 23, 24). Onesimus moreover accompanied both letters (Col. 4:9; Philem. 11, 12). Such a collocation of coincidences can only be explained on the supposition that the letters were sent together. That Ephesians was written also at this time appears from its similarity in contents to Colossians, and from the fact that Tychicus was the bearer of both letters, and in both is commended in almost identical words (Col. 4:7, 8; Eph. 6:21, 22).[454]

We have already brought out that the imprisonment that these letters would most likely have been written was during a time that is *Beyond Acts*, and therefore beyond Paul's Roman imprisonment mentioned therein. Most scholars agree. But what they don't agree upon is whether or

[454] Ernest De Witt Burton, *The Records and Letters of the Apostolic Age* (New York: Charles Scribner's Sons, 1895), 222-3.

not Paul was alive to write them. And true to form, most scholars give a thumbs down on Paul being alive and therefore on Pauline authorship.

The letters to the *Ephesians* and the *Colossians* may have been encyclicals to be read, not just to the Ephesians, but to the "seven churches of Asia" that are mentioned in the *Book of Revelation*: Ephesus, Smyrna, Pergamos, Thyatira, Sardis, Philadelphia and Laodicea. Just as the Apostle John had sent his "revelation" to these churches in the mid-fifties, Paul is now revealing for the first time the doctrine of the "Mystery," which was a "secret" that had been hid "from the ages and from the generations" which is now revealed to God's apostles and prophets by the Spirit (Eph 3:5). Dr. Bullinger long ago recognized these letters as encyclicals:

> In some of the oldest MSS, the words "At Ephesus" (Gr. *en Ephesō*) are not found. And the writings of some of the early Christian apologists show that these words were not in their copies, e.g. Origen (fl. A.D. 230) and Basil (fl. A.D. 350). The explanation of the omission is probably that the Epistle was encyclical, and that the space now occupied in other of the MSS, by the words *en Ephesō* was originally blank, so that the names of the various churches to which it was sent could be filled in. From Col. 4. 16 we learn that Paul wrote a letter to the Laodiceans. There can be little doubt that this is the one as was believed by Marcion, an early Christian writer (but one much tinged by Gnosticism). If *Ephesians* is not the letter, then an epistle has been lost, which is unthinkable.[455]

As we brought out in chapter seven, these three letters were written from the city of Ephesus in an imprisonment that the Apostle Paul endured there around the year of 64 C.E.[456] Therefore, we assign the date of the writing of these Epistles to the spring of 64 C.E.

FIRST THESSALONIANS

PAUL'S FIRST LETTER TO THE CHURCH AT Thessalonica was written not long after Paul made his first visit to the

[455] E. W. Bullinger, *The Companion Bible* (London: Samuel Bagster & Sons, 1969), 1759.

[456] This is one of the most important contributions in New Testament chronology that has come along on the scene in recent years, and we owe it to the shrewd insight of Dr. Ernest L. Martin (see chapter 7 for details on this).

congregation there (1 Thess 1:9, 10; 2:17-3:6). Paul first visited Thessalonica on what is called his second apostolic journey (Acts 17:1-2), shortly after he had spent Pentecost in Philippi (1 Thess 2:2).

There is also evidence that this letter was written after Paul had visited Athens (1 Thess 3:1). It was at Athens that Paul had sent Timothy back to Thessalonica to bring to him information concerning the state of the church there (1 Thess 3:2), which Timothy accomplished (v. 6). From Acts 18:15, we see that Timothy, as well as Silas, rejoined Paul at Corinth. This would indicate that it was from the city of Corinth that Paul wrote this letter, a fact that is corroborated in 1 Thess 1:7-8.

Paul's stay at Corinth lasted a year and six months (Acts 18:11-17). By our chronology Paul arrived in Corinth around November of 49 C.E. and left there in May of 51 C.E. From 1 Thess 1:8-9 we learn that sufficient time had elapsed that the fame of the Thessalonian's faith had spread throughout Achaia and Macedonia. Yet, it cannot be too far away from Timothy's return to Corinth, as we have noted above. Therefore, a date in the spring of 50 C.E. would seem justified by this evidence.

SECOND THESSALONIANS

SINCE THE NAME OF SILAS AND TIMOTHY ARE connected with Paul's in the salutation of this letter (1:1), like the that of the first letter, scholars have generally agreed that this letter was written soon after the first letter. Indeed, there appear to be references to a previous letter (2:2, 15; 3:17), which would only fit the description of *First Thessalonians.*

The character of the letter itself also lends support for this view, since the theme of the coming of the Lord (chapter 2) appears to be a continuation of what was brought out in the first letter, and the second letter seems to be clearing up some misunderstandings that may have developed from the first letter (chapter 2). With these facts in mind, then, we place the writing of *Second Thessalonians* in the summer of 50 C.E.

HEBREWS

THE EPISTLE TO THE HEBREWS, ANONYMOUSLY

written most likely by a companion of Paul well versed in temple Judaism of the time, was written, no doubt, when the temple was still functioning in Jerusalem. It also appears to be written before Paul's revelation of the Mystery, thus pre-63 C.E.

The *Epistle to the Hebrews* is definitely in the circle of the Apostle Paul's purview, although not specifically written by Paul himself. The early scholar, Origen, noted that it could be something of a collection of sermon notes by either Clement or Luke, but admitted that God only knows who actually penned the Epistle:

> In the epistle entitled *To the Hebrews* the diction does not exhibit the characteristic roughness of speech or phraseology admitted by the Apostle [Paul] himself (2 Cor 11:6), the construction of the sentences is closer to Greek usage, as anyone capable of recognizing differences of style would agree. On the other hand the matter of the epistle is wonderful, and quite equal to the Apostle's acknowledged writings: the truth of this would be admitted by anyone who has read the Apostle carefully ...If I were asked my personal opinion, I would say that the matter is the Apostle's but the phraseology and construction are those of someone who remembered the Apostle's teaching and wrote his own interpretation of what his master had said. So if any church regards this epistle as Paul's, it should be commended for so doing, for the primitive Church had every justification for handing it down as his. Who wrote the epistle is known to God alone: the accounts that have reached us suggest that it was either Clement, who became Bishop of Rome, or Luke, who wrote the Gospel and the Acts (Eusebius, *Hist. eccl.* 6.25.11-14).

Martin Luther proposed that the actual writer of Hebrews was Apollos,[457] who is described in Acts, the eighteenth chapter in the following terms:

> Now there came to Ephesus a Jew named Apollos, a native of Alexandria. He was an eloquent man, well-versed in the scriptures. He had been instructed in the Way of the Lord; and he spoke with burning enthusiasm and taught accurately the things concerning Jesus, though he knew only the baptism of John. He began to speak boldly in the synagogue; but when Priscilla and Aquila heard him, they

[457] E. F. Scott, *The Literature of the New Testament* (New York: Columbia University Press, 1959), 198, writes: "Perhaps the happiest guess was that of Luther, who suggested that the Epistle may have been the work of Apollos," but then noted that "there must have been a number of men in the early church who would answer to it as well as Apollos" (ibid.).

> took him aside and explained the Way of God to him more accurately. And when he wished to cross over to Achaia, the believers encouraged him and wrote to the disciples to welcome him. On his arrival he greatly helped those who through grace had become believers, for he powerfully refuted the Jews in public, showing by the scriptures that the Messiah is Jesus (Acts 18:24-8).

This description of Apollos as being the author of *Hebrews* has merit for the following reasons:

1) The author is no doubt a Christian of Jewish background, which fits the description of Apollos that he was a "Jew";

2) His many exhortations belie a preaching style that fits the description that he was "eloquent" and "spoke with burning enthusiasm," that he "spoke boldly," and the he "powerfully refuted the Jews in public";

3) Scholars have noted that the method of interpretation in the Epistle reflects an Alexandrian exegesis style, that he may have even knew Philo of Alexandria, where Apollos was from;

4) The author displays a knowledge of the Old Testament, which fits exactly with the description of: "WELL versed in the Scriptures."

The *Epistle to the Hebrews* tries to deal with the fact of why temple worship is still going on, and that Jesus "has now obtained a more excellent ministry, and to the degree he is the mediator of a better covenant, which has been enacted through better promises" (Heb 8:6). The author tries to explain things through the prism of the "New Covenant" (vs. 7-13).

What prompted such a letter? It is most likely trying to deal with the fact that the Apostle James and his type of Christianity is gone. And in that vacuum, explanations of this type must have been on the minds of many in the Jerusalem church. This would place the writing after the death of James at Passover of 62 C.E. Could it be that when Paul returned from his western campaign in Spain, Gaul and Britain, and he found out about the death of James, he wanted to submit to the Jerusalem brethren an explanation in a "word of exhortation" (Heb 13:22) that helped them focus on the better promises of the New Covenant?

Also, if this letter was written after Paul's western campaign, then it was written at a time when Paul was now absolutely convinced that the events in John's Revelation were for a future generation. However, many within the Jerusalem Church may still have wondered why prophetic events were not happening. At any rate, it seems that the comparison of the Sabbath day rest (Heb 4:4) that the people under Joshua did not achieve (v. 8) was still something that was well in the future (v. 11), then we have the beginning of the teaching that the seventh millennial day "rest" period was yet future (cf. 2 Pet 3:8; Ps 90:4; Barnabas 15:1-5). In other words, the time setting of Revelation 20 was at least another two millennia into the future.

HEBREWS AND JOHN'S CIRCLE

FROM THE WORDING WITHIN THE EPISTLE OF HEBREWS itself we can see that it was a "word of exhortation" (Heb 13:22) specifically written to the Apostle John and John's circle of friends that were discouraged over the developments that rendered John's prophecy a dismal failure. We should remember that John's initial Revelation, given in the 50's, was now seen to be a failure due to the fact that the Roman Empire was crushing the Jewish people, and not the other way around. This may have even caused a rift in the church between the Jewish Christians, who still believed in these prophecies to the bitter end, and those who could now see, as the Apostle Paul did, that the prophecies were for a future generation.

A personal word of encouragement may be directed specifically to the Apostle John himself in the following words:

> Even though we speak in this way, beloved, we are confident of better things in YOUR case, things that belong to salvation. For God is not unjust; he will not overlook YOUR work [the Apocalypse?] and the LOVE that YOU showed for his sake in serving the saints, as YOU still do (Heb 6:9-10).

The person that is addressed here is referred to as "beloved" (v. 9). He was one who served the saints and still was so doing at the time of the writing of the Epistle.

Many in John's circle were beginning to be disillusioned and some were falling away altogether. Paul is appealing to them:

> And we want each one of you to show the same diligence so as to realize the full assurance of hope to the very end, so that you may not become sluggish, but imitators of those who through faith and patience inherit the promises (Heb 6:11-12).

Chapter 13 of *Hebrews* begins with "Never let your *brotherly* love fail" (Heb 13:1, *Phillips*). Paul continues his encouragement, quoting

Psalm 118:6, that God "will never leave you or forsake you" (v. 5). Then Paul concludes:

> I appeal to you, brothers and sisters, bear with my word of exhortation, for I have written to you briefly. I want you to know that our brother Timothy has been set free and if he comes in time, he will be with me when I see you. Greet all your leaders and all the saints. Those of Italy send you greetings. Grace be with all of you (Heb 13:22-25).

The *Epistle to the Hebrews* may have been part of the package that Paul had John Mark deliver to Peter and the other Jerusalem-based apostles. Paul wanted Peter, and maybe even John, to come to see him in Rome to discuss with him the importance of putting together a testament of literature that would inspire the future church.

Clement of Alexandria (ca. 195 C.E.) wrote:

> In writing to Hebrews already prejudiced against him and suspicious of him, he was far too sensible to put them off at the start by naming himself ...Now, as the blessed presbyter [Clement's teacher, Pantaenus?] used to say, the Lord, the apostle of the Almighty, was sent to the Hebrews; so through modesty Paul knowing that he had been sent to the Gentiles, does not describe himself as an apostle of the Hebrews, first because he so reverenced the Lord and secondly because he was going outside his province in writing to the Hebrews too, when he was an ambassador and apostle of the Gentiles (Eusebius, *Hist. eccl.* 6.14.3-4).

Thus, a date that is after the death of James the Just in 62 C.E. and prior to the revelation of the Mystery in 64 C.E. places the writing of the *Epistle to the Hebrews* would make the most sense from our perspective of the history of the times.

First and Second Timothy and Titus

These SO-CALLED PASTORAL EPISTLES REFER TO the apostolic itineraries of the Apostle Paul in Asia, Macedonia, Greece, and Crete that scholars have a hard time identifying in the events that are covered in the *Book of Acts.* Since many scholars believe that Paul was executed shortly after the *Book of Acts* concludes, then they likewise believe that they were written by someone other than Paul. Yet, once we understand that Paul did not die until the year of 67 C.E., then there is nothing that should force us into such a conclusion.

As we have brought out in our story, after Paul was released from his first Roman imprisonment in the summer of 58 C.E., Paul journeyed to Spain (maybe), Britain and Gaul (definitely). We thus place these Epistles conjecturally as follows in the following summary.

SUMMARY

IN SUMMATION, WE PROVIDE THE FOLLOWING table (in canonical order) of our conclusions for the dates of the writing of the New Testament books:

Book	*Date*	*Redaction*	*Place*
Matthew	40	–	Jerusalem
Mark	45	67	Rome
Luke	58	–	Rome
John	68	–	Ephesus
Acts	58	67	Rome, Rome
James	40	67	Jerusalem
1 Peter	66	–	Jerusalem
2 Peter	67	–	Rome
1 John	68	–	Ephesus
2 John	69-?	–	Ephesus
3 John	69-?	–	Ephesus
Jude	68	–	Asia Minor
Romans	54	67	Corinth, Rome
1 Corinthians	53	–	Ephesus
2 Corinthians	54	–	Ephesus
Galatians	50	–	Corinth
Ephesians	64	–	Ephesus
Philippians	58	–	Rome
Colossians	64	–	Ephesus
1 Thessalonians	50	–	Corinth
2 Thessalonians	50	–	Corinth
Hebrews	58	–	Rome
1 Timothy	64	–	Rome
2 Timothy	66	–	Rome
Titus	63	–	Nicopolis

Philemon	64	–	Ephesus
Revelation	56	96	Jerusalem/Ephesus

APPENDIX 6

The Gospel unto Israel

UPON THE RELEASE OF THE APOSTLE PAUL from his house arrest in Rome in the early summer of 58 C.E., tradition tells us that Paul left Rome and traveled westward. During this imprisonment Paul wrote the *Epistle to the Philippians*. We can see in this Epistle the excitement that Paul expressed in getting the gospel before the "household of Caesar" (Phil 1:12-13, 4:22). Note, also here, that Paul is still fervent in his conviction that "the Lord is near" (Phil 4:5).

Most scholars believe that Paul also wrote his other Prison Epistles of *Ephesians*, *Colossians* and *Philemon* during this first Roman imprisonment mentioned in Acts. But this is a mistake which we have already addressed elsewhere. These letters were not written during Paul's fifth imprisonment at Rome, but rather during his sixth imprisonment in the city of Ephesus.

As far as the *Epistle to the Philippians* is concerned, we must note that this is the last time in Paul's writings that he expressed the conviction that "the Lord is near." It was this conviction that gave Paul and the other apostles the impetus to fulfill Jesus' injunction of the "Gospel of the Kingdom" being preached in all the world for a witness unto all nations before the end of the age (Matt 24:14).

To the original twelve apostles Jesus had commanded:

> Go nowhere among the Gentiles, and enter no town of the Samaritans, but go rather to the lost sheep of the house of Israel (Matt 10:5-6).

Most people today believe that this means that they were to go to "Jews" in the so-called "Diaspora." Yet, the term "lost sheep of the House of Israel" is very clear in that it refers to "the Lost Ten Tribes of Israel."

Also, many people today do not understand that there is a distinction between Israel and the Jews even within the pages of the Hebrew Scriptures. The distinction is made in scripture when it uses the word "Jews" who are at war with Syria and the nation of "Israel." How can the

Jews be at war with themselves if the word "Jews" was also a word that denoted the same people as "Israel?" The answer is that the word "Jews" in this sense was applied to the separate Kingdom of Judah, but not to the Kingdom of Israel. The Bible is very clear that these are two very distinct and separate nations.

The Kingdom of Judah, from which the Jews are descended, are basically made up of three tribes of Israel, i.e., the tribes of Judah, Levi and Benjamin. Under King David, and then later under his son, King Solomon, all twelve tribes of Israel were united as one nation known as Israel. But after King Solomon's death the Kingdom was divided into two separate and distinct nations. The tribe of Judah split off from the nation of Israel in order to retain its own King, Rehoboam, who the other tribes of Israel had rejected. The tribe of Levi, and parts of the tribe of Benjamin, split off from the rest of the nation of Israel and followed the tribe of Judah in its schism. A new nation was thus formed, with its capital at Jerusalem. It became known as the "House of Judah." And the people who made up this Kingdom of Judah all became known thereafter as "Jews."[458]

Most standard Bible dictionaries acknowledge the distinction between "Jew" and "Israel," for example, one may typically read the following:

> Israelites was the usual name of the twelve tribes, from their leaving Egypt until after the death of Saul, but after the defection of the ten tribes, they arrogated to themselves the name of the whole nation (II Sam. 2:9, 10, 17, 28; 3:10, 17; 10:40-43; I Ki. 12:1). The kings of the ten tribes were called kings of Israel, and the descendants of David, who ruled over Judah and Benjamin were known as kings of Judah; and in the prophets of that period Judah and Israel are put in opposition (Hos. 4:15; 5:3, 5; 6:10; 7:1; 8:2, 3, 6, 8; 9:1 7; Amos 1:1; 2:6; 3:14; Mic. 1:5; Isa. 5:7). ...After the Babylonian captivity [of Judah] the returned exiles, though mainly of Judah, resumed the name of Israel as the

[458] It may come as a complete shock to a lot of people, even to many modern Jewish people, that before the division of Israel, the only "Jews," so to speak, were strictly only those people who were descended from the tribe of Judah. Although, after the return of Jewish exiles under Nehemiah and Ezra, the tribes of Judah and Levi were assimilated into one nationality of Jewish people, the other tribes never did return to Jerusalem. This even means that it is entirely wrong to refer to Moses as a "Jew" because he was, technically, from the tribe of Levi long before this event. Moses was a Levite — but never was he a "Jew!" This means that all the Israelites of the other tribes, were likewise, non-Jews. This even means that Abraham, Isaac and Jacob also could not possibly be "Jews" because Judah, whose name the word "Jew" was derived from, was not even born yet. Nevertheless, even many Jews of today consider these patriarchs to be "Jews." It is a lack of understanding this point that is responsible for so much misunderstanding of the entire subject today. The point that we must realize here is that Jesus was not talking about Jews when he referred to the lost sheep of the "House of Israel."

designation of their nation, but as individuals they are called Jews in the Apocrypha and New Testament.[459]

The Ten tribes that went into captivity never did return as a nation of Israel. As a result, most historians believe that they were absorbed into the Gentile nations that they were captive within and then merely disappeared from history (hence, the designation "lost" Ten Tribes). The Jewish historian, Heinrich Graetz, was one such Jewish scholar who believed that this was the case:

> The kingdom of the ten tribes of Israel, had in one day disappeared, leaving no trace behind ... But there can be no doubt that the ten tribes have been irretrievably lost among the nations.[460]

Even the *Encyclopedia Britannica* also gives us this same conclusion:

> Following the conquest of the northern kingdom by the Assyrians in 721 B.C.E., the 10 tribes were gradually assimilated by other people and thus disappeared from history.[461]

This view is also maintained by the authoritative *Interpreter's Dictionary of the Bible:*

> This displacement of populations was, it seems, complete so far as the identity of the N ten tribes is concerned; for they eventually assimilated beyond the point of return to any historical continuum with their Israelite origins."[462]

Yet, this "irretrievably lost" belief has two major flaws. For one, Jesus declared quite emphatically that he was sent by the Father to the lost sheep of the "House of Israel" (Matt 15:24). Those who say that this is a designation for the spiritually lost Jews fail to see that Jesus said that he came to his own [the Jews] and his own received him not (John 1:11). With this rejection he did not turn to the Gentiles. That commission was later assigned to Paul and Barnabas. Instead, Jesus said to the Gentile woman that it was to the lost sheep of the "House of Israel" that he would turn (Matt 15:24). But Jesus himself did not go to the lost sheep of Israel, for he was soon to be slain at Golgotha. It would be his disciples that were

[459] Merrill F. Unger, ed., *Unger's Bible Dictionary* (Chicago: Moody Press, 1970), 541.

[460] Heinrich Graetz, *History of the Jews* (Philadelphia: Jewish Publication Society of America, 1891), 1:265.

[461] *Encyclopedia Brittannica*, 1991 ed., vol. 11, art. "Ten Lost Tribes of Israel."

[462] J. Alvin Sanders, "Exile" in *The Interpreter's Dictionary of the Bible*, George Arthur Buttrick, et al., eds. (New York: Abingdon, 1962), 2:187.

sent on this mission.

A second major flaw in the "irretrievably lost" theory is that there are many prophecies in the Old Testament concerning Israel which have never been fulfilled. Although many modern commentators apply these prophecies to the modern Jewish nation, which today calls itself "Israel," this would be exclusive of the descendents of those peoples to whom Jesus sent his disciples. The *Jewish Encyclopedia* recognizes this important point in the following quote:

> According to the Bible, Tiglath-pileser (II Kings xv. 29) or Shalmaneser (*ib.* xvii. 6, xviii. 11), after the defeat of Israel, transported the majority of the inhabitants of the Northern Kingdom to Assyria, and placed them in Halah and Habor, on the stream of Gozan, and in the towns of Media. In their stead a mixed multitude was transported to the plains and mountains of Israel. As a large number of prophecies relate to the return of "Israel" to the Holy Land, believers in the literal inspiration of the Scriptures have always labored under a difficulty in regard to the continued existence of the tribes of Israel, with the exception of those of Judah and Levi (or Benjamin), which returned with Ezra and Nehemiah. If the Ten Tribes have disappeared, the literal fulfillment of the prophecies would be impossible: if they have not disappeared, obviously they must exist under a different name.[463]

Another source says:

> The captives of Israel exiled beyond the Euphrates did not return as a whole to Palestine along with their brethren the captives of Judah; at least there is no mention made of this event in the documents at our disposal... The return of the Ten tribes was one of the great promises of the Prophets, and the advent of the Messiah is therefore necessarily identified with the epic of their redemption. ...The hope of the return of the Ten Tribes has never ceased among the Jews in Exile. ...This hope has been connected with every Messianic rising.[464]

It was to his twelve disciples that Jesus commissioned to go to Israel. He told them specifically to go not to the Gentiles, but rather, to the "Lost Sheep of the House of Israel" (Matt 10:5-6; 15:24). It is quite clear here that the distinction that Jesus made between these two groups of

---

463 Joseph Jacobs, "Tribes, Lost Ten," *Jewish Encyclopedia*, ed. Isidore Singer and Cyrus Adler (New York: Funk & Wagnalls, 1925), 12:249.

464 Adolphe A. Neubauer, "Where Are the Ten Tribes?" *Jewish Quarterly Review* 1 (1889): 15, 17, 21.

people is that he was referring to actual ethnic classes, and not simply to the same ethnic peoples of which some were spiritually lost. This becomes even more crystal clear when we see that James addressed his Epistle to the "Twelve tribes that are scattered abroad" (James 1:1). This is a definite reference to a literal body of people that are scattered among the nations. This also shows us that Jesus and his disciples were, in their day, well aware of the existence of these peoples and where they were scattered.

Indeed, Josephus, writing after 70 C.E., was certainly aware of the existence of one major branch of scattered Israelites when he recorded that

> the entire body of the people of Israel remained in that country, wherefore there are but two tribes [Judah and Benjamin] in Asia and Europe subject to the Romans, while the Ten Tribes are beyond the Euphrates till now, and are an immense multitude, and not to be estimated by numbers (Josephus, *A.J.* 11.5.2 [133]).

Such testimony tells us that the scattered tribes were not only known, but that they had, by the end of the first century C.E., amassed into an "immense multitude." The people that Josephus was particularly writing about were those peoples who were then living in the Roman Province of Parthia.

Who Were the Parthians?

WHO WERE THE PARTHIANS? WHERE DID THEY originally come from? Their ancient ethnic origin's derived from the same area as where Israel was taken captive. The Bible itself tells us where the Israelites were taken captive:

> The King of Assyria took Samaria, and carried Israel way into Assyria and placed them in Halah and in Habor by the River Gozan, and in the cities of the Medes (2 Ki 17:6).

Notice the statement: "in the cities of the Medes." The significance of this is made clear in what the Greek historian Diodorus of Sicily recorded in this regard:

> Many conquered peoples were removed to other homes, and two of these became very great colonies: the one was composed of Assyrians and was removed to the land between Paphlagonia and Pontus, and the other was drawn from

Media and planted along the Tanais [River] (Diodorus, *Histories*, 2:43).

The Tanais River is the modern River Don which lay in ancient Scythia – the modern Ukraine, north of the Black Sea, in southern Russia. This should be no surprise to students of ancient history. Historians have long understood that western Europe was eventually populated from peoples of this region, the foothills of the Caucasus Mountains. Indeed, this is where the term "caucasian," as an ethnic descriptive identity, derives its name.

The Ancient geographer, Strabo, referred to these peoples as "White Syrians" instead of Assyrians (Strabo, *Geography*, 12:3:9). "Syrian" was the general Greek name for all of the peoples who lived along the eastern Mediterranean coastal strip north of Judaea. But in Strabo's description he recognized the need to make a distinction for the northern colonists of Asia Minor as "white" Syrians which were in contrast to the swarthy Aramean populace in southern Syria. And to this day the term "white" is synonyms with the term "caucasian" in reference to race identification.

When Babylon conquered Assyria in 609 B.C.E., the Assyrians were themselves compelled to migrate north. Seventy years later, in the year of 539 B.C.E., the Babylonian Empire fell to the Persian Empire who still held these territories in the grip of slavery. Yet, when Alexander conquered the Persians in 331 B.C.E., the people of these areas were finally released from the Persian grip. Ezekiel was given a vision in which he saw the House of Israel finally being released from their enslavement after a period of 390 years (Ezek 4:3-5). And it was precisely 390 years from 721 B.C.E., when the siege against Samaria began, to 331 B.C.E., the date of the final overthrow of Persia and the deliverance out of captivity of the Israelites.

At this time some of these peoples immediately commenced a migration from Scythia to Western Europe. Scotland was a recipient of some of these peoples and their nation bears to this day the signature of the "land of the Scyths" – alias Scotland.[465] Much of Israel, however, remained for several centuries in the region of Northern Asia Minor.

With this information we can better understand references in the New Testament that reached out to these areas as the descendants of the Lost Tribes of Israel. Peter addressed his first Epistle to: "The Exiles of the Dispersion in Pontus, Galatia, Cappadocia, Asia, and Bithynia" (1 Pet 1:1).

Remember that we just read from Diodorus who identified these very

---

[465] There is an abundant amount of literature available that one could read that identifies the ancient tribes of Israel have migrated into the western areas of Europe. For example, see the research of Steven M. Collins, *The "Lost" Ten Tribes of Israel ... Found!* (Boring, Oregon: COA Books, 1992) and Yair Davidy, *Lost Israelite Identity – The Hebrew Ancestry of Celtic Races* (Jerusalem: Russel-Davis Publishers, 1996).

regions as the area where the Assyrian migrations went to. It is time that we abandon the false notion that "exiles" was merely a reference to the so-called Jewish Diaspora. Peter used the specific term "exiles." These were hardly Gentile Greeks in those areas.[466]

The *Jewish Encyclopedia* also records that:

> In the Apocrypha it is presumed that the Ten Tribes still exist as tribes. Thus Tobit is stated to be of the Tribe of Naphtali, and the Testaments of the Twelve Patriarchs assume their continuous existence. In the Fourth Book of Ezra (xiii. 39-45) it is declared that the Ten Tribes were carried by Hosea, king in the time of Shalmaneser, to the Euphrates, at the narrow passages of the river, whence they went on for a journey of a year and a half to place called Arzareth. Schiller-Szinessy pointed out that "arzareth" is merely a contraction of "erez aheret," the "other land" into which the Lord says He "will cast them [the people] as this day" see Deut. xxix. 27, which verse is referred by R. Akiba to the Lost Ten Tribes (Sanh. x. 4; comp. "Journal of Philology," iii. 114).[467]

This source goes on to state that

> the identification of the Sacae, or Scythians, with the Ten Tribes because they appear in history at the same time, and very nearly in the same place, as the Israelites removed by Shalmaneser, is one of the chief supports of the theory which identifies the English people, and indeed the whole Teutonic race, with the Ten Tribes. Dan is identified sometimes with Denmark, and sometimes with the Tuatha da Danaun of Irish tradition; but the main argument advanced is that the English satisfy the conditions of the Prophets regarding Israel insofar as they live in a far-off isle, speak in a strange tongue, have colonies throughout the world, and yet worship the true God.[468]

Ezekiel, nearly two centuries after Israel went into captivity, recorded:

---

[466] Whether Peter's exiles are the exiles of Ancient Israel or the recent exiles from Judea who fled before the advancing Roman armies is a legitimate question. The likelihood is that these areas comprised of both recent and ancient exiles. Also note that this was the northern region of Asia Minor where Paul did not travel to. Indeed, he was expressly forbidden to preach in Mysia, the northern district of the Roman Province of Asia (Acts 16:7, 8). These regions were obviously assigned to Peter, the Chief apostle to the Circumcision, because they were not predominantly Gentiles in that area, but Israelite. And it is exactly these areas that Diodorus said were settled by new peoples drawn from Media.

[467] Jacobs, "Tribes, Lost Ten," *Jewish Encyclopedia*, 12:249.

[468] Ibid., 12:250.

> Son of man, prophesy and say unto them, Thus saith the Lord God unto the shepherds. Woe be to the shepherds of Israel that do feed themselves! Should not the shepherds feed the flocks? Neither have you sought that which is lost; but with force and with cruelty have you ruled them. My sheep wandered through all the mountains, and upon every high hill: yea, my flock was scattered upon all the face of the earth, and none did search or seek after them (Ezek 34:2, 4, 6).

Jesus also said in a similar vain:

> And other sheep I have which are not of this fold [of Jews living in Judaea]; them also I must bring, and they will hear My voice; and there will be one flock and one shepherd (John 10:16).

Was Jesus referring to the Gentiles? Obviously, not! He was using the exact same type of wording that Ezekiel used in describing the lost tribes of Israel as "lost sheep." But more importantly is the fact that Jesus said that there would eventually be one flock, just exactly as Ezekiel had prophesied. Ezekiel said this in the context of "lost sheep," just like Jesus did, i.e., that one day "Judah" – referring to the Jews – and "Joseph" – referring to the lost tribes of Israel – would once again be joined as one nation (Ezek 37:15-28).

How could "Joseph" be rejoined to Judah if "Joseph" is "irretrievably lost?" The answer is that the Israelites were scattered, but not irretrievably lost at that time (nor should they be considered as such today).

PARTHIA AND ISRAEL

ANOTHER POINT TO UNDERSTAND IS THAT not all of the tribes migrated out of their captive territories. Those who stayed were finally freed when Persia fell. The city of Babylon in the first century was in the Roman Province of Parthia. Who the Parthians were has long remained a mystery. But actually, it is not hard to determine. They suddenly appear near the Caspian Sea around 700 B.C.E. as slaves of the Assyrians. The Historian George Rawlinson wrote:

> According to Diodorus, who probably followed Ctesias, they passed from the dominion of the Assyrians to that of the Medes, and from dependence upon the Medes to a similar

position under the Persians.[469]

The Parthians as a nation didn't rise to power until around 250 B.C.E. What has puzzled historians is that these peoples were neither Persians, nor Medes, nor even Assyrians. Indeed, they could not be identified with any other known indigenous people of all of that region. According to Rawlinson, the term Parthian itself means "exile."[470] And the only exiles in this area that history records were the exiled Tribes of Israel.

When the Apostle James wrote his Epistle around 40 C.E., he addressed his letter to the twelve tribes "scattered" abroad. And he warned the Israelites that he was admonishing against the "wars" being waged amongst themselves. At this time in Roman history the entire Roman Empire was at peace except for only the areas of Parthia and Britain.

THE MISSION OF THE TWELVE APOSTLES

THE APOSTLE THOMAS IS RECORDED AS BRINGING the gospel to

> Parthia, after which Sophornius, and others inform us, that he preached the Gospel to the Medes, Persians, Carmians, Hyrcani, Bactrians, and the neighbor nations.[471]

Bartholomew shared with Thomas the same area according to the Greek historian Nicephorus and then spent time in neighboring Armenia and a portion of Upper Phrygia in Asia Minor. This area was also blanketed by the Apostle Andrew.

Jude, also known as Libbaeus Thaddaeus, ministered to Assyria and Mesopotamia, which was in the heart of Parthian territory. Philip went to Scythia and Upper Asia (Asia Minor).[472] Thomas also went to India East of Persia where the "White Indians" dwelt. These "White Indians" were known as "Nephthalite Huns" in later records. One of the Tribes of Ancient Israel was Naphtali. These people were overthrown in the sixth

---

[469] George Rawlinson, *The Sixth Great Oriental Monarchy or the Geography, History, and Antiquities of Parthia* (New York: Dodd, Mead & Co., 1882), 26, quoting Diodorus, 2, §3; 34, §1 and §6. Rawlinson, however, here expressed that he felt that the balance of evidence was against the view of Diodorus.

[470] Ibid., 19.

[471] Cave, William. *A Complete History of the Lives, Acts, and Martyrdom's of the Holy Apostles* (Philadelphia: Solomon Wiatt, 1810), 2:331.

[472] Ibid., 2:168.

century and migrated into Scandinavia.

William Cave relates concerning Simon the Zealot:

> He is said to have directed his journey towards Egypt, thence to Cyrene, and Africa...and throughout Mauritania and all Libya, preaching the gospel to those remote and barbarous countries. Nor could the coldness of the climate benumb his zeal, or hinder him from shipping himself and the Christian doctrine over to the Western Islands, yea, even to Britain itself. Here he preached and wrought many miracles...[473]

This same source quotes both Nicephorus Gregoras (fl. 14th century C.E.) and Dorotheus (bishop of Tyre, fl. 290 C.E.), who stated that Simon "went at last into Britain, and... was crucified...and buried there."[474]

Notice that Simon is to have also gone to North Africa. Why North Africa? The *Universal History* declares that the ancestors of the white Nordics:

> ...were driven out of Asia by a powerful enemy, and pursued into Greece; from whence they made their escape" to North Africa. But this... was to be understood only of the white nations inhabiting some parts of western Barbary and Numidia.[475]

We need to ask, what white nation was driven from the shores of western Asia by a powerful enemy? Could it be the remnants of the Israelite tribes who managed escape from the Assyrians and fled to the shores of Africa?

James, the son of Alphaeus, we are told went into Spain.

> The Spanish writers generally contend, after the death of Stephen he came to these Western parts, and particularly into Spain where he planted Christianity.[476]

Why Spain? Notice from the Scottish Declaration of Arbroath, written

---

473 Ibid., 2: 203, quoting Nicephorus, *Hist. eccl.*, 8:100.

474 Dorotheus, *De septuaginta domini discipulis* (PG 92:1063-74). The Martyrologies state, however, that he died in Persia.

475 *Universal World History*, ed. John Alexander Hammerton and Harry elmer Barnes, (London, Educational Book Co., 1930. Originally published in 1748), 17:194. Geoffrey of Monmouth, *The History of the Kings of Britain* [xi. 8, 10], tr. Lewis Thorpe [London: Penguin Books,1966], 263, 265), records how Goramund, King of the Africans, came to Ireland with a vast fleet of 160,000 "Africans" and then invaded Saxon England. Yet, there is no trace of a black settlement in Ireland during the Saxon period. The "Africans" were actually exiled Israelites who passed through the northern regions of Morocco before settling in Ireland.

476 Cave, *Lives*, 2:148.

in 1320:

> Most Holy Father and Lord, we know and from the chronicles and books of the ancients we find that among other famous nations our own, the Scots, has been graced with widespread renown. They journeyed from Greater Scythia (where Israel was once captive) by way of the Tyrrhenian Sea and the Pillars of Hercules (Gibraltar), and dwelt for a long course of time in Spain among the most savage tribes, but nowhere could they be subdued by any race, however barbarous. Thence they came, twelve hundred years after the people of Israel crossed the Red Sea, to their home in the west where they still live today.[477]

Now we have a reason for Paul wanting to go to Spain. In his third commission to go to Israel, Spain also was an area that harbored remnants of ancient Israel. The *Declaration* continues:

> The King of kings and Lord of lords, our Lord Jesus Christ, after His Passion and Resurrection, called them (the Scots), even though settled in the uttermost parts of the earth, almost the first to His most holy faith. Nor would He (Christ) have them confirmed in that faith by merely anyone but by the first of His Apostles – by calling, though second or third in rank – the most gentle Saint Andrew, the Blessed Peter's brother, and desired him to keep them under his protection as their patron forever. [478]

And, as we have already brought out, there is strong tradition that Joseph of Arimathea brought the gospel to England. Joseph of Arimathea was a Jew who undertook the burial of Jesus.

> The striking character of this single appearance of Joseph of Arimathaea led to the rise of numerous legends. Thus William of Malmesbury says that he was sent to Britain by St Philip, and, having received a small island in Somersetshire, there constructed "with twisted twigs" the first Christian church in Britain – afterwards to become the Abbey of Glastonbury.[479]

---

[477] *Declaration of Arbroath*, para. 1. The full text can be found online: http://www.geo.ed.ac.uk/home/scotland/arbroath_english.html. The Declaration of Arbroath was prepared as a formal Declaration of Independence in Arbroath Abby on the 6th April, 1320, most likely by the Abbot, Bernard de Linton, who was also the Chancellor of Scotland. In this declaration, on the authority of King Robert Bruce and his noble Barons, the King appeals to Pope John XXII to persuade England to allow the Scots to live in peace.

[478] *Declaration*, para. 3.

[479] *Encyclopedia. Britannica*, 1911 ed., art. "Joseph of Arimathaea." 15:514.

People are often under the impression that the gospel was only a story spun in the hillsides of Judaea. Yet, Britain was an important Province of the Roman Empire in the first century and travel to that area was not only feasible, but historians tell us that there was much traffic to that area:

> Mediterranean traders had been visiting the country (Britain) from at least as early as the fourth century B.C.E.... There was a good deal of cross-channel trade and migration in the centuries before the Roman conquest.[480]

Indeed, in 589 C.E., when the bishop of Rome sent St. Augustine to bring Catholicism to England he found that many of the inhabitants were already professing Christians.

The Bible tells us that Israel was indeed "scattered" among the heathen exactly as was prophesied:

> Behold, the eyes of the Lord God are on the sinful kingdom. And I will destroy it from the face of the earth; Yet I will not utterly destroy the house of Jacob," Says the Lord. "For surely I will command and will sift (the people of the) house of Israel among all nations as grain is sifted in a sieve; Yet not the smallest grain shall fall to the ground (Amos 9:8-9, NKJV).[481]

James' Epistle was addressed: "to the twelve tribes that are scattered over the world" (James 1:1, *Goodspeed* translation). The general tone of James' Epistle shows us that he was not addressing his letter to converted Christians. Rather, he was writing to unconverted members of Israel's scattered tribes (James 4:1-4). It's intent was to provide some preliminary teaching to unconverted Israelites (and Gentiles) before getting into Christian doctrine. The apostles may have taken the *Epistle of James*, the brother of Christ, to the Israelites in the various nations that they were then living.

Many do not realize this, but the Apostle Paul was also commissioned to eventually preach among the scattered nations of Israel. First, however, Paul was to teach the Gentiles, which he did in Cyprus, Asia Minor, Greece and Italy. Secondly, he was to appear before kings, which he did during his two year imprisonment at Rome.[482] But Paul's third commission was not yet accomplished. Paul's threefold commission was "to hear (Christ's) name before the Gentiles, and kings, and the children

---

[480] T. W. Potter, *Roman Britain* (London: British Museum Publications Ltd., 1983), 5.

[481] See also, e.g., Ezek 22:15; Deut 28:63-64; Lev 26:33; 1 Ki 14:15 and Ezek 12:15.

[482] Paul not only appeared before Nero Caesar, but also testified before British royalty captive in Rome.

of Israel" (Acts 9:15).

Clement of Rome confirms that Paul did journey to the West and Theodoret, in the year 435, reported that

> Paul, liberated from his first captivity at Rome, preached the Gospel to the Britons and others in the West.[483]

Earlier historians, before the modern age of skepticism had set in, had collected a wealth of information on the subject, which lead them to conclude:

> The true Christian Religion was planted here most anciently by Joseph of Arimathea, Simon Zelotes, Aristobulus, by St. Peter, and St. Paul, as may be proved by Dorotheus, Theodotetus and Sophronius.[484]

Thus, the story of *Beyond Acts* is one in which a world wide evangelistic campaign eventually reached out to the scattered remnants of the ancient Tribes of Israel.

---

[483] Theodoret, *De. Civ. Graec. Off.*, lib. ix. Quoted from Richard Williams Morgan, *St. Paul in Britain* (London: Covenant Publishing Co., 1948, originally published in 1861), 160.

[484] William Camden, *Remaines Concerning Brittaine* (London: A. I. for Symon Waterson, 1629), 5.

APPENDIX 7

A Lost Chapter of Acts Found?

THERE ARE SOME PEOPLE TODAY WHO ARE OF the firm belief that the final missing chapter of the *Book of Acts* has actually been discovered. Yet, one can only wonder why this discovery has never made front page news. Stop and think about it! Why would one of the greatest finds in history be a little known fact to the general public? Indeed, one would think that if such a discovery were remotely true, scholars would have mentioned it somewhere in the mountains of literature on the Bible. Yet, curiously, there apparently is no manuscript in the hands of qualified scholars and the whereabouts of such a manuscript seems to be as unknown as the golden tablets of Joseph Smith.

So far as can be ascertained by the present author, the contents of this manuscript first appeared in a 25 page tract, published around 1913 by the British Israel Association of Greater Vancouver, entitled: *These are Ancient Things*.[485] In it is contained the astonishing article by one "late" T. G. Cole entitled: "The Long Lost Chapter of the ACTS OF THE APOSTLES, Containing the Account of Paul's Journey in Spain and Britain, also a remarkable prediction of Britain's Glorius Inheritance, Translated by: C. S. Sonnini."[486]

The contents of this manuscript was later republished in 1982 by E. Raymond Capt.[487] This "Long Lost Chapter of Acts," has now also became known as the "Sonnini Manuscript." We are told that it had been

---

[485] *These are Ancient Things: Selected Articles.* (Vancouver: The British Israel Association, n.d., ca. 1913, based on data within the tract).

[486] Ibid., 1. It is interesting that this tract caveats that: "The following is the English translation of the Manuscript, *the authenticity of which cannot be vouched for*" (page 2). The authority for the introduction of the "Sonnini Manuscript" is given by T. G. Cole, who, unfortunately, provides us with no sources.

[487] E. Raymond Capt, *The Lost Chapter of Acts of the Apostles*, 2d. ed., (Thousand Oaks, Calif.: Artisan Sales, 1983). Interestingly, Capt's apparent source for his book is directly lifted from the Cole article in the 1913 tract, with no evidence that he had before him anything other than that article. Indeed, he copies virtually verbatim the introduction given in that tract by T. G. Cole, yet, curiously, without a single reference to the Cole article.

found in the Archives of Constantinople, by one C. S. Sonnini, travelling in Turkey on orders from Louis XVI.

T. G. Cole informs us:

> It [the Lost Chapter of Acts] was found interleaved in a copy of "Sonnini's Travels in Turkey and Greece,"[488] and purchased at the sale of the library and affects of the late Right Hon. Sir John Newport, Bart., in Ireland, whose family arms were engraved on the cover of the book, and in whose possession it had been for more than thirty years, with a copy of the firman of the Sultan of Turkey, granting to C. S. Sonnini permission to travel in all parts of the Ottoman dominions. The document was translated by C. S. Sonnini from an original Greek manuscript found in the Archives at Constantinople, and presented to him by the Sultan Abdoul Achmet.[489]

Who is this mysterious C. S. Sonnini? From the Virtual American Biographies website online we read:

> SONNINI DE MANONCOURT, Charles Nicolas Sigisbert, French traveller, born in Luneville, France, 1 February, 1751; died in Paris, France, 9 May, 1812. Although, from deference to his father's wishes, he studied law, his fondness for natural history and his passion for travel led him to

[488] C.[harles] S.[igesbert] Sonnini (1751-1812), *Travels in Turkey and Greece Undertaken by Order of Louis XVI, and with the Authority of the Ottoman Court* (London: Printed for T. N. Longman and O. Rees, Paternoster Row, 1801). A search for a copy of this book on the internet and Libraries by the author has not yielded any results. However, a similarly titled book was found: C. S. Sonnini, *Travels in upper and Lower Egypt: Undertaken by Order of the Old Government of France.* Trans. Henry Hunter. (London: Printed for J. Debrett, 1800, see online http://library.tamu.edu/cushing/onlinex/africa/) and reprinted seven years later (London: Stockdale, 1807). The description for this later edition on the Alibris website [http://www.alibris.com], which was on sale on December 5, 2002, for $494.95, stated: "This expedition was made with the intention of collecting rare Egyptian birds, however Sonnini includes some unusual and fascinating details of native life and customs such as female and male circumcision and homosexuality, leprosy and other diseases, serpent eating etc." Isn't it interesting that in the year of 1807 Sonnini, who was still alive, republishes his sensational work, but is more interested in discussing "homosexuality" than discussing anything on what would be the greatest find of modern times — the discovery of the final Chapter of Acts?

[489] Cole, *Ancient Things,* 2. There was no Sultan Abdoul Achmet at this time, nor any other time. There was a Sultan Abdulhamid Khan I (1774-1789), son of Ahmed Khan III (1703-1736), who was succeeded by Sultan Selim Khan III (1789-1808). It is interesting that Abdulhamid the First is said to have been "a calligrapher who was well educated and who read all the historical chronicles in existence in his time" (see online: http://www.naqshbandi.org/ottomans/khalifa/s27_detail.htm). So here we have a Sultan who dabbled in calligraphy, and who was well read in all the historical chronicles, and who just so happens to pass off an ancient Greek manuscript to an adventurer, that now is mysteriously lost. The picture that is forming here is one that seems to point to a clever and ingenious hoax.

> enter the navy in 1772, shortly after he had been called to the bar at Nancy. He went to Cayenne in 1773, and soon acquired reputation for his daring journeys into the interior. The government employed him several times in expeditions that were of the greatest advantage to the colony. In 1774 he traversed Guiana its entire breadth as far as Peru. In another expedition he discovered, after wandering through immense marshes, a water route through which he reached the Gabrielle mountain. He made a valuable collection of rare birds, which he presented to the Paris cabinet of natural history. An attack of fever obliged him to return to France, and he selected Montbard as his residence, near the home of Buffon, by whose direction he described twenty-six species of American birds, comprising those belonging to the gallinaceous order, and the water-fowl. He afterward served in the French navy, travelled extensively in Asia and Africa, and wrote numerous books of travel and agriculture and natural history, among others 'Histoire naturelle des reptiles' (4 vols., Paris, 1802-'26), and 'Histoire naturelle des poissons et des cetaces' (14 vols., 1804) See 'Eloge historique de Sonnini,' by Arsdne Thiebaud de Berneaud (1812).[490]

Again, we read here that Sonnini made no important discovery concerning the long lost chapter of Acts. One curious fact, however, to be noted is the fact that E. Raymond Capt tells us that Sonnini was a "member of several scientific or literary societies of the Society of Agriculture of Paris, and of the Observers of Men."[491] What on earth are "The Observers of Men?" Is there not a hint here of a certain amount of Masonic, or Demolay, or even Illuminati mystique surrounding this individual – the kind of which was prevalent in those times?

Also, E Raymond Capt,[492] quotes a "Major Samuels" (sic!),[493] in his book *Far Hence unto the Gentiles*, chapter 29, who refers to the author of the "Book of Travel in Turkey and Greece" as being, not C. S. Sonnini, but rather now as one M. Sonnini, the "M" apparently designating the "Manoncourt" portion of his name. This is curious because also in 1801, there was a certain M. Sonnini who just so happened to discover a another secret manuscript in Egypt, which was translated by a person by the name of H. Kirchenhoffer in 1822, entitled the *Book of Fate*.[494] In the 1927 edition, the title page informs us that the English translator, H. Kirchenhoffer, was a "fellow of the University of Pavia, Knight Grand

---

[490] See online: http://www.famousamericans.net/chariesnicolassigisbertsonninide-manoncourt/.

[491] Capt, *Lost Chapter*, 4.

[492] Capt, *Lost Chapter*, 27.

[493] Samuel J. Lumen, *Far Hence unto the Gentiles* (London: Sumpkin, 1915).

Cross of the Annunciade of Sardinia; and Chevalier of the Legion of Honour." There seems to be an auspicious pattern here. It would appear from this that this C. S. Sonnini and M. Sonnini are none other than one and the same person and his works were part of a mysterious line of secret organizations.

The flavor of the times was the discovery of occultish types of manuscripts which were then peddled among secret societies. Also, it is interesting that Sonnini was able to translate Hieroglyphics (with the aide of a "learned Copt")[495] a quarter century before the Egyptian language code had been broken. There is no mention of the Rosetta Stone, which was also discovered in 1799 by Napoleon's army, and which, in reality, provided the true key to unravelling the Hieroglyphics two decades later. Already, there is too much suspicion cast on the authenticity of Soninni's discoveries. Again, what we have is a supposed Egyptian manuscript for which we have no originals to verify or to authenticate.

The Credibility of the Sonnini Manuscript

As FOR THE CONTENTS OF THE "SONINNI MANUSCRIPT" itself, it reportedly describes the Apostle Paul's trip to Britain. Since it states that the ancestors of the British were "certain of the children of Israel" who fled the Assyrians (v. 2), it has become an important document to those who believe in British/Israelism today. Whether or not it contains any authentic material from the first century is certainly open to question.[496]

The Sonnini manuscript contains some rather blatant historical absurdities. It reports that certain of the Druids that Paul meets claim that they are descended from the "Jews" (not Israelites) that escaped the Egyptian bondage under Moses (v. 13). After leaving Britain, Paul goes to Atium (Atrium?) in Gaul, then into Helvetia (Bassel, Switzerland?), where there is a "Mount Pontius Pilate." And, guess what? Pontius Pilate is there

[494] This was later republished in English in 1927 under the following title: *The Book of Fate: Formerly in the possession of and used by Napoleon, rendered into the English language by H. Kirchenhoffer from a German translation of Ancient Egyptian Manuscript found in the year 1801 by M. Sonnini in one of the Royal Tombs Near Mount Libycus in upper Egypt* (Scranton, Penn.: Personal Arts Co., 1927).

[495] Ibid., x.

[496] That the Apostle Paul did go to Britain after his release from his house arrest in Rome in 58 C.E. is the personal belief of the present author, however, reliance on the "Sonnini Manuscript" as back up material cannot be supported, nor endorsed.

and is alive, until Paul arrives and then he is dashed "head-long" into a pit and dies (vv. 17-20).[497]

Then occurs a great earthquake in which it changes the form and shape of a lake to appear like that of "the Son of Man hanging in an agony upon the Cross" (v. 21).[498] Then Paul journeys to "Mount Julius" where there are two pillars said to have been erected by Augustus Caesar, and supposedly will stand "throughout all generations" as a testimony to Paul's journey through Britain and Gaul (vv. 24-5). Where these pillars are, of course, no one apparently knows, so such testimony is obviously lost.

Where is the "Sonnini Manuscript" today? If it is in the hands of a private individual, scholars should be allowed to inspect it and analyze its worth. Until then, we will have to pass on its validity and charge that it is worthless as any kind of proof text. Indeed, on the surface, it appears to be an eighteenth century "Pilt-down Man" like hoax, in the same vein as the other Sonnini rip-off, the *Book of Fate*. Indeed, if P. T. Barnum knew of this manuscript, he would have made a fortune on it based upon the number of advocates that there are today who believe in its authenticity.

It is interesting that a number of British/Israelite authors in the past, such as R. W. Morgan,[499] J. W. Taylor,[500] George F. Jowett,[501] have produced some well documented research on the subject without ever appealing to this dubious "Sonnini Manuscript." Modern authors that do resort to this source appear oblivious of the fact that this is an obvious eighteenth century hoax, and their refusal to see this fact makes it a joke that appears to be on them.[502]

---

[497] Eusebius, *Hist. eccl.* 2.7.1, reports that Pilate committed suicide in the year of 39 C.E. (See also Rudolph Helm, *Eusebius Chronik* [Berlin: W. de Gruyter, 1924], 178).

[498] "The Son of Man hanging in an agony on the Cross" would be a very uncharacteristic representation of the risen Lord.

[499] R. W. Morgan, *St. Paul in Britain* (London: Covenant Publishing Co., 1948).

[500] J. W. Taylor, *The Coming of the Saints* (London: Covenant Publishing Co., 1969).

[501] George F. Jowett, *The Drama of the Lost Disciples* (London: Covenant Publishing Co., 1961).

[502] There are a number of sites online that appeal to this manuscript. A few examples are: http://www.hope-of-israel.org/sonnini.htm; http://www.geocities.com/regkeith/rkeith7.htm; http://www.theseason.org/acts/acts29.htm; http://asis.com/~stag/paulbrit.html.

APPENDIX 8

Canon Expansion Today?

BEFORE WE CONCLUDE THESE APPENDICES, we need to ask a big "what if" question, especially in the light of the last appendix. What if we were to legitimately find a lost chapter of Acts or another genuine work of one of Jesus' apostles? Should we immediately consider them "canonical" by virtue of their authorship, i.e., material that should be added to the New Testament today? The answer is a resounding no! Why? Because it is the canon itself that is the "fence around the Torah," so to speak, that barricades that which is within from being removed and protects its contents from the invasion of intrusive elements that were rejected by the Apostle Peter and John in the first place. This is a hard concept for many people to understand because of their "gradual acceptance" mentality, but it is true, despite pedantic views to the contrary.

The canon is not just a list of the books that are contained therein, but represents the binding decision of the only two apostles of Jesus that had the authority to pick and choose what the make up of the New Testament would be. Indeed, Peter and John may have actually considered such works [if they existed] and rejected them.

The principle that should guide us in correctly understanding the canon is associated with the "holy" temple. Jesus stated:

> Woe to you, blind guides, who say, 'Whoever swears by the sanctuary is bound by nothing, but whoever swears by the gold of the sanctuary is bound by the oath.' You blind fools! For which is greater, the gold or the sanctuary that has made the gold sacred? And you say, 'Whoever swears by the gift that is on the altar is bound by the oath.' How blind you are! For which is greater, the gift or the altar that makes the gift sacred? (Matt 23:16-19).

This example could not reflect the real meaning of the canon any better. It is not the books in the canon that make the canon sacred, it is the canon (the binding decision of Peter and John of which books to include in the New Testament) that give the books within the canon its sanctity.

Another principle that should guide us here is one concerning the temple. Jesus, in the parable of the stone that the builders rejected, actually gives us some biblical insight that we need in order to understand the correct criteria concerning the biblical canon. The example pertains to the master builder of the temple in search of an important structural cornerstone, but rejected a particularly beautiful stone because he found cracks and flaws that structurally would not support the weight of the building (Matt 21:42, quoting Ps 118:22; see also 1 Pet 2:4-7 and Eph 2:20).

Jesus likened himself to the stone that the builders rejected because he had superficial imperfections by their standards, and thus was rejected by the religious experts to be the prophesied Messiah. Even today more than ever, Jesus undergoes unbelievable scrutiny of every little nit-picking objection conceivable by scholars who believe that he was no more than an ordinary religious teacher of his day. The end result, of course, is that he is rejected by those who look at Jesus through a magnifying glass for any flaws that they can find. Nevertheless, it makes not a bit of difference what these scholars think because he was the one chosen by God to fulfill the role of Messiah, including whatever flaws that critics can imagine.

Thus, it is the same principle as with the books that were chosen to be within the New Testament by Peter and John. These two men were the only ones who had the "binding" authority to choose the books that would make up the canon of New Testament literature. What they accepted was accepted and what they rejected was rejected.

Athanasius of the fourth century (367)[503] did not compile the New Testament, he merely made a table of contents of the existing New Testament books. The entire idea of a canon that was made up by a later Gentile church is a total oxymoron. The very thing that the apostles wanted to prevent was that the later church would be left to decide what were the authoritative works of the apostles and what were not.

And even though Peter and John chose works which had flaws,

---

[503] Athanasius (ca. 296-373) was the arch enemy of the Arian party at the Nicene Council in 325. F. F. Bruce (*The Canon of Scripture* [Downers Grove, Ill.: Inter-Varsity Press, 1988], 77) notes: "One of the minor decisions of the Council of Nicea (AD 325) was that, to guard against any disagreement about fixing the date of Easter, the bishop of Alexandria should have the privilege, year by year, of informing his brother bishops (well in advance) of the date of the following Easter. Throughout his long tenure of that see (328-373) Athanasius issued forty-five such 'festal letters'. In each he took the opportunity of dealing with some other matter of current importance. In the thirty-ninth letter, announcing the date of Easter in 367, he dealt with the canon of the Old and New Testaments." This letter is preserved in *NPNF*², 4:551.

imperfections of grammar, misstated facts, bickering, and other details that scholars are quick to point out which should give rise to doubts of canonicity, it is the *decision* of these two apostles which constitutes the canon. In other words, a proper definition of the canon of the New Testament would be to call it "the decision of Peter and John." So, these so-called microscopic flaws, however, are the twigs that do not destroy the beauty of the tree. They represent the flaws that cause great concern amongst our esteemed experts in the field, but they make not one shred of difference to the subject of canonicity.[504]

Therefore, the many works that some scholars would wish to add to the canon of the New Testament, such as the *Gospel of Thomas, 1 Clement*, the *Gospel of Peter*, the *Gospel of the Hebrews*, the *Protevangelium of James*, the *Secret Gospel of Mark*, the *Magdalene Gospel*, the *Diatesseron*, the totally imagined *Gospel of Q*, even, should we dare say, the *Book of Mormon*, or any other writing that modern scholars should wish to add to the canon today, do not meet the criteria of being chosen for the canon by the Apostles Peter and John. The canon must be understood to represent the binding decisions of the Apostles of Peter and John. The notion that it is just a list of books within the canon is simply the erroneous deduction of modern day scholars.

Indeed, let us thoroughly embrace the sentiments of Ernest L. Martin in this regard:

> To me, Ezra, Peter and John had an infallible commission to produce a canon of Scripture by the infallible Yahweh Elohim (though they of themselves were fallible men). And it is the books of the canon that allow the details within the books to be holy, and not the details themselves.[505]

This last statement is so profound in its importance, it requires further discussion. Scholars write books today on how the canon was formed based upon a host of suppositions that are unsupported. In the absence of scholar's lack of knowledge on how the New [and the Old] Testament was created, they fill in the gaps with pure guess work. One of those modern day scholarly myths that must be demolished is the entire concept of the "criteria for canonization." Let's move on to see why!

---

[504] We thus can ask, as Ernest L. Martin, *Restoring*, 468, has: "Is the Bible inerrant? It is indeed inerrant, including all of its errors!"

[505] Martin, *Restoring*, 464.

THE CRITERIA FOR CANONICITY

THE FALSE ASSUMPTION OF THE GRADUAL ACCEPTANCE theory leads to a whole scenario of speculative reasoning, not the least of which is the so-called "criteria for canonicity." Indeed, most books on the canon will undoubtedly include an entire chapter entitled: "The Criteria for Canonicity."[506] This entire line of reasoning assumes that sometime in the second, third, and fourth centuries there existed a body of canon deciders who all had before them the same list of requirements and worked toward evaluating canonicity of certain works that were floating around against that list. That such a list ever existed is entirely conjectural and is beside the point. It is the natural outgrowth of a premise that appears on the surface to be true and therefore all scholars subscribe to it blithely. But then, the whole idea of "criteria for canonicity" is itself a false notion that keeps spawning new false notions, *ad infinitum*, that tangle the web further and further.

The point is that the whole idea of "Criteria for Canonicity" assumes that it is the intrinsic value of the book that defines it as canonical material.[507] This reasoning is entirely backwards. It is not the book within the canon that is decisive concerning a work's canonicity, it is the canon itself that decides a book's canonicity! Again, it is only when we understand that the definition of the canon is the decision of Peter and later John as to what should be included in the canon that the entire subject will be approached correctly.

Let us look at a simple illustration. If the Apostle Peter, and later the Apostle John, had decided to place *Aesop's Fables* into the canon, then these fables would have then been elevated to the status of sacred literature by virtue of Peter and John's decision.[508] Scholars, of course, will reject this idea, but that is to be expected based upon their subjective and idiosyncratic ideas of what the Bible should be.[509]

Therefore, the so-called "criteria for canonization" principle is entirely a frivolous adventure based upon a total misunderstanding of the biblical

---

[506] For example, see Arthur G. Patzia, *The Making of the New Testament* (Downers Grove, Ill.: Inter-Varsity Press, 1995), 102-110: [1. Authority of Jesus, 2. Apostolicity, 3. Usage in the Church, 4. Orthodoxy, 5. Inspiration]; F. F. Bruce, *The Canon of Scripture* (Downers Grove, Ill.: Inter-Varsity Press, 1988), 255-69 [1. Apostolic Authority, 2. Antiquity, 3. Orthodoxy, 4. Catholicity, 5. Traditional use, 6. Inspiration]; Bruce M. Metzger, *The Canon of the New Testament* (Oxford: Clarendon, 1987), 251-3, [1. Orthodoxy, 2. Apostolicity, 3. Consensus among the Churches].

[507] If we were to apply the test of canonicity, for instance, to the *Epistle of Jude*, it would undoubtedly fail the test, as it has from time immemorial (Eusebius, *Hist. eccl.* 6.14.1).

principles that are there to guide us into the truth. No such list of criteria has ever been found. And even if one did emerge, so what? The latter church did not have the authority to make the decision of the canon of the New Testament. And there exists no evidence whatsoever that they ever did.

Thus, we cannot escape the conclusion that the canon is complete and sealed. What we have in our possession today is a canon of divine literature that Peter and John ultimately collected and bound together for the instruction of the future church. Everything else remains on the side lines of ancient literature, as it should.

---

[508] Paul quotes a proverb in First Corinthians 15:33 that scholars have identified as being from Menander's work called *Thais,* which he in turn quoted from a lost play of Euripides. He also refers to a rabbinical midrash in 1 Corinthians 10:4, a heathen poet in his speech at Athens (Acts 17:28), and names the magicians who withstood Pharaoh as Jannes and Jambres (2 Tim 3:8), which he obviously derived from some non-canonical source. Jude cites the Jewish apocryphal work, *1 Enoch,* almost verbatim and makes reference to another pseudepigraphon, the *Assumption of Moses,* according to the testimony of Clement, Origen and Didymus. Even in the Old Testament books non-canonical works are cited, such as the *Book of Jasher* (Joshua 10:13; 2 Sam 1:18), the *Acts of Solomon* (1 Ki 11:14), and numerous others. Thus, portions of such non-divinely inspired works have now been elevated to the status of divine literature by virtue of being in the canon, and not the other way around. Indeed, they only enrich the canon of divine literature by virtue of the fact that they have been chosen to be included within the canon by the decision of those that have been given the charge to produce the canon, namely Ezra, Peter and John.

[509] Robert W. Funk, "The Once and Future New Testament," in *The Canon Debate,* (ed. Lee Martin McDonald and James A. Sanders, Peabody, Mass.: Hendrickson, 2002): 541-57, is one such scholar who feels that the canon today is still open to alteration: "People are largely ignorant of its [the Bible's] contents or poorly informed about its history and development. The positive side of this ugly scene is that the authority of the Bible is eroding by leaps and bounds. The canon is shedding its canonicity. ...Unless we rightly divide the word of truth and raise the literacy level, the Bible is destined for oblivion in the third millennium. My own solution to the problem is to issue a revised canon, a new New Testament, by both shrinking and expanding the texts to be included," 549. This quote shows where the notion of "criteria for canonicity" ultimately leads.

APPENDIX 9

Design of the Canon of Scripture

ONE OF THE GREATEST TESTIMONIES THAT THE Bible is the complete word of God is to be found in its structure and design. To even say that the Bible was a product of "design" implies that there was a definite plan and purpose as to how the books of the Bible were to be specifically arranged as a complete entity, and not by any gradual acceptance process that took three centuries.

That premise, in itself, flies in the face of so-called "gradual acceptance" theories. Indeed, gradual acceptance theories cannot account for such a phenomenon, and therefore avoid any discussion of it and confuse the issue by showing all the different arrangements that have come down to us from various lines of textual transmission.

Yet the Bible, as a whole, from beginning to end, resounds in the fact that it is a completed book from Genesis to Revelation, just by its very structure, design, and form. And it is this fact that we offer as further evidence that the New Testament was designed to compliment and complete the Old Testament revelation. Once we see the beauty and symmetry of the entire biblical structure, we can be further strengthened in the idea that the Bible that we possess is a completed canon.

Modern translations have obscured the beauty of the design of the original canonical arrangements in favor of later church arrangements. This obfuscation has resulted in the false impression that the Bible is just a haphazard conglomeration of books, which can still be added to or subtracted from, based on modern decisions of supposed canonical worthiness. Yet, the matter is not one of indifference. Nor should we say that it is a modern construct just invented to merely defeat present day theories of canon expansion or reduction. The structure of the canon should be as important a facet of biblical studies as any today.

The earliest full table of contents of the New Testament was published by the bishop of Alexandria, Athanasius, in 367 (*NPNF*[2] 4:551). The critical edition of the Greek New Testament presented to us by the nineteenth century scholars, Westcott and Hort, arranged the New

Testament in this same exact manuscript order, stating that:

> In the order of the different books we have for various reasons not thought it advisable to depart from traditional arrangements. We should have defeated our own purpose had we needlessly mixed up such disputable matter as the chronology and authorship of the apostolic writings with the results of textual criticism, obtained by different methods from evidence of an entirely different kind. We have however followed recent editors in abandoning the Hieronymic order, familiar in modern Europe through the influence of the Latin Vulgate, in favour of the order most highly commended by various Greek authority of the fourth century, the earliest time when we have distinct evidence of the completed Canon as it now stands. It differs from the Hieronymic order in two respects. First, the Acts are immediately followed by the Catholic Epistles. The connection between these two portions, commended by its intrinsic appropriateness, is preserved in a large proportion of Greek MSS of all ages, and corresponds to marked affinities of textual history. ...Secondly, the Epistle to the Hebrews stands before the Pastoral Epistles.[510]

THE PROPER ORDER OF THE BIBLICAL BOOKS

IT SHOULD BE NOTED THAT THE HEBREW SCRIPTURES are divided into three Grand Divisions – The Law, the Prophets, and the Writings. Jesus acknowledged this scheme in Luke 24:44-5:

> Then he said to them, "These are my words that I spoke to you while I was still with you – that everything written about me in the law of Moses, the prophets, and the psalms must be fulfilled." Then he opened their minds to understand the scriptures.[511]

Besides the three Grand Divisions, there exists subdivisions according to categories within these divisions. The Law Division consists of five books (1. Genesis, 2. Exodus, 3. Leviticus, 4. Numbers, and 5.

[510] B. F. Westcott and F. J. A. Hort, *Introduction to the New Testament in the Original Greek* (New York: Harper & Brothers, 1882), 320. It is unfortunate that the direction in the nineteenth century to return to the original manuscript order never took hold. Hopefully, a new revival of this proposal will once again be initiated.

Deuteronomy).

In the Prophets division there is the "Former Prophets," (6. Joshua-Judges and 7. Samuel-Kings). Then there is the "Latter Prophets." This division is further subdivided into the "Major Prophets," (8. Isaiah, 9. Jeremiah and 10. Ezekiel) and the "Minor Prophets," (11. Hosea, 12. Joel, 13. Amos, 14. Obadiah, 15. Jonah, 16. Micah, 17. Nahum, 18. Habakkuk, 19. Zephaniah, 20. Haggai, 21. Zechariah and 22. Malachi).

The third Grand Division, known as The Writings or the Psalms Division, is broken down into three subdivisions: The Poetic books, (Psalms, Proverbs and Job); the Festival Scroll or Megilloth, (Song of Songs, Ruth, Lamentations, Ecclesiastes, and Esther), and the Restoration books, (Daniel, Ezra-Nehemiah and Chronicles).

Thus, as the earliest testimony informs us, the number of books within the Hebrew canon amounts to 22 books[512] contained within three Grand divisions written on seven sub-divisional scrolls: 1) the Law; 2) the Former Prophets; 3) the Major Prophets; 4) the Minor Prophets; 5) the Poetic books; 6) the Festival books; 7) the Post-Exilic books.

When we turn to the structure of the New Testament we can see a similarity in the fact that the books contained therein are assembled into

---

[511] Since the Psalms is the first book of the third Grand Division, it is obvious that Jesus is talking about the same canon as we have it today, since it is still the leading book of third Grand Division of Scripture in the Masoretic tradition. F. F. Bruce, *New Testament History* (New York: Doubleday, 1971), 31, also notes: "There is evidence that Chronicles was the last book in the Hebrew Bible as Jesus knew it. When he said that the generation he addressed would be answerable for 'the blood of all the prophets, shed from the foundation of the world', he added, 'from the blood of Abel to the blood of Zechariah, who perished between the altar and the sanctuary' (Luke 11:50f.). Abel is the first martyr in the Bible (Gen. 4:8); Zechariah is most probably the son of Jehoiada, who was stoned to death 'in the court of Yahweh's house' because, speaking by the Spirit of God, he rebuked the king and people of Judah for transgressing the divine commandments (2 Chron. 24:20-22). Zechariah (*c* 800 BC) was not *chronologically* the last faithful prophet to die as a martyr; some two centuries later a prophet named Uriah was put to death in Jerusalem because his witness was unacceptable to King Jehoikim (Jer. 26:2-23). But Zechariah is *canonically* the last faithful prophet to die as a martyr, because his death is recorded in Chronicles, the last book in the Hebrew Bible." Bruce notes (ibid., n. 7), however, that although Matthew's parallel passage (Matt 24:35) has Zechariah being 'the son of Barachiah' instead of Jehoiada, "the Zechariah of 2 Chronicles 24:20-22 is most probably meant."

[512] See Ernest L. Martin, *Restoring*, 57-61. Today, the Jewish Bible consists of 24 books, not because there have been added two extra books, but because the way the Jews now divide up the books of the Hebrew canon. This is the same situation in what we see in the Protestant Old Testament with its 39 books. Although the content is the same, the way the books have been divided and arranged are different. For instance, in the Hebrew Bible, the twelve minor prophets are considered one book. Likewise, Samuel, Kings, Chronicles and Ezra-Nehemiah are treated as one book a piece. Originally, Joshua-Judges and Samuel-Kings also were counted as a single book each. The Jewish change from a 22 book canon to a 24 book canon may have been done deliberately so as to avoid any numerical significance by adjoining the Christian canon to the Hebrew canon (22+27=49 vs. 24+27=51).

a particular order that compliments the Old Testament canon. In the New Testament we can clearly see four Grand divisions containing: 1) The historical books, 2) the General Epistles, 3) the Epistles of Paul, and 4) the *Book of Revelation.*

These Grand divisions of the New Testament can also be subdivided into seven sub-categories: The Historical Division consists of the four Gospels: 1) Matthew, Mark, Luke, and John, plus 2) the *Book of Acts.* The General Epistles division consists of 3) the Epistles of James, 1-2 Peter, 1-3 John and Jude. The Epistles of Paul division consists of the church Epistles and the Pastoral Epistles, which can be further broken down into 4) Epistles to the seven Churches: i) Romans, ii) 1-2 Corinthians, iii) Galatians, iv) Ephesians, v) Philippians, vi) Colossians and vii) 1-2 Thessalonians. Then follows the General church Epistle, 5) the Epistle to the Hebrews. Then, the Pastoral Epistles 6) 1-2 Timothy, Titus, and Philemon. And finally, 7) the *Book of Revelation.*

Thus we can see that the three Grand Divisions of the Old Testament, coupled with the four Grand Divisions of the New Testament represent a seven-fold Grand divisions of the entire Word of God. Each Testament contains seven sub-divisions. And when we combine these 22 books of the Old Testament with the 27 books of the New Testament, we come up with a complete Bible of 49 books (7 x 7).[513]

The number seven is the stamp of completeness.[514] Once we see this sevenfold arrangement shine through the original disposition, then we can see the truth of a complete and final canon that we have in our possession today.[515]

---

[513] For a beautiful graphical display of the design and structure of the Bible, see *The Symmetrical Bible* online: http://www.centuryone.com/bible.html.

[514] The Protestant Bible reckons 39 OT books, which, when added to the 27 NT books amount to 66 books, which has the curious mark of man's number. The Catholic Church eventually corrected this matter by adopting the Apocrypha into their Bible at the Council of Trent in 1546. This was done to be distinct from the Protestants, obviously, but also, since the Protestants were calling the Apocrypha spurious, the Catholic Church wanted to demonstrate its superior authority over the Protestants in proclaiming books that the Protestants rejected. This also had the advantage of making the Catholic canon to consist of 77 books — a far more pleasing complexion than that of the Protestants. Both groups, however, have jumbled up the original arrangement, producing a version that is contrary to the intent of the original canon.

[515] It is time that Bible publishers produce a 49 book Bible that represents the arrangement of the original canonical edition. One such project that is underway is the Original Bible Project's *Transparent English Version,* editor-in-chief, professor James D. Tabor. For information on this project, see online: http://www.centuryone.org/obp.html

APPENDIX 10

The Text of the New Testament

THE SUBJECT OF WHICH TEXTUAL TRADITION we should follow is a vast one. However, some recent observations by specialists in the field can help guide us in the proper direction. This subject is as important as any to understand in regard to the story behind *Beyond Acts*.

First of all, we should draw our attention to the 50 Bibles that Emperor Constantine commissioned to be made. Now why is this fact significant to the subject? It is significant in that it helps us understand the true origin of the New Testament text. Eusebius stated that he sent to the Emperor the completed Bibles in "magnificent and elaborately bound volumes of a threefold and fourfold form" (Eusebius, *Vit. Const.* 4.36-37).

Jack Finegan comments on the expression "threefold and fourfold" (*trissa kai tetrassa*) as probably meaning "having three columns and four columns" and points out that the pages in codex Vaticanus were written respectively in three columns and four columns.[516]

Dr. Finegan further brings out:

> Two great vellum codices of the Bible, dating probably about the middle of the fourth century A.D., are still extant, Codex Vaticanus and Codex Sinaiticus. ...it is interesting to find that they have three and four columns of writing per page respectively. We also learn that about the middle of the same century the famous library of Origen (d. A.D. c.254) and Pamphilus (d. A.D. 309) at Caesarea had fallen into decay and was restored by two priests, Acacius and Euzoius, who replaced what were probably damaged papyrus rolls with copies written on parchment (in membranis) and presumably in codices. From this time on, parchment or vellum remained the chief writing material until the general establishment of the use of paper in the fourteenth century; and the codex was retained permanently

[516] Jack Finegan, *Light from the Ancient Past* (Oxford: Oxford University Press, 1974), 2:397-8.

as the prevailing form of books.[517]

The codex Vaticanus and Sinaiticus manuscripts certainly bear witness that these great codices were the result of great projects of a significant expenditure of funds. Certainly, the Emperor Constantine would have [and could have] spared no expense in such a project. Is it conceivable that all 50 of these Bibles would have now disappeared and that none have survived?

One thing to note is that the manuscript order of codex Vaticanus follows the original manuscript order according to Westcott and Hort, and other authorities.[518] If the codex Vaticanus is one of Eusebius' fifty Bibles, it may well be the most accurate in terms of faithfully representing the text from the great library of Caesarea, where Eusebius worked.

Although the textual scholars Westcott and Hort placed the Vaticanus on a pedestal, later scholars have brought the prestige of this great manuscript down, claiming that it represented a recension rather than a pure line of manuscript tradition. But now, some have challenged this view due to the recently found papyrus manuscripts that have surfaced in the last century. These manuscripts show remarkable agreement to codex Vaticanus.

Philip Wesley Comfort, visiting professor of New Testament Literature and Interpretation at Wheaton College, and senior editor of the Bible Department at Tyndale, is one such scholar. He is co-translator (along with Robert K. Brown) of *The New Greek-English Interlinear New Testament.*[519] His literal translation is one of my principle study guides – an excellent contribution. In his book: *The Quest for the Original Text of the New Testament,*[520] Dr. Comfort evaluates the impact of early papyrus fragments on textual studies.

One of the papyruses designated P^{75} [Bodmer Papyrus XIV-XV) has been dated to 175 C.E. by Barbara Aland. Dr. Comfort remarks on this important papyrus:

> Unquestionably, $\mathbf{P^{75}}$ is the best extant copy of any substantial portion of the New Testament. ...$\mathbf{P^{75}}$ is the work

[517] Ibid., 398.

[518] F. F. Bruce, *The Canon of Scripture* (Downers Grove, Ill.: InterVarsity Press, 1988), 205-6. Unfortunately, Codex Vaticanus is missing the latter part of Hebrews, the Pastorals and Revelation. Codex Sinaiticus follows the exact same order, except for the curious fact that Acts and the Catholic Epistles follow after Philemon. It also has appended the Letter of Barnabas and the Shepherd of Hermas.

[519] Robert K. Brown and Philip W. Comfort, *The New Greek-English Interlinear New Testament* (Wheaton, Ill.: Tyndale, 1990).

[520] Philip W. Comfort, *The Quest for the Original Text of the New Testament* (Grand Rapids: Baker, 1992).

> of a professional scribe – a scribe who very likely labored in a scriptorium in Alexandria or in another scriptorium influenced by Alexandrian scriptoral practices. $\mathbf{P}^{75}$ displays the penmanship of a professional. ...$\mathbf{P}^{75}$ is eminently recognized as an extremely accurate copy. ...All in all, $\mathbf{P}^{75}$ is a thorough literary production of the highest quality. This carefully made manuscript is an excellent copy of the original text.[521]

So what does this have to do with codex Vaticanus? Dr. Comfort continues:

> It should not surprise us that another accurate manuscript, Codex Vaticanus [B], is quite close to $\mathbf{P}^{75}$. ...Studies have shown a high percentage of agreement between $\mathbf{P}^{75}$ and B. ...Seldom do we see the scribe of B adopting a variant reading from a different tradition.[522]

What this all means is that

> prior to the discovery of $\mathbf{P}^{75}$, certain scholars thought Codex Vaticanus was the work of a fourth-century recension; others (chiefly Hort) thought it must trace back to a very early and accurate copy. Hort said that Codex Vaticanus preserves 'not only a very ancient text, but a very pure line of very ancient text' (Westcott and Hort 1882: *Introduction* pp. 250-51). $\mathbf{P}^{75}$ appears to have shown that Hort was right. Prior to the discovery of $\mathbf{P}^{75}$, many textual scholars were convinced that the second- and third-century papyri displayed a text in flux.... But $\mathbf{P}^{75}$ has proven this theory wrong. What is quite clear now is that Codex Vaticanus was simply a copy (with some modifications) of a manuscript much like $\mathbf{P}^{75}$, not a fourth-century recension.[523]

Another New Testament textual scholar, who has similarly viewed the evidence, is Gordon O. Fee, professor of New Testament at Regent College in Vancouver, British Columbia, and has served as the editor of *The New International Commentary on the New Testament.* He states:

> As to $\mathbf{P}^{75}$, it can be shown to be precisely what Hort considered B [codex Vaticanus] to be: a very pure line of very ancient text. For example, when tested along with all other witnesses in Luke 10 and 11 for variants reflecting possible harmonization to Matthew, Mark, or the LXX, $\mathbf{P}^{75}$ and B stood alone in their "comparative purity." Codex D,

[521] Ibid., 96, 98.
[522] Ibid., 99.
[523] Ibid., 121.

> for example, had thirty-six such harmonizing variants, the Byzantine majority had twenty-seven, while $\mathbf{P}^{75}$ and B had six, and some of theirs were more likely the result of other factors than harmonization.[524]

Still, another prominent specialist in the field of textual criticism, Eldon Jay Epp, has also contributed to the discussion. He is the Harkness Professor of Biblical Literature at Case Western Reserve University, Cleveland, Ohio. He states:

> The place to begin a description of the "B" textual cluster is with the striking and highly significant fact that the texts of $\mathbf{P}^{75}$ and Codex Vaticanus (B) are almost identical, a fact which demonstrates that there is virtually a straight line from the text of a papyrus dated around 200 to that of a major, elegant MS of 150 years later. ...the close affinity of $\mathbf{P}^{75}$ and B is ...striking, for it demonstrates that an early papyrus can stand very near the beginning point of a clearly identifiable and distinctive textual group that has been preserved with a high degree of accuracy over several generations and through a period that often has been assumed to have been a chaotic and free textual environment.[525]

The stability of the text is due to the fact that it was not maintained in local church archives, as many have assumed. The chief guardian of the text was the archive at the Caesarean library. Once it is appreciated that this is a fact of history, then we can better understand the trustworthiness of the true Caesarean text type.

Eldon Epp has also narrowed down the textual families of the early witnesses based upon what he calls two textual streams or trajectories:

> Although we are told that text-types, subsequent to the discovery of these early witnesses, should no longer be classified according to the much later codices B and D, it is true nonetheless that our extant materials and our much enhanced hindsight reveal *only two clear textual streams or trajectories* through all of our material from the first four centuries or so of textural transmission, and these two trajectories are what we have long called the Neutral (or

---

[524] Gordon D. Fee, "Rigorous or Reasoned Eclecticism — Which?" in *Studies in the Theory and Method of New Testament Textual Criticism,* ed. Eldon J. Epp and Gordon D. Fee (Grand Rapids: Eerdmans, 1993), 128.

[525] Eldon J. Epp, "The Significance of the Papyri for Determining the Nature of the New Testament Text in the Second Century: A Dynamic View of Textual Transmission" in *Studies in the Theory and Method of New Testament Textual Criticism,* ed. Eldon J. Epp and Gordon D. Fee (Grand Rapids: Eerdmans, 1993), 289.

> Alexandrian/Egyptian) and the Western text-types. The Neutral line is the clearest, plotted first from **P^{75}**, then perhaps through **P^{23}**, **P^{25}**, 0220, **P^{50}**, etc., to Codex B and thence on through the centuries, e.g., to Codex L (eighth century), MSS 33 (ninth century), 1739 (tenth century), and 579 (thirteenth century).[526]

Now, we should take note of a very curious thing going on here. Where is the Caesarean text type in all of this? This is a most important question because we believe that it is the great library of Caesarea where the "elders" of the Apostle John[527] had ultimately delivered the completed canon of the New Testament. In other words, if we are going to seek the original text, it should ultimately draw a line back to the Caesarean Library. And if that is the case, then the true text type should be called the "Caesarean" text, the true "neutral" text type.

It is unfortunate that the so-called "Neutral Text" that Westcott and Hort identified should have been also dubbed as the "Alexandrian Text" type. Why? Because this has only given the "King James Version Only" movement[528] ammunition in their arsenal of trying to preserve a non-text – the so-called "Textus Receptus." The reality is, however, that they are the ones championing a text that is the result of numerous recensions and eclectic borrowing from dubious sources.[529] Furthermore, because the B manuscript is also called the "Vaticanus," anti-Catholic bias is all too ready and willing to throw suspicion on this codex as a Roman Catholic production. Obviously, clearer heads must prevail. Such prejudice has no place in any honest research.

---

[526] Eldon Jay Epp, "The Twentieth-Century Interlude in New Testament Textual Criticism" in *Studies in the Theory and Method of New Testament Textual Criticism*, ed. Eldon J. Epp and Gordon D. Fee (Grand Rapids: Eerdmans, 1993), 93. Dr. Epp goes on to say: "The Western line takes us, for example, from P^5 and P^{29} through P^{48}, P^{38}, P^{37}, and 0171, then to codices D and D_p, and thence on through the centuries to F_p and G_p (ninth century) and MSS 614 and 383 (thirteenth century)." Epp goes further on to describe a "midway" trajectory which ultimately formed the Byzantine line and most of the miniscules.

[527] Irenaeus, *Haer.* 2:22:5 [*ANF* 1:391-2], also see 5:5:1; 5:30:1; 5:33:3; and 5:36:1-2.

[528] Online, see: http://www.tegart.com/brian/bible/kjvonly/; http://www.angelfire.com/hi2/graphic1designer/hushbeck_article.html; http://hometown.aol.com/ibss2/kjv.html;

[529] One only has to go online to "www.google.com" and type in "Westcott and Hort' to see evangelical idiosyncratic ideology at its very worst. The war waged is not so much against text type categories as it is a naive advocacy of theological indoctrination— one that defends a corrupt text at any cost which supports the high christological Jesus – the imagined pre-existent Divine Being of later church councilor decrees. Once it is understood that theology is the real underlying motive behind the entire tempestuous "KJV Only" movement, then one can see that it is a defecation of false rhetoric rather than an honest appraisal of the facts.

THE ALEXANDRIAN TEXT TYPE MYTH

WE MUST NOW LAY ASIDE THE MYTH OF THE so-called Alexandrian Text Type.[530] It is entirely a misnomer. The Codices Vaticanus and Sinaiticus are not Alexandrian at all – they are Caesarean! Indeed, around the turn of the twentieth century specialists in the field of textual studies were leaning toward labeling these two great manuscripts as Caesarean.[531] But then it seems, scholars, for some strange reason, were compelled to label Vaticanus and Sinaiticus as Alexandrian and not Caesarean. And what was the compelling reason for this change? Hang onto your seats, the answer will floor you. In the final analysis, all the arguments boiled down to the fact that the order of the books in the codex Vaticanus is exactly the same order as that given by Athanasius, bishop of Alexandria, in his "Festal Letter" of 367.[532] But has it never dawned on scholars that Athanasius was merely citing a tradition of the order of books that had come down to him from the beginning of the second century?

Is this the kind of reasoning that supports the entire Alexandrian text type? Indeed, notice how some scholars cleverly try to tip the scales in favor of an Alexandrian provenance in the face of data to the contrary:

> Attempts have been made to associate the great codices Sinaiticus and Vaticanus with Caesarea as their place of origin, but on rather slender data. In the first place, it would seem plausible after the paleographical work of Milne and Skeat[533] that the same scribe had worked upon both

[530] Text types were based on what scholars believed to be recensions, i.e., a deliberate revision of the entire textual apparatus, based on a critical study of its sources. Gordon Fee has adequately demonstrated that there was not any kind of Alexandrian recension in the second, or even third century (Gordon D. Fee, "P75, P66, and Origen: The Myth of Early Textual Recension in Alexandria" in *Studies in the Theory and Method of New Testament Textual Criticism*, ed. Eldon J. Epp and Gordon D. Fee (Grand Rapids: Eerdmans, 1993), 247-273.

[531] The dramatic story of this change in scholarly opinion is told in the brilliant article by Theodore C. Skeat, "The Codex Sinaiticus, the Codex Vaticanus, and Constantine," *Journal of Theological Studies* 50:2 (1999): 583-625. Anyone doing study in this area must not fail to read and understand the thrust of Skeat's important contribution. One of the revealing points brought out in this article is that the imminent textual Harvard University scholar, Kirsopp Lake (1872-1946), originally was of the opinion that Sinaiticus and Vaticanus were of Caesarean provenance, but later changed his mind in favor of an Alexandrian one. The reasons which changed Lake's mind on this important point seem to be a mystery rather than due to rigorous investigation. Nevertheless, scholars today seem to be in a paralysis on this point based mainly on opinions of scholars of the stature of Kirsopp Lake.

[532] Ibid., 587.

[533] H. J. M. Milne and T. C. Skeat, *Scribes and Correctors of the Codex Sinaiticus*, (London: British Museum, 1938).

> manuscripts, scribe A of the Vaticanus being probably identical with scribe D of the Sinaiticus. Hence any datum bearing upon the origin of the one may well be valid for the other. The Sinaiticus has at Matt. 13:54 for *Patrida* (homeland) the curious variant *Antipatrida* (an unknown word), which may spring from *Antipatris*, a place-name of the Caesarean region: similarly it has *Kaisareias* for *Samareias* at Acts 8:40 [sic! Acts 8:5]. ...On the other side there are two weighty points which argue for the Alexandrian origin of the Vaticanus at least (and the Sinaiticus probably comes from the same scriptorium): first, that the order of books is identical with that found in Athanasius' statements about the Canon of scripture, and secondly, that a striking variant in Heb. 1:3 is known elsewhere only in a Coptic source.[534]

Notice that the detailed paleographical data provided by Milne and Skeat for a Caesarean provenance is dismissed with a prejudicial slant of being "slender," but on the side of an Alexandrian provenance we have "weighty points." And what are these so-called weighty points? They are the order of Vaticanus' New Testament books as being the same as that of Athanasius and a unique reading of Hebrews 1:3 only paralleled in Coptic sources. That's basically it! In other words, in the above quote, if we were to exchange the words "slender data" with "weighty points," would our judgment on the provenance of these two manuscripts not be prejudiced in the opposite direction?[535]

In point of fact, the slender data is in reality that in favor of Alexandria, and the weighty points for a Caesarean provenance are those of Milne and Skeat. Indeed, Theodore Skeat has recently reiterated the following:

> I think future generations may be puzzled to understand why it has taken so long for the significance of these two readings, 'Αντιπατπρίδα for πατρίδα and Καισαρίας for Σαμαρίας, to be appreciated. They are in fact first-hand direct evidence of a kind rarely available. *The scribe is, in effect, himself telling us where he is writing.* Short of a colophon saying that Sinaiticus was written in Caesarea, I do not see how this could have been more clearly expressed.[536]

---

[534] J. Neville Birdsall, "The New Testament Text" in *The Cambridge History of the Bible*, ed., P. R. Ackroyd and C. F. Evans, (Cambridge: Cambridge University Press, 1979), 1:359-60.

[535] Indeed, how can the order of books argument for Alexandria be even considered as being "weighty" when both the codex Vaticanus and the codex Sinaiticus differ in order of the books?

[536] T. C. Skeat, ibid., 598.

Today, scholars are still burdened with old, false stereotypes that are in fact really supported by the slenderest of data, and not the other way around as they would have you believe by prejudicial adverbs. It is time that a new generation of scholars begin a fresh study of the problem and render a decision based on the evidence and not on opinions that seek to overthrow the truth in favor of ideas that suit a post-apostolic origin of the New Testament. The true neutral text of the New Testament should be rightly called the Caesarean Text. This is because ancient Caesarea in Palestine is where the true text type originated – not Alexandria!

THE VANISHING CAESAREAN TEXT TYPE

THE CAESAREAN TEXT TYPE IS GRADUALLY FALLING by the wayside in scholarly discussions, which is an unfortunate direction. How do scholars categorize texts into certain groups in the first place? Eldon Jay Epp has gives us some insight in this:

> When J. A. Bengel long ago placed MSS into classes or groups, the development of text-types was under way in the textual critic's mind, reaching its classical formulation in the system of Westcott-Hort, though the more elaborate classifications of von Soden were still to come. As new MSS were analyzed, they were placed into a Westcott-Hort or a von Soden framework; this was appropriate enough if the MSS in question were generally later in time than the cornerstone MSS of each text-type. When, however, much earlier MSS – primarily papyri – began to appear (particularly those well beyond the fragmentary stage), we began to recognize the anachronism of placing these earlier MSS into groups whose nature had been determined on the basis only of the complexion of later MSS (see Birdsall 1960: 8-9, 171 Klijn 1969: 33-38, 50).[537]

This being said, then the resultant deduction was soon to follow:

> The identification of text-types and of the MSS comprising them was a controversial matter for two centuries from Bengel to the discussion about the Caesarean text (roughly 1735-1935), but it was the analysis of papyri like $\mathbf{P}^{45}$, $\mathbf{P}^{46}$,

[537] Eldon Jay Epp, "Decision Points in Past, Present, and Future New Testament Textual Criticism," in *Studies in the Theory and Method of New Testament Textual Criticism*, ed. Eldon J. Epp and Gordon D. Fee (Grand Rapids: Eerdmans, 1993), 17.

> P66, and P75 that brought a new dimension to the controversy, namely, whether the established text-type categories any longer made sense or were even useful for the earliest period, or – to push the question even further – whether there were, in fact, any identifiable text-types at all in that period.[538]

As early as 1945 Bruce Metzger was stating that: "It must be acknowledged that at present the Caesarean text is disintegrating."[539] Why is it disintegrating? Because, the evidence of the papyri showed much overlapping, especially in what was called Alexandrian and Caesarean. Unfortunately, however, scholars maintained the term Alexandrian at the expense of the true identifier – the Caesarean text type. But notice what F. F. Bruce observed long ago:

> The great centres of Christianity in the early centuries tended, in the course of copying and recopying, to have distinct types of text associated with them. Textual students have been able to distinguish among our sources of evidence for the New Testament text groups of manuscripts, versions and citations associated in particular with Alexandria, Caesarea, Antioch and the West (and the West means primarily Rome). The Alexandrian family is represented in particular by Codices א, B, and C, and a few other uncials and minuscules; also by the Coptic (Bohairic) version and by Biblical citations in the Alexandrian writers, Origen, Athanasius, and Cyril. The works of Origen, however, reveal the use of two types of Biblical text. When this was first pointed out (as it was in 1924 by B. H. Streeter in *The Four Gospels*), it was thought that the year 231, in which Origen left Alexandria for Caesarea, marked the time when he exchanged the use of the Alexandrian type of text for the other, which was accordingly called Caesarean. It was later pointed out, however, that Origen may have used this second type of text EVEN BEFORE HE LEFT ALEXANDRIA; and that he certainly used the Alexandrian type of text for a time after he went to Caesarea. Then, when the Chester Beatty papyri were discovered and studied, it appeared that they, too, constituted a witness for the New Testament text which Streeter had called Caesarean, so that this text was current in Egypt in the first half of the third century – that is to say, in the time of Origen. But WHEREVER IT ORIGNINATED, THIS TEXT WAS CERTAINLY USED AT CAESAREA, AND RADIATED FROM THERE, AND IT MAY CONTINUE TO BE CALLED THE CAESAREAN TEXT.[540]

---

538 Ibid.

539 Bruce M. Metzger, "The Caesarean Text of the Gospels," *Journal of Biblical Literature* 64 (1945): 483.

This remarkable observation further confirms our thesis – that the true neutral text type should be identified as the Caesarean text group. A change in terminology is thus called for in order to correctly identify what should be regarded as the standard by which all other text groups should be judged.

A chief witness to the Caesarean text type can be found in the beautiful tenth century codex Athous Laurae 184, now known as manuscript 1739.[541] Also, from the above citations we can see that scholars now feel that there is a direct trajectory from **P**^{75} through Vaticanus and to 1739 that shows remarkable agreement. From the critical notes in the margins that the scribe of this manuscript (who names himself Ephraim) copied, we learn some very important facts about this manuscript:

> (1) They contain no reference to any writer later than Basil of Cappadocia (A.D. 329-379).
>
> (2) A note on James ii. 13 refers to a manuscript written by Eusebius of Caesarea "with his own hand." This suggests the possibility that the original compilation was made in Caesarea, where, of all places, such a codex is most likely to have been preserved. It is obvious that this library would also possess copies of Origen's commentary.
>
> (3) A hint in the same direction may also be found in a note, unfortunately very much mutilated, on Gal. v. 15, which seems to refer to a manuscript written in prison. We are reminded of the colophon in the Codex Sinaiticus which refers to a manuscript written "in prison" by Pamphilus and preserved at Caesarea.
>
> Thus, ...there is a possibility that Ephraim, the scribe of Codex Athous Laurae 184, in the tenth century copied a critical edition of the New Testament which had been made in Caesarea from manuscripts and patristic writings preserved in the great library of Pamphilus.
>
> This evidence, linking up our MS. with Origen and Caesarea,

[540] F. F. Bruce, *The Books and the Parchments* (London: Pickering & Inglis, 1950), 175-6. Bruce goes on to say that "Its chief representatives [the Caesarean text type], in addition to the Chester Beatty papyri and the New Testament citations in some works of Origen, are Codices W and θ, some 20 minuscules (To wit: Codex I and allied minuscules [118, 131, 209, 1582], Codex 13 and allied minuscules (69, 124, 346, 543, 788, 826, 828, 983, 1689, 1709], and Codices 28, 565, and 700), and the Old Georgian version" (ibid.). Oddly enough, Bruce fails to mention manuscript 1739, which is a primary Caesarean witness.

[541] This manuscript contains the New Testament in the correct manuscript order from Acts to Philemon, with the unfortunate loss of the Gospels and the Apocalypse.

> is strikingly similar to that which has made it possible to identify the text of family θ as the Caesarean text. With little doubt the text of Romans in Codex 1739 is that which Origen used, while the text of the other epistles is based on an ancient copy which the compiler of the archetypal text, who seems to have had an intelligent and accurate interest in textual questions, identified as agreeing with the text used by Origen in his commentaries. Thus, considering the way in which our MS. and its archetype were made, codex 1739 may well represent the Origenian-Caesarean text of the epistles more accurately than any MS. in family θ represents the corresponding text of the gospels.[542]

Thus, based on this information it may be time that the so-called trajectory from P^{75}, Vaticanus, and 1739 be identified as the true Caesarean text type. It is ultimately derived from the great library of Caesarea and not from Alexandria in Egypt, as many scholars had originally believed. Eldon Jay Epp, further notes in this regard:

> As we have observed, $\mathbf{P}^{75}$ had an antecedent whose existence can be established even though that MS itself is not extant, and the same kind of text appears later in Codex Vaticanus. The result is that a genuine trajectory can be drawn from a very early (though non-extant) MS to P^{75}, and then to Codex Vaticanus, and on to later witnesses [especially 1739]. Moreover, since no canonical NT books were authored in Egypt, the texts had to travel to Egypt; hence, MSS copied anew in Egypt have trajectories reaching back to their antecedents in other parts of the very early Christian world [i.e., Caesarea].[543]

These other parts of the "early" Christian world, we submit, is the great library of Caesarea, where the canonical assistants, (i.e., the elders of the Apostle John) deposited the original canon for the safe keeping of the future church. It is because of the great Library of Alexandria and its professional scriptorium that scholars have surmised that many of the best manuscripts came from this area. In contrast, Caesarea has been considered virtually a hick town in comparison. But that is not the case.

The Library of Caesarea rivaled that of any great library of its day. Indeed, the noted New Testament scholar, Origen, left Alexandria to go to

[542] Lake, Kirsopp, J. de Zwaan and Morton S. Enslin, "Codex 1739" in *Six Collations of New Testament Manuscripts. Vol. 17 of Harvard Theological Studies* (Cambridge: Harvard University Press, 1932. Repr. New York: Kraus Reprint Co., 1969), 144.

[543] Eldon Jay Epp, "The Significance of the Papyri for Determining the Nature of the New Testament text in the Second Century: A Dynamic View of Textual Transmission" in *Studies in the Theory and Method of New Testament Textual Criticism*, ed. Eldon J. Epp and Gordon D. Fee (Grand Rapids: Eerdmans, 1993), 296.

Caesarea to do his most scholarly work there. Why? Well, for one reason, it was in Caesarea that the best manuscripts of the New Testament resided. Also, when Eusebius made his fifty Bibles for the Emperor Constantine, he used the resources of Caesarea, not Alexandria. And the Codex Vaticanus just may be one of those great Bibles.[544]

Base Text versus Eclecticism

TODAY MANY NEW TESTAMENT TRANSLATIONS rely on a scholarly reconstruction that is called eclectic. This is a process that selects from various sources readings that one believes is the original based upon a discipline called Textual Criticism. Obviously, such a procedure produces a text that is subjective, and therefore, controversial. One good outcome of textual criticism, however, is that it identifies and classifies various manuscripts into various text-types,[545] such as Alexandrian, Western, Caesarean, and Byzantine or Majority Text. Since there are so many New Testament manuscripts extant, and no manuscript is free from what is called scribal error, then it is natural to try to identify these errors and eradicate them from the text. But how does one do this? Ah, therein lies the rub, for no matter what approach is taken, in the end there cannot be an eclectic text that is in itself free from the error of subjective manipulation. We note that texts, such as the Nestle-Aland text and the United Bible Society's text, continually go through revisions in a kind of evolutionary process that is becoming more estranged from the Vaticanus text cluster. P. W. Comfort remarks in this regard:

> There is another disturbing element in NA26. In an effort to make NA26 different from the Westcott and Hort text, the editors rejected nearly 400 readings supported by B that were previously included in the twenty-fifth edition of the Nestle text. What is noticeable about NA26 is that the formation of this edition was more influenced by the praxis

[544] Again, on this see T. C. Skeat, "The Codex Sinaiticus, The Codex Vaticanus, and Constantine." *Journal of Theological Studies* 50 (1999): 583-625. See also Günther Zuntz, *The Text of the Epistles: A Disquisition upon the Corpus Paulinum.* (London: The British Academy, 1953). This important work includes a large section on manuscript 1739, its ancestry, and its relationship to **P**[46] and B, as well as observations about its relation to Origen. His conclusion was that "the archetypal *Corpus [Paulinum]* was produced about the year of A.D. 100" (279).

[545] Eldon Jay Epp, "Issues in New Testament Textual Criticism," in *Rethinking New Testament Textual Criticsim.* (Grand Rapids, Baker Academic, 2002), 35, prefers the term *Textual clusters.*

of eclecticism than the preference for documentation.[546]

The eclectic method places textual critics in an esoteric position of deciding which readings represent the original and discarding the rest. However, it is now being observed that this method is breaking down by bias on the part of textual critics rather than on purely professional criteria. Although Dr. Comfort advocates the papyrus supported readings as a means to obtaining the original text, he is fully aware that the eclectic method used by the Alands forces them to make internal judgements which "often took precedence over external evidence and there was a conscious movement away from Westcott and Hort."[547]

This same criticism could be lodged against Comfort's method as well. For instance, even if one were to attempt an unbiased eclectic approach based upon the earliest papyri, clear cut decisions are not always apparent. Here's an example. In 1 Peter 2:21 there is a textual variation in the verse as to whether Christ "suffered" for sins or "died" for sins. The first reading is supported by $\mathbf{P}^{72}$, A, B, C, 33, 1739 and the second by $\mathbf{P}^{81}$ and א. So on one side we have an early papyrus and a great Uncial in opposition to another early papyrus and a great Uncial. Astonishingly, Dr. Comfort himself notes that "this creates the situation with $\mathbf{P}^{72}$ and B versus $\mathbf{P}^{81}$ and א in a virtual standoff."[548]

Also note that the "Majority Text" crusade is not supported in most early textual evidence and the entire movement is highly charged with more religious bias than scholarly discipline.[549] Indeed, the Textus Receptus[550] is derived from later recensions and is, from its very

---

546 Philip W. Comfort, *Quest*, 126.

547 Ibid., 127.

548 Ibid., 154.

549 For a good run-down of the entire movement, one should read Gordon D. Fee's "The Majority Text and The Original Text of the New Testament" in *Studies in the Theory and Method of New Testament Textual Criticism*, ed. Eldon J. Epp and Gordon D. Fee (Grand Rapids: Eerdmans, 1993), 183-208. See also Maurice A. Robinson, "The Case for Byzantine Priority," in *Rethinking New Testament Textual Criticsim.* (Grand Rapids, Baker Academic, 2002), 125-39, and "Response," idem, 141-50. Also, we should note another remark by Gordon Fee, ("The Theory and Method of New Testament Textual Criticism" [*Studies*, ibid., 12]), that seems pertinent here: "The papyri have generally confirmed [the] opinion as to the late character of the Byzantine text-type. One does find an occasional variant in the early papyri which supports the later text-type, but none of the early papyri is even remotely related to the Byzantine MSS." Such testimony should be fully weighed in evaluating a variant reading of a Byzantine text.

550 The terms "Textus Receptus" and "Majority Text" are often used interchangeably, even though the Textus Receptus is in reality a recension that was published in the work of the kinsmen Bonaventure and Abraham Elzevir, who said in their 1633 edition, "Textum ergo habes, nunc ab omnibus receptum" -- "So [the reader] has the text which all now receive." See an interesting discussion of this online: http://www.skypoint.com/~waltzmn/TR.html.

inception, an eclectic text in its own right, since it too mixes together words and phrases from different manuscripts without any identification of its sources. One only has to read the literature that supports the TR and it is evident that the entire movement is more concerned with preserving false orthodox corruptions that support Trinitarianism, than relinquishing prejudice for the truth!

So which text should we use as a base text for translation? Based upon what we have already established the decision should be an easy one. First, codex Vaticanus from Matthew to Hebrews 9:13 (where it breaks off), then codex 1739 from Hebrews 9:14 to the end of Philemon, and finally codex Sinaiticus for the Book of Revelation. Coupled with this, all the different readings found within these three major manuscripts, along with the evidence of the papyri, especially P^{75} for Luke and John, should be noted.[551]

We should finally observe that the recently published four volume set of Matthew, Mark, Luke, and John entitled: *New Testament Greek Manuscripts: Variant Readings Arranged in Horizontal Lines Against Codex Vaticanus*,"[552] used the codex Vaticanus as the base text, printed with all significant text variants in full, identified by their manuscript witnesses.

Thus, the precedent is already under way. The codex Vaticanus is becoming once again accepted [at least in some enlightened scholarly circles] as the purest textual transmission that exists today. This being said, a new movement should thus be championed that breaks away from the false traditions of the so-called "Textus Receptus" and the eclectic abortion of the NA27, in favor of the true neutral text type – the Caesarean Text – that we have described herein.

Once we have a New Testament that is based upon this text, and the true manuscript order, then at last we will have a Bible that is the closest as we can get to the original New Testament that was deposited in the great library of Caesarea some nineteen centuries ago. Thankfully, the seeds have been sown and efforts will soon be underway to do just that.

---

[551] The Original Bible Project (see online: http://www.centuryone.org/obp.html) headed by professor James D. Tabor, had also wrestled with the question as to which base text to use in their translation. I had submitted my above proposal to them back in 1995, but Dr. Tabor decided to go with codex Sinaiticus because it represented a complete New Testament text.

[552] Edited by Reuben J. Swanson (Sheffield, England: Sheffield Academic Press, 1995).

BIBLIOGRAPHY

Abraham, William J. *Canon and Criterion in Christian Theology: From Fathers to Feminism*. Oxford: Clarendon, 1998.

Achtemeier, Paul J. *The Inspiration of Scripture: Problems and Proposal*. Philadelphia: Westminster, 1980.

———. "Some Things in Them Hard to Understand: Reflections on an Approach to Paul." *Interpretation* 38 (1984): 254-67.

———, ed. *Harper's Bible Dictionary*. San Francisco: HarperSanFrancisco, 1985.

———. "An Elusive Unity: Paul, Acts, and the Early Church." *Catholic Biblical Quarterly* 48 (1986): 1-26.

———. *The Quest for Unity in the New Testament Church*. Philadelphia: Fortress, 1987.

Achtemeier, Paul J., Joel B. Green, Marianne Meye Thompson, eds. *Introducing the New Testament: Its Literature and Theology*. Grand Rapids: Eerdmans, 2001.

Ackroyd, Peter R. "Original Text and Canonical Text." *Union Seminary Quarterly Review* 32 (1977): 166-73.

———. "The Open Canon." Pages 209-24 in *Studies in The Religious Tradition of the Old Testament*. Edited by P. R. Ackroyd. London: SCM, 1987.

Africanus, Sextus Julius (ca. 170 - ca. 240). *Chronography* (Fragments). Pages 130-8 in vol. 6 of *The Ante-Nicene Fathers*. Edited by A. Roberts and J. Donaldson. Grand Rapids, Mich.: Eerdmans, 1957.

Akenson, Donald H. *Surpassing Wonder: The Invention of the Bible and the Talmuds*. New York: Harcourt Brace, 1998.

Aland, Barbara, and Kurt Wachtel. "The Greek Minuscule Manuscripts of the New Testament." Pages 43-60 in *The Text of the New Testament in Contemporary Research*. Edited by Bart D. Ehrman and Michael W. Holmes. Grand Rapids: Eerdmans, 1995.

Aland, Kurt. *The Problem of the New Testament Canon*. London: Mowbray, 1962.

———. "The Greek New Testament: Its Present and Future Editions." *Journal of Biblical Literature* 87 (1968): 179-86.

Aland, Kurt, and Barbara Aland. *The Text of the New Testament: An Introduction to the Critical Editions and to the Theory and Practice of Modern Textual Criticism.* Translated from the German edition, *Der Text des Neuen Testaments*, Stuttgart: Deutsche Biblegesellschaft, 1981, by Erroll F. Rhodes. 2d. ed., Grand Rapids: Eerdmans, 1989.

Aland, Kurt, Matthew Black, Carlo M. Martini, Bruce M. Metzger, and Allan Wikgren, eds. *The Greek New Testament.* Münster: Institute for New Testament Textual Research. 2d ed., 1968.

Alexander, Loveday C. A. "Chronology." Pages 115-23 in *Dictionary of Paul and His Letters.* Edited by Gerald F. Hawthorne, Ralph P. Martin, and Daniel G. Reid. Downers Grove, Ill.: InterVarsity Press, 1993.

Alexanian, Joseph M. "The Armenian Version of the New Testament." Pages 157-72 in *The Text of the New Testament in Contemporary Research.* Edited by Bart D. Ehrman and Michael W. Holmes. Grand Rapids: Eerdmans, 1995.

Alford, Henry. *The Greek Testament; with a critically revised Text, a digest of various readings, marginal references to verbal and idiomatic usage, Prolegomena, and a critical and exegetical Commentary. For the use of Theological Students and Ministers.* Vol. 1, containing the four Gospels. London, 1849; 2d ed., 1854; 3d ed., 1855; Vol. 2, containing the Acts of the Apostles, the Epistles to the Romans and Corinthians, 1852; 2d ed., 1855. Vol. 3, containing Galatians to Philemon, 1856. Vol. 4, containing Hebrews to Revelation, 1859 and 1860 (issued in two parts).

Allert, Craig D. "The State of the New Testament Canon in the Second Century: Putting Tatian's *Diatessaron* in Perspective." *Bulletin for Biblical Research* 9 (1999): 1-18.

Anderson, Charles P. "The Epistle to the Hebrews and the Pauline Letter Collection." *Harvard Theological Review* 59 (1966): 429-38.

The Ante-Nicene Fathers: Translations of the Writings of the Fathers down to A.D. 325. Edited by Alexander Roberts and James Donaldson. 10 vols. 1885-87. Rev. by A. Cleveland Coxe. Repr., Peabody, Mass.: Hendrickson, 1994.

Argyle, A. W. *The Cambridge Bible Commentary.* 4 vols. Edited by P. R. Achroyd, A. R. C. Leaney, and J. W. Pacher. Cambridge: Cambridge

University Press, 1963.

Aschough, Richard S. *What Are They Saying About the Formation of Pauline Churches?* Mahwah, New Jersey: Paulist Press, 1998.

Attridge, Harold W., ed. *The Formation of the New Testament Canon.* New York: Paulist, 1983.

———. "Christianity from the Destruction of Jerusalem to Constantine's Adoption of the New Religion: 70-312 C.E." Pages 151-94 in *Christianity and Judaism: A Parallel History of Their Origins and Early Development.* Edited by Hershel Shanks. Washington, D.C.: Biblical Archaeology Society, 1992.

Aus, D. E. "Paul's Travel Plans to Spain and the 'Full Number of the Gentiles' of Rom. XI 25." *New Testament* 21 (1979): 232-62.

Baarda, Tjitze. "The Syriac Versions of the New Testament." Pages 97-112 in *The Text of the New Testament in Contemporary Research.* Edited by Bart D. Ehrman and Michael W. Holmes. Grand Rapids: Eerdmans, 1995.

Bacchiochi, Samuele. *From Sabbath to Sunday: A Historical Investigation of the Rise of Sunday Observance in Early Christianity.* Rome: The Pontifical Gregorian University Press, 1977.

———. "Rome and Christianity until A.D. 62." *Andrews University Studies* 21 (1983): 3-25.

Bacon, Benjamin Wisner. "The Chronological Scheme of Acts." *Harvard Theological Review* 14 (1921): 137-66.

Baigent, M., Richard Leigh, and Henry Lincoln. *The Holy Blood and the Holy Grail.* New York: Delacorte, 1982.

Balla, Peter. "Evidence for an Early Christian Canon (Second and Third Century)." Pages 372-385 in *The Canon Debate: On the Origins and Formation of the Bible.* Edited by Lee Martin McDonald and James A. Sanders. Peabody, Mass.: Hendrickson, 2002.

Balz, Horst, and Gerhard Schneider, eds. *Exegetical Dictionary of the New Testament.* 3 vols. Grand Rapids, Mich.: Eerdmans, 1991-94.

Barclay, William. *The Master's Men.* Nashville, Tenn.: Abingdon, 1959.

Barker, Ethel Ross. *Rome of the Pilgrims and Martyrs.* London: Methuen, 1913.

Barnes, Arthur Stapylton. *St. Peter in Rome and His Tomb on the Vatican Hill.* London: Swan Sonnenschein & Co., Ltd., 1900.

———. *The Martyrdom of St. Peter and St. Paul.* London: Oxford University Press, 1933.

———. *Christianity at Rome in the Apostolic Age: An Attempt at Reconstruction of History.* London: Methuen, 1938.

Barnes, Timothy David. *Constantine and Eusebius.* Cambridge: Harvard University Press, 1981.

Baronius (Cardinal Cesare Baronio, 1538-1607). *Annales Ecclesiastici. Denuo Excusi et ad Nostra usque Tempora Perducti. Ab A. Theiner. Ejusdem congregationis Presbytero, sanctiorum tabulariorum Vaticani praefecto, etc., etc.* Originally published 1588. 37 vols. Paris: Bar-le Duc, 1864-1883.

Barnett, Paul William. *Is the New Testament History?* Sidney: Hodder & Stoughton, 1986.

———. *Is the New Testament Reliable?: A Look at the Historical Evidence.* Downers Grove, Ill.: InterVarsity Press, 1986.

———. *Bethlehem to Patmos: The New Testament Story.* Sidney: Hodder & Stoughton, 1989.

———. *Behind the Scenes of the New Testament.* Downers Grove, Ill.: InterVarsity Press, 1989.

———. *Jesus & the Rise of Early Christianity: A History of New Testament Times.* Downers Grove, Ill.: InterVarsity Press, 1999.

Barr, James. *Holy Scripture: Canon, Authority, Criticism.* Philadelphia: Westminster, 1983.

Barret, Charles Kingsley. *The Gospel of John and Judaism.* London: SPCK, 1975.

———. *The Gospel According to St. John.* Philadelphia: Westminster, 1978.

———. *The New Testament Background: Selected Documents.* London: SPCK, 1956. Rev. and enl. ed. San Francisco: HarperSanFrancisco, 1989.

———. *A Critical and Exegetical Commentary on the Acts of the Apostles.* 2 vols. Edinburgh: T&T Clark, 1994.

Barrick, W. B. "The Rich Man from Arimathea (Matt 27:57-60) and 1QIsa^2." *Journal of Biblical Literature* 96 (1977): 235-39.

Barton, John. *The Spirit and the Letter: Studies in the Biblical Canon.* London: SPCK, 1997.

———. *Making the Christian Bible*. Oxford: Oxford University Press, 1998.

———. "Marcion Revisited." Pages 341-354 in *The Canon Debate: On the Origins and Formation of the Bible*. Edited by Lee Martin McDonald and James A. Sanders. Peabody, Mass.: Hendrickson, 2002.

Bassler, Jouette M. "Grace: Probing the Limits." *Interpretation* 57 (2003): 24-33.

Bauckham, Richard. "The *Acts of Paul* As a Sequel to Acts." Pages 105-52 in *The Book of Acts in Its Ancient Literary Setting*. Edited by Bruce W. Winter and Andrew D. Clarke. Vol. 1 of *The Book of Acts in Its First Century Setting*. Edited by Bruce W. Winter. Grand Rapids: Eerdmans, 1993.

———. "James and Jesus." Pages 100-137 in *The Brother of Jesus: James the Just and His Mission*. Edited by Bruce Chilton and Jacob Neusner. Louisville: Westminster John Knox Press, 2001.

Bauer, Walter. *Orthodoxy and Heresy in Earliest Christianity*. 2d ed. Edited by Robert A. Kraft and Gerhard Krodel. Translated by the Philadelphia Seminar on Christian Origins. Mifflintown, Penn.: Sigler Press, 1971.

Baxter, Margaret. *The Formation of the Christian Scriptures*. Philadelphia: Westminster, 1988.

Beare, G. W. "Canon of the NT." Pages 520-32 in vol. 1 of *Interpreter's Dictionary of the Bible*. Edited by George Arthur Buttrick, Thomas Samuel Kepler, John Knox, Herbert Gordon May, Samuel Terrien and Emory Stevens Bucke. 4 vols. Nashville: Abingdon, 1962.

Bede (The Venerable of Jarrow, 673-735). *The Ecclesiastical History of the English Nation*. Translated by J. A. Giles. London: Dent/Everyman, 1970.

Bell, Albert A., Jr. "The Date of John's Apocalypse. The Evidence of Some Roman Historians Reconsidered." *New Testament Studies* 10 (1977-78): 93-102.

———. *Exploring the New Testament World: An Illustrated Guide to the World of Jesus and the First Christians*. Nashville: Thomas Nelson, 1999.

Benedictine Monks of St. Augustine's Abbey, Ramsgate. *The Book of Saints. A Dictionary of Servants of God Canonized by the Catholic Church: Extracted from the Roman & Other Martyrologies*. London: A & C Black, 1921.

Benko, Stephen. "The Edict of Claudius of A.D. 49 and the Instigator Chrestus." *Theologische Zeitschrift* 25 (1969): 407-18.

———. *Pagan Rome and the Early Christians*. Bloomington, Ind.: Indiana University Press, 1986.

Benoit, P. "La deuxième visite de Saint Paul à Jerusalem." *Biblica* 40 (1959): 778-92.

Bercot, David. *A Dictionary of Early Christian Beliefs*. Peabody, Mass.: Hendrickson, 1998.

Best, Ernest. "Scripture, Tradition and the Canon of the New Testament." *Bulletin of the John Rylands University Library of Manchester* 61 (1979): 258-89.

———. "Review of R. Jewett, Dating Paul's Life." *Scottish Journal of Theology* 33 (1980): 487-8.

Bettenson, Henry, ed. *Documents of the Christian Church*. 2d ed. London: Oxford University Press, 1963.

Beyer, David W. "Josephus Reexamined: Unraveling the Twenty-Second Year of Tiberius." Pages 85-96 in *Chronos, Kairos, Christos II: Chronological, Nativity, and Religious Studies In Memory of Ray Summers*. Edited by E. Jerry Vardaman. Macon, Ga.: Mercer University Press, 1998.

Bickerman, Elias J. *Chronology of the Ancient World: Aspects of Greek and Roman Life*. Edited by H. H. Scullard. Ithaca, N. Y.: Cornell University Press, 1968.

Beinert, W. A. "The Picture of the Apostle in Early Christian Tradition." Pages 5-27 in vol. 2 of *New Testament Apocrypha*. Edited by Wilhelm Schneemelcher. English translation edited by R. McL. Wilson. 2 vols. Philadelphia: Westminster, 1965.

Birdsall, J. Neville. "The New Testament Text." Pages 308-77 in vol. 1 of *The Cambridge History of the Bible*. Edited by P. R. Ackroyd and C. F. Evans. Cambridge: Cambridge University Press, 1979.

———. "The Georgian Version of the New Testament." Pages 173-88 in *The Text of the New Testament in Contemporary Research*. Edited by Bart D. Ehrman and Michael W. Holmes. Grand Rapids: Eerdmans, 1995.

Black, David Alan, ed. *Rethinking New Testament Textual History*. Grand Rapids: Baker, 2002.

Blackwood, Andrew W. "Paul, The Apostle." Pages 636-41 in *New 20th-Century Encyclopedia of Religious Knowledge*. Edited by J. D. Douglas. Grand Rapids: Baker, 1991.

Bligh, P. H. "The Pauline Chronology of John Knox." *Expository Times* 83 (1972): 216.

Blomberg, Craig L. "Where Do We Start Studying Jesus?" Pages 17-50 in *Jesus under Fire: Modern Scholarship Reinvents the Historical Jesus*. Edited by Michael J. Wilkins and J. P. Moreland. Grand Rapids: Zondervan, 1995.

Bloom, Harold. *The Western Canon: The Books and Scrolls of the Age.* New York: Harcourt Brace, 1994.

Blosser, Donald Wilford. "The Sabbath Year Cycle in Josephus." (A review of B. Z. Wacholder's 1973 article). *Hebrew Union College Annual* 52 (1981): 129-39.

Blowers, Paul M., ed. and trans. *The Bible in Greek Christian Antiquity*. Notre Dame, Ind.: University of Notre Dame Press, 1997.

Bock, Darrell L. "The Words of Jesus in the Gospels: Live, Jive, or Memorex?" Pages 73-100 in *Jesus under Fire: Modern Scholarship Reinvents the Historical Jesus*. Edited by Michael J. Wilkins and J. P. Moreland. Grand Rapids: Zondervan, 1995.

Bornkamm, Günther. *Paul, Paulus*. Translated from the German by D. M. G. Stalker. New York: Harper & Row, 1971.

Bournis, Archimandrite Theodoritos. *"I Was in the Isle of Patmos ..."* Athens: Alex. Matsoukis, 1992.

Bovon, François. "The Canonical Structure of Gospel and Apostle." Pages 516-27 in *The Canon Debate: On the Origins and Formation of the Bible.* Edited by Lee Martin McDonald and James A. Sanders. Peabody, Mass.: Hendrickson, 2002.

Bradley, K. R. "The Chronology of Nero's Visit to Greece AD 66/67." *Latomus* 37 (1978): 61-72.

———. "Nero's Retinue in Greece AD 66/67." *Illinois Classical Studies* 4 (1979): 152-7.

Brakke, David. "Canon Formation and Social Conflict in Fourth-Century Egypt: Athanasius of Alexandria's Thirty-Ninth *Festal Letter*." *Harvard Theological Review* 87 (1997): 395-419.

Brehm, H. Alan. "Reconstructing New Testament History: Ritschl Reconsidered." Pages 141-67 in *Chronos, Kairos, Christos II: Chronologi-*

cal, Nativity, and Religious Studies In Memory of Ray Summers. Edited by E. Jerry Vardaman. Macon, Ga.: Mercer University Press, 1998.

Bright, John. "Felix." Page 783 in vol. 2 of *Anchor Bible Dictionary.* Edited by David Noel Freedman. 6 vols. New York: Doubleday, 1992.

Brock, Sebastian P. "The Use of the Syriac Fathers for New Testament Textual Criticism." Pages 224-36 in *The Text of the New Testament in Contemporary Research.* Edited by Bart D. Ehrman and Michael W. Holmes. Grand Rapids: Eerdmans, 1995.

Bromiley, Geoffrey W., Everett F. Harrison, Roland K. Harrison. William Sanford LaSor, Edgar W. Smith, Jr., eds. *The International Standard Bible Encyclopedia.* Rev. ed. 4 vols. Grand Rapids: Eerdmans, 1979.

———. "Apostolic Age" Pages 195-98 in vol. 1 of *The International Standard Bible Encyclopedia.* Edited by Geoffrey W. Bromiley, et al., Rev. ed. Grand Rapids: Eerdmans, 1979.

Brown, Harold O. J. "The Inerrancy and Infallibility of the Bible." Pages 37-47 in *The Origin of the Bible.* Edited by Philip Wesley Comfort. Wheaton, Ill.: Tyndale, 1992.

Brown, Raymond E. *The Churches the Apostles Left Behind.* New York: Paulist Press, 1984.

Brown, Raymond E., Karl P. Dornfried, and John Reumann, eds. *Peter in the New Testament: A Collaborative Assessment by Protestant and Roman Catholic Scholars.* Minneapolis: Augsburg; New York: Paulist: Toronto: Paramus, 1973.

Brown, Raymond E., and John Paul Meier. *Antioch and Rome: New Testament Cradles of Catholic Christianity.* London: Geoffrey Chapman, 1983.

Brown, Raymond E., Joseph A. Fitzmeyer, and Roland E. Murphy, eds. *The New Jerome Biblical Commentary.* Englewood Cliffs, N. J.: Prentice Hall, 1990.

Bruce, Frederick Fyvie. *The Books and the Parchments.* London: Pickering & Inglis, 1950.

———. *The Acts of the Apostles.* London: Tyndale, 1951.

———. "Christianity under Claudius." *Bulletin of the John Rylands University Library of Manchester* 44 (1961/62): 309-26.

———. *New Testament History.* New York: Doubleday, 1971.

———. "Acts of the Apostles." Pages 33-47 in vol. 1 of *The International*

Standard Bible Encyclopedia. Edited by Geoffrey W. Bromiley, et al. Rev. ed. Grand Rapids: Eerdmans, 1979.

———. *Peter, Stephen, James, and John*. Grand Rapids: Eerdmans, 1980.

———. *The Epistle of Paul to the Romans*. Grand Rapids, Eerdmans, 1982.

———. "Some Thoughts on the Beginning of the New Testament Canon." *Bulletin of the John Rylands University Library of Manchester* 65 (1983): 37-60.

———. "Chronological Questions in the Acts of the Apostles." *Bulletin of the John Rylands University Library of Manchester* 68 (1986): 273-95.

———. *The Canon of Scripture*. Downers Grove, Ill.: InterVarsity Press, 1988.

———. *The Acts of the Apostles: Greek Text with Introduction and Commentary*, 3d ed. Grand Rapids: Eerdmans, 1990.

———. "Peter, The Apostle." Page 648 in *New 20th-Century Encyclopedia of Religious Knowledge*. Edited by J. D. Douglas. Grand Rapids: Baker, 1991.

———. "The Bible." Pages 3-12 in *The Origin of the Bible*. Edited by Philip Wesley Comfort. Wheaton, Ill.: Tyndale, 1992.

———. "Tradition and the Canon of Scripture." Pages 59-84 in *The Authoritative Word: Essays on the Nature of Scripture*. Edited by Donald K. McKim. Grand Rapids: Eerdmans, 1993.

Bullinger, Ethelbert William. *The Companion Bible: Being the Authorized Version of 1611 with the Structures and Notes, Critical, Explanatory and Suggestive and with 198 Appendixes*. London: Oxford University Press, 1913. Repr. London: Samuel Bagster & Sons, Ltd., 1969.

Bunson, Matthew. *A Dictionary of the Roman Empire*. New York: Oxford University Press, 1995.

Butler, Alban. *Lives of the Saints For Everyday In the Year*. New York: Benziger Brothers, Inc., 1878. Repr. Rockford, Ill.: Tan Books, 1995.

Butler, B. C. *The Originality of St. Matthew: A Critique of the Two-Document Hypothesis*. Cambridge: Cambridge University Press, 1951.

Cadbury, Henry J. *The Book of Acts in History*. New York: Harper, 1955.

Cadoux, Cecil John. "A Tentative Synthetic Chronology of the Apostolic Age." *Journal of Biblical Literature* 56 (1937): 177-91.

———. *The Early Church and the World.* Edinburgh: T&T Clark, 1955.

Caird, George Bradford. *The Apostolic Age.* London: Gerald Duckworth & Co., 1955.

———. "The Chronology of the New Testament." Pages 599-607 in vol. 1 of *The Interpreter's Dictionary of the Bible.* Edited by George Arthur Buttrick, Thomas Samuel Kepler, John Knox, Herbert Gordon May, Samuel Terrien and Emory Stevens Bucke. 4 vols. Nashville, Tenn.: Abingdon, 1962.

Camden, William (1551-1623). *Remains Concerning Britain: Their Languages, Names, Surnames, Allusions, Anagramms, Armories, Moneys, Impresses, Apparel, Artillerie, Wise Speeches, Proverbs, Poesies, Epitaphs.* 1st ed. 1605. Written by William Camden Esquire, Clarenceux, King of Arms. 8 vols. London, at the Flowers de Luce: For Charles Harper and John Amery, 1674.

———. *Remains Concerning Britain.* ed. R. D. Dunn. Toronto: University of Toronto Press, 1984.

Campbell, Douglas A. "An Anchor for Pauline Chronology: Paul's Flight from 'The Ethnarch of King Aretas' (2 Corinthians 11:32-3)." *Journal of Biblical Literature* 121:2 (2002): 279-302.

Campenhausen, Hans von. *The Formation of the Christian Bible.* Translated by J. A. Baker. Mifflintown, Penn.: Sigler Press, 1997.

Capgrave, John (1393-1464). *The Chronicle of England.* Edited by the Rev. Francis Charles Hingeston. Published by the Authority of the Lord's Commissioners of Her Majesty's Treasury, under the Direction of the Master of Rolls. 1st ed. London: Longman, Brown, Green, Longmans & Roberts, 1858.

Capt, E. Raymond. *The Lost Chapter of Acts of the Apostles.* Thousand Oaks, Calif.: Artisan Sales, 1982.

———. *The Traditions of Glastonbury.* Thousand Oaks, Calif.: Artisan Sales, 1983.

Carlson, Stephen C. "Clement of Alexandria and the 'Order' of the Gospels." *New Testament Studies* 47 (2001): 118-125.

Carrington, Philip. *The Primitive Christian Calendar. A Study of the Making of the Marcan Gospel.* Vol. 1. Cambridge: Cambridge University Press, 1952.

Cassius Dio Cocceianus. *Dio's Roman History,* with an English translation by Ernest Cary on the basis of the version of Herbert Baldwin Foster. 9 vols. The Loeb Classical Library. London: William Heinemann, 1914-27.

Cave, William. *Antiquitates Apostolicae: or, The History of the Lives, Acts, and Martyrdoms of the Holy Apostles of Our Saviour, and the Two Evangelists, SS. Mark and Luke. Being a Continuation of Antiquitates Christanae, or the Life and Death of the Holy Jesus.* 3rd ed. London: R. Norton for R. Roylston, 1677.

Chadwick, Henry, ed. *Alexandrian Christianity.* Library of Christian Classics. Philadelphia: Westminster, 1954.

———. "St. Peter and St. Paul in Rome: The Problem of the memoria apostolorum ad catacumbas." *Journal of Theological Studies*, New series, 8 (1957): 31-52.

———. *Early Christian Thought and the Classical Tradition: Studies in Justin, Clement, and Origen.* New York: Oxford University Press, 1965.

———. *The Early Church.* New York: Penguin, 1967.

Charles, R. H., ed. *The Apocrypha and Pseudepigrapha of the Old Testament in English: With Introductions and Critical and Explanatory Notes to the Several Books.* 2 vols. Oxford: Clarendon Press, 1913.

Charlesworth, James H., ed. *The New Testament Apocrypha and Pseudepigrapha: A Guide to Publications with Excursus on Apocalypses.* Metuchen, N. J.: Scarecrow, 1987.

Chestnut, Glenn F. "Radicalism and Orthodoxy: The Unresolved Problem of the First Christian Histories." *Anglican Theological Review* 65 (1983): 292-305.

———. *The First Christian Histories: Eusebius, Socrates, Sozomen, Theodoret, and Evagrius*, 2d rev. ed. Macon, Ga.: Mercer, 1986.

Cheyne, T. K., and J. Sutherland Black, eds. *Encyclopedia Biblica.* London: Adam & Charles Black, 1914.

Childs, Brevard S. *The New Testament as Canon: An Introduction.* Philadelphia: Fortress, 1979.

Chilton, Bruce. "James in Relation to Peter, Paul, and the Remembrance of Jesus." Pages 138-60 in *The Brother of Jesus: James the Just and His Mission.* Edited by Bruce Chilton and Jacob Neusner. Louisville: Westminster John Knox Press, 2001.

Chilton, Bruce, and Jacob Neusner, eds. *The Brother of Jesus: James the Just and His Mission.* Louisville: Westminster John Knox Press, 2001.

Chisholm, Hugh, ed. *Encyclopedia Britannica.* 11th ed. 29 vols. New York: The Encyclopedia Britannica Co., 1910.

Clarke, Kent D. "Original Text or Canonical Text? Questioning the Shape of the New Testament We Translate." Pages 281-322 in *Issues in Biblical Translation: Responses to Eugene A. Nida.* Edited by S. E. Porter and R. Hess. Journal for the Study of the New Testament: Supplement Series 173. Sheffield: Sheffield Academic Press, 1998.

———. "The Problem of Pseudonymity in Biblical Literature and Its Implications for Canon Formation." Pages 440-68 in *The Canon Debate: On the Origins and Formation of the Bible.* Edited by Lee Martin McDonald and James A. Sanders. Peabody, Mass.: Hendrickson, 2002.

Collet, Sidney. *The Scripture of Truth.* Edinburgh: Marshall, Morgan & Scott, 1955.

Collins, Adela Yarbro. "Apocalypses and Apocalypticism. Early Christian." Pages 288-92 in vol. 1 of *Anchor Bible Dictionary.* Edited by David Noel Freedman. 6 vols. New York: Doubleday, 1992.

Collins, Raymond F. *Introduction to the New Testament.* Garden City, N.Y.: Doubleday, 1983.

Colwell, Ernest C. *Studies in Methodology in Textual Criticism of the New Testament.* Grand Rapids, Eerdmans, 1969.

Comfort, Philip Wesley, ed. *The Origin of the Bible.* Wheaton, Ill.: Tyndale, 1992.

———. "Texts and Manuscripts of the New Testament." Pages 179-207 in *The Origin of the Bible.* Edited by Philip Wesley Comfort. Wheaton, Ill.: Tyndale, 1992.

———. *The Quest for the Original Text of the New Testament.* Grand Rapids: Baker, 1992.

———. "History of the English Bible." Pages 261-288 in *The Origin of the Bible.* Edited by Philip Wesley Comfort. Wheaton, Ill.: Tyndale, 1992.

Comfort, Philip Wesley, and David P. Barrett, eds. *The Complete Text of the Earliest New Testament Manuscripts.* Grand Rapids: Baker Books, 1999.

Conybeare, Frederick Cornwallis. *The Origins of Christianity*. New York: University Books, 1958.

Conybeare, W. J., and J. S. Howson. *The Life and Epistles of St. Paul*. London: Longmans, Green & Co., 1889. Repr., Grand Rapids: Eerdmans, 1968.

Conzelmann, Hans. *History of Primitive Christianity*. Translated from the German by John E. Steely. Nashville, Tenn.: Abingdon, 1976.

Craig, Clarence Tucker. *The Beginning of Christianity*. New York: Abingdon-Cokesbury Press, 1943.

Craig, William Lane. "Did Jesus Rise from the Dead?" Pages 141-76 in *Jesus under Fire: Modern Scholarship Reinvents the Historical Jesus*. Edited by Michael J. Wilkins and J. P. Moreland. Grand Rapids: Zondervan, 1995.

Creasy, Sir Edward S. *History of England*. 2 vols. London: James Walton, 1869.

Cressy, R. F. [Hugh Paulinus, afterward] Serenus (of the Holy Order of S. Benedict). *The Church History of Brittany, from the Beginning of Christianity to the Norman Conquest under Roman Governors, British Kings, The English Saxon Heptarchy, The English — Saxon (and Danish) Monarchy*. Rouen, France: Printed for the Author, 1668.

Crooks, George B., and John F. Hurst, eds. *Library of Biblical and Theological Literature*. 8 vol. New York: Eaton and Mains, 1900.

Crossan, John Dominic. *The Birth of Christianity: Discovering What Happened in the Years Immediately after the Execution of Jesus*. San Francisco: HarperSanFrancisco, 1998.

Cruttwell, Charles Thomas. *A Literary History of Early Christianity*. 2 vol. London: Griffin & Co., 1893.

Cullmann, Oscar. *Peter: Disciple, Apostle, Martyr*. Translated from the German by Floyd V. Filson. Philadelphia: Westminster, 1953.

———. *The Johannine Circle*. London: SCM, 1976.

Cunningham, Philip J. *Exploring Scripture: How the Bible Came to Be*. New York: Paulist, 1992.

D'Ancona, Matthew, and Carsten Peter Thiede. *Eyewitness to Jesus: Amazing New Manuscript Evidence about the Origins of the Gospels*. New York: Doubleday, 1996.

Danielou, Jean, and Henri Marrou. *The Christian Centuries*. London:

Darnton, Longman & Todd, 1964.

Davids, Peter H. "James's Message: The Literary Record." Pages 66-87 in *The Brother of Jesus: James the Just and His Mission.* Edited by Bruce Chilton and Jacob Neusner. Louisville: Westminster John Knox Press, 2001.

Davies, Edward. *Celtic Researches on the Origin, Traditions, and Language of the Ancient Britons; With some Introductory Sketches on Primitive Society.* London: Printed for author by J. Booth, 1804.

Davies, Philip R. "The Jewish Scriptural Canon in Cultural Perspective." Pages 36-52 in *The Canon Debate: On the Origins and Formation of the Bible.* Edited by Lee Martin McDonald and James A. Sanders. Peabody, Mass.: Hendrickson, 2002.

Davis, Raymond (Translation). *The Book of Pontiffs. (Liber Pontificalis). The Ancient Biographies of the First Ninety Roman Bishops to AD 715.* 1st ed. Liverpool: Liverpool University Press, 1989.

Deissmann, Adolf. *Paul: A Study in Social and Religious History.* Translated by William E. Wilson. 1st ed., 1912. 2d rev. and enl. ed., 1927. Repr., New York: Harper Torchbook, 1957.

Diodorus Siculus. *Diodorus of Sicily,* with an English translation by C. H. Oldfather and others. 12 vols. The Loeb Classical Library. London: William Heinemann, 1933.

Dockx, Stanislas J. "Chronologie de la Vie de Saint Paul depuis sa Conversion Jusqu'à son Séjour a Rome." *Novum Testamentum* 13 (1971): 261-304.

———. "Chronologique paulinienne de l'année de la grand collecte." *Revue Biblique* 81 (1974): 183-95.

———. "Chronologie de la vie de saint Pierre." Pages 129-46 in *Chronologies néotestamentaires it vie de l'église primitive: Recerches exégétiques.* Paris-Gembloux: Duculot, 1976.

———. "The First Missionary Voyage of Paul: Historical Reality or Literary Creation of Luke?" Pages 209-21 in *Chronos, Kairos, Christos: Nativity and Chronological Studies Presented to Jack Finegan.* Edited by Jerry Vardaman and Edwin M. Yamauchi. Winona Lake, Ind.: Eisenbrauns, 1989.

Dodds, E. R. *Pagan and Christian in an Age of Anxiety: Some Aspects of Religious Experience from Marcus Aurelius to Constantine.* New York: Norton, 1965.

Doig, Kenneth F. *New Testament Chronology.* San Francisco: EMText,

1991.

Dornfried, Karl Paul. "Chronology: New Testament." Pages 1011-22 in vol. 1 of *Anchor Bible Dictionary*. Edited by David Noel Freedman. 6 vols. New York: Doubleday, 1992.

Douglas, J. D., ed. *The New Greek-English Interlinear New Testament: A New Interlinear Translation of the Greek New Testament United Bible Societies' Fourth, Corrected Edition with The New Revised Standard Version, New Testament.* Translated by Robert K. Brown and Philip Wesley Comfort. Wheaton, Ill.: Tyndale, 1990.

———. *New 20th-Century Encyclopedia of Religious Knowledge.* Grand Rapids: Baker, 1991.

Drane, John W. "Review of R. Jewett, Dating of Paul's Life." *Journal for the Study of the New Testament* 9 (1980): 70-6.

Duff, Jeremy. "P^{46} and the Pastorals: A Misleading Consensus?" *New Testament Studies* 44 (1998): 581-2.

Duncan, George S. *St. Paul's Ephesian Ministry: A Reconstruction with Special Reference to the Ephesian Origin of the Imprisonment Epistles.* London: Hodder & Stoughton, 1929.

Dungan, David L. "The New Testament Canon in Recent Study." *Interpretation* 29 (1975): 339-51.

Dunn, James D. G. "Levels of Canonical Authority." *Horizons in Biblical Theology* 4 (1982): 13-60.

———. "Once More, Pistis Christou." In *Society of Biblical Literature 1991 Seminar Papers*, ed. Eugene H. Lovering, Jr., 730-44. Atlanta: Scholars Press, 1991.

———. *The Theology of Paul the Apostle.* Grand Rapids: Eerdmans, 1998.

———. "Pauline Theology." Pages 100-9 in *The New Testament Today.* Edited by Mark Allan Powell. Louisville: Westminster John Knox, 1999.

———. "Has the Canon a Continuing Function?" Pages 558-79 in *The Canon Debate: On the Origins and Formation of the Bible.* Edited by Lee Martin McDonald and James A. Sanders. Peabody, Mass.: Hendrickson, 2002.

Dupont, Jacques. "Notes sur les Actes des Apôtres; V, Chonologie Paulinienne." *Review Biblique* 62 (1955): 55-59.

Dyck, E. "What Do We Mean By Canon?" *Crux* 25 (1989): 17-22.

Edersheim, Alfred. *The Life and Times of Jesus the Messiah*. 13th ed. London: Longmans, Green & Co., 1884. Repr., Peabody, Mass.: Hendrickson, 1994.

Edmundson, George. *The Church in Rome in the First Century: An Examination of Various Controversial Questions Relating to Its History, Chronology, Literature, and Traditions*. Bampton Lectures for 1913; London: Longmans, Green, 1913.

Edwards, Ormond. *A New Chronology of the Gospels*. London: Floris Books, 1972.

———. *The Time of Christ: A Chronology of the Incarnation*. London: Floris Books, 1986.

Ehrhardt, A. A. T. *The Apostolic Succession in the First Two Centuries of the Church*. London: Lutterworth, 1953.

Ehrman, Bart D. *The Orthodox Corruption of Scripture. The Effect of Early Christological Controversies on the Text of the New Testament*. New York: Oxford University Press, 1991.

———. "The Text as Window: New Testament Manuscripts and the Social History of Early Christianity." Pages 361-79 in *The Text of the New Testament in Contemporary Research*. Edited by Bart D. Ehrman and Michael W. Holmes. Grand Rapids: Eerdmans, 1995.

———. *After the New Testament: A Reader in Early Christianity*. New York and Oxford: Oxford University Press, 1999.

———. *The New Testament: A Historical Introduction to the Early Christian Writings*. 2d ed. New York and Oxford: Oxford University Press, 2000.

Ehrman, Bart D., and Michael W. Holmes. *The Text of the New Testament in Contemporary Research: Essays on the Status Quaestionis*. Grand Rapids: Eerdmans, 1995.

Eisenman, Robert. H. *James the Brother of Jesus: The Key to Unlocking the Secrets of Early Christianity and the Dead Sea Scrolls*. New York: Viking Penguin, 1997.

Elder, Isabel Hill. *Celt, Druid and Culdee*. Foreword by Lord Brabazon of Tara. London: Covenant Publishing Company, 1973. Repr., Thousand Oaks, Calif.: Artisan Sales, 1990.

Elliott, J. Keith, ed. *The Apocryphal New Testament: A Collection of Apocryphal Christian Literature in an English Translation based on Montague R. James*. Oxford: Clarendon Press, 1993.

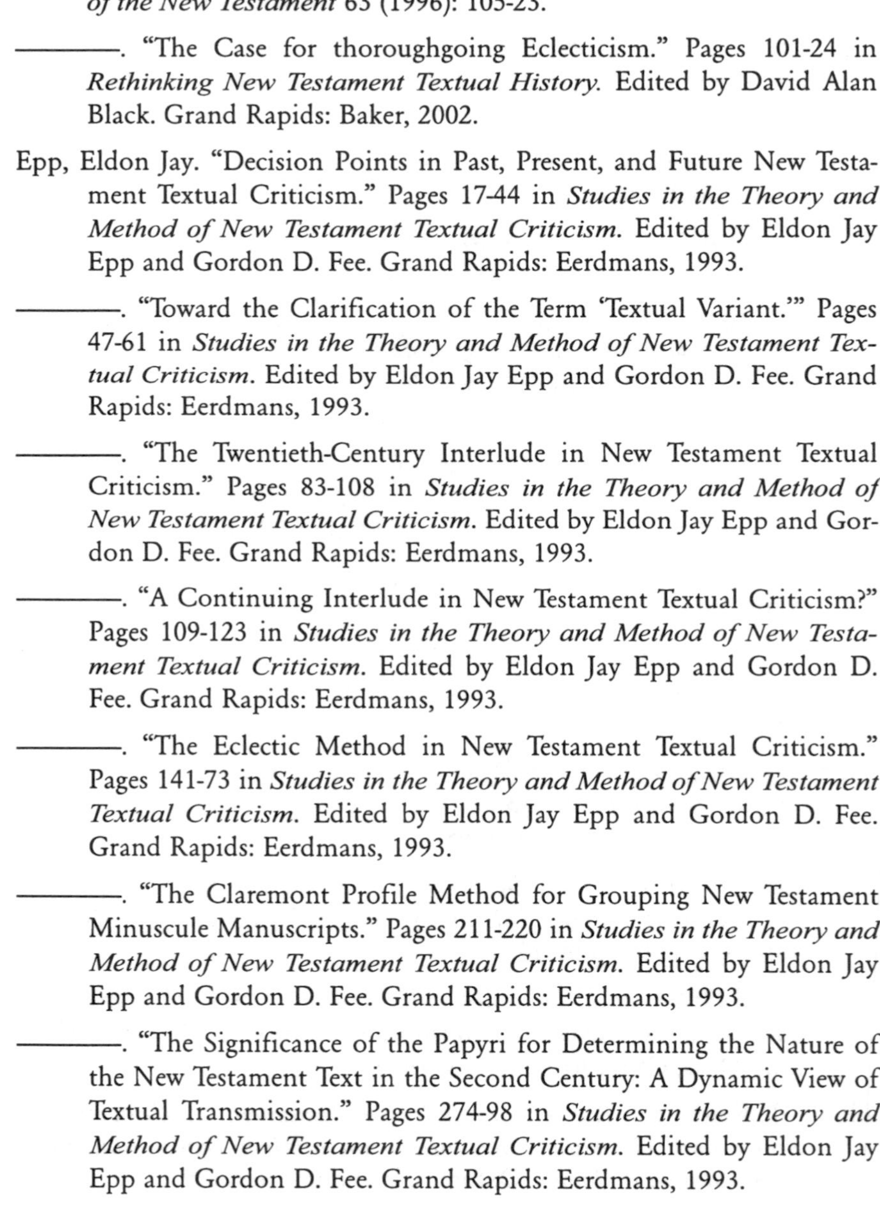

———. "Thoroughgoing Eclecticism in New Testament Textual Criticism." Pages 321-35 in *The Text of the New Testament in Contemporary Research.* Edited by Bart D. Ehrman and Michael W. Holmes. Grand Rapids: Eerdmans, 1995.

———. "Manuscripts, the Codex, and the Canon." *Journal for the Study of the New Testament* 63 (1996): 105-23.

———. "The Case for thoroughgoing Eclecticism." Pages 101-24 in *Rethinking New Testament Textual History.* Edited by David Alan Black. Grand Rapids: Baker, 2002.

Epp, Eldon Jay. "Decision Points in Past, Present, and Future New Testament Textual Criticism." Pages 17-44 in *Studies in the Theory and Method of New Testament Textual Criticism.* Edited by Eldon Jay Epp and Gordon D. Fee. Grand Rapids: Eerdmans, 1993.

———. "Toward the Clarification of the Term 'Textual Variant.'" Pages 47-61 in *Studies in the Theory and Method of New Testament Textual Criticism.* Edited by Eldon Jay Epp and Gordon D. Fee. Grand Rapids: Eerdmans, 1993.

———. "The Twentieth-Century Interlude in New Testament Textual Criticism." Pages 83-108 in *Studies in the Theory and Method of New Testament Textual Criticism.* Edited by Eldon Jay Epp and Gordon D. Fee. Grand Rapids: Eerdmans, 1993.

———. "A Continuing Interlude in New Testament Textual Criticism?" Pages 109-123 in *Studies in the Theory and Method of New Testament Textual Criticism.* Edited by Eldon Jay Epp and Gordon D. Fee. Grand Rapids: Eerdmans, 1993.

———. "The Eclectic Method in New Testament Textual Criticism." Pages 141-73 in *Studies in the Theory and Method of New Testament Textual Criticism.* Edited by Eldon Jay Epp and Gordon D. Fee. Grand Rapids: Eerdmans, 1993.

———. "The Claremont Profile Method for Grouping New Testament Minuscule Manuscripts." Pages 211-220 in *Studies in the Theory and Method of New Testament Textual Criticism.* Edited by Eldon Jay Epp and Gordon D. Fee. Grand Rapids: Eerdmans, 1993.

———. "The Significance of the Papyri for Determining the Nature of the New Testament Text in the Second Century: A Dynamic View of Textual Transmission." Pages 274-98 in *Studies in the Theory and Method of New Testament Textual Criticism.* Edited by Eldon Jay Epp and Gordon D. Fee. Grand Rapids: Eerdmans, 1993.

———. "The Papyrus Manuscripts of the New Testament." Pages 3-21 in *The Text of the New Testament in Contemporary Research.* Edited by Bart D. Ehrman and Michael W. Holmes. Grand Rapids: Eerdmans, 1995.

———. "Issues in the Interrelation of New Testament Textual Criticism and Canon." Pages 485-515 in *The Canon Debate: On the Origins and Formation of the Bible.* Edited by Lee Martin McDonald and James A. Sanders. Peabody, Mass.: Hendrickson, 2002.

———. "Issues in New Testament Textual Criticism: Moving from the Nineteenth Century to the Twenty-First Century." Pages 17-76 in *Rethinking New Testament Textual History.* Edited by David Alan Black. Grand Rapids: Baker, 2002.

Epp, Eldon Jay, and Gordon D. Fee. *Studies in the Theory and Method of New Testament Textual Criticism.* Grand Rapids: Eerdmans, 1993.

Eusebius Pamphilus, Bishop of Caesarea (260?-339). *The History of the Church from Christ to Constantine.* Rev. and ed. with a new introduction by Andrew Louth. Translated by G. A. Williamson. London: Penguin, 1965; revised edition, 1989.

———. *The Church History of Eusebius.* Pages 82-387 in volume 1 of *Nicene and Post-Nicene Fathers.* 2d series. Edited by Philip Schaff and Henry Wace. Peabody, Mass., Hendrickson, 1994.

———. *The Life of the Blessed Emperor Constantine.* Pages 481-559 in volume 1 of *Nicene and Post-Nicene Fathers.* 2d series. Edited by Philip Schaff and Henry Wace. Peabody, Mass., Hendrickson, 1994.

———. *The Oration of the Emperor Constantine, which He Addressed "To the Assembly of the Saints."* Pages 562-80 in volume 1 of *Nicene and Post-Nicene Fathers.* 2d series. Edited by Philip Schaff and Henry Wace. Peabody, Mass., Hendrickson, 1994.

———. *The Oration of the Eusebius Pamphilus in Praise of The Emperor Constantine.* Pages 581-610 in volume 1 of *Nicene and Post-Nicene Fathers.* 2d series. Edited by Philip Schaff and Henry Wace. Peabody, Mass., Hendrickson, 1994.

———. *Proof of the Gospel (Demonstratio Evangelica).* Edited and translated by W. J. Ferrar. London: SPCK, 1920. Repr., Grand Rapids: Baker, 1981.

———. *Preparation for the Gospel (Praeparatio Evangelica).* 2 Parts. Translated by Edwin Hamilton Gifford. Oxford: Clarendon, 1903. Repr., Grand Rapids: Baker, 1981.

———. *The Onamasticon by Eusebius of Caesarea: Palestine in the Fourth Century A.D.* Translated by G. S. P. Freeman-Grenville. Jerusalem: Carta, 2003.

Evans, Craig A. "Where Do We Start Studying Jesus?" Pages 17-50 in *Jesus under Fire: Modern Scholarship Reinvents the Historical Jesus.* Edited by Michael J. Wilkins and J. P. Moreland. Grand Rapids: Zondervan, 1995.

———. "Comparing Judaisms: Qumranic, Rabbinic and Jacobean Judaisms Compared." Pages 161-83 in *The Brother of Jesus: James the Just and His Mission.* Edited by Bruce Chilton and Jacob Neusner. Louisville: Westminster John Knox Press, 2001.

Faillon, M. *Monuments inédits sur l'apostolat de Sainte Marie-Madeleine en Provence, et sur les autres apôtres de cette contrée Saint Lazarre, Saint Maximin, Sainte Marthe, les saintes Maries Jacobé et Salomé, ouvrage orné d'un grand nombre degravavures it publié ... etc.* 2 vols. Paris: Montréjeau, Soubiron, 1847.

Farkasfalvy, Denis M. "The Early Development of the New Testament Canon." Pages 97-160 in *The Formation of the New Testament Canon* by William R. Farmer and Denis M. Farkasfalvy. Edited by Harold W. Attridge. New York: Paulist, 1983.

———. "The Ecclesial Setting of Pseudepigraphy in Second Peter and Its Role in the Formation of the Canon." *Second Century* 5 (1985-86): 3-29.

Farmer, William R. *The Synoptic Problem: A Critical Analysis.* Macon, Ga.: Mercer University Press, 1981.

———. *Jesus and the Gospel: Tradition, Scripture and Canon.* Philadelphia: Fortress, 1982.

———, ed. *New Synoptic Studies: The Cambridge Gospel Conference and Beyond.* Macon, Ga.: Mercer University Press, 1983.

———, ed. *The Gospel of Jesus.* Louisville, Ky.: Westminster John Knox, 1994.

———. "A Dismantling of the Church's Canon." Pages 35-55 in *The Gospel of Jesus.* Louisville, Ky.: Westminster John Knox, 1994.

———. "The Church's Gospel Canon: Why Four and No More?" Pages 1246-50 in *The International Bible Commentary.* Edited by William R. Farmer. Collegeville, Minn.: The Liturgical Press, 1998.

———. "Further Reflections on the fourfold Gospel Canon." Pages 107-13 in *The Early Church in Its Context: Essays in Honor of Everett*

Ferguson. Edited by J. Malherbe, F. W. Norris, and J. W. Thompson. Leiden: Brill, 1998.

———, ed. *Anti-Judaism and the Gospels*. Valley Forge, Penn.: Trinity Press, 1999.

———. "Reflections on Jesus and the New Testament Canon." Pages 321-340 in *The Canon Debate: On the Origins and Formation of the Bible*. Edited by Lee Martin McDonald and James A. Sanders. Peabody, Mass.: Hendrickson, 2002.

Farmer, William R., and Denis M. Farkasfalvy. *The Formation of the New Testament Canon: An Ecumenical Approach*. Edited by Harold W. Attridge. Introduction by Albert C. Outler. New York: Paulist, 1983.

Farrar, F. W. *The Early Days of Christianity*. New York: Funk & Wagnalls, 1883.

Fee, Gordon D. "Textual Criticism of the New Testament." Pages 3-16 in *Studies in the Theory and Method of New Testament Textual Criticism*. Edited by Eldon Jay Epp and Gordon D. Fee. Grand Rapids: Eerdmans, 1993.

———. "On the Types, Classification, and Presentation of Textual Variation." Pages 62-80 in *Studies in the Theory and Method of New Testament Textual Criticism*. Edited by Eldon Jay Epp and Gordon D. Fee. Grand Rapids: Eerdmans, 1993.

———. "Rigorous or Reasoned Eclecticism – Which?" Pages 124-40 in *Studies in the Theory and Method of New Testament Textual Criticism*. Edited by Eldon Jay Epp and Gordon D. Fee. Grand Rapids: Eerdmans, 1993.

———. "Modern Textual Criticism and the Synoptic Problem: On the Problem of Harmonization in the Gospels." Pages 174-182 in *Studies in the Theory and Method of New Testament Textual Criticism*. Edited by Eldon Jay Epp and Gordon D. Fee. Grand Rapids: Eerdmans, 1993.

———. "The Majority Text and the Original Text of the New Testament." Pages 183-208 in *Studies in the Theory and Method of New Testament Textual Criticism*. Edited by Eldon Jay Epp and Gordon D. Fee. Grand Rapids: Eerdmans, 1993.

———. "Codex Sinaiticus in the Gospel of John: A Contribution to Methodology in Establishing Textual Relationships." Pages 221-244 in *Studies in the Theory and Method of New Testament Textual Criticism*. Edited by Eldon Jay Epp and Gordon D. Fee. Grand Rapids:

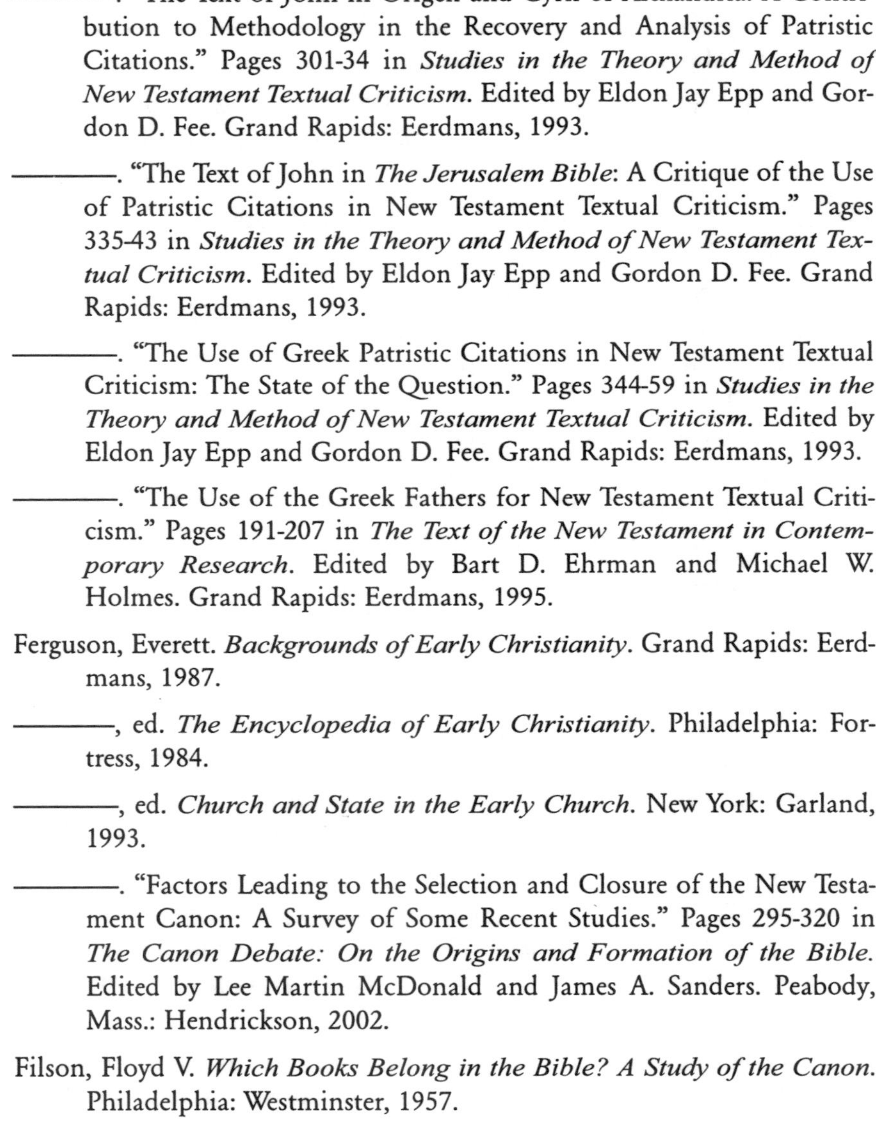

Eerdmans, 1993.

———. "P75, P66, and Origen: The Myth of Early Textual Recension in Alexandria." Pages 247-73 in *Studies in the Theory and Method of New Testament Textual Criticism.* Edited by Eldon Jay Epp and Gordon D. Fee. Grand Rapids: Eerdmans, 1993.

———. "The Text of John in Origen and Cyril of Alexandria: A Contribution to Methodology in the Recovery and Analysis of Patristic Citations." Pages 301-34 in *Studies in the Theory and Method of New Testament Textual Criticism.* Edited by Eldon Jay Epp and Gordon D. Fee. Grand Rapids: Eerdmans, 1993.

———. "The Text of John in *The Jerusalem Bible*: A Critique of the Use of Patristic Citations in New Testament Textual Criticism." Pages 335-43 in *Studies in the Theory and Method of New Testament Textual Criticism.* Edited by Eldon Jay Epp and Gordon D. Fee. Grand Rapids: Eerdmans, 1993.

———. "The Use of Greek Patristic Citations in New Testament Textual Criticism: The State of the Question." Pages 344-59 in *Studies in the Theory and Method of New Testament Textual Criticism.* Edited by Eldon Jay Epp and Gordon D. Fee. Grand Rapids: Eerdmans, 1993.

———. "The Use of the Greek Fathers for New Testament Textual Criticism." Pages 191-207 in *The Text of the New Testament in Contemporary Research.* Edited by Bart D. Ehrman and Michael W. Holmes. Grand Rapids: Eerdmans, 1995.

Ferguson, Everett. *Backgrounds of Early Christianity.* Grand Rapids: Eerdmans, 1987.

———, ed. *The Encyclopedia of Early Christianity.* Philadelphia: Fortress, 1984.

———, ed. *Church and State in the Early Church.* New York: Garland, 1993.

———. "Factors Leading to the Selection and Closure of the New Testament Canon: A Survey of Some Recent Studies." Pages 295-320 in *The Canon Debate: On the Origins and Formation of the Bible.* Edited by Lee Martin McDonald and James A. Sanders. Peabody, Mass.: Hendrickson, 2002.

Filson, Floyd V. *Which Books Belong in the Bible? A Study of the Canon.* Philadelphia: Westminster, 1957.

———. *A New Testament History: The Story of the Emerging Church.* Philadelphia: Westminster, 1964.

Finegan, Jack. "The Original Form of the Pauline Collection." *Harvard Theological Review* 49:2 (April, 1956): 85-103.

———. *Encountering New Testament Manuscripts: A Working Introduction to Textual Criticism*. Grand Rapids: Eerdmans, 1974.

———. "The Fall of Jerusalem in A.D. 70." *Biblical Illustrator* 11:3 (spring, 1985): 2-3, 9-12.

———. *Handbook of Biblical Chronology: Principles of Time Reckoning in the Ancient World and Problems of Chronology in the Bible*. 1st ed, Princeton: Princeton University Press, 1964. 2d ed. Peabody, Mass.: Hendrickson, 1998.

Finegan, Jack, and W. P. Armstrong. "Chronology of the New Testament." Pages 686-93 in vol. 1 of *The International Standard Bible Encyclopedia*. Edited by Geoffrey W. Bromiley, et al. Rev. ed. Grand Rapids: Eerdmans, 1979.

Fisher, George Park. *History of the Christian Church*. London: Hodder & Stoughton, 1896.

Fisher, Milton. "The Canon of the New Testament." Pages 65-78 in *The Origin of the Bible*. Edited by Philip Wesley Comfort. Wheaton, Ill.: Tyndale, 1992.

———. "Literature in Bible Times." Pages 97-108 in *The Origin of the Bible*. Edited by Philip Wesley Comfort. Wheaton, Ill.: Tyndale, 1992.

Fletcher, Ivor C. *The Incredible History of God's True Church*. No pages. Online: http://www.giveshare.org/churchhistory/fletcherindex.html.

Foakes-Jackson, Frederick John. *Peter, Prince of the Apostles: A Study in the History and Tradition of Christianity*. New York: George H. Doran, 1927.

———. "Evidence for the Martyrdom of Peter and Paul in Rome." *Journal of Biblical Literature* 46 (1927): 74-8.

Folkert, K. W. "The 'Canons' of Scripture." Pages 170-79 in *Rethinking Scripture: Essays from a Comparative Perspective*. Edited by M. Levering. Albany, N.Y.: SUNY Press, 1989.

Fox, Robin Lane. *Pagans and Christians*. New York: Alfred A. Knopf, 1987.

Freedman, David Noel, editor-in-chief. *The Anchor Bible Dictionary*. 6 vols. New York: Doubleday, 1992.

Frere, Sheppard S. *Britannia: A History Of Roman Britain*. London: Routledge & Kegan Paul, 1969.

Fuller, Thomas. *The Church History of Britain. From the Birth of Jesus Christ until The Year MDCXLVIII. [with] The History of The University of Cambridge since The Conquest.* 1st ed. London: Printed for John Williams, 1655.

Froelich, Karlfried. *Biblical Interpretation in the Early Church.* Philadelphia: Fortress, 1984.

Funk, Robert W. "The Enigma of the Famine Visit." *Journal of Biblical Literature* 75 (1956): 130-6.

———. "The New Testament as Tradition and Canon." Pages 151-86 in *Parables and Presence*. Philadelphia: Fortress, 1982.

———. "The Incredible Canon." Pages 24-46 in *Christianity in the 21st Century*. Edited by D. A. Brown. New York: Crossroad, 2000.

———. "The Once and Future New Testament." Pages 541-57 in *The Canon Debate: On the Origins and Formation of the Bible.* Edited by Lee Martin McDonald and James A. Sanders. Peabody, Mass.: Hendrickson, 2002.

Gager, John. *The Origins of Anti-Semitism: Attitudes Toward Judaism in Pagan and Christian Antiquity.* New York: Oxford University Press, 1983.

Gamble, Harry Y. *The New Testament Canon: Its Making and Meaning.* Guides to Biblical Scholarship. Philadelphia: Fortress, 1985.

———. "The Canon of the New Testament." Pages 201-43 in *The New Testament and Its Modern Interpreters*. Edited by Eldon J. Epp and G. W. MacRae. Atlanta: Scholars Press, 1989.

———. "The Pauline Corpus and the Early Christian Book." Pages 265-80 in *Paul and the Legacies of Paul.* Edited by William S. Babcock. Dallas: SMU Press, 1990.

———. "Canon. New Testament." Pages 852-61 in vol. 1 of *Anchor Bible Dictionary*. Edited by David Noel Freedman. 6 vols. New York: Doubleday, 1992.

———. *Books and Readers in the Early Church: A History of Early Christian Texts*. New Haven: Yale University Press, 1995.

———. "The New Testament Canon: Recent Research and the Status Questionis." Pages 267-94 in *The Canon Debate: On the Origins and Formation of the Bible.* Edited by Lee Martin McDonald and James A. Sanders. Peabody, Mass.: Hendrickson, 2002.

Gardner, Laurence. *Bloodline of the Holy Grail: The Hidden Lineage of Jesus Revealed.* Foreword by Prince Michael of Albany. Dorset, England, Boston, Mass., and Melbourne, Australia: Element Books, 1999.

Geer, Thomas C., Jr. "Analyzing and Categorizing New Testament Greek Manuscripts: Colwell Revisited." Pages 253-67 in *The Text of the New Testament in Contemporary Research.* Edited by Bart D. Ehrman and Michael W. Holmes. Grand Rapids: Eerdmans, 1995.

Geivett, R. Douglas. "Is Jesus the Only Way?" Pages 177-206 in *Jesus under Fire: Modern Scholarship Reinvents the Historical Jesus.* Edited by Michael J. Wilkins and J. P. Moreland. Grand Rapids: Zondervan, 1995.

Gentry, Kenneth L., Jr. *Before Jerusalem Fell: Dating the Book of Revelation.* Tyler, Tex.: Institute for Christian Economics, 1989.

Geoffrey of Monmouth (?-1155). *The History of the Kings of Britain.* Edited by L. Thorpe. London: Penguin, 1966.

Gibbon, Edward. *The History of the Decline and Fall of the Roman Empire.* 2 vols. The Modern Library. New York: Random House: n.d. Originally published 1776-88.

Gildas III (c.516-c.570). *The Ruin of Britain and Other Documents.* Translation of *De Excidio ie Conquestu Britanniae* by Michael Winterbottom. Chichester, England: Phillimore, 1978.

Gill, David W. J., and Conrad H. Gempf, eds. *The Book of Acts in its Graeco-Roman Setting.* Grand Rapids, Eerdmans, 1994.

Gillman, Florence Morgan. "James, Brother of Jesus." Pages 620-21 in vol. 3 of *Anchor Bible Dictionary.* Edited by David Noel Freedman. 6 vols. New York: Doubleday, 1992.

Gnuse, Robert. *The Authority of the Bible. Theories of Inspiration, Revelation, and the Canon of Scripture.* New York: Paulist, 1985.

Godwin, Francis (Bishop of Llandaff, 1601-1617). *A Catalogue of the Bishops of England since the First Planting of the Christian Religion to this Island, Together with a Briefe History of Theire Liues... Whereunto is Prefixed a Discourse Concerning the First Conuersion of Our Britaine vnto Christian Religion.* London: Printed for Thomas Adams, 1615.

Gontard, Friedrich. *The Chair of Peter: A History of the Popes.* Translated by A. J. and E. F. Peeler from the German ed. (*Die Päpste.* Munich: Verlag Kurt Desch GmbH, 1959). New York: Holt, Rinehart and

Winston, 1964.

Goodrich, Norma Lorre. *The Holy Grail.* New York: HarperCollins, 1993.

Goodspeed, Edgar J. *The Formation of the New Testament.* Chicago: University of Chicago Press, 1926.

Gorak, J. *The Making of the Modern Canon: Genesis and Crisis of a Literary Idea.* London: Athlone, 1991.

Goudoever, J. van. *Biblical Calendars.* 2d ed. Leiden: E. J. Brill, 1961.

Grabbe, Lester L. *Judaism from Cyrus to Hadrian.* vol. 1: *The Persian and Greek Periods.* vol. 2: *The Roman Period.* Minneapolis: Fortress, 1992.

Graham, William A. *Beyond the Written Word: Oral Aspects of Scripture in the History of Religion.* New York: Cambridge University Press, 1987.

Grant, Robert McQueen. *The Formation of the New Testament.* New York: Harper & Row, 1965.

———. *After the New Testament.* Philadelphia: Fortress, 1967.

———. "From Tradition to Scripture and Back." Pages 18-36 in *Scripture and Tradition.* Edited by Joseph F. Kelley. Notre Dame, Ind.: Fides, 1976.

———. *Early Christianity and Society.* New York: Harper & Row, 1977.

———. *Greek Apologists of the Second Century.* Philadelphia: Westminster, 1988.

———. *Jesus After the Gospels: The Christ of the Second Century.* Louisville, Ky.: Westminster John Knox, 1990.

———. *Heresy and Criticism: The Search for Authenticity in Early Christian Literature.* Louisville, Ky.: Westminster John Knox, 1990.

Gray, Andrew. *The Origin and Early History of Christianity in Britain from its Dawn to the Death of Augustine.* London: Skeffington & Son, 1897. Repr., London. Thousand Oaks, Calif.: Artisan Sales, 1991.

Green, H. B. "Matthew, Clement, and Luke: Their Sequence and Relationship." *Journal of Theological Studies* new series 40 (1989): 1-25.

Gregory, Caspar René. *Canon and Text of the New Testament.* International Theological Library. Edinburgh: T&T Clark, 1907.

Griffin, Miriam T. *Seneca: A Philosopher in Politics.* London: Oxford University Press, 1976.

———. *Nero: The End of a Dynasty*. New Haven: Yale University Press, 1984.

Groh, Dennis E. "Hans von Campenhausen on Canon: Positions and Problems." *Interpretation* 28 (1974): 331-43.

Guest, Edwin. *Origines Celticae (A Fragment) and Other Contributions to the History of Britain.* Facsimile print of the text and maps of the 1883 ed. Port Washington, N. Y.: Kennicat Press, 1971.

Gunther, John J. *Paul: Messenger and Exile: A Study in the Chronology of His Life and Letters*. Valley Forge, Penn.: Judson Press, 1972.

Guthrie, Donald B. *New Testament Introduction.* 3d ed. Downers Grove, Ill.: Inter-Varsity, 1970.

Habermas, Gary R. "Did Jesus Perform Miracles?" Pages 117-40 in *Jesus under Fire: Modern Scholarship Reinvents the Historical Jesus.* Edited by Michael J. Wilkins and J. P. Moreland. Grand Rapids: Zondervan, 1995.

Hagner, Donald A., and Murray J. Harris, eds. *Pauline Studies: Essays Presented to F. F. Bruce*. Grand Rapids: Eerdmans, 1980.

Hahneman, Geoffrey Mark. "The Muratorian Fragment and the Origins of the New Testament Canon." Pages 405-415 in *The Canon Debate: On the Origins and Formation of the Bible.* Edited by Lee Martin McDonald and James A. Sanders. Peabody, Mass.: Hendrickson, 2002.

Hall, Edward H. *Papias and His Contemporaries: A Study of Religious Thought in the Second Century*. Boston: Houghton, Mifflin & Co., 1899.

Hall, Stuart G. *Doctrine and Practice in the Early Church.* Grand Rapids: Eerdmans, 1992.

Halley, Henry H. *Halley's Bible Handbook: An Abbreviated Bible Commentary*. Grand Rapids: Zondervan, 1984. (Originally published in 1924).

Hammond, N. G. L., and H. H. Scullard, eds. *Oxford Classical Dictionary*. 2d ed. Oxford: Clarendon, 1970.

Haran, Menahem. "Archives, Libraries, and the Order of the Biblical Books." *Journal of the Ancient Near Eastern Society* 22 (1993): 51-61.

Hardinge, Leslie. *The Celtic Church in Britain.* London: SPCK, 1972.

Harrington, Daniel J. "Introduction to the Canon. Pages 7-21 in vol. 1 of

The New Interpreter's Bible. 12 vols. Nashville: Abingdon, 1994.

Harris, R. Laird. *Inspiration and Canonicity of the Bible: An Historical and Exegetical Study*. Grand Rapids: Zondervan, 1969.

Harris, William. "Why Did the Codex Supplant the Book-Roll?" Pages 71-85 in *Renaissance Society and Culture: Essays in Honor of Eugene F. Rice, Jr*. Edited by John Monfasani and Ronald G. Musto. New York: Italica, 1991.

Harrison, R. K. "Old Testament and New Testament Apocrypha." Pages 79-94 in *The Origin of the Bible*. Edited by Philip Wesley Comfort. Wheaton, Ill.: Tyndale, 1992.

Harnack, (Karl Gustav) Adolf von. *The Mission and Expansion of Early Christianity in the First Three Centuries*. Translated by James Moffat. 2 vol. New York: Putnam's, 1908.

———. *The Date of Acts and the Synoptic Gospels*. Crown Theological Library: New York: G. P. Putnam's Sons, 1911.

———. *Marcion: The Gospel of an Alien God*. Translated by John E. Steely and Lyle D. Bierma. Durham, N. C.: Labyrinth Press, 1990.

Hastings, James, ed. *A Dictionary of the Bible, Dealing with its Language, Literature and Contents*. 5 vols. New York: Scribner's, 1898-1904.

———. *Dictionary of Christ and the Gospels*. 2 vols. Edinburgh: T&T Clark, 1906.

Hatch, William H. P. "The Position of Hebrews in the Canon of the New Testament." *Harvard Theological Review* 29 (1936): 133-51.

Hawthorne, Gerald F., Ralph P. Martin, and Daniel P. Reid, eds. *Dictionary of Paul and His Letters: A Compendium of Contemporary Biblical Scholarship*. Downers Grove, Ill.: InterVarsity Press, 1993.

Hedrick, Charles W., and Robert Hodgson, eds. *Nag Hammadi, Gnosticism, and Early Christianity*. Peabody, Mass.: Hendrickson, 1986.

Hemer, Colin J. "Observations on Pauline Chronology." Pages 3-18 in *Pauline Studies: Essays Presented to F. F. Bruce*. Edited by D. A. Hagner and Murray J. Harris. Grand Rapids: Eerdmans, 1980.

———. *The Book of Acts in the Setting of Hellenistic History*. Edited by Conrad H. Gempf. Winona Lake, Ind.: Eisenbrauns, 1990.

Hengel, Martin. "Jacobus der Herrenbruder – der erste 'Päpts?'" in *Glaube und Escatologie: Festschrift für W. G. Kümmel zum 80. Geburtstag*. Edited by E. Grässer and O. Merk. Tübingin: J. C. B. Mohr (Paul Siebeck), 1985.

———. *The Pre-Christian Paul.* London: SCM Press, 1991.

———. *Paul Between Damascus and Antioch: The Unknown Years.* Louisville: Westminster John Knox, 1997.

———. *The Four Gospels and the One Gospel of Jesus Christ.* Harrisburg, Penn.: Trinity, 2000.

Hennecke, Edgar. *New Testament Apocrypha.* Edited by Wilhelm Schneemelcher. English translation edited by R. McL. Wilson. 2 vols. Philadelphia: Westminster, 1963, 1965. 2d ed. 2 vols. Louisville, Ky.: Westminster John Knox, 1991, 1992.

Henry, Carl F. H. "The Authority of the Bible." Pages 13-27 in *The Origin of the Bible.* Edited by Philip Wesley Comfort. Wheaton, Ill.: Tyndale, 1992.

Hermer, C. "The Name of Felix Again." *Journal for the Study of the New Testament* 31 (1987): 45-9.

Hill, Charles E. "Justin and the New Testament Writings." Pages 42-8 in *Studia Patristica* 30. Edited by E. A. Livingstone. Leuven, Belgium: Peeters, 1997.

———. "What Papias said about John (and Luke). A 'New' Papian Fragment." *Journal of Theological Studies* 49 (1998): 582-629.

Hinson, E. Glenn. *The Early Church: Origins to the Dawn of the Middle Ages.* Nashville, Tenn.: Abingdon, 1996.

Hirsch, Emmanuel. "Petrus und Paulus." *Zeitschrift für die neutestamentliche Wissenschaft* 29 (1930): 63-76.

Hodges, Zane C., and Arthur L. Farstad, eds. *The Greek New Testament According to the Majority Text.* 2d ed. Nashville: Thomas Nelson, 1985.

Hoever, Hugo. *The Lives of the Saints.* New York: Catholic Book Publishing Co., 1967.

Holmes, Michael W. "Reasoned Eclecticism in New Testament Textual Criticism." Pages 336-60 in *The Text of the New Testament in Contemporary Research.* Edited by Bart D. Ehrman and Michael W. Holmes. Grand Rapids: Eerdmans, 1995.

———. "The Case for Reasoned Eclecticism." Pages 77-100 in *Rethinking New Testament Textual History.* Edited by David Alan Black. Grand Rapids: Baker, 2002.

Hoover, R. W. "How the Books of the New Testament Were Chosen." *Bible Review* 9 (1993): 44-7.

Hophan, Otto. *The Apostles*. Translated from the German and edited by L. Edward Wasserman. Westminster, Md.: The Newman Press, 1962.

Horn, Siegfried H., and Lynn H. Wood. *The Chronology of Ezra 7*. Washington, D. C.: Review & Herald Publishing Association, 1973.

Howard, George. *Hebrew Gospel of Matthew*. 2d ed. Macon, Ga.: Mercer University Press, 1995.

Hughes, J. *Secrets of the Times: Myth and History in Biblical Chronology*. Journal for the Study of the Old Testament: Supplement Series 66. Sheffield: JSOT Press, 1990.

Hunt, Robert. *Popular Romances of the West of England; or, the Drolls, Traditions, and Superstitions of Old Cornwall*. Collected and Edited by Robert Hunt. 1st [and Second] Series. 1st ed. of each part, 2 vols. London: John Camden Hotten, 1865.

Hunter, A. M. *Introducing the New Testament*. London: SCM, 1957.

Hurst, L. D. "Apollos, Hebrews, and Corinth: Bishop Montefiore's Theory Examined." *Scottish Journal of Theology* 38 (1985): 505-13.

Hyldahl, N. *Die Paulinische Chronologie*. Leiden: E. J. Brill, 1986.

Jeffers, James S. *Conflict at Rome. Social Order and Hierarchy in Early Christianity*. Minneapolis: Fortress, 1991.

Jeremias, Joachim. *Jerusalem at the Time of Jesus*. Translated by F. H. and C. H. Cave. Philadelphia: Fortress, 1969.

Jewett, Robert. *A Chronology of Paul's Life*. Philadelphia: Fortress, 1979.

John of Glastonbury. *Cronica sive Antiquitates Glastoniensis Ecclesie*. Edited by James P. Carley. 2 vols. Oxford: British Archaeological Reports 46, 1978.

Johnson, Luke Timothy. "Luke-Acts, Book of." Pages 403-20 in vol. 4 of *Anchor Bible Dictionary*. Edited by David Noel Freedman. 6 vols. New York: Doubleday, 1992.

———. *The Acts of the Apostles*. Collegeville, Minn.: Michael Glazier/ Liturgical Press, 1992.

———. *The Real Jesus: The Misguided Quest for the Historical Jesus and Truth of the Traditional Gospels*. San Francisco: HarperSanFrancisco, 1997.

———. *The Writings of the New Testament: An Interpretation*. Minneapolis: Fortress Press, 1999.

Jones, G. D. B., and D. Mattingly. *An Atlas of Roman Britain*. London:

Oxford University Press, 1990.

Jowett, George F. *The Drama of the Lost Disciples.* London: Covenant Publishing Co., 1961.

Jung, Emma and Mary Louise von Franz. *The Grail Legend.* Translated by Andrea Dykes. Boston: Sigo, 1986.

Kalin, Everett R. "The New Testament Canon of Eusebius." Pages 372-85 in *The Canon Debate: On the Origins and Formation of the Bible.* Edited by Lee Martin McDonald and James A. Sanders. Peabody, Mass.: Hendrickson, 2002.

Kaufman, Peter I. *Church, Book, and Bishop: Conflict and Authority in Early Latin Christianity*. Boulder: Westview Press, 1996.

Keresztes, Paul. *Imperial Rome and the Christians*. Vol. 1. *From Herod the Great to about 200 A.D.* Lanham, Md.: University Press of America, 1989.

Keyser, John D. "1st Century Britain and the Gospel of Christ." No pages. Cited 23 Mar 2003. Online: http://www.hope-of-israel.org/1stcent.htm.

———. "When Did the Apostle Peter Meet His Death." No pages. Cited 23 Mar 2003. Online: http://www.hope-of-israel.org/petdeath.htm.

———. "Joseph of Arimathea and David's Throne in Britain." No pages. Cited 23 Mar 2003. Online: http://www.hope-of-israel.org/i000111a.htm.

Killen, W. D. *The Ancient Church: Its History, Doctrine, Worship, Constitution, Traced for the First Three Hundred Years*. Edited by John Hall. New York: Anson D. F. Randolph, 1883.

Kim, Young Kyu. "Paleographical Dating of P46 to the later First Century." *Biblica* 69 (1988): 248-57. (Also online: http://members.aol.com/egweimi/p46.htm).

King, Charles. "The Outlines of New Testament Chronology." *Catholic Quarterly Review* 139 (1945): 129-53.

Klijn, A. F. J. *Jewish-Christian Gospel Tradition*. Leiden: E. J. Brill, 1992.

Knox, John. "Fourteen Years Later: A Note on the Pauline Chronology." *Journal of Religion* 16 (1936): 341-49.

———. "The Pauline Chronology." *Journal of Biblical Literature* 58 (1939): 15-40.

———. *Marcion and the New Testament. An Essay in the Early History of the Canon*. Chicago: Chicago University Press, 1942.

———. *Chapters in a Life of Paul*. New York: Abingdon, 1950.

Koester, Helmut. "Apocryphal and Canonical Gospels." *Harvard Theological Review* 73 (1980): 105-30.

———. *Introduction to the New Testament*. Vol. 1, *History, Culture, and religion of the Hellenistic Age*. Vol. 2, *History and Literature of Early Christianity*. Philadelphia: Fortress, 1982. 2d ed., 1994, 1996.

———. *Ancient Christian Gospels: Their History and Development*. London: SCM, 1990.

Kraft, Robert A. "The Use of Computers in New Testament Textual Criticism." Pages 268-82 in *The Text of the New Testament in Contemporary Research*. Edited by Bart D. Ehrman and Michael W. Holmes. Grand Rapids: Eerdmans, 1995.

Kuchinsky, Yuri. *The Magdalene Gospel. A Journey Behind the New Testament*. Toronto: Roots Publishing, 2002.

Kümmel, Werner Georg. *Introduction to the New Testament*. Translated from the German by A. H. Mattill, Jr. Nashville: Abingdon, 1966.

———. "The Formation of the Canon of the New Testament." Pages 475-510 in *Introduction to the New Testament*. Edited by W. G. Kümmel. Translated by H. C. Kee. London, SCM, 1975.

Lagorio, Valerie M. "The Evolving Legend of St. Joseph of Glastonbury." *Speculum* 44:2 (April, 1971): 209-32.

Laing, Lloyd, Jennifer Laing, Stephen Johnson, and John Wacher. *Britain Before the Conquest: An Archaeological History of the British Isles 1500 BC - AD 1066*. 5 vols. London: Routledge & Kegan Paul, 1990.

Lake, Kirsopp. *The Text of the New Testament*. New York: Edwin S. Gorham, 1900. 6th ed., Revised by Silva Lake, London: Rivingtons, 1928.

———. "The Chronology of Acts." Pages 445-74 in volume 1 of *The Beginnings of Christianity*. Edited by F. J. Foakes Jackson and Kirsopp Lake. Grand Rapids: Eerdmans, 1966.

———. "Simon Cephas, Peter." *Harvard Theological Review* 14 (1921): 95-7.

Lake, Kirsopp, and Silva New, eds. *Six Collations of New Testament Manuscripts*. Vol. 17 of *Harvard Theological Studies*. Cambridge: Harvard University Press, 1932. Repr. New York: Kraus Reprint Co., 1969.

Lake, Kirsopp, J. de Zwaan and Morton S. Enslin. "Codex 1739." Pages 141-219 in *Six Collations of New Testament Manuscripts*. Edited by Kirsopp Lake and Silva New. Vol. 17 of *Harvard Theological Studies*. Cambridge: Harvard University Press, 1932. Repr. New York: Kraus Reprint Co., 1969.

Langer, William L., ed. *An Encyclopaedia of World History*. 5th ed. Boston: Houghton Mifflin, 1972.

Layton, Bently. *The Gnostic Scriptures*. Garden City, N. Y.: Doubleday, 1987.

Levick, Barbara. *Claudius*. New Haven: Yale University Press, 1990.

Lienhard, Joseph T. *The Bible, The Church, and Authority: The Canon of the Christian Bible in History and Theology*. Collegeville, Minn.: Michael Glazier/Liturgical Press, 1995.

Lietzmann, Hans. *Petrus und Paulus in Rom*. 2d ed. Berlin: W. de Gruyter, 1927.

Lightfoot, Joseph Barber (1828-1889), and J. R. Harmer. *The Apostolic Fathers. Revised Greek Texts with Introductions and English Translations*. 3 vols. London: MacMillan & Co., 1891.

————. *The Apostolic Fathers*. 2d ed. Revised and edited by Michael W. Holmes. Grand Rapids: Baker Book House, 1994.

Lingard, John. *The History & Antiquities of the Anglo-Saxon Church. Containing An Account of its Origin, Government.* London: C. Dolma, 1845.

————. *History of England, From the First Invasion by the Romans to the Accession of William and Mary in 1688.* 10 vols. London: J. C. Nimmo & Bain, 1883.

Linnemann, Eta. *Is There a Synoptic Problem: Rethinking the Literary Dependence of the First Three Gospels*. Translated by Robert W. Yarbrough from the original German edition, *Gibt es ein synoptisches Problem.* Grand Rapids: Baker, 1992.

————. *Historical Criticism of the Bible: Methodology or Ideology? Reflections of a Bultmanian Turned Evangelical.* Translated by Robert W. Yarbrough. Grand Rapids: Baker, 1998.

————. *Biblical Criticism on Trial: How Scientific is "Scientific Theology?"* Translated by Robert W. Yarbrough. Grand Rapids: Kregel, 2001.

Livingston, E. A., and F. L. Cross, eds. *The Oxford Dictionary of the Chris-*

tian Church. 3d ed. Oxford: Oxford University Press, 1997.

Loisy, Alfred Firmin. *The Birth of the Christian Religion*. London: George Allen & Unwin Ltd., 1948.

———. *The Origins of the New Testament*. London: George Allen & Unwin Ltd., 1950.

Luedemann, Gerd. *Paul, Apostle to the Gentiles: Studies in Chronology*. Foreword by John Knox. 2d ed. Translated from the German and edited by F. Stanley Jones. Philadelphia: Fortress, 1984.

———. *Opposition to Paul in Jewish Christianity*. Minneapolis: Fortress, 1989.

Lysons, Rev. Samuel. *Our British Ancestors: Who and What Were They?* Oxford: John Henry and James Parker, 1865.

MacDonald, Dennis R. *The Legend and the Apostle: The Battle for Paul in Story and Canon*. Philadelphia: Westminster, 1983.

Mack, Burton L. *Who Wrote the New Testament?: The Making of the Christian Myth*. San Francisco: HarperSanFrancisco, 1989.

———. *The Lost Gospel: The Book of Q and Christian Origins*. San Francisco: HarperSanFrancisco, 1993.

MacKinnon, Albert G. *The Rome of Saint Paul*. London: Religious Tract Society, 1930.

MacMullen, Ramsey. *Christianizing the Roman Empire A.D. 100-400*. New Haven: Yale University Press, 1984.

Martin, Ernest L. "Design and Development of the Holy Scripture." Ph.D. diss., Ambassador College Graduate School of Theology, 1965, 1971.

———. *Restoring the Original Bible*. Portland, Oreg.: ASK Publications, 1994.

———. *Secrets of Golgotha: The Lost History of Jesus' Crucifixion*. 2d ed. Portland, Oreg.: Associates for Scriptural Knowledge, 1996.

———. *The Star that Astonished the World*. Portland, Oreg.: Associates for Scriptural Knowledge, 1996.

Matlock, R. Barry. "'Even the Demons Believe': Paul and pistis christou." *Catholic Biblical Quarterly* 64 (2002): 300-318.

Mauck, John. *Paul on Trial*. Nashville: Thomas Nelson, 2001.

Mays, James L., ed. *Harper's Bible Commentary*. San Francisco: HarperSanFrancisco, 1988.

McBirnie, William Steuart. *The Search for the Twelve Apostles*. Wheaton, Ill.: Tyndale, 1973.

McDonald, Lee Martin. *The Formation of the Christian Biblical Canon*. Nashville: Abingdon, 1989, 2d ed. Peabody, Mass.: Hendrickson, 1995.

———. "Canon (of Scripture)." Pages 169-73 in *Encyclopedia of Early Christianity*. Edited by E. Ferguson. New York: Garland, 1990.

———. "The Origins of the Christian Biblical Canon." *Bulletin for Biblical Research* 6 (1996): 95-132.

———. "Identifying Scripture and Canon in the Early Church: The Criteria Question." Pages 416-39 in *The Canon Debate: On the Origins and Formation of the Bible*. Edited by Lee Martin McDonald and James A. Sanders. Peabody, Mass.: Hendrickson, 2002.

———. "Primary Sources for the Study of the New Testament Canon." Pages 583-4 in *The Canon Debate: On the Origins and Formation of the Bible*. Edited by Lee Martin McDonald and James A. Sanders. Peabody, Mass.: Hendrickson, 2002.

———. "Lists and Catalogues of New Testament Collections." Pages 591-598 in *The Canon Debate: On the Origins and Formation of the Bible*. Edited by Lee Martin McDonald and James A. Sanders. Peabody, Mass.: Hendrickson, 2002.

McDonald, Lee Martin, and Stanley E. Porter. *Early Christianity and its Sacred Literature*. Peabody, Mass.: Hendrickson, 2000.

McDonald, Lee Martin, and James A. Sanders, eds. *The Canon Debate: On the Origins and Formation of the Bible*. Peabody, Mass.: Hendrickson, 2002.

McEvedy, Colin. *The Penguin Atlas of Ancient History*. London: Penguin Books, 1967.

McGiffert, Arthur Cushman. *A History of Christianity in the Apostolic Age*. Edinburgh: T&T Clark, 1897.

McLaren, James S. "Ananus, James, and Earliest Christianity. Josephus's Account of the Death of James." *Journal of Theological Studies*, n.s. 52:1 (April, 2001): 1-25.

McKnight, Scot. "Who is Jesus? An Introduction to Jesus Studies." Pages 51-72 in *Jesus under Fire: Modern Scholarship Reinvents the Historical Jesus*. Edited by Michael J. Wilkins and J. P. Moreland. Grand Rapids: Zondervan, 1995.

McRay, John. *Paul: His Life and Teaching*. Grand Rapids: Baker, 2003.

Meade, David G. *Pseudonymity and Canon: An Investigation into the Relationship of Authorship and Authority in Jewish and Earliest Christian Tradition*. Grand Rapids: Eerdmans, 1986.

Meier, John Paul. *A Marginal Jew: Rethinking the Historical Jesus*. Volume 1: *The Roots of the Problem and the Person*. The Anchor Bible Reference Library. New York: Doubleday, 1991.

Metzger, Bruce Manning. "Seventy or Seventy-Two Disciples?" *New Testament Studies* 5 (1959): 299-306.

———. "Canon of Scripture." Pages 123-27 in *Hasting's Dictionary of the Bible*. 2d ed. Edited by F. C. Grant and H. H. Rowley. Edinburgh: T&T Clark, 1963.

———. *The New Testament: Its Background, Growth, and Content*. New York and Nashville: Abingdon, 1965.

———. *A Textual Commentary on the Greek New Testament*. New York and Stuttgart: United Bible Societies, 1971, 2d ed. 1994.

———. "Literary Forgeries and Canonical Pseudepigrapha." *Journal of Biblical Literature* 91 (1972): 3-24.

———. *The Canon of the New Testament: Its Origin, Development, and Significance*. Oxford: Clarendon, 1987.

———. "Canon of Scripture." Pages 149-51 in *New 20th-Century Encyclopedia of Religious Knowledge*. Edited by J. D. Douglas. Grand Rapids: Baker, 1991.

———. *Manuscripts of the Greek Bible: An Introduction to Palaeography*. New York: Oxford University Press, 1992.

———. *The Text of the New Testament: Its Transmission, Corruption, and Restoration*, 3d ed. New York: Oxford University Press, 1991.

Metzger, Bruce M., and Michael D. Coogan, eds. *The Oxford Companion to the Bible*. New York and Oxford, England: Oxford University Press, 1993.

Meyers, Eric M., and James F. Strange. *Archaeology, the Rabbis, and Early Christianity: The Social and Historical Setting of Palestinian Judaism and Christianity*. Nashville, Tenn.: Abingdon, 1981.

Migne, Jacques-Paul, ed. *Patrologiae Cursus Completus*, 382 vols. Paris: Garnier, 1928-1967.

Miller, J. W. *The Origins of the Bible: Rethinking Canon History*. Theological Inquiries. New York: Paulist, 1994.

Miller, Robert J., ed. *The Complete Gospels: Annotated Scholars Version.* San Francisco: HarperSanFrancisco, 1992.

Milne, H. J. M., and Theodore C. Skeat. *Scribes and Correctors of the Codex Sinaiticus.* London: British Museum, 1938.

Milner, W. M. H. *The Royal House of Britain: An Enduring Dynasty.* 1st ed. 1902. 15th ed. London: The Covenant Publishing Co., 1991.

Milton, John. *The History of Britain, that Part Especially Now call'd England. From the First Traditional Beginning, Continu'd to the Norman Conquest.* 2d ed. 8 vols. London by John Milton for John Martyn, 1677.

The Mishnah. Translated, with introduction and explanatory notes, by Herbert Danby. London: Oxford University Press, 1933.

Morgan, Richard Williams (1814-1899). *St. Paul in Britain or, the Origin of British as Opposed to Papal Christianity.* 10th ed. London: Covenant Publishing Co., 1948 (originally published in 1860).

————. *St. Paul in Britain.* Abridged ed. Repr. [from 1860 ed.], Thousand Oaks, Calif.: Artisan Sales, 1984.

Momigliano, A. D. *Claudius: The Emperor and His Achievement.* Cambridge: Oxford University Press, 1961.

————. "Herod of Judaea." Pages 316-339 in vol. 10 of *Cambridge Ancient History.* Edited by S. A. Cook, F. E. Adcock, and M. P. Charlesworth. Cambridge: At the University Press, 1966.

Moody, Dale. "A New Chronology for the New Testament." *Review and Expositor* 78 (1981): 211-31.

————. "A New Chronology for the Life and Letters of Paul." Pages 223-40 in *Chronos, Kairos, Christos: Nativity and Chronological Studies Presented to Jack Finegan.* Edited by Jerry Vardaman and Edwin M. Yamauchi. Winona Lake, Ind.: Eisenbrauns, 1989.

Morby, John E. *Dynasties of the World: A Chronological and Genealogical Handbook.* Oxford: Oxford University Press, 2002.

Morgan, R. L. "Let's Be Honest about the Canon: A Plea to Reconsider a Question the Reformers Failed to Answer." *Christian Century* 84 (1967): 717-19.

Morris, Leon. "Acts of the Apostles." Pages 4-5 in *New 20th-Century Encyclopedia of Religious Knowledge.* Edited by J. D. Douglas. Grand Rapids: Baker, 1991.

————. "Gospel and Gospels. Introduction." Pages 364-7 in *New 20th-*

Century Encyclopedia of Religious Knowledge. Edited by J. D. Douglas. Grand Rapids: Baker, 1991.

———. "Disciples of Jesus." Pages 112-128 in *Jesus of Nazareth: Lord and Christ. Essays on the Historical Jesus and New Testament Christology*. Edited by Joel B. Green and Max Turner. Grand Rapids: Eerdmans, 1994.

Moule, Charles Frances Digby. *The Birth of the New Testament*. London: Adam & Charles Black, 1976.

Mowry, Lucetta. "The Early Circulation of Paul's Letters." *Journal of Biblical Literature* 63 (1944): 73-86.

Murphy-O'Connor, Jerome. *St. Paul's Corinth: Texts and Archaeology.* Wilmington: Michael Glazier, 1983.

———. "Paul and Gallio." *Journal of Biblical Literature* 112, no. 2 (1993): 315-7.

———. *Paul the Letter-Writer.* Collegeville, Minn.: Liturgical Press, 1995.

———. *Paul: A Critical Life*. Oxford: Clarendon, 1996.

Murray, Robert. "How Did the Church Determine the Canon of the New Testament?" *Heythrop Journal* 11 (1970): 115-26.

Musurillo, Herbert A. *The Fathers of the Primitive Church*. New York: The New American Library, 1966.

———, ed. *The Acts of the Christian Martyrs.* Oxford: Clarendon, 1972.

Neusner, Jacob. *Jews and Christians. Judaism in the Beginning of Christianity*. London: SPCK, 1984.

———. *The Mishnah: A New Translation*. New Haven: Yale University Press, 1987.

———. *The Myth of a Common Tradition*. London: SCM, 1991.

———. "Introduction: What is a Judaism?" Pages 1-9 in *The Brother of Jesus: James the Just and His Mission*. Edited by Bruce Chilton and Jacob Neusner. Louisville: Westminster John Knox Press, 2001.

———. *Judaism When Christianity Began.* Louisville: Westminster John Knox Press, 2002.

Newman, B. "The Fallacy of the Domitian Hypothesis. Critique of the Irenaeus Source as a Witness for the Contemporary-Historical Approach to the Interpretation of the Apocalypse." *New Testament Studies* 10 (1962-63): 133-39.

Newman, Dorman. *The Lives and Deaths of the Holy Apostles.* London: Kings Arms in the Poultry, 1685.

Newman, R. C. "Daniel's Seventy Weeks and the Old Testament Sabbath-Year Cycle." *Journal of the Evangelical Theological Society* 16 (1973): 229-34.

North, J. Lionel. "The Use of Latin Fathers for New Testament Textual Criticism." Pages 208-21 in *The Text of the New Testament in Contemporary Research.* Edited by Bart D. Ehrman and Michael W. Holmes. Grand Rapids: Eerdmans, 1995.

North, Robert. "Maccabean Sabbath Years." *Biblica* 34 (1953): 501-15.

O'Connor, Daniel Wm. *Peter in Rome: The Literary, Liturgical, and Archeological Evidence.* New York and London: Columbia University Press, 1969.

Ogg, George. "Chronology of the New Testament." Pages 728-32 in *Peake's Commentary on the Bible.* Edited by Matthew Black and Harold H. Rowley. London: Nelson, 1962.

———. *The Chronology of the Life of Paul.* London: Epworth, 1968.

Orchard, Bernard. *Matthew, Luke & Mark.* 2d ed. Manchester, Eng.: Koina Press, 1977.

Orchard, Bernard, and Harold Riley. *The Order of the Synoptics: Why Three Synoptic Gospels?* Macon, Ga.: Mercer University Press, 1987.

Orr, James, and Geoffrey W. Bromiley. "Christianity." Pages 657-63 in vol. 1 of *The International Standard Bible Encyclopedia.* Edited by Geoffrey W. Bromiley, et al. Rev. ed. Grand Rapids: Eerdmans, 1979.

Osburn, Carroll D. "The Greek Lectionaries of the New Testament." Pages 61-74 in *The Text of the New Testament in Contemporary Research.* Edited by Bart D. Ehrman and Michael W. Holmes. Grand Rapids: Eerdmans, 1995.

Packer, J. I. "The Inspiration for the Bible." Pages 29-36 in *The Origin of the Bible.* Edited by Philip Wesley Comfort. Wheaton, Ill.: Tyndale, 1992.

Pagels, Elaine. *The Gnostic Scriptures.* New York: Random House, 1976.

Painter, John. *Just James: The Brother of Jesus in History and Tradition.* Minneapolis: Fortress Press, 1999.

———. "Who Was James? Footprints as a Means of Identification." Pages 10-65 in *The Brother of Jesus: James the Just and His Mission.* Edited by Bruce Chilton and Jacob Neusner. Louisville: Westminster John Knox Press, 2001.

Pansini, Francis David. *Our First Gospel: The Doctrinal Argument for Mark's Priority is Inadequate; The Traditional View of Matthew's Priority Remains in Possession.* Washington: Catholic University of America Press, 1946.

Parker, David C. "The Majuscule Manuscripts of the New Testament." Pages 22-42 in *The Text of the New Testament in Contemporary Research.* Edited by Bart D. Ehrman and Michael W. Holmes. Grand Rapids: Eerdmans, 1995.

———. *The Living Text of the Gospels.* New York: Cambridge University Press, 1997.

Parker, Matthew, Archbishop of Canterbury (1504-1575). *De Antiquitate Britannicæ Ecclesiæ, Et nominatim De Privilegiis Ecclesiæ Cantuariensis, atque de Archiepiscopis eiusdem LXX. Historia. Antehac non nisi semel, nimirum Lonini in dibus Ioannis Daii Anno M.D. LXXII. excusa: Nunc ver boni publici ergo reco.* Hanover, Germany: Typis Wechelianus, apud Claud. Marinium & hredes Ioannis Aubrii, 1605.

Parker, Pierson. *The Gospel Before Mark.* Chicago: University of Chicago Press, 1953.

Parvis, Merrill M., and Allen P. Wikgren, eds. *New Testament Manuscript Studies.* Chicago: The University of Chicago Press, 1950.

Pattingale, Jerry A. "Arimathea." Page 378 in vol. 1 of *Anchor Bible Dictionary.* Edited by David Noel Freedman. 6 vols. New York: Doubleday, 1992.

Patzia, Arthur G. "Canon." Pages 85-92 in *Dictionary of Paul and His Letters.* Edited by Gerald F. Hawthorne, Ralph P. Martin, and Daniel G. Reid. Downers Grove, Ill.: InterVarsity Press, 1993.

———. *The Making of the New Testament: Origin, Collection, Text & Canon.* Downers Grove, Ill.: InterVarsity Press, 1995.

Peddie, John: *Invasion: The Roman Conquest of Britain.* New York: St. Martin's, 1987.

Pelikan, Jaroslav. *The Riddle of Catholicism.* New York: Abingdon, 1959.

Perkins, Pheme. *Gnosticism and the New Testament.* Minneapolis: Fortress, 1993.

———. "Spirit and Letter: Poking Holes in the Canon." *Journal of Religion* 76 (1996): 307-27.

———. "Gnosticism and the Christian Bible." Pages 355-371 in *The Canon Debate: On the Origins and Formation of the Bible*. Edited by Lee Martin McDonald and James A. Sanders. Peabody, Mass.: Hendrickson, 2002.

Petersen, William L. *Tatian's Diatessaron: Its Creation, Dissemination, Significance, and History in Scholarship*. Leiden: Brill, 1994.

———. "The Diatessaron of Tatian." Pages 77-96 in *The Text of the New Testament in Contemporary Research*. Edited by Bart D. Ehrman and Michael W. Holmes. Grand Rapids: Eerdmans, 1995.

Petzer, Jacobus H. "The Latin Versions of the New Testament." Pages 113–130 in *The Text of the New Testament in Contemporary Research*. Edited by Bart D. Ehrman and Michael W. Holmes. Grand Rapids: Eerdmans, 1995.

Polydore Vergil. *Polydore Vergil's English History*. Edited by Henry Ellis. London: Camden Society, 1846. Repr. Dyfed, Wales: Llanerch, 1996.

Popkes, Wíard. "The Mission of James in His Time." Pages 88-99 in *The Brother of Jesus: James the Just and His Mission*. Edited by Bruce Chilton and Jacob Neusner. Louisville: Westminster John Knox Press, 2001.

Porter, Stanley E. "Joseph of Arimathea." Pages 971-2 in vol. 3 of *Anchor Bible Dictionary*. Edited by David Noel Freedman. 6 vols. New York: Doubleday, 1992.

———. "Pauline Authorship and the Pastoral Epistles: Implications for Canon." *Bulletin for Biblical Research* 5 (1995): 105-23.

Price, Robert M. *Deconstructing Jesus*. Amherst, N.Y.: Prometheus Books, 2000.

———. "Eisenman's Gospel of James the Just: A Review." Pages 186-97 in *The Brother of Jesus: James the Just and His Mission*. Edited by Bruce Chilton and Jacob Neusner. Louisville: Westminster John Knox Press, 2001.

Pritz, Ray A. "The Jewish Christian Sect of the Nazarenes and the Mishna." *Proceedings of the Eighth World Congress of Jewish Studies*, 1982, Division A:125-30.

Pritz, Ray A., A. F. J. Klijn, and G. J. Reinink. *Nazarene Jewish Christianity: From the End of the New Testament Period until Its Disappearance in the Fourth Century*. Jerusalem: Magnes Press of Hebrew University, 1995.

Pryce, John. *The Ancient British Church: A Historical Essay*. London:

Longmans, Green & Co., 1878.

Ramsay, William Mitchell, Sir. *St. Paul the Traveller and the Roman Citizen.* New York: Hodder & Stotten, 1903.

Reicke, Bo. *The New Testament Era: The World of the Bible from 500 B.C. to A.D. 100.* Translated by David E. Green from the German ed. *Neuetestementliche Zeitgeschichte.* Berlin: Adolpf Töpelmann, 1964. Repr. Philadelphia: Fortress, 1968.

———. *The Roots of the Synoptic Gospels.* Philadelphia: Fortress Press, 1986.

Riesner, Rainer. *Paul's Early Period: Chronology, Mission Strategy, Theology.* Translated by Doug Stott from the German ed. *Die Frühzeit des Apostles Paulus.* Tübingen: J. C. B. Mohr, 1994. Repr. Grand Rapids: Eerdmans, 1998.

Rist, M. "Pseudepigraphy and the Early Christians." Pages 75-91 in *Studies in New Testament and Early Christian Literature: Essays in Honor of Allen P. Wikgren.* Edited by D. E. Aune. Novum Testamentum Supplement 33. Leiden: Brill, 1972.

Roberts, L. G. A. *British History Traced from Egypt & Palestine and other Essays.* London: The Covenant Publishing Company, 1927.

———. *Drudism in Britain: A Preparation for the Gospel.* Repr., Readrunner Aeris, www.readrunneracerie.com, 2001.

Robbins, Gregory Allen. "'Fifty Copies of Sacred Writings' (*VC* 4.36): Entire Bibles or Gospel Books?" Pages 91-98 in *Studia Patristica* 19. Edited by E. A. Livingstone. Leuven, Belgium: Peetrs, 1989.

———. "Eusebius' Lexicon of 'Canonicity.'" Pages 134-41 in *Studia Patristica* 23. Edited by E. A. Livingstone. Leuven: Peetrs, 1993.

Roberts, C. H. "Books in the Greco-Roman World and in the New Testament." Pages 48-66 in vol. 1 of *Cambridge History of the Bible.* Edited by P. R. Ackroyd and C. F. Evans. Cambridge: Cambridge University Press, 1970.

———. *Manuscript, Society, and Belief in Early Christian Egypt.* New York/London: Oxford University Press, 1979.

Roberts, C. H., and Theodore C. Skeat. *The Birth of the Codex.* Oxford: Oxford University Press, 1983.

Robinson, J. Armitage. *The Glastonbury Legends: King Arthur and St Joseph of Arimathea.* Cambridge: Cambridge University Press, 1927.

Robinson, James M., ed. *The Nag Hammadi Library in English.* 3d ed. San

Francisco: HarperSanFrancisco, 1988.

Robinson, John Arthur Thomas. *Twelve New Testament Studies.* London: SCM, 1962.

———. *Redating the New Testament.* London: SCM, 1976.

Robinson, Maurice A. "The Case for Byzantine Priority." Pages 125-40 in *Rethinking New Testament Textual History.* Edited by David Alan Black. Grand Rapids: Baker, 2002.

Ropes, James Hardy. *The Apostolic Age in the Light of Modern Criticism.* New York: Charles Scribner's Sons, 1912.

Royse, James R. "Scribal Tendencies in the Transmission of the Text of the New Testament." Pages 239-52 in *The Text of the New Testament in Contemporary Research.* Edited by Bart D. Ehrman and Michael W. Holmes. Grand Rapids: Eerdmans, 1995.

Ryken, Leland. "The Bible as Literature." Pages 109-148 in *The Origin of the Bible.* Edited by Philip Wesley Comfort. Wheaton, Ill.: Tyndale, 1992.

Salmon, George. *A Historical Introduction to the Study of the Books of the New Testament: Being an Expansion of Lectures Delivered in the Divinity School at the University of Dublin.* London: John Murray, 1885. 2d ed. New York: E & JB Young & Co., 1889.

———. *Infallibility of the Church.* Grand Rapids: Baker, 1959.

Salway, Peter. *A History of Roman Britain.* Oxford: Oxford University Press, 1997.

Sanders, James A. "Spinning the Bible." *Biblical Research* (June, 1998): 22-29, 44-45.

Sanders, James N. "The Literature and Canon of the New Testament." Pages 676-82 in *Peake's Commentary of the Bible.* Edited by Arthur S. Peak, Matthew Black, and Harold H. Rowley. London: Thomas Nelson & Sons, 1962.

Sandmel, Samuel. *The First Century in Judaism and Christianity.* New York: Oxford University Press, 1969.

Schaff, Philip. *History of the Christian Church.* New York: Charles Scribner's Sons, 1858. Repr., Grand Rapids: Eerdmans, 1995.

Schaff, Philip, and Henry Wace, eds. (original editor Archibald Robertson). *Nicene and Post-Nicene Fathers.* Peabody, Mass.: Hendrickson, 1994.

Schiffman, Lawrence H. *Who Was a Jew? Rabbinic and Halakhic Perspectives on the Jewish — Christian Schism.* Hoboken, N. J.: Ktav, 1985.

Schmidt, Daryl D. "The Greek New Testament as a Codex." Pages 469-484 in *The Canon Debate: On the Origins and Formation of the Bible.* Edited by Lee Martin McDonald and James A. Sanders. Peabody, Mass.: Hendrickson, 2002.

Schnabel, Eckhard. "History, Theology, and the Biblical Canon: An Introduction to Basic Issues." *Themelios* 20 (1995): 16-24.

Schoeps, Hans-Joiachim. *Jewish Christianity: Factional Disputes in the Early Church.* Translated by Douglas R. A. Hare. Philadelphia: Fortress, 1969.

Schürer, Emil. *The History of the Jewish People in the Age of Jesus Christ.* 4 vols. Edited by Geza Vermes and Fergus Millar. Edinburgh: T&T Clark, 1973, 1978, 1986, 1987.

Schwartz, Daniel R. *Agrippa I: The Last King of Judea.* Tübingen: J. C. B. Mohr [Paul Siebeck], 1990.

Scott, Ernest Findlay. *The Literature of the New Testament.* New York: Columbia University Press, 1932.

Scrivener, Frederick Henry Ambrose. *A Plain Introduction to the Criticism of the New Testament,* 4th ed. by Edward Miller, 2 vol. London: George Bell & Sons, 1894.

Scullard, H. H. *From the Gracchi to Nero: A History of Rome from 133 B.C. to A.D. 68.* London: Methuen & Co., 1977.

———. *Roman Britain: Outpost of the Empire.* London: Thames & Hudson, 1979.

Seifrid, Mark A., and Randall K. J. Tan. *The Pauline Writings: An Annotated Bibliography.* Grand Rapids: Baker Academic, 2002.

Shedinger, R. F., "The Textual Relationship Between P^{45} and Shem-Tob's Hebrew Matthew." *New Testament Studies* 43 (1997): 58-71.

Sherwin-White, A. N. *Roman Society and Roman Law in the New Testament.* Oxford: Clarendon Press, 1963.

Shotwell, James T., and Louise R. Loomis. *The See of Peter.* Records of Civilization: Sources and Studies 7; New York: Columbia University Press, 1927.

Silva, Moisés. "Modern Critical Editions and Apparatuses of the Greek New Testament." Pages 283-96 in *The Text of the New Testament in*

Contemporary Research. Edited by Bart D. Ehrman and Michael W. Holmes. Grand Rapids: Eerdmans, 1995.

———. "Response." [A response to Maurice A. Robinson's "The Case for Byzantine Priority" cited above]. Pages 141-50 in *Rethinking New Testament Textual History*. Edited by David Alan Black. Grand Rapids: Baker, 2002.

Skarsaune, Oskar. *In the Shadow of the Temple: Jewish Influences on Early Christianity*. Downers Grove, Ill.: InterVarsity Press, 2002.

Skeat, Theodore C. "The Codex Vaticanus in the Fifteenth Century." *Journal of Theological Studies* 35 (1984), 454-65.

———. "Irenaeus and the Four-Gospel Canon." *Novum Testamentum* 34 (1992): 194-99.

———. "The Oldest Manuscript of the Four Gospels." *New Testament Studies* 43 (1997): 1-34.

———. "The Codex Sinaiticus, The Codex Vaticanus, and Constantine." *Journal of Theological Studies* 50 (1999): 583-625.

Slingerland, Dixon. "Acts 18:1-17 and Luedemann's Pauline Chronology." *Journal of Biblical Literature* 109:4 (1990): 686-90.

———. "Acts 18:1-18, the Gallio Inscription, and Absolute Pauline Chronology." *Journal of Biblical Literature* 110:3 (1991): 439-49.

Smallwood, E. Mary. *The Jews under Roman Rule from Pompey to Diocletian: A Study in Political Relations*. Boston: Brill Academic Publishers, Inc., 2001.

Smith, Ashbury. *The Twelve Christ Chose*. New York: Harper & Brothers, 1958.

Smith, D. Moody. "Why Approaching the New Testament as Canon Matters." *Interpretation* 40 (1986): 407-11.

———. "When Did the Gospels Become Scripture?" *Journal of Biblical Literature* 119 (2000): 3-20.

Smith, John Holland. *Constantine the Great*. New York: Charles Scribner's Sons, 1971.

Smith, Robert W. "New Evidence regarding Early Christian Chronology: A Reconstruction." Pages 133-9 in *Chronos, Kairos, Christos II: Chronological, Nativity, and Religious Studies In Memory of Ray Summers*. Edited by E. Jerry Vardaman. Macon, Ga.: Mercer University Press, 1998.

Smith, William A., ed. *A Dictionary of the Bible, Comprising its Antiquities, Biography, Geography, and Natural History*. 3 vols. Hartford, Conn.: S. S. Scranton & Co., 1900.

Sonnini de Manoncourt, Charles Nicholas Sigisbert (1751-1812), G. A Roberts, M. Savage, and T. G. Cole (Members of several Scientific and Literary Societies). *These Are Ancient Things: Selected Articles*. (Including The Long Lost Chapter of the Acts of the Apostles. Containing the Account of Paul's Journey in Spain & Britain; also a Remarkable Prediction of Britain's Glorious Inheritance. Translated by C. S. Sonnini from an original manuscript found in the archives of Constantinople, presented to him by the Sultan Abdoul Achmet, with notes and comments by the late T. G. Cole; The Early British Church and its Continuity to the Present Time by L. G. A. Roberts; The Flags of Freedom by Miss M. Savage). Vancouver B.C.: British-Israel World Federation of Greater Vancouver, n. d. (ca. 1913).

Souter, Alexander. *The Text and Canon of the New Testament*. New York: Charles Scribner's Sons, 1917.

Sparks, H. F. D. *The Formation of the New Testament*. London: SCM, 1952.

Spelman, Henry, Sir. *Councils and Ecclesiastical Documents Relating to Great Britain and Ireland.* 4 vols. Edited, after Spelman and Wilkins, by Arthur Haddan and William Stubbs. Oxford: Clarendon Press, 1869-73.

Spence-Jones, H. D. M. *The Early Christians in Rome*. New York: John Lane, 1911.

Spong, John Shelby. *Liberating the Gospels: Reading the Bible with Jewish Eyes: Freeing Jesus from 2000 Years of Misunderstanding*. San Francisco: HarperSanFrancisco, 1996.

Staniforth, Maxwell, ed. and tr., *Early Christian Writings: The Apostolic Fathers*. New York: Dorset, 1968.

Stanton, Graham N. "The Gospel of Matthew and Judaism." *Bulletin of the John Rylands University Library of Manchester* 66 (1984): 264-84.

Stark, Rodney. *The Rise of Christianity*. Princeton: Princeton University Press, 1996.

Stendahl, Krister. "The Apocalypse of John and the Epistles of Paul in the Muratorian Fragment." Pages 239-45 in *Current Issues in New Testament Interpretation*. Edited by W. Klassen and G. F. Snyder. New

York: Harper & Row, 1962.

Stein, Robert H. *The Synoptic Problem: An Introduction.* Grand Rapids: Baker Books, 1987.

Stevenson, James. *A New Eusebius: Documents Illustrating the History of the Church to AD 337.* Revised and edited by William H. C. Frend. London: SPCK, 1993.

Stillingfleet, Edward. *Origines Britannicae: Or, the Antiquities of the British Churches.* London: M. Flesher for Henry Mortlock, 1685.

Stough, Henry W. *Dedicated Disciples.* Thousand Oaks, Calif.: Artisan Sales, 1987.

Strack, Hermann. L., and Paul Billerbeck. *Kommentar zum Neuen Testament aus Talmud und Midrasch.* 4 vols. Munich: C. H. Beck, 1922-28.

Strecker, Georg. "Die sogenannte zweite Jerusalemreise des Paulus." *Zeitschrift für die neutestamentliche Wissenschaft* 52 (1962): 67-77.

———. "On the Problem of Jewish Christianity." Pages 241-85 in Walter Bauer, *Orthodoxy and Heresy in Earliest Christianity.* 2d ed. Edited by Robert A. Kraft and Gerhard Krodel. Translated by the Philadelphia Seminar on Christian Origins. Mifflintown, Penn.: Sigler Press, 1971.

Styger, Paul. *Die römischen Katakomben: Archäeologische Forschungen über die Bedeuting der altchrislichen Grabsätten.* Berlin: Verlag für Kunstwissenschaft, 1933.

Sundberg, Albert C., Jr. "Toward a Revised History of the New Testament Canon." Pages 452-61 in *Studia Evangelica IV. Texte und Untersuchungen* 89. Berlin: Akademie-Verlag, 1964.

———. "The Making of the New Testament Canon." Pages 1216-24 in *Interpreter's One-Volume Commentary on the Bible.* Edited by Charles M. Laymon. New York: Abingdon, 1971.

———. "Canon Muratori: A Fourth-Century List." *Harvard Theological Review* 66 (1973): 1-41.

———. "The Bible Canon and the Christian Doctrine of Inspiration." *Interpretation* 29 (1975): 352-71.

———. "Canon of the NT." Pages 136-40 in *Interpreter's Dictionary of the Bible: Supplementary Volume.* Edited by Keith Crim. Nashville: Abingdon, 1976.

Suetonius. *The Twelve Caesars.* Translated by Robert Graves. London:

Harmondsworth, Penguin Books, 1957.

Suggs, M. Jack. "Concerning the Date of Paul's Macedonian Ministry." *Novum Testamentum* 4 (1960): 60-8.

Tacitus. *The Annals of Imperial Rome.* Translated by Michael Grant. London: Harmondsworth, Penguin Books, 1956.

Talmud. [Soncino English Translation]. Edited by Isidore Epstein. 34 vols. London: Soncino, 1935-48.

Taylor, Gladys. *Our Neglected Heritage: The Early Church.* 1st ed. London: Covenant Publishing Co., 1969.

Taylor, J. "The Making of Acts: A New Account." *Revue Biblique* 97:4 (1990): 504-24.

Taylor, James. "British Israelitism." Page 123 in *New 20th-Century Encyclopedia of Religious Knowledge.* Edited by J. D. Douglas. Grand Rapids: Baker, 1991.

Taylor, John W. *The Coming of the Saints: Imaginations and Studies in Early Church History and Tradition.* 1st ed. London: Methuen & Co., 1906. Rev. ed. London: Covenant Publishing Co., 1969.

Taylor, Vincent. *The Formation of the Gospel Tradition*, 2d ed. London: Macmillan, 1935.

———. *Gospels: A Short Introduction.* London: Epworth, 1952.

Theron, Daniel J., ed. *Evidence of Tradition.* Grand Rapids: Baker, 1980.

Thiede, Carsten Peter. *Simon Peter: From Galilee to Rome.* Exeter: Paternoster, 1986.

———. "Babylon, der andere Ort: Annermerkungen zu 1 Petr 5, 13 und Apg 12, 7." *Biblica* 67 (1986): 532-8.

Thorne, E. A. "The Earlier Missionary Journeys in Acts of Apostles." *Catholic Quarterly Review* 121 (1935-6): 109-17.

Toit, Andrie B. du. "Canon: New Testament." Pages 102-4 in *The Oxford Companion to the Bible.* Edited by Bruce M. Metzger and Michael D. Coogan. New York: Oxford University Press, 1993.

Torrey, C. C. *Documents of the Primitive Church.* New York: Harper, 1941.

Toynbee, Jocelyn M. C. "Review of *De Pythagore aux Apôtres: Etudes sur la conversion du monde romain*, by Jérôme Carcopino." *Gnomon* 29 (1957): 261-70.

Toynbee, Jocelyn M. C., and John Ward Perkins. *The Shrine of St. Peter and the Vatican Excavations.* New York: Pantheon Books, 1957.

Treharne, R. F. *The Glastonbury Legends: Joseph of Arimathea, The Holy Grail, and King Arthur*. London: The Cresset Press, 1967.

Trobisch, David. *Paul's Letter Collection: Tracing the Origins*. Philadelphia: Fortress, 1994.

———. *The First Edition of the New Testament*. Oxford: Oxford University Press, 2000.

Turner, Cuthbert Hamilton. "Appendix to W. Sanday's Article: 'The Cheltenham List of the Canonical Books, and the Writings of Cyprian.'" *Studia Biblica* 3 (1891): 304-25.

———. "Latin Lists of the Canonical Books: 3. From Pope Innocent's Epistle to Exsuperius of Toulouse (A.D. 405)." *Journal of Theological Studies* 13 (1911-12): 77-82.

———. "The Papal Chronology of the Third Century." *Journal of Theological Studies* 17 (1916): 338-52.

———. "The Early Episcopal Lists." *Journal of Theological Studies* 18 (1917): 103-34.

Twysden, Sir Roger (1597-1672). *Historiæ Anglicanæ Scriptores X.* 1st ed. London: Typis Jacobi Flesher, Sumptibus Cornelii Bee, 1652.

Ulrich, Eugene. "The Notion and Definition of Canon." Pages 21-35 in *The Canon Debate: On the Origins and Formation of the Bible*. Edited by Lee Martin McDonald and James A. Sanders. Peabody, Mass.: Hendrickson, 2002.

Urquhart, John. *The Bible: Its Structure and Purpose*. 2 vols. New York: Gospel Publishing House, 1904.

Vassiliadis, Petros. "The Nature and Extent of the Q-Document." *Novum Testamentum* 20 (January, 1978): 49-73.

Wacholder, Ben Zion. "The Calendar of Sabbatical Cycles during the Second Temple and the Early Rabbinic Period." *Hebrew Union College Annual* 44 (1973): 153-96.

———. "Chronomessianism: The Timing of Messianic Movements and the Calendar of Sabbatical Cycles." *Hebrew Union College Annual* 46 (1975): 201-18.

———. "The Calendar of Sabbath Years during the Second Temple Era: A Response" (A response to Don Blosser's 1981 article, cited above). *Hebrew Union College Annual* 54 (1983): 123-33.

Wagner, Walter H. *After the Apostles: Christianity in the Second Century*. Minneapolis: Fortress, 1994.

Walker, Larry. "Biblical Languages." Pages 211-231 in *The Origin of the Bible*. Edited by Philip Wesley Comfort. Wheaton, Ill.: Tyndale, 1992.

Walker, William O., ed. *The Relationships Among the Gospels: An Interdisciplinary Dialogue*. San Antonio, Tex.: Trinity University Press, 1978.

Wall, Robert W. "The Acts of the Apostles in Canonical Context." *Biblical Theology Bulletin* 18 (1986): 1-31.

———. "The Significance of a Canonical Perspective of the Church's Scripture." Pages 528-40 in *The Canon Debate: On the Origins and Formation of the Bible*. Edited by Lee Martin McDonald and James A. Sanders. Peabody, Mass.: Hendrickson, 2002.

Wall, Robert W., and Eugene Lemcio. *The New Testament as Canon. A Reader in Canonical Criticism*. Sheffield: Sheffield Academic Press, 1992.

Wallace, Daniel B. "The Majority Text Theory: History, Methods, and Critique." Pages 297-320 in *The Text of the New Testament in Contemporary Research*. Edited by Bart D. Ehrman and Michael W. Holmes. Grand Rapids: Eerdmans, 1995.

Walter, Victor. "Versions of the Bible." Pages 289-308 in *The Origin of the Bible*. Edited by Philip Wesley Comfort. Wheaton, Ill.: Tyndale, 1992.

Webster, Graham A. *Boudica: The British Revolt against Rome, AD 60*. London: B. T. Batsford Ltd., 1978. Rev. ed. 1993. Repr., London: Routledge, 1999.

———. *The Roman Invasion of Britain*. London, 1980.

———. *Rome against Caractacus: The Roman Campaigns in Britain, AD 48-58*. London, 1981

Weiss, Johannes. *Earliest Christianity: A History of the Period A.D. 30-150*. 2 vols. Originally published in 1937 under the title: *Das Urchristentum*. Translated and edited, with a new introduction and bibliography by Frederick C. Grant. New York: Harper & Brothers, 1959.

Welborn, L. L. "On the Date of First Clement." *Biblical Research* 29 (1984): 35-54.

Wellesley, Kenneth. *The Long Year: A. D. 69*. Boulder: Westview, 1976.

Wenham, John W. "Did Peter Go to Rome in A.D. 42?" *Tyndale Bulletin*

23 (1972): 94-102.

———. *A Fresh Assault on the Synoptic Problem: Redating Matthew, Mark & Luke*. Downers Grove, Ill.: InterVarsity, 1991.

Westcott, Brooke Foss. *A General Survey of the History of the Canon of the New Testament*. Cambridge: Macmillan, 1866, 4th ed. 1881. Repr., Grand Rapids: Baker, 1980.

———. *Introduction to the Study of the Gospels*. New York: Macmillan & Co., 1885.

Westcott, Brooke Foss, and Fenton John Anthony Hort. *Introduction to the New Testament in the Original Greek: With Notes on Selected Readings*. New York: Harper & Brothers, 1882. Repr., Peabody, Mass.: Hendrickson, 1988.

Whitehead, John. *Guardian of the Grail: A New Light on the Arthurian Legend.* New York: Barnes & Noble, 1993.

Wilhelm-Hooijbergh, A. E. "A Different View of Clemens Romanus." *Heythrop Journal* 16 (1975): 266-88.

Wilken, Robert. *The Christians as the Romans Saw Them*. New Haven: Yale University Press, 1984.

Wilkins, Michael J., and J. P. Moreland, eds. *Jesus under Fire: Modern Scholarship Reinvents the Historical Jesus*. Grand Rapids: Zondervan, 1995.

William of Malmesbury. *Chronicles of the Kings of England.* London: Bell & Daldy, 1866.

———. *The Antiquities of Glastonbury.* Translated by F. Lomax. Repr. Dyfed, Wales: Llanerch, 1980.

Williams, Hugh. *Christianity in Early Britain.* Oxford: Clarendon Press, 1912.

Wilmshurst, Edwin. *St. Paul & Britain: Notes on the Dedication Stone of the Temple of Neptune and Minerva, At Chichester Which Connects the Roman Senator Pudens, the British Princess Claudia, and St. Paul with the City of Chichester.* Chichester: T. G. Willis & Co., 1910.

Wilson, Ian. *Jesus: The Evidence*. San Francisco: HaperSanFrancisco, 1985.

Wilson, Neil S., and Linda K. Taylor. *Tyndale Handbook of Bible Charts & Maps*. Wheaton, Ill.: Tyndale, 2001.

Wilson, R. McL. "Gnosticism (Gnosis)." Pages 358-9 in *New 20th-Century*

Encyclopedia of Religious Knowledge. Edited by J. D. Douglas. Grand Rapids: Baker, 1991.

Wisse, Frederik. "The Coptic Versions of the New Testament." Pages 131-41 in *The Text of the New Testament in Contemporary Research*. Edited by Bart D. Ehrman and Michael W. Holmes. Grand Rapids: Eerdmans, 1995.

Witherington, Ben, III. *The Paul Quest: The Renewed Search for the Jew of Tarsus*. Downers Grove, Ill.: InterVarsity Press, 1998.

———. *New Testament History: A Narrative Account*. Grand Rapids: Baker, 2001.

Yamauchi, Edwin M. "Jesus Outside the New Testament: What is the Evidence?" Pages 207-30 in *Jesus under Fire: Modern Scholarship Reinvents the Historical Jesus*. Edited by Michael J. Wilkins and J. P. Moreland. Grand Rapids: Zondervan, 1995.

Zahn, Theodor B. *Introduction to the New Testament*. Trans. J. M. Trout, et al. 3 vols. New York: Scribners, 1909.

Zuntz, Günther. *The Text of the Epistles: A Disquisition upon the Corpus Paulinum*. The Schweich Lectures of the British Academy, 1946. London: The British Academy, 1953.

Zuurmond, Rochus. "The Ethiopic Version of the New Testament." Pages 142-56 in *The Text of the New Testament in Contemporary Research*. Edited by Bart D. Ehrman and Michael W. Holmes. Grand Rapids: Eerdmans, 1995.